The Shell Guide to Wales

Cover picture: **Harlech Castle**   *W. A. Poucher*
End-papers: **Moel Hebog from Llyn Dinas**   *W. A. Poucher*

The Shell Guide to Wales

Introduction by Wynford Vaughan-Thomas
Gazetteer by Alun Llewellyn

Book Club Associates London

This edition published in 1977 by
Book Club Associates
by arrangement with Michael Joseph Ltd

© Shell U.K. Ltd 1969

This book was designed and produced by
George Rainbird Ltd, London

House Editor: Yorke Crompton
Editorial assistant: Julia Trehane
Designer: Michael Mendelsohn
Cartographer: John Flower

The maps on pages 345–52 are based on the
Ordnance Survey Map with the sanction of
H.M. Stationery Office (Crown Copyright reserved)

The picture research was done by Patricia Vaughan
and Frances Latty

Contents

Colour Plates

Forewords by the Authors

No guide can ever be complete. Wales today is undergoing change at an unprecedented rate. The Forestry Commission spreads its work over the hills and alters whole landscapes within a year. Valleys are no sooner described than a Bill is approved by Parliament to drown them, in a desperate attempt to keep pace with the thirst of our ever-increasing industrial areas. Every little town in rural Wales seems to have a scheme to double or treble its inhabitants, whether the local people approve or not. Overnight, power stations and pylons seem to leap up to confound the guide-writer.

His only hope must be that certain basic things will remain, whatever may still be lying in wait for the unsuspecting community on official drawing-boards. And not all change is for the worse. A country is a living thing, which alters in response to the needs of the inhabitants – and of the visitors. Exciting new things are to be seen in Wales, as well as the fascinating heritage of the past. This guide will try to cover both.

We have taken as our model the *Shell Guide to Scotland* by Moray McLaren, who in turn acknowledged his debt to the *Shell Guide to Ireland* by Lord Killanin and Michael V. Duignan. We have retained the system used in the Gazetteer of the Scottish Guide when describing places, lakes, and mountains. Thus all lakes are entered under their second name and not under Llyn (Lake); Llyn Vyrnwy, for instance, is entered under Vyrnwy. The same is true of mountains. We omit the Mynydd (Mountain) printed on the Ordnance Survey maps and go straight to the main name.

Unfortunately one can do nothing about the Welsh practice of naming places with Llan (Church). This goes back to the mists of history, so that the biggest proportion of the entries in the Gazetteer come under the Llan heading. Most Welsh place-names, however, have the advantage of being descriptive. Llanrhaeadr-ym-Mochnant becomes comparatively simple when you translate it as the Church of the Waterfall at the Brook of the Pig. The vocabulary of the place-names is not extensive. It does not take long to learn, for example, that "aber" means mouth and "tre" a town or settlement. Immediately after the historical part of the Introduction, therefore, the reader will find a short guide to the language and a glossary of common words. A few minutes spent in reading this last will help him to look at his map without confusion.

Some names printed on the older editions of the Ordnance Survey maps appear in this guide under new spelling. The early Ordnance Survey was not altogether accurate or consistent about the orthography of place-names. In recent years, many of these early mistakes have been officially corrected, and this guide attempts, so far as the matter has been decided, to give Welsh names with their correct spelling; thus Llanelli has replaced Llanelly and Dolgellau amends Dolgelly.

Wales is a comparatively small country, and it is possible for two men separately to travel over most of it, either on foot or by car. But no two men can amass all the facts that must be included in a guide such as this. They have to depend on their forerunners, the travel writers who have already covered much of the ground;

on the official guides prepared by the municipalities; on the hand-outs of Government offices and big industrial firms. In certain areas I myself have received special help from Mr Dilwyn Miles of the Pembrokeshire Community Council. I am also indebted to the admirable collections of the National Library of Wales at Aberystwyth and the Cardiff Public Library. The Welsh Office and the Welsh Tourist Board have been unfailing in their support. A list of books consulted and useful for further study follows the Gazetteer. In a volume of 250,000 words there are bound to be mistakes. We hope that readers of the guide will point them out so that they can be corrected in later editions.

Wales has only recently become a tourist area on a big scale. North Wales and the mountains of Snowdonia have always been a great attraction, but only since the Second World War have Pembrokeshire and South-West Wales shared in the tourist inrush. Hotel accommodation may not always be on a scale sufficient to meet the ever-increasing demand. This matter is receiving attention. The tourist trade is now Wales's biggest industry, and the Welsh Tourist Board is tireless in improving tourist facilities.

But, whatever changes are made, one thing remains changeless – the unique charm and distinctive personality of Wales.

W.V.-T.

In drawing together something from what has been a life's labour of love, I should like to thank many who have helped me with companionship and guidance.

Foremost are members of the Company of Sunday Tramps, founded in 1879 for pursuing the delights of the British countryside: Dr C. Doree (No. 69); Sir Assheton Pownall (No. 150); Lord Samuel, O.M. (No. 105), whose affection for the Welsh borderland was deep and active; Sir G. M. Trevelyan, O.M. (No. 3), whose interest in and encouragement of my attempts to resolve the mysteries of the Arthurian period in Wales I hope one day to justify; Mr L. S. Elton (No. 170), of the Association of Architectural Historians, whose introduction to Mr Arnold Taylor and his research into the inspiration for King Edward I's building of Caernarfon Castle was of great value; Mr David Davies, of Llangynfelyn and Thailand (No. 182), who led me through the depths of the Cors Fochno and suffered himself to be led in turn to the mysterious burial mounds of Pen Creigiau'r Llan.

My thanks are also due to the Librarian of the University of London Law Library for help in following some of the more obscure points in constitutional law and history; and to Mr Griffiths, of a famous bookshop, whose enthusiasm in tracking down and providing certain of the ancient books of Wales in their original form I can never adequately repay. Thomas Lewis of Caersaer and Garthgwynion, my great-grandfather, left an invaluable collection of accounts and memoranda covering both the mining and the shipping interests of the Dovey valley in the early nineteenth century; and my grandfather, Llewelyn Llewellyn of Brynhyfryd (Llewellyn Ddu o Lantawe), a life's collection of Welsh memorabilia.

My wife, who made everything possible, deserves more than acknowledgment.

A.Ll.

Introduction

The Shape of the Land

Their Lord they will praise,
Their speech they will keep,
Their land they shall lose,
Except Wild Wales.

So runs the most cherished of the numerous prophecies that kept the patriotism of the Welsh at burning point through the troubled ages before the rise of the Tudors and the accession, at last, of a Welsh-born prince to the throne of England. No matter if the prophecy is a late affair and the prophet had the advantage of prophesying after the event. The verse sums up the one overriding fact about the very existence of Wales – its unexpectedness.

Within fifty miles of many of the big cities of England – Liverpool, Birmingham, Bristol – is a country whose inhabitants speak another language and who feel themselves, in every way, to be a separate nation. In spite of over fifteen hundred years of constant pressure from its powerful neighbour, and of the complete political and legal union of Wales and England, this separate character of the Welsh continues to show through. There is no demarcation line to indicate the border, except an occasional sign set up by the Tourist Board on certain main roads, proclaiming "Croeso i Gymru", "Welcome to Wales". But an Englishman in Lleyn, or in a village in north Cardiganshire, can sometimes feel himself in a country more foreign to him than France or Germany. The folk around him speak another language. The place-names seem all consonants, and he has no clue to their pronunciation. The laws, the traffic regulations, the everyday things may be exactly those he is used to in England, but below the surface all is changed. He has only to listen to the singing in chapel on Sunday to sense how foreign a land Wales can be. Even the powerful new factors that make for the obliteration of local differences – television, pop culture, the motor-car and aeroplane – have not yet made Wales the mass-produced, standardized, easily handled unit dear to the heart of the modern administrator. This separate quality of Wales is the secret of the contribution it has made to the general life of Great Britain – a contribution out of all proportion to the size of the country. It is also the source of the attraction that Wales has for the visitor.

Solid geographical and geological facts made possible the survival of Wales. The mountains were the hard core of resistance, the keep into which the Welsh retired when all their outer barriers had fallen, the inner defence line that made nationality possible. This mountain keep is not so conspicuous as the celebrated Highland Line that so dramatically divides Gaelic from Lowland Scotland. In the extreme north and south, coastal plains make entry into Wales easy for an invader. The wide valleys of the Severn, the Wye, and the Usk form pathways into Central Wales. But the modern motorist, driving towards the west, sooner or later becomes aware that the hills lie ahead of him barring the horizon. Wild Wales is still very much there.

Geographically, the nature of this mountain mass changes as you move from north to south, and these changes have had important effects on the character and history of the people of Wales. It is not altogether fanciful to see the North Walian, with his strong sense of duty, his solidarity in opposition to change, his deep devotion to the Welsh language, reflected in the rugged peaks of Snowdonia; and the South Walian, easy-going, more willing to accommodate himself to the outside world, sharing the character of the rounded hills and the lush valleys of the Towy, the Usk, and the Vale of Glamorgan. But man, after all, is a late-comer to this landscape. We can date his arrival to a mere three hundred thousand years ago at the most. For millions of years before the first small band of primitive hunters wandered westward, maybe in the wake of the retreating ice, the land we now call Wales had been preparing for their coming.

The oldest rocks in Wales lie in Anglesey and along the Menai Straits. There are other pre-Cambrian outcrops, notably in the far west of Pembrokeshire. But it is in Anglesey that you see the remains of that ancient, hard core of worn and twisted rock beds against which the rest of Wales has been constructed. South of Anglesey lie the wild mountains of Snowdonia, the Rhinogs and Cader Idris, that are the peculiar glory of North Wales. Geologically, they are complex in the extreme – made up of a vast variety of slates, lavas, sedimentary rocks, grits, and shales. What we see now is not the actual mountains but the roots of mountains. The core lies south in the great dome that rises behind Harlech, carved into some of the toughest mountains in Wales. About three hundred million years ago, the rocks became subject to the powerful pressure from the south that we associate with the Caledonian earth movements. The rocks of Arfon and Merioneth were squeezed remorselessly against the hard core of Anglesey, with the result that all the main lines of the hills and valleys on the map of North Wales – and indeed West Wales as well – run from north-east to south-west. You can see this trend in the line of the Lleyn peninsula, the Menai Straits, the Dovey, and indeed as far south as the valleys of the Teifi and Towy. It has left a permanent mark on the very structure of Wales, hardening the silts into the slates that made the fortune of the quarry owners of Llanberis, Bethesda, and Blaenau Ffestiniog. Earlier in the period came the eruption of lava that lies at the heart of the Mynydd Preseli, and the rocky outcrops of Central Wales.

After this whirling burst of mountain pressure, volcanic outpourings, and rock upheavals, the mountains south of Merioneth give a calmer, more gentle impression. All over Central Wales are the Ordovician and Silurian shales and mudstones, which seem relatively undisturbed after North Wales. The grey, rounded moorlands of Plynlimon set the tone; and for thirty miles southwards the high, lonely hills continue. Until recently this could be regarded as one of the unknown areas of Great Britain, a land of sheep-walks, lost valleys, and treeless wastes – the Desert of Wales. Today the Forestry Commission has moved in, and the extreme loneliness has been modified. But the big rivers of South and Central Wales still rise in this central wilderness. The Wye and the Severn flow out from Plynlimon, the Teifi and the Towy rise further south; their valleys widen as they go. They become lush, green, beautiful – fat farming country, with pleasant little towns, strongholds of Welsh-speaking in the west and pathways of English entry in the east. Away in the extreme south-west lies Pembrokeshire, with the magical range of the Mynydd Preseli dominating the northern landscape of the county, with its old rocks around St David's and a gloriously wild coastline from Strumble Head to Ramsey Island.

With southern Pembrokeshire, we come to the third great geological area into which Wales can be divided. Here are the rims of Old Red Sandstone and limestone that form the underlying rocks of the great saucer of the South Wales coalfield. The coal was formed in the steaming hot deltas of the shallow seas that succeeded the deserts of the Old Red Sandstone period. In North Wales as well, on the edge of the mass of the older rocks further west, the same thing occurred.

The coal measures of South Wales are thin and compressed in Pembrokeshire, but widen and thicken as you go eastward. Here, in Glamorgan and Monmouthshire, you come to the extraordinary landscape of the "Valleys", where the long lines of terraced houses lie in the narrow slots made by the rivers, and the waste from the mines is carried up by long ropeways to be dumped on to the moorlands. Coal meant power, certainly until the First World War. In and around the valleys is clustered over two-thirds of the population of Wales. If you include the less intensively developed coalfield of North Wales, you can say that three-quarters of the total number of Welshmen live concentrated in a comparatively small part of the country. This is the source of some of the most vexing problems that beset modern Wales. Rural Wales is basically Welsh-speaking. Industrial Wales, the Wales of all the big towns, is far more mixed in population and language. Are the two drifting irretrievably apart? The deep seams of coal, laid down millions of years ago, carried unguessed-at complexities for the men who mine them today.

There are younger rocks in Wales. You meet the Triassic beds, for example, in the Vale of Glamorgan and in Flintshire, but they lie on the perimeter of the heartland formed by the mountains of Wales. At the end of the Carboniferous period came the second great period of land movement that left its mark mainly on South Wales. This was the Armorican or Hercynian folding, so called because it is most noticeable in Brittany and the Hartz mountains in Germany. The line of folds ran right across Europe from the Ukraine to southern Ireland. In South Wales they affect the line of Milford Haven, the limestone of south Pembrokeshire and Gower, and the lower valley of the Towy.

Two more major geological forces put the finishing touches to the present landscape of Wales. Strange as it may seem, Wales sank in its turn under that sea in which was formed the chalk beds that cover so much of southern England. The chalk extended westward to cover most of the principality. Then, when the earth was uplifted again sixty to thirty million years ago during the great "earth storm" that give birth to the Alps, new rivers flowed down the slope of the chalk. They cut across the ancient, buried north-east, south-west folds. As the chalk in its turn weathered away, so the rivers continued to cut down deeply. Thus the hard rocks have been seamed by those river trenches and mountain passes that appear to cut right across the obvious lie of the land.

Then came the latest of all the forces that had a hand in carving out the face of Wales – ice. At the height of the greatest extension of the ice, there was not a single foot of Welsh soil that did not lie under this cold winding-sheet. There is something chilling to the imagination in the picture of the great glaciers forming on the high ground of Snowdonia, Plynlimon, and the Brecon Beacons and steadily flowing outwards from the hills, linking together, grinding the harder rocks into cliff-faces, spokeshaving the softer ones, and finally pushing before them the vast moraines and the sheets of boulder clays that were to alter the whole courses of rivers like the Dee and the Severn.

The great Scottish glacier came down the Irish Sea and overrode West Wales, thrusting aside the local ice and carrying its debris over Pembrokeshire, Gower, and the Vale of Glamorgan. The ice ebbed and flowed in successive Ice Ages. At last it retreated, leaving behind moraines, valleys carved into U-shapes, and a debris of clay and rounded boulders smeared over the country. Today, in Snowdonia, you can see spectacular evidence of the power and weight of the ice. The whole landscape around the Pass of Aberglaslyn, Moel Hebog, and Cwm Croesor, for example, was torn by the glaciers. Then, as the ice retreated, man advanced.

The first tiny bands of hunters appeared, following the enormous herds of game that must have roamed the tundras where now roll the seas of the Bristol Channel and the waters of Cardigan Bay. We can hardly call these hunters Welshmen. But with them we leave the world of geology and enter that of history.

Prehistoric Wales

These primitive newcomers may have first arrived in one of the many interglacial periods of warmer weather that interrupted the ebb and flow of the ice. Britain in this Old Stone (or Palaeolithic) Age was part of the continent of Europe, and man had no English Channel to cross. The first arrivals must have been extremely few. The first relics of man found in Wales are mere fragments – a molar tooth amongst animal bones in the Pont Newydd cave in Denbighshire, and relics from similar caves at Coygan, near Laugharne in South Wales. These hunters were Neanderthalers: one of the earlier species of man, who walked less erect and possessed heavy jaws and receding chins. But they had large brains and could use tools for hunting and dressing the skins of the animals they killed. It was the Neanderthalers who found the plentiful caves of the limestone country in Denbighshire, Flintshire, the peninsula of Gower, and southern Pembrokeshire that must rank as the first homes created by man in Wales. Flint, primitive man's best raw material, is rare in Wales, and this may have accounted for the sparse population.

The Neanderthalers did not remain in undisputed possession. A new race of Palaeolithic hunters appeared, who were far more akin to ourselves in physique, and even in their thinking. They were related to the Cro-Magnon race identified in the painted cave region of southern France, and may have reached Wales somewhere around twenty-two thousand years ago. The Cro-Magnons supplied the most spectacular evidence of their presence in Wales in the Paviland cave in Gower. Here, in 1823, the pioneer archaeologist Dean Buckland of Oxford created intense excitement by uncovering a human skeleton, in association with the bones of mammoths, woolly rhinoceroses, and other long-extinct species. The skeleton seemed to be daubed with red ochre. Dean Buckland christened his find the "Red Lady of Paviland", but in fact the burial is that of a young man, about twenty-five years old, who was placed against the wall of the cave with full ritual. For the first time in Wales we know we are in the presence of some primitive form of religion. The red ochre on this huddled body is the only painting we know from the caves of Wales. Certain marks in Bacon Hole, also in Gower, have been claimed as designs made by primitive men, but this is doubtful. We have no Altamira or Lascaux in Wales. But Paviland seems to give us our first clear link with the Continent and the general tide of human development.

Meanwhile the climate changed. We are nearing the end of the successive advances of the glaciers. About 10,000 B.C. the retreat of the ice became general. The melting polar caps released the water, and the sea-level around Wales gradually rose again. About 8000 B.C. there were still large areas of land uncovered up to the 120-foot line in the Bristol Channel and Cardigan Bay. There was a pause at the 60-foot line about 5000 B.C., and then a renewed advance towards our present coastline.

Is this advance of the sea reflected in the many tales in Welsh folklore of the drowned kingdoms that lie under Lavan Sands, the Drowned Hundreds of Cardigan Bay, and the rest? There is no proof. We do know, however, that about 5000 B.C. a change was taking place in the conditions of human settlement. The Old Stone Age was giving place to the Mesolithic or Middle Stone Age. New techniques of stone-chipping appear. The folk who lived in Nanna's Cave on Caldey Island made small, neatly trimmed blades. Those on Burry Holms, an islet off the Gower coast, also used this type of tool. Until recently, it was assumed that most of the microlithic hunters were cave dwellers on the sea-coast or within easy reach of the sea. But the discovery, in 1960, of a hoard of microliths high up on the mountains of Glamorgan's Craig y Llyn showed that the microlithic folk dared to venture far inland after their prey. Many more of these hunting camps probably lie hidden amongst the peat high in the central hills. The gradual warming up of the climate may have encouraged these hunters to move further afield. It seems clear that, for over two thousand five hundred years after 5000 B.C., the climate of Wales was much as it is today, with forests of oak, elm, and lime extending into the sheltered valleys. The stage is set for the next act of the drama.

The Coming of the Celts

While the hunters were roaming the coastal plains of Wales and the lands now drowned beneath the Bristol Channel and Cardigan Bay, decisive events were taking place in the Middle East. In Egypt and Mesopotamia man had learnt to domesticate animals and plant cereals. The Neolithic revolution was in full swing. This New Stone Age farming technique spread through Europe. By 3000 B.C. there must have been peasants living by mixed farming over most of the western half of the Continent. Only the English Channel, formed in comparatively recent times, kept them from entering Britain. Soon they adventured across these swift tidal waters, and Britain's first farmers, the Windmill Hill people, were moving with their flocks and their carefully guarded stores of grain over the chalk downs of southern England. We know that they reached Wales, for, on the rocky outcrop of Clegyrfwya in the impressive Land's End of Wales beyond St David's, these Windmill Hill folk built their simple houses – a sign that the Cave Age was ending at last. The hunters were in retreat before the farmers.

The Windmill Hill people were only the advance guard of the successive waves of invaders that moved westward across Europe. Wales was not quite the end of the line for the wanderers. Ireland still lay beyond. And Ireland had two possessions that made her a magnet for invaders – her gold and her copper. So along the coastline, from Spain and Brittany, came the bearers of the Megalithic culture, the builders of the cromlechs and stone circles that lie in such impressively isolated sites on our moorlands. The peninsulas of Wales, jutting far out into the sea, were naturally attractive to these adventurers. The Megalithic monuments they left seem to be of two classes. Those invaders who settled in Gower (Glamorgan) and the Black Mountains of Monmouthshire seemed to have come from southern Brittany and the lower Loire valley. Others, who colonized Pembrokeshire and Anglesey, may have come from Spain and Portugal. Two of the great Anglesey monuments, Bryn-celli-ddu and Barclodiad y Gawres, have carvings – complicated spirals and zigzags that may be stylized representations of the Mother Goddess whose cult originated from the far-distant Mediterranean. Were these early cromlech-builders linked in some way with the builders of Stonehenge, or was it the Beaker Folk who came after them?

In the nineteen-twenties, Dr H. H. Thomas of the Geological Survey made an astonishing discovery. He proved, beyond all possible doubt, that the bluestones at Stonehenge must have come from one particular outcrop on the Mynydd Preseli in Pembrokeshire. The builders must have dragged the stones down to the shores of Milford Haven, floated them around the South Wales coast, and then up the Wiltshire Avon to the edge of Salisbury Plain. Such an extraordinary feat could only have been performed under the stimulus of a profound religious faith.

This was a Bronze Age culture. Bronze held the field until the arrival of iron – and with iron came the Celts. Some time after 500 B.C. the Bronze Age ends and the Iron Age begins. Three successive waves of invaders eventually reached Wales. The newcomers, with their powerful new iron weapons, brought war and trouble. The Iron Age forts that crown so many of the hill-tops all over Wales tell their own story.

The Celts were a warrior race, an aristocracy that delighted in fighting and raiding, and in the glory of battle celebrated by their bards. We can picture them from the descriptions left by the classical writers – bold men wearing long trousers and cloaks, plastering their hair with lime before battle until it stood out like a lion's mane; great drinkers and story-tellers, generous to a fault, quick to pick a quarrel or make a friend, honouring the smiths who made their weapons and the poets who sang their prowess. Their shields, weapons, and chariots were decorated with rich, flowing designs. Some of the greatest treasures of Celtic art found in Wales are the Trawsfynydd cup and, above all, the great hoard of chariot fittings, weapons, and collars found at Llyn Cerrig Bach in Anglesey.

The religious leaders of the Celts were the Druids, and we know from Tacitus that Anglesey was a great centre of Druidic lore. Young men of promise were sent to Anglesey, even from far-away Gaul, to be instructed in religion, history, philosophy, and poetry. The discipline was strict, and the candidate had to learn everything by heart. There was a dark side to the Druidic cult, including human sacrifice. Says Tacitus of the woods and sacred groves of Anglesey: "In these recesses the natives smeared their altars with blood from their prisoners and sought the will of the gods by exploring the entrails of men".

This irresistible combination of mystery, horror, and esoteric lore has fascinated many latter-day Celts, especially during the Romantic Revival of the late eighteenth century. But in truth we know very little of what the Druids taught, or indeed what they actually looked like. One thing, however, is certain. Druids, warriors, bards were all Celts and therefore the remote ancestors of the modern Irish, Highland Scots, and Welsh. These were the people who now had to face the best organized invasion yet to land in Britain – that of the Romans.

The Discipline of Rome

The Romans began their serious assault on the island of Britain in A.D. 43. It took them a bare four years to overrun most of southern Britain. Wales and the north were far tougher. It was thirty years or more before Wales was held down in the web of forts, roads, and camps with which the Romans enmeshed the peoples they conquered. Right to the end, two legions had to be stationed on the borders of Wales, at Chester in the north and Caerleon in the south. This does not seem to bear out the usual picture of the Welsh tribesmen in the hills eventually going back to their village-forts under the protection of the Pax Romana.

The five main tribal areas of Wales all had their share of fortified camps and military roads. The Romans clearly still felt they had to keep a stern eye on these reluctant tribesmen. In the south-east, in modern Monmouthshire and Glamorgan, were the Silures, who had offered a particularly stubborn opposition to the Roman advance. In the south-west (modern Pembrokeshire and Carmarthenshire), the Demetae were the leading tribe. The stern Ordovices held the hill country of Mid-Wales and the upper Severn; the Degeangli, Denbighshire and Flint.

Only in the extreme south-east of Wales do we find the sort of civilian settlement that was common all over the lowland zone of Roman Britain. Here, Caerwent (Venta Silurum) is the showplace, a *colonia* settled by the veterans from nearby Caerleon (Isca Silurum). Venta had fine public buildings, baths, and a shopping centre. The wall that was built around it in the troubles of the third century A.D. is still one of the most impressive Roman remains above ground in Britain. For the rest, Rome in Wales means forts and military roads – the network along which the legions could move at speed to check any trouble.

The four hundred years of Roman occupation were bound to leave some mark. Words were borrowed, and the nature of this acquisition is interesting. Many of the military weapons – sword, javelin, and shield – stay Celtic, but "saeth" (arrow) comes from the Latin *sagitta*. Most of the words connected with writing are Latin, but poetic terms remain Celtic. Words about building are naturally taken from the Romans, like "ffenestr" (window). But, surprisingly enough, the natives clung to their own law terms. Piggott may have exaggerated when he wrote that the "Celtic cowboys and shepherds, footloose and unpredictable, moving with their animals over rough pasture and moorland, could never adopt the Roman way of life", but certainly a strong Celtic substratum remained in Wales unaffected by the Roman Conquest.

Perhaps this was just as well, for the natives were to need all their old fighting spirit in the troubled times that fell upon Roman Britain, while the Roman power faltered and grew feeble at the centre. The Picts and Scots began to prey on the Empire in the north and west. The shore-forts at Caernarfon and Cardiff were strengthened. The civil wars that racked the Empire at its very heart tempted ambitious military chiefs to denude Britain of troops in a bid for power. In A.D. 383 Magnus Maximus led the legions, including no doubt men from Caerleon and Chester, over into Gaul. After four dazzling years of success, he was defeated and slain by Theodosius at Aquilea. He left a legend that haunted the Welsh – the legend of Macsen Wledig, who came from Rome to the golden castle of Caernarfon to wed Helen ("Helen of the Legions"), the daughter of a Welsh chief, and returned in triumph to the Imperial City. Thus, as Rome collapsed, she still left a story of power and splendour behind her to lighten men's spirits through the Dark Ages.

The curtain of darkness was indeed coming down rapidly over the land.

The Emergence of Wales

Left to their own devices, the Britons now faced invasion on three fronts. The Saxons were beginning to press along the eastern shores. The Picts swarmed in from the north. From Ireland came the Scotti in their skin boats, "whose hulls," says Gildas, "might be seen creeping across the glassy surface of the main like so many insects awakened from torpor by the heat of the noonday sun and making with one accord for some familiar haunt". Whatever may have happened on the eastern shore against the Saxons, there is no doubt that the western Britons struggled to acquit themselves like men. When the mists of history part again a hundred years later, we can see the dim outline forming of the nation we can now call Wales. And that Wales would never have appeared if the Britons had not achieved a partial success at least in checking the Saxon advance.

Heroic names – half myth, half history – sound through the sparse chronicles of the times. Cunedda and his eight doughty "sons" are supposed to have come from south-east Scotland to expel the Irish who had swarmed into the north and south-west of the land. This story has the ring of truth. The settlement of outside warrior tribes, as a defence against invaders, was an old Roman practice, and the advance of the Saxons had not yet cut a wedge between the Britons of southern Scotland and their fellow countrymen in western Britain.

Then there is Arthur himself. In spite of the later legends that have accumulated around the name, it is hard not to believe that the defence of the west must have had some valiant leader who put heart into the Britons. Maybe it was Arthur, or some figure like him, who won the great battle of Mount Badon, fought about A.D. 500, and checked the Saxon advance for a good fifty years.

We have only one guide through the darkness of the time – Gildas, the querulous yet learned monk who wrote the *De Excidio*, a rip-roaring denunciation of the evil rulers of Wales about the middle of the sixth century. For a moment we have a flash of illumination. We see the sinister figure of Vortigern, the traitor ruler who let in the Saxons: Maelgwn Gwynedd, Lord of the North, the "Island Dragon" and a mighty warrior, but a prince who "closes his ears to the music of Heaven and listens only to the flattery of the bards". Gildas looks back in longing to the great days of Rome, but he shows us clearly that the unity imposed upon the island by Rome is gone for ever. Wales emerges as a country ruled by petty kinglets, occupied in expelling the Irish from the west and holding off the English in the east. The link with southern Scotland is still strong. Above all, a new language is forming.

Just as colloquial Latin in France was beginning to change into something like French, so – even more rapidly – the old Brythonic tongue changed into something that can now be recognized as unmistakably Welsh. Maybe the removal of the Roman administration started the change, which was helped by the social chaos that followed the first inroads of the Saxons. The early date of the change is important, for, by the seventh century, we are beginning to hear of the great early poets of Wales – Aneurin, Taliesin, and others. Although their poems were written down very much later, the material they contain could still be sixth century in its essence.

The heroic epic of the *Gododin* celebrates the disaster that overtook a war band from eastern Scotland, who met glorious death at Catterick in Yorkshire fighting against the advancing Saxons. It has a Homeric ring about it.

> The men who went to Catraeth,
> Merry was the host; the grey mead was their drink.

But one by one the gay warriors went down to death. That distinguished Welsh historian, the late Sir John Lloyd, described the *Gododin* as "wearing the aspect of a genuine relic of a long-forgotten strife – a massive boulder left on its rocky perch by an icy stream which has long since melted away".

There were still men who valued learning. The famous stone at Llangadwaladr in Anglesey celebrates in Latin the virtues of King Cadfan, "most learned and renowned of all kings". Above all, there was the Church. This is the Age of the Saints.

Christianity was already established in Roman Britain, and we have some archaeological evidence of its existence around Caerleon and Caerwent. Exactly how much survived, and was carried over into the new world that followed the collapse of Rome, is not certain. Some elements of the Celtic Christianity that now arose in the sixth century may have come from across the water, reintroduced by Gallo-Roman Christians. One thing at least is clear. The sixth and seventh centuries were the great age of missionary activity in Wales. The wandering monks travelled the length and breadth of the country. They left a profound and ineffaceable impression.

Alas, we do not know anything certain about most of them. These saints were never officially canonized by the Roman Church. Their lives were usually written six hundred years later by monks who wished to enhance the glory of their monastic houses, and who did not hesitate to add a goodly percentage of miracles to edify the faithful. But we can see some of these holy figures clearly. The learned St Illtud was at the very heart of the missionary movement. He founded his monastery at Llantwit Major, in the Vale of Glamorgan. It became a centre from which bands of monks set out to proselytize the heathen.

The leader would set up a cross at a chosen spot, and, if the people were responsive, a little church would be built of wattle and daub, with some simple cells for the company. The whole settlement would then be surrounded with an earthen rampart against wild beasts – maybe against wild humans as well. Such a settlement was known in ancient Welsh as a "llan", and eventually "llan" was used for the church itself. Illtud's fame was international. One of the lives known to be of an early date, that by St Samson of Dol in Brittany, acclaims Illtud as the most learned of the Britons in the scriptures, a philosopher, an authority on grammar and rhetoric and, curiously enough, a man gifted with the power of foretelling the future. One is reminded of the fame of the Druids as soothsayers. Perhaps in that uncertain world, compounded of the new Christianity, the learning of pagan Rome, and the living memory of Druidic lore, a holy man could draw on the three sources of inspiration together and be all the better for it.

Near St Illtud, St Cadoc set up his own seat of learning at Llancarfan. Cadoc's family is said to have been ultimately descended from the Emperor Augustus, and he himself was famous for his love of Virgil and the pagan poets. In St Cadoc, St Illtud, and St Dubricius we seem to sense a deep respect for the achievements of Rome. These men were the bridge over which the best of the pagan world was carried to the newly emergent Celtic Church.

St David and St Teilo, who became the dominant saints of the west, and St Beuno in the north, were men of a different stamp. We do not hear of David as a man of learning. He won fame for his asceticism and his gentle but persuasive character. The monastery he founded in the remote corner of West Wales was noted for its hard discipline. Dewi Sant (St David) drank only water. He was Dewi Ddyfrwr (David the Water-Drinker), the first Welshman who is known to have been pledged to teetotalism. His monks had to harness themselves to the plough. All work was carried on in religious silence. No one claimed any property for himself. The man who accidentally said "my book" or "my plate" had to expiate the offence with severe penance. Yet, in spite of this stern discipline, disciples flocked to David. He early became the national saint of Wales. May we suspect that his eloquence as well as his holiness gained for him the principal place in the hearts of a nation of brilliant talkers?

We hear of his being summoned to combat heresy at the Synod of Llanddewi-brefi in Cardiganshire. None of the bishops there assembled could make themselves heard amid the vast throng. St David, who seems to have been a stocky little Welshman, had no trouble at all. He produced a miracle. The ground on which he stood conveniently rose into a little hill (the church of Llanddewibrefi was built upon it), and his voice carried to the furthest corners of the crowd. St David died on the 1st March, and this day has become the National Day of Wales.

In the stories that were told of St David and many of the early saints – of St Brynach, who had a mystic power over animals, and of other saints who preached to the birds and lived lonely and holy lives deep in the heart of the countryside – we detect a peculiar sweetness and charm, which is totally different from the atmosphere that surrounded similar saints in Europe and, above all, in Rome.

To the men busy organizing the new structure of the Roman Church, codifying its laws and asserting its claims against the secular power in the heart of the old Empire, the Celtic Church must have seemed a strange survival, lost in the mists on the rim of the civilized world. A clash was inevitable.

The Celtic Church had been cut off from the rest of the Christian community for nearly a hundred and fifty years. The Anglo-Saxons were steadily advancing, and a new forward movement by the invaders had begun in the second half of the sixth century. The check administered at Mount Badon had only a temporary effect. Everywhere the British were again under heavy pressure. The Celtic saints had no heart for missionary work among the hated and triumphant heathens. They would probably have had short shrift if they had tried. There was a barrier of blood, slaughter, and destruction between the two races.

"He who acts as a guide to the barbarians, let him do penance for thirteen years. If there follows the shedding of blood, captivity and the slaughter of Christian folk, let the man abandon his arms and spend the rest of his life in penance." Such was the stern edict obeyed by the Welsh. St Beuno, in his cell at Berriew, not far from the Severn, one day heard an Englishman's voice on the other side of the river, urging on his dogs in chase of a hare. Beuno hurriedly called his monks together and ordered instant departure. "The kinsmen of yonder strange-tongued man will surely obtain possession of this place." An Englishman of any sort was held to pollute the very air of Britain. A saint could only hurriedly remove himself from the contaminating influence. A man who preached to the invaders was no religious hero. He was a traitor to his race and to civilization.

This, then, was the position when St Augustine landed in Kent in A.D. 597, sent by the Pope to convert the English to Christianity. He had an impressive success. Clearly a meeting between himself and the Celtic Church could not be long delayed. It came in about 602 at Aust (Augustine's Oak), on the estuary of the Severn. Augustine may have been a saint and an organizer of genius. But he was no diplomat. The Celtic bishops saw in him a man who had been sent to the hated enemy, and who stubbornly stood on the authority of Rome. The ritual differences between the Churches over such things as tonsures and the correct date of Easter were mere quibbles. What stuck in the gizzard of the Celtic Church was Augustine's tone of legal superiority, his demand for submission to Rome when cooperation would readily have been given. Subsequent conferences failed to remove the painful impression left by that first meeting. It was not long before religious isolation was followed by political isolation as well.

The Isolation of Wales

In the history of Wales, the seventh and eighth centuries are at once tragic, heroic, and decisive. The English were now solidly organized in the kingdoms that successively competed for the overlordship of the island. The rise of Northumbria under the formidable Aethelfrith was the first danger signal. He it was who struck the long-remembered blow at the Welsh at Bangor-on-Dee in 615, when the monks praying in support of the Welsh army were mercilessly slaughtered. Worse was to come. Edwin of Northumbria was as tough as his predecessor Aethelfrith. He drove the final wedge between the Britons of southern Scotland and those of Wales by his destruction of the old kingdom of Elmet, with its centre around Leeds. For a time he even threatened to seize North Wales itself, but the Welsh rallied under the doughty Cadwallon and, by allying themselves with the rising power of Mercia, defeated and killed Edwin.

So the struggle went on, swaying this way and that, with sometimes the Welsh winning a victory or two but continually giving ground because of the sheer numbers against them. By now we can certainly call them Welsh, not Britons, although the word Welsh comes from the Anglo-Saxon *wealeas*, a foreigner. The Welsh actually called themselves the Cymry. The derivation of the word has been disputed, but it probably means "our set of people" or "our fellow-countrymen".

After Northumbria came the threat of Mercia, this time right on the Welsh doorstep. There was no hope now of ever reversing the decision of history. The dream of recovering eastern Britain had seemed possible right up to the middle of the seventh century. It was now abandoned, for all practical purposes, although the bards kept it alive in the imagination of the people. The English were established in Shropshire and Herefordshire. The border had moved steadily westward. Yet the closer it came to the hill country, the slower became its advance. The Welsh had been driven back towards their mountain keep, and this they held – stubbornly, desperately, successfully.

Their success was indicated by the construction of Offa's Dyke. This celebrated earthwork runs, with certain gaps, from the coast of North Wales at Prestatyn to the Wye in the south. There can be no question that the dyke was built by Offa, the great King of Mercia, but the interesting thing about it is the reason for its construction. It could not be a serious defence line like Hadrian's Wall. Rather was it an attempt to mark the boundary for all time. Maybe penalties would be inflicted for anyone found on the wrong side of it, although the theory that any Welshman found to the east of it would have his hand cut off seems to date from the twelfth-century chroniclers. There is no doubt, however, that the dyke was accepted by both sides as a firm demarcation line. The Welsh to this day speak of going to England as "crossing Offa's Dyke". The place-names show its effectiveness. On one side we find the English villages, with "ham" and "ton"; on the other the Welsh "Tre" and "Llan". Besides, it was not long before Wessex wrested the overlordship from Mercia. The heat was off along Offa's Dyke. Wales could breathe again.

But not for long. No sooner had the English danger receded than the Danish danger began. This was a miserable stab in the back for the Welsh. They had beaten off the English in the east. Now came the Vikings, harrying the west coast, burning the monasteries, and giving their names to the headlands around the Welsh coastline, from the Great Orme to Worms Head and the Holms in the Bristol Channel. As in Wessex, so in Wales. The hour produced the man. In Wales the hero who checked the advance of the Danes was Rhodri Mawr, Rhodri the Great.

He made a profound impression on his contemporaries. Not only did he crush the Viking hordes in Anglesey, for which he earned the thanks of Charles the Great himself. He was also the first man to unite Wales politically – not by conquest but rather in the manner of the Hapsburgs, by a highly successful marriage policy. Both the emergence of Rhodri and the building of Offa's Dyke were signs that an independent Wales was going to survive.

The age of Rhodri was followed by the age of Alfred the Great in Wessex. Alfred had Welshmen in his service. His life was written by a learned Welshman, Bishop Asser, and he pursued a policy of diplomatic relations with the Welsh. There were dangers in this on the Welsh side. The English might now obtain by peaceful penetration more than they ever obtained by open war. Alfred himself was taken as an example by Rhodri's grandson, Hywel Dda (Hywel the Good), the only Welsh ruler to be given such a title. Hywel is famous in Welsh history for his codification of the law. Some thirty-five Welsh law-books have survived from the period 1250 to 1500 – as many as the most important manuscripts of Glanvil and Bracton, the great source-books of English medieval law. All these manuscripts ascribe their authority to Hywel. So there is a strong probability that Hywel did initiate some sort of movement towards setting down the law as it then stood. But, as with so much else in this period, modern historians always qualify their account by saying "We cannot at present be sure". We know quite a good deal about Hywel himself, however. He was one of the few Welsh rulers to go on pilgrimage to Rome and return to find his kingdom intact. No wonder the chroniclers styled him the "head and glory of all the Britons".

By Hywel's day the main political divisions of Wales had become fixed, with names that were to become familiar all through the Middle Ages. They are even being resurrected in our own day to cover the big county regrouping that is about to take place.

In the north was the land of Gwynedd, which included Anglesey, the mountains of Snowdonia, the peninsula of Lleyn, and the Conway valley. Further east, facing the English danger, was the land of Powys, with its strength in the upper valley of the Severn. Along the western coast was Ceridigion (Cardigan), then as now a land somewhat apart from the rest of Wales. The province of Dyfed embraced the present counties of Carmarthenshire and Pembrokeshire. The land of Gwent covered the rich country between the lower Wye and the Usk. Morganwg (Glamorgan), to the west of Gwent, included both the "Blaenau" or hilly area and the "Bro" or Vale of Glamorgan. Each of these areas had its small princedoms, each with its story of quarrels, of fluctuating fortunes in battle against fellow Welshmen and the ever present menace of the English.

Alas, after Hywel the Welsh world again falls into confusion. The petty princes come and go. Sometimes South Wales predominates and sometimes North. The Church still has its monasteries, although with no illuminated manuscripts to rival those of Ireland. Celtic crosses are set up by rulers with obscure names and complicated pedigrees. These princes, however, do not live in castles of stone, but rather in courts of wood, surrounded by their retainers and praised by their bards. There are alliances made and broken, constant wars and raids into other princes' territories. The great figures of Rhodri Mawr and Hywel Dda seem to be accidents – men not typical of the Welsh scene.

Thus we see Wales in startling contrast to England. England had become united; the Danish menace had been overcome. There was a strong monarchy. The kingdom that Earl Harald took over from Edward the Confessor was solidly based; political institutions were complex and efficient. Wales, on the face of it, remained a welter of small squabbling princedoms. A great variety of reasons has been produced for this failure of the Welsh to maintain the unity they won at such cost under Rhodri: tribal feeling, the custom of dividing royal inheritances, the very geography of the country where the mountain masses keep people apart. But many of these factors originally applied to England, and yet unity was achieved.

The real reason lies in the very presence of this united England on the border of Wales – a powerful neighbour who would always find it in her interest to oppose any attempt by the Welsh to unify their country. The Welsh could not conduct their politics in isolation. England was always there to back the discontented, and her opposition to the unification of Wales remained constant to the very end of Welsh independence three hundred years later.

The Coming of the Normans

The year 1066 was as important for Welsh history as it was in the history of England, although the Welsh took no part in the Battle of Hastings. Indeed, most of them may never have heard of it. Yet the result of the battle profoundly affected Wales. When William the Conqueror took possession of his new kingdom, he had to make arrangements to control his turbulent western border. He and his followers cared nothing for Offa's Dyke and agreed boundaries. These powerful, efficient freebooters had just completed one of the quickest and most successful land grabs in history. Wales was clearly next on the list.

There was no swift Norman Conquest of Wales, no seizing of a kingdom after a dramatic battle. Rather was there a Norman penetration into the Welsh heartland, in a series of border forays and skirmishes, a hundred years of steady gnawing away at Welsh territory. The Normans held down the newly gained lands with yet another castle, until South Wales became the most becastled sector of the British Isles. William, and the kings who immediately succeeded him, had perforce to entrust the business to some of their most powerful followers. William FitzOsbern, the Conqueror's cousin, established himself as Earl of Hereford and began pushing up the Wye valley. He was soon firmly set at Strogoil, the modern Chepstow, and began his advance into Gwent. Further north, Roger of Montgomery operated the same tactics, with Shrewsbury as his base and Central Wales as his prey. The north was handed over to the tender mercies of Hugh of Avranches, moving out of Chester. We are now in the presence of the Marcher Lords, who were to have such a powerful influence upon English as well as Welsh history all through the Middle Ages. Here were men with private armies, who operated almost as independent powers outside the limits of the kingdom. The March derives from the old French word meaning "border", and the Lords Marchers were the barons of the borderlands, whose rights far exceeded those of their brethren in settled England.

The technique of their advance was soon standardized. The Normans had two enormous advantages over the Welsh: they were armoured and they knew how to build castles. The mailed knights and their followers would push their way along the lines of the old Roman roads, where they still existed. The Welsh might harass them from the woods and crags, but these closely knit bands usually got through to some strategic point where they could construct their castle. This was of wood, not stone. A mound, or "motte", would be thrown up, surrounded by a moat. On it would be a shell made of stout palisades in which the garrison could live secure from surprise. The castle would become the centre of a district, in which the fighting men who accompanied their lord would receive grants of land in return for military service. Thus a series of defensive cells would be set up in the most desirable parts of the countryside, and the Welsh would be slowly forced back into the inhospitable hills.

The Welsh chief lived among his own people. He had no need to defend himself from them. He kept open court in his wooden-built "llys" or court. The Norman had to be on guard as a foreigner amongst a hostile population. He soon replaced his original wooden castle with a stone one, which became not only his defence but also the centre of administration for the surrounding country.

Under the protection of the castles, the little towns grew and flourished. The town was a new concept in Wales and one foreign to the Welsh mind. The Normans created most of the towns on the map today, with the exception of the new towns that grew up with the Industrial Revolution. Swansea, Newport, Cardiff, Carmarthen, Pembroke, Haverfordwest – they all started life at the foot of the castle. And with the town came the churches and abbeys. The old Welsh saints were replaced with dedications to St John or St Peter. Remorselessly this pattern of conquest spread across South Wales. There seemed to be no way of stopping it.

The Normans might be checked by geographical difficulties as much as by Welsh resistance. In the south the Normans crawled irresistibly forward. By the reign of Henry I, the castles had spread all along the Vale of Glamorgan and into Pembrokeshire. Henry himself took a decisive hand in the game. Gerald of Windsor held the great castle of Pembroke in the King's name. The whole of southern Pembrokeshire and Gower, and parts of the Vale of Glamorgan, were so thoroughly settled by immigrants that the Welsh speech was no longer heard in the land. The very place-names were changed, and a language frontier, the Landsker, runs to this day north of Haverfordwest and splits the countryside into a Welsh Pembrokeshire and a "Little England beyond Wales". The waters of Milford Haven, winding far inland, gave the Normans and their followers an easy pathway to conquest in this part of the world. Even Cardigan and Aberystwyth, on the far west coast, had their castles. The thirty-five years of Henry I's reign were a woeful time for the Welsh. They must have asked themselves where it would all end. The Welsh Church was the final victim. Canterbury marched in behind the Norman men-at-arms. The sees of Llandaff and St David's were occupied by Norman bishops. Bangor at last recognized the supremacy of Canterbury. St Asaph was simply put into abeyance. The old monastic structure of these Welsh bishoprics was briskly broken up. The new bishops set about building cathedrals to the glory of God and certainly to the glory of the conquerors.

Then, on the 1st December 1142, Henry I died from his celebrated surfeit of lampreys. Nowhere was the news received with such lack of grief as in Wales.

The Welsh Revival

Henry's death meant a disputed succession, with Stephen fighting for the crown against the Empress Matilda. The Marcher Lords, led by Robert of Gloucester, backed Matilda. Once again England's troubles gave Wales her opportunity. In the north, Owain Gwynedd swept the country almost to the walls of Chester. In the south, Cardigan and Dyfed saw a great Welsh revival. The Norman grip on Pembrokeshire was too strong to be shaken, but the Welsh had recovered confidence. They felt that piecemeal conquest by the Normans was not inevitable. Even the coming of Henry II did not destroy their morale. Henry was a strong king. He moved fast, when the Pembrokeshire barons, following Strongbow, began to play a part in the politics of Ireland. But even Henry II could not contemplate a full-scale conquest of Wales. In the south Rhys ap Gruffydd became the dominant power, from his castle at Dynevor, outside Llandeilo. Both Rhys and Owain Gwynedd had eventually to come to terms with Henry, but not before Henry had suffered defeat in his turn. One expedition was long celebrated by the bards.

Henry made a tremendous attempt at invasion in 1165, "with a host beyond number", as a chronicler says, drawn from all parts of his English and French domains. This army started to cross the high, lonely range of the Berwyns. And then the heavens opened. To this day the scene of the disaster is known as Heol-y-Saeson (Englishmen's Road). The great armament foundered in the bogs and on the rain-sodden moorlands nearly 2,000 feet above sea-level. The Berwyn disaster was the graveyard of Henry's Welsh policy. Henceforth Gwynedd in the north was safe from invasion. Owain died in 1170, and was buried in the cathedral church of Bangor after sixty vigorous years of service to his country. In the south the Lord Rhys had been equally successful. Patron of the arts, he held the first gathering of bards – at Cardigan in 1177 – that could be called an Eisteddfod. Henry II, at the Council of Oxford, treated him with respect. Wales had been restored to the map again.

This new breed of Welsh princes acted in the belief that the Welsh revival would be permanent. The Lord Rhys endowed the monastery at Strata Florida, among the wild hills at the top of the Teifi valley. It became a centre of Welsh literature and patriotic inspiration. With political revival came a new artistic achievement. The bards now perfected that complicated system of musical alliteration, of giving pattern to a line by means of echoing vowels and consonants, which Welsh poets call "cynghanedd", harmony. Meilwr, Gwalchmai, Cynddelw, Hywel the son of Owain Gwynedd himself are some of the great names: poets who were honoured to praise their chiefs and who delighted in the sheer joy of living. Here is a passage from Gwyn Williams's literal translation of Gwalchmai's *Boast*. It catches the spirit of the poem, though no translator, however skilful, can convey in another language the brilliant word-juggling of the "cynghanedd".

> Quick rising the sun, summer hurries on.
> Splendid the song of birds; fine, smooth weather.
> I am of golden growth, fearless in battle.
> I am a line, my attack a flash against a host.
> I watched through the night to keep a border.
> Murmuring ford water in heavy weather,
> The open grassland green, the water clear,
> Loud the nightingale's familiar song;
> Gulls play on the bed of the sea,
> Their feathers glistening, their ranks turbulent. . . .

A new note, not only in Welsh but in European literature.

Outside the Welsh language, works were produced in Latin that attained to European celebrity – in one case to notoriety.

Gerald de Barri (Gerald the Welshman) we know intimately, as we know few figures in the Middle Ages, when men were not given to self-revelation in prose. But Gerald had a sprightly pen, and he sets himself down with all his weaknesses, vanities, hopes, and boundless curiosity. He was born about 1146 in Manorbier, on the south Pembrokeshire coast, of the mixed Norman-Welsh stock that played

an important part in the history of the Marches. He was a cleric who hoped in vain
to become the first independent archbishop of St David's. He was proud of his
Welsh and Norman descent. The mere English he regarded with contempt. He was
a scholar, educated in Paris, and a man of consequence in the Church, who toured
Wales as chaplain to Archbishop Baldwin to preach the Third Crusade. The result
was a marvellous picture of the country through which the preaching team passed.
It is Gerald who relates for us the story of the old Welshman at Pencader, in the
days when Henry II was marching through South Wales. Asked by the King if the
rebels would continue to resist, the old man replied in words that seem to sum up
the whole spirit of the Welsh revival: "This nation, O King, may now, as in former
times, be harassed, and in a great measure weakened and destroyed by your and
other powers, and it will often prevail by its laudable exertions; but it can never be
totally subdued through the wrath of man, unless the wrath of God shall concur.
Nor do I think that any other nation than this of Wales, or any other language,
whatever may hereafter come to pass, shall, on the day of severe examination
before the Supreme Judge, answer for this corner of the earth".

The other twelfth-century Welshman who made a European reputation is not
so easy to write about in terms of undiluted praise. With Geoffrey of Monmouth
we are on tricky ground. His *History of the Kings of Britain* burst like a bomb on
an astonished world around 1136. Geoffrey's purpose, as he frankly admits, was
to glorify the Britons and to show that they too possessed a glamorous past. Once,
he claimed, they dominated Europe; let them remember the prophecies of Merlin
about the triumphs of the Welsh yet to come. Why shouldn't the Welsh triumph,
if only they remember and draw inspiration from their ancient history?

And what a history! Geoffrey claimed to have taken his facts from an old Welsh
book lent to him by Walter, Archdeacon of Oxford. Geoffrey ultimately became
Bishop Elect of St Asaph, but he played ducks and drakes with the facts of British
history in a way most unbecoming to a bishop. He gives us an astonishing chronicle
of how the British were descended from Brutus the Trojan. He speaks of the
glorious and improbable career of Prince Belerius, who captured and sacked Rome;
of the tragedy of King Lear; of the giants Gog and Magog; of Lud, who built
London; of Cymbeline and a host of other dubious heroes, who have become so
firmly fixed in our minds that it is difficult to believe that Geoffrey invented them.
Above all we encounter Arthur and Merlin. It was Geoffrey who launched the
pair on their triumphant career, through the romances of the Middle Ages and on
to our own day. The whole *Historia Regium Britanniae* passed as serious history,
and the "Matter of Britain" continued to bedevil historians down to the days of
Charles II.

Geoffrey may have been a liar, as even some of his contemporaries suspected.
Gerald the Welshman relates with dry relish: "It is worthy of observation that
there lived in the neighbourhood of this City of the Legions (Caerleon) a Welshman
named Melerius who acquired the knowledge of occult events. . . . If the evil spirits
oppressed him too much, the Gospel of St. John was placed on his bosom, when
like birds, they immediately vanished. But when that book was removed and the
History of the Britons by Geoffrey Arthur was substituted for it, they instantly
reappeared in greater numbers and remained a longer time than usual on the body
and on the book".

Geoffrey may have had the last laugh. He was, after all, a great literary artist.
The man who practically created King Arthur and Merlin has surely contributed
something permanent to the literature of Europe. His heroes still go riding on.

The Age of the Two Llywelyns

Wales entered the thirteenth century with high hopes. The Norman menace had been faced, and the nation had survived. Land might be lost again, but it did not seem possible that an independent Wales would ever disappear completely. The Welshman in his hills had proved himself a hardened warrior. Despite the wave of feudalism that beat against it in the south and east, Welsh society remained based upon the pasturing of flocks and herds. It possessed a resilience under strain.

Gerald paints an attractive picture of life among the hills. Houses were flimsy affairs, built of woven osiers and replaced when necessary with no trouble. The Welsh existed on a main diet of meat, oats, milk, butter, and cheese. They were moderate eaters – they had to be, since they did not depend upon intensive agriculture. Hospitality was a duty, and guests were entertained also with music on the harp. At night a simple bed of rushes was spread on the floor. Both sexes cut their hair in a circle level with the eyes. A hazel twig served as a toothbrush.

All Welshmen took a profound interest in the matter of descent, a trait that has survived to this day. Their faults? They could be treacherous to outsiders. They could lose heart in pitched battles, but soon recovered. And they had an unbreakable addiction to lawsuits. They were firm believers in prophecy, above all in the prophecy that a time would come when the Welsh would drive the invaders out of the land for ever, and regain their ancient supremacy over the whole island. Patriotic Welshmen might have been forgiven if they thought that the prophecy had every chance of becoming at least partly true as the thirteenth century began. For there appeared on the scene the most powerful and successful of the princes of medieval Wales. Llywelyn ap Iorwerth began as the ruler of Gwynedd, but extended his power over almost the whole of Wales and fairly earned the title of Llywelyn the Great.

Once again the weakness of England gave Wales her opportunity. Richard Lionheart was away on his crusade and his foreign wars. John, his successor, had his hands full of baronial troubles. Llywelyn could consolidate his power unchecked. He first set about annexing the neighbouring lands by force of treaty. He clearly saw that Welsh disunity was the national weakness, and that unity, if it was to come at all, would have to be imposed. This did not endear Llywelyn to many of his fellow-countrymen, but the more far-sighted accepted the Llywelyn revolution because of its future potentialities.

And we can speak of a "revolution" since Llywelyn deliberately speeded up the process by which the old tribal and pastoral world depicted by Gerald was changing in Wales to a more manorial and feudal pattern. He tried to break down the age-old custom of divided succession in favour of accession by a single heir. He pressed forward a more durable agricultural settlement; the richer part of the land became, for the first time, dotted with hamlets and traced with fixed boundaries. He gathered a nucleus of permanent administrators around him – lawyers who were keen supporters of centralized authority. Most of the old manuscripts of the Laws of Hywel Dda date from this period. Small boroughs received charters. Clearly Llywelyn and his successors saw the work that had been accomplished under the Norman kings and realized that Wales would have to follow suit. The Llywelyns represented a new theory of government in Wales. If they had been given time to develop their policies, they would undoubtedly have created a state with the sort of structure that made England great under Edward I or France under St Louis. On a far smaller scale, it is true; but the root of the matter was in them.

Llywelyn the Great was lucky; he had Richard I and John to deal with. Llywelyn the Last was unlucky – and Wales with him. He came up against Edward the First.

Moreover Llywelyn the Great, at the height of his power, was married to the daughter of King John. But he saw the advantage of allying himself with the rebel barons. Magna Carta contained reassurances that the Welsh should have restored to them all lands annexed by the King. Llywelyn took the opportunity to make himself supreme also in South Wales. When John died and the young Henry III came to the throne, the King's advisers judged it best to recognize Llywelyn's power. From time to time Llywelyn was challenged both by Welsh princes and Marcher Lords, but never shaken. When he died at last in 1240, the Cistercian annalist of Aberconwy could write of him as "that great Achilles the Second . . . he kept peace for men of religion, to the needy he gave food and raiment, he gave justice of all . . . and by meet bonds of fear and love bound all men to him".

Not quite all men, perhaps. There was always an irreconcilable core of Welshmen who resented Llywelyn's innovations and whose resistance played a part in the tragedy that overtook his successor.

In spite of Llywelyn's care, there was the usual period of disputed succession after the death of his son Dafydd. But the foundations of the state had been firmly laid, and later the second Llywelyn, Llywelyn ap Gruffydd, was able to seize the state in his capable hands. Henry III was in trouble with his barons, and the second Llywelyn could once again play the profitable Welsh game of benefiting from the difficulties of England. He went so far as to assume the official title of Prince of Wales. We have referred to the Welsh rulers as princes, but most of them wisely did some sort of homage to the kings of England. They might style themselves Prince of Powys or of Gwynedd, but never used the title of Prince of Wales. By the treaty of Montgomery, Henry III was forced to recognize the title. Llywelyn ap Gruffydd is thus the first native Prince of Wales. He was also the last.

The pace of the manorial and administrative revolution continued to increase. On the surface, all seemed to be set fair for the future of an independent Wales, developing alongside England in the same way as Scotland, paying some sort of homage, no doubt, but free to make its own laws, to become a Welsh state with all the inspiration and pride in achievement that only national independence can give. For the moment, the glittering dream seems on the verge of fulfilment. Llywelyn is seated in his noble hall at Aberffraw on the coast of Anglesey, in correspondence with the Pope, recognized as Prince of Wales from the banks of the Taff to the shores of North Wales, praised by his bards, surrounded by gifted administrators, a founder of monasteries and builder of courts and castles. He looks the golden man of the future. Then, within a few years, comes humiliation; within ten years, downfall and death.

The end of independent Wales was dramatic. It left a nation stunned by the tragedy – in some respects a nation that even now, six hundred years later, has not completely recovered from the events of 1282.

The End of Independence

Once again the cause of the disaster is easy to find. England had a strong king, one of the strongest she has ever had. Edward I was a very different man from his father or John. He had the hard, dry mind of a legalist, the skill of a general long trained in the wars, the pride of a ruler who saw greatness in himself and in his country. He would not long tolerate the dangers, the sheer administrative untidiness, of a small semi-independent state on his border. Llywelyn had his enemies at home, including his own brother Dafydd. The Prince of Wales, for reasons we can never know, also made a series of diplomatic slips. He refused to pay tribute or homage, although bound to do so by treaty. He also insisted on marrying the daughter of Simon de Montfort, a demand that hardly endeared him to the King. Was Llywelyn over-confident of the position he had built up with such care? Did he underestimate the King? If so, he made a fatal miscalculation. Edward decided to finish with the Welsh. In 1277, after Llywelyn had been formally declared a rebel, the attack began.

Edward first cut Llywelyn's ground from under him in southern, eastern, and central Wales, by launching a three-pronged attack from Chester, Montgomery, and Carmarthen. By the summer of 1277, he had Llywelyn neatly shut up in Gwynedd. Then he made a methodical advance along the northern coastline towards Conway, with the Welsh resisting fiercely all the way. Finally Edward played his trump card – his fleet. This cut Llywelyn off from the farm lands of Anglesey, and he had no option but to sue for terms.

They were hard. Llywelyn could keep on calling himself Prince of Wales, but he was stripped of his lands east of the Conway, of all his mid-Wales territories, and of his overlordship of the other Welsh princes. He was, however, allowed to marry Eleanor de Montfort, though he had to pay homage in London. We have a vivid description of this visit. The courtiers laughed at the strange dress of the barons of Snowdon who accompanied the Prince and were quartered at Islington, "where the milk supply ran short". The Welsh hated the London wine. "They were still more offended by the crowds of people that flocked about them when they stirred abroad, staring at them as if they had been monsters, and laughing at their uncouth garb and appearance."

The Welsh returned, with hatred in their hearts, to their sadly reduced principality. The inevitable reaction was bound to come. The King's new officials in the ceded districts were not tactful. People who had been used to independence found it hard to conform to new laws. By 1282 the country was in turmoil. Dafydd, Llywelyn's brother, started it by seizing Hawarden. There was a general rising. Llywelyn, as the national leader, could not stand aside. So he went to his doom.

Again Edward advanced from three points. Again his fleet cut off Anglesey. Llywelyn might burn the bridge of boats across the Menai Straits, but the pincers closed in on him once more. In a desperate attempt to raise new support from the south, he slipped through the ring with a small escort. He was cut off from his men during an obscure skirmish near Builth, and run through the body by one of a band of English knights. His killer did not at first realize whom he had killed. Today, a great slab of North Wales granite has been placed near the spot at Cilmery where Llywelyn died. It seems a fitting memorial to the man whom the Welsh were later to call "Ein Llyw Olaf", Our Last Guide.

Dafydd was soon run to ground, and then hanged, drawn, and quartered at Shrewsbury. Llywelyn's unfortunate wife, Eleanor, had died giving birth to a daughter, Gwenllian. The child was packed off to a distant English nunnery at Sempringham. With one swift stroke, the pride and hope of an independent Wales had been decisively crushed. No wonder the poet Gruffydd ab yr Ynad Coch poured out his cry of despair in that wintry, unhappy December:

> O God, that the sea might engulf the land!
> Why are we left to long-drawn weariness?

It was not long, however, before the men of Gwynedd received proof that they were indeed a conquered race. The great Edwardian castles began to rise, almost as prison walls ringing the wilds of Snowdonia. Conway guarded the mouth of the Conway valley. Beaumaris and Caernarfon blocked both ends of the Menai Straits. Harlech and Criccieth watched from the west. Today the castles are part of the glories of North Wales. Then, they appeared as symbols of oppression.

Edward regulated his conquest of Wales with the Statute of Rhuddlan. The story that he promised to give the Welsh a new prince who would not speak a word of English, and then presented his infant son to them at Caernarfon, is a pretty legend. Edward was not much given to romantic gestures. Moreover Edward, his heir, was not made Prince of Wales until 1301. The conqueror was more intent on tidying up Welsh administration. He made most of Llywelyn's principality into English-type shires. Thus were created Anglesey, Caernarfonshire, Merioneth, Cardiganshire, and part of Carmarthenshire and Flint. The rest of Wales was not Edward's to play around with. It was in the jealous hands of the Lords Marchers, and they would tolerate no abatement of their privileges. English law prevailed in the boroughs. Edward did not intend to be harsh, but Welshmen were now excluded from many of the offices of the administration. The dream of independence was over. Welshmen had to make the best they could of the new world.

The Changing World of Wales

A curious calm seems to settle down over the affairs of Wales after the drama of the rise, glory, and death of Llywelyn the Last and the final flurries of revolt that followed. Was it the calm of despair? Or were there enough Welshmen who had decided to make the best of a bad world and come to terms with the new régime? The truth seems to lie half way between the two poles.

There were plenty of the court officials of Llywelyn – administrators from the family of Ednyfed Fychan, the famous seneschal of Llywelyn the Great – who were prepared to go on serving under Edward, or at least to compromise with him. And from the family of Ednyfed Fychan eventually sprang those supreme political realists, the Tudors. Llywelyn had himself encouraged a change in the direction of an administrative structure on English principles. The line of de-marcation between opposition and cooperation must have seemed very thin for both officials and the "uchelwyr", the high-placed men. They could bide their time. By the end of the fifteenth century we shall see them getting control of the ad-ministrative machinery of North Wales once again.

Outside Gwynedd, there must have been many small rulers who positively rejoiced at Llywelyn's fall. The full consequences of the loss of independence would take a hundred years to seep into the Welsh mind. With that realization came the wild explosion of protest that was the rising of Owain Glyndwr.

Even now, although the patronage of the princes had been removed, there was no falling off in the development of poetry. There were still enough powerful landowners and monasteries left to encourage the bards. Into the returning sun-light steps the jaunty figure of Dafydd ap Gwilym, one of the greatest poets that Wales ever produced, handling like a master a new, seductive metre, the "cywydd". The highly complicated, sonorous, aristocratic verse that was the cult of the Welsh court had now to give way to something far more popular. Dafydd was not alone as a practitioner of this new verse form. Others were before him. Even the trouba-dours of France may have influenced it. Of course, Dafydd was learned in the old forms as well. No one could be educated, and of noble birth, who did not have the classical metres at his tongue-tip. But the new form suited his mood like a glove.

He regards the English with disdain, their new towns as places to avoid. He sings the seagull scudding over the white waves, the free life in the woodland glades, and the adventures of love with more than willing women. He is nothing if not personal, a man made for the pleasures of the moment. Hear how, in Gwyn Williams's fine translation, he lures his love to the bracken with irresistible verve.

> Beauty, come to the hillside,
> Our bed be high on the hill,
> Four ages under fresh birches,
> The mattress of green leaves,
> Valanced with brilliant ferns,
> A coverlet, against beating rain,
> Of trees that check the shower.

That voice hardly comes from a nation in despair.

It was now, too, that the *Mabinogion*, the supreme achievement of Welsh medieval story-telling, was set down in writing in the Red Book of Hergest. These stories embody material that must go back to the twilight of Celtic history and to the magic before Christianity, even before Rome. Later heroes like Arthur are woven into the fabric. The *Mabinogion* stories cast a spell as you read them. Where were they written down? We do not know; perhaps in one of the Cistercian monasteries that still influenced Welsh life.

The Cistercians, or white monks, had always been the favourite order of the Welsh. The Benedictines clung cautiously to the skirts of the Norman castles and towns, but the white monks went out to cultivate the lonely places and to create the great moorland sheep-walks that were the basis of Welsh woollen production. Their monasteries are in ruins today, but the names of Strata Florida, Margam, Valle Crucis, and Cymer are still music to Welsh ears. Here were the scriptoria in which the monks laboured to copy the poetry, the chronicles, the prose romances that enabled Welsh literature to survive. No university grew up in Wales, although one was later projected by Owain Glyndwr. The place was far too poor and troubled to attract students in big numbers. Welshmen of talent trekked to Oxford and Paris. There were plenty of them.

The fighting men also had to enter the service of the English crown if they were to make any sort of a career. The Welsh borderlands in Gwent had been the home of the long bow, the weapon with which Edward III beat down the French at Crécy. Welsh archers made a major contribution to that famous victory. When the Black Prince was thrown from his horse, the banner of the Red Dragon of Wales was wrapped over him for protection. It was at Crécy, too, that the Welsh first plucked leeks and wore them in their hats as a mark of distinction.

This was the beginning of that continual emigration of men of talent and enterprise from Wales which has remained a feature of the national life. Yet all the time, behind this apparent acquiesence in the English conquest, something strange, fierce, and desperate was stirring.

The Glyndwr Revolt

Owain Glyndwr, Shakespeare's Owen Glendower, is still a magic name in Wales. He is the Welsh William Wallace, if you like – the last of the great men who had a chance to create an independent Wales. Shakespeare's Glendower boasted that

> All the courses of my life do show
> I am not in the role of common men.

Henry IV, in the same play, cries out against "that great magician, damned Glendower".

Indeed, there is something strange, almost inexplicable, in the sudden eruption of Glyndwr's revolt and in its staggering success. On the face of it, Glyndwr seems an unlikely man to have created a devastating social and political explosion. He was a member of the mixed society of the Marches. He had studied at the Inns of Court and been a witness at a court of chivalry with none other than the poet Geoffrey Chaucer. Glyndwr served against the Scots in 1385. He had an estate bringing him in a comfortable £200 a year, a very large income for the period. At the age of forty, he was a man of distinction, of proved loyalty to the English crown. True, he had a dispute with his neighbour, Lord Grey of Ruthin, and had lost the ear of the new king, Henry IV. But this was a typical Marcher quarrel. Why did it turn into a national revolt?

There were deeper forces at work, pressures building up around Owain, of which he may not have been aware at first. The Marches of Wales had suffered the same disasters that caused the Peasants' Revolt in England. The Black Death had also devastated Wales. The old tribal and pastoral bonds were loosening all through the century of English rule. A new class of rich peasants was forming, as the germ of the later gentry class. The burden of production and payments fell upon the "unfree", the lowest orders of society. In the minds of the oppressed there was only one way out of an intolerable situation – to go back to the rosy days when all Welshmen had apparently been free and independent under the princes of the past. The bards were there to lend irresistible power to the appeal. They could remind Owain that he was far more than a mere English-educated gentleman. The blood of the Princes of Powys ran in his veins. The Tudors were his cousins. They had been pledged to Richard II and bore no love for his supplanter. Siren voices surrounded Owain, whispering revolt.

On the 16th September 1400, a band of Welsh rebels boldly met at Glyndyfrdwy and declared Owain Glyndwr the rightful Prince of Wales. There was panic in London. Henry IV was feeling none too secure on his throne. He came rushing down to Wales, and for the moment the rebellion seemed checkmated. But then violent anti-Welsh legislation was forced through Parliament. The flames flickered again in Wales. Welsh students began to leave Oxford to join the rising, and on Good Friday 1401 it began in earnest. The Tudor brothers captured Conway Castle. Owain himself switched towards South Wales and won a brilliant victory on the slopes of Plynlimon. By 1402 the rebellion was in full swing.

A brilliant comet encouraged the Welsh, and Owain captured his old enemy, Lord Grey. He had a further success when he next captured Edmund Mortimer, one of the most powerful of the Marcher Lords. Henry tried once again to pin down this will-o'-the-wisp of a rebel, but his army floundered hopelessly in drenching rain – which only confirmed Glyndwr's reputation as a wizard. In vain Prince Henry burnt Sycharth, that pleasant seat of Owain's, so movingly celebrated by the Welsh poets, "girdled by its moat of shining water". Even the defeat of Hotspur at Shrewsbury did not affect the rise of Owain's power, which reached its zenith between 1404 and 1406. There was an extraordinary deal with Henry's enemies, Mortimer and Percy, Earl of Northumberland, which gave Glyndwr a Wales that was to run in a line from the Severn mouth to the Mersey. Harlech and Aberystwyth had fallen to him.

The intelligentsia now joined him, and Owain's schemes took on an impressive amplitude. Backed by men like John Trevor, Bishop of St Asaph, and the keen-minded lawyer Dr Gryffydd Young, Owain summoned two parliaments, at Machynlleth and Harlech. He had himself crowned Prince of Wales in the presence of envoys from France, Scotland, and Castile. He made St David's the metropolitan church of Wales and, by an imaginative stroke, planned to set up two universities, one in the north and one in the south, to train the administrators of his new Welsh state. The French sent a force to support him, and with it he marched into England as far as Worcester – and then fell back. He did not yet feel strong enough to abandon his guerilla tactics for pitched battles.

But by 1407 the impetus was dying out of the revolt. In 1408 Harlech and Aberystwyth were lost and many of Owain's family taken prisoners. The superior resources of England were now beginning to tell, for they were marshalled under a prince who was proving himself a master of war. The marvel was that Owain had been able to keep the revolt going at all. Few medieval social rebellions lasted more than a few months. Owain's lasted for years. The destruction it brought in its train was crippling.

By 1410 Owain was on the run, hunted as an outlaw. Henry V offered a pardon, but this was greeted with a disdainful silence. No one knows what happened to Glyndwr. Some say he took refuge with his relatives, the Scudamores, in the remote Golden Valley of Herefordshire. It would be pleasant to think of the old rebel, at his sunset, finding a country peace. Wherever he may have gone, Wales never forgot him. His is a name like Arthur's, with a peculiar magic attached to it. He would come again, men said, and the support that ultimately went to Henry Tudor was a direct result of the rebellion. One morning, so the story goes, Owain was walking on the hills near Valle Crucis Abbey, when he met the Abbot. "You are up betimes, Master Abbot," said Owain. "Nay, sire," replied the Abbot, "it is you who have risen too early – by a hundred years."

On the face of it, Glyndwr's rebellion appears to have failed completely. The dream of independence had vanished once again. Wales woke to a picture of a countryside in ruins, trade at a standstill, monasteries and manors plundered and burnt, towns devastated, castles wrecked, and cattle driven off or destroyed. The English adopted a scorched-earth policy; the Welsh had to levy toll on the population to find money for the struggle. We must beware of exaggeration, but it does seem that Owain's revolt left an appalling legacy of destruction and misery.

The social changes against which the revolt had been in some ways a despairing protest were speeded up. Wales of the squires emerged, with gangs of broken men taking to the wastes and moors. There was a legacy of hatred between the races as well. The authors of *The Libell of English Policye* could write, as late as 1436,

> Beware of Wales; Christ Jesu must us keep
> That it makes not our child's child to weep.

The poets, such as Lewis Glyn Cothi, were equally bitter on the Welsh side.

But, terrible though the experience had been, Welshmen were well aware that Owain had changed the course of their history. He had rekindled the flame of nationality. Owain may have departed into the mists, but the Welsh thereafter were never to lose the feeling that, come what might, they would remain a separate people – even when the laws bound them ever closer to England. Modern Wales, it has been truly said, really begins in 1410.

The Tudors

The wreckage left by the revolt of Glyndwr cluttered Welsh life throughout the fifteenth century. Strict penal laws against the Welsh remained on the statute book. The only career that seemed open to the adventurous was service with the English crown in the French wars. Many a Fluellin won distinction in the armies of Henry V. And soon there were other struggles nearer home. In the long anguish of the Wars of the Roses, Wales was a reservoir of men, a factor that could upset the balance of power. The Yorkists drew much of their support from the vast Mortimer estates on the border; the Lancastrians were stronger in South Wales. The major battles took place in England, but the repercussions of each victory and defeat were sorely felt in Wales. When Sir William Herbert of Raglan, who had been the most powerful figure in the government of Edward IV, was slain at Banbury, the number of prominent Welshmen who were killed with him made the battle a national disaster.

These wars were the swan song of the old-style barons, of those powerful Marcher Lords who had their own private armies and could afford to defy the royal writ. They committed suicide as a class in the treacherously shifting alliances, blood feuds, pointless battles and betrayals that make up the history of Wales as well as England for twenty years. And through it all the bards still nourished the hope that not even the anguish of the Glyndwr revolt had succeeded in killing: the hope that, one day, the deliverer – Arthur, Glyndwr, call him what you will – would appear and lead the nation back to recover the lands unlawfully stolen from them by the perfidious Saxon a thousand years before.

The Welsh clung to this hope with the fervour of the exiled Jews looking for their Messiah and their return to Jerusalem. It sustained them in their darkest hour. It might be totally irrational, improbable, laughable even, to the sober political realists among the Welsh themselves. Logic did not enter into it. The dream was important because it was believed in. And, as the miseries of civil war deepened, these hopes crystallized around one man – Henry Tudor.

The rise of the Tudors to the throne of England was one of those unlikely events that gave colour to the most extravagant claims of the bardic prophecies. Every card seemed stacked against the accession of this family from Anglesey to supreme power in London. The whole romantic story could have occurred only in a period of political chaos, when chance can play a more important part in life than the most careful planning.

The Tudor family were not exactly obscure in Wales. They took their origin from Ednyfed Fychan, who had been seneschal to Llywelyn the Great. This did not prevent the family from playing a double part throughout the fifteenth century. One branch became career men with the new English power. Others were "out" with Glyndwr and played a major part in the rising. Meredith Tudor was steward to the Bishop of Bangor. Amongst other property, he owned the estate of Pen-mynydd in Anglesey, the so-called "home of the Tudors", although the rather disappointing farmhouse was only part of the estate. Meredith survived the scandal of the family's connection with Owain Glyndwr – so successfully that his son Owain, anglicizing his name to Owen and leaving out the vast array of "ap"s (sons of) that traced his ancestry back to the Celtic mists, took service under Henry V.

Never was sexual attraction more potent in the history of Britain. This young Welshman, of no great fortune, was on the spot when Henry V died early, leaving his young widow, Katherine of France – beautiful, unsatisfied, and clearly in need of romance. The handsome Welshman bowled her over. The latest researches have still not decided the tricky point of whether they were married or not. But Katherine's son, Henry VI, obviously did not object, for he took Owen's sons, his step-brothers, into high favour.

Edmund became Earl of Richmond, and Jasper became Earl of Pembroke. Edmund married Margaret Beaufort, who was a descendant of John of Gaunt. Their son was Henry Tudor. It was through his mother, Margaret, that Henry inherited his extremely tenuous claim to the throne. And this claim would never have become important, or even have been made, if the Wars of the Roses had not developed into a series of massacres that thinned out the potential claimants. Owen Tudor himself, the founder of the family fortune with his incomparable gifts as a lover, was beheaded. He laid down his head on the block with a word to his executioner to be careful of a head that was "wont to lie in a queen's lap".

Jasper Tudor swiftly whipped off young Henry to the safety of Brittany. There he lived as an exile for fourteen years, while the bards never ceased to hail him as the ultimate heir to Arthur and Glyndwr. Dafydd Llwyd of Mathafarn was the chief prophet, and his words reverberated across Wales. Henry Tudor, born in Pembroke Castle, nursed by a Welsh nurse who may have taught him to speak the language, was the new Messiah.

In 1485 the Messiah actually landed near Dale on the west shores of Milford Haven. He had made some earlier attempts, but this time all was ready. Richard III was vulnerable. He was able but suspect. There were great lords like the Stanleys, with their land holdings on the Welsh border, who were wobbling in their loyalty. Henry's march from Dale was surrounded with the sort of incidents that glamorized Napoleon's return from Elba.

Sir Rhys ap Thomas, the magnate of South Wales, joined him. Sir Rhys had sworn to Richard that Henry would advance only over his body. Rhys got out of the difficulty, so the legend goes, by crouching under Mulloch bridge while Henry rode over it. Alas for the legend, Rhys appears to have joined Henry much later.

The Welsh flocked to Henry's standard as he marched up the west coast. Dafydd Llwyd, the bard, was waiting for him at Mathafarn, near Machynlleth, and prudently prophesied victory, on his wife's advice: "If he wins he'll never forget you, if he loses you can forget him." So, with an escort of Welsh magnates and droves of Welsh cattle following his army for supplies, Henry's motley array confronted Richard at Bosworth. The treachery of the Stanleys gave Henry the victory. Against all probability, a descendant of the chief administrator of Llewelyn the Great sat on the throne of England. His greatest achievement was that he stayed on it until he died. Bosworth was the last battle of the Wars of the Roses, and the nation was duly grateful.

For the Welsh the event was decisive. The whole nation felt that the long struggle with the English had ended in a glorious victory. The victory was an illusion, of course, and it was not long before some Welshmen were voicing their disappointment. But, all through the Tudor period and even under James I, Wales as a whole basked in the glow of Henry's astonishing adventure. There was no further call for another Owain Glyndwr. The successor of Arthur was now safely installed in Windsor, surrounded by his Yeomen of the Guard, many of them Welsh. The King's eldest son was christened Arthur, and his court was wide open to his countrymen. A Welsh job-rush followed. So many Welshmen came to London to seek their fortune that the somewhat atrabilious poet Skelton circulated the story that St Peter, tired with the clamour for better jobs of the Welshmen in Heaven, arranged for an angel to shout "Caws pobi" ("Toasted cheese") outside. Whereupon the Welshmen rushed out in a body, and St Peter slammed the Golden Gates behind them.

Largely on the authority of his *Life* by Bacon, Henry has come down to us as a cunning administrator with an eye for money, but with a skill in chopping magnates down to size. Welsh sources see him in a more attractive light: a lover of music, a patron of learning, an encourager of the new craft of printing who amply rewarded his Welsh supporters. Maybe he remained more of a medieval king than a man of the Renaissance, but he proved to be the one sort of king that both Wales and England needed at the time – a successful one.

The Union of Wales and England

The Wales that the Tudors won by battle was an administrative mess. It could be inconveniently divided into two parts. First, there was the principality set up by Edward I after the conquest, with shires on the English model. Here, in theory, English law was administered, and the King had direct power over his new and unwilling subjects. Second, there was the March – that complicated pattern of individual lordships, each with its own courts, its own legal system, and its fierce insistence on rights and privileges. The Wars of the Roses and the cunning of Henry VII had placed most of these Marcher lordships in royal hands, by the time Henry VIII came to the throne. But this did not lessen the determination of the Marcher officials to stay separate. The whole tenor of life in the Marcher lordships made the inhabitants unwilling to recognize any lord other than their local baron. It was high time that someone appeared who could bring order into this legal chaos. The man who did it – as he did so much else of vital significance in our history – was the formidable Thomas Cromwell, adviser of Henry VIII. He was able to do it because, although Henry VIII did not worry overmuch about Wales, Wales still worried about him. Henry was a Tudor. That, in the long run, made all things bearable.

Cromwell, in eight drama-packed years, had already transformed the administration of England. The break with Rome, the end of the monasteries, the establishment of the royal authority over the Church, had dragged the country out of the Middle Ages into the world of the modern nationalistic, sovereign states. In 1536 came the turn of Wales. There was, in fact, more than one Act uniting the two countries under a single administration. The Act of 1536 is usually given as the one by which Wales was firmly linked to England, but the Act of 1543 was far more detailed and comprehensive. No matter which you take, the final outcome was crystal clear. Henceforth Wales and England were indissolubly tied together. As the *Encyclopaedia Britannica* used to print, "For Wales, *see* England".

The changes were sweeping. All the Marcher lands were converted into shires. Some of the older shires were extended to take in neighbouring Marcher estates, but new shires were created in Monmouth, Brecon, Denbigh, Radnor, and Montgomery. Welshmen were granted political equality with Englishmen. Where it still survived, Welsh law was replaced by English law. The language of the courts was to be English. Wales would be represented in Parliament by her knights of the shires and burgesses of the boroughs.

Although the codes of law were assimilated, Wales was to have her Court of Great Sessions, her special system of law courts separate from Westminster. The country was divided into circuits. Monmouthshire alone was attached to West-minster by the Act of 1536. This was done merely for administrative convenience, "it being the nearest part of Wales to London and suitors could therefore appear in London without undue expense and hardship". But this exception placed Mon-mouthshire in the anomalous position in which it has continued to this day. In ecclesiastical affairs it is part of the Church in Wales. It has been included in Wales for the purpose of most subsequent Acts of Parliament – Licensing Acts, Education Acts, and the rest of them. Monmouthshire men are proud to play in the Welsh rugby team. But the county has also been given special treatment in other parliamentary Acts, with the result that it remains a place slightly apart, facing both ways.

The Council of Wales, originally set up by Henry VII, was given a statutory basis and centred at Ludlow. Welsh geography made it impossible to find a capital for Wales conveniently placed for both North and South. So Ludlow became the centre of Welsh legal and administrative life. Throughout Tudor times, the noble castle of warm red stone, where Milton's *Comus* would receive its first performance, was the local place of power. Here came the men with political and legal ambitions as their first step to Westminster. The great Presidents of the Council, men like Bishop Rowland Lee or Sir Henry Stanley, made their office effective. The Council of Wales at Ludlow seemed at times to be that separate government of which Welsh patriots had dreamt so long. And yet the whole of the Tudor settlement has received a distinctly bad press from nineteenth- and twentieth-century Welshmen.

But the intention of Henry VIII had been to give Welshmen what was conceived to be the best gift in his hands – total equality of opportunity with Englishmen. The new men, the Welsh gentry, became justices of the peace as the gentry did in England, and local administration was placed in the hands of the local families of importance. True, as one distinguished Welsh historian has remarked, many of them neither administered justice nor kept the peace. But even in turbulent Elizabethan Wales the new system proved itself efficient and popular.

The real danger in the Act to the national life was certainly never perceived by the Welshmen of the day or intended by the King. The provision that English would be the language of the courts and administration meant that inevitably the gentry, on whom the burden fell, turned to English – the language of success, promotion, and careers at top level in government. The process was begun that, in a hundred years, would anglicize the Welsh ruling class and separate it, linguistically and emotionally, from the bulk of the population, which remained Welsh-speaking. When, in the eighteenth century, the Welsh speakers were carried out of the Church of England by the Methodist revival, the gulf between gentry and people became deep indeed. The men who should have been the leaders of Wales were out of sympathy with all things Welsh. Their ambitions turned to England, to the excitement of careers in a far wider field than Wales. Their language could be a drawback to such men. "Speak no Welsh," wrote one North Wales squire to his son at Oxford, "to any that can speak English, no, not to your bedfellows, that thereby you may attain and freely speak the English tongue perfectly."

Welshmen had to change not only their tongue, but their style of nomenclature as well. The old style did not fit into the English pattern. In the old days a man's status depended upon his ancestry. He had been proud to trace it back in his own name, embellished with many an "ap" (son of). Thus a Welshman of breeding would announce himself as Hywel ap Iorwerth ap Llywelyn ap Rhys – and so on through as many generations as he cared to remember. This was far too cumbersome a system to fit into the new structure of English law. Henry VIII suggested that men might care to take their names from their place of residence. A few followed this system. Most simply selected their two most easily understood names or had them selected for them by lawyers. It was safer, when a man might have to appear in the new law courts. Ap Ivan became Bevan; ap Hywel, Powell. And the hordes of Thomases, Joneses, and Evanses sprang up throughout the land.

This change to English manners did not happen overnight. Rather was it a steady sapping of the gentry's Welshness – a process that went on into the time of the early Stuarts. The change wasn't visible immediately. The bards were still welcomed in many homes and great houses. Sir John Wynn, the North Wales magnate, may have sent his sons to be educated at Westminster School, but he made his daughters-in-law learn Welsh. One of the greatest Welsh poets, William Llyn, was an Elizabethan. Under Elizabeth the squirarchy was still notably Welsh and proud of its pedigrees – to the mockery of the English. They told the story with relish of the day when James I was surrounded by a crowd of Welshmen on horseback. To get out of the dust, James ordered that the best gentlemen should ride ahead. All immediately rode on, except one. "Are you not a gentleman?" asked James. "Oh, yes, so please Your Majesty," came the reply, "as good as the rest, only my horse is not so good."

Well mounted or not, the leading Welshmen were now solid Crown supporters. How could they be otherwise, when the Tudors had offered them a government that was both lucrative and emotionally satisfying? When Henry VIII did away with the monasteries, he met no opposition in Wales. They had long ceased to be a power in the land. They were not dens of vice; rather were they comfortable snuggeries for monks who made no particular contribution to the national life. True, there were one or two monks whose conduct demanded some explanation. One of the five monks who remained in Strata Florida was put in Carmarthen jail, charged with counterfeiting in his monastic cell. Abbot Salisbury was arrested for highway robbery at Oxford. But these men were not typical. The average monastery had the air of an institution that had seen better days. These Welsh monks, one senses, were almost glad to be pensioned off.

Even the destruction of the wonder-working shrines failed to produce any violent popular reaction. The shrine of the Virgin at Penrice in the Rhondda was broken up at night, but the burning of the wooden image of St Devel the Mighty from Llandderfel, the end of the miraculous image of the Virgin with her Taper at Cardigan, and the closing of St Winefride's Well created no disturbance. Bishop Barlow of St David's was an active suppressor of pilgrimages and destroyer of relics. He also stripped the lead from the roof of the bishops' palace in St David's, thus ruining one of the finest ecclesiastical buildings in Wales. But not even Barlow's activities succeeded in disturbing the supine quiet with which the Reformation was received by the bulk of the population in Wales.

There was some compensation in the fact that Sir John Price of Brecon later translated the *King's Primer* into Welsh. This contained the Lord's Prayer, the Creed, and the Ten Commandments. His work had no title. It is simply known by its first words, "Yny lhyvyr hwnn" ("In this book"). When the type was set up, the author found that he had left out the eighth commandment. But this was the first book actually printed in the Welsh language.

The faster pace of religious change under Edward VI caused some concern in Wales, and there was no real resistance to the restoration of Catholicism under Mary. The principality supplied only three martyrs, the most notable one being Robert Farrer, Bishop of St David's who was sent to Carmarthen to be burnt. When Elizabeth came to the throne, Wales once again obligingly turned about with no trouble. Prominent Catholic clergy were given permission to go into exile, and there was no great inclination to protest at any of the terms of the Elizabethan Church settlement. Some gentry still clung to Catholic practice, but showed no desire to be martyred for the faith. In many of the remoter parishes, Catholic ritual still went on simply because it seemed the natural thing. No one in Wales wanted change for the sake of change in matters of religion. The Methodist awakening was two hundred years away.

Wales had its share of the attempts by the Catholic exiles, under the inspiration of the Counter Reformation, to rekindle the old devotion of the country to Catholicism. Welsh priests, trained abroad, were smuggled back into the country. Some were caught and executed, but again the net results of their effort must have seemed very discouraging to the men of zeal who sent them. The return of 1603 gives the number of communicants with the Established Church as over two hundred thousand. The figure of recusants is only eight hundred and eight. Catholics formed less than half of one per cent of the religious population.

The extreme Puritan cause had even fewer adherents, in spite of the fiery advocacy of John Penry, who took a hand in the notorious Martin Marprelate tracts that so vexed the heads of the Church of England in Elizabeth's day. Penry can, however, claim to have made one important contribution to the future of Wales. He was one of the chief advocates of a full translation of the Bible into Welsh.

There had been part translations before, notably the efforts of William Salesbury. But this pioneer scholar had unfortunate ideas about orthography. He latinized Welsh words wholesale and made his translations virtually unintelligible even to scholars. Finally, a new and definitive translation did appear in 1588, the work of Dr William Morgan, the vicar of Llanrhaeadr-ym-Mochnant, assisted by two other scholars. Morgan eventually became a bishop, but it is hard not to picture him at work in his lonely vicarage at Llanrhaeadr, with the dark mountains of the Berwyns all around, far from the libraries of Oxford and Cambridge, and yet producing that miracle of powerful and poetic Welsh we call Y Beibl Cymraeg.

The Welsh Bible has the same merits as the English Authorized Version, issued under James I. The language is unforgettable; the sentences sang themselves into the hearts and minds of the people of Wales. This translation appeared at a time when the status of Welsh was in dispute. At one stroke it established the language. Whatever happened to Welsh from now on, there was no danger that it would degenerate into an ill-considered dialect spoken by a peasantry without power. The lower orders had been given a guide to the greatness of the tongue they spoke.

This triumph was possible only because Wales too, in spite of its remoteness, had felt the stirring of the Renaissance. The movement came to Wales as a direct result of her closer contact with England. A strong school of humanists grew in Wales. They felt, indeed, a double loyalty. The enormous prestige of Latin and Greek overwhelmed them, yet they had inherited from Geoffrey of Monmouth the claim that the Welsh were themselves descended from the Trojans, and their language had thus the prestige of measureless antiquity. The Welsh of the Bible represents the final triumph of the humanists. They had also done a service to their country in the grammars they produced, and the magnificent manuscript collections they made of the remains of old Welsh writing wherever they found it. Yet, inevitably, the tide of anglicization grew in strength. Jesus College in Oxford was founded in 1571 and became the Welsh centre of the university, but not a centre of Welsh speaking or scholarship. The Elizabethan grammar schools had no place for the language in their curriculum. As the Age of Elizabeth ended and the Age of the Stuarts began, Wales was getting ready to sink her individuality totally in her union with England.

The Civil War

The almost mystical loyalty that Wales had shown to the Tudors was now easily transferred to their successors, the early Stuarts. The gentry, the leaders of the nation, were now firmly linked to England. There lay their fountain of honour, their hopes of a career on the stage of the big world. Squire William Vaughan of Llangyndeyrn declared roundly: "I rejoice that the memorial of Offa's Ditch is extinguished with love and charity: that our green leeks, somewhat offensive to your dainty nostril, are now tempered with your fragrant roses . . . God give us grace to dwell together without enmity, without detraction". Common British citizenship was now something to be guarded with enthusiasm. When James ascended the throne, it was that prolix Welshman Sir William Maurice, M.P. for Caernarfonshire, who bored his fellow-members with his long-winded exhortations to hail James as King of a new country – not England but Great Britain. The Welsh distinguished themselves from the newer Britons by giving themselves the curious hybrid title of Cambro-Britons. James sniffed their Welsh incense with high approval.

He was also one with the Welsh in continuing to support the Council of Wales at Ludlow. The lawyers in London, who were becoming consolidated with the Parliamentary opposition, disliked it as being outside the orbit of the common law; the border counties protested that, by being tied to it, they were being deprived of their "birthright to the laws of this kingdom". The Welsh felt nothing but affection for it. James might strain Welsh loyalty a little by his use of monopolies, and Charles I still more by his arbitrary government, but Wales on the whole was a pro-Stuart part of the country. The Welsh paid ship money with none of the outcry made by John Hampden. The Spanish pirates were rampant along the coast; Catholic Ireland was just across the water. The Welsh saw the point of a strong, efficient fleet.

This does not mean that Wales went along quietly as a passenger when the Stuart ship ran into the storms that led to the Civil War. As Charles I applied the financial screws necessary to govern without Parliament, the new Welsh M.P.s were far more critical of Stuart policy than in the past. But the real test of their loyalty was now ahead, and when Charles in 1642 raised his standard at Nottingham there was no doubt which way most of Wales would turn. All those long years of favour from the Tudors and James I paid off. Wales became the "nursery of the King's infantry".

The great explosive force that impelled the Parliamentary party to rebellion – Puritanism – had no great roots in Wales. The merchant class, which supplied the sinews of war for Parliament, was weak in Wales. The economics of the country were still simple. There was some wealth in the lead mines of Cardiganshire, ready money came from the exports of the black Welsh cattle, and the trading class was growing in the little coastal towns. But there was nothing to compare with the City of London, the rich agricultural area of East Anglia, the great fleets of merchantmen sailing out of the Thames and the Humber. Wales was poor and therefore royal. The two main centres of Parliamentary effort in the principality were both exceptions to the general economic structure.

Sir Thomas Myddelton held Chirk Castle and Ruthin for Parliament, and would prove himself a thorn in the Royalist side, but his family roots lay with the money-men in the City of London. In West Wales, the merchants of Haverford-west and Pembroke were linked with Bristol and had control of the Irish trade. They were the strong point of Parliamentary resistance in the county. The Earl of Pembroke, with his stronghold at Cardiff Castle and his influence in the Vale of Glamorgan, was anti-Royalist; but the opposition of this ill-tempered man probably rose out of personal pique. In the opening moves, these Parliamentary centres were naturally on the defensive in face of the overwhelming Royalist feeling in the rest of the country. At Raglan, the Catholic Marquis of Worcester was prodigal in pouring out his wealth for his King. Before the struggle ended he would have spent over £400,000 in the cause of Charles – an enormous sum for those days. It was to Raglan that Charles dispatched his son, Prince Charles, for safe keeping. King Charles himself moved to Chester and made certain of his supply line to North Wales and Ireland. North Wales provided a big contingent of the foot that marched to Edgehill as the King began his first major move on London. They did not behave with much distinction in the battle, but proved their worth later at Brentford.

Considering the important part they played in all the major campaigns of the war, we know curiously little of the feelings and origin of these Welsh soldiers. They seem to have been looked upon as cannon-fodder, something on which the Royalists could always rely. None of them kept a diary. Many could not speak a word of English, a fact that caused their undoing at Naseby, when the Welsh camp-followers got their noses cut and throats slit under the impression that they were the hated Irish. These peasants from Carmarthenshire or Anglesey must have wondered at times what it was all about and for whose cause they were fighting. They took time to get hardened to the discipline that was now demanded. As raw levies they frequently broke, but, once experienced in the business, they formed a hard, reliable core to the Royalist armies.

The major moves of the first year of the Civil War inevitably took place outside Wales. The King could be reasonably sure of his Welsh base, and his aim was to strike directly at London, the seat of rebellion. After Edgehill, he pushed on to the outskirts of the city. But here he was held, and fell back to the west. In 1643 he still had the initiative, and he struck for London again, with a three-pronged advance. For its success he needed to capture the three great Parliamentary strongholds of Bristol and Gloucester in the west and Hull in the north. Prince Rupert carried Bristol with the help of a large contingent of Welsh troops under Sir John Owen of Clenennau, who was severely wounded. Encouraged by this victory, Richard Vaughan, Lord Carbery, attacked south Pembrokeshire, cap-tured Tenby and Haverfordwest, and penned the Parliamentarians into Pembroke. But these successes were offset by the failure to capture Hull in the north, and above all by the resistance of Gloucester in the west.

Gloucester's resistance had serious repercussions for the whole of the Royalist cause in Wales. Lord Herbert of Raglan laid siege to it, but he was utterly defeated in the Forest of Dean at Highnam, and, even when the King himself took over,

Essex and the Parliamentary army succeeded in reprovisioning the city with the heroic march of the London train-bands. This has been called the psychological turning-point of the Civil War. If Gloucester had gone, the King would have had uninterrupted access to his Welsh recruiting grounds. Now, the rich south-east corner of Wales was isolated by the wide Severn and hostile Gloucester. Even worse, Pembroke in the far west still threatened the royal supply route to Ireland.

And Ireland was now becoming an important factor in the calculations of the King. As Parliament turned to Scotland, so Charles looked across the Irish Sea for help. Here Pembroke played a critical role, since Parliament had the fleet and could reinforce Pembroke, recapture Tenby and Pembrokeshire, and interrupt the Irish supply route. With the line through South Wales lost, Charles in 1644 had to make certain of his North Wales route to Ireland. At first his troops were successful. Archbishop Williams forgot his cloth, seized Conway Castle, and helped the contingents from Ireland onward. The Parliamentarians fell back from their recent conquests of Wrexham, Hawarden, Flint, and Mold. The Royalists advanced into Cheshire, but again all hopes were dashed when Fairfax routed them at Nantwich.

Prince Rupert had been given a completely free hand to try to reorganize the royal resources in Wales, but the dashing commander had found it an ungrateful task. One of his officers lamented: "If your Highness shall be pleased to command me to the Turk, or Jew or Gentile, I will go on my bare feet to serve you, but from the Welsh, good Lord, deliver us." The Welsh might have uttered the same prayer for delivery from Rupert's exactions, for the civil population was getting increasingly hostile to the demands of the army. There was even less enthusiasm when Rupert himself was heavily defeated at Marston Moor in July 1644. He came back to Wales to learn of yet another Royalist disaster. In September, outside the walls of Montgomery Castle, the Royalists were hopelessly crushed in the biggest battle fought in Wales during the Civil War. A wedge was driven between the Royalists in North and South Wales, and 1645 dawned drearily for the King.

The Parliamentary forces had been reorganized. The New Model Army was getting ready to take the field. In vain a flash of hope came to the royal army as the able professional soldier Sir Charles Gerard marched down to South-West Wales and swept the Parliamentarians under Laugharne back to their bases at Pembroke and Tenby. Charles's main and last big army was crushed by Fairfax and Cromwell's Ironsides at Naseby. The King's Welsh Infantry fought stubbornly, then surrendered. The patient cannon-fodder had had enough.

Gerard had no option. He fell back and rejoined the unhappy Charles at Raglan Castle. In vain they tried to raise new armies. The Welsh were alienated by the behaviour of the royal professionals, brutalized in Continental wars. The gentry themselves were restive. Charles went north and looked out from the walls of Chester, to see his last hope smashed on Rowton Heath. The Parliamentary forces mopped up the castles in North and South. Harlech was the last fortress in England and Wales to haul down the royal flag, on the 15th March 1647.

The second Civil War did not last long. In Wales it began in Pembrokeshire, where there had been much mutual recrimination among the victors. Poyer refused to surrender Pembroke Castle to Fleming, who had been appointed to relieve him. The revolt swept South Wales, but a section of the formidable New Model Army was sent down under Colonel Horton. It crushed the insurgents in a furious fight at St Fagan's, just outside Cardiff. Cromwell himself came and took charge of the siege of Pembroke Castle. It surrendered after forty-eight days. Poyer was shot. The rising in North Wales was quickly stamped out. Wales was now at the mercy of Parliament, or rather of the Army. Charles I himself was executed in 1649. Two Welshmen were among those who signed the death warrant – Colonel John Jones of Maesygarnedd, in Merioneth, and Thomas Wogan, M.P. for Cardigan boroughs.

The economy of Wales recovered fairly speedily from the Civil Wars. There was much "slighting" of castles. Raglan was deliberately destroyed; some private houses were burnt. But there had been no scorched-earth policy on the scale of the Glyndwr revolt. The main battles of the Civil Wars had been fought outside Wales. The fighting had interrupted the great cattle drives that brought in so much of Wales's badly needed ready money; but the wounds of war, as Professor Dodd has pointed out, are soon healed in an agricultural and pastoral community. It was the social, religious, and moral wounds that took time to heal. The gentry suffered; their world seemed in ruins. The victors were faced with re-organizing a country in which they knew they were unpopular.

In a spirit of grim dedication, the Army and Cromwell began to rule Wales. They meant well. They would have preferred to have the cooperation of the conquered. Cromwell sighed with frustration: "I am as much for government by consent as any man, but where will we find consent?" Not, on the whole, from the Welsh.

The first task, the Commonwealth rulers felt, was to encourage the advance of Puritanism. From 1650 to 1653 one of Cromwell's ablest officers, Colonel Harrison, held power under the Commission for the Propagation of the Gospel, and Wales had an astonishing measure of administrative autonomy. There was even a plan to give Wales a separate University. But nothing could disguise the fact that it was government by a minority. The gentry held aloof or were excluded. And there was a thorough purge of the Welsh Church – although it was remarkable how many clergymen succeeded in retaining their livings after a little judicious stretching of their conscience. The attempt to spread the Puritan gospel, however, produced disappointing results.

There had been small nonconformist movements in Wales before the Civil Wars, notably those associated with the names of Walter Cradock, Vavasor Powell, and Morgan Llwyd. In 1649 John Miles had established the first Baptist chapel at Ilston in Gower. And it was to these men, and others like them, that the Commissioners first turned. Some of these Commissioners were powerful in the eyes of the London authorities: Colonel Philip Jones of Llangyfelach was the force in South Wales, as Colonel John Jones, the regicide, was in North. But, despite all the efforts of the itinerant preachers, the cause did not seem to prosper. George Fox came to Wales, and had a remarkable vision on Cader Idris, convincing him that "God would raise up a people to himself in that area". All in vain. Vavasor Powell was disillusioned when Cromwell turned out the Rump and proclaimed himself Lord Protector. "Cromwell," declared Powell, was the "dissemblingest purjured villain." Cromwell replied with the experiment of the Major Generals; and Wales was allotted to Major General James Berry, a fair-minded man who was equally unsuccessful in getting calm and goodwill in Wales.

Yet the longer the Commonwealth lasted, the more the gentry and other opponents came to terms with it. Wales, said one diehard Royalist bitterly, had become a nation of trimmers. Many a man now felt, with Howell Gwynne of Carmarthenshire: "Heigh god, heigh devil, I will be for the strongest side". And it is easy to see that most of the country would have settled for the *status quo* if Cromwell had not died in 1658 at the age of fifty-nine. In the year of crisis that followed, everything went into the melting-pot. As the Welsh said, "When a kingdom is tossed in a blanket, happy are they who are out of it".

The tossing ended in 1660. King Charles II enjoyed his own again. The conduits in Carmarthen town ran with wine. Vavasor Powell was flung into jail; Colonel John Jones met the death of a regicide with impressive courage; Thomas Wogan escaped overseas. John Miles led his congregation off to America to found the settlement of what was then called Swanszey, Massachusetts.

As for Colonel Philip Jones, of Llangyfelach, not only did he escape with his life, but he performed the remarkable feat of keeping all the land he had confiscated from the Royalists, ending up as High Sheriff of Glamorgan in 1671.

The Supine Century

On the face of it, the hundred years that followed the Restoration of Charles II are the least eventful years in Welsh history. The wars, revolts, high tragedies, and dramatic reversals of fortune that had been the pattern of life in Wales from the Dark Ages fade away into a grey lassitude. The forces that were to transform the national life in the late eighteenth and the nineteenth centuries were not yet stirring. In politics, Wales drifted in the wake of England.

The Civil Wars had ruined the smaller gentry. The Restoration exalted the big lords. What national cause was there now left to stir the blood? England's enemies were the Dutch or the French. Neither threatened the Welsh coast in the way the Spaniards had once done. The rulers of Wales had become completely anglicized. Their lives were linked with the power game in London. The country continued to produce outstanding men, but they won their fame on a bigger stage than Wales. In the post-Restoration period Wales produced a Lord Chancellor, two Secretaries of State, two Speakers of the House of Commons, and a host of lesser but nevertheless distinguished people. Sir John Vaughan, of Trawscoed, was the judge who established the freedom of juries to decide according to their consciences. Even Judge Jeffreys now has his apologists. But all this took place outside Wales.

Within the principality, politics was simply a rivalry for lucrative places and positions. The followers of the great men looked to their leaders for their reward. Elections became occasions for glorious corruption, seats in Parliament the preserve of prominent families. Bulkeleys represented Anglesey for fifty-three years after the Restoration. The Harleys ruled Radnorshire. Myddeltons were always elected for Denbighshire, and Vaughans for Montgomeryshire. Carmarthen borough sent a scion of the Vaughans of Golden Grove to represent the burgesses in Parliament for a solid sixty-two years.

No political principles were really involved in the election battles. A certain amount of religious anxiety appeared when James II made his attempt to gain toleration for Catholicism, but on the whole Wales behaved like the Vicar of Bray – all things to all kings. James planned to raise a Prince of Wales regiment of ten thousand men, and met with a favourable response. Yet when the same King went to Ireland to recover his throne, Wales cheerfully raised the force now known as the Royal Welch Fusiliers to help his rival, William of Orange. When William died and Anne reigned, the Welsh dutifully applauded. The Hanoverians were hardly a dynasty to inspire enthusiasm. There was a certain amount of toasting of the Old and Young Pretenders among such societies as the Cycle of the White Rose in the North and the Circle of Sea Serjeants in the South, but, when the Jacobites were put to the test, few of them were prepared to risk life and limb in the cause.

The Welsh magnate of North Wales, Sir Watcyn Williams Wynn, was confidently expected by Prince Charles Edward to raise North Wales in his favour. The Prince wrote to him from Preston as he advanced southwards: "I am persuaded that you will not break my expectation". And indeed Sir Watcyn might have led a party of Welsh Jacobites to join Bonnie Prince Charlie if the Prince's letter had not gone astray. Or would he have contented himself with waiting on the result before he declared himself? We shall never know. A few Welshmen did join, and some fought at Culloden. But the long-awaited Welsh Jacobite rising never took place, and Wales turned back to her slumbers. One Jacobite, Henry Lloyd, took service with Catherine the Great of Russia and became one of the most celebrated writers on military tactics of the day. His books influenced the young Napoleon, who read them at his military academy.

The Church in Wales as well seemed to snore through the supine century. It is fatally easy to collect examples of slothful, corrupt, and even criminal bishops, for the Welsh Church offers an astonishing gallery of oddities. There was William Beaw, who had been a soldier of fortune in Europe and "picked up the little bishopric of Llandaff in expectation of quick preferment". He never got it, and for a quarter of a century he neglected his bishopric – "a disease," as he called the bishopric, "which none of my predecessors were suffered to labour under so long". James's nominee to St David's, Thomas Watson, was tried for simony and found guilty. A Bishop of Bangor begged the Archbishop to transfer him before induction to his benefice "just to save me the trouble of a long journey". Few of the Georgian bishops laboured long in their remote and unpopular dioceses. Candidates for ordination often had to journey over the border to find their appropriate bishop. The Bishop of Gloucester was amused to be importuned by a "little Welsh deacon who fled hither from his native mountains by accident, like a wood cock in a mist". It was amusing for the Bishop, but hardly for the "little Welsh deacon" and his distant flock.

Of course there were good prelates like George Bull, the saintly bishop whom Anne appointed to St David's. And it must not be forgotten that the founder of the Society for Promoting Christian Knowledge, Dr Bray, was born just across the border from Welshpool and was educated at Oswestry Grammar School. Two of his closest collaborators were Sir Humphrey Mackworth, the Neath industrialist, and Sir John Philipps, the Pembrokeshire magnate. The S.P.C.K. opened charity schools in Wales and helped to stir the national conscience.

But the general tone of the Georgian Church and the general religious background in Wales are not inspiring. No bishop appointed between the accession of George I and 1870 was capable of preaching in Welsh. The greatest Welsh poet of the period, Goronwy Owen, was left to break his heart as an obscure curate.

Social life was hardly better. The squirarchy was totally cut off from the lower orders. The rift, begun under the Tudors, was now complete. The peasantry were by no means brutish and broken in spirit, but they lived their own life; they knew little and cared less about the world above them. The nation, if it still thought of itself as a nation, seemed to be waiting. But no one could be quite certain for what event it waited. There were no bards to prophesy another Arthur or Glyndwr. That would have seemed absurd in the Age of Reason.

But, when the event occurred, it was seen not to have any connection with cold reason. No national revival in Wales ever had.

The Methodist Revival

Once again Wales displayed her extraordinary powers of recovery, but this time the first impetus came from an unexpected source – religion; and from an unexpected quarter – the peasantry and lower orders of society. The Methodist Revival, the first of the two great forces that created modern Wales, had been in gestation for some time before the 1730s. After the experiment of Commonwealth rule, nonconformist communities had continued to develop in Wales. They were always small, but Baptists and other dissenters had passed through the fire of persecution under the Test Acts, and their leaders were men of quality. The standard of the educational academies they set up was high – even Anglicans sent their sons to them in preparation for the universities. These held the seeds of hope for the future.

The S.P.C.K., and the Welsh Trust formed to distribute Welsh bibles, had already entered the field. Above all, Griffith Jones, the vicar of Llanddowror in Carmarthenshire, had begun his remarkable work in creating his circulating schools, which spread through West Wales, using Welsh as the medium of instruction and comparatively humble men as teachers. Griffith Jones is the link between the older reformist spirit and the remarkable group of young men who, in a relatively short time, launched a Methodist movement in South Wales. Howell Harris, the gifted organizer; William Williams of Pantycelyn, who gave it a battle cry with his hymns; and Daniel Rowland, the preacher who could move vast audiences to terror and exaltation – these were the three first giants of the revival. A later generation, headed by Thomas Charles, spread the movement in the North and consolidated the administrative structure. Inevitably the leaders were drawn into the orbits of Wesley and Whitfield, who, in England, were beginning to penetrate the Church of England with their new fervour for mystical religious experience.

But Welsh Methodism always maintained its own character and independence. The men who began the revival had no intention of breaking away from the Church, but the Church could not possibly hold such enthusiasts. The final break was long in coming, but was devastating for the Church of England when it came. The new Methodist Church took with it great numbers of the Welsh people. And not only that. The older dissenting bodies were stirred into emulation of Methodist ways. They too began to grow in numbers. Every one of the converts – Methodist or otherwise – came from the "hen Eglwys Lloegr", the old Church of England.

Within fifty years the land became dotted with chapels, rivals to the churches – little "causes" in remote villages, each with its memory of the stalwarts who founded it, of the financial and social sacrifices they made, of the "saints" who sustained it in the early days. The chapel, not the church, now held the loyalty of the people. Architecturally, it might not compare with the older building, although the early chapels that survive have a moving simplicity. Too often the inscription "ail-adeiladwyd" (rebuilt) appears above the door, showing that the chapel has moved away from the whitewashed walls towards pillars and even spires in some cases, as the land grew richer and the faithful more prosperous. But Chapel and Church confront each other all through the Wales of the nineteenth and early twentieth centuries. The Church stood for the gentry, the landowners, the alien traditions of England and Toryism. The Chapel sprang from the people. It was democratic in form, radical in politics, and Welsh in thought and speech.

The Methodist Revival, and the other religious movements that accompanied it, gave Wales new leaders to replace the anglicized gentry. It gave an impetus to the use of the Welsh language. It gave the peasantry a new respect for itself, new standards of conduct, new habits of industry. But there were losses, too. Wales after the revival was a sterner place. The dancers, the fiddlers, the carefree interlude-players, the laughter in the ale-houses died before the strict admonition to men that their first duty was to save their souls from Hell. In the walls of the porch of the little church of Llanfair Discoed in Monmouthshire is the inscription:

> WhoEver hear on Sunday
> Will Practis Playing At Ball
> it May Be before Monday
> The Devil Will Have you All.

Before such disapproval, the old boisterous games around the churchyard on the day of rest would disappear. The Welsh Sunday was on its way.

The Church would not stay in its eighteenth-century stupor for long. There would be a strong reform movement in the mid-nineteenth century. The Church would turn back to Wales again. There would be church-rebuilding, new schools, churchmen and bishops who could speak in Welsh, a new determination to get closer to the people. But all this lay in the future. For the moment, the ordinary people of Wales were going to live their lives outside the Church and in the Chapel.

The Methodists were no revolutionaries in social and political life. Their concern with the inward life made them conservative in outward affairs. But the other dissenting bodies had a more radical temper and a more intellectual cast of mind. At the same time as the Methodists were stirring the emotional life of Wales, the Dissenters, who had already been outside the Church for two hundred years, were turning their attention to the question of political as well as religious liberty. From their ranks came Dr Richard Price, the greatest political theorist Wales has produced. Price was the man who published the *Observations on the Nature of Civil Liberty*, which had such a profound influence on the political thinking of the revolutionary Americans. He hailed the French Revolution, and his sermon "On the Love of Country" provoked Edmund Burke to reply with his "Reflections on the Revolution in France". David Williams became a deist and an honorary citizen of the French Republic. Rousseau declared himself Williams's most devoted disciple. The men of the literary romantic movement, which was now budding in Wales as well as England, felt the excitement. Iolo Morgannwg (Edward Williams), a remarkable stonemason who was also a historian, a collector of manuscripts, and a dazzling literary forger, sang with determination:

> If a tyrant King I meet,
> Clench fist and knock him down!

Iolo was deeply influenced by David Williams's cult of Nature, as Robespierre was when he established his cult of the Supreme Being. Iolo anticipated Robespierre by inventing the esoteric ritual of the Gorsedd, compounded of nature worship and the supposed lore of the ancient Druids, with a dash of Christianity thrown in. The first Gorsedd met at the summer solstice of 1792 and the improbable place of Primrose Hill in London. And the visitors who gaze fascinated on the Archdruid, leading his white-robed brethren to crown and chair the bard at the modern Eisteddfod, would be distinctly surprised to find that the whole ceremonial had its roots in such revolutionary theorizing.

But any remote chance that the Welsh would develop a real revolutionary movement ended in 1797 with the French invasion of Pembrokeshire.

This was a somewhat farcical episode, in which a French expeditionary force, consisting mainly of men liberated from prison and of galley convicts, under the command of an American named Tate, landed near Fishguard – in default of Bristol. The plan of the invasion, however, was not entirely absurd. The brilliant young French general, Lazare Hoche, had hopes that he could start a sort of peasants' rising of the poor against the rich if only a token force set foot on British soil. Perhaps the ideas of David Williams were bearing fruit in France after all.

The winds prevented the two ships of the expedition from sailing up the Bristol Channel. The only alternative was to go ashore in Pembrokeshire. Tate proved an incompetent leader. He disembarked his men on the wildest part of Strumble Head. They immediately began looting, drinking, and terrorizing the farms. The first British commander on the scene, Colonel Knox, was too cautious, and Tate was able to get his men into some sort of order and advance towards Goodwick. But now the energetic Lord Cawdor was racing up with the Castlemartin Yeomanry. Legend maintains that before his arrival the crowd of Welsh countrywomen in their red petticoats and tall hats were mistaken by the French for red-coated soldiers coming up as reinforcements. Tate's men were in no condition to fight. When Cawdor moved into the attack, Tate sued for terms. The French laid down their arms on Goodwick Sands and the "last invasion of Britain" was over.

It had one important effect in Wales. The shock of it killed all sympathy with France and any taste the Welsh might still have for revolution. The next wave of radical revolt was to come from another area – the new industrial towns and villages of the developing South Wales coalfield.

The Arrival of Industry

Methodism was the first, and industry the second, of the two forces that remoulded Wales in the late eighteenth century. Wales, before the new mines and factories started to rise among the hills of Glamorgan and Monmouthshire and along the coalfield of Flint, was basically an agricultural country. There were lead mines in Cardiganshire and small industries scattered here and there in South Wales, but nearly all the people lived directly off the land as their forefathers had done. The sheep on the uplands produced wool that went for export, and the black cattle of Cardigan and the western counties were driven into England for sale. As London and the Midland cities grew, the cattle became of prime importance to Wales. Vast herds were driven across the countryside on the lonely mountain tracks that avoided the big towns. The bellowing cattle swam rivers, with the drovers mounted on their sturdy ponies following them like Wild West cowboys. Rural Wales today has, in out-of-the-way places, many inns called the Drover's Arms. The drover was the banker, the postman, or the adventurer of the countryside. The "cattle fleet" brought back ready money.

The Industrial Revolution came to break up this simple economy. It came later to Wales than to England. The country was isolated, its roads were poor, and its landowners had little capital to finance new industries. The big money and the big iron-men arrived from England. All along the northern outcrop of the South Wales coalfield, iron-smelting started to grow with impressive swiftness. From Hirwaun, through Merthyr Tydfil and Tredegar to Blaenafon (a strip eighteen miles long and one mile wide), the ironworks filled the air with the clang of their hammers and the smoke of their furnaces. By 1801, the little village of Merthyr had become the biggest town in Wales, with a population of over seven thousand.

It beat Swansea by at least a hundred and seventy heads. Cardiff and Newport had not yet begun their explosive growth. A customs official could say of Cardiff: "We have no coal exported from this port, nor ever shall, as it would be too expensive to bring it down here from the internal part of the country". But soon the canals, and later the railways, would let coal move down to the sea as easily as iron. The strange industrial landscape of South Wales, with its strings of houses wedged into narrow valleys and its coal tips crawling up the hill-sides, was in process of formation.

In North Wales the slate industry was starting to become important. New houses, rushed up to accommodate the workmen, needed slate roofs on a big scale. The quarries started to bite into the mountains of Snowdonia, the modest beginnings of the excavations we see today at Bethesda and Llanberis.

With all this industrial growth came the rise of an industrial proletariat, up-rooted from the countryside not only of Wales but of the English border counties as well. The new industrial areas had a life separate from the rest of the country: "raw, bawdy, and boisterous", as it has been described – a soil for revolutionary activity. But not straight away. The big labour movements came in South Wales in the 1830s, when the whole balance of the population was changing, and Glamorgan and Monmouthshire were the magnets that drew all the enterprising and discontented to the coalfield.

The coming of the railways was a turning-point. Half the world ran its first trains on the rails made in South Wales. And coal was growing to be as important as iron. The growth of coal-mining and then coal-exporting was to be the central fact that eventually came to govern, and then to distort, the whole economy of Wales. But this would not occur until the second half of the nineteenth century. In the early days iron was king, with other industries such as tinplate growing in its shadow. The growth of organized labour movements, and the dramatic and some-times bloody incidents that accompanied this growth, also took place in the new towns and villages created by the iron kings. Some of the incidents are indeed memorable. In the riots at Merthyr in May 1831, the battle between rioters and soldiers was on a scale that Britain was never to see again, with over twenty dead at the end of it all. The rioters stormed the town and clashed with the Argyll and Sutherland Highlanders. The dead lay before the Castle Hotel, and the riot grew into an insurrection. More troops were poured in. Pitched battles were fought with the troops, before Merthyr and the district around could be pacified. A young and apparently innocent man, Dic Penderyn, was convicted and hanged in Cardiff jail. He became the martyr of the movement.

Organized unions were still some way off, but the miners and ironworkers were now becoming aware of the power of unity. Chartism thus made a powerful appeal in industrial Wales. The movement had the textile workers of Llanidloes in a ferment that led to their taking over the town for a week, but the biggest manifesta-tion of Chartism in Wales occurred at Newport in 1839. Three long columns of Chartists marched on the town, with an ex-mayor of Newport, John Frost, leading one of them. Once again the demonstrators were met with military force. A detachment of soldiers was drawn up before the Westgate Hotel. The columns received a volley of rifle fire, and the crowd scattered, leaving several dead.

These bloody encounters with the military produced a legend. When, later on, organized labour became a force in the coalfield, the South Wales workers had a tradition of militancy and of martyrdom for the cause that lent a special fiery quality to the trade disputes in the coalfield.

For now we can begin to see that coal indeed was entering on its period of power. The next sixty years found coal outdistancing all its competitors as the biggest export of the country and the source of a great deal of its employment and wealth. The rise of coal was accompanied by the collapse of the iron industry and its replacement by steel, backed by a whole series of new processes in steel-making. It was now that the population of South Wales really began its expansion.

Dr Brindley Thomas has pointed out that, at the date of the Great Exhibition of 1851 (in which Wales was represented by a few lumps of coal and some pit-gear), Wales had a population of about one million, and two-thirds lived in the country-side and not in the towns or industrial areas. But at an astonishing rate the whole pattern of the population started to change. The deeper coal seams began to be exploited in the Rhondda. A coal rush took place. In 1851 the population there was about a thousand. The valleys were wild, lonely places, tree-covered, with crystal-clear streams flowing down from the romantically beautiful uplands. By 1921 there were over a hundred and sixty thousand people crowded into these slots in the hills. The woodlands had gone, and the streams ran choked with coal-dust down to the Taff and the sea.

On the coast, towns like Cardiff, Newport, Barry, and Swansea started to burst with the newcomers, as coal exports leapt and South Wales became the biggest coal-exporting area in the world. Cardiff exported seven hundred and five thousand tons in 1851 and nearly ten million tons in 1911.

This population expansion was not a matter of uninterrupted progress. The rise of coal was accompanied by strikes, trade depressions, tragic explosions, battles over wages between the coal-owners and the unions, as well as by export success and technical triumphs. But this inrush of people to the Klondike of coal had one important effect for the rural population of Wales. The Welsh peasantry had no need to migrate beyond their borders to find work as the Irish had to do. The promised land lay in Glamorgan, Monmouthshire, and Flintshire rather than America. Of course there was a considerable movement overseas as well. The Welsh went to America, to Australia, and – in one interesting case – to Patagonia. There, on bare, inhospitable plains, a settlement was established where it was hoped that Welsh culture and the Welsh language would be paramount. The "Wladfa" had a desperate struggle for survival. Today it is politically part of Argentina, and the inhabitants speak Welsh and Spanish.

It is calculated that about a hundred thousand people left Wales during the great period of emigration in the nineteenth century. Not a high figure, but important for a small country. And the emigrants were people of quality, whose descendants played a part out of all proportion to their numbers in places like America, or Australia and the other British colonies of the period. But, when all is said and done, the Welsh coalfields were the areas that received the overflow population of rural Wales.

This had its effect on the future of Welsh-speaking. If the Welsh had indeed migrated far afield as the Irish were forced to do, there is not the slightest doubt that Welsh would have gone the way of the Irish language. But the immigrants into the coalfields brought the language with them and kept it alive there. The Rhondda at the beginning of the century was still intensely Welsh; the second generation of new arrivals were brought up in the tradition of their fathers. Even as late as 1951, when the forces making for anglicization had already become extremely powerful, fifty-four per cent of the population that had registered as being able to speak Welsh lived in the coalfields.

Plate 1   At the mouth of the Afon Soch (see p. 82)   *British Travel*

Welsh nonconformity was also given a much stronger economic basis. With the immigrants came the chapels, and from the chapels came the early leaders of the new communities. And, without the wealth of the industrial areas, would there have been any money on a big scale to support those institutions so typical of the new feeling of Welsh nationalism in the late nineteenth century – the Welsh university colleges, the National Library, and the National Museum? The story changed as Wales entered the twentieth century. The rise of the Labour movement and the troubles that beset King Coal began to make industrial Wales a place apart from rural Wales. But, in the great days of coal, one nurtured the other.

In the first half of the nineteenth century rural Wales and Ireland present the same picture, with a population expansion for which no completely satisfactory explanation has been found. It could not be the improved methods of medicine and sanitation – everything goes to show that sanitary conditions in the country-side were grim. Perhaps, as in Ireland, the potato, with its fatally easy method of cultivation, made it possible to raise larger families, with earlier marriages. We are not certain. All we know is that, until the railways expanded and allowed the excess rural population to be siphoned off to the coalfields, pressure on the land was building up. During the Napoleonic Wars this pressure had been concealed by the demand for agricultural products. In the depression that followed the end of the wars, the over-populated countryside suffered.

In vain the farms climbed ever higher on to the moorlands; there was no real escape for the rural poor. The explosion-point was reached with the curiously named Rebecca Riots, between 1839 and 1844. The immediate cause was the new stringency in toll-collection that accompanied the general improvements along the turnpike roads that preceded the arrival of the railways. Tolls fell hard on small farmers struggling to survive. As good nonconformists, they remembered their Bible before they began their riots. Didn't Genesis 24:60 say: "And they blessed Rebekah, and said unto her, Thou art our sister, be thou the mother of thousands of millions, and let thy seed possess the gate of those which hate them"? Naturally the farmers didn't look at the next verse in Genesis, which said: ". . . and they rode upon the camels". They elected their leader as Rebecca, dressed themselves up in women's clothing as Rebecca's daughters, and rode in the night to smash the hated toll-gates. The whole countryside entered into a conspiracy of silence to protect the rioters. Rebecca and her daughters grew bold enough, at one point, to ride into the town of Carmarthen and ransack the workhouse. At last the authorities had to use troops to smash the movement, which was finally put down in 1844. Soon the railways spread into the area and enabled Rebecca's daughters and sons to move out to the coalfields. The great migration began that led to the depopulation of the countryside.

The New Nationalism

There can be no question that the Wales of the nineteenth century had once again become conscious of its separateness from England in a way that would have seemed inconceivable to the men of the seventeenth and eighteenth centuries. They would have agreed with the dictum that "Wales is a geographical expression". The new leaders in the cultural awakening that followed the growth of nonconformity and the rise of industry felt far differently. It was in this atmosphere of renewed national feeling that the patriotic song written by Evan and John James of Pontypridd, "Hen Wlad fy Nhadau", became the Welsh national anthem.

The Pass of Aberglaslyn (see p. 79)   *J. Allan Cash*

The elections of 1868 saw Welsh nonconformity triumphant. Henry Richards could boast: "The Nonconformists are the People of Wales". The Liberal Party benefited by this rising fervour and dominated Welsh politics until the Labour Party created a new loyalty in the industrial areas. The Eisteddfod entered a new period of development. Matthew Arnold attended it and set the seal of intellectual approval upon the Celtic creative spirit.

Thus, while industry was binding Wales closer to England on the economic front, emotional forces insisted on keeping alive a separate feeling of nationality. There was a moment in the 1880s when this feeling might even have expressed itself in political action on the Irish model. In the stormy atmosphere of "tithe wars" in North Wales, young politicians like Tom Ellis and Lloyd George looked across the Irish Sea. This was, in a way, an act of sentimental courage. The Catholic Irish and the Protestant Welsh were both Celts, but no great emotional bonds have ever linked them in modern times. To the nineteenth-century Welsh, the Irish were a menace – a flood of poor labourers, rushing into Wales to take the bread out of people's mouths.

To the Irish, the Welsh seemed curiously unaware of their Celtic heritage – they were just as unsympathetic as the English. Thirty years later, after the Treaty negotiations, the Irish were to sing:

Lloyd George, when he dies,
Will go up to the skies
Borne in a fiery chariot,
Seated on slate
On a red-hot plate
Next door to Judas Iscariot.

But in the 1880s the young Lloyd George and his associates dreamt of Home Rule and the rise of a Welsh Parnell. The whole movement of "Cymru Fydd" (Wales of the Future) fell apart after the Liberal defeat in 1895. It had no hope of again capturing the national imagination once the Labour Party started to sweep triumphantly through the industrial areas.

The career of Lloyd George himself showed the weakness of the position of Cymru Fydd. This son of a poor man, brought up in the remote village of Llanystumdwy, had within him such fire and such transcendent ability that, inevitably, he had to reject the narrow career offered him by Wales. He could sway the House of Commons at the moment when England was at the height of her world power. He saw the world as his stage. And he was triumphantly justified. So the Welsh revolt expended itself, eventually, on issues that were basically non-political – on education, local government, the language problem, and above all the disestablishment of the Welsh Church. After a battle of great bitterness, the Church in Wales, with her own Archbishop, came into being in March 1921. The career of David Lloyd George, however, highlights the whole dilemma of modern Wales. As surely as in Tudor times, her gifted sons move out from her boundaries and play their part in a wider world. Can the new Wales of our own time hold them closer?

For this new Wales is a country in the throes of change. Industrial Wales, after being the Klondike of the whole nation, faced a crisis following the First World War. King Coal was violently dethroned in the Great Depression. A tremendous migration took place away from the coalfield. Since then industrial Wales has, with success, gone through a period of readjustment, seeking continually to broaden the basis of her industrial structure. Now a new world lies before Wales.

How will this nation of fewer than three million people fit into the pattern of the future? Can it indeed retain its individuality in the face of the great political, social, and economic pressures making for steam-rollered unity?

Come what may, the words of the old Welshman who talked to Henry II over eight hundred years ago remain in the mind: "Nor do I think that any other nation than this of Wales . . . shall, on the day of severe examination before the Supreme Judge, answer for this corner of the earth".

The Welsh Language

Welsh has a totally undeserved reputation among English speakers as a mysterious and complex language, written entirely in consonants and presenting insurmountable problems of pronunciation. The first sight of such place-names as Cwmrhydyceirw or Llanerchymedd convinces many visitors that they have indeed entered a foreign land whose tongue is bound to be incomprehensible. Nothing could be further from the truth.

Welsh, in common with English, French, German, and Italian, is descended from the original Aryan stock that lies at the heart of most European languages. It belongs to the Celtic subdivision of the original Aryan, which itself divided into two – the Q-speaking Celts and the P-speaking Celts. In the Q group are Irish, Scottish Gaelic, and Manx; in the P group are Welsh, Cornish, and Breton. The development of the two groups proceeded separately, and today they are as far apart as English is from Dutch or German. A Welsh-speaker cannot make himself understood in the Gaeltacht of Ireland or the Western Isles, although he might learn Breton fairly easily.

It is probable that the language assumed its present form some time in the sixth century, amid the chaos that attended the fall of the Roman Empire and the advance of the Saxons. It was then that the Old British language – that branch of P-Celtic origin which was spoken from southern Scotland through the rest of the island – began rapidly to lose its case-endings and to streamline itself.

The earliest Welsh texts appear in the second half of the eighth century, and it was then that Welsh became a written language, although it must be confessed that there is no real corpus of Welsh writing until many centuries later. But these stray survivals from the dark and distant past prove one interesting point – the Welsh language has not changed fundamentally from this Old Welsh period to the present day. The spelling is different, and the text can look different, but, if it is read aloud, sense begins to emerge for an educated Welshman in a way that it would not for a modern Englishman when reading a text in Anglo-Saxon.

This does not mean that any Welshman can follow the stanzas of the old epic of the *Gododin*, which is ascribed to Aneirin, a bard of the seventh century. You need to be a scholar to tackle Aneirin. But the reader can see that the language is unmistakably Welsh. And the bardic discipline helped Old Welsh to survive and develop into Middle and Modern Welsh.

The grammar of Welsh is thus more regular than that of German, for example, and its pronunciation, in some respects, is nothing like as difficult as that of French. Many so-called difficulties are more apparent than real.

Take Welsh orthography first. Spelling becomes much simpler once you realize that, as a rule, w and y are vowels. *W* is pronounced like *oo* in the English "pool". *Y* is a little more complicated; it can become *ee*, usually in words of one syllable, but in some cases it can be a short *i*. One strong tip about *y*. Whenever you see it between hyphens in place-names (Betws-y-coed is a well-known case), do not pronounce that particular *y* as *ee*. Pronounce it like *u* in the English "fur". The result is more euphonious and will please all Welshmen who hear you.

Some of the consonants may be unfamiliar. The *dd* is, however, the same as *th* in English; *ph* is *f*; *f* is always *v*; and *h* is always aspirated. In fact, there are only two consonants that can cause trouble, and they have acquired a notoriety out of all proportion to their actual difficulty. First *ch*. This has nothing to do with the *ch* you find in the English "cheese". It is precisely the same sound that you find in the Scottish "loch". There is a similar sound in German, and most people find little trouble in getting to terms with words like *Nacht*. Place the tongue in the position for making the sound of *k*, but do not quite touch the roof of the mouth as you pronounce the letter.

The *ll* sound needs more practice. It seems difficult because there is no equivalent in English, although there are approximate sounds in Spanish and certainly more complex sounds in Portuguese. The elaborate instructions given in many books on Welsh grammar are not really necessary. Put the tip of your tongue against your upper gums and breathe out. If you can place the tongue on the right side of the mouth so much the better. One curious statistic unearthed by the experts shows that two-thirds of the population of Wales pronounce the *ll* through the right side of the mouth.

All syllables are clearly pronounced, and in words of more than one syllable the stress falls on the syllable next to the last in nearly every case.

There is, however, one problem that has to be squarely faced – the vexed problem of the mutations. Welsh has a practice, fascinating to philologists but infuriating to beginners in the language, of sometimes changing the initial consonants of words. Nine consonants are mutatable: *c*, *p*, *t*, *g*, *b*, *d*, *ll*, *m*, *rh*. The mutations take place according to fixed laws. For example, the Welsh for "brother" is "brawd", but, when you put "ei" ("his") before it, "brawd" becomes "frawd". "Father" is "tad" in Welsh, but "my father" is "fy nhad". The laws governing the mutations can be learnt easily enough. The main worry for the student comes when he tries to look up an unfamiliar word in his dictionary. How is he to know what the root spelling of a word is when he can encounter it with four different letters? The only encouragement one can give is that practice makes even mutations easier.

Welsh, well spoken, is a delight to hear, and in the mouth of a master orator or preacher (Wales has produced plenty such) it can be an instrument of great power. This very power of the language has led the Welsh to value the spoken almost as much as the written word. The vocabulary is rich, although, in common with many other tongues, Welsh has for some time had to face an invasion of foreign words, mostly expressing the new technical age in which we all live.

As in English, there are numerous dialects and accents. A Welshman has no trouble in distinguishing a man of Caernarfon from a man of Carmarthen. They are as far apart in the sound of their speech as a Yorkshireman and a Devonian or a Texan and a New Englander. There is, moreover, a clearly marked division between the Welsh spoken in North Wales as a whole and that spoken in South Wales. The dividing line is formed by the Plynlimon range in Mid-Wales. But there is also a classical Welsh – based on the long traditions of the court bards and prose-writers, and brought to splendid fruition in the great translations of the Bible in Tudor and Jacobean times – that is written and understood by all educated Welshmen.

Welsh never developed a distinctive script, as Irish did. True, Ogham inscriptions are found in Pembrokeshire and elsewhere, but this strange method of writing by making strokes and notches on the edges of memorial stones came from Ireland and had died out by the end of the fifth century A.D. The "coelbren y beirdd" (the so-called bardic alphabet) was a simplification of conventional characters adopted for cutting on wood. It was largely a product of the romantic inventors at the end of the eighteenth century, and never had any currency. You can still come across it in nineteenth-century memorial inscriptions.

The Welsh language is at present facing a crisis. The last census, in 1961, showed a drop in the number of people who could speak it. In 1953 over nine hundred thousand returned themselves as Welsh-speaking. By 1961 the number had fallen to six hundred and fifty-six thousand, or twenty-six per cent of the population. There are numerous reasons for this decline, ranging from the break-up of the old rural society to the coming of television and the influx of people from over the border, who now find Wales a delectable place to live in. The great question for Welsh seems to be: can the language adapt itself quickly enough to the needs of a modern technological society?

The language has its vigorous defenders. Welsh has been accorded an important place in the educational system of Wales. Both the B.B.C. and the independent television companies broadcast a statutory number of hours in Welsh. There are still writers and poets who use Welsh as magnificently as in the past, although Welsh publishers have an uphill struggle compared with their opposite numbers in England.

Against the language are all the familiar pressures for conformity, for using English as a passport to the wider world of mass culture. If Welsh dies, or is reduced to the present status of Scottish Gaelic, something of profound value will have gone with it. The defenders of the language can take some comfort from the fact that Welsh has been given up for lost at many stages in the recent history of Wales. It has refused to obey the prediction of philologists and tactfully die out.

In the meantime, the visitors will hear it spoken in many parts of the country, particularly the north and west, and will still need his dictionary to interpret the place-names and even the political slogans painted on the walls. To help him, here is a list of words he is likely to meet on his travels. Most are connected with place-names.

Glossary

n., noun. *adj.*, adjective. *pl.*, plural. *fem.*, feminine. Lat., Latin. Cf., compare.

Abaty. Abbey.
Aber. River mouth, confluence.
Aderyn (*pl.* **adar**). Bird.
Afanc. Beaver.
Afon. River.
Allt. Hill-side.
Amgueddfa. Museum.
Ap, ab. Son of.
Arglwydd. Lord.

Bach (*fem.* **fach**). Small.
Ban (*pl.* **bannau**). High place, peak.
Bardd. Bard, poet.
Bedd. Grave.
Betws. Oratory, chapel.
Blaen. Point, upper reaches of a valley or river.
Braich. Arm.
Brân. Crow.

Bras. Rich, large.
Brenin. King.
Bro. Country, lowland, vale.
Bron. Breast of a hill.
Brwyn. Rushes.
Bryn. Hill.
Bwlch. Pass, gap.

Cadair. Chair.
Cadno. Fox.

Cae. Field.
Caer. Fort.
Cain. Fine, elegant.
Calch. Lime.
Cam (*n*.). Step.
Cam (*adj*.). Crooked.
Cant. One hundred.
Cantref. A hundred (division of land).
Capel. Chapel.
Cariad. Lover.
Carn, carnedd. Cairn.
Carreg. Stone.
Castell. Castle.
Ceffyl. Horse.
Cefn. Back, ridge.
Ceiliog. Cock.
Cennin. Leek.
Ceunant. Ravine.
Cigfran. Raven.
Cil. Recess, retreat.
Cistfaen. Prehistoric grave.
Clas. Cloister.
Clawdd. Dyke, embankment.
Cleddau. Swords.
Clogwyn. Precipice.
Clwyd. Gate.
Cnwc. Hillock.
Cob. Embankment.
Coch. Red.
Coed. Wood.
Cors. Bog, fen.
Corwg. Coracle.
Craig. Rock, crag.
Crib. Comb, a narrow ridge.
Croes. Cross.
Crug. Mound.
Cwch. Boat.
Cwt. Shed, hut.
Cymro. Welshman.
Cywydd. Poem in one of the strict metres.

Da. Good.
Dafad (*pl.* **defaid**). Sheep.
Dan. Under.
Dau. Two.
Dewi. David.
Dinas. Fort, city.
Dol. Meadow.
Draen. Thorn.
Drwg. Evil, bad.
Drws. Door.
Du. Black.

Dŵr. Water.
Dyffryn. Valley.
Dyn. Man.

Eglwys. Church.
Eisteddfod. Competitive festival for poetry and music.
Esgair. Hill spur.

Ffair. Fair.
Fflur. Flowers.
Ffordd. Road.
Ffos. Ditch, trench.
Ffridd. Mountain pasture, sheep-walk.

Gafr. Goat.
Garth. Enclosure, hill, ridge.
Gefail. Smithy.
Ger. Near, by.
Glân (*adj*.). Clean.
Glan (*n*.). Bank, shore.
Glas. Green.
Glyn. Glen, valley.
Gorsaf. Station.
Gorsedd. Throne, bardic order.
Grug. Heather.
Gwastad. Plain, flat.
Gwaun Meadow. (Cf. **Waen**.)
Gwely. Bed.
Gwern. Swamp; also alder-trees.
Gwig. Wood.
Gwylan. Seagull.

Hafod. Summer dwelling.
Helyg. Willows.
Hendre. Winter dwelling, established settlement.
Heol. Road.
Hir. Long.
Hiraeth. Yearning, nostalgia.
Hwyl. Mood, inspiration.

Iarll. Earl.
Isaf. Lowest.

Llam. Leap.
Llan. Church.
Llech. Slate.
Llethr. Slope.
Lloer. Moon.

Llwybr. Path.
Llwyn. Grove.
Llyn. Lake.
Llys. Court.
Llythyrdy. Post office.

Mab. Son.
Maen. Stone.
Maes. Field.
Mam. Mother.
Mawn. Peat.
Mawr. Big.
Melin. Mill.
Melyn. Yellow.
Min. Edge, brink.
Moch. Pigs.
Moel. Bare, rounded hill.
Môr. Sea.
Morfa. Bog, sea-marsh.
Mur. Wall.
Mynach. Monk.
Mynydd. Mountain.

Nant. Stream.
Neuadd. Hall.
Newydd. New.
Nos. Night.

Oen. Lamb.
Oer. Cold.
Ogof. Cave.
Olaf. Last.

Pandy. Fulling-mill.
Pant. Valley, hollow.
Parc. Park.
Pen. Top, head.
Pentref. Village.
Pistyll. Waterfall.
Plaid. Party.
Plas. Mansion.
Pont. Bridge.
Porth. Port.
Prifysgol. University.
Pump. Five.
Pwll. Pool.

Rhedyn. Bracken.
Rhiw. Hill.
Rhos. Moor, plain.
Rhyd. Ford.
Rwan (N. Wales). Now.

Saesneg. English language.

Sant. Saint.
Sarn. Causeway.
Sir. County.
Swyddfa. Office.
Sych. Dry.

Tad. Father.
Tal. Forehead, front.
Taran. Thunder.
Taren. Knoll, rock.
Tarw. Bull.
Teg. Fair.
Tir. Land.
Tomen. Mound.
Traeth. Beach.

Traws. Across.
Tre, tref. Town, home.
Tri. Three.
Trum. Ridge.
Twll. Hole.
Tŷ. House.
Tylwyth Teg. The "fair family", the fairies.

Uchaf. Highest.
Undeb. Union, religious denomination.
Urdd. Order of Urdd Gobaith Cymru (Welsh League of Youth).

Uwch. Higher.

Waen. Meadow. (Cf. **Gwaun.**)

Y. The, of the.
Yn. In, at.
Ynys. Island.
Ysbryd. Spirit, ghost.
Ysbyty. Hospital.
Ysfa. Craving.
Ysgol. School.
Ysgubor. Barn.
Ystrad. Vale.

The Spirit of Wales

On the 24th May 1738 John Wesley, at a Bible reading in Aldersgate Street, London, experienced a sudden warming of the heart that was to give his own life a fresh direction and profoundly change the course of religious feeling in Britain. His preaching by day and night touched in turn the hearts of country folk. The delights of ritual dance and of half-pagan, half-Christianized ceremonies to honour the growing and reaping of the corn were converted into yearnings for the bread of Heaven. In Wales, more deeply and durably than in any other part, this conversion was complete. And among those who threw off the husk of worldliness was the Harper of Abergwesyn, skilled and honoured in his time, who renounced his instrument for ever. It was as symbolic an act for Wales as Wesley's own conversion had been for England.

The extreme effect of the Methodist revival of religion in Wales sprang from the fact that the Second Civil War and the collapse of the Royalist cause had put the whole of Britain under the Protectorate. Colonies of Roundhead settlers had been placed in strategic positions, particularly in the province of Powys, with curious effects upon the native language; for still in W. Montgomeryshire people mop the floor with a "clwt" (clout), rather than a rag, and a woman no better than she should be is a Rocsan (Roxana). The Wesleyan movement blew a spark in embers that had smouldered grimly since the Restoration, and in the 19th cent. the flame of Spurgeon lit the grimy skies of the industrialized South.

And yet it was the precursor of all this, the Vicar of Llandovery, Rhys Prichard, who in his *Seren Foreu* or *Canwyll y Cymry* (The Welshman's Candle), written in the 17th cent., lit a candle for Welshmen from an earlier fire. Unlike his Puritan contemporary Morgan Llwyd, or his Catholic contemporary Richard Gwyn, the Vicar accepted reformation in the terms agreed by the official Church. But, like them, he spoke to the people in the forms of poetry laid down by the bards of the Middle Ages, and he opens his series of admonitory verses with an appeal to "hill Brutus fab Silfus, Brutaniaid brwd hoenus" (the seed of Brutus, son of Silvius, the blithe sap of Britain). Royalist in politics, yet deeply influenced by Puritan respect for the sanctity of the Word, his sympathy extended not only to both contending factions in his time but also to the common people, ready to welcome the last descendants of the wandering bards, whose songs have survived as a living influence among the Welsh. One of these songs, "Codiad Yr Hedydd" (Rising of the Lark), said to have been spontaneously sung in the dawn upon the mountain-side where the harper had slept, is today the regimental march of the Welsh Guards. Another, "Gwenith Gwyn" (White Wheat), is even more famous:

Mi sydd fachgen ieuangc ffol	(I'm a lad of lazy days,
Yn byw yn ol fy ffansi;	And all my ways are lonely;
Myfi'n bugeilio'r gwenith gwyn	I come to count the curving corn,
Ac arall yn ei fedi. . . .	I in the morning only. . . .)

The translation, though inadequate, may give some idea of the writer's skill in construction, and of the vagrant delight that the Vicar felt must be controlled. But he used the same unforced language, for he knew the people sang. And in his opening line he recalled their origin. He appealed to the legend that Geoffrey of Monmouth had taken from such collections as the Red Book of Hergest, where the traditional epics of Rome and Greece – above all the tale of Troy, with its wonder at how the fate of men is ruled by the heavens – had been applied to the tale of Britain. From fallen Troy, Aeneas had fled to found the greatness of Rome; and from Rome had come Brutus, a descendant of Aeneas, to settle Britain under the will of heaven, which his race, the British, was to establish on earth. Geoffrey of Monmouth, in the 12th cent., was thinking in the terms of his own time, yet he crystallized a direct memory of the Roman connection with Britain, and a less precise one of earlier contacts with Mediterranean civilizations and the traditional meaning of the stone circles of Wales and the monument at Stonehenge, into the theme based on that distant knowledge by the philosophers of Greece and Rome and reintroduced by scholars taking refuge in Britain from the invasion of the West, about A.D. 410, by the Goths. He called it the theme of Arthur; and it was to Wales that Europe looked for the source of that theme throughout the Middle Ages.

The most considered attempt to set up a state reflecting those ideas was that of Henry VII. The incursion that was to end the Wars of the Roses was accompanied by the publication of Malory's *Morte d'Arthur*. Henry's landing was in that part of Wales which had accepted an Anglo-Norman settlement. Bosworth was won under the Red Dragon of Wales, which then became part of the insignia of England. Wales owes its identity today much more to the institution of a Court and Council of Wales and her marchlands by Henry, under his eldest son Arthur, Prince of Wales, than to the recognition of her right to such identity by Edward I. But even Edward, when setting up the fortress of Caernarfon, realized that in taking Wales he had taken something that Wales uniquely represented. His castle was modelled on the Theodosian fortifications at Constantinople, the new capital of the Roman world that the British-born Constantine, leaving with British troops from Britain, had in the middle of the 4th cent. established as a Christian city. Near the site of the Roman fort of Segontium, Edward raised his new Byzantium to make plain that in overcoming the Prince of North Wales he had won the right to the Rome of the West.

The contentions between Wales and England had always been treated, particularly by the Welsh rulers of Powys, as a rivalry for a common cause. The heritage from the fallen days of Rome belonged to each; it was largely a dispute about how far the Stoic principle that all men were free and subject only to universal justice should be applied to politics. This was the theme of Gerald de Barri, the 12th-cent. Welshman whose genius is more acknowledged on the Continent than in his own country. Praising his people for their courage and skill, and above all others for the art of music, he blamed them for denying that they could live independently and yet in harmony with England. This was the policy of the Lord Rhys of the South who, while ruler in his own right, agreed to serve as Justiciar for Henry II. It was the policy of Llywelyn the Great, who at Runnymede joined with the Norman baronage to reassert in Magna Carta the supremacy of justice over government, in the same way that the last Llywelyn found an ally in Simon de Montfort, who first created a genuinely representative parliament in Britain.

In the 13th cent. this theme was by no means new. When Hywel the Good in the 10th cent. refused to join the alliance of Celts and Danes, from the Scots islands to Brittany, that might have overthrown Saxon England, and when the Welsh cleric Asser went to the court of Alfred of Wessex to develop written records among the Saxons, it was in recognition of something that went back to the 3rd cent. in Roman Britain.

When the Saxons and the men they called Welsh fought the 150-year battle that ended with the loss of Chester and Bath by the Roman-British, the symbol of what they struggled for across the English Midlands was the sign of sovereignty that, as Bede reports, the English called the Thuuf, the Welsh Twff, and the Romans the Tufa. It was the standard of three ostrich plumes carried before the monarch; Edwin of Northumbria took it after his triumph over the North to show that he was Bretwalda, or successor to the Roman Duke of the Britains. So too the Dragon (as it is called) of Wales was a survivor of the imperial legionary symbols in the days of Augustus; a red one for Wales, say the old records, a white one for the Saxon. It was not so much a struggle between two opposed races as between two rival successors to the same inheritance, though certainly with a different interpretation of purpose. Modern archaeology has established that Saxons were present in large areas of Britain as early as the 4th cent. and perhaps the 3rd. Nor did Rome ever speak of Britain, but always of the several Britains, since she understood that many differing peoples dwelt here. At the end of the 3rd cent. one Carausius, seizing the fleets of Britain, declared his independence, and caused Britain to be recognized, for ten years, as an independent empire. He was probably from the Netherlands; he favoured the people of the North Sea from whom he sprang, and habitually wore their dress. He manned his own fleets from them, and was the first British ruler to have a base in the Low Countries and to realize the importance of Gibraltar. Much of the later provincial development within Britain, including that of the Saxon heptarchy, may have been originated by him as a means of interior organization and defence. Rome destroyed his Britain in the end; but the idea of a Britain that must either control the North Sea for itself or control the West of Europe remained to dominate her policy for centuries. Britain again became independent for a while within the Gallic Empire of Romanized Celts; and successive leaders, both before and after Constantine, used Britain as a base for the attempt to take the whole Empire of Rome. The last record is of Riothamus, who sailed from Britain in the 5th cent. on a final attempt to save the falling government of Rome. A Briton (for all contemporary records call him so), he went with his ships and unruly British forces up the Loire into the Lyonnaise, the lost land of Lyonesse, as the Arthur who stood for Rome against the pagan and one day would come again.

The intelligent strategy used by both sides in the long conflict between Welsh and Saxon does not suggest the conflict of barbaric tribes. Whether Britain should live for herself or decide to come again into a reunited Europe was to be settled otherwise. The unity of Europe would turn on the unity of its religion; Europe was slowly reuniting on the basis of the Catholic Church in the West. In Britain, and particularly around the shores of the Irish Sea, Christianity had found another expression.

The assumption of Victorian school-books that all Romans left Britain in the calamitous 5th cent. has not borne examination. Whatever the difficulties in Britain, the disturbed conditions in Europe could hardly have offered anything better. Subjects of the Empire had for generations been made Roman citizens, regardless of race or origin. For the Britain of the time, Rome meant the Gallic Prefecture of which Britain was part and whose capital was in France. The desperate need was to re-establish its stability; and the Agitius to whom the records of the time say the British rulers turned for assistance is most likely to have been the

Peter Baker

Roman Wales: the amphitheatre at Caerleon

Aegidius of Soissons who kept the Empire of the West in being and Brittany free from attack.

But the Saxon who drove a wedge between the Roman-British and the Channel was inspired by motives other than political. From Brittany, Gildas had called on the rulers of Britain to renounce forms of Christianity that had been influenced by heathen wonder at the intelligence of the heavens. From the islands and the land outposts of the Severn Sea, the missionaries of the Celtic Church had gone into Wales. What kind of people they met is shown by the memorial stones, still surviving from the 5th and 6th cents.: men with Roman names, mourning their children in words no longer of correct Latin; forgotten kings who call themselves Augustus; Roman ex-servicemen, the Emeriti, settled among the people they had guarded; native auxiliaries who had learnt Roman ways; merchants who had traded under Roman licence; labourers who had worked in the mines for silver and on the villas for grain. It was this frontiered legacy of Rome, and the cities still standing with their Roman roofs and tiles, that the rulers of Powys guarded. The Church that was cut down at Chester and Bangor-Is-Coed in 615 survived in another form. But Wales, like Geoffrey of Monmouth, still remembered an earlier time when the British seas were first made open to sail from the Mediterranean, before the voyage of Pytheas, about 500 B.C., when those who took the stones of Preseli to stand at Stonehenge, and Irish gold to travel down the Dee and Severn, brought the first mastery of navigation to her shores and with it the worship of the Thought beyond the stars. This was what legend made into the tale of Brutus and conceived as the story of Arthur; this was what Edward I and Henry VII had in mind when they considered the spirit of Wales. It inspired Gerald de Barri to fight against all odds for the honour of his country, and formed the theme of harp-men in their tunes. And, though the harp of Abergwesyn waits to be taken up again, it has never ceased singing to itself.   A.Ll.

Gazetteer

Map references will be found in the Index.

ABBEYCWMHIR, *Radnorshire.* This lonely hamlet, set among the high, newly forested hills, 5 m. E. of Rhayader, once sheltered the largest abbey in Wales. The "Abbey of the Long Valley" was a Cistercian foundation, the second in Wales, and one that was always held in special favour by the Welsh. The abbey was built on an ambitious scale; only York, Winchester, and Durham had naves longer than the 242-ft one at Abbeycwmhir. The monastery was sacked during Glyndwr's rising and was never completed. At the Dissolution in 1542, the building was demolished, and some of the arches of the nave were almost certainly incorporated in Llanidloes church. Enough of the ruins were still erect at the time of the Civil War for the place to survive a short siege. Today only the bare outline of the walls, the bases of columns, and the altar steps can be seen among the trees in the meadow beside the Clywedog stream. A thorn tree grows over the spot where once the high altar stood. Here the headless body of Llywelyn, the last Prince of independent Wales, was supposed to have been secretly buried, after he was killed near Builth in 1282. His head was sent to London to be exhibited on Cheapside as a symbol of Edward I's victory.

Later, part of the abbey lands passed into the possession of the Fowler family, about whom the well-known Radnorshire rhyme was written:

Alas! Alas! Poor Radnorsheere,
Never a park, nor never a deere,
Never a man with five hundred a year,
Save Richard Fowler of Abbey Cwm Hir.

The present mansion and church were built in 1867 in a Gothic style of truly marvellous spikiness. Nearby is the Happy Union Inn, with a sign showing a Welshman riding a goat. The whole place has an atmosphere of remote charm.

To the N. of Abbeycwmhir the road goes over the mountains to the little village of Bwlch-y-Sarnau (Pass of the Causeways). Here are traces of the Roman road that ran from the camp at Castell Collen, near Llandrindod, to Caersws.

ABER, *Caernarfonshire,* is a pleasant village, tucked under the towering outlines of the high Carnedd range, 4 m. E. of Bangor. Its full name in Welsh is Abergwyngregyn (River Mouth of the White Shells). Llywelyn the Great had a palace here, and it was a favourite residence of the Princes of Gwynedd. The building was probably of wood and stood around the mound known as Y Myd. The mound was probably first constructed by the Normans during their early invasion of North Wales. Here, according to the romantic story, Llywelyn's wife Joan, the daughter of King John, fell in love with Llywelyn's prisoner, the Marcher Lord William de Braose. After De Braose had been ransomed and freed, Llywelyn invited him back to a banquet. The Prince of Gwynedd is supposed to have taken his revenge by hanging De Braose, and then showing his lifeless body to Joan. The story is the theme of one of the finest dramas written in Welsh in our day – *Siwan* by Saunders Lewis. Joan seems to have made her peace with her husband, for she was buried with honour later in Llanfaes Priory in Anglesey.

Inland from Aber are the celebrated Aber Falls. They can be reached in an easy hour's walk up a particularly narrow and beautiful valley. The small stream of the Afon Goch rises on the wide slopes of Llwytmor and tumbles over a precipice at the Rhaeadr Fawr (Big Fall). There are actually two falls. The first is the higher, with a drop of 120 ft, broken up into a series of cascades; the second can be reached by a 5-min. walk along the foot of the mountain-side to the SW. The falls can be reached only by walking, and this has preserved the lonely beauty of the spot. The power-lines that now run along the lower slopes of the hills behind Aber join the line of the old Roman road that crosses the high pass of Bwlch-y-Ddeufaen, some 4 m. due E. over the mountains from Aber.

Rhaeadr Fawr

Peter Baker

The harbour, Aberaeron

Aber looks out northwards, over the northern end of the Menai Straits. At low tide the wide Traeth Lafan (Lavan Sands) are exposed. Robert Morden's maps of 1668 make them a prominent feature, and the coach-ways of that and later centuries took Aber as the place from which the best passage across them could be made for the short ferry to Anglesey and its then important copper and coal production, its wheat and gracious cattle. In Aber church is still preserved the bell that used to be rung in foggy weather to warn travellers of the rising tide. Lavan Sands are also the site of one of the numerous legends of drowned lands common along the coasts of Wales. A noble palace, Llys Helig, is supposed to be buried under the sand and sea. Unfortunately Dr North showed that the stones, which are exposed at low tide and look like the foundations of buildings, have a natural origin.

ABERAERON, *Cardiganshire.* The name is also spelt Aberayron. This small port on the Cardiganshire coast at the mouth of the Afon Aeron is a rarity in Wales, a town that was built to a set plan and laid out, moreover, in the early 19th cent. during one of the best periods of British architecture. The result is wholly delightful. Aberaeron, however, contains no masterpiece of the Regency. The houses are generally small and two-storeyed, but they are grouped round a square, or in terraces overlooking the harbour against a background of green hills. The present inhabitants are aware of their heritage. In common with many of the smaller towns of Wales, Aberaeron is under pressure to expand with the growth of the tourist trade, and there are caravan parks N. and S. of the town. But there is every hope that future expansion will be orderly, in keeping with the spirit that first created the town.

Aberaeron was a place of little importance until about 1807, when Susannah and Alban Thomas Jones of Ty-Glyn, who had inherited a fortune, obtained parliamentary sanction to build piers and a harbour at the mouth of the River Aeron. The little town grew swiftly. The names Regent Street and Waterloo Street indicate the date of their construction, although one of the pleasantest parts of the town, Alban Square, was not built until the 1850s. By this time the pattern was set. Inevitably the plans have been attributed to John Nash, who was known to have visited the neighbourhood. But there is no evidence firmly connecting him to the place. The present Harbourmaster Hotel, one of the first buildings to be put up, was originally the Harbour Master's house. The Town Hall, which overlooks the harbour, is an elegant brown-stone building.

The harbour itself dries out at low tide. The once-celebrated box-ferry in which visitors were slowly cranked across a wire cable suspended over the water, has been discontinued. The harbour is now entirely devoted to yachting, but in the 19th cent. was a busy centre of shipbuilding. Aberaeron made a reputation for its schooners, especially those constructed by the master builder, David Jones. The great days of the port ended when the railways destroyed the coastal trade of West Wales. Aberaeron is now a holiday and residential place, and the old breed of retired sea captains who seemed to be the main inhabitants in the old days is dying out. The houses have been painted in light colours according to a plan. The churches and chapels are not quite in the Regency tradition. The church seems a little out of character in its Gothic garb of the 1870s. The beach is a storm beach, composed of rounded pebbles.

About 1 m. N. of Aberaeron is the place it supplanted, Aberarth. The village is tucked into a hollow, with a stream tumbling through it. The village church of Llandewi Aberarth contains the graves of Susannah and Thomas Jones. Between Aberarth and Aberaeron, on the coast, is the site of Castell Cadwgan, one of the castles of that lax and unfortunate 12th-cent. prince, Cadwgan ap

Bleddyn, whose son Owain abducted Nest, the glamorous wife of Gerald of Pembroke, and let loose a series of feuds and petty wars that were to trouble South-West Wales for thirty years.

ABERAMAN, *Glamorgan*, is a mining township in the Cynon valley 1 m. below Aberdare. The church, St Margaret's, was built in 1883. It contains Munich glass in the chancel. Antony Bacon, one of the early pioneers of the South Wales coalfield, lived at the old Aberaman House. Beyond Aberaman, and the village of Abercwmboi next to it in the Cynon valley, a side valley cuts back deep into the hills to the W. that separate the Cynon valley from the Rhondda Fach. At the end of this side valley, Cwmaman is a typical South Wales colliery village in a typical setting: long rows of houses dominated by the headgear of pits and the tips of colliery waste. Above are the high hills, at this point deeply wooded with the new plantations of the Forestry Commission. No road leads out of the top of the valley.

ABERAVON, *Glamorgan*. The oldest part of the great industrial complex that has grown up between the sea and the hills, Aberavon lies 12 m. E. of Swansea, at the mouth of the narrow Afan valley. The municipal borough of Aberavon has been merged into the newer borough of Port Talbot, and together they now form one of the most important manufacturing areas of South Wales. Aberavon claimed to have been granted its first charter in 1158. Gerald the Welshman passed this way when he accompanied Archbishop Baldwin on his tour through Wales to preach the Third Crusade. He gives a vivid description of the difficulties of the passage across the quicksand between Aberavon and Neath. There are a few traces of the small castle of the local Welsh rulers on Mynydd Dinas, the craggy hill at the mouth of the Afan river. The old Church of St Mary was rebuilt in 1860. In the graveyard is the grave of Dic Penderyn (Richard Lewis), who was hanged for complicity in the Merthyr Riots of 1831, although he was certainly innocent of the crime. The body of the unfortunate youth was refused burial in Cardiff, Llantrisant, and Bridgend. Finally it was interred at dead of night at Aberavon. Dic Penderyn was regarded as the first martyr of the Labour movement in South Wales. In the borough municipal offices is preserved the hollowed block of wood in which the municipal charters were hidden from the Parliamentarians during the Civil War. Aberavon has spread out in recent years, along the sand-dunes and seashore to the NW. A new promenade has been built fronting the fine, sandy Aberavon beach, and a comprehensive entertainment centre, the Afan Lido, constructed to include swimming-pools, assembly halls, and restaurants. The Lido is owned by the municipality.

Linked firmly to Aberavon is Port Talbot, where now the Margam steelworks of the Steel Company of Wales stretch for over 3 m. eastwards from the dock-side. This was a £100,000,000 project, and the blast furnaces, steel furnaces, rolling-mills, and strip-mill form one of the most impressive industrial spectacles in southern Britain. S.C.O.W. is now nationalized, and an important harbour development is in full swing, which will allow big ore-carriers to dock at Port Talbot for the first time. The breakwater runs 1 m. out to sea. The first dock was built here in 1835. Port Talbot will soon be one of the biggest ports in the Bristol Channel. The town was named after the Talbot family of Margam Abbey, who were pioneers in its industrial development.

A new motorway sweeps round the town from Margam on the eastern side to Briton Ferry on the W. The road is cut along the hill-side and carried over the mouth of the Afan valley on a viaduct. The road gives a splendid view over the whole industrial area, especially impressive at night, when the blast furnaces are being tapped.

The Afan valley runs inland from Aberavon. This is one of the narrowest valleys of the coalfield, beset with high hills, many of them now under the plantations of the Glamorgan forest. The road, railway, and river struggle for space as the valley cuts back towards the highest summits of the mountains of the coalfield. The first village of the valley, Cwmafan, was once the site of copper-works. The fumes were carried up a tunnel on the side of Foel Fynyddau to a stack 1,200 ft above sea-level. Cwmafan could claim to have the tallest factory chimney in the world. The stack on the summit was demolished during the Second World War. Beyond Cwmafan is Pontrhydyfen, once noted for the variety of its viaducts, and now as the birthplace of Richard Burton, the actor. The valley becomes narrower. A road goes over the cleft in the hills to the NW., to descend at Neath. Beyond Pontrhydyfen is the old farm of Pen-hydd. This was once a grange of Margam Abbey, celebrated in Welsh folklore as the home of a monk whose gift of foretelling the future earned him the nickname of Twm Celwydd Teg (Tom of the Fair Lies). A young man going bird's-nesting once chaffed him with: "Well, Tom, what lies have you got for me today?" Said Twm: "You will die three deaths before nightfall". The young man laughed, for who can die three deaths? But, as he climbed a tree over the river to rob a kite's nest, his hand was bitten by a viper the bird had brought back to feed her young; he tumbled out of the tree, broke his neck, fell into the river, and was drowned. The lonely valley of Twm Celwydd Teg was changed by industry in the late 19th cent. Today, as the collieries face closure, the valley is regaining some of its former rural beauty.

There is a particularly attractive stretch between Pontrhydyfen and Cymer. From Cymer a road goes over a tow-pass in the hills into Maesteg. Cymer itself is a village all on a slope, a tangle of terraces and houses jammed in the bottom of the valley. A tablet on the wall near the inn at the bridge commemorates the Eisteddfod held there in 1735; one competitor was Wil Hopkin, to whom are attributed the words of "Bugeilio'r Gwenith Gwyn" (Watching the Wheat).

A branch road leads off the main road, after a hair-raising bend, to follow the Corrwg valley. At the head of the valley, which is a dead-end, lies the secluded village of Glyncorrwg, which has the reputation of being the wettest village in Glamorgan. No wonder, for it is overshadowed by the highest point in the county, Craig y Llyn (1,969 ft). The mountain-sides all around are now forested.

The main road continues up the ever-narrowing Afan valley, through a stretch that is deeply wooded, to Blaengwynfi, a colliery village that, from its remoteness, used to be known to the old miners as the Cape. The railway dives through the mountains in a tunnel that emerges into the upper reaches of the Rhondda valley. The road goes up over the mountains in an impressive climb that brings you out at the summit of the moorlands. This road is part of the inter-valley links, built after the First World War.

The pass is worth driving through for the views over the whole of the Glamorgan hills, with a glimpse of the mining villages, sunk far below in the narrow valleys. At the summit of Bwlch-y-Clawdd the road forks; one branch goes down the face of the mountain into the Rhondda, the other swings sharply westwards and drops steeply under a line of cliffs into the forested head of the Ogmore valley. These inter-valley passes are a surprise for the visitor. They are remarkable pieces of road-engineering in themselves.

ABERCARN, *Monmouthshire,* is an industrial township 9 m. from Newport in the lower part of the Ebbw valley. It possesses a modern church, which stands above the centre of Abercarn in a grove of trees, rather like a fortress set on a hill. A long flight of steps leads up to the W. door from the road. An equally long flight of stairs within the church brings you up into the nave with dramatic effect. The interior is bare but impressive. The plaster, peeling in corners, indicates that the church could do with some help. The peal of eight bells, presented in 1947 on the twenty-first anniversary of the church's consecration, are splendidly named Love, Joy, Peace, Long Suffering, Gentleness, Goodness, Faith, and Meekness. It would be interesting to hear which virtue sounds most clearly when the peal is rung. Just before the church, a road turns off to the right from the main road up the Ebbw valley. This side road takes you into a picnic-place about 4 m. in the heart of the Ebbw forest. The South Wales coalfield specializes in these unexpected contrasts between stark industrialism and unexpected beauty. Here the deep pine-woods make a magnificent showing. The Ebbw forest now covers most of the lower slopes of the mountain area E. of Abercarn. As the hills rise to 1,500 ft, these steep, wooded valleys are striking in their garment of green. Far beneath the mountains lie the workings of the old Prince of Wales colliery at Abercarn. Here, in September 1878, 268 miners lost their lives in one of those tragic explosions that were part of the price of coal in the heyday of the South Wales coal trade.

ABERCUCH, *Pembrokeshire.* The village straggles along the road that runs S. of the River Teifi 3 m. W. of Newcastle Emlyn. There is not much to see, but the map shows that Abercuch is on the exact junction of the three counties of Pembroke, Carmarthen, and Cardigan. The Afon Cuch flows into the Teifi, and it forms a beautiful and secluded valley southwards into the hills. The valley has the additional attraction of being densely wooded. It was once famous as the home of one of the finest wood-turners in Wales. The workshop has unfortunately been burnt down. Further up the valley is Cwm Cuch, a hamlet with a few houses, a telephone box, and a quiet bridge over the stream. Beyond Glyn Cuch the woods close in, and the valley becomes a place for the walker, not the motorist. It was in Glyn Cuch that Pwyll, Prince of Dyfed, went hunting, as related in that great collection of Welsh medieval stories, the *Mabinogion.* Pwyll's hounds pulled down a stag hunted by the King of the Underworld, with strange results. The whole area still has a feeling of remoteness from the ordinary world.

ABERCYWARCH, *Merioneth.* This is something less than a hamlet, and at present it makes a sad comment on the change overtaking so much of the true Welsh life. In the place itself and on the way from Dinas Mawddwy, the stone-pile houses, which in this district replace the slate structures of the region around Machynlleth, are often empty, eyeless, and falling. Yet Abercywarch and its subsidiary, the community living along the lengthy valley of Cwm Cywarch, had once a vigour, physical and mental, and a social identity from which the Welsh character drew its varied and stubborn strength.

It is reached by a rising road that at first skirts the ruined wall of an estate. The great house is gone, though its grounds in their present wildness, as yet no more than threatened by afforestation development, preserve something of the oaken woodlands once dominant throughout Wales.

Built on the banks of the wild Cywarch stream, the grey walls of Abercywarch echo a memory honoured in Welsh literature. For Borrow exultantly assumed, when passing through this place, that here Ellis Wynne composed the immortal *Y Bardd Cwsg* (The Sleeping Bard), a prose-poem that Borrow himself had translated a short while before. Ellis Wynne lived from 1671 to 1734. In a sense, he marks the end of a period in the development of Welsh literature. The effect of the exclusion of the Welsh language from official use by Henry VIII was gradually making itself felt. Rhys Prichard, Vicar of Llandovery (1579–1644), had had, and still has, great influence in maintaining the tradition of independent Welsh culture, but his notable work, the *Canwyll y Cymry* (The Welshman's Candle), was both in style and purpose based on the simple, wholly genuine tastes of the common people, and no longer on the intellectual dexterities used by the poets of older times. Ellis Wynne seems to stand half way on this course, using a strength of

Aberdovey: the Dovey estuary, looking towards the Plynlimon hills   Peter Baker

philosophic thought lit with the charm and directness of the harp-men of the early 18th cent. whose work lives in many of the famous songs of Wales, and who caught their tune from the larks that rose from hill-sides much like those of Cwm Cywarch.

As Abercywarch is neared, a lane leads to the left; it goes into the Cywarch cwm and reaches at last the foot of Aran Fawddwy. But the better way to the Arans, at least for cars, runs from Abercywarch itself. It can now be taken through Bryn Sion, Terwyn, and Tyn-y-twll (House in the Hole). For the walker, the lane before the hamlet on the western side of the valley passes through farmsteads where sheep and sheep-dogs, hens, goats, and pigs move under ancient oaks and among walls almost as ancient. It is doubtful whether anything there has altered significantly for several hundred years. The track is impossible for cars, but at the ford-bridge in Fawnog Fawr it joins the motorable road from Abercywarch. This almost immediately gives a view of the hanging rocks of Craig Cywarch, severe enough to serve the purpose of commando training, usually in winter. But for some time the eye is taken up with the evidences of farm and saw-yard, mill and chapel, that remain as monuments of the self-contained life of a valley that, in some ways, is now unique. Unfortunately, one of the chapels, the centre for the religious and social life of the scattered cottages here, is now in ruins, its pews tumbled with its rafters, and its ornamental furnishings abandoned. After a century and a half the tide of faith has ebbed away from it. At the end of its route the road swings out to cross the river and fades entirely at the ford. This part of the valley, known as Blaencywarch, has flat fields, black cattle unwelcoming to strangers, and one or two houses of the manor type, well settled into their centuries of age, and begins the first step in the ascent of the Arans.

It is possible to follow a footpath up the Terwyn valley to reach the shoulder of Pumryl. It is also possible to climb by the stream that falls between Craig Cywarch and the Great Aran, the Afon Camddwr. Considerable care, however, must be taken on this unmarked route. The Camddwr shows a striking feature in the cascade of tumbled rocks, large and dangerous, that line its course and lie in a heaped spill over the fields at its foot. A great overflow of water must once have poured these heavy stones in tumult from the top. They are loosely laid one on the other, and, the angle of the slope being sharp, genuine risk is run in attempting the climb. But, if the danger is successfully avoided, something of value can be had. At the crest (2,248 ft) lies an ankle-deep swamp that offers no further obstacle to the head of Aran. Though unattractive in itself, it gives a remarkable view of the Cwm Cywarch as you look down it. This point lies fairly accurately in the centre of the two valley-sides, straight and long and parallel. They form a perfect bowl-shape with the valley floor, and give a vivid picture of the glacial action that scooped this hollow and dried away. Possibly the bog is the relic of some lake that once lay here but burst with a torrent of rocks into Blaencywarch.

A steadier but equally interesting way is to take the sheep-track that rises over the Hengwm stream. Penfolds for washing and watering stand about the river, and scattered sheep observe you half with alarm, half with indignation. Three mountain springs of clean, icy water cross the track as you ascend. On the last height of this ascent, a bare and level moor spreads until suddenly it falls away and, half way up the folds of earth between Aran Fawddwy and Aran Benllyn, the blue lake, Creiglyn Dyfi, shines in silence 300 ft below you.

To reach the Great Aran, the curious ridge must be followed from Drysgol to Drws Bach (Little Gate). On a reduced scale, but with much the same effect, this ridge resembles Striding Edge on Helvellyn; there is the same narrow footway between two steeply inclined slopes and the same sense of being suspended in mid-air. The Drws Bach is a place where the ridge narrows so much that under the constant action of wind and rain it has decayed away. There is little if any danger normally; but the Arans are subject to mist and heavy rain, and you can take false footing and fall steeply.

The shoulder and head of Aran Fawddwy are covered with grey granite boulders, heaped irregularly together and sunk treacherously in the grasses. A persistent local legend asserts that they were assembled there, with painful industry, by a man of Mawddwy who made many journeys to tip them from his wheelbarrow. Oddly enough, this is not offered as a piece of humour. It is probably a worn-down variant of the many legends that associate the placing of such monumental crags on the hill-tops with saints of the Church and the "giants" of even remoter days.

Winds on the Aran Fawddwy are stiff at times, often too stiff for one to stand upright. Its most impressive characteristic is its habit of gathering thunderclouds about it; and the sight of the storm steadily sheering over the summit and discharging its lightnings as it comes is memorable. The peak itself overhangs the drop of the valley where the Creiglyn lies, and several of its boulders have in past years gradually fallen away. The Aran Benllyn, slightly lower, lies northward and is easily reached. Close at hand, it seems, and again a little lower, the back of Cader Idris gathers itself like a crouching dog. Rhobell Fawr, over Llanfachreth, the Tafolog behind Cemaes, and the sides of Plynlimon above Llanbrynmair can be made out.

A relatively easy descent leads to Dolgellau, or by the Llaethnant to Llanymawddwy, though the more interesting way there is by Pistyll Gwyn or Foel Clochydd. Whichever route from Abercywarch has been taken, it is always worth while, on returning, to take the other.

Magpies, jays, hares, and buzzards haunt Cwm Cywarch, and the beautiful slow-worm is often seen. Snake-like in seeming, it is entirely harmless and will without resentment allow you to stroke its coppered and steel-seamed skin.

Plate 2 One of the old cottages at Berriew (see p. 106)   Tom Wright

ABERDARE, *Glamorgan,* an industrial town, lies at the head of the Cynon valley, 12 m. N. of Pontypridd. The valley here begins to open out a little, and Aberdare lies in a bowl of hills, which guard but do not oppress it. Most of the collieries still working in the area are placed in side valleys, such as Cwmaman, so that the centre of Aberdare gives the impression of a market town rather than an industrial centre. Even the new opencast coal-mining, at Bryn Pica on the mountains to the E., does not altogether alter this feeling. The grass-grown mounds on the hills N. of Bryn Pica on the Merthyr road are the remains of the old coal-working in the early days of the Industrial Revolution. They convey the promise that the Bryn Pica opencast workings will also be smoothed over and absorbed into the landscape.

Aberdare started on its first period of expansion in the late 18th cent. Then the emphasis was on the iron-workings, but with the growth of the coal trade in the mid-19th cent. the town expanded fast. It is the centre of a district that produced the best steam coal in the world. When the demand for coal fell, Aberdare turned gallantly to other industries.

It has always been a Welsh town, even if the language is not as prominent in the streets as once it was. It has also a proud record for its interest in the arts. The poet Alun Lewis was born here. Aberdare is probably the only town in Britain that has raised a statue to a choir conductor. It stands in Victoria Square, in front of the Black Lion Inn, which has translated its name into Welsh as Gwesty'r Llew Du. The bronze statue, by Sir William Goscombe John, represents Caradog (Griffith Rhys Jones) with baton raised conducting the Great Choir (South Wales Choral Union), 500 strong, which won the chief choral prize at the Crystal Palace in 1872 and 1873.

In Victoria Square, behind the statue, is the small, well-designed Victoria Hall, and a little further on the successfully modern Public Library.

Near the Library the classical façade of the English Wesleyan chapel (1859) confronts the florid Constitutional Club, with its remarkably complicated wrought-iron crown over the small tower in the centre. Close to this group of buildings the old Church of St John stands in a daffodil-filled churchyard, surrounded by trees. This was one of the oldest churches in Glamorgan, but has been extensively restored. In the churchyard, David Williams of Aberaman, in 1789, insisted on being buried standing upright, to be ready at the Day of Judgment.

The other large church in the town is St Mary's, Maesydref, built in the French Gothic style in 1865. The novelist Thomas Hardy, who was apprenticed to the architect in his youth, is supposed to have had a hand in preparing the plans.

Aberdare Park, on the road out towards Hirwaun, has a statue of Lord Aberdare, set in a pool with a fountain.

ABERDARON, *Caernarfonshire.* This still remote and very attractive village is set in the curve of the last hook of Lleyn, the western peninsula of Caernarfonshire reaching out to Ireland. It is in a bay with the name of Aberdaron, separated from the greater bay of Porth Neigwl, commonly called Hell's Mouth, by the head of land called Trwyn y Penrhyn and its small scatter of islands, Ynys Gwylan-Fawr and Gwylan-Fach. Once lost in the Land's End of Wales, it has now been rediscovered. This restores some of the importance it had in

Y Gegin Fawr, the 14th-cent. pilgrims' rest-house at Aberdaron

Peter Baker

the Middle Ages, when it was the point of embarkation for the pilgrims to Bardsey Island, a place of many buried saints. The rest-house they used in Aberdaron is still shown – a small whitewashed cottage, probably a genuine relic of the times. The bridge over the Daron stream, a narrow curve of stone between arched parapet walls, is also probably the original one.

The church had an older foundation than the one seen now, though the earlier plan can still be made out. With Bardsey, it shares its origin in the "Celtic" expression of Christianity that claims precedence over the mission of St Augustine to Britain in the late 7th cent. It has been described as forming with the church on Bardsey Island a centre of faith as important as the Scots Iona with which it formed part of the same missionary movement. Bardsey Island is believed to have been the place of refuge for the monks of the great Christian college at Bangor-Is-Coed, not far from Chester, after the decisive battle of A.D. 615, when the armies of Northumbria severed the Britons of what is now Wales from those of Strathclyde and all the territory lying between Chester and Carlisle. The existing church at Aberdaron has a door of Norman style to show how, even in this westernmost refuge, the early faith was overtaken. But it always kept a position of special sanctity, and was the scene of an incident in which the politics of medieval Wales was curiously concentrated. For in the 12th cent. the Prince of South Wales, Gruffydd the son of Rhys, fled there for sanctuary from the diplomatic intrigues of Gruffydd son of Cynan, Prince of the North, who proposed to hand him over to Henry I of England. The military force sent to take him was met by the united clergy of Aberdaron and Lleyn and dared not set foot within the holy place. The young Prince of the South escaped by night and found refuge in his own territory.

Aberdaron has always fished the deep waters, and its engaging old inn can provide crab and lobster of remarkable size. The streets are narrow; all the lanes, rising steeply from the place, are narrow and winding. This is entirely proper. The width of view over sea and mountain is more than compensation, and the nearness of the houses to one another gives, against that background, a sense of human community. The countryside surrounding the village is rich with the colours of gorse and heather, and the cliffs of the promontory cut into it with stark contrast. From Aberdaron the crossing can be made by boat over Bardsey Sound to Bardsey Island, whose Welsh name Ynys Enlli (Island of Tides) is a warning of very real dangers, even though an alternative meaning is possible for Enlli as a place of good provender.

About 1 m. from Aberdaron, on the road to Pwllheli, Bodwrdda was built as a farmhouse in the 15th cent.; about 2 m. N. the old quarries of stone, once much in demand for their blood-red jasper and pink marble, lie abandoned; but evidence of their output can be seen here and there in the local roadways. SW. for just over 2 m.

is the route to the cape stretching from the arm of land curved over the pool of sea, Braich y Pwll. Here the cliffs, notably the Parwyd (Great Wall), are at their best; and the holy water of Ffynnon Mair (Mary's Spring) justifies its sanctity by keeping itself always fresh, however often overrun by the strength of the salt tides.

A local worthy, still remembered as Dic Aberdaron, was one Richard Robert Jones, who died at St Asaph in 1845. He is respected as a self-educated man who contrived to learn at least fourteen languages. He put this effort to little further use, content to be possessed so widely of the world without wishing to change it in any way. The spirit of the Dark Age monks, who worshipped God in the works of nature they chose to live among, was perpetuated in him.

ABERDOVEY, *Merioneth,* called Aberdyfi in Welsh, is a small town, beautifully placed at the mouth of the Dovey (Dyfi) estuary. The hills of Cefn Rhos, gorse-covered and rugged, shelter it from the north wind. There are some older houses clustered along the quay, but the main town rises in pleasant Victorian and Edwardian terraces round a curve of the lower slope of Cefn Rhos, and looks across over the wide sands of the estuary to the wilds of Plynlimon in the S. A small ferry takes the visitor over to Borth and its sands on the Cardiganshire side of the estuary. Aberdovey, however, has plenty of sand to itself. The wide beach curves round the steep plunge of Cefn Rhos and runs northwards towards Towyn. The well-known golf course of Aberdovey is laid out in these sandhills.

Aberdovey is now firmly in the holiday business, but 100 years ago there was a different atmosphere here. The little quay was thronged with the trading schooners that made all these small Cardigan Bay ports into lively places, full of the adventure of seagoing and trade. The young men of Aberdovey went to sea as a matter of course, but – as the historian of seagoing Aberdovey, the Rev. D. W. Morgan, suggested by the title of his book – it was a *Brief Glory.* Documents survive to throw a good deal of light on the ships and shipping that used the Dovey waters 150 years ago. They were held by partnerships that divided the interest in them into as many as sixteenth parts or, in one case, sixty-fourth parts. In 1828, four of these last were sold for £35, or about £350 of present value. Owners were not always mariners themselves; one partnership included also a farmer, a ropemaker, a timber merchant, a spinster, a tanner, and even an ostler. But the ostler would be one of those who owned an inn and had a stable of horses on hire for the coaching-roads. Lime, timber, culm, hides, and wool went aboard for shipment, and the sloops would not only touch in at Gareg, as the Dovey shore between Eglwys-fach and Derwenlas was then known, but were often built at wharfs both there and at Llugwy on the opposite bank. Today the heirs of this tradition are the members of the Outward Bound Sea School, which has its headquarters in Aberdovey.

Peter Baker

The sea-front, Aberdovey

Aberdovey's early story is also quickly summarized. It had the happy knack of keeping out of the more dangerous events of Welsh history. After all, the road along the estuary was not completed until 1827, and the railway had to tunnel industriously to get here. But from Penhelyg, the true port of Aberdovey, can be seen, and for some distance walked along, a roadway cut at the base of the rocky hill-sides through which the railway line burrows. It reaches a fair distance into the estuary; but it is rarely safe to use, for the tide drowns it at intervals. Local belief is that this is a roadway cut to serve the coach-routes of the 18th and 19th cents. but one can scarcely believe that vehicles in those days would have risked such a perilous journey. It seems to have been engineered when the estuary lay further below its present level, which would have been a considerable time before the silt and sand affected the river mouth. The Romans used Pennal as a military station; and there could have been for them no alternative way to reach it except at the foot of the rocks. Llywelyn the Great, however, did summon an assembly of all the leading men of Wales to meet him at Aberdovey in 1216, in what was virtually the first Welsh parliament. Llywelyn succeeded in settling, with statesmanlike moderation, the claims of all the lords who owed him homage. The main outlines of this settlement were not disputed in his lifetime, and they became the main base of his power.

If history has been largely silent about early Aberdovey, legend has more than made up for this reticence. The name of the little town has rung round the world on the notes of the popular song "The Bells of Aberdovey". This is no folk-song. The music was composed by Dibdin for his opera *Liberty Hall*, and the original words have a period charm, with the refrain in Welsh: "If you love me as I love you, the Bells of Aberdovey ring one, two, three. . . ."

> Do salmon love a lucid stream,
> Or thirsty sheep love fountains?
> Do Druids love a doleful theme,
> Or goats the craggy mountains?
> If it be true these things are so,
> As truly she's my lover,
> And os wyt ti yn carri fi,
> Fel wyf fi yn caru di,
> As un, dau, tri, pedwar, pump, chwech
> Go the bells of Aberdovey.

Other lyricists have added other words to the tune, but the theme remains the same. A city lies off Aberdovey, sunk beneath the waves, and the bells can be heard, "in the quiet even time", swinging softly in the swell of the sea. The story is a common one all along the Welsh coast-line and is known in Brittany as well. It may reflect some far-off folk memory of the advance of the sea after the Ice Age. Geologists date some of this advance to as late as 5000 B.C., and there were certainly hunters wandering over the drowned areas at that date.

There could be a second source for the story. Not many miles N. of Aberdovey, near Towyn, one of the "sarnau" or causeways that are such a strange feature of Cardigan Bay runs out to sea. This is Sarn-y-Bwch. Even stranger is the long bank of stone and sand called Sarn Badrig (St Patrick's Causeway), which stretches over

12 m. into the sea from the sandy point of Mochras, near Harlech. This dries out in patches at very low tide. A third sarn begins 7 m. S. of Aberdovey at Sarn Gynfelyn. There are even traces of a fourth sarn starting to form off Llanrhystyd S. of Aberystwyth.

The origin of the causeways is still uncertain. At one time it was suggested that they might be moraines deposited by the glaciers of the Ice Age in retreat. Maybe the swirl of the tides into the circling arms of the Lleyn peninsula has something to do with it. And does each sarn reach a certain limit, and then act as a breakwater to turn material to the next sarn growing further S.? Nothing is sure, but the sarnau have always impressed the sailors of Cardigan Bay with the regularity of their structure. This could have suggested some vast defence work protecting fertile lands from the sea. Thomas Love Peacock gave memorable literary form to the story told in the old Triads of the drowning of Cantref y Gwaelod (Bottom Hundreds). Seithenyn, one of the "three immortal drunkards of Wales", had been entrusted by Prince Gwyddno Garanhir with the guardianship of the great dyke and sluices that protected the most fertile land of Wales. Gwyddno himself had his palace somewhere on Sarn Gynfelyn. Seithenyn saw no reason to disturb himself about the state of his charge. To every warning that the embankment had become rotten, he laughed and gave the immediate order: "Cupbearer, fill!" Nemesis arrived on a night of great storm. The embankment was overwhelmed and Seithenyn with it. Gwyddno escaped to spend his life in lamentation over his lost province.

Aberdovey's concern with the sea is now in fishing. It has rivals in this activity along the estuary. And of one of them a tale is told that is bitterly resented. It alleges that this other community of toilers in the sea had the habit of thieving whatever was thrown up as flotsam and jetsam, including men cast away by wreck. One unlucky Portuguese was washed up, alive and wearing a pair of remarkable sea-boots. To get them, runs the slanderous tale, his legs were cut off. "And they are cursed down to the ninth generation," say the seamen of Aberdovey; repeating, however little they are aware of it, the doom pronounced by the earliest Welsh tribal law.

The present church of Aberdovey is modern, and so are the bells. Until it was built, Aberdovey folk had to walk to Towyn, and the spot on the road from which they first caught sight of the building is still called Bryn Padria, from the paternosters pronounced by the devout.

Behind the Cefn Rhos ridge lies Cwm Dyffryn, a fine, somewhat rugged valley that the old guidebooks insisted on calling Happy Valley. Apparently no Welsh resort was considered respectable in late Victorian days unless it had a Happy Valley close at hand. This one has luckily been left in its natural state. On the hills near the top of the pass lies Llyn Barfog (Bearded Lake), a somewhat melancholy tarn.

ABEREDW, *Radnorshire*, is placed in an enviable position at the point where the small Edw stream tumbles into the Wye 6 m. S. of Builth. Here the Wye runs through steep hills in one of the most beautiful stretches of its long and memorable course. Aberedw stands on the Radnorshire bank of the river, away from the traffic that follows the main road on the Breconshire side.

The church, in its wooded dingle above the little Edw stream, is a beauty. It possesses a 15th-cent. screen, a fine and ancient wooden roof over the nave, and a porch with clover-leaf ornaments. Until the 18th cent. the populace used to stage sports meetings round the two old yew trees before the porch, on the day of their patron saint in June. Immediately S. of the village the hills rise to over 1,000 ft, and on the steep plunge down to the Wye are the Aberedw rocks, a fine terraced formation that runs for 1 m. above the river. They may not quite be a "gorge of Alpine proportion", as they seemed to the old traveller Malkin, but this rocky and wooded steep inspired Parson Kilvert to a rhapsody in his celebrated diary, as he looked up from the river and saw the cliff castles and marked the green woods waving and the wild roses clinging to the crags.

The narrow and beautiful valley of the Edw runs eastwards under the high Rhulen hills. The road squeezes onwards between hedges. It brings you, within a short distance, to Llanbadarn-y-Garreg. Here the church stands, whitewashed and clean, in a meadow beside the rushing stream. A church of lonely charm – as, indeed, is Rhulen church, a few miles further on. Rhulen is perched high up on the mountain-side in a site of remote splendour. It dates from the 14th cent., has only two windows, and boasts a wooden belfry. The valley continues with increasing rural beauty to Cregrina. Here again is a church difficult to get to but perfectly suited to its lonely setting. It has a Norman font, a 15th-cent. screen, and an ancient wooden roof. It was restored with the help of a grant from the Pilgrim Trust in 1958. Cregrina is one of the many places that claim to be the spot where the last wolf in Wales was killed. In Cregrina's case, the event is claimed for the reign of Elizabeth I. The paws of the animal were nailed to the church door.

From the little bridge over the Edw a mound is visible called Pennar Mount. This was the home of a celebrated soldier of the 15th cent., a great patron of the poets, who rejoiced in the euphonious name of Maredudd ap Dafydd ap Hywel ap Meilyr. Luckily for the English, and for the poets who had to find rhymes to sing his praises, he was also known as Bedo Chwith. Lewis Glyn Cothi, one of the best Welsh poets of the 15th cent., celebrated his prowess and hospitality in ringing verse. Just beyond Cregrina the road forks. One branch goes through the hills to Hundred House; the other turns E. to the hidden valley of Glasgwm. Both are worth travelling.

High up among the rocks by Aberedw, and rather difficult to find, is the cave of Llywelyn the

Last, where that unfortunate prince is supposed to have hidden just before he met his death. A persistent tradition asserts that he came to the blacksmith when the snow lay on the ground, and ordered him to reverse the shoes of his horse, so that he could mislead the English. The blacksmith is said to have betrayed the fact to the English, who were able to follow Llywelyn's tracks in the snow. To this day, local folk are rightly sensitive if you refer to this unfounded story.

On the height that looks above the village of Aberedw at the Brecon hills are the ruins of a castle. The old Cambrian Railway, now closed, cut through its site, and the stones were used to ballast the track between Aberedw and Llanelwedd. That castle – although far into what was for him enemy territory – was the seat of the last Llywelyn; it was used by him as a place from which to take his sport at hunting when the sterner affairs of his principality in the North allowed it. Here he stayed not long before his death in 1282.

In 1240, the Llywelyn called the Great had died and been buried at Aberconwy (Conway). His success had lain not simply in asserting an effective supremacy over the other ruling houses of Wales, and making the North the foremost of the Welsh provinces, but in establishing a principle even greater than the recognition of the unity of Wales internally. With both the King of Scotland and the feudal baronage of England, he had been in 1215 a signatory of Magna Carta under which King John of England had been required to acknowledge that the only true definition of a state was the supremacy of law over power. Llywelyn the Great had joined with the baronage to establish the fact that the laws of Wales, like the laws of Scotland, must be looked on as equal in worth with those of England. Llywelyn the Last joined with Simon de Montfort to push the principle further, and make the identity of Wales as a distinct national personality within the British community permanently accepted. The ancient and persistent policy of Powys was to establish as an association of equals the common descent from Roman jurisdiction in Britain that both England and Wales enjoyed.

It was not as an act of political intrigue among dissident barons, but as a seal of common purpose in a matter of high policy, that Llywelyn became engaged to marry the daughter of Simon. Llywelyn was identified with the North of Wales, in which English influence had least penetrated. But, in conjunction with Simon de Montfort, he reached out to the South and defeated the Earl of Mortimer at Builth. De Montfort, however, was overthrown and killed at Evesham in 1265, and in 1267 Llywelyn, despite earlier successes, was forced to agree to the Treaty of Montgomery. This, however, recognized his title as Prince of Wales and his right to the allegiance of all other Welsh rulers. Nine years later, Edward I, the new King of England, marched a large force into Wales, laid waste Anglesey, and imposed a new treaty on Llywelyn that reduced his control to the Isle of Anglesey alone and left him with that only on condition of his paying a tribute of 1,000 marks yearly. But the Treaty of Rhuddlan, which laid down these terms, added that even this scrap of sovereignty would be lost if Llywelyn died childless. But he married Eleanor, De Montfort's daughter, in 1278, and two years later he had a daughter of his own, Gwenllian. It was then that Edward accused him of still insisting that Welsh matters should be settled by Welsh laws. Again the King's forces invaded the country, and got as far as Anglesey, the granary of Wales. Across the Menai Straits, they laid a wooden bridge capable of taking men sixty abreast, to invade what was the last piece of Welsh soil belonging to a Welsh prince. The English were driven back with heavy loss; and they were compelled to retreat rapidly to the S. They fell back on Builth, and Llywelyn pursued them.

What happened is still largely a mystery. To Aberedw came the Prince, and somehow in the woods there was a chance skirmish. It may have happened at the small place of Cilmery, where the monument of Llywelyn stands. An English man-at-arms cut down a knight as he might have cut down any other. It is sometimes said that he came upon this knight with his helmet off, drinking at a stream. Only after he went over the corpse for what he might find did the Englishman realize that he had killed the Prince of Wales. The head was cut off and sent for public display in London in derision of the claim of Wales to have the only just right to the crown of Britain. And Edward built his castle at Caernarfon in deliberate imitation of the Theodosian fortifications at Constantinople, the capital once of the Roman world; for in overthrowing the last successor of Cunedda, founder of Powys and of the Roman-British tradition in the West of Britain, Edward felt the Empire of the West of Europe had passed into his hands.

What is less well known about this tragedy that Aberedw remembers is that upon Llywelyn's body was a sacred relic, one that perhaps his slayer discovered and so realized whom he had slain. It is the Croes Nawdd (Cross of Protection), a fragment of the True Cross, whose ultimate fate is also a mystery.

The sequel was not, however, what the Treaty of Rhuddlan of 1277 had foreshadowed, the total extinction of Welsh nationality. The rising of Rhys ap Maredudd in 1287–90, and the capture of Caernarfon Castle by Madoc, son of Llywelyn, in 1294, resulted in the continuance of the principality as Magna Carta and the ideals of Simon de Montfort required. The castle at Aberedw is in ruins, but the spirit that raised it is immortal.

ABERERCH, *Caernarfonshire.* Lying between Criccieth and Pwllheli, Abererch is reached by side roads from the main way. It is secluded and quiet, and is almost a model village, with neatly balanced cottages fronting each other. The church is large and distinguished for so small a place. The lanes around it are heavy with flowered hedges. Its greatest attraction is its nearness to the wide and lonely beach of the Morfa Abererch. From its sands, the fragments of rock called Cerrig y Baredy stand out of the sea. Small families of seals are known to haunt it, and they seem to have no fear of boats that are rowed there for fishing.

ABERFAN, *Glamorgan*. This mining village in the narrow valley of the Taff, 4 m. S. of Merthyr Tydfil and now within the borough boundaries, made a tragic entry into history on the 21st October 1966. Just after 9.15 a.m., while the morning mists still clung to the 1,500-ft mountain above Aberfan, a section of one of the seven big tips of the Merthyr Vale colliery suddenly slipped. It poured a strange black flood of sludge and mine-waste down the mountain-side. It raced forwards for 500 yds, crushing a small farm in its path. It swept away terraced houses and fell upon the Pantglas Junior School. The pupils were gathered in their classrooms when the flood of slimy rubbish burst over the building. In all, 116 children and twenty-six adults perished on the spot.

The news sent a wave of sympathy round the world. The accident seemed to symbolize all the risks and tragedy of coal-getting. A memorial to the children now stands in the cemetery on the hill-side. It is visible from the main Merthyr to Cardiff road on the other side of the valley. The killer tip has been extensively landscaped, levelled, and planted, and an intensive survey made of the other tips of the coalfield. Tips, however, present grave problems. The removal of one large tip, built up during fifty years, could cost millions of pounds. Where tips lie on the valley floor, they can be levelled, but in the narrower valleys the mine-waste had to be carried up on to the mountain-side by ropeways. These mountain tips still stand grimly against the skyline. The National Coal Board is not complacent about them. It is simply the heir of 150 years of ruthless mining in South Wales.

ABERFFRAW, *Anglesey*. Pronounce the name with the accent on the second syllable.

Around this charming little sea-coast village there is little to see now but the westward rocks of Anglesey that fall into the sliding sea, to the SE. the long glimmer of Malltraeth Sands, and to the NW. the piled stones of Barclodiad y Gawres. Of Aberffraw itself, the glory has departed. But here was the seat of the legendary kingdom that was the birth of Britain.

The last years of Rome saw a sudden and successful burst of energy; the Rescript of Honorius in A.D. 410 delegated the defence of Britain and Brittany to the cities themselves, though Roman generalship was available to be called on in times of real need. The reaction against Scots and Irish incursion, as Bede states, resulted in fifty years of peace and prosperity for Britain. This period is associated with the name of one Cunedda and his successors, with a force that gathered itself about Carlisle in the North, held the Walls and swept the Irish Sea clear. It is only later opinion that has assumed Cunedda to have been some Scots tribal leader hired to keep firm the coasts of Gwynedd and Strathclyde. Sir John Rhys makes no doubt that he wore the regalia of a Roman commander and had regiments of horse, ridden with the knee-stirrup that in the 5th cent. had been introduced to give greater control of one's mount, and headed with

Aberffraw

Peter Baker

legionary standards. The names of his "fore-fathers" – Paternus, Aeturnus, Tacitus – are in fact names of the Roman para-Mithraic hierarchy that the legions in their later days had adopted; a Mithraic temple has in recent years been found at the Segontium that was the first Caernarfon, for one example.

At Aberffraw the "sons" of Cunedda made their capital and gathered their fleets to dominate the seas of Anglesey and Man between Westmorland and Ulster. It was at Aberffraw, too, that Gwynedd, the North of Wales, made its administrative centre for generations, and in Anglesey that the people of Gwynedd were supplied by the agriculture first founded on that island under direct Roman control. And it was at Aberffraw that the Maglocunos, or Maelgwn, whom Gildas singled out in the 5th cent. as chief of all the rulers of Britain, had his ships centred and rallied the Britons of the West against the Saxon onslaught. While it lasted, the Roman-British state fostered on both sides of the Irish Sea that distinctive Celtic Christianity which has left its monuments widely scattered through the heart of Wales. The fall of that state, which proceeded piecemeal after the loss of Chester in A.D. 615, left in the command of the western waters a gap that the Viking fleets were only too ready to fill. Aberffraw left its memorials only in the names of the great saints – Patrick, David, Columba, and many others – who made their impression on the story of the Irish Sea. Of its court and castle nothing remains, though Llywelyn the Great, in the 13th cent., still kept the title of Prince of Aberffraw.

A mysterious link in that story stands at Barclodiad y Gawres. The Gawres (Giantess) its name suggests is, as usual, some memory of a woman of princely birth. When excavated, the chamber showed itself to be a curious parallel with that other chamber of Bryn-celli-ddu only 10 m. away and not far from Llanfair P.G. The stones are incised with spirals, chevrons, and other geometrical figures by which men of that time tried to express the divine mathematic system of the stars. But these at Barclodiad are allied closely with those patterns found in Ireland; at Bryn-celli-ddu they follow fashions found elsewhere. Two cremation burials were found in it. Its builders seem to have followed ritual forms that had come, and perhaps they had brought, from the eastern Mediterranean and from the intermediate point of Spain, 4,000 years ago, when the Wessex Culture that set up Stonehenge traded in Irish gold and Baltic amber, and the excellent timber of Britain, with the centres of Bronze Age civilization on the other side of Europe.

The only relics of Aberffraw's past are on the islet rejoined to the shore at low tide and called St Cwyfan's after the church that possesses it, where a service is held once a year. This, like most churches in Anglesey, can claim its first foundation in the Age of Saints. But the evidence for that period is best found in the nearby church of Llangadwaladr. This is now built in the style that affected Welsh church architecture after the Edwardian Wars, being Perpendicular in style and belonging to the 1400s. It has old glass and, even more strikingly, a monument to the legend-beset era when Rome withdrew from centralized control of its empire, and native governments attempted to maintain the Roman-British culture they had inherited. This monument is of the 7th cent. It is therefore part of the later "Arthurian" period, when that Roman-British tradition was being forced back into what was to be its last refuge in Wales. *Catamanus rex sapientissimus opinatissimus,* the inscription is reported to read. "Cataman, king most wise" is a phrase to be expected. The second adjective may be a misreading of some other word, since, as it stands, it means that the king was entirely imaginary. Either it was intended to convey that he was a man filled with thought, or perhaps that he was *opimus,* of great wealth. He is supposed to be Cadfan, the war leader of the Cymry or Welsh and father of the Cadwallon who, about A.D. 660, revenged the fall of Chester and overthrew the Northumbrian forces at Hethfield, and so for a while regained British control of Strathclyde and even from Yorkshire up to Edinburgh.

ABERGAVENNY, *Monmouthshire,* is proud of its title, the Gateway to Wales, and has an incomparable setting. Here the Usk emerges from the mountains and swings southwards on its new course towards the distant sea. Four noble hills stand sentinel round the town. To the N. is the graceful cone of the Sugar Loaf, just under 2,000 ft and an outlier from the main mass of the Black Mountains of Monmouthshire. Some 2,130 acres of the Sugar Loaf were given to the National Trust as a memorial to Lord Rhondda. Across the Usk rises the massive Blorenge, 1,834 ft, a mountain of Old Red Sandstone capped with limestone cliffs. To the NE. is Ysgyryd Fawr (the Skirrid, 1,596 ft), where another 205 acres belong to the National Trust. Ysgyryd Fach (the Little Skirrid, 886 ft) completes the ring of hills to the E. Abergavenny lies in the lush green bowl in the centre of this ring. Not even the new line of tall pylons, ruled across the landscape from the mouth of the wooded valley of the Usk, can mar this fine composition of mountain and river scenery. The town itself may not be remarkable architecturally, but it has the life and bustle of a country market centre and contains some ancient monuments that make it worthy of its setting.

As can be expected from its position at the point where the Usk leaves the mountains, Abergavenny has always been a strong base for anyone trying to invade South Wales. The Romans seem to have had a fort here, Gobannium, but the town enters fully into history with the arrival of the Normans. Rufus gave it to Hamelin de Balun. Later it became the stronghold of the famous Marcher family of De Braose. It was a William de Braose, one of the most notable of the clan, who made Abergavenny a place hateful for 200 years in the eyes

Abergavenny, across the Usk valley to the Skirrid

of the Welsh. This powerful baron, who combined unctuous piety with ruthlessness in a way peculiar to the Normans, succeeded to the inheritance in 1177. He signalled his entrance into history by inviting Seissyll, the most important of the neighbouring Welsh rulers, together with numerous other prominent Welshmen from Gwent, to a banquet in the castle. He had them mercilessly put to death as they feasted. Not content with this, he sent his retainers post-haste to Seisyll's castle. Here they seized his wife and killed his young son, Cadwaladr, in his mother's arms. The Welsh took revenge by capturing Abergavenny Castle, but William de Braose, in the way of the wicked, flourished for thirty years, until he met his match in wicked King John. John stripped him of his lands and left him to die a beggar. Abergavenny Castle, with its memories of blood and border tragedy, is now a ruin, set on the wooded hill that dominates the town. The gatehouse, some walls, the motte, and the foundations of the keep are all that is visible. The town museum is in the park. The Castle came into the possession of the Neville family in the 15th cent. The barony of Abergavenny is not created, but is attached to the possession of the Castle, in the same way as Arundel Castle carries with it the enjoyment of the earldom of Arundel. The townsfolk now pronounce the name of their town with the accent on the penultimate syllable. The Marquess of Abergavenny prefers to retain an older pronunciation and calls himself – to the confusion of foreigners and most Welshmen – "Aberghenny". Whichever way you pronounce the name, the view from Abergavenny Castle westwards is magnificent. The wooded domain is now a public park.

The main street of Abergavenny is an epitome of its history. It has collected buildings from the Tudor period onwards, and they all seem to fit in, including the fine early 19th-cent. Angel Hotel. The level of the road has risen continuously through the centuries, so that, by searching at ground level, you can spot the occasional Tudor archways and windows that survive. The old tower, with its battlements, belonged to the former Parish Church of St John. Beside it is the Masonic Hall, built on the site of the old grammar school. Among the churches of the town is the Roman Catholic one, built opposite the new grammar school at Pen-y-Pound. It contains a painting of St George slaying the dragon, interesting as the work of Sir Kenelm Digby, who was killed in 1648, during the Second Civil War. The Town Hall is a 19th-cent. Gothic triumph of red stone with a green-topped tower and a large clock presented by the ironmaster Crawshay Bailey.

Abergavenny today is hardly a stronghold of Welsh-speakers, but in the 19th cent. the efforts of Sir Benjamin Hall and his wife, later Lord and Lady Llanover, made the town an important centre in the movement to revive Welsh culture. At the little Sun Inn, in the main street, the literary society of Cymreigyddion y Fenni was inaugurated, and for nearly thirty years the annual Eisteddfodau drew all that was best in the literary world of Wales to Abergavenny. Here, in 1848, Thomas Stephens won the prize for his essay on the literature of the Cymru, which became the authoritative textbook on the subject throughout Europe. The impetus behind the Eisteddfod died with the passing of Lord Llanover. Abergavenny returned to its natural vocation as a pleasant, busy market town. The River Usk flows under the old bridge, with its fifteen arches, undisturbed by the music and poetry of the bards.

Monk Street leads out of the main street to the great glory of Abergavenny, St Mary's Church. This was originally the church of the Benedictine priory founded by Hamelin de Balun. The Benedictines were the favoured monks of the Norman Marcher barons, as the Carthusians were of the Welsh. The priory grew under the protective shadow of the Castle. It was naturally sacked by Owain Glyndwr's men, when they set fire to the town during the wild Glyndwr Revolt. Little remains of the priory buildings. Some of the walls run alongside the little River Gavenny, from which the town gets its name. Two noble trees, a chestnut and a sycamore, give shade to the site. The great tithe barn of the priory still stands, and the prior's house adjoins the S. transept. It was rebuilt in the 17th cent. Henry VIII dissolved the priory in 1543 and used the income to found the grammar school. He converted the priory church into the Town Church of St Mary.

From the car park that now lies inside the wall immediately to the right of the W. end of the church, you can see something of the massive strength of the walls and the 14th-cent. tower, which made these great churches of the borderland as much fortresses as houses of prayer. The present W. front is new and was rebuilt in 1882, as well as the five arches within the church that now separate the nave from the N. aisle. The church, however, still contains a remarkable collection of ancient treasures. The two outstanding features are the choir-stalls and the tombs in the Lewis and Herbert chapels. There are twenty-four choir-stalls dating from about 1380. In view of the many Welsh sackings, Puritan cleansings, and Victorian rebuildings to which this church has been subjected, their survival is a small miracle. Yet here they are to gladden the eye, with the stalls of the prior and sub-prior under tall, pointed canopies, rich in elaborate tracery, at the end of each row.

The Lewis Chapel flanks the sanctuary to the N. At the base of the E. wall of this chapel has been placed one of the most impressive monuments in St Mary's, a huge wooden figure of the patriarch Jesse. The nobly bearded patriarch lies asleep, clasping the tree branch growing from his body. The figure may have been the base of a huge Jesse tree that formed the reredos of the old high altar. Near at hand is the tomb of Dr David Lewis, who became the first Principal of Jesus College, the Welsh college at Oxford. He was also one of Queen Elizabeth I's Commissioners of Admiralty. A wide arch separates the Lewis Chapel from the chancel. Under it are the two earliest tombs in the church, one of Eva de Braose (1246), the other of Christian Herbert (1307).

The rest of the Herberts lie in the Herbert Chapel itself. The family possessed the great estate of Coldbrook on the Usk road. In the chapel to the left of the sanctuary the Herberts are numerous indeed. The altar tomb at the back of the stalls is that of Laurence de Hastings (1348). His half-brother Sir William Hastings (1349) lies on the beautifully carved tomb below the three-light window. In the centre of the chapel is the proud last resting-place of Sir William ap Thomas of Herbert (1446), with his wife Gladys beside him. She was the daughter of the famous soldier Sir David Gam, who died at Agincourt. The fine alabaster tomb of Sir William's son, Sir Richard, is nearly under the

great arch. He was a Yorkist, executed after the Battle of Banbury in 1469. So many border notables followed him into defeat that the battle was looked upon by the Welsh as a national disaster. His wife Margaret rests beside him. A final Herbert, Sir Richard Herbert of Ewyas, lies under a crocketed arch under the window. So the Herberts lie in the dignity of death on their elaborately carved splendours of stone and alabaster. There is one effigy in the church that seems to make more impression than even the Herbert glories. This is the wooden effigy of a young nobleman, placed on a simple trestle. There are only about 100 similar figures in the churches of Britain. The Abergavenny figure is regarded as one of the finest. It represents a young warrior clad in mail, noble and dignified. There is no certainty about who he was. He may have been George de Cantelupe, who died in 1273 at the age of twenty. There are other tombs and monuments in the church, but none to rival this simple image.

Abergavenny is now the starting-point of the new Heads of the Valleys road that runs from the outskirts of the town, up through the Clydach vale under the Blorenge, and so on to the tops of the mining valleys to the W. The Usk valley to the W., the Black Mountains, and the Brecon Beacons are now all part of the Brecon Beacons National Park. Abergavenny is the natural gateway to the park. The information centre of the Monmouthshire Park Planning Committee is in Monk Street.

ABERGELE, *Denbighshire.* The old market town of Abergele lies 1 m. from the sea, half way between the bigger coastal resorts of Rhyl and Colwyn Bay. The new motor road along the coast now by-passes it. The wooded hills rise behind it; to the E. are the long levels of the great Morfa Rhuddlan. The church is double-naved. The main structure dates from the reign of Henry VIII and was tactfully restored in 1879. The initials and dates on the screen were probably carved by the pupils when the church was used as a school in Tudor times. The marks on the pillars were made by archers who used the pillars to sharpen their arrows. Other treasures include some 15th-cent. stained glass, a 13th-cent. stone cross within the communion rails, a wooden chest carved out of a single log, and a chalice dated 1601. The churchyard contains memorials of the shipwreck of the *Ocean Monarch* in 1848 and the Irish Mail disaster of August 1868, when the train ran into petrol trucks at Llanddulas station, with the loss of thirty-three lives.

Abergele is connected with its seaside suburb, Pensarn, by the wide Dundonald Avenue. Pensarn has the usual promenade and sea-front of boarding-houses. The sands along this stretch of coastline are firm and welcoming, although the railway runs close to the shore, and the station for Abergele is in Pensarn. With the sands go the caravans. The extent of the caravan sites and holiday camps, which now stretch along the whole length of the North Wales coastline from Point of Air past Rhyl to near Abergele, is breathtaking. This must be one of the most intensively caravanned parts of Britain. As a result, there is heavy traffic in the Abergele district all through the summer on the new main road and the side roads as well. It is a relief to get up on to the hills behind to Castell Cawr, claimed to be a Roman stronghold. A little further S. on the road to St Asaph is Kinmel Park, with its fine tree-filled grounds. The house is now a girls' school, but the park became well known during the First World War as the main Army training centre for North Wales.

To the W. of Abergele the hills begin to come nearer the sea. About ½ m. away, at the foot of these wooded slopes alongside the old main road, is Gwrych Castle, once the home of the Earl of Dundonell, who won fame as a soldier in the South African War. Gwrych is an imposing mock antique (half the towers are sham), and can be enjoyed in the spirit in which it was built. If you care to risk the traffic, you can stop to read the long array of historic events inscribed on the tablets at the gates as having taken place in the neighbourhood. Gwrych Castle is now a holiday centre. Beyond the Castle the gap narrows between the hills and the sea. There are extensive quarries in the area, and long jetties run out from the high coastline to allow coasting vessels to load the stone easily. At the village of Llanddulas the Earl of Northumberland lured Richard II to capture, after Richard had returned from Ireland to Conway Castle. From Llanddulas he was taken on his unhappy journey to Flint, where he was handed over to his enemy, Bolingbroke.

The countryside inland from Llanddulas is impressive. The limestone hill of Cefn yr Ogof offers caves and fine views over the coast. The Dulas river runs back into the high ground that guards the valley of the Elwy further S. The roads and lanes become narrower, steeper, and more twisting the further you go inland. Moelfre Isaf (Lower Rounded Hill) makes a fine and exhilarating viewpoint.

ABERGLASLYN, Pass of, *Caernarfonshire.* This miniature pass, through which the turbulent Glaslyn river cuts its way out of the fastnesses of Snowdon towards the meadowlands of the Traeth Mawr and the sea, is one of the justly praised showplaces of North Wales. The cliffs on either side are only 700 ft high, but they make a splendid effect as they lift their pine-clad rocks out of the tumbling stream. Maybe the old 18th-cent. traveller John Cradock was slightly carried away when he declared that Aberglaslyn was the "noblest specimen of the Finely Horrid the Eye can possibly behold . . . 'tis the last Approach to the mansion of Pluto through the regions of Despair". But the pass is fine enough, especially when you stand on the rough stone bridge, with the heights of Moel Hebog hemming you in on the N. Standing on the bridge, however, is hardly possible with the tourist traffic in high summer. The old Welsh Highland Railway tunnelled through the rocks on the S. side. It is

now disused. The meadows stretch westwards, under the long range of wooded cliffs that line the roadway between Aberglaslyn and Tremadoc. The whole of this level area is reclaimed land. It seems hard to believe it today, but, before the Portmadoc embankment was built in the early 19th cent., small ships sailed up to the entrance to the pass – and Aberglaslyn really was the mouth of the Glaslyn. The whole landscape immediately to the S. of the pass after you have crossed the bridge is wild and strangely torn with tumbled rock, ice-scraped by the glaciers that once passed down through Nantgwynant. Away from the road, this is one of the roughest regions of North Wales.

ABERGORLECH, *Carmarthenshire,* is a quiet village 8 m. N. of Llandeilo on the Cothi river. This is remote pastoral country, with the Forestry Commission well established in the area. The Cothi has a reputation as a fishing stream. The church has been restored; it was remarkable for the splendour of its polished oil-lamps. The old three-arched bridge across the Cothi is a delight to the eye. For the rest, Abergorlech is unknown to the great world, and perhaps all the happier for it.

ABERGWESYN, *Breconshire,* a small place, lies at the end of a 14-m. walk from Tregaron over the empty moors of the Ellennith region of Central Wales; or by way of country roads from Llandrindod Wells, going westward until you reach the opening of the Irfon valley; or from Builth Wells till you come to Llanwrtyd Wells and find yourself at the same spot, where the Irfon runs out from under Cefn-coch (1,642 ft) and Mynydd Trawsnant (1,695 ft). The valley is beautiful and lonely; but its most interesting feature, 2½ m. further on, is the church named Llanddewi after the David who was patron saint of Wales, and who is said to have preached here himself in his proselytizing days of the 5th cent. Certainly the Celtic cross in the church, a rough monolith incised with an oval circumference round a cross-like figure that seems almost a face with a mitred cap, suggests that it was made at a very early date.

Like many another church in Wales, this can probably trace its original foundation to the first days of Christianity in Britain; but its present structure is a later development. It is extended away from the single-chambered oratory that the Age of Saints chose to set up. One of its windows, near the pulpit, is pre-Norman; others were put into the walls in early Norman times, and of these one has parts of a Roman altar built in to form its framework. The credit for discovering the virtues of the waters at Llanwrtyd Wells goes to one of the vicars: Theophilus Evans, incumbent between 1732 and 1767. But an earlier vicar deserves more particular notice.

This was Thomas Howell. He had two sons. The elder, Bishop of Bristol, died in 1645. The other was James Howell, born perhaps in 1594 and dying in 1666, five years after his appointment as Historiographer-Royal to Charles II. This post was given him as a reward for having been, through the long years of the Protectorate, a determined Royalist supporter, imprisoned in the Fleet between 1642 and 1651. He deserved the honour, being a prolific writer on many things and always with distinction. Poems, of which the most important was the political allegory *Dodona's Grove*; studies in political science such as the *Survey of the Seignorie of Venice*; and above all his *Epistolae Hoelianae* (Familiar Letters) established his reputation in his own time. His letters keep it alive today. He was also a learned philologist in French, Italian, and Spanish as well as in his native Welsh; his earlier official appointments included the Secretaryship to the English Embassy to Denmark, diplomatic missions to Sardinia and Spain, and some work for the Government at home in Scotland. He was a close friend of Ben Jonson and Sir Kenelm Digby, and his interests ranged from physics and medicine to astrology and the arts.

His letters were favourite reading for Defoe, Swift, Addison, Scott, Browning, and Thackeray; they are delightful, discursive, and informatively worldly, giving a sharp insight into the politics of Britain and western Europe in his day. He took a deep interest in the Welsh language and literature, and in his origins in the valley of the Irfon. He found time when in Spain to inquire into the relationship of Basque with Welsh, concluding that the "Biscaynians" were the same people as his own. He finds a Welsh origin for words in the native tongue of the West Indies, and was one of the first to assert the discovery of North America, centuries before Columbus, by Madoc, who (he says) set sail from Milford Haven four years before the Norman Conquest and so established a primary British right to the New World. His literary style is a permanent delight. Excusing the relatively rapid fall of the Gauls before the advancing strength of Caesar, he says of France: "It is a passable and plain pervious continent". The Gallic tongue, he insists, was an offshoot of Welsh as much as Basque, and what preserved the ancient tongue in each case was the mountains, cast up by Nature as "propugnacles of defence".

Into his handling of the English language had crept a certain imaginative and bardic quality, even to the extent of inventing words unknown in English literature before or since. For one political opponent, a hack in the Parliamentary cause, James Howell reserved some of his best inventions. "Sterquilinous rascal!" he explodes. "A meer triobolary pasquiller!" The object of his attack was worthy of this unprecedented eloquence. It was John Milton, author of *Paradise Lost*.

ABERGYNOLWYN, *Merioneth*. This village, 7 m. inland from Towyn and 3 m. from the end of Tal-y-llyn lake, is also the terminus of the Tal-y-llyn Railway. The station is up on the hill-side, and Abergynolwyn lies in the valley below, a pleasant collection of old quarrymen's

G. Douglas Bolton

Approaching Abergynolwyn:
the Tal-y-llyn Railway

cottages and new council houses. It owes its existence to the Bryneglwys (Church Hill) slate quarries, now closed. These lie due S. of the village, high up in a hollow between the peaks of Taren Hendre (2,076 ft) and Taren y Gesail (2,187 ft), the highest points of a range that starts near Towyn and runs for over 12 m. to the pass above Corris. A great part of the Tarens range is now under forest, and some of the tracks marked on older Ordnance Survey maps as crossing the range from Abergynolwyn are now difficult to follow. The walk up to the quarries through the Wild Ravine is impressive. As the track comes out on to the open mountain, a small bridge crosses the stream. This is Pont Llaeron; it is commonly called the Roman Bridge, but it was probably a pack-horse bridge of comparatively recent date. The quarries, with their deep, water-filled pits, the ruined buildings, and the long incline driving down into the valley far below, have a forlorn but strongly evocative atmosphere.

ABERHOSAN, *Montgomeryshire*, is a tiny village on the River Carog reached by a turning from the mountain road between Machynlleth and Dylife. The by-road goes no further than Aberhosan, but it takes you on a curve over an unexpectedly impressive valley of gorse and heath. Aberhosan depends on the neighbouring hill-farms, for which it is a communal centre, and it is the best point from which to go on foot to the top of Foel Fadian, the highest point in Montgomeryshire. The drove-track leading to it is often used by the local hunt, since the startling rocks of Esgair Fochnant that rise here are a favourite resort of foxes for evading pursuit. The same track leads to Glaslyn lake and Bugeilyn.

A little while ago, Aberhosan was famed for the craftsman who made, carved, and ornamented the bardic chairs for the Eisteddfodau both national and local.

ABERLLEFENNI, *Merioneth.* From Lower Corris, coasting the side of the sharp ascent to the right as you cross the bridge, the road runs 2 m. through a long, afforested valley that seems to drive straight into the heart of the Cwm Celli hills. Aberllefenni – in origin, occupation, and lay-out – makes something of a twin to Lower Corris, and its slate-workings are an obvious feature. Once, with its quiet pools and its streams edging through rocky slopes, it was the end of the road, and the sheep-walks surrounded and surveyed it. But now the hills have been laid open. Great files of fir march the valleys, and beyond Aberllefenni opens a series of spectacular mountain roads. The Forestry Commission has recognized their character and provided several observation-points over the deep cwms. Motorable tracks mount the hills, crossing and criss-crossing in a way that calls for care in navigation, and following the banks of streams that formerly knew only the fox, the marten, and the otter. Not often can the walker find openings in the marshalled plantations, but, when he does, the views across the country are startlingly vivid. Perhaps the best of several descents from the height is from the Black Hendre down to Aberangell, following the mountainous stream called the Angell (Angel). This takes you through forests whose very uniformity has an attraction, varied by the river's contours; it is a more manageable way for walkers than the

precipitous chances of the crags towards Dinas Mawddwy. Aberangell is now a lonely but pleasing outpost of the forests, with shops typical of the deep countryside and well worth a visit. Beyond it, the main roads lie open to Dolgellau or Machynlleth.

ABERMULE, *Montgomeryshire,* a small village 4 m. NE. of Newtown, is set in a particularly lush part of the Severn valley. Across the river to the W., on a green hill, is the site of Castell Dolforwyn. This was built by Llywelyn, the last native Prince of Wales, almost as a challenge to the royal stronghold of Montgomery. It was granted to Roger Mortimer after the fall and death of Llywelyn. There is little left of the castle. The meadow below it along the Severn is called Dolforwyn (Maiden's Meadow). Local tradition places here the scene of the drowning of the unfortunate nymph Sabrina, the daughter of Locrine. The story comes from the fertile imagination of Geoffrey of Monmouth, who relates in convincing detail that Locrine, when King of Britain, fell in love with Estrildis and had a daughter by her, which roused the envy of Gwendolen, his own queen. Gwendolen seized power and threw Sabrina into the river, "whereby it comes that down to our own time this river is called Habren in the British tongue, although by a corruption of speech it is called Sabrina in the other tongue". The story was used by Milton in his masque *Comus,* where Sabrina is invoked as the goddess of chastity.

The cast-iron bridge over the river was built

The beach, Llangrannog, near Aberporth

G. Douglas Bolton

Peter Baker

By Abersoch: the ancient church of Llanengan

in 1852 and carries an inscription pointing out that it was the second iron bridge constructed in the county of Montgomery. Railway enthusiasts will remember that Abermule was the scene of one of the few accidents that ever occurred on the old Cambrian Railway.

ABERNANT, *Carmarthenshire*. This village has no special character, but it stands in unspoilt and unfrequented country 5 m. NW. of Carmarthen. The church, which has a few 13th-cent. features, was practically rebuilt in 1706, and stands in a surprisingly large church-yard of over 3 acres. For some unknown reason, Abernant became a sought-after place of burial over a wide area of South Wales. Bodies were interred here from parishes in remote Cardiganshire and Pembrokeshire. The countryside a little further N., especially around Talog, is a pastoral land of wooded hills and small trout streams, off the beaten track.

ABERPORTH, *Cardiganshire*, is a large village, popular with holiday-makers; it stands on the heights that look down on two sandy coves. There is grand bathing, and the coast to the N. is cliffed round to Tresaith. The headland of Ynyslochdyn, beyond Llangranog, closes the view in this direction. Westwards the fine headland of Pencribach, which rises to over 400 ft, is forbidden ground. The towers and other constructions on the head belong to the R.A.F. missile range. The range extends out to sea for a good distance into Cardigan Bay. Shipping is warned to keep clear.

ABERSOCH, *Caernarfonshire*, a small village, lies on the S. coast of the Lleyn peninsula, about 7 m. SW. of Pwllheli towards

Trwyn Cilan (Penkilan Head) and Porth Neigwl.

The trout stream of the Afon Soch runs an extraordinary course. It rises some miles to the W. near the lumpy hill of Mynydd Cefnamwlch, tries to get into the sea, swings N. again, cuts through higher ground, and finally flows out to the open water at Abersoch. These diversions are the product of the landscape reshaping at the end of the Ice Age.

Abersoch has grown fast in recent years; in summer it is a crowded holiday resort, complete with boarding-houses, caravans, and golf course. It offers pleasant opportunities, too, for deep-sea fishing, at least to the extent of spinning for eager mackerel and occasionally for more unexpected hauls. The sands are shallow but extensive, and the yachtsmen have annexed the small shelter at the mouth of the stream, with its old houses at the water's edge. Southward lies the fine, bare peninsula, speckled with small farms, that reaches its climax in Trwyn Cilan. Here the bay of Porth Ceiriad is walled in with perpendicular cliffs that give point to the name of the nearby Porth Neigwl (Hell's Mouth), from the currents that destroyed so many ships. Offshore lie the two islets of St Tudwal, haunted by guillemots and puffins above the cliffs and deep, sea-surged caves. St Tudwal was apparently Tugdual, a Breton who, like many of his contemporaries in the 6th cent., reached the shores of the Irish Sea, to escape the disturbances in western Europe during the collapse of Rome and to establish faith among the people. He was a bishop of Treguier, and the remains of a 12th-cent. chapel on one of the islands may represent an oratory he founded. The other island has an abandoned lighthouse. Both islands were bought in 1934 by Clough Williams-Ellis to save them from "development".

The 17th-cent. mansion of Castellmarch, just outside Abersoch, has dwindled in status to a farmhouse, but still retains its thick oak rafters. The Castellmarch family produced a long line of lawyers, doctors, and M.P.s. Legend maintains that this was the site of the castle of King March, the King Mark of the Tristan story that inspired Wagner to write his most lyrical opera. King March was cursed with horse's ears, and had every barber who cut his hair put to death, to keep the dreadful secret. But reeds grew thickly on the place where the unhappy barbers lay buried. A piper happened to make pipes out of the reeds, and no sooner did he play on them than they sang out King March's secret shame. This story has arisen from the fact that "march" in Welsh happens to mean a stallion.

W. of Abersoch and 1½ m. away is Llanengan, with a church considered the oldest in the Lleyn peninsula. Its screen is beautifully carved, though belonging to much later than the time of Tugdual, and it has holy vessels brought from the great abbey that once stood on Bardsey Island. The coffer of solid oak was the strong-box in which the congregation placed its coins of tribute to the church. Also to the W., crouched under the shelter of a small hill, is Llangian, which on past occasions has won the prize for the neatest village in the county. The church here is of 6th-cent. foundation and dedicated to Gian, a fellow of Tugdual's. It has been restored, but the churchyard contains the ancient stone with the inscription *Meli Medici Fili Martini Iacit*, "[The mortal part] of Meluc the Doctor, Son of Martinus, Lies Here". This must be the earliest mention of a doctor in Wales.

ABERTHAW, *Glamorgan*, is a village, 7 m. from Barry on the coast of the Vale of Glamorgan. It is divided into East and West Aberthaw by the mouth of the little River Thaw. Both hamlets are now overwhelmed by the cement-works, with the basin-like quarry next to it, and by the still bigger power station, which has filled the Thaw valley with a new wirescape. The chimneys of both works are visible for miles over the lower land of the Vale. The power station has swallowed up a great deal of the low burrows of the Leys, where once the little port of Aberthaw traded across the channel to Somerset and even further afield. In the 17th cent. the 100-ton *Great Thomas* of Aberthaw sailed to St Kitts in the West Indies for tobacco and sugar. Later, limestone from the shingle on the shore near Watch House Point was the main export. For the building of the Eddystone lighthouse between 1756 and 1759, the engineer Smeaton picked Aberthaw lime because it made an exceptionally hard mortar to resist the sea. Throughout the 18th cent., limestone for agricultural purposes was a far more important cross-channel export than coal. As so often happened to the little coastal ports of Wales, the coming of the railways finally killed the Aberthaw trade. A very ancient village inn is the only sign of past renown.

The parish church of the district is at Penmarc, 2 m. inland from Aberthaw in the valley of the little Kenson stream. The church has a plain embattled tower and a chancel arch decorated with zigzag mouldings. Against the churchyard is part of the wall of the old castle. This must once have been of considerable extent. It belonged to the De Umfraville family of Glamorgan knights, who were prominent in the local opposition to King John. Penmarc Place, like so many similar old manor houses in Glamorgan, is now a farm. Cement-works are also prominent at Rhoose, the next village eastwards and the site of Cardiff's modern airport. Between Rhoose and Aberthaw is Fontygarry, framed in low cliffs, where the sandy bay draws the crowds in summer.

ABERTILLERY, *Monmouthshire*, with **BLAINA**, **NANTYGLO**, and **BRYNMAWR**, *Breconshire*. Abertillery, in the valley of the Ebbw Fach, has a population of over 40,000, and is therefore the second largest town in Monmouthshire after Newport. Together with its neighbouring villages, it forms an almost continuous strip of houses and coal-mines, beginning at Aberbeeg, where the little Ebbw valley splits from the Ebbw Fawr. Railway Terrace, Aberbeeg, is reputed to be built along the line of a Roman road. With few breaks, and with the newly forested hills closing in on every hand, the valley runs through Six Bells into Abertillery itself. Here the streets all seem to be on a tilt. Abertillery grew somewhat later than the older industrial settlements higher up the valley. Its great period of expansion came with the prodigious growth of the coal trade in the second half of the 19th cent. The population stood at about 8,000 in 1891, but had exploded to 40,000 some twelve years later. The whole area suffered when coal began its decline, and today there are few mines working. Abertillery, and its district, have gallantly set out to bring in new industries. The line of housing continues up through Blaina to Nantyglo (Coal Brook). Here the valley widens a little, as it comes out on to the high uplands that mark the rim of the coal-

Abertillery

G. Douglas Bolton

field. This was the area in which heavy industry first developed. At Nantyglo were the celebrated ironworks of the Bailey brothers. Crawshay Bailey (1782–1872), one of the outstanding leaders in the iron industry, the coal trade, and railway construction in the coalfield, impressed himself so vividly upon the imagination of his workmen that he has entered folklore as the hero of a song sung all over South Wales, especially at rugby club reunions:

> Crawshay Bailey had an engine,
> She was puffin' and a-blowing,
> And she had such mighty power
> She could go a mile an hour.

Chorus: Did you ever see,
Did you ever see,
Did you ever see
Such a funny thing before?

> And when Crawshay Bailey died,
> How all the people cried!
> And they raised two hundred
>   pound,
> Just to put him underground.

And so on, for forty-three verses, printable and unprintable. The glories of the ironworks have long since departed, and only the slag-heaps remain on the hills. Nantyglo is on the border of Monmouthshire. By some freak of boundary-drawing, the county of Brecon comes down over the mountains that continue the Beacons range to annex the township at the top of the valley, Brynmawr. At nearly 1,300 ft, it is the highest town in Wales. It has always been a dormitory-place, with the men working at Nantyglo and further down the valley. The high, bleak moorlands roll away to the N. Before the new inter-valley roads, Brynmawr must have seemed rather out of the world. This made it a self-reliant township with strong local loyalties, which stood up to the savage strain of the Depression in the 1930s, when over 74 per cent of the population were unemployed. Now a new factory area has been established between Brynmawr and Nantyglo. The rubber factory, designed by the Architects Cooperative Partnership, was a notable landmark in industrial building in Britain.

The whole area has a vigorous political tradition. Rehoboth Chapel, in King Street, has a history of a congregation of Independents that goes back to 1646. The Chartists were strong here. They held their secret meeting at Nantyglo, when they made the decision to march on Newport in 1838. John Frost, the principal leader, harangued the Chartist "army" in Brynmawr, and one of his local lieutenants, King Crispin, a shoemaker, lived in Boundary Street. Zaphaniah Williams, who led one of the columns, kept a beerhouse in Nantyglo. He was sentenced to death, but the sentence was afterwards commuted, and he was banished to Van Diemen's Land.

From Brynmawr the new road sweeps swiftly eastwards, down the beautiful Clydach valley into the area of Abergavenny, the Usk, and another and totally different world.

ABERTRIDWR and **SENGHENNYDD,** *Glamorgan.* These two mining villages adjoin each other in the side valley of the Nant yr Afon N. of Caerphilly. On the hill 1 m. to the W. of Abertridwr is the old church of Eglwysilan, which was the mother church of the whole Caerphilly area. The building has been heavily restored, but the registers record the marriages of two distinguished leaders of Nonconformity – Christmas Evans and George Whitfield, who married an Abergavenny widow at Capel Martin near Caerphilly. The mysterious 14th-cent. character known as Sion Kent, or John O'Kent, was believed to have been born in the parish. Sion was half priest, half wizard, and became the centre of a remarkable series of folk-tales celebrating his contests with the Devil. His fame, however, is more properly associated with Grosmont in Monmouthshire and Kentchurch in Herefordshire. Senghennydd lies at the top of the Nant yr Afon valley. Senghennydd is a name of sadness to anyone associated with the South Wales coal industry. Here, on the 4th October 1913, occurred the explosion that has been described as the greatest disaster in the annals of British mining. The Universal colliery at Senghennydd had long been known as a particularly "fiery" pit. This explosion killed 439 men, 2,000 ft underground. Seldom has the "price of coal" been so terribly made clear. The Universal colliery has now been closed and dismantled. A narrow road leads up over Mynydd Eglwysilan (1,169 ft) to Nelson.

ABERYSTWYTH, *Cardiganshire.* This seaside town, placed almost half way round the long curve of Cardigan Bay, seems poised between North and South Wales. The massive moorlands of Plynlimon lie behind it to the E., and the threatened railway takes a long time to reach it through the valleys and hills of Central Wales. The town is a long way from any of the big centres of population in the principality. Aberystwyth, now the administrative centre of the county of Cardigan, thus seems to have a character of its own, Welsh and independent despite the flood of visitors that swamp it in summer. "Aber" is a fascinating amalgam of holiday resort and university town, with a national library as well. Less than justice has been done to its architecture. It may not be the "Brighton of Wales", as the old guides dubbed it, but the curve of houses and hotels along the sea-front, each with its double bow-windows, has charm, even distinction. The same early 19th cent. saw the construction of the South Marine Terrace, the pleasing houses around Queen's Square, and the attractive Laura Place near St Michael's Church.

There is plenty of history here as well. The earliest settlement lies on the summit of Pen Dinas, the shapely hill that rises just S. of the town, between the rivers Rheidol and Ystwyth, whose waters eventually unite in Aberystwyth harbour. Pen Dinas is crowned by a column in a form of a cannon on end, set up by a local landowner who fought at Waterloo. But the

Plate 3   Nant Ffrancon, looking towards Moel Perfydd (see p. 107)   Pix Photos

summit ridge of the hill has been fashioned into a fort, or rather a double fort, of the Iron Age. This is one of the largest forts in West Wales. Pottery discovered here linked this remote fortress on the far coast of Wales with Iron Age people in Gloucestershire and even Spain and Portugal. The Normans built the next fortifications at Aberystwyth, as they advanced up the coastline from Cardigan in the reign of Henry I. The first of these Norman castles (the Welsh destroyed them from time to time) was S. of the present town in the Ystwyth valley. Later the strong position overlooking the sea at the mouth of the Rheidol was firmly occupied. Edward I rebuilt the castle on this spot. Glyndwr captured it in 1404, and its loss to Prince Henry in 1408 marked the beginning of the decline in Glyndwr's fortunes. During the reign of Charles I, Thomas Bushell received permission to establish a mint here in 1637. Bushell had taken over the mining concession of the Plynlimon lead-mines from Sir Hugh Middelton, who had already made a fortune out of the enterprise. Middelton used the money to finance the New River project, which brought London its first reliable water supply. For a while Bushell also did well. His new process of refining silver from the ore made the Aberystwyth mint important The Civil Wars eventually ruined Bushell. The castle was held for the King, but surrendered to the Parliamentary forces in 1646. After that it fell into decay. The ruins are now in the care of the Aberystwyth Corporation, and the promontory on which they stand is pleasantly laid out with seats and gardens. In the castle courtyard is a stone circle, prepared for the Gorsedd ceremonies when the National Eisteddfod was held in the town in 1952. Overlooking the sea is the tall column of the war memorial, surmounted by a figure representing the Angel of Peace. From the castle grounds, in clear weather, the peak of Snowdon can be seen 44 m. to the N.

S. of the castle is the harbour. Aberystwyth was a busy port until the middle of the 19th cent. At one time it could boast 2,000 small vessels, and in 1801 it was still the fourth largest town in Wales. Inevitably the Railway Age brought a slow decline in the trade of the port. Now it is a yachting harbour that dries out at low tide.

To the N. of the castle are St Michael's Church and the extraordinary complex of buildings that was the first home of the University College. The core is formed by the neo-Gothic hotel – a connoisseur's piece of Victoriana – built by the railway engineer Thomas Savin about 1860. He was a man with ideas on tourism far ahead of his day. He conceived a brilliant scheme for popularizing Aberystwyth, and his own railway line to the coast, by offering a week's board free to anyone who bought a return ticket at Euston. He built the hotel (and planned two others at Aberdovey and Borth) to accommodate the rush of tourists he confidently anticipated. Unfortunately, the whole speculation failed after Savin had spent £80,000 on his dream hotel.

From the ruins of Savin's dream, another dream came to fulfilment. The 1860s were also the period of a great awakening in Welsh education, and of the voluntary movement to establish a university college in Wales. Funds were collected from the patriotic, and Savin's empty building seemed just what was wanted. The committee paid down £10,000, and the first constituent college of what afterwards became the University of Wales was established, with Thomas Charles Edwards, the great-grandson of Thomas Charles of Bala, as its first Principal. The college fought its way through the financial difficulties that surrounded its origin, and survived by the "pennies of the people". This was a college for which a whole country had fought. The seal of royal approval was set on the college in 1896, when the future King Edward VII, then Prince of Wales, came to Aberystwyth to be installed as first Chancellor of the University of Wales. This was also Mr Gladstone's last appearance in public. The college has now become involved in the post-war "university explosion". The old buildings are now mainly a museum, where, among many other interesting exhibits, a collection of the silver coins minted at Aberystwyth by Thomas Bushell is on display. The main buildings of the college now lie on Penglais Hill, on the road that leads N. out of the town. Here is an ever-growing series of lecture halls, laboratories, halls of residence, and appurtenances considered essential for a college in the mid-20th cent. The college has almost become a small town in itself, looking down over the old town and the first "college by the sea".

In the centre of this new development stands the somewhat older, imposingly Edwardian building of the Llyfrgell Genedlaethol Cymru (National Library of Wales). Until the new college construction after the war, the Library stood out in lonely white splendour on its hill above Aberystwyth, as another symbol of the Welsh people's determination to create their own national institutions. The movement to establish a national library began as far back as 1873, and Aberystwyth, with its new college, seemed the right place for this second venture in spite of its remoteness from the main centres of population. The first section was finished in 1911, to the designs of Sidney Greenslade and later additions made by Sir Charles Holden. The whole scheme was completed in 1955.

Here is housed the most complete collection of Welsh books and MSS. in the world. The nucleus of the MS. collection was brought together by Sir John Williams (1840–1926), the Royal Physician. Apart from the Havod MS. which belongs to Cardiff Library, there is hardly a Welsh MS. of importance that is not at Aberystwyth. Here is the Black Book of Carmarthen, the earliest MS. in Welsh, together with the White Book of Rhydderch, the Book of Taliesin, and the earliest complete text of the *Mabinogion*. Here also is the Hengwrt Chaucer, one of the most important texts of Chaucer's *Canterbury Tales*. Copies of the earliest books printed in Welsh are also among the treasures of the Library.

Aberystwyth: (top) *the promenade and first University building ;* (bottom) *the new University buildings*   Peter Baker

The printed book section expanded rapidly
after the passing of the Copyright Act of 1911,
when Aberystwyth became one of the six libraries
in the British Isles (including Ireland) entitled to
receive a copy of nearly all the books, periodicals,
pamphlets, maps, and sheet music published in
this country. Today the Library contains over
2,000,000 printed works and about 30,000 MSS.
It is also the repository of over 3,500,000 Welsh
historical records of all kinds, including certain
valuable ones from the Church in Wales. The
Library has an outstanding department of
maps, prints, and drawings, and its binding
department was a pioneer in the difficult art of
treating damaged volumes and MSS.; in some
cases this involved splitting a fragile leaf into
two leaves so that a strengthening sheet could be
inserted between them. A changing selection of
the Library treasures is on display to the public
in the exhibition gallery.

Descending the hill from the Library and the
University precinct back into the town, we come
to the tree-lined North Parade, the principal
shopping centre. The new Town Hall is in
pleasant Queen's Square, near at hand. Beyond
the square is the sea-front, sweeping round from
Castle Hill to the precipitous Constitution Hill
(485 ft) on the N. This is the Aberystwyth of
tourism, although the days are long past when a
visitor (in 1803) could praise the town by saying
that "the ladies' and gentlemen's machines are
placed nearly a quarter of a mile asunder; and the
indecency of promiscuous dipping, so disgusting
at more fashionable resorts, is in consequence
avoided . . .". Today the front still has all the
trimmings expected from a Victorian promenade
– a pier with the end broken, a bandstand, a
disused lifeboat slip, glass shelters, and the
County Council offices in a gloomy-looking
hotel near the Alexandra Women's Hostel, where
the "prom" ends with a rail. It used to be the
established ritual among visitors and students
to touch the rail with the foot before walking
back along the promenade. Behind Alexandra
Hall, the funicular cliff railway gallantly hauls
passengers up a 2-in-1 gradient to the glorious
viewpoint of Constitution Hill. From here a path
leads round the coast for 2 m. to the beach at
Clarach, set between two steep hills. Clarach
has sand; Aberystwyth beach is mainly shingle.
Clarach is also choked by caravans, for it can be
easily reached by road through the quaintly
named village of Bow Street. The Clarach valley
holds the little church of Llangorwen, surprisingly connected with the subtleties and religious
anxieties of the Oxford Movement. Isaac
Williams, the poet and one of the leaders of the
Movement, lived in the house of Cwm Cynfelin,
behind the church. Here Keble wrote the last
section of his *Christian Year*. The church was
built in 1841, and the chancel is a replica of the
church that Newman himself built at Littlemore.
Keble presented the lectern. Unusual, too, is the
altar, constructed of stone. Cwm woods are
part of the public attractions of Aberystwyth.
The golf course is nearby.

Eastwards from Aberystwyth, the remarkable
Rheidol valley reaches inland to the wilds of
Plynlimon. One of its delights is the Light
Railway that runs to Devil's Bridge.

The valley parallel to the Rheidol northwards is
not only the traditional birthplace of Dafydd ap
Gwilym, but also contains Plas Gogerddan, the
home of the powerful Pryse family, one of the
last county families to keep a private harper.
The Pryses ruled the political life of northern
Cardiganshire throughout the 18th cent.; so
much so that in 1714 one Pryse was automatically
elected in his absence and without ever being
consulted about his candidature. He resolutely
refused to regard himself as an M.P., and defied
all Parliament's attempts to punish him until
another Pryse nominee was duly elected in his
place. No wonder the old mayors of Aberystwyth
were supposed to administer the loyal oath with
the formula: "I swear to be faithful to the King
and the House of Gogerddan". The house today
is the centre of the university plant-breeding
station, which carries on the tradition of agricultural research established at Aberystwyth by
Sir George Stapleton, the great authority on
mountain grasslands. (*See also* Elerch.)

One other valley comes down to the sea near
Aberystwyth – that of the Ystwyth itself. The
Rheidol is more prominent from the town.
The Ystwyth rather sneaks in apologetically
around Pen Dinas. Its lower reaches at the sea's
edge are bleak and open. After Llanfarian bridge,
about 2 m. from the town, the valley becomes
wooded and pastoral. It continues past Abermad,
with its well-known preparatory school, the
only "prep" school that has made Welsh the
central subject of instruction. Llanilar, beyond
Abermad, has a church with a tower like that of
Llanbadarn-Fawr, a fine wood roof over the
nave, and several chalices, one of which was
brought from Stockholm by John Parry, a
Messenger to George I and George II and a native
of the parish. The parish account book has some
appealing entries, such as: "1801. Paid Richard
Evans for shooting rafens, 2.0. 1805, paid for ye
ale, £2.15.0."

In a fold between the lower courses of the
Ystwyth and the Rheidol is the estate of Nanteos.
(Nightingale Brook). In this mansion was once
kept a wooden cup said to be the Holy Grail (see
p. 324), taken there by the monks of Strata Florida
when threatened by the Dissolution. It left
Nanteos, however, with its owners in 1967. Legend
had it that Joseph of Arimathea brought it to
Glastonbury, either as having been used at the
Last Supper or part of the Cross. The very name
Grail and the belief that it was a Cup belong to
Malory's *Morte D'Arthur*. Earlier romances called
it a precious stone. It is recognized as having
originated with a religious philosophy belonging
to the oldest interpretations of Christianity and as
being the symbol of all Creation, an idea on which
the visitor could well reflect even in the absence of
the Cup.

The coastline S. of Aberystwyth, after the
mouth of the Ystwyth river, becomes high and

Near Acrefair: the River Dee spanned by the Pontycysylltau aqueduct

rather remote, with one showplace in the Monk's Cave or Twll Twrw (Thunder Hole). On the ridge behind is the Blaenplwyf transmitter of the B.B.C. The main road southwards to Llanrhystyd runs high here. Look NE. on a clear day for a panorama of the Plynlimon range, rolling away to the far horizon.

ACREFAIR, *Denbighshire*, stands on the Ruabon-Llangollen road near the beginning of the entry to the lovely Vale of Llangollen. It is industrial, however, rather than rural, the last fling southwards of the North Wales coalfield. Nearby, the chemical-works at Cefn-mawr stand above the winding Dee. The woods help to conceal them from the southern side. Acrefair can boast of one splendid sight, described by Sir Walter Scott as the most impressive work of art he had ever seen. This is the Pontycysylltau aqueduct, which carries the Shropshire Union Canal over the Dee on its way to Llangollen. It was built by Telford between 1795 and 1805. Telford was proud of it and spent £47,018 on its construction: "a very moderate sum", in his own words. The length of the embankment on either end of the bridge is 1,500 ft; the length of the bridge itself, 1,007 ft. It stands 121 ft above the river. The canal it carries is 11 ft 10 in. wide. The bridge has nineteen arches, each with a span length of 48 ft. But cold statistics do not reveal the grace of the bridge. Together with the railway bridge further down, it makes a splendid, many-arched entrance to the delights of the Vale of Llangollen ahead. Hazlitt tramped this way on the journey to Llangollen so vividly described in one of his essays. He stopped to look out over the view of Trefor, Froncysylltau, and Pontycysylltau, and admired this "Roman Amphitheatre of hills". This was in the days before Acrefair and Cefn-mawr had felt the touch of industry. But the effect is still splendid as you look towards Llangollen.

AMBLESTON, *Pembrokeshire*. About 7 m. NNE. from Haverfordwest, this village is grouped round a church with a Norman tower and a stair-way projecting outside. The rest of the church has been rebuilt. In a field near Scollock West farm, 1 m. to the S., is a curious and rather touching monument to the yeoman farmer John Llewellin and his wife Martha. The worthy couple arc depicted with the realism of folk art dressed in their Sunday best. The inscription proudly declares: "By the blessing of God on their joint understanding and thrift they bought this farm and hand it down without encumbrance to their heirs. Endeavour to pull together as they did. Union is strength".

AMLWCH, *Anglesey*. On the NE. edge of Anglesey, Amlwch is now a pleasant resort with hotel accommodation. The place has excellent bathing in waters rounding cliffs of rock not too dangerous and yet giving a sense of wildness and remoteness.

The first sign that Amlwch was used for human habitation is given by the evidence of industrial occupation around Parys Mountain in the period that followed the withdrawal of direct Roman rule, when the working of the copper in Parys Mountain was continued by the natives under their own British governors. This continued economic activity throws light on the political importance the island had. The Romans them-selves were experts in the detection, mining, and smelting of copper no less than other ores; their interest in Wales as a whole was largely in the use to which its natural resources could be put. But others had long preceded them in this; the people of the Bronze Age who traded across to Ireland for precious metals took copper to be the most useful of all things, and it is unlikely that the riches of Parys Mountain would be ignored by them. For students of early literature, Amlwch is famous; for it was here that, as a tale in the *Mabinogion* tells it, Branwen, daughter of Llyr, looked back across the sea to the Ireland she had sailed towards to be its queen, and re-membered the treachery of her husband and how her brother Bran had gone with a mighty fleet to rescue her, and how so many men of might had died. She wept that two such noble islands as Ireland and Britain should have been ruined by her own evil fate. And her heart broke, and they buried her by the banks of the Alaw in a four-sided grave.

The story is allegorical, like most of the early epics. The similar collection of verses known as the *Gododin* makes use of the tale and calls the Alaw the "stream of Amlwch". Curiously enough, in 1821 it was reported that eight years previously, at a spot called Ynys Branwen, a farmer, digging for stones to mend a wall, laid bare just such a four-sided grave with an urn in it containing cremated bones. From the description of the find, the urn seems to have been typical of the Iron Age folk who settled in Anglesey after the Age of Bronze. Both the *Gododin* and the *Mabinogion* contributed directly to the growth of the Arthurian legend, and the facts reveal how far back goes the theme on which the great British epic is based.

Amlwch is the biggest place on the N. coast of the island. It was the terminus of the old railway line that meandered across the centre of Anglesey, but it owed its growth originally to its position as the nearest port to the copper-mines of Parys Mountain. The mines lie about 2 m. S. of Amlwch and are now deserted in a strange upland speckled with little lakes and reservoir ponds. The mines of Parys played an important part in the Industrial Revolution. In the late 18th cent., Thomas Williams, a local solicitor from Llanidan, became the Copper King of the whole country. He established the copper smelting trade in Swansea, where he used South Wales coal to smelt North Wales ore. In 1811, the vein of copper in Parys Mountain was said to be 74 ft thick. With the

exhaustion of the Parys mines in the middle of the 19th cent., Amlwch's industrial importance declined. But the harbour, wedged between high rocks and built at enormous expense for those days, still reminds us of Amlwch's 100 years of glory under copper. Today the little town has a chemical-works and a tourist trade and has developed as a market centre. The 20th cent. has marched firmly into Anglesey not only with its atomic power station at Wylfa, but with the stride of the giant pylons bearing power to Amlwch's new aluminium industry, a sudden revival of its industrial importance under the Romans and their British successors. The concrete Catholic church, with its nave rather like the hull of an upturned boat, is a surprising architectural concept. About 1 m. to the W. of Amlwch is Bull Bay, with fine headlands and safe bathing in their coves. The bay affords shelter for shipping between tides, which run strongly offshore along this coast. Westwards the cliffs become higher and even more precipitous.

Eastwards from Amlwch the coast is equally rugged and interesting round to the well-sheltered inlet of Eilian Bay, with its sands and the tourist developments that accompany them. Point Lynas juts out to sea to the E. This is the pilot station for ships making up to Liverpool and the Mersey. On the point is a modern lighthouse and a semaphore and coastguard station. Near the point is Ogof y Saint (Saint's Cave), which runs a long way inland.

Just inland from Point Lynas is one of the treasures of Anglesey, the remarkable church of Llaneilian. This church is one among many in the near neighbourhood of Amlwch, and has various highly important architectural features that illustrate the first growth of Christian

The coastal village of Cemaes Bay, west of Amlwch

Peter Baker

foundations around the Irish Sea. St Eilian, "the Bright", was one of the seven patron saints of Mona, and was honoured for his sanctity by St Patrick himself. The oldest part of the church is the little chapel, connected by a passage to the main church, which may even be built on the actual site of the saint's cell. The church-tower, with its rectangular roof, is 12th-cent.; the nave and chancel date from the 15th. The roof of the nave and chancel is of carved oak. The corbels are finely carved, with angels playing trumpets and bagpipes. The altar is also of carved oak, but it is eclipsed by the rood-screen, rare in Anglesey churches, with its strange folk-art painting of a skeleton under an inscription in Welsh, "The sting of death is sin". Other curiosities of the church are the tongs, dating from 1748, used by the churchwardens to remove unruly dogs during service, and the Cyff, an iron-studded chest made in 1667, in which all the offerings were locked. The chest was officially opened once a year on St Thomas's Day.

In medieval times the fame of the church largely depended upon the curative powers of Ffynnon Eilian, the healing well set among the rocks on the coast N. of Llaneilian. The well now seems to be dry, but in addition to its healing power Ffynnon Eilian had a reputation as a cursing well. The technique employed was either to stick pins into floating corks, or else to write your victim's name on a slate and attach the slate to a cork. As long as the cork floated, the victim was bound to have ill-health. Some of the slates are still preserved.

AMMANFORD, *Carmarthenshire*, is called Rhydaman in Welsh. Until about 1880, this mining village at the edge of the high country of the Black Mountain of Carmarthenshire consisted of a few houses grouped round the Cross Inn, which still stands in the centre of the township. The name Ammanford replaced that of Cross Inn when the place expanded with the growth of the anthracite-mines. Ammanford is the centre of a district christened locally the "Land of the Pyramids". The countryside is dotted here and there with high, triangular coal-tips. But the "Land of the Pyramids" is far greener and more open than the mining valleys further E. and is backed by moorland and unspoilt hills. Here the individual house, with its small garden, is the rule. The long rows of miners' terraces, so characteristic of the Rhondda, are the rare exceptions. Coal-mining seems to be part of agriculture, and has not swallowed the whole landscape. Ammanford, in the heyday of the anthracite coalfield at the beginning of the century, was also renowned through Wales as the home of Gwynfryn School, now the English Congregational chapel. Under Watcyn Wyn and the Rev. John Jenkins, later better known as Gwili, the Archdruid of Wales, the school produced a remarkable number of men who later made their mark in the public and religious life of the principality. Today the demand for the hard anthracitic coal has declined, many of

the pits of the area are closed, and the "pyramids" are losing their sharp points.

The Afon Aman joins the Loughor at Ammanford, and united they flow through an unspoilt green valley down to Pontardulais. The upper reaches of the Aman are wide and open, holding the mining villages of Glanaman, Garnant, and Brynaman. From Brynaman the main road goes over the Black Mountain to take you out of the coalfield into the lush valley of the Towy. The views from the top of the road are splendid. George Borrow tramped over the pass in 1854 and spent an eventful night at the Farmers' Arms in Brynaman, then known as the Gwter Fawr. Gwauncaegurwen, just S. of Brynaman, is shortened in local speech to "G-C-G". It has a gaunt welfare hall and stands in Glamorgan, since the Aman stream forms the boundary between the two counties.

AMROTH, *Pembrokeshire*. In this seaside village 5 m. from Tenby, the few houses face their enemy the sea and a long bank of pebbles, beyond which lie fine sands at low tide. When the tide comes in during winter storms, it has a habit of washing the road and an odd house or two into the sea. Long lines of groynes try to protect the road. Amroth is growing in popularity. New holiday bungalows climb the green hill behind the beach. They are well designed and an example to other "developments" along this coast. The Amroth Inn is Georgian. Amroth Castle is a late 18th-cent. house with castellated trimmings, behind a long wall on the sea-front. It is one of the numerous places in these parts that were proud to welcome Lord Nelson during his South Wales tour of 1802. The Castle grounds are now a caravan park. At very low tide the stumps of a submerged forest are visible in the sands. The old practice of bathing in the nude on a certain day of the year, referred to by Sir John Rhys, the great Celtic scholar, has long since been discontinued; all ablutions are now very proper in Amroth. The church lies some way inland. It has been restored and enlarged, but still contains some interesting monuments. Colby Lodge, in a charming little wooded valley, was designed by John Nash.

ANGLE, *Pembrokeshire*. A few years ago, this was an unfrequented dead-end at the tip of the long peninsula on the southern side of Milford Haven. Long oil-piers now run out into the haven from Popton Point. Popton Fort, built in 1863, has been adapted as offices. Rhoscrowther church, overlooked by silvery oil-tanks, is worth a visit. It is dedicated, under his Latin name of St Decumanus, to St Tegfan, well known in Somerset as St Decuman. Tegfan apparently sailed out of Milford Haven up the Bristol Channel on a raft of twigs, to settle as a hermit near Watchet. Here he was nurtured on milk supplied free "by a kindly cow", as his monkish biographer put it, until a pagan Dane martyred him by cutting off his head. St Tegfan, however, surprised the Dane by walking away with his head tucked under his arm. His church at Rhoscrowther has a strong tower, a large N. porch with a cobbled floor, and a remarkable figure of the risen Christ over the pointed arch of the doorway. The interior of the church is curious, with a "walk-through" squint and a medieval figure of a woman in a cusped recess in the S. chancel chapel. The E. window of this chapel has a modern stained-glass picture of the Holy Family. About ¼ m. to the NW. is the small, ruined manor house of Eastington, marked as a castle on the map. It is now converted into a farm. The bay beyond it is Angle Bay, with a rather gritty foreshore but a good anchorage for small craft.

Pwllcrochan, to the E. of Rhoscrowther, has also been changed by oil installations. The ancient church now possesses a background of oil-tanks. A big power station overlooks the Pwllcrochan Flats, once renowned for their cockles.

To recapture the old charm of this peninsula, continue along the ridgeway road into Angle itself. The village consists of a single delightful street, with the colonnaded front of the old Globe Hotel as the centrepiece. Angle church has had a rough time from restorers, but the church-yard retains a small detached chapel founded in 1447. The outside steps lead up to a tiny room with narrow lancet windows. The castle ruins lie N. of the church and consist of a single rectangular peel-tower. Over the door of an old house nearby is a carved head, said on uncertain authority to represent Giraldus Cambrensis, the 12th-cent. cleric, author, and quarrelsome patriot who was born at Manorbier. Continue through the village westwards, and you come at last to West Angle Bay at the road's end. When it is not crowded, West Angle Bay forms a fine climax to the southern arm of the haven. The fort on Thorn Island, now a hotel, guards the N. Across the water is St Ann's Head. A fine line of cliffs leads round to Sheep Island southwards; they front the open Atlantic with indents, and have strange names like Parsonsquarry Bay and Guttle Hole. Within 3 m. you reach Freshwater West, a grand sweep of sand backed by dunes. The Atlantic rollers make a glorious display here when the western wind gets behind them, but the undertow is dangerous in certain states of the tide.

ANGLERS' RETREAT, *Cardiganshire.* This lonely spot, consisting of a single fishing-lodge, is one of the most important for fishermen. Long established as an angling centre, it has become through recent developments an attraction for the less professionally minded tourist. It can best be reached by the long mountain road from Llangynfelyn or Taliesin, a road that takes you steadily through long-backed moors into the upland vales spreading to the foot of Plynlimon Fawr. The road ends at the New Pool spread below the sparse tree-clumps of Esgair Fraith, with its prehistoric tumulus. A short way NW., the crags of Moel-y-Llyn fall away from Llyn Conach and Llyn Dwfn, both excellent for trout. To the NE. the grassy bogland runs to the lake at Penrhaeadr (Head of the Falls), a sheep-grazed run of fells and peat-marsh that is also a garden of whin and gorse, bog-orchid and sun-dew, starmoss and flax-feather. This area is now pressed upon by the terraces of fir-plantation; but the drainage these schemes impose has greatly helped the spread of wild flowers; and the heron, which has left the lower valleys by reason of afforestation, still haunts these rivers, and the jay and magpie, the buzzard, falcon, and sea-mew slant across the sky.

The Rhaeadr lake leads to the falls that drop into the valley of the same name. They are interesting to geologists, since the slate-formations through which the water wears have been thrust by some upheaval from the horizontal through a full angle of 90 degrees. Only here are the branches of the falls seen for what they are. Artists can find no worthier study of natural beauty. But the greatest care must be taken not to challenge the falls too closely; there have been deaths even among experienced mountain-walkers and anglers, for with one slip you are at the mercy of the falls. The new forestry-track can be taken past Hafod Wnog to the immense view over the head of Cader Idris towards Snowdon, the Wrekin, the Black Mountains, and the Irish Sea that can be had from the sharp summit of Rhiw Goch, where the rock-strata strike through the ancient drove-way over the peak in a wave of frozen convulsion, and the hills fall sheer to the white incline of the Hengwm Falls, from which the expert can pick his trout with advantage.

Now roadways can be followed down to the new reservoir over Nant-y-moch, and further to the one at Clywedog; both have brought a beauty of wide silence to the empty valleys. But the quietude of the Eye of Rheidol that opens under the crater of Plynlimon Fawr has still a unique and austere loveliness. N. of it, beyond Hyddgen, the streams of Mawnog give lively fishing; but the bog here is treacherous, and one must keep to the banks. The height of Mawnog, covered with heath and ling, is a most beautiful observation-post upon the scars of Bwlch Gwyn.

ARANS, The, *Merioneth.* The long range of the Arans runs from the head of Bala Lake southwards to Dinas Mawddwy. Aran Fawddwy is the highest peak (2,970 ft); its northern neighbour, Aran Benllyn, is only 69 ft lower. Aran Benllyn (Peak at the Head of the Lake) is thus the mountain that makes such a fine climax to the view up the lake from Bala. Aran Fawddwy is the highest peak S. of Snowdonia, overtopping Cader Idris by 43 ft. Seen from the W., the whole range seems an expanse of heathery moorland. To the E., however, the Arans present a splendid array of crags and lonely mountain hollows, set in wild country. The road that runs from Llanuwchllyn over the heights to Dinas Mawddwy gives a fine glimpse into the heart of the Arans. As the narrow track traverses Cwm Cynllwyd, Aran Benllyn rises on the right

G. Douglas Bolton

Looking south from Bwlch-y-Groes: the road to Dinas Mawddwy

in a line of dark cliffs. The road climbs over a high spur thrown out from the main ridge.

This is the celebrated pass of Bwlch-y-Groes (Pass of the Cross), at 1,790 ft the highest pass in Wales. For many years Bwlch-y-Groes was the great test for car and motor-cycle trials. The road has now been well surfaced, but it still drops very steeply to the S. – 1 in 4½ for 200 yds. It has not lost all its challenge, especially in wet weather. From the summit a track leads away over the moors to Llyn Vyrnwy. The valley S. of the pass is spectacular.

On the right, the infant Dovey comes foaming down through a fine gorge. The Dovey rises in the lonely tarn of Creiglyn Dyfi, under the summit cliffs of Aran Fawddwy. The southern section of the range is deeply penetrated by the dark and narrow valley of Cwm Cywarch. At the head of the cwm is the impressive crag of Craig Cywarch, which has been recently explored by rock-climbers. The best track to the summit of Aran Fawddwy curves away up Hengwm to the narrow ridge of Drysgol. (For ascent of the Arans, *see* Abercywarch.)

ARENNIGS, The, *Merioneth.* These mountains stand on either side of the head of the Tryweryn valley, now drowned under the waters of Llyn Celyn. Arennig Fach (2,264 ft) is a round hump of a mountain with a steep face overlooking the little Llyn Arennig-fach. It is the highest point of the wide, heathery wilderness of the Migneint. Arennig Fawr (2,800 ft) is more interesting as well as being higher. It has a fine cliff overlooking a tarn high up on the eastern side. On the summit is a moving memorial to the

crew of an American Flying Fortress that crashed a few feet below the summit in August 1943. Arennig Fawr fascinated the painter J. D. Innes, the friend of Augustus John. Innes died young, but not before he had left a fine series of canvases in which the mountain is the central theme.

ARTHOG, *Merioneth,* is a small village on the S. shore of the Mawddach estuary, opposite Barmouth and upstream from the long railway bridge that crosses the estuary. Tyrau-mawr (2,167 ft), the westerly summit of the Cader Idris range, rises immediately behind; its beautifully wooded lower slopes are the chief glory of Arthog. The Arthog Falls, in the grounds of the castellated Arthog Hall, are impressive after rain, and the woods that surround Tyn-y-Coed House are delightful. The steep lane up to Cader Idris comes out on to the open moorlands at the point where the Ffordd Ddu (Black Road) comes over the open hill-side to the W. This grass-grown track may be an old Roman road. The drovers certainly used it. It curves round the western slopes of the Cader range for 7 m. to descend into the Dysynni valley at Llanegryn. It is a memorable walk. The Llynau Cregennen, 800 ft up behind Arthog, are two enchanting tarns with high crags of Tyrau-mawr in the background.

BAGILLT, *Flintshire,* lies between Flint and the Point of Air, overlooking the Dee estuary and not far from the Bay of Mostyn, the chief port on this part of the coast. To some extent, it shares the industrial development belonging to the area of Liverpool on the other side of the estuary. Mostyn has its blast furnaces, Bagillt has lead-works and the Bettisfield colliery, and there are abandoned soap-works nearby. But this is by no means all a modern phenomenon, since "John Ogilby Esq, His Majestie's Cosmographer," marked on his road-map 200 years ago the lead-mines of Flintshire; and lead was a commodity the Romans eagerly sought after. In the neighbourhood of Bagillt there are many places to visit. Among them (now admittedly a little confused with the abandoned soap-works) are the remains of Basingwerk Abbey, founded about 1131 for monks of the Order of Savigny and amalgamated with the Cistercians in 1147. Curiously enough, Gerald de Barri, who passed that way in 1188 on a campaign of recruitment for the Third Crusade, refers to it only as a little cell, though he adds two points of modern relevance. It was here that men mined the earth for its mineral riches; it was here that he and his Archbishop had to cross the dangerous Sands of Dee and their race-tide dangerous to men, where Henry II had come to grief in his attempt to invade Wales. The present ruins show fragmentary walls of church, cloisters, refectory, dormitory, and gatehouse. In the 12th cent. the spot had already had a long history of border warfare behind it, since Wat's Dyke, an earthwork thrown up to mark the strategic line from Dee to Severn that dates to mysterious centuries as early as the 5th or even 4th, found its terminus here.

Rather to the S. of Mostyn is the site of the mansion of Downing, noted by Daniel Paterson in his *Direct and Principal Cross Roads* (1811) as the birthplace of the traveller and historian Thomas Pennant. He was born there in 1726, and lived till 1798. He was buried in the neighbouring Whitford church, where he has a monument. He travelled widely in Europe, and was the first man to open up Scotland to English attention; before he went there and wrote of what he found, the place, a contemporary said, was as unknown as Kamchatka. He also made a pair of most interesting volumes of his journeys through his native Wales. He was a notable correspondent, was placed on a level with the great naturalist Linnaeus, and earned the approval of Dr Johnson as the best travel writer he had known. His birthplace was burnt in 1922 and awaits restoration.

A further monument is very much older. In a field at Whitford is the Stone of Chwyfan, the tallest Celtic cross S. of Scotland. It dates from the 10th cent.; all its sides are covered with the detail typical of Celtic workmanship.

The Point of Air, where the Dee estuary finally meets the sea, has a lighthouse, now disused, and a wide stretch of sandhills overgrown with the plants that haunt the lonely strands: sea-holly and horned poppy.

BAGLAN, *Glamorgan*, is 2 m. NW. of Port Talbot on the road to Swansea. The old village has been overwhelmed by a new housing estate, which shows in places an imaginative use of the open spaces and older houses on the site. Behind rise the wooded slopes of Mynydd y Gaer. This was a place of great natural beauty even thirty years ago. Today Baglan looks out over the big new industrial developments that are taking place on Baglan Burrows. Baglan House has now been pulled down, and the grounds, which possess a sycamore tree claimed to be the largest in Wales, are a public park. The poet Thomas Gray was a frequent visitor here in the days of its glory. The Baglan Social Club is good architecture of the mid-20th cent.

The present Baglan church is modern. The shell of the old church can still be seen among the trees in the steep upper part of the churchyard. It had a plain, small western door and a double bell-cote, and is reputed to date from Norman times. St Baglan himself settled here in the 6th cent. He was a disciple of the great St Illtud at the famous monastic centre of Llantwit Major in the Vale of Glamorgan. According to one of those charming legends that enliven the history of the early Welsh saints, Baglan had been told to build his church wherever he found a tree bearing three kinds of fruit. He found his tree near the spot where, today, a little stream still runs down from Mynydd y Gaer past the new and old churches. A crow nested in the upper branches, bees swarmed in the tree-trunk, and a sow and her piglets rooted below. Baglan refused to accept the omen. He began to build in a better position but everything he built by day fell down by night. At last he admitted defeat and built his church on the present spot.

The fine modern church is dedicated to St Catherine. It is in the Decorated style and is known locally as the Alabaster Church, from the lavish interior use of alabaster quarried at Penarth. The E. window contains glass by Burne-Jones. The representation of the Crucifixion is unusual. The figure is beardless and the cross is an unhewn tree. The church also possesses a cross slab inscribed with the name of Brancu. It may date from the 9th cent. Mynydd y Gaer (Hill of the Fort, 1,028 ft), is well named. A large Iron Age fort crowns the summit. The Victorianus stone, a Roman milestone dated A.D. 265, formerly stood at the side of the main road between Baglan and Briton Ferry. It is now in the museum at Swansea.

BALA and **BALA LAKE,** *Merioneth*. This little town of Bala at the eastern end of the lake of the same name is the centre of an intensely Welsh countryside. The town itself has charm. The one main street is wide and tree-lined, with the Town Hall in the centre. The White Lion Royal Hotel is built on the rambling scale that Victorian tourism demanded. Just off the main street, behind the grammar school, is the grassy mound known as Tomen y Bala, the site of a Norman motte-and-bailey castle, probably the one captured by Llywelyn the Great in 1202. The Tomen used to be a favourite resort of the knitters of Bala on summer days.

Peter Baker

The High Street, Bala

At the end of the 18th cent., Bala and the whole surrounding district was famous for its knitted stockings. Everyone knitted them and George III, when he suffered from rheumatism, insisted on wearing Bala stockings. The trade has long since disappeared.

Bala retains a more enduring fame in Welsh life as one of the great generative centres of the Methodist Revival in North Wales, although Howell Harris, when he first came here in 1741, had a rough reception and was badly beaten by the irate inhabitants. The key figure in the North Wales movement, Thomas Charles, lived in Bala, and his statue now stands before Capel Tegid, on the road to the lake. His sympathies with the Methodists lost him his curacy. His organizing ability created a system of Sunday schools and circulating schools for the education of the peasantry. In 1800 Mary Jones, a girl of sixteen from Llanfihangel-y-Pennant, under Cader Idris, walked barefoot across the mountains to obtain a Bible from Charles. Charles had to give her his own Bible. The incident made him realize that a vast unsatisfied hunger for the Scriptures existed not only in Wales but throughout the world. This led ultimately to the formation of the British and Foreign Bible Society. Charles's work continued after his death. His grandson, David Charles, joined with Lewis Edwards to found the Bala Calvinistic Methodist College in 1837. The buildings are just outside Bala, above the Tryweryn river. The memorial to Dr Edwards stands in front of the College. The parish church of Bala lies 1 m. outside the town on the N. side of the lake at Llanycil. The little church is set among fine yew trees. Here are the graves of Thomas Charles and Lewis Edwards.

Bala has also a tradition of sturdy independence in politics. It was a Congregational minister of Bala, Michael D. Jones, born at Dolhendre at the other end of the lake, who was the inspiration behind the extraordinary settlement of the Welsh in Patagonia. He dreamt of a colony where the emigrating Welsh could maintain their national identity, and fixed on the wilds of the Chabut river in South America, now part of Argentina, as the ideal place to plan a new Wales. The colony had a stormy history of hardship, and difficulties with Indians and the Argentinian authorities, but it exists today; the inhabitants speak Welsh and Spanish, but not English.

In the main street, the statue of T. I. Ellis (1859–99), who was born on the small farm of Cynlas, about 3 m. outside Bala, and played a prominent part in the development of the Radical wing in the Liberal Party in the last decades of the 19th cent. He won the spectacular election of 1886 to become M.P. for Merioneth, and was appointed Chief Liberal Whip in 1894. The Welsh inscription on the statue's base, taken from the works of Morgan Llwyd of Gwynedd, can be translated: "A man's time is his inheritance, and woe to him who wastes it". The poor boy who made such a mark in Welsh life in so short a time certainly lived up to his favourite quotation.

Bala has another side to its history, typified by the career of Squire Price of the Rhiwlas estate, whose entrance gate stands beyond the bridge over the Tryweryn past the site of the railway station. Prices had held Rhiwlas for over 200 years, but it is safe to say that no Price was more of an original than R. J. Lloyd Price. He was sportsman, author, enthusiast for cottage industries, and above all the determined promoter of

Welsh whiskey. In 1889 he founded a company to make the whiskey, and built a massive distillery at Frongoch on the banks of the Tryweryn. The promotional material was splendidly florid: "Welsh whiskey is the most wonderful whiskey that ever drove the skeleton from the feast or painted landscapes on the brain of man. It is the mingled souls of peat and barley washed white within the waters of the Treweryn." Unfortunately, the enterprise did not survive the First World War. The Frongoch distillery was used for a short time as a camp for the prisoners of the Sinn Fein Rising, among them Michael Collins. It was finally pulled down after the War. Lloyd Price lies buried in the family vault in Llanfor churchyard 1 m. to the E. of Bala. Eccentric to the end, he caused an inscription to be cut over the vault commemorating the horse Bendigo, which got him out of financial difficulties by romping home in the Cambridgeshire.

> As to my latter end I go
> To meet my Jubilee,
> I bless the good horse Bendigo
> Who built this tomb for me.

The lake remains Bala's greatest attraction for visitors. By Scottish standards it is small – only $4\frac{1}{3}$ m. long and $\frac{2}{3}$ m. wide, but it is the largest natural sheet of water in Wales. The view from the tiny promenade at the Bala end is impressive. Aran Benllyn rises on the left and Cader Idris closes the far distance. The lake varies in depth, being shallow in some parts though over 150 ft at its deepest point. Its Welsh name is Llyn Tegid, but it also features as Pimbermere in the older travel books. The usual legends of drowned palaces are attached to Bala as to many Welsh lakes. A wicked prince was celebrating the birth of his son when his harpist heard a voice pro-

A lamb-shearing competition at sheepdog trials near Bala

Peter Baker

nouncing: "Vengeance will come". He turned and saw a little bird beckoning him. He followed the bird; then, thinking he had been foolish, tried to return. Next morning he reached the spot where the palace had lain. All he saw was the placid lake and his harp floating on it. The Dee was also supposed to flow through the lake without their waters mingling. The lake does, however, contain one mysterious fish, the gwyniad, a species of salmonid (genus *Coregonus*) that is found only in Bala Lake. It is rarely taken on the line, but is sometimes cast up on the shore after storms. A specimen is displayed in the White Lion Royal Hotel. Bala has become an important sailing centre, and the British Long Distance Swimming Association has held its Welsh championships here. Extensive works have recently been completed at the point where the Dee leaves the lake, designed to control the flow of the river water to the valley lower down and prevent flooding.

Bala has been the subject of studies to enlarge its population by 10,000. If this occurs, the whole character of the district will of course change considerably.

BANGOR, *Caernarfonshire*. The town faces Anglesey across the Menai Straits, and is about 2 m. NE. of the suspension bridge across them. Its present importance is largely that of a university town and centre of learning. Its earliest origin is suggested by its name. "Bangor" is explained as meaning either a great circle or a wattle enclosure; perhaps the two have a common source in a circular enclosure designed to surround a place of worship or of communal habitation. Its possibly religious significance is supported by the well-attested facts that the Mona (Anglesey) known to the Romans on their first serious invasion of Britain was the centre of the schools of learning called Druidic, and that the other Bangor, near Chester, named Bangor-Is-Coed (Bangor This Side of the Woodlands) was in the 5th and 6th cents. a college of the Celtic Church, destroyed at the Battle of Chester in 615 by the victorious Aethelfrith, leader of Northumbria. It is possible that this Bangor by the Menai waters was founded as an offshoot of the Bangor on the Dee, since the first account of it is as a monastery created in the 5th cent. by St Deiniol, a son of the Abbot of Bangor-Is-Coed. The rules of the Celtic Church did not follow those of the later medieval Church; its saints were not necessarily clerics, but often laymen of standing who protected its foundations; its monasteries were independent bodies with considerable freedom of discipline, and their Abbots do not seem to have been bound by any requirement of celibacy.

The Cathedral of Bangor, an attractive building, gives an impression of decorous antiquity. The earlier structure was assailed in 1402 by Owain Glyndwr, in his assertion of Welsh independence as a separate kingdom; rebuilding was undertaken between 1496 and 1532. Its look now dates from a restoration by Gilbert Scott, 1866–70 and by Caroe, 1966–71. But it houses memorials to Owain of Gwynedd, King of North Wales, who died in 1169 and was buried in front of the high altar, and to a later celebrity, Goronwy Owen, poet and native of Anglesey, who died in 1769 in Virginia, U.S.A. In spite of its precedence among the churches of Wales, it keeps a pair of wooden tongs of the kind once used in remoter and smaller foundations for dealing with outbreaks of discord among the dogs who accompanied their masters into the place of worship.

The University College was one of the four constituents of the University of Wales in 1884; the present buildings spring from those opened in 1911 and are set in Upper Bangor, the newer part of the town. The older and lower part where the Cathedral stands – much crowded upon, in medieval style, by shops and houses – can still show the Archdeacon's dwelling in which Shakespeare set the scene of Glendower's declaration that he could "summon spirits from the vasty deep". It now forms part of a bank; whether this institution can make the same claim is perhaps a matter of opinion.

Ecclesiastically, Bangor was once renowned for the activities of its Bishop, Benjamin Hoadly, who in 1717–20 – by the publication of his pamphlets *The Nature of the Kingdom or Church of Christ* and *A Preservative Against the Principles and Practices of Nonjurors* – aroused what is still referred to as the Bangorian Controversy.

Lower Bangor drops down to the straits at Garth, where a pier leads out for over 500 yds, two-thirds of the passage across the water. And Porth Penrhyn near at hand still serves as a place of dispatch for the slate quarries at Bethesda. But these places once played a part in history.

From Bangor, more than from any other place, the command of the Island of Anglesey and the seas around it can be established. The fate of the Royalist uprising in the Second Civil War against the Parliamentary forces, after the capture and imprisonment of Charles I in Carisbrooke, was decided between Bangor and Beaumaris. This Second Civil War was, in some respects, a more serious and delicate matter than the First; not only Wales but the Marches along the English border, and Scotland too, were implicated. Montgomeryshire and Merioneth saw the gathering of Royalist malcontents particularly in Machynlleth, Pennal, and Llanidloes; Pembroke, Chepstow, and Shrewsbury were involved, and the invading Scots marched as far S. as Preston. Denbigh, Flint, and Conway were in arms; and the Royalist Welsh forces, under the main command of Sir John Owen of Clenennau, were able to rely on support both in Beaumaris and Bangor. But Sir John could neither organize his campaign competently nor accommodate himself with the Archbishop Williams who held Conway for the King. Cromwell showed no such incompetence; he beat the Scots soundly and left the decision in North Wales to an equally effective commander, one of the Welsh family of Mytton.

On the 5th June 1647, the Parliamentary forces under Twistleton and the Royalists under Sir John Owen met at a place called Dalar Hir, between Bangor and Aber on level ground near the shore. Since neither side wore distinctive battle-dress, passwords were used to distinguish friend from foe. As might be expected, the Puritans cried "Religion!" and the Royalists "Resolution!" Unluckily the two words were often mistaken for each other. The first encounter, between the "forlorns" or outriders of both sides, gave advantage to the King's cause; but, the main body of the Parliamentary troops coming up, the result was a rout of Owen's forces and his own wounding, unhorsing, and capture. His captor, as a reward, was granted the rents from Owen's estates. The immediate result seems to have been a general retreat of the Cavalier regiments from Mallwyd and Llanrwst upon Beaumaris. The defence of Anglesey was in some dispute between Byron, whom the Royalist command approved, and Bulkeley, the son of the local chief family, who suggested that his own generalship would do more honour to Wales than that of the Scot, Byron. Byron was given little choice in the matter, and with native foresight he decided to wait for a favourable wind and betake himself to Man. Mytton, for Parliament, had ships sent from Conway to Bangor, and when they arrived he crossed to invade. On the outskirts of Beaumaris the two sides engaged, young Bulkeley having made no attempt to contest the passage of the ships. A Parliamentary cavalry charge scattered the defenders from the field; and the Second Civil War was over. Among those who that day smote mightily for the Lord (of course on the Puritan side) was Vavasor Powell, a man devoted to Puritan evangelism, which he pursued both in writing and in the work of his hands. Born in Radnorshire and a schoolmaster at Clun, he had Cromwell's licence to preach and oversee the faith in Wales, and in that service he opposed Cromwell's appointment as Lord Protector of the Realm and suffered imprisonment.

Beaumaris surrendered, and its castle did so shortly afterwards. The citizens of the town neither embroiled themselves in the affair nor received any particular penalty. They and many others of the population seem to have looked on the war with indifference. More than once, Cavalier and Roundhead in the Welsh marchlands agreed on the site of battle, only to be laid about by the farming community with pitchfork, flail, and other discouragements and told to take their war somewhere else.

In the Civil War, Welsh poets and literary men were engaged on both sides. Contrary to Vavasor Powell (1617–70), his near contemporary Huw Morus (1622–1709) took the Royalist side; so did George Herbert, the cleric who was one of the greatest poets of the Anglo-Welsh Metaphysical school. The Goronwy Owen commemorated in Bangor Cathedral belonged to the 18th cent. He was born in Anglesey, and, through the encouragement of the antiquarian Morris brothers, this tinker's son had his education at the Friars' School in Bangor. He became a cleric in the Church of England, which at that time was

G. Douglas Bolton

Bangor-Is-Coed bridge over the River Dee

the official Church in Wales; but he made no headway. Perhaps his great interest and skill in his native language obstructed him. Many people think him the greatest Welsh poet of modern times. Undoubtedly he began the revival of the country's literature, which was beginning to fall into the hands of the wandering harp-men, who retained an unaffected lyricism but never attempted the heights that Goronwy Owen reached. He considered his *Cywydd y Farn Fawr* (Ode on the Great Judgment at the End of the World) his best work; it has been ranked with Milton's best. Bangor has his memorial; Virginia has his bones.

BANGOR-IS-COED, *Flintshire.* This is a famous place; the modern Bangor-on-Dee with its racecourse represents it. A monastery and college of the Celtic Church, active in Britain before the mission of Augustine at the end of the 6th cent., may have flourished here. Founded in A.D. 180, if the legendary date is accepted, by 596 it had 2,400 monks. It played a great part in the refusal of the Celtic Church to accept the authority of Rome, as Augustine demanded, at a place of meeting called Augustine's Oak, in 602. The Anglo-Saxons were encouraged to reprimand them, and at the Battle of Chester in 615 the matter was put to the trial. Monks from Bangor-Is-Coed, after several days of fasting, came to attend the British forces and pray for their victory and the triumph of their Church. Apparently they were left, apart from the actual battle, in the charge of a young British leader named Brochuael. Aethelfrith, leader of the Northumbrian forces, sent a detachment to dispose of the monks; the young war leader entrusted with their safety took alarm and left them to their fate. The British lost both the battle and control of the area lying between Chester and their kinsmen in Strathclyde to the N. of it.

The monks were slain as they prayed, and the monastery was destroyed. Bede claims that several thousands of its members were massacred.

The only name that has survived in connection with this monastery is that of its Abbot, Dunawd (Bede calls him Dinoot), who took the lead in rebutting the claims of Augustine.

BARDSEY ISLAND, *Caernarfonshire.* About the coast of Wales lie many islands, all with their special sources of interest, whether the wildlife that inhabits them or the history they hold encased from time in the circle of the sea. Indeed, much that is distinctive of the ancient Welsh culture, shared by many provinces and differing peoples, comes from these islands. The memory of this fact, rooted in prehistory, inspired a Welsh claim centuries ago to the island of Lundy.

Ynys Enlli (as Bardsey Island is called in Welsh) has among them all a particular claim. The learned Thomas Richards, Curate of Coychurch, published in 1759 a survey of the British tongue that was much praised at the time. In it he points out that the name Bardsey may not be correct, and that the island should be called Birdsey (Isle of Birds). Similarly, he gives no authority for the derivation of Enlli from "eddies", though his vocabulary implies that it may have meant refreshing to the soul or body. Certainly the tides dominate the life of Bardsey; the race through the sound always affects boats seeking the island, and they may be marooned there for a week or so. It has a lighthouse. It even has a harbour, though the wharf channelled in the rock-shore is scarcely distinguishable from the natural fissures. The harbour has to be on one side of the island, which falls into two contrasted sections. Part is a stone-strewn level, still holding the few farms. The rest is a mountain-rise sheering from the flatland and standing with a round green head and grey, torn

Reece Winstone

Bardsey Island from Braich y Pwll on the Lleyn peninsula

flanks above the heave of spray. On that summit, you can well believe, from the strange speech of the gulls and sea-mews steering on their wing-lift in the bluster of winds, that this is indeed the Isle of Birds. But Bardsey's 444 acres, largely taken up by the hill (548 ft), have long been populated with sheep, and a dwindling number of farms tended them. Fishing, including the catch of crab and lobster, is perhaps the main industry. There are still enough people to justify a church that stands in the precincts of the ancient Abbey of St Mary, founded by St Cadfan in A.D. 516. Here St Dubricius died in 612; his bones were removed in 1120 to Llandaff Cathedral, of which he was reputedly the founder.

Twenty thousand saints are said to have their resting-place in the island, since it was here, according to ancient chroniclers, that the monks of the college at Bangor-Is-Coed, near Chester, came to re-found their institute of Christian learning, after the Battle of Chester in 615 had thrown their form of Christianity, and the British power that protected them, out of the English Midlands. They have no kind of memorial in the shape of gravestones, though many bones have from time to time been disinterred. Yet the presence of these saints seems to have made the air itself holy; and Gerald the Welshman, observing the extent of Wales in the 12th cent., says about Bardsey that none died there except of extreme old age, so healthy was it both of soil and water, and so much removed from the contentions of the rest of the world.

It probably did not earn its original importance by being a place of refuge from the disastrous times of the 7th cent.; the record confirms that its abbey was set there at least 100 years earlier, when, as Bede states in his *Ecclesiastical History* of about 750, Britain had recovered much of its stability after the withdrawal of direct Roman

rule; and fifty years of peace and prosperity made 6th-cent. writers, including the acrimonious Gildas, describe it as an island of ideal pastoral beauty. It was in this period, when the succession to Rome was being disputed, that missionaries of the Celtic Church of both sides of the Irish Sea went about their task of converting the heathen, some of them penetrating deep into Europe and leaving their memoried names as far afield as the Alps. It was in the islands about the coasts of Britain that they first set up their sanctuaries for the faith, and from these islands that they invaded the mainland with no greater weapon than fortitude and belief.

One such area of penetration was to the S. of Bardsey, in the Dovey estuary where Cynfelyn has left his name. In the Lleyn promontory and the shoreland from which it strikes, the number of early Christian churches still retaining their primitive development in building is considerable; they are thickly set, and Anglesey is filled with them. Puffin Island, off Anglesey; Llantysilio in the Menai Straits; near St Cybi on Holy Island; at Llangwyfan and Llanddwyn on the western shore of Anglesey; Ramsey Island off St David's, and Caldey off the Pembrokeshire coast are some examples of early settlement. Llanrhychwyn, near Llanrwst, contains evidence of the earliest structural forms; in Anglesey, Tregaean, Rhosbeirio, Llechylched, Llanfair-yn-y-cwmwd and Llanfair-yn-neubwll, Bodedern, Cerrigceinwen, Llanfwrog, Llanddeusant, and others show the single-chamber plan by which these first churches were distinguished. Llanfair P.G., Llanfair, Mathafarn Eithaf, Llangristiolus, and others are somewhat later structures making additions to the primitive form. Not till the 14th cent. did any major alteration in plan begin to affect the native and simple design.

The institution of a "King of Bardsey" must

be mentioned. The liability of the island to be cut off at times from the mainland shore made it necessary, as it still is to some extent, for the islanders to have their own means of deciding disputes. The practice of setting up an islander to judge any question was a commonsense step of the kind that organized the Courts of Strays in the sheep country around Plynlimon. The "Gothick" whimsy of a member of the Wynn family, owners of the island, is responsible for the "crown", the "treasure", and the wooden effigy that stood in place of the "army", and for the title of "king". When appeal was made to this office later, it was to a president.

BARFOG, Llyn, *Merioneth.* This lake is small, but of outstanding interest. It is advertised as part of a picnic attraction in the neighbourhood of Aberdovey. The approach to it is through some of the most sequestered valleys in the most beautiful part of Wales. But it also has far nobler qualities.

The way from Aberdovey is either by the footpath from Bwlch Gwyn to Cwrt or by the motor roads running past Botalog through Cwm Dyffryn as far as Tyddyn Gwylim. It can also be reached by driving to Cwrt and taking the Cwm Dyffryn road from the opposite direction.

Lake Barfog lies in a fold of the Briddell hill, a spur looking directly down the Dovey valley to the estuary, and commanding a wide view of the sea. The name Barfog means Bearded; a satisfying derivation has been found in the rushes that stand thickly towards one end of it, interspersed with water-lily and haunted by wild birds. The area around it is boggy and set with small hillocks. Against many of these are laid circles of craggy stone, the remains of hutments whose coverings have disappeared. Overgrown with grasses and scattered over a well-defined area, they lead to a green track on the height of the Briddell hill. What they originally were seems to be decided by the occurrence, again at logically determined spots, of upright stone slabs, anvil-like and surrounded with a litter of stone fragments splintered to significant size. This is characteristic of the ancient stone factories that shaped the agricultural tools of a simple economy. (*See* Bugeilyn.)

Such tool-making was one of mankind's first industries, belonging to the peoples that inhabited Britain even before the Celtic folk crossed from the Continent. Like other lakes in Wales, this one has its own legend, which Sir John Rhys mentions in his *Celtic Folk-Lore.* It is that of the young local farmer who finds near the lake a girl of great beauty but from a fairy race. She agrees to marry him, and she brings as dowry a number of cattle, different in kind from his own but rich in yield. She makes conditions, such as that she must have a special sort of food and, above all, must never be brought within touch of iron. When he breaks these conditions, she is taken back into the depths of the waters by her own people, together with the fairy cattle, and is never seen again.

The 18th cent. decided to treat these legends as "fairy-tales". Modern archaeology takes a different view. The reference in folk-memory was to settlements like the one around Barfog, established before the iron-using communities of Central Europe invaded the country. Still making stone implements and, among metals, knowing the use only of bronze, they were part of the wide archaic civilization that flourished about 2000 B.C. in the eastern Mediterranean. To dismiss them as primitive is entirely wrong. Their bronze-work was skilled and beautiful. Examples of outstanding interest can be seen in the Carmarthen museum. The manufacture and casting of bronze is a highly sophisticated operation. Nor, as the arrow-heads of Bugeilyn show, was much less skill needed for the shaping of flints. The extensive trade, by sea as well as land, in the exchange of stone products required knowledge that can be called scientific.

A further point of interest is the now-tumbled and prostrate cairn called the Carn March Arthur. The name seems to mean Arthur's Horse, and on this stone the eye of faith can see a hoof-mark made by King Arthur's horse when the hero took off in a leap that landed him across the estuary into Cardiganshire. But the metaphor of the horse was widely used among peoples who first studied the time-schedules laid down by the sun. The cairn, standing on the northward alignment from the Bedd Taliesin on the opposite shore of the estuary, is probably much older than the "Arthurian" period. Sir John Rhys, however, scholar though he was, made a curious error in failing to note that, in the 12th-cent. romance by Geoffrey of Monmouth that initiated the accepted version of Arthur, Barfog is the name given to Arthur's foster-father. The lake of Barfog, like much else round the Dovey, is typical of all that is connected with the name of Wales.

From the same Cwm Dyffryn road, the Gaelic graves near Erw-faethlon can be traced. They have received much learned comment; and no part of this lovely district should be left unvisited.

BARMOUTH, *Merioneth.* In Welsh Abermo, but more correctly called Aber Mawddach, Barmouth stands in the estuary of the Mawddach river, where it stretches to the sea from the valley under the shoulder of Cader Idris. Across this estuary stands Barmouth Bridge, $\frac{1}{2}$ m. long and of wood except where it passes over the bed of the river. There, for 400 ft, it is carried on girders supported by steel cylinders driven into the Mawddach. Apart from the railway track, there is also a foot-bridge.

Barmouth town has few ancient monuments, but is fitted with everything required for sport and entertainment. It is terraced against the steep sides of the mountains and has a curiously other-worldly appearance. Its chief attraction lies in the splendid scenery of coast and valley and the high hills that crowd upon it, the range of the Llawllech. Most of the town is modern, but on the quay dominating the strand, where

The harbour, Barmouth

the sea covers the shore completely at high tide, is the Ty Gwyn (White House) reputed to have been built by one of the Vaughan family of Gors-y-Gedol for Henry Tudor, Earl of Richmond, when he landed to begin his campaign against Richard III that ended at Bosworth. It has been converted into cottages, but the ancient door remains. A less well-known episode concerns the part Barmouth played in the Second Civil War of the 17th cent. Royalist forces were strong in the area and were preparing to outflank the triumphant Parliamentary troops in North Wales by joining sympathizers in Anglesey. Under the command of a Cardiganshire man (one Lloyd), the Cavaliers, mainly on foot, had gathered at Machynlleth and quartered themselves at Pennal in the neighbouring Dovey valley. Twistleton, the Roundhead Governor of Denbigh, took a company of no more than eighty horse and rode into the Ardudwy, that part of Merioneth which lies just N. of Barmouth. The enemy, however, had for the moment been too quick for him and had got away from Dolgellau to Harlech. The regiment at Pennal was making its way to reinforce them; but, as they waited to make the crossing by Barmouth ferry, he surprised them into surrender. The encounter was decisive: it broke the whole of the offensive at the start.

To have a view of the place of engagement and the impressive land- and seascapes, Dinas Olau is a place to reach. It is a cliff above the town, and in 1895 was the first possession acquired by the National Trust.

Llanaber church, the foundation of Barmouth, is now nearly 2 m. away from its centre. It is an unusual church for this part of Wales, but a perfect specimen of its date and kind. Begun in 1200, and finished in fifty years, it has remained unaltered. In it, evidence of some forgotten Barmouth of even earlier date is preserved: an inscribed stone apparently bearing the words *Coelextus monedo regi*. What or whom it refers to is a matter of doubt. It was found on the shingle beach not far from Barmouth, and was used by a farmer as a foot-bridge over a stream. It may have had some connection with the Egryn Abbey that once stood just over 1 m. away from Llanaber but has now vanished entirely.

BARRY, *Glamorgan*, on the shores of the Bristol Channel 8 m. SW. of Cardiff, is a 19th-cent. boom town, based on the coal-mining bonanza of the Rhondda and neighbouring valleys in the 1880s. Before 1884 the total population of the place was eighty-five. Barry Island was separated from the mainland and held the Chapel of St Baruch, a contemporary of St Cadoc of Llancarfan, who probably gave the place his name. A few walls of the church can be seen near the holiday camp. The island also contained a remarkable bellowing cave, which was regarded as one of the Wonders of Wales. The nearest churches were at Cadoxton and Merthyr Dyfan. Cadoxton is now near the eastern entrance to the docks. The old church has an ancient font, a rood-loft staircase behind the pulpit on the S. wall, and traces of medieval painting. Merthyr Dyfan is also now inside the borough boundaries. The church is small and restored, with a tower holding three bells.

In 1844 the rural peace of Barry was shattered by the arrival of an army of workmen who set about building the largest dock until then built in Wales. The first dock was completed in 1889, and Barry's population leapt to 13,000. The building of the dock was a triumph for the redoubtable David Davies, the "top sawyer" and former railway magnate who had become a pioneer of the Rhondda coal-mines. Coal was in its heyday, and David Davies and his supporters found the delays and changes at Cardiff docks intolerable. After one of those epic battles with the Bute interests who controlled Cardiff, so characteristic of robust Victorian capitalism, Davies got his Bill through Parliament to make new docks at Barry. The island was joined to the mainland by a causeway, and dock basins were built to the E. By 1900 Barry was exporting

6,000,000 tons of coal a year. New entrance locks were built – a remarkable engineering feat in itself, for Barry has a rise of tide of over 40 ft, one of the highest in the world. The gates allow ships to enter at any state of the tide. In 1898 a second dock was built, and later three graving docks were added. Behind the town new railway lines were constructed, with great viaducts that allowed the coal of the Rhondda and valleys further E. to be siphoned off to the new docks. The impressive viaduct in Porthkerry Park to the W. of Barry is part of this system. In 1911 Barry exported 11,000,000 tons of Welsh coal, an all-time record for any port. The statue of David Davies, poring ruggedly over his plans, stands before the dock offices.

Then came decline. By the 1930s coal was in the doldrums. It is still exported from Barry, but most of the coal-hoists have been closed down and many dismantled. The harbour has turned to other commodities – from oil to, surprisingly enough, bananas. An important chemical industry has grown on Cadoxton Moors. Industrially and as a port, Barry has moved with the times.

There is a second Barry that has always been an expanding asset – the holiday and pleasure resort. Barry Island has one of the largest fun fairs in the country, set along Whitemore Bay. Beyond the island and its popular attractions is Cold Knapp, with the largest swimming-pool in Wales. To the W. runs the Pebble Beach, a remarkable geological formation consisting of an accumulation of pebbles, 1 m. long, that falls steeply to the water's edge. The "Golden Stairs" at the far end of the beach lead up to Porthkerry Park, a valley left in its natural state and making an open space of 225 acres through which runs the Porthkerry viaduct. Barry is expanding inland, and has become increasingly popular as a residential area for Cardiff.

BEAUMARIS, *Anglesey.* This most beautiful town on the side of the Menai Straits that belongs to Anglesey has an apparently pure Norman name. Beau Marais (Lovely Flatland) was what the invaders called it; and the description remains true. The pronunciation of the word may also remain purely Norman, for it is always called "Bew Marris".

The Menai Straits seem to have good weather all the time, though admittedly this is a matter of personal experience. At Beaumaris, the blue waters between the wooded beach of Anglesey and the dark strength of the mountains of Snowdonia open out to the wider reaches of Conway Bay. And, standing guard at the entrance to the narrows, Beaumaris Castle shows a perfect and symmetrical example of medieval military architecture. In 1295, soon after the death of the last Llywelyn, it was set up by Edward I as a warder of the Welsh in the chain of such fortifications bounding the N. from Conway to Caernarfon and to Criccieth and Harlech. More than any of its associate fortresses, it is built with a sense of balance and proportion that appears to have come not from military needs but from apprecia-

Peter Baker

Beaumaris Castle

tion of the site. The inner ward, or main castle stronghold, is squared with gatehouses that held the state apartments of the chamberlain. The outer defence is an eight-sided wall strengthened with drum-towers. The ancient defensive device of right-angled structure to put a flanking fire on the attacker is very noticeable in its inner and outer gateway. The great hall and the chapel are excellent examples of their kind; and the essential moat was connected with the sea by a canal.

The Tudors were a family from Anglesey, and the first act of Henry VII was to give possession of Beaumaris to his son by a Breton lady. It was then, and still remains, the chief centre of administration for the island. But the Edwardian castle was not in fact the first invading stronghold set up in medieval times. In the private grounds of a house a little way out of the town, there is another castle. It is largely ruined and stands obscured by woodland on the slope of a small hill. It is a knight's castle – a minor structure with a single central tower and a circular surround of battlement; one of the most perfect examples of this outpost type is the knight's castle at Restormel in Cornwall. This one near Beaumaris is said to have been set there in the earlier days of the Norman invasion by a feudatory of Hugh the Wolf, Earl of Chester. If it has a history, no one seems to remember it. You have the impression that the knight who built it decided after all to forget about the war and surrender himself to the quiet that drops in bright air over land and sea about Beaumaris.

The church of the town is also an invader. It is contemporary with the great Castle, but has additions from the 14th and 16th cents. It is not a church belonging to Anglesey, for in this always holy island the churches possess a deeply

Top: *The church at Beaumaris*   *G. Douglas Bolton*
Bottom: *Beddgelert on the River Glaslyn*   *Jane J. Miller*

indigenous character. The houses have a calm reserve that, for many of them, survived unruffled the taking of Beaumaris Castle during the Second Civil War, an event that followed directly on the Royalist defeat across the Straits of Menai, close to Bangor.

BEDDGELERT, *Caernarfonshire*, has charm and magnificent scenery. Yet it is associated with an 18th-cent. ballad that casts a slur on one of the noblest men in Welsh history. The too-familiar story goes that Prince Llywelyn the Great, having left his hound Gelert to guard his infant son, returned from the chase to find the animal covered with gore. In the panic of the moment he assumed that it had eaten the child, and he slew it in revenge. The unfortunate hound did not, apparently, have time to explain that it had saved the child from a wolf. Thus was the name Bedd Gelert (Gelert's Grave) explained.

The story is typical of the late 18th cent. both in its unreality and its commercial inspiration. MacPherson's *Ossian*, which romantically distorted Gaelic traditions in Scotland, began a series of mishandlings of Celtic literature from which it is barely recovering today. Before 1798, the tale about Llywelyn was unknown in the village. It seems to have been originated by one David Prichard, who migrated from South Wales to become the first landlord of the Royal Goat Inn at Beddgelert. He was interested in folklore, and he attached this tale to the village for a reason not unconnected with his trade. Helped by the parish clerk and some other person unnamed, he supported the fiction with a "primitive" cairn that they set up in a meadow close to the church. It was from Prichard that the author of the ballad obtained the detailed history he immortalized.

More probably the name was given by a St Kelert in that form to the village, which kept it until Prichard changed the spelling and largely obliterated the history. Perhaps one of Wales's many champions of faith in the Age of Saints, Kelert was held in memory by a priory of the Augustinians, provided for pilgrims to Bardsey and Ireland. The priory is now represented by the church at Beddgelert.

SW. of the village stands Moel Hebog (Hawk Hill, 2,566 ft), which is, however, more easily reached from Llanfihangel-y-Pennant on the road from Dolbenmaen; the eastern side of the mountain is a toothed escarpment difficult to climb. The approach from the Royal Goat Hotel at Beddgelert is the shortest; but the Llanfihangel route can be recommended for the sight it gives of the lake Cwmystradllyn, lying like a shale of blue slate between the heights of Hebog and Moel Ddu. Hebog is a most satisfactory hill to climb, the long ridge that runs in a tumbled scree of rock to Moel Lefn (2,094 ft) giving a wild background to the point known as the Cave of Owain Glyndwr, where the fallen King of Wales is supposed to have hidden when hunted by the English. From this ridge, the Snowdon massif rises as if upon another level of

air and holds the whole horizon of the NE. with its head.

Beddgelert stands at the confluence of the Gwynant and the Colwyn, and from it the road is short to Llyn Gwynant and the upper stream of the Glaslyn river. Before the Gwynant lake is reached, you pass another one, called Dinas. This is Welsh for a fortified position, and the word seems to relate directly to the Duns that the Romans found used by the British, and that still remain as place-names in England and Scotland. Dinas Emrys (Fort of Emrys) is the name given to the height from which the lake takes its own. It recalls the Arthurian legend invented by Geoffrey of Monmouth in his romance *The History of the Kings of Britain*, which he spent ten years in writing and published about A.D. 1140. For the Fort of Emrys is said to have been granted to the great Merlin, called Emrys, by Vortigern, the luckless ruler of Britain who summoned Hengist and Horsa to his aid in the hope of repelling incursions by the Picts and the Scots. The myths into which the history of Britain between A.D. 400 and 600 have collapsed were not in themselves invented by Geoffrey; handlers of history had used them before him. Of the three Merlins who still haunt the imagination from that time, the Emrys seems to have been some commander of imperial forces, or of garrisons that tried to continue the system of Roman control, while the Scots and the Irish Merlins seem to have been junior commanders, in charge respectively of the northern and the western fronts in Britain. At all events the tale of Dinas Emrys impressed local memory deeply enough to impose its name on the mountain and the lake.

BEGUILDY, *Radnorshire*. This is the Bugeildy (Shepherd's House), and its setting is appropriate to the name. It lies in the valley of the Teme, running parallel to the course of the Clun river as it comes from the high uplands dominated by Kerry Hill. The wide hills are famous for their sheep, which once had the whole of these heights for their own, and can be said to be the true founders both of Beguildy and the Church of Fleeces at Betws-y-crwyn, 1,300 ft above Beguildy on the Black Mountain ridge that stands between the Clun and the Teme. Today, though the flocks are as large as ever and the sheep themselves remarkable and beautifully clad creatures, the tops are widely over-marched with long ranks of afforestation – fir-plantations that seem large and lofty when you walk through them, but prove to be only a green cloak over the mountain-shoulders when you stand in the open and see them laid beneath the long sky that drops distantly to the plains of Severn. There is no more beautiful place in Wales – the old Wales of Powys that disregards the political incidents of such constructions as Offa's Dyke, the border castles, and modern administrative boundaries – than these valleyed hills where sheep and men live under the clouds that are similarly careless of frontier restrictions. The Teme and the Clun go

Plate 4 Caernarfon Castle (see p. 124)   W. A. Poucher
Plate 5 Harlech: the Castle, against the Snowdon range (see p. 183)   W. A. Poucher

down into the Shropshire fields where Castle Idris looks across at Spoad Hill, and Beguildy in Wales looks along its narrow vale to Llanfair Waterdine and Skyborry Green in England, and both know, whatever maps may demarcate, that it is all Powys still. Beguildy is best known by its church, one of those remoter places in Wales that contrived to keep intact its 13th-cent. rood-screen, intricately carved and panelled, through all the changes of faith. It has a striking Jacobean pulpit and an altar-table of the same period, and a bench-end of much earlier date.

Opposite Beguildy, where the road crosses the Teme to traverse the Black Mountain and reach the Newtown road, is a tumulus that has companions along the valley above Dutlas and shortly before Llanfair Waterdine. That the Teme was a very ancient trackway is shown by the standing stone about 1 m. SE. of Beguildy, and, as you take the hill-path past Quabbs and Betws-y-crwyn, you can find what it pointed to. There were grey stones – or, as the Welsh know them, "maeni llwyd" – 1,500 ft up on the western side of the head of the Black Mountain; a little below them where the hills fall sharply into a wooded valley lies the Bryn Amlwg site. And, on the greater height rising again from the valley close to the minor road to Newtown, is the stone circle that men set up to trace the working of the sun and stars. The rich valleys and the hills, as fruitful then as now, attracted one of the earliest of civilized human settlements. The peace and the identity between man and man that this borderland seems to confirm make Beguildy a place deserving of pilgrimage.

BERRIEW, *Montgomeryshire*. "Berhiew," says Daniel Paterson in 1811, "5 miles from Montgomery; or you may go forward through the Rhiew river to Glanhafren in dry weather, crossing the Canal twice and the Severn river." In this way he confirms the meaning of the name as Aber-rhiw, or the place where the Rhiw flows into the Severn, and gives an explanation of its former importance. Nowadays it would be said that you take the road S. from Welshpool and go over the Severn hard by Garthmyl and so approach Berriew village and the Union Canal. Berriew is set in an area that was one of the most fertile districts of the old Kingdom of Powys, that province of Wales which stretched along the rich valleys running eastwards from the uplands of the Plynlimon range. Berriew lay at the junction of the sheep-walks of the hills and the lush farms of the lowlands; it was on the routes of the cattle-drovers into England, and it was a place where the wool shorn from sheep could be conveniently stored and baled. The forward-looking policy of Charles II in the 17th cent. proposed to make use of the Severn valley and the sheep-rearing industry on which it drew by building a series of canals concentrating on Manchester, a project carried out by the Duke of Bridgewater and culminating in the middle of the 18th cent. Welshpool became an important centre of this development, and Berriew flourished in consequence. Manchester,

Montgomeryshire might well claim, owed the foundation of its prosperity to the canal that took its products and its keenest commercial brains from the valleys of Wales into Lancashire. Berriew was, in its way, the bridge-head of supply, and it remained so until the woollen industry in the early 19th cent. transferred the breeding of sheep to Australia. Berriew retains the evidence of its past in the charming cottages of the 1700s and 1800s still looking over the confluence of the Rhiw and the Hafren (Severn) and the run of the Union Canal as it goes in sober restriction to Welshpool. It stands almost exactly on the English border, but in its peace and beauty it keeps alive the distinctive spirit of Powys.

BERSHAM, *Denbighshire*. Though surrounded by places with Welsh names, whose inhabitants speak Welsh, Bersham has been called the most English village in Wales. The language of its people is English; so are their most typical surnames. Some of the families seem to have originated in Cornwall, being drawn to Bersham when a paper-mill was active there. Others probably arrived earlier, to work in the foundry of Isaac Wilkinson, the father of the ironmaster John Wilkinson who made Bersham memorable by producing parts for James Watt's engines and cannon for Wellington to fire in Spain. Today the village is quiet and rural. In spite of open-cast coal-working in the park nearby, the countryside has come secretly back and claimed Bersham as its own. The six-sided mill of the old Wilkinson works has become a farm barn. The small waterfall supplied power for the mill.

There was a long tradition of ironwork in the area before Wilkinson arrived. Not far away is Groes Foel, now a large farmhouse, but famous as the workshop of the brothers Davies in the early 18th cent. Robert and John Davies won fame as the craftsmen who created the splendid iron gates that add distinction to so many of the churches and mansions in the area. The gates of Chirk Castle are especially notable. They were set up between 1719 and 1721.

Bersham lies between Offa's Dyke and Wat's Dyke. Both are well seen in the neighbourhood.

BERWYNS, The, *Montgomeryshire, Denbighshire, Merioneth*. These belong to Corwen. The high, heathered tops look down upon the town from Moel Fferna and swing towards Bala over the course of the Dee with Cader Fronwen (2,572 ft), Cader Berwyn (2,712), and Moel Sych (2,713), to Milltir Cerrig (1,638). The names speak of Wales in many aspects, and the moor is set with cairns that use the name of Arthur to confirm the significance of that other name of romance, Branwen. About these hills Owain Gwynedd, Owain of Cyfeiliog, and Rhys son of Gruffydd summoned the greatest force that Wales had yet raised to meet and throw back the march of Henry II from Shrewsbury in 1169, when Wales for once was united in all its ruling Houses. And from these hills the other Owain, Glyndwr, looked north and south to see the extent of his own landed heritage before he widened his rule to take in all Wales. Pistyll Rhaeadr is to the S. of them, and to the E. is the pleasant place Llanarmon Dyffryn Ceiriog, where the poet who was also a railwayman is commemorated. Llandderfel, with its ancient church, and the wide sheet of Bala Lake lie to the W. But in the shoulder of Moel Sych (Dry Hill) is a smaller lake called Lluncaws, or sometimes Llyn Caws (Lake of Cheese). The name most probably comes from the shape of the lake, which is almost circular and, when it catches the moon, looks like a round of yellow milk against the darkness. But the magnificence of the circuit of rock in which it lies has supplied another explanation. Helen of the Legions, the queen after whom the Roman roads striking through the heartland of Wales are named, sat here once to rest after leading her troops over the Berwyns, and she lost her provisions in the waters. Any angler today who comes here for sport can bring his own sandwich and feel in royal company.

BETHESDA, *Caernarfonshire,* is a quarryman's village where slates are hewn to be sent by rail to Porth Penrhyn for shipping. The first name of Bethesda was Glan Ogwen, for the Ogwen river runs by it. Nonconformism set a chapel here, and its name has superseded the old one. George Borrow summarized the place in a note: "If its name is scriptural, the manners of its people are by no means so". Time, of course, has changed this. The Penrhyn slate quarries dominate the town; their 1,000-ft incision into the mountainsides is worth examining. Facilities are given to watch the blasting, splitting, and dressing of the slates. Their variety of colour is remarkable, ranging through blue, grey, green, and red; and they are greatly in demand.

The village stands in what is probably the most impressive region of Snowdonia. The upper part of the Ogwen valley is called Nant Ffrancon; one interpretation of the words is Brook of Beavers. This is not impossible, since the beaver was once familiar among the Welsh mountain-streams, and Gerald de Barri, in his *Itinerary of Wales* (1188), has passages of considerable interest about them. He had obviously watched them with delight; and he tells us how some cut wood, while others carried it to the stream, and a further group set the stakes and wound them about with willows, so that the dam was efficiently formed; and how they would then lift a further tier of logs until their castle had the look of a natural, treed island in the river.

Nant Ffrancon is remarkable for the press of great heights around it. Carnedd y Filiast (Cairn of the Greyhound Bitch, 2,694 ft); Moel Perfydd (Central Hill, 2,750); Elidir Fawr (perhaps Riven Hill, 3,029); Foel Goch (2,726); Y Garn (3,104); and the Glyders, Fawr and Fach (perhaps the Slippery Ones, 3,279 and 3,262) surround it and make it one of the most rewarding valleys for those who love the heights. Nor does this finish the roll; Carnedd Ddafydd and Carnedd Llywelyn (3,426 and 3,484 ft) thrust their heads here to look at Snowdon almost with level eyes. They are peaks named after the two last defenders of independent Gwynedd against Edward I of England in the 13th cent. And Craig Ddu (Black Rock, 3,169 ft) stands high over the lake.

Ogwen is a lake of great interest both to anglers and students of folklore. It is 1 m. long, 984 ft above sea-level, and the source of the Ogwen river, which streams from it in a series of falls to the Bwlch y Benglog. On the S. side, the black triangle of the three points of Tryfan (3,010 ft)

The Penrhyn slate quarries, Bethesda

J. Allan Cash

stand with a challenge to the climber. From Tryfan, years ago, a landslide fell upon Ogwen lake; and the river that once ran to Capel Curig was forced to find a new outlet into Nant Ffrancon. Ogwen was originally called Ogfanw; and this early name survives in the locality as Ogwan rather than in the form the maps accept. It suggests a covered cave; and legend has it that such a cave does exist in the tumble of rocks at the foot of Tryfan known as Pen Bryn Melyn. A coach was often seen there, setting down a passenger who entered the fissure among the boulders where no mortal could ever follow. The coach was always brightly lit within and vanished when approached. Only one fortunate explorer ever found the opening; he discovered great riches in it, and laid a trail of pebbles behind him as he left it so that he might find it again next day. But, when he returned, the secret and immortal folk who dwell there had removed all trace of them. Legend has set the grave of Bedivere, the last knight of Arthur, on the slopes of Tryfan; and Ogwen is the lake into which he must have cast Excalibur, the potent sword of light that Arthur bore. It does not matter that Arthur and Bedivere and the sword meant more than romance allows them. Ogwen can impose its own truths on anyone who walks beside it.

But, magnificent and mysterious as it is, Llyn Ogwen is no equal of Llyn Idwal. This lake is higher still than Ogwen, being 1,223 ft above sealevel and cupped in the hands of Glyder Fawr. Its name comes from a son of Owain Gwynedd, Prince of North Wales in the days of Stephen of England and one of the most powerful princes Wales ever knew. No bird will fly across its dark waters, people say, because here, by the treachery of his guardian Nefydd Haradd, or of his fosterfather Dunod, the young prince Idwal was drowned. According to some accounts, the church at Llanrwst was built by Rhun son of Nefydd to expiate his father's crime. Any fisherman who has walked the sides of Idwal lake will be prepared to exonerate both Nefydd and Dunod. At the end of the lake furthest from its outfall is a pool overgrown with weeds and called Llygad Glas (Green Eye). It is a malevolent eye, to be avoided at all costs. More than one man has found himself in danger of being sucked into that morass; and Idwal's death may have been due to the treachery of his footing rather than of his guardians.

Storms on Idwal are frequent. The winds cut through the peaks carrying clouds that writhe and resist like living creatures; the rain can fall in ranks of silver like the lances of a threatening host, and water whips from the surface of the lake in curtains 20 ft high. Nowhere else in Britain can so tremendous or so savage a beauty be found.

One of the most adventurous walks around it is the track that leads to Twll Du (Black Hole), more commonly called the Devil's Kitchen, a chasm between the Garn and the Great Glyder, whose rock-walls seem to touch. It is a natural feature unique in its grim strength; and the tale of Idwal has been varied to say that down this he was hurled from the wall of mountain to his death.

BETWS GARMON, *Caernarfonshire.* "Betws" is said to be a Welsh adaptation of the English "bede-house", and to date from the days of faith and pilgrimage; and Garmon is a name identified with the heroic missionary age of the Celtic Church. The village is set in one of the most impressive areas of Snowdonia. The approach from Caernarfon and Llanbeblig is over a three-arched bridge, with the first dominant heights of the mountain area in Moel Eilio and Mynydd Mawr to right and left. The place itself is something of a straggle, as befits a habitation adjusting itself to the narrow valley that falls into the Cwellyn lake. But, remote as it seems from the world, it gave birth to one of Wales's most curiously employed and far-travelled sons.

In 1804 the President of the United States, Thomas Jefferson, was deeply interested in the future of the new territory of Louisiana, only recently acquired by purchase from France. To explore and survey the area, he relied in the main on a man of apparently Welsh extraction, one Meriwether Lewis, his own secretary. But Lewis was not to go unsupported by experienced travellers already knowledgeable in the region. Among them was another Welshman of undoubted ancestry.

"I enclose," wrote Jefferson on the 13th January 1804, "a map of the Missouri as far as the Mendans, 12 or 15 hundred miles I presume above its mouth; it is said to be very accurate having been done by Mr. Evans by order of the Spanish Government.... Mr. Evans, a Welshman...whose original object I believe had been to go in search of the Welsh Indians said to be up the Missouri. On this subject, a Mr. Rees of the same nation established in the western part of Pennsylvania will write to you."

John Thomas Evans was a native of Waunfawr, a place lying between Llanbeblig and Betws Garmon. He was – oddly enough, in view of his later employment in the New World by the Spaniards – of a stock deeply committed to the outlook and purposes of Welsh Methodism. His earlier life was given to the society of poets, antiquarians, and writers of imaginative history, including Iolo Morgannwg (Edward Williams), who created out of scanty material the bardic lore of modern Wales. One of the subjects most eagerly considered by this circle was the story – approved by Humphrey Lhuyd of Denbigh, a learned Tudor antiquary; by Hakluyt in his tale of British voyages; and by Howell, the Royalist writer of the *Familiar Letters* from the recesses of the Fleet prison; and subsequently made into an epic poem by Southey – of the journey made by Owain Gwynedd's son Madoc over the waters to the West and his discovery of the land later known as the Americas.

There is little to substantiate this medieval anticipation of Columbus, at least in the chief person of the drama. Evidence for the extent of early skill in navigation is being accumulated, however, and American learning today is inclined to suggest a contact between the Old World and the New antedating by several centuries not only

Columbus but Madoc. Evans, like many Welshmen of his time, paid attention to the story by one Morgan Jones, a minister resident in a wild region of the Plantations close to New York. Jones reported in 1686 that he had been captured by savage Indians but, though tied to a tree for slaughter, had managed to escape because he had consoled himself by uttering a few words in Welsh, and the Indians had understood him perfectly. These were Indians of the Doeg tribe. Another report mentioned the nation of the Padoucas, who also had excellent Welsh, and were traced back by way of their name to Madogwys, or people of Madoc.

This was the summons that Evans heard and obeyed. Service with the Spanish government or with the President of the United States was a means to an end. The nations of western Europe might war as they would over control of the North American continent; the fate of Madoc and his followers was the absorbing interest of the man from Betws Garmon and Llanbeblig.

With regret, one must repeat his last words on the subject: "I have only to inform you that I could not meet with such a people, and from the intercourse I have had with Indians from latitude 35 to 49 I think you may with safety inform our friends that they have no existence".

The settlement of the New World by Welshmen was reserved for a 19th-cent. colonization of the district of Trelew in Argentine Patagonia.

Peter Baker

Betws-y-coed: the Swallow Falls

BETWS-Y-COED, *Caernarfonshire,* became famous as a beauty-spot through its discovery by the artist David Cox on his tour of North Wales in 1805–6. It can be reached from Llanrwst, Ffestiniog, or Cerrigydrudion. It lies in a narrow valley, deeply wooded, against hills that are of no great height but stand so close upon it that they bar the sight of taller mountains.

It is a village whose recollections go a long way back. The grey stone architecture – very like that of the isolated farmsteads in the area, built of scattered hill-stones – gives the sense that Betws is of primitive origin, if not actually sprung from the soil. This is not to suggest that it lacks modern amenities; but the past serves it well. The bridge across the Llugwy, Pont-y-Pair, a 15th-cent. four-arched structure, is one of the best examples of ancient bridge-building in North Wales. Another, called the Waterloo Bridge and made of iron, goes over the Conway river and dates from the end of the Napoleonic Wars, though in 1811 Daniel Paterson's *Direct and Principal Cross Roads* makes Conway Bridge and the Salmon Leap the two outstanding points for which the traveller by stage-coach should look. But the roads to Betws are much older even than the 15th cent. The great Roman chain of routes that traversed the Ellennith, the stretch of moor and lake set in the centre of Wales, runs towards Betws from Pont-y-pant, shortly after Dolwyddelan; as the Sarn Helen or Elen, it passes over Mynydd Cribau, leaving the Llyn Elsi reservoir on its eastward side.

The church at Betws is one of Wales's ancient foundations, and for historical interest can compare with the church at Llanrwst. The font is in Norman style, and therefore later and of less purely native inspiration than the one at Llanrhychwyn; but Betws has the grave-effigy of Gruffydd son of Dafydd the Red and grandnephew of Llywelyn ap Gruffydd. Much of the attraction of the district lies in the scenes that David Cox made so well known. One cannot easily forget the Machno Falls, coming under the woods that skirt the small height curiously called Iwerddon (Ireland) S. of Betws; or the site of Jubilee Bridge, washed away by the flood of the Conway, where the bouldered stream makes a show of its strength. Dolwyddelan to the W., an isolated quarryman's village, has a church dating from about 1500, standing much as it originally did, and a castle, only one of its towers remaining, that was a Welsh construction of the 13th cent. and looks as if the rocky soil had spontaneously rooted it. At Pentrefoelas (Town among the Bowed Hills), the inns are for those who follow the grouse upon the moors that dominate the area. But the range of Snowdonia rises magnificently to the N.

For the mountaineer, Dolwyddelan (Meadland of the Gael), opens the best paths to ascend Carnedd Moel-Siabod (2,860 ft) and Y Cribau, with their razored crags, and the trackway that lies below the Diwaunedd lake. Llyn y Foel under Siabod was once perhaps the best trout-fishing lake in all Wales, the cold, deep water breeding fish that were strong and heavy. Great care must be taken to approach it from the easterly side; the 1-m. stretch of boulder and crag sweeping down to it is dangerous to anyone, however experienced. Capel Curig is in some ways the better centre for the lakes in this region.

BISHOPSTON, *Glamorgan.* This place in Gower has just succeeded in staying outside the western boundaries of Swansea. The Swansea suburbs are spreading, and new housing is springing up all around. But the Bishopston Valley is National Trust property and retains its beauty. The stream rises on Fairwood Common and goes underground after it passes Bishopston church. St Teilo's Church, in the valley-bottom, has a sturdy tower with 18th-cent. bells, a Norman font, and in the churchyard the remains of a stone cross. Bishopston remained under the control of Llandaff diocese long after the other Gower churches had gone to St David's. From Bishopston, the valley winds down to the sea. In dry weather the stream goes underground most of the way and can be heard flowing beneath the earth at Guthole. It enters the sea at Pwll-du, after seeping through the pebble bank of the beach. The headland of Pwll-du has been seamed with the trenches left by the 19th-cent. limestone quarries, but they only add to its impressive appearance. (*See* Gower.)

BLACK MOUNTAIN, *Carmarthenshire,* is the most westerly of the two Black Mountains of South Wales. The other is the range between the valleys of the Usk and the Wye on the borders of Monmouthshire and Herefordshire. The highest point of the long escarpment of the Carmarthenshire Black Mountain is formed by the Carmarthen Van (2,632 ft), which is actually in Breconshire. The ridge runs for 10 m. from the top of the Tawe valley to the top of the valley of the Loughor. The highest section has impressive, layered cliffs carved out of the Old Red Sandstone. The cliffs of Fan Hir dominate the upper reaches of the Tawe river, which rises in the boggy land just below the lonely lake of Llyn y Fan Fawr. The ridge curves westwards for 1½ m. to the dark hollow that hides the smaller of the two Fan lakes, Llyn y Fan Fach. This is one of the finest pieces of mountain scenery in South Wales. Further W. the Old Red Sandstone gives place to limestone. The ridge is still high at Garreg Las (2,076 ft). Further W. still the road between Brynaman and Llangadog has to climb to over 1,600 ft to cross the mountains.

The Black Mountain is a splendid viewpoint, and the great prow of Fan Hir is also splendid to contemplate from over the rolling moors to the N. Southwards the mountain slopes down more gradually, but the upper valley of the Twrch is extremely rough going for walkers.

Llyn y Fan Fach is now a reservoir for Llanelli, but it still retains its romantic atmosphere as a setting for the legend of the fairy who rose from the lake. The son of the nearest farm fell in love with her. She married him after warning him that, if ever he struck her three times, she would have to return to the lake. They lived happily and had five sons. Inevitably the husband did strike her, though only in play. The fairy returned to the lake, with all the cattle of the farm, leaving the broken-hearted husband and her sons lamenting on the shore. The descendants of the marriage became physicians, wise in the fairy remedies taught to them by the Lady of the Lake. They lived at Myddfai 5 m. to the N. of the lake. The physicians of Myddfai were famous throughout medieval Wales, and the line did not end until the death of Rhys ap Williams of Aberystwyth in 1842.

The lake can be reached from Llanddeusant, a hamlet on the road that crosses the foothills of the Fan from Trecastle and the big reservoir at the headwaters of the Usk. Llanddeusant has a small church with an unusual roof, and a youth hostel that used to be the Old Red Lion. The Sawdde stream comes down from the lake, and the track leads up along it. Cars cannot be taken further than the waterworks house.

BLACK MOUNTAINS, *Breconshire, Herefordshire, Monmouthshire.* These have a distinctive a character as Radnor Forest. Although of Old Red Sandstone, they are properly called black since, from the levels of the Hereford and Monmouth plain, they stand in a long, dark wall that by some trick of light is always black. To the S. is Abergavenny; on the N., Hay-on-Wye; on the E., the Golden Valley, and on their western flank the lake of Llangorse. The red of their essential structure shows through the gorse and heather, where crow and pipit, hawk and raven,

The Black Mountains

Barnaby/Mustograph

are more plentiful than men; only the high Pen Cerrig-calch (Chalk Rock), shows a touch of limestone white. Waun Fach (2,660 ft) and Penygader-fawr (2,624 ft) are the highest summits, seen only from the upper levels of the ridges that stand over Talgarth and Llanthony. There are 80 sq. m. to walk through, with the Malverns and the Clee Hills, the Fanau and the Brecon Beacons, for distant companions, and reach Pont yr Escob, the Bishop's Bridge that remembers how in 1188 Gerald de Barri and his Bishop, calling men to the Third Crusade, stayed there to preach to the crowd upon the hill. This was the country that Gerald loved for its woods and water, its deer, crops, and flowers, and above all for its Welshness and the peace of its valleys.

BLAENAU FFESTINIOG, Merioneth, the largest town in the county, must not be confused with the village of Ffestiniog 3 m. or so to the S. of it. Both are named from the valley in which the village lies, but Blaenau has the additional word meaning that it rises among the sharp mountain points that close the valley in from both sides, the Moelwyn and the Manod ranges curving in like a horseshoe and reaching over 2,500 ft.

Blaenau has no architecture to distinguish it, but seems to grow out of the hills themselves and form part of their walls. It is a town of bluish slate; buildings, roofing, fencing, paving – all are made from this, the town's major source of wealth. The mountains around it are deeply bitten into by quarries, which export slate of high quality all over the country. Permission can be obtained to visit the working-chambers, deep in the heart of the hills and reached by steep and galleried inclines. The largest of these is the Palmerston. A mountain railway with exceptional engineering features at Tan-y-bwlch and Minffordd was built in 1836 to run between Blaenau and Portmadoc. The station at Tan-y-bwlch was closed in 1946 but later reopened.

The area has magnificent mountain scenery and lakes with notable fishing. Of these, Llyn y Morynion (which is also Blaenau's reservoir) lies at 1,300 ft and can be easily reached by car. Trout are its stock; the lake is Crown property, but fishing can be done by payment. The shore is gravelly, the bottom peaty. Its name of the Maidens has had a legend built round it. Long ago the men of Ardudwy, the area of Merioneth around Ffestiniog, raided the Vale of Clwyd and bore back a number of women. But the men of Clwyd, in pursuit, came up with the raiders by this lake and slew them all. The women apparently had had no objection to being abducted; indeed, they had fallen in love with their captors, and on seeing them slain they plunged into the lake and drowned. A series of unexplained grave-like mounds 1 m. away to the W. was once shown as the place where the raiding men of Ardudwy had been buried. Nothing remains of these graves or the headstones marking them; the spot, however, can be found from the Ordnance Survey maps. Another version of the story says

that a traitress to the lord of the district conspired against him with some sea-raiders and, when they were defeated, drowned herself in Morynion.

Manod, the Garnedd, Edno, Conglog, and Barlwyd are also excellent for trout. Edno has magnificent views around it. Barlwyd has to be carefully dealt with; the best fish choose to lie close in to floating mounds of peat, a characteristic of many Welsh mountain lakes and the source of many legends. If you step on one of them, the result may be disastrous. Manod is exceptionally deep and seems to lie in a crater between the greater and lesser Manod hills. It is strewn with boulders, many of which can be seen lying at great depths in the waters.

BLAEN-Y-PANT, Montgomeryshire. Now that new roads and road surfaces are penetrating the remoter valleys of Montgomeryshire, one can visit this scattered community, which is typical of a kind still surviving from the days of Borrow and earlier. The great house, Bryn Llwydwyn, stands above its level lawns against the trees that skirt Cefn Modfedd, the hill behind it. It is now a simple farm. On the small road leading to it from Forge is a line of cottages, untouched by time, in which the activities of the society round about the great house were carried on: shoemaker and saddler, watchmaker and baker, maintained the medieval tradition of self-sufficiency well into the 20th cent. The school, converted into a bungalow, stands a short way beyond the chapel, which in turn overlooks the site of the vanished Ceniarth, another great house now replaced by a farm. From Blaen-y-pant a narrow lane, enough for the traffic of the 1700s, climbs and falls to the stream and bridge at Dol Caradog; another steeply descends to the ford on the Machynlleth road. Anyone interested in seeing the Wales of 200 years ago would be well advised to take these tracks. From Blaen-y-pant, green drove-tracks rise to Cefn Modfedd, excellent for walking or riding, where above the new afforestation one of the most complete views of the Five Summits of Plynlimon, Cader, and the Arans can be had.

BODNANT, Denbighshire. About 4 m. S. of Conway, the house of Bodnant stands above the Conway river. To reach it means to climb the steep Croesau Hill; the views of Snowdon are exceptionally good. Bodnant Gardens, laid out in 1874 and given to the National Trust by Lord Aberconway in 1949, are among the finest and most famous anywhere. They are renowned for their conifers and rhododendrons laid out over $\frac{1}{2}$ m. Terraces of yews, roses, and water-lilies, azalea beds, and rock-gardens with gentian and meconopsis and other rarities make them an outstanding illustration of landscape modelling. From spring to autumn they are open to the public on specified days. Members of the Royal Horticultural Society have free admission. The only bridge over the river between Conway and Llanrwst is at Tal-y-cafn nearby.

Peace and water-lilies in Bodnant Gardens

BORTH, *Cardiganshire*. A century ago, this was called by some unfortunate visitor "no more than a miserable cottage". But it attracted the attention of artists well known at that time, and they left excellent impressions of the Welsh homesteads – lime-washed and with the door stoutly porched against the wind – to be found in Borth then and now.

The name should mean a port; but, although Borth has always had some reputation as a fishing village, there is no evidence that it acted as a port for the Dovey valley. That position was reserved for Aberdovey, with its considerable coasting traffic in the late 17th and early 18th cents., and for the inland wharf-stages about what is now called Glandyfi. More probably the word carries its wider Welsh meaning of an opening-out. This would fit its position on level and firm sands, free from the quicksands found occasionally at Aberdovey, and facing the wide stretch of sea, and with the broad level of the Dovey estuary behind.

It is essentially one long street of cottages, small and still picturesque, looking towards the smooth, sandy beach and keeping much of their character as homes of working fishermen. Northward, on the way to the railway station, is an accumulation of hotels and lodging-houses. In the fields at the back of the village a car-caravan camping site has recently developed on a scale that seems immense. Further N. still, the lonely beach and ragged dunes of Ynyslas face across the Traeth Maelgwn to Aberdovey; the sands in the river mouth receive sudden influxes of tide that race in upon the unwary. Ynyslas (Blue Island), like Borth, has safe bathing. It is uninhabited except for the congregation of cars in summer. But the development of yacht clubs in Aberdovey gives Ynyslas a further advantage as a viewing-point.

Borth itself stops rather abruptly at the foot of the small cliff Craig yr Wylfa (Watch-Place Rock) to the S. It begins a stretch of small hills that take you to Bow Street or Aberystwyth. The road to Llangorwen is worth singling out, since it can lead by a side lane to the curious coastal point of Sarn Gynfelyn, the causeway associated with St Cynfelyn and with the Llangynfelyn standing on the way to Ynyslas and Borth from Taliesin. It is another of the mysterious causeways into the sea that, legend says, mark a series of embankments to keep unflooded the lands lost long ago by the negligence of their guardians. The legend may well have derived from Borth, since – at low tide, far below the ridge of pebbles that guards the village from its sands, and far out to sea among these sands themselves – the stone-like stumps of ancient trees can be seen. They are known as the Submerged Forest; but the Sarn Gynfelyn, like the Craig yr Wylfa, was more probably a lookout for shipping and a landmark for seamen.

BRECHFA, *Carmarthenshire*. Although only 9 m. NE. of Carmarthen, Brechfa, hidden in a bend of the Cothi valley, might be one of the most out-of-the-way villages in South Wales. It has an air of secluded happiness. The little hamlet consists of a small bell-cote Victorian church, built by Lingen Baker in 1891; the four-square rectory beside a lane leading down to a ford; the Forest Arms fishing inn, covered with creeper; a remarkable, thick-walled medieval house; a well-proportioned chapel; and some additional dwellings, which include council houses. All seem to fit into the deeply wooded landscape. The roads that lead out of Brechfa go through lonely woods or valleys. The Forestry Commission has been active in this area for many years, and the Brechfa Forest is now mature. The road to the E. follows the Cothi up to

Brecon Cathedral

Abergorlech; the one to the N. climbs up through the plantations and Gwernogle out to the open mountain behind Llanybydder in the Teifi valley. The western road makes a narrow cut through a hill-side, deeply wooded, over to the headwaters of the Afon Gwili. About 5 m. W. of Brechfa is Llanllawddog, with a simply proportioned Victorian church and a polite notice: "This Churchyard is committed to the tender care of all who enter". The southern exit from the wooded bowl of Brechfa passes over the hill to Nantgaredig in the Towy valley. There is a group of standing stones 1½ m. due S.

BRECON, *Breconshire*. "An ancient town," says Daniel Paterson's *Direct and Principal Cross Roads* of 1811, "called by the Welch Aber Honddey, being seated at the conflux of the Honddey and Uske rivers. Several Roman coins have been dug up at this place. Here are three Churches, one of which is collegiate; and a considerable trade in clothing is carried on. A little east of the town is a large Lake, abounding in fish."

As usual in that work, the information is concise. Each shire-town in Wales has its own character, and Brecon, or Brecknock, is outstanding. It is a town apart from the rest of Wales and, to some extent, from Welsh history. Brecon concentrates upon its own cathedral, the Priory Church of St John, the centre of the diocese of Swansea and Brecon since 1923.

Its first connection with history seems to belong to the Iron Age hill-fort, Pen-y-crug, immediately to the N. on a hill above the town, watching the valley-rivers. Otherwise there is no nearer human settlement than a probable lake-village at Llangorse and a Roman station at Y Gaer, about 3 m. out, excavated in the 1920s and still showing masoned walls and warded gates. The ridge

on which Aberhonddu (as the Welsh call Brecon) stands was not seen with a strategic eye until the Norman drove into Wales after his conquest of England. But the older name of Brecknock is a link with that time between the relaxation of direct Roman rule and the crystallization of British rule in Wales upon Aberffraw in Anglesey, Dynevor in the South, and Pengwern Amwythig (Shrewsbury) on the Severn. For Brecknock is derived from the original Welsh word Brycheiniog, which described the whole district ruled by the Brychein who, as one of the "sons" of Cunedda, reorganized the West of Britain in the 5th cent. A thrust of Powys into the restive uplands of Wales founded Brecknockshire; the Roman station may well have been reoccupied for that purpose, but this has not yet been proved. When Bernard of Neufmarché pushed his forces from the S. into the Ellennith in the days of Henry I, and set his castle on the high ridge of Brecknock, he seems to have been the first to see it as a position of strength. He made it a town of Norman identity, with a bridge and a priory (the present cathedral), which was to be served by Benedictine monks brought from Battle Abbey, set up near the site of Senlac Hill where the Conqueror had, by a single stroke, defeated Saxon England and its King. But Brecknockshire had its own attitude to the Saxon. Like Cardiganshire, when both Wales and England were at odds with the Dane, it had sought alliance with Alfred; and whatever resentment it felt against the Norman it shared with Englishmen.

Today, Brecon is an English-speaking town with the sense of being an English cathedral city. It remembers Nest, the fatal princess who involved Bernard and his son in the feuds of the South when family hatreds made no distinction between Welsh and Norman; it remembers the Norman overlord, William de Braose, who succeeded to the Neufmarchés and had the young Trahaiarn of Wales treacherously mocked and slaughtered in its streets. But, after the total defeat of Henry I in the NE. and the collapse of Anglo-Norman England itself under Stephen about 1150, Brecon town seems to have remained an unassailed island outpost, protected perhaps by the sanctity of its churches. Gerald de Barri visited it in 1188, shaking his head at the villainies that De Braose had perpetrated a generation before, but pointing out that at least the Norman overlord never failed to preface them by invoking the name of the Lord; and he adds a note on the miraculous powers lodged in the neighbouring Church of St David at Llanfaes, a suburb just over the river from the town. A boy who had chased a pigeon into the holy place found this sin punished when his hand stuck to a stone; it was not released until he had repented. The impression of the boy's fingers were there for all to see. The mistress of a Church dignitary in England, adds Gerald, had been similarly punished by finding herself stuck to a stone in his church. She had been more embarrassed than the boy, for she had sat on the stone, and could be removed only with damage to her underwear and what it clothed.

From Brecon Sir John Price, a true Welshman, sent his petition to Henry VIII, Tudor King of England, for the union in legal matters between Wales and England. The "maggotty-headed" John Aubrey, antiquarian under the Stuarts, lived here and lost the Welsh estates he had inherited; and in the 18th cent. the great actor and actress Charles Kemble and his sister Sarah, later known as Mrs Siddons, lived at 47 High Street, then the Shoulder of Mutton Inn.

A pleasant and prosperous place, the market for the farming valleys in the area and curiously unfrequented by tourists, Brecon still holds itself apart. It is a centre for education; there is a training college for Congregational students and a public schools in Llanfaes – Christ's College, founded in 1541 as part of the great Tudor experiment in education and refounded in 1855. Its museum is of great interest for its Roman and medieval relics; but even here Brecon insists on its apartness, for none of the Ogham stones and inscriptions that are scattered widely in the South and appear frequently in the North belong to its area.

The Cathedral still dominates the town and sets a note of bright respectability over its streets and people. Massively cruciform, it has a choir in Early English style, and a nave in the still later Decorated style. The font suggests some foundation older than that of the main building; its side chapels are evocative of the Middle Ages with their names of the corvizors (shoemakers), tailors, weavers, tuckers, and fullers. Apart from this reminder of the trade guilds, a chapel to the men of Battle and one to the red-haired men seem to speak of the first Norman intrusion. Although a small place called Battle is not far off, the name almost certainly derives from the Abbey near Senlac Hill; and there, if anywhere, the red-

haired men must have been Normans. The Parish Church of St Mary is also of Norman foundation, with at least one pillar of Norman style, though the tower is 16th-cent. Of the castle only fragments remain, part in the gardens of the Castle Hotel and part in the Ely Tower, a residence of the Bishop where the overthrow of Richard III and accession of Henry VII was plotted.

Brecon is a monument to peace and beauty. Of all its inhabitants, Gerald de Barri, Archdeacon of the Priory of St John, seems to have left the deepest mark. Charles I entered the place, more for meditation and despair than for war; and Brecon apparently escaped the Roundheads. Around it are the hills that Gerald loved: the Beacons and the Fanau, the Fforest Fawr and the Black Mountains, with the sight of Cader Idris to the N. and the heads of Plynlimon beside it if the air is clear. Farm land and woodland lie around it, and the Usk, shaded with trees, runs by it as it did 150 years ago, when officers of Napoleon, spending their captivity here, went contemplatively by its side on the path still known as the Captains' Walk.

At Llwynllwyd, about 5 m. NW. of Brecon, one of the most famous of the Nonconformist academies was founded, probably by Vavasor Griffiths, minister and schoolmaster at Maesgwyn, Beguildy, Radnorshire. He refused to have his academies in any town, but preferred the remoter countryside for the better moral growth of his pupils. He was a native of Beguildy, born there about 1688.

BRECON BEACONS, The, *Breconshire.* These mountains look down upon the Wye from a height of nearly 3,000 ft. On their eastern side, the lakes run from Vaynor and the Taf Fechan reservoir to Tal-y-bont and Llangorse with its lake, called Syfaddan in Welsh. To the W., the Fan hills of the Fforest Fawr carry the Roman road, the Sarn Helen, that supplied the forts set above the Wye. From Pen Milan, you can see against the sky the Black Mountains that drop to Hay-on-Wye and the Mynydd Epynt that rise over Builth and just detect the fingers of Radnor Forest reaching for the skirt of the clouds.

Camden in 1586 called the Beacons "Arthure's Hill, three good Walsche miles from Brecknock; and in the veri toppe is a fair well-springe". It seems he meant by this a tiny pool above Cwm Llwch, cold and believed to be unfathomable. No fish swim in it, though other creatures are busy about it. The tarn is the best place from which to judge the structure of the Beacons themselves, for the springs that feed it come from the feet of great cliffs of red sandstone worn into deep clefts. The scientist Murchison wrote: "In no other tract of the world visited by me have I seen such a mass of red rocks so clearly intercalated between the Silurian and Carboniferous strata". The tarn, in fact, is some 700 ft below the "veri toppe"; but it is a place that under the solitary sky makes for legend. It had an enchanted island, and you could visit it by a tunnel running

A storm gathering over the Brecon Beacons

from the shore. The island was seen only on May Day. The folk living there offered music, flowers, and fruit. But one man from our world brought a flower back with him; and the island has never been seen again. For such a tale to have been born, lake-dwellers in the innocent Bronze Age that knew no iron must have lived by Llwch. The Beacons look southward to Aberdare, Mountain Ash, and Merthyr Tydfil; but they belong to a later day.

The flooding of the valley to make the Taf Fechan reservoir changed the character of the area from farm land to afforested slopes, falling to a white water where the voices of sheep are few. Even the small railway that used to serve Dol-y-gaer (Meadow Where the Roman Fort Was), with its 15th-cent. church and community of living folk, the last sign that once it was a living place, was closed in 1962, nearly forty years after the valley was drowned. Silence and beauty stay beside the 2½ m. of water, and Dol-y-gaer is now a centre for the discovery of the Brecon Beacons as a National Park.

BREIDDENS, The, *Montgomeryshire*, are on the borderline of what is officially Welsh; and yet, as they look over Shropshire, they carry Wales on their shoulders. The best view of them is from the tiny place called Coedway (a word half-English and half-Welsh), set on the border itself. Its peaks are relics of volcanic action, with Moel y Golfa (1,324 ft) somewhat higher than Middletown Hill and Breidden. Cones thrust upwards from the grass and huddled trees; they form a saddleback between them, the Breidden having added to its height Rodney's Pillar, a column in honour of Admiral Rodney, victor of St Vincent Cape and Dominica, who died in 1792, pensioned off by the Government in a somewhat miserly fashion. The monument was set up by the voluntary action of local landowners. The view from here is one that perhaps Caratacos had of the eastern plains over which the Romans

marched to drive him deep into Wales. It is the view so warmly recommended by the expert in the coach-roads of Britain, "Mr. Daniel Paterson", who thought that to ride over the Breiddens was to have the finest sight in the world. Buttington, to which he rode, and Arddleen lie below them; and Cefn-y-castell, which is the right name for Middletown Hill, nurses the home of Old Parr, who was born in the reign of Edward IV and died in that of Charles I at the age of 153. Even then, it was the journey to London to be presented to the King, and the encounter with unseemly lowland air, that killed him. It was small amends that in exchange for the Breiddens he was given a grave in Westminster Abbey.

BRIDGEND, *Glamorgan*. Today, Bridgend is described as an urban district and market town, some 20 m. W. of Cardiff at the western end of the Vale of Glamorgan. It is exceptionally favoured among towns of the South, since its population, instead of falling steeply after the Depression of the 1930s, climbed from 10,000 to 14,000. The coal and iron mined to the N. of it, supplemented by the stone-quarrying industry, were very much reinforced by the establishment of a Royal Ordnance factory during the Second World War. But Bridgend, in any event, has been and remains an important administrative centre for its area.

Travellers have always noted it as an attractive place, largely brick-built and with the relics of a Norman castle. An ancient town, and set among ancient and beautiful places, its name of Pen-y-bont ar Ogwr describes its function as the point of passage over the Afon Ogwr and as the principal place in the Ogmore valley. "This part of the Country," says Christopher Saxton in 1610, "is most pleasant and fruitful, beautified also on every side with a number of Townes." The rough mountains above it gave way, as he notes, to a plain that stretched towards the sun and had a mild and better soil. Daniel Paterson, 200 years later, notes its surrounding features: at Tayback, the extensive work of coal and copper; at Ewenny Bridge, 2 m. off, the Pelican Inn, of much assistance to coaches and their passengers; at Newbridge, 2 m. on the other side, the ruins of Ogmore Castle across the river; and at Cowbridge (a "pleasant mercate Towne", as Saxton calls it, with some claim to be thought of as the Roman Bovium) the castles of St Lythian and Pen Lyne. But he singles out Ewenny Priory in particular. Saxton goes a little further into these matters, relating how "the river Ogmore, maketh himself way into the Sea, falling from the mountaines by Coitie [Coety] which belonged sometimes to the Turbevilles; also by Ogmore Castle which came from the family of London"; and "a little from hence," he adds, "in the very bout-well, neere of the shore, standeth Saint Donat's Castle, a faire habitation of the ancient and notable family of the Stradlings." In this way he notes the descendants of those companions of Robert FitzHamon who came into Glamorgan on the tide of the Norman Conquest and set the castles that still remain dominant in the landscape. St Donat's, a structure of the 14th to 16th cents., was acquired in the 20th cent. by the American lord of newsprint, William Randolph Hearst, who made it a centre for antiquities gathered from all over Britain. Ogmore Castle, which stands where stepping-stones cross the stream, has dwindled into little more than a companion to some pleasant cottages; but it was a stronghold of the hated William de Braose and, with the new Castle of Bridgend and the fortress at Coety, held down the line of the Ogmore and Ewenny in three points of power.

Bridgend's neighbourhood contains Newton Nottage, a "little towne in a sandy plain", says Saxton; with a well, in his day, pure enough and good for use – "it never springeth and walmeth up to the brinke, but by certaine staires folke goe downe into the Well." It has a church with a massive tower, and leads to Porthcawl and the stretch of sand-dunes between there and Neath, where the lost city of Kenfig lies hidden.

Betws, in the N. of the valley, has a curious 19th-cent. charm.

BRYNMAWR, Breconshire. To the N. of Ebbw Vale, and 1,250 ft high in the hills, the small town of Brynmawr has something worth notice in its recent record. Like the whole area of the South Welsh field of coal and iron, it was left stranded by the receding tide of prosperity in the disastrous 1930s. Its population, small by comparison with many of its neighbours, dropped by 13 per cent, and its pit-heads and steel-works dropped out of service. Chances of employment could be found, and can still be found, by leaving the little township and taking up with industry in other valleys and on other hills. But Brynmawr, which was threatened with total dereliction, came under the survey of a study council led by a group of Quakers between 1929 and 1932. Brynmawr decided that Brynmawr must help itself, and do so at once, rather than go elsewhere or accept

relief. Something of the ideas of the co-operative community dreamt of by Robert Owen was brought in, and something, too, of old Welsh native industry. Brynmawr began its own communal activity with small furniture-making activities, tweed-cloth weaving, stocking and boot enterprises, and the task of creating out of the huddle of barrack-houses a town of beauty and pleasure. It was a scheme that ran counter to many other well-intentioned programmes for the district. Brynmawr does in fact now rely on support from new light industries introduced on a scale its self-help programme could not cope with. But the resurgence of its spirit stays as a model for the future.

BUGEILYN, Montgomeryshire. This is a lake and a farm; but it is also the centre in this part of Wales for a distinctive way of life, which it shares with its distant neighbour, Hyddgen.

It can be most easily reached by turning off the Dylife road and following the roughish track towards Glaslyn. The turn is made close to the shoulder of Foel Fadian, the highest point in Montgomeryshire and one of the Five Summits of the Plynlimon escarpment. A short way off the track, the craggy rocks known as Esgair Fochnant drop precipitously between the branches of the River Dulas. These rocks are well known among climbers, but for local inhabitants they have a special significance. Here foxes, followed by hounds from packs maintained in various parts of the district, make their way from the lower valleys. It is done with deliberate purpose, and so often that two packs from widely separated areas have been known to run into each other at this spot. Regrettably, the fox does not aim just at evasion. Nimble, alert, keen-sighted, he takes to the ledges knowing that, though his scent will quickly dry from them, the hounds will relentlessly follow. The hounds, bred for detecting scent, have developed their sense of it at the cost, above all, of sight. Broad-footed and short-sighted, yet hot in pursuit, they fall from these rocks to their death 500 ft below.

The lake at Glaslyn is very well worth a visit, although the ground is private. Grouse were once maintained here in numbers, but are less often met with now. It is advisable to watch for the keepers and obtain permission from them.

Notices also warn the visitor that fishing in the lake is private. This surprises people who know Glaslyn and the legends attached to it. No fish, the local shepherds say, will ever swim its waters, because no weed can grow in it. And certainly the lake seems weedless; it has a slate-shale shore, and waves disturb its surface under the winds that sweep it as it lies on the rim of sky level with the distant heads of Cader Idris and the Aran Fawddwy. It catches all the colours of the sun and moon and is one of the most beautiful things anywhere in Wales. But it belongs entirely to the moor and drains its waters from the peats. The hidden lode of lead under its shores is what supposedly prevents the growth of greenstuff in the lake.

To walk from its N. side over a slow rise of heather and whin brings you to the peak (1,656 ft) that faces Taren Bwlch Gwyn (1,909 ft) across one of the most striking valleys among the Five Summits of Plynlimon. Bwlch Gwyn measures 1 m. across; its sides are sheer and rocky. A precarious path, advisable only for sheep, climbs upwards from Rhosygarreg and the lovely woodlands around it to end at last at Bugeilyn farmhouse. Striking as the peak by Glaslyn is, the wild magnificence of the Bwlch is better appreciated from the Taren itself. To reach this Taren, however, you should start from Hyddgen and Carn Gwilym; even so, the approach is through difficult peatland, and the sheep-path along the head of the Taren is dangerous for those without heads as steady as the sheep's. But the results can be very rewarding.

The buzzards are constant companions to anyone who walks these hills. They can be seen hanging in the air with effortless strength, sometimes swooping on their prey, sometimes crying to startle it into reaction, sometimes hawking indignantly at a trespassing crow or gull. And sometimes with a tremendous wing-clap one of them will steer itself from the ground into the air, as you unsuspectingly get near. They hunt all the lesser valleys below, and in times of bitter winter can be found hopefully lining the hedges and fence-posts of farm lands miles away from their principal habitat. But it is in Bwlch Gwyn that they raise their young. At the proper season you can lie quiet on the head of the Taren, and look down at the succession of ledges set in its side, and watch the young birds being cajoled or compelled to leave the nest and launch into the air for the first time – never to return, for that is the rule of growth.

Lesser hawks can be found among the Five Summits. Notably the merlin, with its distinctive plumage, may be seen about the Hengwm valley below Hyddgen, usually near the point of Rhiw Goch above the recently founded fir-plantations. But, regrettably, these conifers, useful as a rule to protect the scree-strewn hill-sides from further crumbling, are affecting the natural wildlife of the area, perhaps irretrievably. Few wildfowl choose for a home the dark and columned corridors of the fir with their needle-covered flooring. The drainage necessary for planting the young conifers has largely abolished the congregations of moorhens and their young that used to gather on nearly every hill-top nearby, so unaccustomed to human beings that you could walk through them without attracting attention. Herons, too, were once a common feature of Bwlch Gwyn, Cwm Rhaeadr, the banks of the Rheidol at the foot of Plynlimon Fawr, and particularly the falls in Hengwm, where they fished constantly. The curlew is now rarely heard; so it is with the stonechat. But the lark stays undefeated, and the buzzard is perhaps undefeatable.

Leaving the Bwlch Gwyn valley and the white sheet of Glaslyn, the track turns somewhat sharply over a scatter of the curious marble-like rock that typifies much of this area, and goes down into a depression filled with the water of Bugeilyn. The farmhouse – still considerable, and with the remains of the high walls inside which the sheep were gathered, the shearing done, and the fleeces stored – can be seen on the near side of the lake with a small grove of trees huddled against it. On the western side of the approach a "twmp" or early burial mound can be seen. This was excavated shortly before the Second World War by the son of Bugeilyn farm, and was found to contain an urn of the kind attributed to the Beaker Folk, a Bronze Age people who settled elsewhere in Britain about 1000 B.C. His interest was to be expected, since some time before then another farmer at Bugeilyn had made a similar discovery. Beyond the farm, set to the E. under the black slopes of the Llechwedd Crin, is a small tarn. The ground surrounding it has for generations provided the household with peat; and the rolls of peat-turves, neatly piled at the end of the dug furrows, still characterize this lonely place. Digging for the peat with his long-handled, heart-shaped spade, the farmer found a number of flint arrow-heads, beautifully worked and flaked and still retaining the natural colouring that makes them seem jewelled works of art. What animals were hunted with them in the distant period of their manufacture, is difficult to tell. This was most probably a hoard, stored for safety and never recovered by the owner. Flint is not a local stone; but as long ago as 2000 B.C. flint-working factories produced axe-heads and similar tools and weapons. Among the most famous are the twin factories of Tievebulliagh and Rathlin in Northern Ireland, whose products have been identified as far afield as Kent, Hampshire, eastern Scotland, and the Hebrides. Some of the arrow-heads so found can be seen at Aberystwyth under the care of the University.

From this evidence we can consider the age of permanent human settlement at Bugeilyn. The slopes of Foel Fadian show definite signs of terracing; on a remote plateau such as that on which Glaslyn spreads itself, protected by natural features from any surprise assault, and with a plentiful supply of pure water, early huntsmen might well have made Bugeilyn a principal resort and done much to establish the ancient ways and pointer-stones crossing the Plynlimon moorland. But there is a curious survival from the past that has given more definite and living proof of itself. The dangerous bogland between Foel Fadian and Bwlch Gwyn has recently come under the attack of the bulldozer and afforestation-drainage. Certain shafts from old mines have now been converted by foxes into lairs of escape. Not long ago one such fox was run to earth by a local pack, and after a considerable struggle was destroyed. It turned out to be something rare – a grey fox, bigger than the common red one and belonging to a different breed. Romans, they say, introduced the red fox. The grey one was a survival of the original native fox, first in these islands but now so infrequently known that this particular specimen was given a special place of honour, again in Aberystwyth.

Bugeilyn means Lake of Shepherds. It is worth noting the word "bugeil" in connection with this way of life; for on sale in many small shops in the lower valleys is a brand of shag tobacco called Baco'r Bugeil. Like the men it is named after, it is strong and sturdy, becoming most agreeable after a little experience, preferably in the open air.

The farm was the last to survive as a living unit on these moors. Many other families once lived, all the year round, in the neighbourhood of Plynlimon. In summer, living conditions can be enjoyable; but in winter they are extremely hard. The snow comes in sudden whirling sheets and lies long and heavy. The last herdsman who dwelt in Bugeilyn, a decade or so ago, had his walls and roof buried beneath the drifts for days. In one such storm, bringing his scattered sheep from the moors, he became suddenly aware through the flurry of white blindness that he and they were walking the frozen surface of Llyn Glaslyn. At Bugeilyn, sheep were gathered for protection during the wintry season about the farm buildings themselves. But often the wandering flocks can be overtaken by a storm and buried. If found soon enough, they may be dug out and saved; they can endure some while, huddled together for warmth and by their united breath melting the snow above their heads to keep there a pocket of unfresh air. One much-recalled memory belongs to a farmer who, sounding for strayed sheep in these conditions, discovered one indeed, but in strange company. A fox was curled up with the sheep, and the two animals, though total enemies, were keeping each other alive. This, as he will tell you in his own words, calls for a new consideration of natural good and evil.

BUILTH WELLS, *Brecknockshire.* About 1 m. below the confluence of the Wye with the Irfon, Builth opens itself at an 18th-cent. bridge across the Wye. The street goes from the six arches of this structure towards the church, considerably restored but keeping its ancient outline and holding Elizabethan memories intimate to the town in the effigy of a knight, Sir John Lloid of Towy, personal attendant of the Tudor Queen; he died in 1585. It is the scenery around Builth that calls most for attention; the Wye towards Glasbury in one direction, and towards Rhayader in the other, offer outstandingly attractive views. The town itself is now no older than the end of the 17th cent., since in 1691, just before Christmas, it was entirely destroyed by a fire that not only startled but roused consternation in England. The Government gave permission to the houseless townsfolk to send out appeals for assistance over the rest of Britain; and record survives of a Lincolnshire parish that was so moved by this petition that it sent "eight shilling one fardin". For those days, this represented a worthwhile donation. One probable survivor of the great fire of Builth was the old wool market of stone set a little way up the hill above the main street.

Buallt seems to have been the earlier name for the place, varied by 17th-cent. cartographers as Buelth or Bealt. Apart from its long-established popularity as a place for medicinal waters, it has always been important as a centre for stock-sales and as a meeting-ground for the two strains of cultural tradition, the English and the Welsh. But, among the Welsh, Builth still remembers that fatal day – in another December, the one of 1282 – when Llywelyn the Last was slain at its outskirts. Tradition says that the Prince was in flight from the pursuing English forces, and came to the town of Builth to seek shelter; and that the townsfolk shut him out to die. The treachery of Builth passed into an adage; but strategically the relationship of the English and Welsh forces did not place Llywelyn in that kind of position. This tale belongs with the one that, to evade pursuit, the Prince had his horse's shoes turned round so

Builth Wells: the 18th-cent. bridge over the River Wye

Peter Baker

that the snow would give prints in reverse a ruse attributed to several legendary figures. (*See* Aberedw.)

Builth now keeps its memories of Llywelyn rather at a distance, with the monument at Cwm Llywelyn by Cilmery and with the ruinous castle at Aberedw, once his hunting-seat. But it is now a spreading town, sedate in the broad green of meadow and wooded hill, thinking more of its early 19th-cent. prosperity than of the embattled past. Of its own castle, nothing remains but the earthwork mound behind the Lion Hotel. The pump-room and the Old Crown Hotel are memorials of the days when Builth came into the fashion set by Beau Nash in Bath during the latter part of the 18th cent. What was once a resort chiefly for the local squires and their ladies, among whom the virtues of the Builth waters were traditionally celebrated, became fashionable in more international circles. This was largely because of a visit paid to the place in 1808 by Lady Hester Stanhope, niece of the younger Pitt and his domestic support during his struggle with Napoleon. Her lively intelligence is preserved in her letters, ranging in subject from her residence in ambassadorial circles at Constantinople to her final retreat from the world into the remote and beautiful home she found for herself at Glan Irfon near Builth. What made her renounce the world of affairs is not clearly known; but Sir John Moore's death at Corunna during the British retreat from Spain in the Peninsular campaign of 1809 seems to have had a disastrous effect on her life. She kept her coach in Builth (at the Royal Oak Hotel, it is said), where she had first known the beauty of the Welsh valleys. Her life at Glan Irfon was one of charity; she gave food and wool to the needy, and encouragement and patronage to the gifted. Among the young men she took on long pony-treks into the hills was Thomas Price, the son of a clergyman and later a parson himself, better known to the present generation of Welshmen as Carnhuanawc, poet and philologist.

Builth is an excellent centre for the discovery of some of the most varied and heart-stirring regions of Wales. Northward, the way to Rhayader is chequered with peaks and valleys that witnessed the long struggles between the Welsh rulers of Powys and the forces of the De Braoses and the Mortimers. On the one hand there are broad stretches of level pasture land, on the other the rolling uplands of Radnor and the Black Mountains. The Wye here has travelled 50 m. from its source in the Plynlimon range, and has settled to a series of wide and wooded arcs through the green; but, at one point near Builth, it is forced into a narrow passage 1 m. long that turns it into streaming rapids where salmon struggle against the rush of water with the same agile strength that Gerald de Barri noted in his *Itinerary of Wales* for the Third Crusade in 1188. Builth Rocks, as the place is known, is famous for its salmon, and they are more eagerly sought after than even the Wells of Builth were in the days of Lady Hester Stanhope.

BURRY PORT and **PEMBREY**, *Carmarthenshire*. Pembrey, the older of these twin townships on Carmarthen Bay, lies about 6 m. W. of Llanelli on the main railway line to Carmarthen. Burry Port has, however, swallowed Pembrey administratively, and the houses run together. Burry Port grew up as a coal port for the nearby mines. It also possessed tinplate-works. This trade has disappeared, and the small harbour has long lost its importance; the Council has made strenuous efforts to attract new industries. A new power station dominates the town. The sands that run westwards along the shores of Carmarthen Bay are an advantage. In 1928 *Friendship*, the first seaplane to cross the Atlantic, came down in the wide Burry Inlet. Amelia Earhart, the first woman to fly the Atlantic, also landed near Burry Port in 1928, after a flight of 20 hrs 40 min. from Trepassey Bay in Newfoundland. The fine Ashburnham golf links lie between Burry Port and Pembrey. A large munition factory was built on Pembrey Burrows in the First World War and used again in the Second.

Pembrey village is now rather straggling, but the heart of it lies around the church. It is 13th-cent. with an impressive 16th-cent. timber barrel roof to the nave and chancel. The strong door to the porch bears the date 1717. There is a fine four-light window of the 16th cent. in the S. wall, and an arch carved with shields and emblems of the Passion. The church also contains numerous memorials to the Butlers, Vaughans, and Mansels, who lived in the old house of Y Cwrt (The Court), now a farm. In the churchyard is a memorial to the passengers and crew of the French ship *Jeanne Emma*, which was wrecked on the Cefn Sidan Sands at the mouth of the Towy estuary. Among the drowned was Adeline, a niece of Napoleon's wife, the Empress Josephine. The Cefn Sidan Sands had a particularly evil reputation in the days of sail. At the churchyard gate is the old pound, now restored. It was useful in the days when Pembrey held its big annual St Barnabas Fair.

Behind Pembrey and Burry Port is Mynydd Pen-bre (Pembrey Mountain). In the late 18th cent. it was haunted by a notorious footpad and murderer named Wil Manney, who had the dubious distinction of being the last criminal in Carmarthenshire to be gibbeted – in 1788, near the scene of his crime.

BUTTINGTON, *Montgomeryshire*, a small place, stands on the road and rail between Shrewsbury and Welshpool. But it is also by the Severn, as it turns N. from its outflow in the Plynlimon range and comes by way of Caersws, Newtown, Montgomery, and Welshpool. Thus it occupies a position on the strategic inlet from the Midlands into the waist of Wales, and that opening in the defences of the old Kingdom of Powys which at last forced back the Welsh frontier from Severn to Wye and created the debated region of the marchlands. A section of Offa's Dyke runs into Buttington. It stands under the Long Mountain (1,338 ft), where the Roman road curved about its northern slopes and Beacon Ring shows the point at which another invader stood to command the military routes over Wales and England.

In 1610 Christopher Saxton wrote: "Right over against this Castle Coch (near Welshpool) on the other side of the river, standeth Buttington, well known by reason of the Danes wintering there; out of which, Ahered, Earle of the Mercians expelled them in the yeere of Christ 894 as Marianus writeth. Severn being past these places turneth by little and little Eastward, that he may sooner entertain the small river Tanet, which being once received into his society, he goeth on forward to Shropshire".

Daniel Paterson, in 1811, breaks away from his thorough-going list of towns and distances, drawn up with a practical eye, into an almost lyric passage: "The traveller on horseback, who wishes for a most exquisite prospect, may have it by going from Shrewsbury to Welch Pool along the Montgomery Road to Westbury, as above $8\frac{3}{4}$ mile, there turn by the Inn on the right hand, keep a track over the hill, inclining to the right, and go down to Buttington, known by a small Church, and just beyond it a wooden bridge over the Severn".

CADER IDRIS, *Merioneth,* though it stands a little lower than the Arans (2,927 ft to their 2,970 ft), gets a special prominence from its shape as a long, continuous heave of earth and rock between the valley of the Mawddach and the valley of the Dysynni. It marks the frontier between what was in old days the chieftainship of Gwynedd, classically called Venedotia, and the country of Powys. Other hills hereabouts chiefly exist as local features, but Cader Idris is the locality itself. Only the Plynlimon moorland shares this quality of being much less a point on

The summit of Cader Idris, from the north

G. Douglas Bolton

the map than an area imposing its character on neighbouring counties.

Cader Idris, all the same, has its own central point, the Craig Lwyd (Sharp Crag) at the summit, reached by a lengthy and scarcely interrupted rise from Llanfihangel-y-Pennant, or even from Llanegryn, taking in the Craig Las and Craig y Llyn cliffs of rock; or by the shorter routes from Minffordd, Arthog, or Cross Foxes. The way from Dolgellau lies either along the pony-track or the Fox's Path. The most direct and challenging approach is from the valley-bottom by the eastern flats of the lake Tal-y-llyn and the house called Llwyn-dol-Ithel. This takes you up a steep ascent among rocks that overhang the falling torrent of water, until more level ground is reached, and stony meadows, picked over by sheep, lead at last to Llyn y Cau. This lies dark and windless under tall escarpments of rock, which curve above and around it as if the relics of volcanic walls. It is a most impressive lake, reputed to have no bottom, and also to hide in its depths a monster like that of Loch Ness. An account was given in the middle of the 18th cent., though not by an eye-witness, of a youth who dared to swim across the depths; half way over, the monster suddenly emerged, seized him in its jaws, and dived from sight. The brooding edges of this lake and the peculiar darkness in its waters incline one to think many things possible. But one need only see its cragged rim against the sky and, in worsening weather, the drift of stubborn cloud along its head to understand its legendary sanctity. The well-worn myth that one who sleeps there by night must wake blind, mad, or a poet need not detain us; it is a fancy embroidered by Mrs Hemans in the last century. Nor can the attribution of the name to some Chair of Arthur be much relied on. "Cader" or "cadair" has for some time been recognized to mean something more than a seat and nearer in meaning to a settled place; and Idris, if here connected with the semi-historical king, seems to be unsupported by such an attribution of the word anywhere else. The association of the place with good fairies might indeed be one of those traditions of an alien, refuge-seeking people that modern archaeologists are prepared to accept as genuine folk-memory.

Such heights were of practical use in those early days, when the calendar had to be checked by daily observation of sunrise and sunset and the wheeling of the stars. In mountainous country the only possible glimpse of the sea-horizon was from such an altitude, and only there could the succession of dawns and the swing from summer to winter solstice and back be accurately gauged.

The Llyn y Gader (Goat Lake) is best appreciated from the head of the mountain, which can be attained from Llyn y Cau by taking, with hands as well as feet, the track to a little "col" at its north-western side. From there, a choice of descent is between the Fox's Path into the Mawddach valley or back to Tal-y-llyn, perhaps by dropping to Llyn y Cau on its eastern edge over the steep rocks and past one of the coldest,

Plate 6   Reflections at Llanwrda, Carmarthenshire   Pix Photos

purest, and most refreshing spring-pools to be found anywhere.

CAEO, *Carmarthenshire.* This little village, called Cynwyl Gaeo in Welsh, is tucked away in a side valley near Pumsaint. Its church, dedicated to the Virgin and St Conwil (Cynwyl) is set against a steep wooded hill-side. A mountain stream comes tumbling through the trees near at hand. The church has a sturdy 13th-cent. tower, and a porch built as a memorial to members of the Hills-Johnes family of Dolaucothi. The main structure has been heavily restored, and all the windows have been renewed. The rows of cottages in front of the church are pleasingly colour-washed. Caeo may have had connections with the Roman gold-mines in the next valley, for Roman objects, including a hoard of medals dug up in 1762, have been found here. The 9th-cent. poems of Llywarch Hên describe it as the place where Cadwallon's army stormed the "red town of the south built of thin red bricks"; there must have been some substantial Roman construction at Caeo. Later history records that this remote Carmarthenshire village sent nine archers to fight at Agincourt. The mounted archers got 6d. a day; the unmounted ones had to be content with 4d.

The most distinguished son of Caeo was the 15th-cent. Welsh poet, Lewis Glyn Cothi. His work is a storehouse not only of fine poetry, but of historical and genealogical information about the Wales of his period. In the 18th cent. Dafydd Jones of Caeo, who learnt his English as a drover travelling the roads, became a hymn-writer of note and one of the greatest translators into Welsh. Joshua Thomas who published his important *History of the Baptists in Wales* in 1778, was born in the Ty Hên (Old House) in Caeo. His younger brother Timothy wrote, in Welsh, that splendidly named devotional work *The Shining White Robe Fit to Enter the Palace of the Heavenly King.*

Above Caeo the hills are covered with Forestry Commission plantations.

CAERLEON, *Monmouthshire,* the City of the Legion, lies 4 m. upstream from Newport, at the first point where the fiercely tidal Usk could be bridged safely in the old days. Caerleon today is having a hard task to retain its ancient reputation for mystery and high romance. The suburbs of Newport creep nearer every year, and the traffic thunders through the streets in what seems to be a one-way racing circuit. No wonder a certain householder in the High Street has christened his house "Chaos". Yet, for all that, Caerleon still reminds us, at every turn, of its two great claims to fame – its associations with the Romans and King Arthur.

The Romans' advance into South Wales met its most determined resistance from the tribe of the Silures, who inhabited the country westwards of the Wye. The legionary fortress of Isca Silurum was established as a base from which this wild country could be finally subjugated. It became the permanent home of the Second Augustan Legion, 5,600 strong, from A.D. 75 to the 4th cent. From Isca in the S., and Deva (Chester) in the N., the Romans extended their network of roads and subsidiary forts westwards to subdue Wales. Isca always remained an active military centre – the soldier, not the civilian, was the man in power. The civilians developed Caerwent on the safer lands SE. from Caerleon. Isca looked towards the hills and possible danger.

The fort covered 51½ acres. The outline of the ramparts can be clearly traced on the SW. and W., but houses have overlain the other sides. The SW. gate stood near the present entrance to the Priory Hotel, which is guarded by a thatched gatehouse, and the centre of the fortress is now marked by the present parish church, built on the site of the old basilica. Sir Mortimer Wheeler carried out extensive excavations at Caerleon in the 1920s, and the National Museum of Wales has been active here for many years, but most of the Roman foundations are hidden under more modern buildings. Two important areas have been preserved for inspection by the Ministry of Public Building and Works. In the Prysg Field, at the NW. corner of the fortress, and reached from the Broadway, the visitor can see the remains of the only legionary barrack block yet found in Britain, as well as turrets of the actual fortress wall. SW. of the gardens of the priory lies the most impressive of Caerleon's remains, the amphitheatre. Like many other buildings, including baths and temples to Mithras, the amphitheatre lay outside the walls of the fort. It is an oval, 184 ft long and 136 ft broad, and was hollowed out of the hill-side. It had timber seats ranged round an earth bank that rose 28 ft above the arena floor. The bank was supported by stone walls. The legionary soldiers, as was usual, constructed the arena themselves, and each cohort left an inscription on the part entrusted to them. The "box" or seat of honour was placed over the large entrance on the SW. side.

Today the amphitheatre is a place of quiet, and of beautifully smooth grass – the best place to get the flavour of Caerleon's second claim to fame. For the arena site, long before excavation, had been locally known as King Arthur's Round Table. That powerful romancer, Geoffrey of Monmouth, sealed Caerleon's connection with King Arthur when he wrote, in his *History of the Kings of Britain,* given to the world in 1136: "On one side, the city was washed by that noble river, so that Kings and princes from the countries beyond the seas might have the convenience of sailing up it. On the other side, the beauties of the meadows and groves, and the magnificence of the royal palaces with gilded roofs that adorned it, made it even rival the grandeurs of Rome". In Geoffrey's day, as we know from the description by Giraldus Cambrensis not very much later, a great deal of the fortress was still standing. Giraldus especially admired the hot baths and the palaces with gilded roofs and the aqueducts. It was easy to associate Arthur with all these visual splendours. The reality now boils down to the broken pottery, the shattered stones, and the incomplete inscriptions that have been carefully preserved in the little museum, with its elegant columns, that stands alongside the church. It is now a branch of the National Museum of Wales, but it was originally established by the Caerleon Antiquarians in 1850. Among the many exhibits are the unique remains of a pipe burial, in which a pipe was left projecting above ground to receive libations from the relatives of the deceased. Next to it is the parish church, dedicated to the 6th-cent. saint Cattwg (Cadoc) of Llancarfan. But there is no possibility that Christianity might have survived on this very spot from Roman times. Caerleon is supposed to be the site of the martyrdom of St Julius and St Aaron about 303, but again there is no evidence to support this. However, it is possible that, as Christianity became the official religion of the Empire before the legions left Caerleon, the basilica might have been adapted for Christian worship when it became the site of the present church. Again we have no positive evidence. These pleasant conjectures seem to come naturally in Caerleon.

The present church was heavily restored, perhaps one should say completely reconstructed, in 1867. A fine round-headed Norman arch is incorporated in the S. wall of the W. end. The graceful, pointed arches of the nave are all that remains of the Tudor church. But the general effect of the new work is pleasing and impressive in itself. The stained-glass windows are part of the Charles Williams bequest.

In the second half of the 17th cent. Charles Williams, a young man belonging to one of the leading families in the district, killed his cousin, Edmund Morgan, in a duel in Caerleon. He fled the country, made a fortune in the Middle East, and returned, rich and respected, to be buried in Westminster Abbey. But, out of remorse, he left a large sum to embellish the church and to establish a school in his native town. This charity school, with its graceful early 18th-cent. windows and cream-coloured walls, now stands opposite the church.

Further along the street to the E. are the long walls of the priory. It was founded in the 12th cent., but was a private house from 1450 until our time. The present building shows Tudor influences. The house is built round a courtyard known as the Nun's Court. The 15th-cent. windows contain portraits and verses about the Roman Emperors. A passage leads under the road to the Bull Hotel in the square. The bull was part of the arms of the Morgan family. Again the building contains Tudor elements.

Further along the High Street, great walls now surround the castle enclosure. Inside the circuit, hidden from the road, are gardens full of fine trees. Among them stands the steep mound, built by the Normans as the motte for the castle keep. Inevitably this mound has gathered a whole cycle of legends. Here, in all its splendour, stood King Arthur's palace. From the top of the battlements you could see the Bristol Channel, in spite of the surrounding hills.

On the river bank, near the arched bridge over

the Usk, is the Hanbury Arms, with a pedigree that goes back to Tudor times. A defence tower stands in the SE. corner of the inn. Tennyson stayed here when he was gathering material for his *Idylls of the King*. Until recently the inn contained an old dog-spit over the kitchen fireplace. Caerleon was the birthplace of the writer Arthur Machen, who described his native town as "noble, fallen Caerleon-on-Usk in the heart of Gwent".

Today Caerleon has developed industries that can prevent the town from ever again being described as "fallen". On the hill to the W. is Caerleon Training College. The Afon Lwyd flows into the Usk just to the N. of Caerleon. About 1 m. away up this valley are important brickworks on the Ponthir road.

CAERNARFON, *Caernarfonshire*, or Caernarvon, in the more or less English spelling is Y Gaer yn Arfon (Fort on the Shore), facing Anglesey. It lies directly on the Menai Straits at their SW. mainland point, where the River Seiont runs into the sea. Like most British river-names, this Seiont is a word going far back in time, at least to the Celtic peoples who settled here before the Romans came. Rome built its fortress on the site, $\frac{1}{2}$ m. from the present town on the Beddgelert road, that is still marked Segontium. The Romans accepted the native word for any place they set their military stations to command, and Segontium preserves a British name close to if not identical with Seiont. This was their most westerly position in Wales, mounting guard over the great line of communication called in medieval times Watling Street, which ran from London to the NW. and formed the main strategic route for the whole island. An outlying fort, watching the ways to Watling Street from the S., is at Dinas Dinlle, not far off. Some Roman remains can be seen in the small museum at Segontium, and the ground has been sufficiently excavated for the plan of the first Caernarfon to be made clear. Whether or not this position was chosen for a town or encampment by the native British folk before the Roman invasion, is not certain; they may have preferred the Tre'r Ceiri in the Rival hills near Llanaelhaearn. "Caer", however, the Welsh for a town or fortress, is now recognized not as a contraction of the Latin *castra*, but as a native word for an enclosure.

The town is overshadowed in every sense by the great citadel set up by Edward I of England between 1285 and 1322. The work was not begun until three years after the last independent Welsh Prince of Wales, Llywelyn, was killed and his principality occupied; the building was done in three stages, with great care. For Edward intended to secure his future footing in Wales beyond any doubt; and the whole of Gwynedd, the northern province of the country, was to be held in a chain of castles from the border with England round to Harlech. Caernarfon Castle was to be the most potent of them all. Probably it replaced a wooden strong-point put there by the Princes of Gwynedd.

The Castle is the finest in Great Britain, only Alnwick in Northumberland coming close to it in magnificence. The area enclosed by the Castle walls is 3 acres, and the walls themselves are from 7 to 9 ft thick. Once they extended to encircle the entire town, but now they surround only a portion of it, crossing the High Street where the original E. gate, bearing the Guildhall, can be seen. There were at first only two main gates into the town, but others were added from time to time as conditions for the garrison became more secure. Although the Castle is now only a shell, the shell is perfect. Entrance is still made through the Gate of the King over what was the Castle ditch and moat. This is a great arch surmounted by an effigy of Edward II, the first English Prince of Wales to be so proclaimed, and set there in 1321. The inner and outer baileys, once chief centres of strength, are now represented by tidily mown lawns. The remains of the kitchen can be seen, where huge cauldrons once rested on the fireplaces, and water-gullies ran to supply them. The Well Tower and the Eagle Tower stand together, this last 124 ft high, with three fine turrets. It is named after a worn figure placed there representing Edward's crest, an eagle; rumour has it that a Roman eagle-standard found at Segontium originated the name. The top of the tower is reached by 158 steps. They pass the room known as the Queen's Oratory, small and dark, where the son of Edward I was supposed to have been born. He was certainly by birth a native of Caernarfon; but this room was not where he first saw the light. The foundations of the existing Castle were not laid till 1285; and the future Prince was born at least a year before that, in the older and native fortress of the rulers of Gwynedd. The entrance on the E. side, called the Gate of Queen Eleanor, is where the infant (legend tells us) was presented to the people as their new Prince by King Edward. He was not installed in that office until 1301; and some important historical facts turn on the point.

At Rhuddlan in 1284 Edward promulgated the Statute of Wales to give the country a new relationship with England. In the preamble he offers thanks to God that at last Wales, which had never until then come under the direct sovereignty of the Kings of England, was now fully part of his sovereignty. The relation between the two countries, in spite of unceasing warfare, was one in which they shared a heritage of Roman and Christian civilization. The Middle Ages, throughout the whole of western Europe, was an attempt to restore the unity its peoples once had under a common law and culture. The institution known as the Holy Roman Empire, founded by Charlemagne, was intended to revive in A.D. 800 the empire that had drifted into dissolution in the 5th cent. The idea that all European sovereigns were bound together within that system lasted long enough for Henry VIII of England in the 16th cent. to think of accepting nomination as Holy Roman Emperor. Between national sovereigns, the medieval mind insisted on a relationship of degree, not of dominance; for, if the Law of God could require observance of the Truga Dei, or Divine Truce, to mitigate the evils of war, the Law of Justice similarly insisted that every

nation had its separate right to exist. In 1284, the Great Charter was barely seventy years old; and Edward I himself is famed for first introducing the parliamentary system based on the distinct privileges and identities of all communities within the realm. Just as Edward I himself owed allegiance to the Holy Empire, so Scotland, Wales, and Man had always had a certain fealty to England, while keeping their right to their own identities. The Baron, or King's man, who was himself King of Man, and that other who was crowned King of Wight and the Channel Islands, attended the English Parliament. So both the King of Scotland and the Great Llywelyn, Prince of Wales, were signatories to Magna Carta. Perhaps Edward at first intended to annex directly to himself the northern land of Gwynedd, which the last Llywelyn had controlled, though the Marcher Lordships, with the possible exception of Monmouth, he was prepared to leave with their own jurisdictions. But the death of Llywelyn did not end the sense of Welsh national distinctiveness. In 1294 Pembroke, Cardigan, and Glamorgan were in revolt; in the same year one Madoc, who claimed to be the son of Llywelyn, seized Caernarfon Castle itself and Denbigh and even succeeded in capturing Oswestry. In 1301, therefore, the son of Edward was proclaimed Prince of Wales, not by way of tactfully abolishing but of tactfully accepting the independent nature of Wales.

This recognition of the right of all people to be different became a guide for the later development of the British political idea. Under the Stuarts, Wales was referred to not as part of England but as a dominion by itself – the first use of the word that in our own time initiated the structure of the British Commonwealth. The same principle was applied by Thomas Jefferson, one of the American Founding Fathers, himself of Welsh descent, to justify the argument for American independence of direct rule from Westminster.

Caernarfon town is now a little grey, as becomes its antiquity, and a little remote in spite of its excellent communications. It is a centre for markets in North Wales and the Lleyn and Anglesey, and for tourists who come to see not only its monuments of the past but the tremendous scenery around the mass of Snowdon, the bright beauty of the Menai Straits, and the scattered churches that touch the last years of dying Rome.

Owain Glyndwr failed to take the place in 1401. The Castle was held in the Civil Wars by Parliament and then captured by Col. Byron for the King. In 1646 it surrendered to Mytton, the Roundhead general, on honourable terms; but, as a storm centre for Royalist attempts at reviving the lost cause, it was dismantled by order of Parliament, which accounts for its present emptied state. Indeed, in 1660 a writ of Parliament was issued to demolish it altogether, but fortunately the order was never carried out. The statue of the man who in modern times did most to re-establish it stands in the Castle Square. That man was David Lloyd George, O.M., Constable of Caernarfon

Castle and one-time Prime Minister of the United Kingdom, who officiated at the initiation of Edward VIII in his younger days as Prince of Wales. The Castle now houses the memorials of the former Royal Welsh Fusiliers.

CAERPHILLY, *Glamorgan*. Some 7 m. N. of Cardiff, this town is famous for its cheese and its castle. The cheese has largely disappeared, but its castle remains – a vast fortification, the second largest in Britain next to Windsor, and really, as Tennyson said, a "ruined town". Caerphilly's strategic position can best be appreciated by driving over Caerphilly Common, the 800-ft ridge, with hidden valleys and plantations, that separates the Caerphilly area from the low plain on which Cardiff is built. From the top of the hill above the town there is a fine view northwards over the mining valleys of Glamorgan and Monmouthshire. In recent years Caerphilly has spread with new housing estates and industrial developments, but you can still see how easily any castle here could command the exits from the tangle of valleys to the N. The Romans were the first to understand the advantages of the site. They built a fort at Caerphilly some time around A.D. 75, as part of their defensive network holding down the hill tribes of South Wales. The fort was well placed, within an easy day's march from Cardiff on a road that led northwards through Gelligaer to Brecon. The camp lay about 200 yds NW. of the present castle, in the area known as the North-East Earthworks. These fortifications, thrown up during the Civil War, have greatly disturbed the site, and nothing is visible of the fort above ground. Further excavations have recently been made.

After the Romans, came the Celtic saints. St Cenydd was active in the district, and his son Fili is supposed to have given his name to the town.

The turning-point in Caerphilly's history was in 1266. Gilbert de Clare, the powerful Lord of Glamorgan, began building the greatest castle so far planned in Wales. The Blaenau (Uplands) of Glamorgan had remained in the possession of the Welsh long after the Bro, the Vale and Lowlands, were in Norman hands. In the middle of the 13th cent. the Welsh cause had greatly revived under the Princess of North Wales; and, with the local Welsh now looking towards the vigorous leadership of Llywelyn ap Gruffydd, the last native Prince of Wales, the Lord of Glamorgan felt bound to do all in his power to overawe the men of the hills. In 1270 Llywelyn destroyed the half-finished structure. Building started again, and the fortifications were completed in spite of Llywelyn's resistance. The Edwardian conquest of Wales did not remove the need for the new castle. It was attacked and besieged during the revolt of Llywelyn Bren in 1316.

Caerphilly Castle also played an important part in the troubles that beset Edward II. His favourite, Hugh le Despenser, had inherited Caerphilly through his marriage to a daughter of Earl Gilbert. Hugh incurred the hostility of neighbouring barons, who seized Caerphilly in 1321. Although Edward reinstated Hugh, disaster in 1326 overwhelmed King and favourite. Queen Isabella led the revolt of the barons that overthrew the King. He fled to Caerphilly, and left his treasury in the Castle as he wandered further westward towards Neath before the avenging Queen and her allies. The Castle held out against her long after Edward had been captured near Llantrisant. Glyndwr captured the Castle during his revolt, but this was its last serious appearance in history. In 1536 it was in decay – a wilderness, as Leland described it, "of ruinous waulles of wonderful thicknes".

An earthwork was thrown up on the site of the Roman fort during the Civil War, and one or other of the opposing armies "slighted" the fortress by blowing up some of the towers. As a result of this treatment, one of them still leans at a remarkable angle. The 3rd Marquess of Bute began the work of restoration in the late 19th cent. by clearing away the houses that had clustered around the walls. His work was continued by the 4th Marquess until the Second World War. The Castle is now in the hands of the Ministry of Public Building and Works. The moat and surrounding lake have been refilled with water. Caerphilly today magnificently demonstrates the power of a medieval stronghold.

It was in fact planned during a great period of castle-building, when England was being influence by the new ideas on fortification brought back to Europe after the Crusades. New siege engines forced the builders to adopt new tactics. Thick walls alone could not be relied on to keep out the enemy. The aim now was to seal off the attackers if they succeeded in breaking in. Hence the "concentric castle", with a double set of defences, each complete in itself. The inner ring would dominate the outer even if the outer fell. Beaumaris in North Wales is a fine example of this style. Caerphilly is even more impressive. The outer and inner wards of Caerphilly are a complete "concentric castle" in themselves, surrounded by a lake. In addition, there is a powerful hornwork of earthen banks on an island in the middle of the water that guarded the castle to the W., and to the E. a great curtain wall, strengthened by towers and buttresses. This huge eastern front not only protected the eastern approaches but dammed the Nant y Gledyr stream, and, by stretching right across the line of drainage, created and defended the lake. It also had a moat before it. The banks of the moats have now been cleared and turfed, and the Castle stands again in the middle of the restored lakes, complete with swans.

The main entrance is on the E. side, across the outer moat. On either side of this gatehouse run the N. and S. platforms. On the S. platform was the mill, worked by water that poured through an outlet under the platform from the S. lake. A strong postern guarded the southern end of this platform. The N. platform is narrower and is also known as the "royal stables". The oubliettes, or pits, opposite each tower were originally covered by trapdoors, which could be opened in case the garrison had to retreat into the inner defences. formed by the "concentric castle" itself.

These were reached by a drawbridge. The walls of the outer ward are comparatively low, to allow them to be dominated from the towers of the inner ward. The inner ward contained the heart of the Castle. In the quadrangle, marked by four great towers at the corners, is the eastern gate-house, with arrangements for a portcullis and with a small vaulted chapel. The smaller western gate-house stands on the other side of the greensward of the inner quadrangle, and next to it is the great hall. This is early 14th-cent. and was probably built for Hugh le Despenser. When the present restoration is complete, the hall will reappear in its old glory as one of the most important build-ings of its kind in Wales. The celebrated "Leaning Tower of Caerphilly" stands on the SE. corner of the inner ward. This fragment of one of the corner drum-towers is 80 ft high and 13 ft out of the perpendicular. It was blown up deliberately during the Civil Wars of the 17th cent.

The Castle dominates Caerphilly, and there are few other ancient buildings that survived the expansion of the town with the development of the coalfield. The remains of the old manor house of the Van lie at the foot of the wooded hills on the road to Rudry. This was once a fine Tudor mansion, built in 1530. Thirty years later the owner. Thomas Lewis, obtained permission to pillage the Castle for stone to enlarge the building. The family of Lewis the Van claimed descent from Ivor Bach, the celebrated Welsh chieftain of Senghennydd, who was a doughty opponent of the Normans in the 12th cent. The Van fell into ruin when the family removed to St Fagan's Castle.

In the SW. of Caerphilly is Watford, where the first synod of the newly formed Welsh Calvinistic Methodist Church was held in 1743. From Wat-ford, George Whitfield married Elizabeth James of Abergavenny in 1741. The marriage took place at Capel Martin, which has now been rebuilt. Near Watford Chapel is Waenwaelod (now the Carpenter's Arms), the birthplace of David Williams, the remarkable pamphleteer who be-came a deist, attempted to establish a cult of Nature, and wrote a litany for it that won the approval of Voltaire, Franklin, and Rousseau. His *Letters on Political Liberty* (1782) in support of the Americans, made him a leader of radical thinking, and he later became an honorary citizen of the French Republic. In 1796 he published his *History of Monmouthshire.* His most enduring memorial is the Royal Literary Fund, which he founded.

Caerphilly cheese also belongs to history so far as the town is concerned. This delicious, light, and crumbly cheese was a favourite with the old miners, and the Caerphilly cheese-market was famous throughout southern Glamorgan. Early in this century production was being overtaken by Devonshire and Somerset, and Caerphilly cheese ceased to be made in the place of its origin. Attempts are being made to ensure that some Caerphilly cheese is again made in Caerphilly.

CAERSWS, *Montgomeryshire.* So far, this small town has kept its rural character unspoilt. It is a centre for the farming interests of the upper Severn valley, where the moors of Plynlimon and the Radnor Forest drop to lush levels of green. Unfortunately, its open fields have attracted the attention of town-planners, and projects are afoot to expand this area so obviously ripe for develop-ment.

It is an ancient place, and its roots in the history of Roman Britain are firmly laid. Here stood a Roman military station – one that concerned itself with the economic development of the region. The men holding it were probably under orders from the Twentieth Legion, which operated in W. Shropshire and even to the N. towards Chester. The main interest of the Empire was to exploit the lead in the Plynlimon heights; at first this was a matter for central government authority, but in course of time the mine-workings were apparently farmed out to local people.

A Roman road can be traced, leaving the modern highway between Newtown and Llanidloes shortly after Penstrowed, on the S. side of the Severn, passing through Maes-mawr Hall on the outskirts of Caersws, and then striking W. across the fields to connect with the farm roads to Trefeglwys. Here the uplands crowd in again on the River Trannon, and no motorable track can follow the ancient pack-way, though a mountain road can be taken to Llawryglyn over Foel Fawr to Stay-little and Dylife. Before the Romans, the route across the hills to Caersws may have been regu-larly used: this is suggested by the standing stones leading to Llawryglyn and by the many encamp-ments on the neighbouring hills.

S. from Caersws, the pleasant village of Llan-dinam is worth seeing. Milton's "Sabrina fair" in *Comus* is said to have been inspired by a visit to the Severn he made when at Ludlow, and by a particular meadow near Caersws.

The church in the small village of Llanwnog, a little to the N. of Caersws, shares its Roman memories. The foundations of the tower are laid on stones believed to have been gathered from an imperial building close by.

CAERWENT, *Monmouthshire.* This is an evoca-tive place. The M4 motorway to Newport, the old by-pass, and a wartime munition factory are all near at hand, yet Caerwent remains a place apart. Its secret lies in its remote past when, 1,800 years ago, Caerwent was Venta Silurum, a Roman city, the biggest civilian settlement in SW. Britain after Bath. Today the Roman walls still encircle the site, and the southern section must be one of the most impressive relics of Roman power left above ground in this country. There it stands, for 500 yds, facing the S. and the Bristol Channel, whence came the dangerous Irish raiders when the Roman Empire was in its death throes. There are six semi-octagonal bastions, and the wall is over 17 ft high. The E. wall has also been restored, and work is continuing under the guardianship of the Ministry of Public Building and Works. Eventually the full circuit will be revealed. The W. wall is also clear, in places up to 17 ft. Systematic excavation has continued on the site since 1845. Most of the finds are in the Newport Museum. In addition to the walls, the foundations of the shops and houses that lay W. of the forum are preserved; they are open to the public at the corner of the main street and Pond Lane.

The main street of Caerwent lies roughly along the line of the old Roman central avenue. The present war memorial marks the centre of the city; the basilica and the forum lay N. of it, with the baths to the S. The temple was E. of the forum. It was not constructed with pillars, in the style familiar in metropolitan Rome. Temples in Britain seldom were. They usually consisted of a rectangular building surrounded by a veranda. The Ministry has acquired the site, and the wall of the temple has been left in full view.

Roman masonry at Caerwent

G. Douglas Bolton

Venta Silurum seems to have been founded about A.D. 75. The Silures were one of the tribes who offered fierce resistance to the first Roman advance. One of their forts lies 1 m. NW. of Venta on the wooded hill of Llanmelin. When, at last, the power of the Silures was smashed and the Romans set up their legionary fortress at Caerleon, they also set up a new town at Caerwent as the administrative capital of the tribal area. It was part of the Roman policy to show the conquered tribes the civilizing mission of Rome as well as her military might. The Silures were expected to leave their hill-forts and settle peacefully in the valleys around the Roman centres. So Venta arose, with the usual rectangular layout and a wooded palisade round it, although it was never a military centre. Perhaps the Silures did not settle down so peacefully after all.

Venta Silurum was never a large city; in its heyday it probably had no more than 2,000 inhabitants. But it contained all the amenities expected in a Roman city, including a small amphitheatre within the walls. The 2nd cent. was the happiest period in the life of Caerwent. The Silures had now accepted it as their tribal capital, and were proud to honour their locally successful men. In the church porch is the base of a statue set up by the decree of the Senate of the Community of the Silures to the commanding officer of the Second Legion, who had been promoted to Governor of Narbonensis and then of Lugdunensis, two of the biggest provinces of Gaul. Quite a transition from the rainy outposts of Caerleon and Caerwent to high office in one of the richest parts of the Empire!

By the end of the 2nd cent., however, the clouds were gathering. In the military reorganization that then took place, Caerwent was enclosed with stone walls. But the towns of Britain, Caerwent among them, continued to decline even if the countryside around them prospered. Soon greater dangers threatened town and countryside alike. The pressure of the barbarian tribes on the Empire increased. The Irish raiders grew bolder all along the Severn shore. To this problem, the military solution adopted by the Romans included the building of special fortified bases for the fleets stationed along the threatened coastline. About A.D. 300 a new, strong fort was built at Cardiff. Caerwent may have obtained some protection from this fort and from the fleet, but about A.D. 340 the little town felt so insecure that a decision was made to strengthen the whole length of the S. wall facing the Severn coast. Six polygonal bastions were built, each capable of mounting *ballistae*, stone-throwing machines that could send a missile 400 yds. The fourth bastion from the W. is the best preserved.

The reorganized defence system did not outlast the 5th cent. By A.D. 400 it seems clear that all Roman troops had been withdrawn from Wales. Darkness closed in on the little city of Venta Silurum. A grim reminder of the fate that may have overtaken the inhabitants was found when the third bastion from the left was being excavated. The debris included a skeleton and a collection of human skulls, perhaps belonging to the victims of some raid in the 5th cent. The darkness lifted for a brief period when a small church-like building was raised late in the 5th cent., amid the ruins of the Roman baths near the present church. Could it have been connected with the Irish St Tathan, who is said to have been persuaded by King Caradog of Gwent to found a monastery here? Christianity must have put down roots very early in this region. Scholars have recently made out a very strong case for the countryside around Caerwent as the original home of St Patrick. We know that he was kidnapped when very young by raiders at a place called Bannaventa "near to the sea" – and the Caerwent area is the only one that fits all the facts. Darkness descended again, and Caerwent faded out of history until the coming of the Normans. The mound on the SE. corner of the defences was probably thrown up by the Normans as they advanced into Gwent in the early stages of the conquest of South Wales.

They probably built here a church that was replaced by the present one in the 13th cent. Caerwent church stands near the centre of the old city. It is now dedicated to St Stephen, because the Normans by custom altered all dedications made to Celtic saints, and this one especially, as St Tathan's festival fell on St Stephen's Day. In 1912 it was claimed that the bones of St Tathan had been discovered. They were reverently re-buried in the S. aisle under an inscribed slab now covered by a carpet. The church also contains numerous Roman relics in the 14th-cent. porch and a section of a Roman mosaic, displayed at the base of the S. pier. The finely carved oak pulpit, with the inscription "Woe unto me if I preach not the Gospel", dates from 1632. There are numerous and interesting memorials, as well as finely carved gargoyles on the 15th-cent. tower.

The double lych-gate is a memorial to Thomas Walker, who was concerned with the building of the Manchester Ship Canal as well as the Severn Tunnel.

The church and the houses of Caerwent seem to huddle together in the centre of what was once Venta Silurum. Much of the old city still lies under the open fields, on which the cows peacefully graze. Nowhere in South Wales are the changes wrought by time more evocative than in quiet, wood-encircled Caerwent.

CAERWYS, *Flintshire*. Caerwis it is called on 18th-cent. maps, and in the early 19th cent. it was noted chiefly as a crossroads junction for mysterious places like Skynyog and Bullafranck. It is now a smallish place reached by relatively minor roads between Holywell and St Asaph or Denbigh and Mold. But it is a striking example of the way in which Wales can preserve its ancient traditions in the 20th cent. In 1968 Caerwys celebrated the 400th anniversary of its unique Eisteddfod.

It seems always to have had an artistic tradition peculiar to itself. The contests of music and poetry known as Eisteddfodau have been an outstanding feature of life among the Welsh for longer than written records have existed. The most important of these gatherings, perhaps the first to be held on a national scale, was the one called in the year 1177 by Rhys ap Gruffydd, Prince of South Wales, who invited all the bards of the country to his castle at Cardigan, or Aberteifi, to prove themselves in competition. Those of South Wales were found to excel in music, those of the North in verse; and for both arts the highly sophisticated rules that have governed them ever since were established. Gerald de Barri, the Norman-Welsh Archdeacon of Brecon, some sixty years afterwards wrote of the great skill the Welsh seemed naturally to have in these things, and of how they were distinguished from all other people he knew by their habit of singing not in unison but in harmony, by some natural instinct.

Caerwys, being set in an area where the political questions between Wales and England were most acute, naturally found in them a theme for its poets; and the death of the last Llywelyn was mourned in an elegy written by a man of Caerwys, Gruffydd ab yr Ynad Coch, who had been a bard under the special patronage of that prince. But there is little record of the place as a fully developed town until 1290, when Edward I of England granted it a charter, making it the only Welsh borough in Flint. Its importance for the district in which it lay was marked by its fairs, held once a week until very recent times. The drovers who brought their cattle to market, and passed through Caerwys on the great cattle-trek into England, had their animals shod in a smithy that once stood at the end of Drovers Lane, and in the market square a bell was hung to ring in the opening of the fair and ring it out again.

In 1568 Caerwys became nationally significant. The ending of the succession of native Princes of Wales did not mean the ending of the Welsh literary tradition; even the ban laid by Henry VIII on the use of the Welsh language in courts of law did not succeed in destroying a tradition that went much further back than the Eisteddfod of 1177. Certainly the language became increasingly confined to the villagers and peasantry, but the wandering harp-men, living by their skills and going from place to place in all seasons and weathers, produced songs that are still known and sung today as outstanding pieces of lyric beauty and literary craftsmanship. The 17th and 18th cents. have many names of such men to prove how strong was the life of the Welsh cultural tradition. The practice of the wandering harp-men continued far into the 19th cent. Caerwys can claim to have made this survival possible.

Queen Elizabeth Tudor granted a commission to twenty gentlemen of North Wales to summon a meeting of all such wandering minstrels at Caerwys. They had been active since the fall of Llywelyn, demanding their ancient privilege of hospitality and payment for their songs; but they were apparently threatened by the competition of vagrant and idle persons calling themselves rhithmers and barthes. The Tudors were anxious to suppress the dispossessed who had flooded the country after the Wars of the Roses and the economic revolution that had overthrown the village systems of the Middle Ages. Under their legislation, even professional actors were classed with rogues, vagabonds, Egyptians (gypsies), and other masterless men. The native harpists of Wales were a considerable problem. The Commission of Caerwys regularized the profession and instituted a system of licences to those who proved their ability, giving the award of a silver harp to the man who came first in the competitions. The date and place of all subsequent Eisteddfodau were announced in advance at fairs and markets throughout the five counties of North Wales. The old town hall, where the first Commission Eisteddfod was held under the branches of an ash tree, has now been replaced by the post office.

The original plan of the town, as laid out in the days of Edward I, is still obvious in the pattern of its long, straight streets. Its influence has passed far beyond Wales. When William Penn was projecting his new town of Philadelphia in the peace-seeking community of Pennsylvania in America, he took the advice of Dr Thomas Wynne, a native of Caerwys, who thought Edward I's designers were no bad masters to follow.

The parish church is one of the ancient Welsh foundations, and a holy well recalls the days before Christianity was introduced. Roman relics are, a little surprisingly, not much in evidence so far; the silver and lead along the Dee estuary were of the sort to attract them. But the medieval village has recently been excavated near at hand, and the grave-mounds of the Bronze Age lie about the area.

CALDEY ISLAND, *Pembrokeshire,* is often included in the excursions that can be made from the resort of Tenby; but, like all the islands lying off the Welsh shores, it has a separate and mys-terious dignity both as an island stormed by the seas and as a point of human settlement when men first learnt to master the ocean and explore the continents from them. Under its present owner-ship it preserves this attitude of standing outside time. For it belongs to a priory of Cistercians, monks of the strictest observance, known as Trappists. When they came to Caldey in 1929, they were a colonizing movement in early medi-eval fashion from Chimay in Belgium. However, they were not pioneers, since a group of Bene-dictine monks had preceded them in 1906 under Dom Aelred Carlyle; they had erected the build-ings that now stand, the priory itself, the gardens, and the farms. The Benedictines themselves had preferred to move to Prinknash in Gloucestershire. Caldey is no more than a fragment of territory $1\frac{1}{2}$ m. by 1 m., its breached coasts and shorn cliffs breasting the channel tides as if they were moving and the seas were still.

But the Benedictines themselves built on earlier foundations. So far as record goes, the first monastery was created in 1113 by Benedictines of St Dogmael's near Cardigan, who remained there until in 1534 Henry VIII dissolved all such foun-dations, and Caldey stood empty after a period of occupation that seems to have begun much earlier than the 12th cent. Theirs was the first to be built of those that survive in use. Church, gate-house, refectory, and the Prior's lodging (which is now in service as the guest-house), stand as they were built in the 12th, 13th, and 15th cents., made singularly solid to withstand the press of gales no less than the severer attacks of time. But the first church of all, whose date is uncertain, has continued a bare existence into the present. It seems from its shape to belong to that period of first Christian proselytization which followed

Giltar Point, which faces Caldey Island across the narrow Caldey Sound

when Roman centralized authority was surrendered and the House of Cunedda took over control of the seas of the West. As in the case of the other islands and offshore points, Bardsey, Seiriol (Puffin Island), and Llanbedr, and Ramsey, the missionary effort led by David, Patrick, and Columba took as dominant positions these secluded sanctuaries in the seas. What men were those it worked among is suggested by another ancient monument on Caldey, the stone inscribed in both Latin and Ogham and preserved in the church. The Ogham writing, although based entirely on the Latin alphabet, does not use Latin signs for vowels or consonants; the five vowels are represented by groups of dots running from one to five; the consonants are shown by a series of grouped lines, upright and oblique. The script made its appearance just when Roman direct control vanished from Britain, and it is found on old stone inscriptions in Ireland, South Wales, and Cornwall. It seems to have belonged to the sea-people about the Bristol Channel and the waters between Pembrokeshire and SE. Ireland. The use of it ceased about 800, when political conditions on the British side of the Irish Sea had suffered a considerable reversal, and the influence of the Latin Church had begun to prevail at last over Celtic Christianity. Many Ogham inscriptions, collected from Wales, are preserved in the Cardiff National Museum. It is a fair conclusion that the script, perhaps one that seamen had developed for themselves, was applied under instruction from devoted missionaries with a knowledge of Latin as well as of native tongues to preserve a record of outstanding men and events. It was common to the coasts and islands of the Irish Sea. In former days the sea was the most practical bridge between peoples, far less of

a barrier than land, and we do not need to assume Irish invasion of any part of Britain.

A little nearer than Caldey to the mainland, St Margaret's Island keeps secret the memory of who built its ruined structures.

Opposite Caldey, where Giltar Point looks at it from the mainland, the village of Penally lies behind the hills called the Burrows. Here St Teilo wrought mightily for the Faith. Although the present church dates from no earlier than the 13th cent., and belongs to the period of conquest, the churchyard has a carved Celtic cross of outstanding beauty that speaks more directly of his time.

Near at hand are Lydstep Haven and Point, looking over the last limestone formations of this coast before they turn towards the Old Red Sandstone hard by Manorbier; and the caves, much admired by the villagers of Lydstep, which can be inspected at low tide.

CAPEL CURIG, *Caernarfonshire.* This village, small and straggling, is prolific in hotels to accommodate the hill-walker and the angler. To this remote and unapproachable spot, hidden in Snowdonia, came Curig, a saint and Bishop of Llanbadarn, perhaps officiating in a church set by the lake that carries the name of Padarn, in the 6th cent. A church, old and little, stands in the village beside a much more modern one built in Norman style. The hill Carnedd Moel-Siabod (2,860 ft) and Pen Llithrig-y-Wrach (Hag Slide, 2,621 ft) hold Capel Curig between them. The Llynau Mymbyr, two large stretches of water linked by a channel, are usually named the Capel Curig lakes; they offer the best of trout fishing and a C.C.P.R. Mountaineering Pursuits Centre.

CAPEL-Y-FFIN, *Monmouthshire.* The name means Chapel on the Boundary; for at this point the Monmouthshire ground runs out from Llanthony into a narrow enclave between Herefordshire and Breconshire. The three counties meet a little higher on the ridge.

The place belongs in many ways to the story of Llanthony priory; it had a 19th-cent. Llanthony Abbey of its own, a special foundation for Anglican Benedictines, later made into a girls' school. There are two chapels here, of similar appearance and structure. One at least may have had some connection with the 12th-cent. priory; beyond Capel-y-ffin, the narrow and tree-lined lane opens into a moorland track as it ascends by the side of the Honddu, here a mountain stream, to reach the Bwlch-yr-Efengel (Gospel Pass, 1,778 ft). It is a wide and open height, besieged with snows in season, but giving sight of Radnor Forest and the hills that follow the Wye. Its name may come from that preaching itinerary for the Third Crusade which Gerald de Barri, as Archdeacon of Brecon, undertook with Archbishop Baldwin in 1188 and described with so much detail; for that laborious undertaking, which summoned crowds all over Wales to hear and take the Cross, has left its mark in many place-names in the area. Of the two chapels,

St David's Church, Caldey Island
Reece Winstone

The church at Capel-y-ffin

Jane J. Miller

one is Baptist; the other is a church, a simple cottage-like building with a wide porch and a tower that has adopted Monmouthshire fashions of design. Yews surround it, and they are of great age; the churchyard is walled with dry-slab stones like any hedge-wall in the district. It commemorates on one of its gravestones the 18th-cent. boy who, though he died at the age of eight, had already conceived a violent repugnance for any desecration of the Sabbath day. The building was noted in the diary of the Rev. Francis Kilvert (1870–9) as the "old chapel, short, stout and boxy, with its little bell-turret – the whole building reminded me of an owl – the quiet, peaceful chapel yard shaded by seven solemn yews, the chapel house, a farmhouse over the way, and the Great Honddu brook crossing the road and crossed in turn by the stone foot-bridge".

Two streams do in fact join here, and, if you choose not to walk to the Gospel Pass, the other stream will lead to Nant y Bwlch, where a path drops steeply to the Wye valley and the ancient coaching inn, the Three Cocks, still famous and a great resort for fishermen.

CARDIFF, *Glamorgan*. The capital of Wales, as it has become under Queen Elizabeth II half way through the 20th cent., is in Welsh Caerdydd. The announcement that the principality should have its independent identity confirmed by the official selection of a capital was answered by three rival claimants for the honour. In a curious way, it reaffirmed the traditional division of Wales into three contending provinces that has coloured all its history.

Caernarfon could argue that it was the centre of Roman administration, which Edward I had accepted as transmitting to him the imperial authority of Rome wrested by him from the Princes of the North. Cardiff, as a city with an equal Roman tradition, and an even earlier connection with Anglo-Norman interests than Caernarfon could show, represented the claims of the South. A third claimant was Machynlleth, whose association with the House of Cunedda through Maelgwn in the 6th cent., and through Owain Cyfeiliog in the 12th with the ancient Kingdom of Powys that created Wales as a national concept, put forward its own request for recognition as the natural capital, reinforcing it with the reminder that it had already been so selected by Owain Glyndwr in 1402. The 19th-cent. prosperity of the South, which had continued some way into the 20th cent., the standing of Cardiff as a centre of easy communication with London, and its position as an industrial exporter with a great system of docks, made the decision inevitable. A torch was lit at Machynlleth to be borne to Cardiff as the due successor to its national prestige.

For Cardiff, too, can claim an important Roman legacy; indeed, there is evidence that its site between the estuaries of the Rhymney, the Taff, and the Ely rivers was of considerable importance in the earliest times when the Bristol Channel was in contact with the Wessex Culture of 1500 B.C. Its more precise historical foundation is in the Roman station that served as the base for the later Norman castle and acted as an intermediary not only for traffic between Neath and Caerwent but also for Carmarthen, Llandovery, Y Gaer, Llandrindod, and Abergavenny. The very name Cardiff may in its form of Caer Did (as the 17th-cent. Christopher Saxton writes it) trace its origin back to the Aulus Didius who commanded it. The castle site still shows the earthworks of this station, and part of its masonry walls, including its N. gate, one of the best-preserved pieces of Roman structure in the country. Saxton points out that, by St Donat's Castle, which he closely associates with Cardiff, many "antique peeces" of Roman coins had been recovered, including the very rare ones of Aemilianus and Marius and the Thirty Tyrants, the period of confusion in the rest of the Roman World that ended in A.D. 268.

When, in the 5th cent., British cities were advised by the imperial government to manage their own defence system, the Kingdom of Morganwg succeeded as a Roman-British state: this "Morganuc", Saxton insists (quoting Ptolemy, the geographer of Rome, as his authority), meant the State by the Sea. Sir John Rhys favoured the idea that Cardiff became part of the Kingdom of Powys in the 5th and 6th cents., and relied on the name of Dinas Powis (Fort of Powys), which still exists with its railway station somewhat to the SW. of the city. This may well be so, though the name Powys means in Welsh something firmly stabilized, and the deduction is not quite conclusive. But we can be certain that Iestyn, Lord of Morganwg, and his son-in-law Einion thought it necessary to call in the Normans, who were adventuring from conquered England on to the Welsh border to assist their revolt against Rhys son of Tewdwr, Lord of the South at the end of the 11th cent.

It was Robert FitzHamon – "sonne to Haimon Dentatus of Corboil in Normandy", writes Saxton – who answered the call with twelve followers, and they resolved the question by taking the whole territory for themselves. The castle was set up about 1090, and it remains dominant in Cardiff still. Saxton thought it "not amisse" to enter a list of these men, Robert and his peers, and set them out as "William de Londres, Richard Granvil, Pain Turbervill, Oliver St John, Robert de Saint Quentin, Roger Beke-roal, William Stradling (or Easterling, for that he was borne in Germanie), Gilbert Humfranvill, Richard Siward, John Fleming, Peter Soore, and Reinald Sully". It is not amiss to quote their names, for they have remained prominent from that time, and have left their mark on many places in and around Cardiff. Saxton, for example, points out that FitzHamon kept Cow-bridge for himself; that the Stradlings founded the Castle of St Donat; and that, of the two small islands of the mouth of the Taff, "the hithermore is called Sullie and also the Towne right over against it", after the Reinald who was peer among the twelve.

"A proper fine Towne," says Saxton of Cardiff, adding the precaution "as Townes goe in this country." But it had a very commodious haven, which FitzHamon fortified when he made Cardiff a centre of military strength and of justice. In 1158, however, one Ivor (a mountaineer) brought his British forces down from the hills, captured the Earl of Gloucester, grandson of FitzHamon, and held him to ransom until conditions of better justice still were agreed between Welsh and Norman. That balance of contract seems to have remained in force throughout the rest of Cardiff's history. It was Owain, King of Wales in the early 15th cent., who seized and almost destroyed the town and castle in 1404. The comment of the 17th cent., "deflor'd by Glendower", which is entered against so many of the churches and towns of Wales, is particularly applicable to Cardiff; and the memory of that intrusive nationalist from Machynlleth is not held in the highest reverence by its people today. Cardiff was so much thought to be a firm stronghold of the early Norman Kings that William the Conqueror's eldest son, Robert Curt-Hose, Duke of Normandy, supplanted by his younger brother, Henry I of England, was imprisoned for life in the castle and remained there, blinded, for twenty-eight years. "You shall understand," says Saxton, "that royall Parentage is never assured either of ends or safe security."

But Cardiff stood so much for the King during the Civil Wars that Charles I was welcomed there in 1645 – a gesture to which Parliament replied by taking the place exactly one month afterwards. Its subsequent history is curious. It was by no means considerable in population, but it was active in pursuit of the commerce of the sea, which still survives in its impressive fishing industry. Its first charter was a Norman grant in 1147; James I confirmed its status as a borough in 1608. But the Bristol Channel, heavy with sea-borne traffic, was designed by nature to favour the activities of pirates, in which Cardiff seems to have had its share. It is even said that culverins and cannon were sent out from Cardiff to supply the Spanish Armada when it was preparing its descent on Britain in 1588.

In 1801 its population numbered 1,018. In 1931 it rose to 223,648. This, as with so many other places in the South, was due to the exploitation of the region's natural resources by the Industrial Revolution. Coal and iron became a major export for Cardiff, and made it the principal point of dispatch for them anywhere in the world. But its prosperity depended on the conditions in the great coalfield and ironfield of the "Valleys". Export figures even after nine years of the Depression stood in 1938 at 5,330,000 tons, of which coal supplied 5,000,000. In 1956 exports were of just under 1,000,000 tons, coal making 600,000 of them. But the population of Cardiff does not show a parallel decline; in this way it is unique compared with its neighbouring industrial communities. In 1931 the figure was 226,937; in 1951, 243,627.

The docks, which handled 45 per cent of the South Wales output of coal, were begun in 1830 by the 2nd Marquess of Bute, who gambled his entire fortune on the project, and not without success. The first to be completed was Bute West

Dock, opened in 1839. The water area is 165 acres, with 7 m. of quays, ten dry docks, and a 125-ton floating crane. They came into the possession of the Great Western Railway, and then of its successor. East Bute Dock, completed in 1854, was followed by Roath Basin (1874) and Roath Dock (1887), and in 1907 by the Alexandra Dock, with an area of over 50 acres, capable of holding the great ships of that day. Coal-hoists can lift 20-ton wagons, and modern hydraulic and electric cranes can take up to 100 tons. A tidal harbour and a low-water pier 1,400 ft long add to the facilities. Penarth docks and Barry extend the system further, the last adding another 114 acres of water. This rapid development enabled Cardiff to outdistance Swansea, which in 1811 was described as the "most important centre in all Glamorganshire", despite the creation of Port Talbot docks below Swansea and Neath. The process began with the opening of the Glamorganshire Canal in 1794, linking Cardiff with Merthyr Tydfil. In 1912 Cardiff was at the peak of its prosperity.

There are other productive industries in Cardiff, concerned with coal, steel, and copper, brewing, biscuits, and chemicals. But ships and shipping have remained an important factor in its life from its earlier piratical days to the more refined present. Perhaps Bute Road by the docks was the most striking evidence of this, above all in the years around 1912. The pirates were still there, though they had become known as Lascars, that community of seamen which from time immemorial had wandered and mingled with other races, turning from prau and felucca to coaster-tramps. It was a colourful, restless, and uncontrollable group, maintaining its own customs against all comers, especially the police. Inter-racial rivalry seethed among its members. Often it was directed against the natives of Cardiff streets, and the record of three-day riots, which can be studied in the journals of the time, anticipated much of what goes on in American cities today.

Cardiff, as capital city, is now much more respectable. The view of it is at first dominated by the long main street, where the castle screens its original grim beauty behind a castellated front invented by one William Burges to make a residence for the Marquess of Bute, who had many such places in Scotland, Wales, London, and Edinburgh, and even in Spain. In 1947, his new Cardiff Castle was handed over to the City Corporation for public use. To enter the grounds is to see one of the finest examples of a Norman keep in Britain. The great walls, awe-inspiring in the exact geometry of their construction, recall the grey eminence of Rochester. In some respects, the workmanship of the 1890s, which surrounds it with its echoes of Victorian Gothic and Scottish Baronial, makes the symmetry of the earlier structure better seen; there are few others that create from such solid strength the sense of an upward-leaping balance from green lawns. The library is outstanding as a reference source for the study of history and architecture.

Peter Baker

Cardiff's Civic Centre: the City Hall and National Museum

There is also a Chaucer Room, so named from its stained-glass windows depicting, in the style of Burne-Jones, the figures of the *Canterbury Tales*.

South of the Castle is the 15th-cent. St John's Church, with its tower of 1443, the rest being in the Perpendicular style. N. of it, Cathays Park has become the focal point of the new Cardiff. Around the City Centre, developed as modern taste demands, stand the City Hall; the Glamorgan County Hall; the buildings of the Welsh Board of Health, opened in 1938; the Assize Courts; the University College of South Wales and Monmouthshire (for Cardiff has its own University); the Welsh National Temple of Peace and Health; the offices of the Welsh Department; and the National Museum of Wales.

This last is a building that, for architecture and content, emphasizes Cardiff's claim to be the repository of Welsh culture. Its most remarkable feature is the collection of Roman and Roman-British standing stones, rescued from their isolation in pasture land and forgotten trackways. Here, for example, you can find the original incised stones of Bryn-celli-ddu in Anglesey and those from around the Harlech district, the Museum being careful to leave on the sites exact replicas. There is considerable advantage in having these monuments of Britain's past assembled for reference in this way. A large number are inscribed in the Ogham script, which appeared suddenly around the coasts of Britain and Ireland immediately after the Roman power handed over its authority to the native cities. Wholly based though it is on the Latin alphabet, this script stands as a sign of the re-

The 15th-cent. tower of St John's
Church, Cardiff

St Fagan's Castle, the home of the Welsh
Folk Museum

emergence of a Celtic culture that had at last found the means of permanent record. The names of rulers and of saints that it preserves are usually difficult to identify with actual men; for, apart from these monuments, there is no other contemporary record. The one to whom we can assign a place in written history is the Uotiporius, or Uotipore, who appears in the list of rulers in Britain denounced by Gildas in the mid-6th cent., and whose inscribed memorial is preserved in the Museum at Carmarthen. No one with an interest in the "Arthurian" period should fail to visit these doubtful evidences of that time, or to make the journey to Carmarthen.

The wide spaces of the City Centre are typical of the Cardiff that is adapting itself to the 20th cent. and its new position as a capital. It is marked by the growth of a new kind of population, with new outlooks and new demands. Queen Street and St Mary's Street reflect the novel kinds of salesmanship belonging to contemporary society, without deserting that inherent Welsh taste in composition and design which the Museum perpetuates in its collection of pictures by Welsh artists such as Richard Wilson, Burne-Jones, Frank Brangwyn, and Augustus John. From the City Hall, with its twelve marble sculptures that, as commissioned by Lord Rhondda, give the history of Wales a concrete expression, the well-disciplined streets, the tidy new-development houses, the 440 acres of parks, congregate upon the Taff and the Rhymney in a way that seems to throw the long shadow of the walls of Castle Bute in its present municipal stateliness further and further, one way over the crowded valleys of the dark South of the recent past, another way towards the horizon of the ageless Ellennith.

The television aerial marks its paces, as the signpost of the wider horizons that reach in to the capital of Wales. For Cardiff is the home of the broadcasting companies through which the native Welsh language finds a novel method of expression and novel matters to express.

Among the enterprises Cardiff has undertaken in the present century, there is one of which it can be specially proud. This is the Welsh Folk Museum, called St Fagan's. The need for water and water-power, timber and wood-pulp, to serve England has not only set dams along the Rheidol and the Clywedog, but has sent armies of firs to march across the moorlands. The Ellennith and the Melienydd have been invaded; the heartland of Wales is increasingly threatened. Marginal farming on the uplands, and the attempt to introduce large-scale farming in the modern style, have resulted not only in the abandonment of many an ancient farmstead to the nettled ruin of neglect, but in destroying a distinctive way of life.

Not the town, but the valley community of houses built by those who would live in them, was the reality of Welshness. Rarely was a town planned as a whole; Machynlleth's Maen Gwyn Street, the Street at Bala, and the centre of Dolgellau are outstanding exceptions. Many cottages remaining on the outskirts of the older villages were put up in a single night under the old Welsh law that a house so built would become at once the freehold property of its maker. Undressed stones hastily assembled by this co-operative effort have stood for generations. But usually more considered techniques were applied, and the results can still be studied in out-buildings and byres along the busy roads of Wales. Lengths of tree, chosen for the limb-curve, form the "cruck" on which the walls and roofs of ancient churches were constructed, in a way used by the Romans and by civilizations before them to counter shifting soil. Many examples of this method have been saved and reassembled at St Fagan's. From the drowned valley of the Claerwen in Radnorshire, the Ty Hir (Long House) of Cilewent, with its byres set alongside the living-quarters, has been taken and placed in a proper setting. From Penley in Flintshire, the 17th-cent. Barn of Stryt Lydan stands under its thatch of wheat-straw. Rhostryfan in Caernarfonshire shows its boulder-walls whitewashed under a slate roof. Llangynhafal in Denbighshire has its Hendre (Lowland Dwelling) of 1490 preserved, with its living-quarters divided from the animals' sleeping-place by a cruck-supported fence of daub and wattle. The 15th-cent. house of Abernodwydd from Llangadfan in Montgomeryshire shows the half-timbered style called in those parts "ty brith" (speckled house), which can claim direct descent from Roman architectural fashions. In this study, Wales is unique.

CARDIGAN, *Cardiganshire.* Aberteifi (Mouth of the Teifi) is the proper name for this place, which carries in English the name of that Ceredig who held the district of Ceredigion by the sea as one of the "sons" of the 5th-cent. Cunedda, honoured as the founder of what is called Wales today. It is the county town, and yet is too small to bear the burdens of office. The Assizes are at Lampeter, and the Council enjoys its prominence at Aberystwyth.

Cardigan is a bright and pleasing town, somewhat withdrawn from the world; and even in 1811 Daniel Paterson's *Direct and Principal Cross Roads* could not find a separate position for it, but entered it under "Cross Road Centres". The bridge over the Teifi is its most remarkable architectural feature. Its life is vigorous, but belongs to its own immediate district of rich farms and forests; the river that once made it an important seaport has withdrawn and left Cardigan to nurse proud memories. The valiant stand against the Danes, and the common cause that Ceredigion made with Wessex against them in the days of Rhodri the Great and after him, were renewed when in 1136 the drive of Norman power into Wales was met by the two Gruffydds, the son of Cynan and the son of Rhys, and defeated outside the town. Its castle had been built by Roger of Montgomery, who held it as a fief for William the Red, Norman King of England; but shortly afterwards it became the home of Cadwgan son of Bleddyn, a Welsh prince of Powys who did more than any other in repulsing the Norman attempt to overrun Wales. Anglesey, Gwynedd, Ceredigion, and most of Brycheiniog were recovered by him, and he successfully carried the war into the lost lands of eastern Powys — Cheshire, Shropshire, and Herefordshire. But for the damaging charms of Nest — bride of Gerald of Windsor, Constable of Pembroke — that led Cadwgan's son Owain to abduct

her and so plunged all Wales into bloody feud, he might well have given Wales real strength and unity. Perhaps it was at the Cenarth, some little way up the river from Cardigan, that Nest had her house, though more probably it was the Cenarth in Pembrokeshire. But it was at Llechryd that Cadwgan found his fatal check, when he engaged the forces of Rhys ap Tewdwr, Prince of the South, and his Irish soldiers in a battle that choked the river with blood.

Until the days of Edward I, Cardigan successfully maintained its Welshness. Gerald de Barri, himself a grandson of Nest, in about 1188 wrote of the Teifi — of the salmon, whose name he learnedly derived from the Latin *salire*, to leap; the beavers, which were then numerous in the river; and Cilgerran Castle, set upon a rock with a great cataract up which the salmon leapt and near which the beavers formed their dams. The Castle was Welsh, apparently built by the Lord Rhys whom Gerald knew; little of it is left but two drum-towers by the bridge. No medieval war destroyed it, but Parliament in 1645 "slighted" it for supporting Charles I. The remains of walls stand by the seven-arched bridge, where tall warehouses speak of Cardigan's former importance as a shipping centre. But the Teifi, one of the loveliest rivers in Wales, has like the fatal Nest betrayed the town. The silting of the river mouth has left Gwbert-on-Sea, by the entry, as not very much more than a pleasant bathing-place with beautiful beaches. Cenarth, where Gerald de Barri and his Bishop preached, has a light and leaping bridge of its own, and claims to use coracles for salmon fishing. The coracle is an ancient British round-boat excellent for hovering on the stream and turning suddenly in a way no other craft can, but is rarely seen now, except at Carmarthen. Like Aberporth, its not too distant neighbour, Cardigan has lost the outgoing importance of the days when it commanded the trade of the Irish Sea; but it remains a solid centre for the life of Wales at its most natively Welsh. Llangrannog, with its wooded and hidden hills, and Llanarth, with its ancient church and recollections of the march of Henry VII to victory, are readily reached from it.

CAREW, *Pembrokeshire.* Carew Castle, set almost exactly half way between Tenby and Pembroke, was near enough neighbour to Manorbier not only to be known to Gerald de Barri but also for him to make note of the outlaw spirit that was the great failing of the Welsh princes.

The Castle was founded, apparently, in the first wave of Norman invasion that, having subdued England, went on almost to complete the conquest of Wales twenty years later. At the death of the Conqueror himself, Brecon, Cardigan, Radnor, Pembroke, Glamorgan were held by Norman force, and the castles of Brecon, Maesyfed (Radnor), Cilgerran, Pembroke, Aberlleiniog stood as monuments to their sovereignty. Under the leadership of Gruffydd ap Cynan and Cadwgan ap Bleddyn, the tide was effectively turned. The invaders were driven out of Anglesey and the North, and Cheshire, Shropshire, and Herefordshire were overrun. In Pembrokeshire and Cardiganshire, the only Norman strongholds left standing were at Pembroke itself and a smaller one at Rhyd-y-gors. Ten years later, the Normans made a counter-attack and settled on the S. shores of Wales at Kidwelly, Loughor, and Swansea. Carew seems to belong to the earlier wave of entry; Manorbier to the second.

But Carew Castle came to its possessor, the Norman Gerald of Windsor, in 1095, by dowry to the woman he married, Nest, daughter of Rhys ap Tewdwr, Prince of South Wales (*see* Cardigan). When she was abducted by Owain, son of Cadwgan, Prince of Powys, the policy of stabilization that Cadwgan had initiated was ruined; Welsh and Norman fell again into conflict, and the family of Cadwgan dissolved into a bitter feud that reached even into Ireland. When Gerald chose to lecture the Welsh on the failings they must overcome if they were to keep their ancient land for themselves, he found no better text than in the story, fresh for him, of Nest and her reckless lover.

Carew Castle is as it was when re-adapted into the style of the Edwardian Conquest. It is chiefly associated with the Rhys ap Thomas whose welcome to Henry Tudor on his first landing sealed the fate of Richard III. At Carew he held the great tournament in celebration of the new dynasty in 1507, and the W. side, great hall, entrance porch, and stair were built by him. It was taken with some ease by Parliament in 1644, and lay quiet in the Second Civil War that ended in 1648.

The church at Carew, and its cross, are at least as important as the Castle. The church is at the turning of the road towards Carmarthen. It dates from what is, for this part of Wales, the recent date of 1400 and is of English style. The tower is even later, of about 1500; but it has the particular interest of the tombs of the family of Carew, keepers of the Castle and perhaps distinguished by kinship with the Kentish-born Thomas Carew who followed Lord Herbert of Cherbury on missions to France and, like him, wrote poems in the style of Donne. But there are even earlier traditions belonging to the place. Its name is properly pronounced Carey and is believed to be no other than the Welsh word "caerau" (forts), a term descriptive of the scattered camps, set up long before history began on the hills around it. The high cross speaks of times that history has forgotten, for it belongs to the age made deliberately dark by religious controversy, the sub-Roman period that did not end, for Wales, until Hywel Dda (the Good), grandson of Rhodri the Great, ally of Alfred of Wessex against the Dane, accepted the ways of the Roman Church and set his face against those who would have overthrown Alfred's successors. The cross, 14 ft high and carved with intricate ornament in the reef-knot fashion of the Celtic Church, is given a date slightly earlier than Hywel's, the 9th cent. It has a Latin epigraph: *Margiteut Recett Rex*. If the inscription could be read as commemorating Maredudd, King of Rheged, it would probably have to fall into the 10th cent., when such a Maredudd, grandson of Hywel, came to power in the South. Whoever he was, this king lives only in his name.

Between Manorbier and Carew runs the long, high Ridgeway, which gives splendid views of the sea and the dark outline of the Mynydd Preseli, known to the English as the Prescelly Hills.

Carew Castle

G. Douglas Bolton

CARMARTHEN, *Carmarthenshire.* Even when seen from the E., amid the clutter of garages, milk factories, and caravan parks, Carmarthen looks an interesting town. The site, on a bluff above the Towy, at the point where the tidal waters begin to fail, is a fine one. The new county offices and the old castle dominate the scene. The usual traffic problem has forced the authorities to remove the old bridge and build some ruthless roads along the river front to get cars in and around the town. Even more ruthless widening plans are on paper. For the moment, Carmarthen still manages to retain its character of an early 19th-cent. county town, anxious to move with the times.

The origins of Carmarthen are wrapped in the usual legends. One thing, however, is certain. This was the site of the Roman Moridunum, the furthest W. of the big Roman bases. There were undoubtedly Roman roads and camps beyond Carmarthen, though Moridunum was more important as a road junction and port. The site has now been built over, but one side of the Roman station probably followed Priory Street. The Avenue, East Parade, and Priory Field formed the rest of the square. The site was occupied from the 1st to the 4th cent. Nothing now remains above ground.

With the Dark Ages, the legends gather. Carmarthen became in Welsh Caerfyrddin (Merlin's City). The great enchanter, who plays a notable part in the Arthurian legends, was supposed to have been born near at hand. He uttered numerous prophecies concerning Carmarthen, including the famous one about the oak tree at the end of Priory Street:

When Merlin's oak shall tumble down,
Then shall fall Carmarthen town.

The stump of the tree is now embedded in concrete and held together with iron bands. The fall of Carmarthen is clearly imminent.

Under the early Welsh rulers of South Wales, Carmarthen retained its importance, and the "clas" (monastery) founded by St Teulyddog lay just outside the Roman walls. It received special mention and protection in the laws of Hywel Dda. With the coming of the Normans in the 11th cent., the "clas" was displaced. William Rufus built the first castle, and the Normans lost no time in setting up a priory. This was linked with Battle Abbey in Sussex and later became a house of Austin Canons. The settlement around the castle became known as New Carmarthen; the one around the priory and the old Roman station was Old Carmarthen. The priory was never large, but had a high reputation for hospitality and learning. Here the famous Black Book of Carmarthen (1105) was written. It is the oldest known manuscript in the Welsh language and contains a priceless collection of early poetry. It is now in the National Museum of Wales at Aberystwyth. The priory was dissolved in 1539, and not a trace of it remains.

There is more to be seen of Carmarthen Castle.

This stood on the high bluff overlooking the river. Although repeatedly captured by the Welsh, the Castle always returned into English hands. Carmarthen was captured by Owain Glyndwr in 1403, and again by his French allies in 1405. The Royalists held it during the Civil War and threw up earthworks, the Bulwarks, which are still visible to the W. of the town. After the capture of Carmarthen by the Parliamentarians, the Castle fell into ruin. The drum-towers of the gatehouse, the old motte or mound, and part of the curtain wall are all that remain. John Nash built a gaol on the site later on. This has now been replaced by the dominating County Hall designed by Sir Percy Thomas, with a high, steep-angled roof covered with West Wales slates.

Carmarthen has always been an important administrative centre. King John gave it a charter in 1201. Edward III made it the staple town for the marketing of wool in Wales. About 1451, Gruffydd ap Nicholas of Dinefwr, who was then Deputy Justice of South Wales, held one of the earliest recorded Eisteddfods in the town, when the bards assembled from all over the principality and, according to tradition, the twenty-four rules for poetic measures were promulgated. Henry VIII gave the Mayor permission to have a sword borne before him on ceremonial occasions, a right still zealously preserved.

During the 18th cent. Carmarthen must have been a lively place. Politics were conducted with the violence of Dickens's Eatanswill. The theatre was strongly supported by the county families, who had their town houses in Carmarthen. There are still many traces of Georgian influences to be seen in the buildings, especially in King Street, Quay Street, and the Parade. John Nash fled to Carmarthen to escape his debts, and he made it his centre for twelve years. Unfortunately, very little remains of his work in the town or county. Most of the buildings in Carmarthen centre are now mainly early Victorian, although they seem to retain a Georgian imprint.

The big event in the history of the 19th-cent. Carmarthen was the invasion of the town by the Rebecca Rioters in 1843. Carmarthen was a centre of road trusts, and the rioters protested against the high tolls charged at the too numerous gates. The Bible had stated that Rebecca's seed should possess the gates of them that hate her. "Rebecca and her Daughters", 400 strong, invaded the town. The protest turned into a riot, in which the gaol was attacked and the mob finally dispersed by dragoons. Later, Victorian Carmarthen became more respectable and an important centre of Welsh education and publishing. Carmarthen Grammar School was first founded on the proceeds of the old Franciscan priory, dissolved at the same time as the Austin house. It was refounded by the 1st Earl of Essex in 1576 as the Queen Elizabeth Grammar School. The boys wear on their caps the cipher and crown of the Queen.

At the top of Priory Street stands St Peter's Church. The tower and nave are 13th-cent., the S. aisle and porch 14th-cent. The S. aisle was

lengthened in the 16th cent. The porch has a moulded doorway, a vaulted roof, and a niche for a figure of the patron saint. The interior, with its elaborate box pew near the door, and stained glass, gives an impression of rich darkness. There are numerous memorials, including the tombs of Sir Rhys ap Thomas, the supporter of Henry VII, which was removed here after the Dissolution from the Grey Friars. The organ covers the burial-place of Walter Devereux, 1st Earl of Essex, who was born at Carmarthen Castle. There is an elaborate epitaph to Lady Vaughan. Sir Richard Steele, the essayist, is buried here. When the vault was reopened in 1876, it was noted that "the skull was in excellent condition, and had a peruke tied with a black bow". There is a brass tablet to his memory on the S. wall. Bishop Farrar is also commemorated.

Farrar was one of the few Welsh martyrs in the Marian persecution. He was burnt at the stake outside the Castle on the spot now occupied by the statue of General Nott (1782–1845). Nott was a distinguished soldier who won fame in the Afghan Wars. His father was the proprietor of the Fry Bush Hotel in Carmarthen. The little square in which the statue stands is named after the General. Near at hand in Quay Street is the County Museum, with an important collection of exhibits drawn from all parts of the shire, including rare books and MSS. The Guildhall stands in the centre of the town. It was built in 1770 and has the classical merits of the period. From the Guildhall the long, main street runs westwards, with its public houses, chapels, and shops, extremely busy on market days. It ends among the early 19th-cent. houses that front the tall column erected to General Thomas Picton, the Pembrokeshire-born soldier who died at Waterloo after a distinguished military career. Among other distinguished men associated with Carmarthen are Brinley Richards, the friend of Chopin, and composer of "God Bless the Prince of Wales", who was born in Hall Street in 1817, and Sir Lewis Morris, the Victorian poet and author of *The Epic of Hades*.

Carmarthen has numerous colleges. The Presbyterian College was founded in 1689 – the oldest institution of higher learning in Wales. Trinity Training College, of the Church in Wales, is in the W. of the town and has a notable complex of modern buildings.

The A40 road E. and W. of Carmarthen is apt to be crowded in summer. About 1 m. out of Carmarthen to the E. is Llangunnor. Sir Richard Steele's wife had an estate here; it is now a farmhouse. The 13th-cent. church stands on a hill with fine views over the Towy valley. Within are box pews and columns instead of arches supporting the aisles. Sir Lewis Morris and David Charles, the hymnologist, are buried here.

Newchurch, 3½ m. NW. of the town, is in pleasant pastoral country. The church dates from 1829. The whole country N. and NE. of Carmarthen is rather off the beaten track, and all the better for it.

CARNO, *Montgomeryshire.* Here the setting is more remarkable than the village. Its early history seems to have been lost. Yet its position must always have been important. Caersws, close by, was set where the tracks from the Dovey could reach the Severn valley; Carno stands on a ridge dividing E. from W. As you descend by the rail or road that leads from Carno towards Machynlleth, you pass from a Severn green, recalling the fields of the English Midlands, into the slate-ribbed hills that speak only of Wales. Carno appears to have taken its name from the Carno river, which probably means the "hard or stony" one; it winds to join the Severn at Caersws and at Carno is itself joined by the Gerniog. Southwards the Waun Garno, a moorland oddly called a meadow because of its broad stretches of whin and heather, forms part of the Trannon upland, which is marked everywhere with the roads and pack-ways of long ago. Not far from Carno is Bryn y Castell. This is not in fact the site of a castle but of an encampment, 1,032 ft up, that may mark the first choice of Carno as a place for settlement. N. of Carno a series of hills all bear the name of Allt, a word for a wooded height, which suggests how much afforested the area was when such a settlement was made. Not far beyond Carno to the W., the railway passes the small stop of Talerddig, and then begins to go down through what was in its day a triumph of bold design. The hill here presented one of the major obstacles to communications; the cutting cleaves the buckled slate that shaped the whole Plynlimon region. Memory of the difficulties in making the line persisted up to the First World War, when a local councillor, considering air-raid precautions, observed that there was no need for them. Zeppelins would never get over Talerddig Top to the Dovey valley – even the Cambrian Railway could only just manage it.

CARREG CENNEN CASTLE, *Carmarthenshire.* About 4½ m. SE. from Llandeilo is one of the most striking castles in Wales. There is neither town nor village crouched before it, where it stands on a height of nearly 900 ft. From one side it is approached by a long and slowly rising mount; on the other it is moated by a sheer drop down to the narrow valley of the Cennen river, the precipice itself falling 300 ft below the walls that not only continue the perpendicular face of the bluff but have their inner passages cut within it. The upthrust of this craggy height is unexpected among the long and rolling hills that run parallel with the Towy valley and rise no higher than 1,360 ft with the knolled head of Trichrug. A little to the W., and almost due S. of Llandeilo, is a standing stone to show that the Cennen valley was an important passageway long before the present Castle of Carreg Cennen was built; on the other side of the river, mounds and circles further prove the point.

No fortress in Wales has a more impressive situation. It is Norman, perhaps first planted by a Marcher Lord. It was held in the days of Henry II

Plate 7 Pistyll Rhaeadr (see p. 222) W. A. Poucher

by the Lord Rhys of the time, and then owned by Hugh le Despenser, favourite of Edward II; its final form belongs to the time of Richard II.

Impregnable from the southern side because of the unscalable cliff, it could be reduced from the other side either by sudden assault or by a long siege. Owain Glyndwr was unable to carry out either operation successfully, and the Castle remains as an ideal example of medieval architecture. It is now in the careful hands of the Ministry of Public Building and Works. The climb, from the farm at the foot of the rock to the entrance works, is steep. The ramped entrance was heavily defended, and clearly an enemy would have an impossible task, before the days of gunpowder, in penetrating to the inner ward. This is guarded by a fine gatehouse and strong corner towers. The most interesting feature of the place is the 150-ft passage that leads steeply down, from the S. side fronting the cliff itself, to a cistern cut deep into the rock. Care is needed to follow this passage in the darkness. But the descent to the well-spring, cold and whispering in the depth of the rock, is lit by arched openings cut successively in the cliff-face through which breathtaking views of the Black Mountain ranges and the tree-grown run of the river appear.

A legend, Arthurian in style but belonging to a historical date, is directly concerned with Carreg Cennen. Along the banks of the river is a cavern called the Ogof Dinas (Castle Cave). And in it a local farmer, many years ago, came upon the cloaked and seated figure of an immortal. It was the sleeping body of Owain Llawgoch, a hero of Wales mentioned in Froissart's *Chronicles*; he was waiting like Arthur to be summoned in the time of danger to his native land.

This Owain is in fact the man whom the French in the 14th cent. called Ywain de Galles (Owain of Wales). While the Black Prince was levying Welsh archers and javelin-men for service in the Hundred Years War, Owain came to the King of France claiming to be the true heir of Llywelyn the Last and the rightful King of Wales. The French welcomed and recognized him, and many times had proof of his mastery in the art of war. A naval expedition was fitted out to support his claim; Guernsey was taken, and an invasion planned of Wales itself. England was greatly alarmed; no Welshman, ordered Edward III, should have charge of any castle or strong-point in Wales, for even in France the number of Welsh deserters to Owain from the English levies was remarkable. But, as Froissart relates, Owain had an esquire, an English prisoner he had saved after one of his victories, called John Lamb. And one day, as Lamb performed his squire-duty of cutting his master's hair, he took the blade and thrust it into Owain's throat, for he was still in the pay of England. No better news had ever been brought to King Edward; but in Wales the mourning was great. Historians can find in this an explanation for the emergence, a generation later, of that Owain Glyndwr who also had the French for allies and found his legendary resting-place in a cavern in the hills.

The quaintly named hamlet of Trapp lies near the narrow road that leads up to the Castle rock. On the mountain beyond, the Afon Llwchwr (Loughor) flows from a fine limestone cavern, called Llygad Llwchwr (Eye of the Llwchwr). As in the district around Craig-y-Nos further to the E., the limestone rock that marks the geological edge of the coalfield could yield some surprises when fully explored by pot-holers.

Carreg Cennen Castle, looking across the Cennen valley

Barnaby/Mustograph

CASGOB, *Radnorshire,* is a small village lying between Knighton and Presteigne. It is mainly significant for its church, though the surrounding country is wild and attractive in its unspoilt beauty. From its general appearance, Casgob church suggests that it is one of the primitive oratory-like structures gradually extended to meet the demands of a growing congregation and variations in faith. It has acquired both a chancel and a tower, half-timbered and squarely roofed, and probably owes its present shape to the 13th cent. Its rood-screen is of the Perpendicular style, the kind introduced into Wales from England after the Edwardian Wars, and may date as late as 1500.

But it has carefully preserved evidence of a different sort of faith, though the date of the Abracadabra Charm, unearthed during altera-tions earlier this century, is (relatively) as recent as 1700. It runs: "In the name of the Father, Son and of the Holy Ghost. Amen X X X and in the name of the Lord Jesus Christ who will deliver Elizabeth Loyd from all witchcraft and from all evil sprites by the same power as he did cause the blind to see the lame to walke the dum to talke. Pater pater pater noster noster noster ave ave ave Maria in secula seculorum X On X Adonay X Tetragrammaton X Amen and in the name of the Holy Trinnity and of Hubert . . . Grant that this holy charm Abracadabra may cure thy survent Elizabeth Loyd from all evil sprites and all ther desises. Amen X X X by Jah Jah Jah".

Experts will find this a medley in which pagan beliefs in evil spirits are blent with several stages of Christian doctrine, from that of the Celtic Church through Catholicism to the expressions familiar in Elizabeth's day. "On" and "Adonay" are found in the Black Book of Carmarthen. But the Tetragrammaton belongs to the Faust of Marlowe and the researches of Dr John Dee, the 17th-cent. Welsh wizard.

CEMAES, *Montgomeryshire,* must not be confused with the Cemaes Road that stands about the railway station at the junction between the Mallwyd and the Newtown roads and near the bridge over the Twymyn river.

Kemis is what old maps call it, and for the coaches it was the next staging-post when you had taken the fork from the Dinas Mawddwy route after Mathafarn. The maps show its church, which remains remarkable to this day, sheltered with yews and ruminating on the centu-ries, a building typical of the still undisturbed Welsh way of life. The village is a centre for the salmon fishing of the Dovey. Its inn is a most attractive survival; it was visited by George Borrow. Here, at the bar, he alarmed the locals by rather threateningly making notes.

The name is curious; in Welsh "cemaes" means games, though the derivation may be from a combination of words meaning ridge-field. The dialect of the district, which is heavily influenced by 17th-cent. English importations, perhaps through the influence of Cromwellian garrisons, prefers "cammocs" for games; the word has been traced to an origin in "gambols", and has a parallel in the local English of Shrop-shire.

Cemaes has recently tended to replace Machyn-lleth in some degree as a centre for grading and stock-sales.

From the inn, and past the rectory, a path can be taken that at first gradually and then steeply rises to the Mynydd y Cemaes, whose highest point, Moel Eiddaw (1,489 ft), looks over its shoulder at Comins Coch, with its inn, and the Bwlch of the Ffridd Fawr, a spot for which the ecstatic language of early 19th-cent. travellers for once is justified. The Twymyn river streams through a narrow gorge, over which the road stands unperceived. The boulders lying in the water seem, in some distant day, to have provided the "meini llwyd" at Darowen and elsewhere along this area. Woodlands of grey and contem-plative oak stand guard there; the buzzard and, more rarely, the heron are known. But new ways have been opened up on the northern side of the river, and new kinds of tree are advancing upon it.

The Mynydd y Cemaes is a long plateau from which a unique view can be had of the long fall of the Dovey towards its mouth; when floods fill the valley from side to side, as they often do in the season of rain and adverse wind, another view, also unique, extends from here. Only the railway line manages to keep its head above water, which is why the motor roads, like the coaching ways before them, climb the hill-sides well above the valley-levels. Trees, writhing their arms like drowning men, are swept rapidly along the flood, and debris of many sorts floats with them. Sometimes it is not merely some unfortunate farm animal, but a man, a woman, or a child. One then remembers the old saying that the Dovey must have one human life every year. This is perhaps a half-lost recollection, from ancient times, of placating such a stream with a human sacrifice. The Carnedd Cerrig (Cairn of Stone) that tops the Hill of Cemaes may have belonged to such a period, but more certainly stands in its place as part of the direction-finding complex necessary here.

The hill is an excellent spot for studying the bird-life of the region – crow and hawk and curlew.

CEMAES HEAD, *Pembrokeshire.* This bold headland guards the S. side of the Teifi estuary, about 4 m. NW. of Cardigan town. The much-frequented Poppit Sands lie at the estuary mouth. Behind them the land slopes steeply up to the high peninsula formed by the head. A maze of lanes makes it difficult to find your way without an Ordnance Survey map, but good walkers – this is strictly a walker's coastline – will find it worthwhile to explore the splendid cliffs that girdle the whole peninsula. The summit is over 600 ft. The cliffs are thrown into remarkable folds, which are also remarkably crumbling in places and definitely not for careless climbing.

At Pwllygranant a stream tumbles straight into the sea. The cliffs and caves continue for 3 m. S. to Ceibwr. Beyond Ceibwr is an equally interesting stretch of cliffs around Trwyn y Bwa into Newport Bay. Pwll y wrach (The Witch's Cauldron) is an enclosed pool carved out of the cliffs and connected by a short tunnel to the sea. The Pembrokeshire Path, for walkers, follows the whole of this coastline. It is a favourite breeding-ground for the grey Atlantic seal. The country is all within the boundary of the Pembrokeshire National Park.

CERRIGYDRUDION, *Denbighshire.* About 10 m. from Corwen on the road to Betws-y-coed and Llanrwst, the village of Cerrigydrudion lies by-passed by the main highway. Although as small in his day as it is now, the village was mentioned by Daniel Paterson among the places of interest to be observed by the stage-coach traveller in the early years of the 19th cent. Within ½ m. of it, says he, is the famous Citadel of the Druids, whither Caractacus retired after his defeat at Caer Caradoc. He refers to the Caer Caradoc shown on Ordnance Survey maps to the SE. of Cerrigydrudion on a spur of hill 1,367 ft high, but known otherwise as Pen-y-gaer. This should not be confused with the Caer Caradoc that lies near Cardington in Shropshire, just over the Welsh border, above the Roman road and between Wenlock Edge and the Long Mynd. This latter Fort of Caradoc is usually accepted as the place where the champion of British resistance to the final advance of the Romans suffered his defeat. Tacitus, the Roman historian, who was no friend of imperialism for its own sake, records how in A.D. 50, as we know the year, the command of the invading forces was given to the brilliant Ostorius Scapula. Caratacos (as the British ruler appears to have been actually named), son of a kingly race, was the only native prince to defend the country to the last. He was pursued to the Welsh border and, either near Cardington or on the edge of Radnor Forest, he chose a hill-top to make his stand. After considerable difficulty, the Romans stormed the hill, and Caratacos was taken to Rome in chains, but still with so defiant a bearing that Rome felt conquered by his spirit. The ancient camp near Cardington may antedate Caratacos by generations, though as a defensive site it would have offered him a position of strength. The Caer Caradoc near Cerrigydrudion is said to have been the place where he fled to seek refuge with the local rulers. But it was from here that Cartismandua, Queen of this part of Wales, betrayed him to the pursuing Roman power. It is a hill-fort of the customary type, ditched and mounded and certainly marking the site of a Celtic encampment. It extends across 6 acres and more. The view from it is over the gentler parts of Denbighshire where Foel Goch (2,004 ft) stretches its broad back towards Llyn Tegid (Bala Lake).

The village has a pleasant inn, an old church, and almshouses dated 1717. The name Cerrig-

ydrudion did not have, as Paterson thought, any connection with Druids. "Drudion" can mean heroes; and the tale of Caratacos inclines one to think that so it must be meant. But "drudion" can also mean starlings; and the charm and peace of the place and the haunt of bird-song above the moors makes that interpretation equally apt.

CHEPSTOW, *Monmouthshire,* perched on its steep hill-side, with its magnificent castle set above the winding Wye, is a glorious point of entry into Wales. Or should one simply say into Monmouthshire? There is a certain amount of border feeling in this delectable part of the country. Before the construction of the great Severn Bridge near by, most motorists entered South Wales through Chepstow, and the steep, winding, narrow streets of the town presented them with a traffic problem that only a bridge could solve. Chepstow, however, rises triumphantly over every problem, even the one of building on its site. The town is set upon the steep western slopes above the River Wye. Immediately to the N., high cliffs begin, which are the glory of this lower reach of the river. Southwards, towards the sea, the marshy banks announce the proximity of the Severn estuary. Chepstow had no option but to climb the hill. The main street twists upwards from the bridge across the Wye, to reach the old town gate, and in between, as the 18th-cent. local poet, the Rev. Edward Davies, proudly declared:

Strange to tell, there cannot here be found
One single inch of horizontal ground.

The name Chepstow is Anglo-Saxon, from *cēap* (market) and *stōw* (place, town). The Welsh know it as Cas Gwent. The Romans probably forded the river here on their way to Isca Silurum, the modern Caerleon. There are traces of the final sections of Offa's Dyke on the English side of the Wye, N. of the town. The Normans recognized the importance of the crossing, and William FitzOsbern, who received the lordship of Hereford from the Conqueror, built the first castle on the site of the present imposing structure. Chepstow was known as Striguil in Norman days, and the Lord of Striguil enjoyed the privileges of the semi-independent Lords Marchers, who guarded the borderland against the Welsh. In the 15th cent. the Earls of Pembroke added Chepstow to their great estates in Wales. The town developed rapidly in the 14th and 15th cents. and received a charter of incorporation in 1524, although this was suspended in the reign of Charles II through a dispute with the all-powerful Duke of Beaufort. The Urban District Council took over local administration in 1894.

The road bridge over the Wye, now the main entrance to the town, is one of the earliest iron bridges in Britain. It was built by John Rennie in 1816 and underwent extensive repairs in 1968. Chepstow Castle lies to the right of the bridge and is one of the show-pieces of the place. It stands on a spur sloping down from the hill to

Chepstow, with its Castle and the iron bridge across the Wye

the westward. The Wye and its cliff made a magnificent defence on the river side, while a deep ditch separated it from the town wall. The site is mentioned in the Domesday Book, and after William FitzOsbern's day the Castle was constantly increased and strengthened, especially by the De Clares in the 12th cent., and the Marshalls and Bigods into whose hands it then passed. Under the Earl of Pembroke it became one of the great country houses. The most stirring days of its history occurred during the Civil War. It was held for the King and surrendered in 1645. In the Second Civil War it was surprised by Sir Nicholas Kemeys, who held out in a memorable siege until the Roundheads, under Col. Ewer, broke in and killed Sir Nicholas and routed the garrison. After the Restoration, the Castle was handed back to Lord Herbert. Jeremy Taylor, the Royalist bishop, was a prisoner here. But the most famous prisoner in Chepstow was Henry Marten, the regicide, who spent twenty years incarcerated in the Castle's drum-tower, which now bears his name. Later the Castle fell into decay. It has been carefully restored and is open to the public.

The entrance is through the gatehouse overlooking the town green alongside the Wye. The Marten Tower is the conspicuous round tower you see to your left before you enter. The Castle has four courtyards. The first and largest contains the state apartments, kitchens, and domestic quarters. From the cellar below the complex of buildings, the garrison was able to maintain communication with the river, a useful channel of supply during siege. The top storey of the Marten Tower has a small chapel with interesting carvings. Beyond the second court lies the Great Tower, which forms the keep of Chepstow. This is an impressive ruin with thick walls on the river side, where it is separated from the cliff by a narrow pathway. Beyond is a further court, with a gatehouse built in the late 13th cent. This defended the western approach to the Castle.

The town walls, known as the Port Walls, began near the top of the Castle ditch, and ran from the

Castle in a circuit that brought them down to the riverside about ¾ m. below the bridge. The river formed an adequate defence to the E. The total length of the walls was just under 1 m., and the defences are still visible for most of the way. A particularly well-preserved stretch starts near the Castle. The town gate stands at the top of High Street and was rebuilt in 1524 by the Earl of Worcester. The battlements and windows are modern. The room over the archway houses the small museum of the Chepstow Society. The bell above the arch was formerly the watch bell of H.M.S. *Chepstow*.

Bridge Street leads up from the Wye Bridge, and is lined with early 19th-cent. bow-windowed houses. They have surprisingly survived the shaking of the traffic. At the turn at the top of Bridge Street are the Powys almshouses, endowed in 1716. In nearby Upper Church Street are the gabled Montague almshouses, dating from 1613. The parish church, at the top of Church Street, which runs parallel to Bridge Street, has been extensively restored and in parts rebuilt. It is dedicated to St Mary and was originally the church of a Benedictine priory. The tower was rebuilt in 1706; after the alterations of 1841, only the nave and W. door remained of the rest of the original structure. The nave is Norman, and the W. door is finely decorated with five concentric arches resting on receding columns. The church has preserved some interesting monuments in spite of the drastic restorations. The font is 15th-cent. The canopied tomb of the 2nd Earl of Worcester and his wife Elizabeth is on the N. side of the nave. On the S. side of the chancel is the characteristically Jacobean monument of Mrs Clayton, a lady who commemorated her two husbands in the same memorial. On the floor just inside the W. door is the gravestone of Henry Marten, inscribed with a verse composed by himself, including the ironic last words of farewell from the old regicide:

My time was spent in serving you and you,
And death's my pay, it seems,
    and welcome too.

In the centre of the town lies Beaufort Square, laid out, like everything in Chepstow, on a slope. The medieval stocks from Portskewett were set up in 1947. Nearby is a gun from a captured German submarine presented as a memorial to Chepstow's V.C., William Charles William, the sailor killed at Gallipoli.

Chepstow is now a town of bridges. The new Severn Bridge is only a few miles away, but the railway bridge over the Wye represents a fine piece of railway history. It was originally built by Brunel, with a main span of 300 ft. The weight of the span was carried by two enormous tubes, a daring idea at the time. The tubes were removed when the bridge was reconstructed in 1962, but they will be remembered by engineers for the ingenious way in which Brunel harnessed the exceptionally high tides of the Wye to lift the tubes into place. It was Brunel's need to solve the difficult problem of bridging the Wye that led to the establishing of the "Shipyard", now the Fairfield constructional engineering works. Fairfield's continued their long tradition of building camions, dock gates, and bridges, when they assembled and launched the deck sections of the Severn Bridge. These floated out to the site in a manner of which Brunel would surely have approved.

Lower down the river from Fairfield's are the Bulwarks, the ramparts of a fine Iron Age fort, although the nearby housing estate detracts a little from its romantic effect.

Some 2 m. SW. of the town is the little village of Mounton. Between 1727 and 1876 this was a busy place, full of small paper- and corn-mills. Some have delightfully unindustrial names – Lark Mill, Lady Mill, Linnet Mill. Mounton was proud to claim that it made the paper for the Bank of England notes. Now the little village is a peaceful beauty-spot, with the gardens of Mounton House perched on the edge of a cliff.

To the N. of the town, on the road to Tintern, is the Chepstow racecourse, laid out on one of the finest sites in the country, Piercefield Park. Proud stone lions still guard the entrance gate. Racing men will have a fellow feeling for Valentine Morris, the 18th-cent. grandee, who laid out the park in its present splendour. He was over-generous in his hospitality, and had to leave for the West Indies to restore his fallen fortunes. The tradesmen of Chepstow rang a muffled peal as he drove through the town for the last time.

The park is surrounded by a long stone wall. Once past it, you enter the splendour of the lower valley of the Wye.

CHIRK, *Denbighshire*. The name of this town has various interpretations; the favourite is that it simply Anglicized the name of the River Ceiriog on which the town grew up. This river is a tributary of the Dee, but at Chirk the aqueduct carrying the Shropshire Union Canal with a ten-arch span of 750 ft is perhaps more remarkable, though it is not so much so as the one of eighteen arches built by Telford for a similar purpose at the beginning of the 18th cent. at Pontycysylltau,

4 m. below Llangollen. The church is worth seeing, since its 15th-cent. roof and tower hold monuments to the Myddelton family, of great note here in the 16th and 17th cents., and to the Trevors of Bryn-kinallt, one of whose daughters was the mother of that Duke of Wellington who, in the words of the song, "thrashed Bonapart".

Chirk and its castle can be reached in several ways; the most attractive is to walk from Llangollen by the 4-m. route past Plas Newydd, for this takes you on a green track smoothly winding up the hills to where a stone offers itself as a font for blessing. Chirk Castle has its Welsh name, Castell y Waun (Meadow Castle), apt enough for its siting. It was built by one of the Mortimer Marcher Lords, Roger, in the reign of Edward I. Roger is said to have been granted the lands of Chirk as a reward for his part in bringing about the downfall of the Llywelyn who was last of the native Princes of Wales. The present extent of the Castle is much greater than the 13th cent. would have foreseen. But as a frontier fortress it needed to have great strength. Rectangular in plan, it has a round tower at each corner; on entering, you have the impression of a great quadrangle in which the companies of its defenders could be drawn up in force, and from which open various storerooms, stables, and other places.

In these storerooms many relics of the Castle's curiously alternating fortunes are preserved. The front is 250 ft long, the principal gateway strong and imposing; the internal quadrangle measures 160 by 100 ft. The battlements are laid so that at least two persons could walk abreast when watching the defences.

Most of the relics housed around the square date from the Civil War. The fortress was bought in 1595 by Sir Thomas Myddelton, who was Lord Mayor of London in 1613. His son, also Thomas, found his castle seized by the Royalist forces and attempted to recover it by arms. He failed. After the end of the Civil War, he managed to acquire it again, but decided to change his allegiance. He took up the cause of Charles II in 1659, and was himself besieged by General Lambert. Again he failed. The Cromwellian artillery played a great part in reducing the defence, and breached many of the walls. For our eyes the examples of the Puritan steeple-crowned hat have an unusual interest. The gunners laid their weapons, applied the match, and handled the cannon-balls still in their sombre broadcloth and white neck-bands. The only concession they made to war was to line the steeple-hat with iron. No more improbable – or inefficient – helmet could surely have been devised. But the gunner felt himself to be a journeyman doing a trade; the dash of Rupert's cavaliers could be left to the highly armoured and proficient horsemen of Oliver.

In the Castle proper, with its chambers and dining-rooms, is a great deal of architectural and historic interest. One immense room, its floor of long single beams, is so wide that it yields rhythmically beneath your feet. Pictures are many; they include the piece by an allegedly

The gates of Chirk Castle (see *Bersham*)

foreign artist whose paintings of the falls at Rhayader includes ships sailing over dry land. The legend is that he was invited to include the sheep on the hills, but misunderstood the request; either he heard, or his Welsh patron actually used, "ships" for "sheep". Certainly local people are still inclined to fumble with the English *sh*. But the effect is to speak of the "seeps" on the hills; and the presence of shipping in the coats of arms belonging to the area may account for the ships in the picture. The portraits from Stuart times include those of Charles I, Charles II, his illegitimate son the Duke of Monmouth, and Dutch William and his wife Mary. But, just as the windows of the Castle show that they were changed to their present form in the days of Elizabeth Tudor, so does one portrait in particular recall them. This is shown as representing Katheryn of Berain; and a word or two about her opens certain forgotten pages of history.

The House of Tudor was formed by Henry, Earl of Richmond, a man very conscious of his Welsh heritage. The family he sprang from was identified with Anglesey. His connection with the ruling dynasty of England restrained him from risking his chances in the War of the Roses, and he followed the example of several Welsh leaders before him and went to live in the anciently related country of Brittany. He loved a Breton lady, and as a result fathered one Roland called Velville. When Henry grasped the crown of Britain at Bosworth, he naturally took steps to secure the legitimate succession to the throne, and he provided himself with an heir first in his elder son Arthur, Prince of Wales, who died too soon, and then in his second son, Henry, later called the Eighth. But he did not forget his earlier-born offspring, and he made Roland Constable of Beaumaris Castle, with other lands in Anglesey. Roland in turn had a daughter by his Welsh wife, and this was the mother of Katheryn of Berain. Katheryn's father, from whom she inherited Berain, was another Tudor. And this may well have disturbed Elizabeth I, who at last succeeded in holding her father's crown against all competition. Perhaps even Henry

VIII may have doubted the strength of the claim to blood royal, since he tried to create the precedent of leaving the throne by appointment in his will. Constitutional practice in England has always insisted that the kingship goes only by choice of Parliament. But Elizabeth clearly preferred to take no chances. The remedy was found, not, as in other cases, by use of the axe, but by arranged marriage. Katheryn is famed for the number of her descendants; but they all came from gentlemen of undoubted loyalty to Elizabeth. The first marriage was to Sir John Salusbury, son of the Chamberlain of North Wales; it took place when Katheryn was twenty-two but her groom still under age. The second, ten years later, was to Richard Clough, Knight of the Holy Sepulchre; in a much later century one descendant was the poet Arthur Hugh Clough. The third was to Maurice Wynn of Gwydir, again representative of a famous family; this was about 1573. The fourth, to Edward Thelwall, took place about 1583. Rumour, elaborating on this record, spoke of Katheryn as an irrepressible lover with notable dexterity in disposing of rejected suitors. But her surprisingly rapid series of marriages seems to have been imposed on her by the court. Her affairs were warily overseen; she underwent some peril by her nearness to Leicester's estates in Wales, and again when one of her youthful descendants showed too intimate an interest in Babington and his pro-Catholic conspiracy. She died at an uncertain date, but was buried next to her first young husband at Llanefydd in 1591. Among her numerous descendants was Mrs Thrale, the blue-stocking and close friend of Dr Samuel Johnson.

CILGERRAN, *Pembrokeshire.* This village on the course of the Teifi, and almost exactly on the border between Pembroke and Cardigan, was once important enough to be a borough. Now it is not very much more than a hamlet, but it is set in a spot of great natural beauty, and over it stands one of the most impressive castle remains that Wales can show. It has something of the timeless majesty of Carreg Cennen; the

Jane J. Miller

Cilgerran Castle, above the River Teifi

to change in character, and the loneliness and remoteness of this country will probably disappear. In return the authorities have promised to develop all the popular amenities that go with modern water schemes. At present the road out of Llandovery to Cilycwm crosses the Towy, then follows the river deep into the hills. Near Dolau Hirion is the graceful single-arched bridge built in the 18th cent. by the self-taught genius William Edwards, architect of the famous and similar bridge at Pontypridd. Cilycwm, in its circle of hills, has an important place in the history of Welsh Methodism. Soar can claim to be one of its first meeting-houses. Cilycwm church is also notable. It is mainly 15th-cent. with family box pews and some frescoes on the wall of the S. aisle, including one of a skeleton holding a spear, which again may date from the 15th cent. The yew trees in the churchyard are massive and noble. The memorial tablets commemorate, among others, David Powell Price, who died while commanding the combined French and English naval squadrons before Petropaulovski in 1851.

From Cilycwm, the valley continues up to Rhandirmwyn, where it narrows. The road on the E. bank now enters a part (the finest) of the upper Towy valley that will be profoundly changed with the building of the new dam. At Ystradffin is the small chapel dedicated to St Peulin or Paulinus. It stands in isolation among the hills; it was rebuilt by the Earl of Cawdor in the 1820s. W. of it rises the steep, craggy, wooded hill that hides Twm Shon Catti's cave.

Twm Shon Catti's story belongs also to Tregaron. He was a real person whose name was actually Thomas Jones (about 1530–1609). The sober facts recorded about him show him to have been born near Tregaron and married to his second wife in 1607. She came originally from Ystradffin. He was a man of substance, a bard, and an authority on heraldry. But he must also have been a bit of an adventurer, for the stories clustered thick and fast around the "Wild Wag of Wales". They passed into popular acclaim when Thomas Llewelyn Pritchard published *The Adventures and Vagaries of Twm Shon Catti* in 1828. The book was a best-seller, although poor Pritchard had no luck; he died in poverty in a fire in his lodgings at Swansea. In the book Twm appears as a sort of Welsh Robin Hood, a master of trickery and adventure. Pritchard was not above fathering on to Twm a whole host of stories told about similar European characters. Twm Shon Catti's cave, which he probably never used, is narrow and difficult to find among the clutter of rocks, but the situation is magnificent.

The good road ends at Ystradffin farmhouse. A formidably rough track, which cars usually find very difficult, follows up the Towy, through the great new plantations of the Forestry Commission, to the old farm of Nantyrhwch, where the track joins the better road that crosses this wilderness from Abergwesyn to Tregaron. The

village of cottages and small shops represents a timeless quality of men and women who live and work beside a flowing river and under hanging woods. The Castle of Cilgerran stands out of time altogether. It was first made by the Clares from Normandy, who took possession of Dyfed and put their fortress to watch the Welsh of Ceredigion. The quarries not far from the village were probably taken into service for the operation. The Castle, with its feet on the edge of the sharp descent to the river, is now a survival from the 13th cent. It had fallen and been raised again many times. Llywelyn the Great, fresh from the capture of Shrewsbury and his part in the dictation of Magna Carta to the English King John, set the seal on his overlordship of all the rulers of Wales by capturing the castles of Llanstephan, Carmarthen, and Aberystwyth; he took Cilgerran and marched from there to subdue the whole of Pembrokeshire. By this victory at Cilgerran he was able to summon a Council of all Wales to Aberystwyth, where as Prince of the North he took allegiance from the sons of the Rhys of the South.

Only two great round towers and parts of a gatehouse now stand; and these are of a time fifty years after Llywelyn the Great. Turner found inspiration in painting it. In the churchyard the 6th cent. left the stone memorial inscribed in Latin and Ogham: "Trenegussi son of Macutreni lies here".

CILYCWM, *Carmarthenshire*, $3\frac{1}{2}$ m. N. of Llandovery, is the gateway to one of the loveliest and most romantic regions of South Wales; until recently it could also be called the most unspoilt. The decision has now been taken to build a new reservoir, Lake Brianne, at the headwaters of the Towy. The whole area is bound

Towy itself rises in a lonely bog some miles beyond the last sheep-farm on the river, Nant-ystalwyn.

Three tributaries of the river cut their way down to join it near Ystraddfin – the Camddwr, the Doethie, and the Pysgotwr. All their valleys are wild and craggy, leading out on to the mountain-side. Somewhere in this area, in sites that are jealously guarded by volunteer wardens, and whose exact locations had best be left vague, the kite has its last stronghold in Britain.

It is profoundly to be hoped that the unique character of this region will in some degree remain after the building of the dam.

CLYDACH, *Glamorgan.* This is an industrial village 4 m. NE. of Swansea in the Tawe valley, dominated by the Mond nickel refinery. The statue of Dr Ludwig Mond, the German chemical genius who invented the process on which the works were founded, stands at the gates. He gazes out over the main road from under a flat-brimmed hat of memorable proportions. Immediately S. of Clydach, the Tawe valley is blocked by the remains of a low moraine, left behind by the glaciers when retreating northwards to the heights of the distant Carmarthen Van. The sharp prow of Mynydd Drumau (893 ft) stands out to the E. behind Glais. The Tawe valley here is industrial, with scattered hamlets, but the hills lend it a saving grace in spite of railways, power-lines, and glimpses of oil-refineries. At Clydach a narrow and surprisingly unspoilt valley cuts back into the moors to the W. The road leads out past Craigcefnparc to the summit of Mynydd y Gwair (1,099 ft), a fine viewpoint over the whole hill country of the West Wales coalfield. Industry is lost in the cracks of the hidden valleys. The hills behind Craigcefnparc acquired a mysterious local reputation between the wars. Here Grindell Mathews, the inventor, had a lonely laboratory in which he was credited with discovering an all-powerful death ray. The stories of the Laboratory in the Mists lost nothing in the telling. Fortunately, or unfortunately, Craigcefnparc failed to enter history as the birthplace of Britain's secret weapon.

CLYNNOG FAWR, *Caernarfonshire,* is a most attractive, whitewashed village of some size, growing still because of its discovery by tourists. Its most impressive feature is the church, which stands on the site of a much older foundation dating from A.D. 606. This example of early Christian activity in the area was replaced by a collegiate building in the time either of Edward IV of England or the Tudor Henry VII. It lost its collegiate character when the son of the latter, Henry VIII, dissolved all monastic foundations. It is probably one of the earliest examples of the Late Perpendicular style in this part of Wales. Its rood-screen and the carvings under its mise-rere seats are excellent of their kind.

The church is dedicated to St Beuno, a saint of much popular appeal, and its character as a place forming part of the everyday life of the community is shown by two things. The first is the pair of wooden tongs that here, as so often in old Welsh churches, were used not to remove dogs from attendance with their masters at divine service, but to prevent their breaking into fights. The second is the Chest of Beuno, an ancient oaken strong-box credited with almost miraculous power, since to break the Chest of Beuno was accepted locally as equivalent to achieving the impossible. The saint was said to set his mark, the Nod Beuno, on the ears of certain calves and lambs born in the parish; and, when it so appeared, the new-born creature was redeemed by the owners on Trinity Sunday in the churchyard. The fees paid were secured in the Chest.

Beuno is said to have come to Clynnog in A.D. 635, and to have founded many oratories in Gwynedd. But Clynnog was his principal field, and his remains were laid in a place for pilgrimage, his own original cell, now a chapel of the existing structure on the S. side of the church and connected with it by a shadowy cloister. His memory is further maintained by a rock standing out to sea and called the Gored (Weir) of Beuno, for it seems he blessed the work of fishermen; and also by his Well, a short way to the W. of the road towards Pwllheli and $\frac{1}{4}$ m. S. of the church, from which villagers can still obtain the benefits of the holy water that cured their ancestors of all evils. A cromlech (to use the convenient term for the stone ribs of a vanished tumulus-grave) stands close beside it.

CLYRO, *Radnorshire,* lies under its own hill, a little more than 1,000 ft high, where the Wye at last breaks out of the Ellennith (or Moruge, as the Normans of Gerald de Barri's day called it), the moor and peat of Central Wales, into the green breadth of the borderlands. It is a very short way from Hay-on-Wye, and it may have been ancestral to that town. For the Romans – striking into the western hills with an eye to the riches they held in lead, copper, silver, and gold – set a station at Clyro between the water-valley and the forests: a station that probably looked along the Roman road eastwards to Brinsop, now in Herefordshire, where the church stands, like that at Caerhun, within the squared earth-embankments of another of their stations, watching the ways from Magnis (Kenchester) to Gobannium (Abergavenny) and Isca (Caerleon).

If you come to it from Kington, you will pass Rhydspence after Brilley, a place on the English side of the border and giving its inn the name of the Last House in England. Its presence in the area is unlikely to be from earlier than Tudor times, though it claims patronage by the Marcher Lords and their princely Welsh rivals.

Clyro itself is a pleasing place some distance from the Clyro Castle built by direction of the Norman William de Braose, but still near to the first fort thrown up by the Romans. The Norman Castle, now ruined, had a successor in the time of Queen Elizabeth Tudor, a mansion unluckily destroyed by fire and replaced by a modern

The River Wye near Clyro

reconstruction, with the original battlemented gateway now serving as entrance to a farm. Further beyond Llowes, a neighbouring village, which has in its churchyard a magnificent Celtic cross dating from about A.D. 600, and close to Glasbury, stands Maes-yr-Onnen (Ash Field), one of the oldest Nonconformist meeting-houses in Wales, founded in 1696; it still has furnishings of the 17th cent.

A more modern connection is that in Clyro Francis Kilvert held a curacy for seven years. His diary opens with the last two of these years, 1870–2, and has many charming anecdotes of the people and sketches of the wind and weather in this hilly district, which seem at a distance of 700 years to echo what Gerald de Barri, the Welshman who served a Norman bishop, felt about other such places.

COETY, *Glamorgan*. This village, 2 m. NE. of Brigend, is worth a visit for its castle and church. Coety Castle is in the charge of the Ministry of Public Building and Works, although the Pencoed Rural District Council has taken over the children's playground on the little green before the ruins. Here the Council has put up a series of gaily painted swings as a contrast to the grey walls of the Castle. The ruins of Coety consist of a roughly circular inner ward, with a gatehouse, keep, and round tower, the whole surrounded on three sides by a ditch. This was the earliest part of the Castle to be built, and the curtain wall and keep probably date from the late 12th cent. The domestic quarters, hall, and chapel stood on the S. side of the inner ward. There was a small E. gatehouse with a drawbridge and portcullis. The slots for the portcullis are still visible. The walls of the outer ward date from the 14th cent.

The Castle was founded by Payn de Turberville, a follower of Robert FitzHamon, the powerful Marcher Lord who first conquered Glamorgan for the Normans. According to tradition, Morgan, the last Welsh ruler of Coety, was confronted by Payn's men-at-arms. Morgan

appeared, leading his daughter by one hand and carrying a naked sword in the other. "I am old," he said to Payn, "If you marry my daughter, you shall have all my lands without bloodshed after I die. If you refuse, we will fight to the last drop of our blood." Naturally Payn accepted the gift. The descendants of this Norman-Welsh marriage played an important part in the history of Glamorgan all through the Middle Ages. In 1404, the Castle withstood a long siege by the followers of Owain Glyndwr. The lordship eventually passed from the Turbervilles to the Gamage family.

By the middle of the 16th cent., Barbara Gamage was the sole heiress, and her wealth, beauty, and landed possessions made her marriage an important affair not only for Glamorgan but for the Crown. Queen Elizabeth ordered her to court. Sir John Stradling of St Donat's, however, spirited her away to his castle until she was safely married to Sir Robert Sidney, the brother of the famous Sir Philip Sidney. In spite of the royal displeasure with Stradling, the young couple eventually succeeded in winning the Queen's favour. Sir Robert Sidney became Earl of Leicester. He and Barbara lived in Penshurst, where Barbara's wifely virtues were highly praised by Ben Jonson in his work *Forest*. The Earls of Leicester held Coety until the line died out in the middle of the 18th cent. The estate was then split up.

Coety church stands next to the Castle, which looks its best from the churchyard. The cruciform church has been little altered since the early 14th cent. The embattled tower, with its remarkable gargoyles, is of a slightly later date. The interior is devoid of arches and thus gives an impression of great spaciousness. There are pointed openings on either side of the chancel arch, and the vaulted crossing has a groined roof; the original font, a massive specimen is now in the S. transept. In the N. transept is an oak chest that has a saddleback top, carved with emblems of the Passion. This may probably be one of the few surviving examples of a portable Easter altar. On either side of the main altar are two miniature effigies of members of the Turberville family.

At Coed-parc-garw, ¼ m. N. of the Castle, is a chambered tomb of the long cairn type, dated between 2500 and 2000 B.C. The wide common of Cefn Hirgoed forms the background to Coety.

COLWYN BAY, *Denbighshire*, received its charter of incorporation in 1934. Within thirty years it had grown from an obscure village into a town of more than 20,000 inhabitants, with two public schools, Rydal for boys, Penrhos for girls. Between two separate villages, Old Colwyn and Llandrillo-yn-Rhos, the modern Colwyn Bay has developed into a 3-m. promenade continuing as far as Rhos-on-Sea. It is a busy holiday resort even in the winter months, for its climate is mild and its situation protects it from rain and wind. It is an entirely modern town with entirely modern resources that have succeeded in overcoming the perils of the approach to it over the headland of Penmaenrhos – so difficult in the old coaching days that it alarmed Dr Johnson and daunted even the intrepid traveller Thomas Pennant, who thought it more dangerous than the cliffs at Penmaenmawr on the other side of the Great Orme. Rhos-on-Sea, at the E. side of the Little Orme, brings you almost into Llandudno. Llysfaen, near at hand, is hilly and beautiful, but has three very large limestone quarries as its most distinguishing feature. Within easy reach are Abergele and Llaneilian-yn-Rhos, with their old churches and quiet old manor houses.

CONWAY, *Caernarfonshire*. Aberconwy is the Welsh name for the town, since it stands at the mouth of the Afon Conwy. The estuary makes a delightful prospect, opening between long hills through which the stream turns from side to side as it comes from its distant source, the small lake also called Conwy, in the Migneint mountains northward from Arennig Fawr. Denbigh, Merioneth, and Caernarfon counties meet at the shores of this lake.

The history of Conway town seems to have begun no earlier than the time of Edward I of England and the castle he set up to make his hold firm on the territories controlled by Llywelyn, last of the independent Welsh Princes. The castle once built, the town grew round it. The estuary, however, was so valuable in itself, and formed so important a strategic point, that earlier strongholds had possessed the place before him. About 5 m. S. of Conway, the small village of Caerhun stands on the site of the Roman station Canovium, and on the other side of the estuary, rather to the N., Deganwy, now a small slate-shipping port, marks with its name the Dinas Conwy (Fort on the Conway) that Llywelyn in his conflict with Edward had to destroy in 1260. On the severe line of defence drawn by this estuary many attacks from England on the independence of Gwynedd were halted.

The town is still contained within its medieval walls. Telford's suspension bridge across the estuary dates from 1827, and is one of his most impressive works. The railway bridge follows it closely, running above the 13th-cent. walls and trying to harmonize with them by throwing up towers in the "Gothic" style. Otherwise Conway still stands much as it did when, in 1295, Edward I was himself besieged by the Welsh in the fortress of his own making, rescued only by the arrival of a ship with provisions from England.

The strength of Conway Castle saved it from any real threat of overthrow, and has preserved it as perhaps the most perfect specimen of its times anywhere in Britain. Only in the Civil War did it suffer alarms, and even then it seems to have imposed a kind of neutrality, or at least a double-sidedness, on both Cavaliers and Puritans. It was held at first for Charles by his Archbishop of York, John Williams, who was chased from his see by the rebels, and came to Conway through "magnetick attraction" (it was said) like that which causes the salmon to seek its place of birth. Williams swore to hold Conway against all comers; he urged all who were for the King to deposit their valuables in the Castle for safe keeping, and all good citizens to spend their days in prayer. But the Sir John Owen who was active in these same parts for the Royalist cause demanded that Williams should surrender the place into better keeping – Sir John's own. Perhaps Williams was in some way suspect, since he was not only acquainted with Oliver Cromwell but was a cousin of his. "Cromwell" was an adopted name; Oliver's true surname was Williams, but his family had formed a connection by marriage with that of Thomas Cromwell, Henry VIII's Minister. The Archbishop had originally no great opinion of this Oliver Williams,

Conway Castle and Telford's bridge

Barnaby/Mustograph

alias Cromwell, for he told King Charles: "He is the most dangerous enemy your Majesty has. I knew him at Bugden but never knew his religion. He loves none that are more than his equals. And above all that live, I think he is the most mindful of injury".

Deeply outraged by Sir John Owen's demands, John Williams wrote to Mytton, the local Parliamentary commander: "Expel me this intolerable Owen; Owen out, I will hold the Castle for Parliament and you. His Majesty would seem to have done with fighting now". Oliver himself wrote to him from Putney: "Your advices will be seriously considered by us. We shall endeavour to our uttermost so to settle the affairs of North Wales as, to the best of our understandings, does most conduce to the public good thereof and of the whole. And that without private respect or to the satisfaction of any humour [prejudice] which has been too much practised on the occasion of our Troubles". He signed himself "Your cousin and servant, Oliver Cromwell".

Mytton's troops took the position without much trouble, the people of Conway being, it was said, as ready to fight for Sir John Owen as for a maypole. The Archbishop then retired to Gloddaeth, an estate not far away. At the news of the King's execution, he fainted. He has been described as the one man who could have averted the Civil War. Afterwards he is said to have lived in a great house at Bethesda in Caernarfonshire. He was buried at Llandegai, a remote spot close to the sea. But he does not seem to have rested in peace. His ghost walked frequently, explaining to one Betty Jones that he was anxious for the security of a treasure he had buried there. Betty, however, refused to have anything to do with its recovery.

Conway's Church of St Mary, in the centre of the town, is believed to incorporate, in its entrance arch to the S. porch and part of the tower's W. wall, portions of the Cistercian Abbey of Aberconwy, which was removed by Edward I to Maenan, lower down the river, when he created his new fortress.

An Elizabethan half-timbered house, Plas Mawr, built in 1585 by Robert Wynn of Gwydir, is now maintained by the Royal Cambrian Academy of Art, and its panelling, plaster-work, and ancient fireplaces are the background for its annual exhibitions. Another timbered building, where Castle Street and High Street meet, is claimed as the oldest house in Wales; the title of the Smallest House in Britain is given to a building by the river-quay.

Conway is no longer a port, though the development of yachting in recent years has made the estuary a place of resort. The Ministry of Agriculture, Fisheries, and Food maintains an oyster- and mussel-breeding centre; beds at the mouth of the estuary are said to produce mussel-pearls.

Local tradition states firmly that the first sweet peas in Britain were grown by Queen Eleanor of Castile, in a little terrace overlooking the river and known as the Queen's Garden.

CORRIS, *Merioneth.* There are two Corrises, Upper Corris and Corris. The latter is reached by the Roman road past Plas Llwyngwern and Esgairgeiliog. Of the two, Corris itself is clearly the older. The name may be no more than a breaking-down into Welsh pronunciation of the English "quarries", for the taking of slate has been from the beginning the chief factor in the life of both villages. But to dismiss the lower Corris as a relatively modern village would no doubt be wrong. The superior value of Welsh slate was recognized in Roman (as in Renaissance) times; and the Roman road may have sought out this remote corner of the world not only to link the Dovey with the Dysynni but also to cart slates from the outcrops on these hills.

Corris repays a visit, preferably by this same Roman road: from there the valley looks its best. Old houses lead to the bridge, perhaps even older; all are built of the local slate. Regrettably, these houses showing much of old Welsh farmstead structure, with byres for cattle and storerooms for wool and straw, are falling into disrepair, and some have already been cleared away. The tortuous main street lies deeply below the more modern highway that rises to Upper Corris. But it is from Corris itself that you can see the curiously sited cemetery, climbing the ravine of the upper Dulas, its tombstones terraced against the hill-fall and seeming embedded among the scattered houses.

The turn towards Tal-y-llyn is made at the very sharp corner by the old inn. Here, high above the valley-level, is the war memorial, which until a few years ago was occupied as a point of ambush by an old farmer expert in the local craft of making rush baskets and platters; for over these marshy slopes the rushes grow in green profusion, and even whips can be made from them by plaiting. This ancient gentleman, at the dangerous curve in the road, would hold motorists to ransom, forcing upon them the sale of his admittedly excellent wares. The road goes on, rising steadily between piles of slate-spoil for several miles, the run of rails and work-sheds lying to one side and, a little later, the rows of quarrymen's cottages firmly retaining their structure of 150 years. Here and there stand the inevitable chapels, though one of them has disappeared. Against the sheer hill-sides that lead to the Taren range, the spoil-stacks reach a considerable height, and their position is precarious. One night of storm and flood a generation ago loosened the piled slates, and they fell upon the village. There was no disaster such as more recently overwhelmed Aberfan; but one of the holy places remains buried beneath the slide with a lone ash tree growing sparsely above it.

At last the road opens to green fields and comfortable farms; the lake of Tal-y-llyn lies gleaming to one side, the giant shoulders of Cader Idris fill the forward horizon, and the long pull to Cross Foxes and Dolgellau begins. As you take this steady climb, cast an eye into the valley on the left, skirting the eastward thrust of Cader Idris. A green track, surviving long enough to be marked with telegraph poles and still serving the uses of the scattered farms, marks the way that Mary Jones in 1800 marched to get her Bible (*see* Bala).

CORS FOCHNO, *Cardiganshire.* This wild tract of sea-land, a deep bog covered with a forest of tall rush-like reeds, lies along the southern side of the Dovey estuary. Geographically and historically, its true point of reference is Llangynfelyn. The bog is no longer what it was only a few years ago, when the path from Glandyfi station forced you to shoulder through the rushes as if through a field of corn, with the heads rustling about your ears. Dykes and drainage have cut into it considerably, and a few farms now operate in its depths. But the area of safe movement about it is still limited, and, unless one is very familiar with the bog, it can be most dangerous. Its estuary edge is a channelled network of sand and stream filled with the wildlife of the sea. Its depths are haunted with wildfowl, which find a natural nesting-place and shelter there. Cormorant and curlew, moorhen and gull, are its favourites. But local report says that the bittern has come there within the last few years.

With so much of the Plynlimon upland that runs towards the Dovey now drained and planted with afforested firs, the fowl that used to be familiar in the Dovey valley have been driven away from their long-established homes. The Penderi Nature Reserve has been established to offer them an alternative chance for survival.

In legend the bog has a hag. It issues only at night, and in nights of mist at that. It rears itself to a height of 7 ft and has an enormous head. When disturbed, it hisses like a snake and returns into the peaty mire.

CORWEN, *Merioneth.* About 10 m. from Llangollen and rather more from Bala, depending on which road you choose, Corwen is set on the junction of the Alwen with the Dee. Northward it looks over the Dee valley, here known as the Dyffryn Edeyrnion, and to what was Corwen's ancient predecessor, the Caer Drewyn, only 1 m. away on a height overlooking the town. Here is the most important of all Welsh prehistoric fortresses. Not less than $\frac{1}{2}$ m. in circumference, with walls about 4 yds thick, and with a NE. sector leading to the remains of circular dwellings, Caer Drewyn represents a settlement of a race still mysterious, though the stone circle close to the old track – the Cam Elin Way under Cader Fronwen, S. of Corwen – may relate it to the first Brythonic penetration of the area.

The same hill was occupied by Owain, Prince of Gwynedd, in 1165 against Henry II of England, who encamped on the Berwyns by the Cader Fronwen and was driven off by the violent weather. But Corwen prefers to remember that other Owain, Glyndwr, who wrested the independence of Wales from Henry IV. He got his name from Glyndyfrdwy, one of his estates,

which lay round about the village of the same name 5 m. to the W. of Llangollen. His other property of Cynllaeth centred on Sycharth, to the S. of the Berwyns; and it is said that, standing on the hill Penypigyn close by Corwen, as he gathered his troops before the Battle of Shrewsbury, he could look across 40 sq m. of his own land.

According to a picturesque tradition, he left his personal mark on the town: the church has on the stone lintel of its S. door, called the Priest's Door, an incised cross that was supposed to have been made by the Welsh King when, in a fit of annoyance, he threw his dagger from the peak of Penypigyn. The sign is more probably a simple mark of consecration.

The church traces its foundation to the 6th cent., the heroic age of Christianity in Wales, and is dedicated to Mael and Sulien, who, in that period, accompanied St Cadfan, the saint of Towyn, on his missionary venture from Brittany to Wales. A legend says that the builders at first intended to put up the church elsewhere, but all work done during the day was mysteriously removed by night. At last they decided to have the church on a site already occupied by a great stone; and this was done, the stone being built into the porch, where it still appears. The story may well have some foundation, since Christian sites were often chosen to be where previous cultures had their venerable places, usually associated with time-and-space calculation by monoliths used as sundials. No other relic of the first church remains. The font, with its cable-patterned decoration, dates from about 1100; the grave of a vicar who died in 1350 is at the N. side of the chancel. On the opposite side the remnant of a Celtic cross can be seen; this also is said to bear the mark of Glyndwr's dagger.

In 1750 a Mr William Eyton of Shropshire caused a row of almshouses, mainly for clergymen's widows and called the College, to be set up immediately behind the church. Other survivals from the 18th cent. are gravestones indented with circular shallows to rest the knees of those who came to pray over the buried.

Near Corwen is Rug, the mansion owned by the Welsh family of Salesburys, then by the Vaughans and by the Wynns. Some 5 m. to the N. is tiny Derwen, a place with an exceptional rood-loft and one of the most perfect Celtic crosses in Wales. A little further off stands Efenechtyd church, its font carved from a single block of oak and its door with a knocker that may have belonged to a nunnery nearby.

Corwen itself is a typical town of Merioneth, a little like Dolgellau in its sober greyness and disciplined ranks of houses. It was once dependent on slate-quarrying, but now relies on its fishing, history, and old inns, and the heathered Berwyn hills, all of which entice the traveller.

COWBRIDGE, *Glamorgan,* called Pont Faen in Welsh, is a little town 12 m. along the main road westwards from Cardiff. It has been christened the Capital of the Vale, and even the Cranford of Glamorgan. Times have changed, and no county town near a big city is safe from traffic. But Cowbridge has now been by-passed to the N., and there are signs that its former peace is returning. In essence the town is one long street running E. to W., with a cross road leading down to the church. Cowbridge is lucky to have escaped "development" – so far.

The town has a long history. It is possibly the Roman Bovium, on the main Roman road to the W., and the town plan is certainly as rectangular as a Roman camp. In Norman times, it developed as the market for the lordship of Llanblethian. It was a borough by the end of the 13th cent., and has remained the smallest and one of the most ancient boroughs in the country. The civic arms show a cow on a bridge, commemorating the old and unauthenticated story that the place got its name from the cunning of a local farmer, who hid his cow under the Pont Faen (Stone Bridge), when the first Norman tax-gatherer arrived. Until the Industrial Revolution, the place rivalled Cardiff in importance.

Cowbridge was also a walled town, and the remains of the town wall can be seen on the S. side. There is a charming group of ancient buildings around the S. gate, which still survives. Turn down from the main street at the Bear Inn, noting the tall chimneys that sprout from the huddle of roofs at the back of the Bear. The S. gate stands before you, with the grammar school immediately to the left. The present buildings of the school date from 1847. Cowbridge Grammar School was founded in the 16th cent., probably by Sir Edward Stradling, of the powerful St Donat's family. It was moved to its present position by his nephew, Sir John Stradling, who is usually regarded as the founder. The school also owed a great deal to Sir Leoline Jenkins (1623–85) who left it in his will to the Fellows of Jesus College, Oxford. Sir Leoline was a great man in his day. Born in Llantrisant, he became Principal of Jesus, fought in the Royalist army in the Civil War, was appointed Judge, Privy Councillor, and in 1680 Secretary of State. Even Pepys, in his secret diary, declared, "I am mightily pleased with the Judge, who seems a very rational, learned and uncorrupt man" – a man, in fact, whom any school would be proud to honour as a benefactor. The church is alongside the school, with the entrance to the small churchyard tucked away against the school buildings. The Church of the Holy Rood is mainly Early English and Perpendicular, and rather odd in construction, both within and without. The 13th-cent. embattled tower is a complicated structure of buttresses and stairways; inside, the aisle of the chancel is on the opposite side of the aisle of the Perpendicular nave. The church contains memorials to distinguished local men, among them Dr Benjamin Heath Malkin (1769–1842), the historian and traveller whose descriptions of South Wales in the early 19th cent. are constantly quoted with appreciation by later guide-book writers. The original sanctus bell was re-hung in 1939, after being used as a fire-bell. The combined Town Hall and Market House, standing in the main street, is a pleasant little building that once served as the house of correction for most of the county, and still contains the cells. The stocks are now in the National Museum of Wales at Cardiff. Cowbridge was once a lively publishing centre, and the first printing-press used in Glamorgan was established here by Rhys Thomas in 1770. The press also has gone for safe keeping to the National Museum.

On the E. of the borough, at the point where the by-pass begins, Stalling Down gives a fine view over the country to the N., through the newly erected mesh of power-lines. Tradition makes the Down the scene of a victory of Owain Glyndwr over the troops of Henry IV in 1405. The monument on the Down, however, commemorates the men of the Glamorgan Yeomanry.

About 1 m. to the S. of Cowbridge is the village of Llanblethian. A certain amount of new building is going on, but Llanblethian still feels itself a separate place from the borough down the road, although the castle at Llanblethian was the cause of Cowbridge's existence. The remains of the fine 14th-cent. gatehouse are still visible. The popular title of the ruin is St Quintin's Castle, but the St Quintin family did not get possession of the estate until much later. Llanblethian church stands apart from the village, looking proud of its isolation: a fine building, with a tower reminiscent of the Jasper Tower of Llandaff Cathedral, containing some medieval effigies and unusual arches in the S. porch. To the W. the hill is crowned by a large Iron Age fort, which has recently been excavated. It has the unusual local name of the Devil's Foot and Knee.

Thomas Carlyle was a frequent visitor here to his friend John Sterling (1806–44), who is regarded as one of the first of the "military experts" in the world of journalism. His articles in *The Times* were eagerly followed, and Carlyle relates that Sterling would be anxiously standing on Llanblethian hill to see the coach, with the latest dispatches, rumbling over Stalling Down into Cowbridge. Sterling's house is the villa with the veranda on the hill leading to the church. Carlyle had an affection for Llanblethian, and described it as a "cheerful group of human homes" and a "little sleeping cataract of white houses with trees overshadowing it and fringing it". His description is not so far wrong for Llanblethian today.

COYCHURCH, *Glamorgan.* The village is 2 m. due E. of Bridgend. The busy road from Bridgend to Llantrisant runs through it, and a big trading estate stretches between Coychurch and Bridgend. This estate began its career as a shell-filling factory before the Second World War. In spite of this nearness to industry, the church has atmosphere and interest, besides being one of the largest in the vale. It is dedicated to St Crallo, and is mostly 13th-cent. in style; the plan is cruciform, though the clerestory extends on the S. side only. The arcading in the nave is especially fine. The roof of the nave is

15th-cent., with intricately carved angels. There are medieval stonemasons' marks on some of the arches of the nave.

In 1877 the tower fell and demolished most of the S. transept. Both the tower and transept have been successfully restored. Tucked away in the N. transept is a recumbent figure of a woman dating from the 14th cent., and a Tudor effigy of "Thomas Ivans, Clerk, Parson of Coychurch". The registers of the church date from 1736 and record that, in 1771, a wedding ceremony was repeated a month later because the bridegroom had placed the ring on the wrong finger of the bride. Other points of interest are the tablet in the church commemorating Arthur J. Williams, the founder of the National Liberal Club; the churchyard cross; and the grave of Thomas Richards in the churchyard. Richards was a curate of Coychurch for forty years and compiled an important Welsh-English dictionary, published in 1753.

The two oldest monuments at Coychurch now stand at the W. end of the nave. The highest is the Ebisar Cross. This was damaged when the tower fell, and it has been reassembled with some obvious bits missing. In its original form it must have been one of the tallest crosses in the country. The second stone also contains the statement "Ebissar, the founder of this church, rests here". It is not certain if the Ebissar or Ebisar referred to was the founder of Coychurch, as the stones may have been brought from elsewhere. About 1 m. to the N. of Coychurch is the Gaer, an old earthwork. To the E. is St Mary Hill, formerly in the possession of Neath Abbey. The old church has no W. door, but contains a massive Norman font and a curious distempered bust of a former incumbent. The cross in the churchyard has its original carved headstone. The annual horse fair was held on the 26th August on the down to the N. of the church. It was once one of the biggest in South Wales, but it lost its importance with the growth of motoring.

CRAIG-Y-NOS, *Breconshire,* stands at the top of the Swansea Valley at the point where the Tawe turns and leaves all trace of the coalfield behind. The limestone crags close in, and beyond the high Old Red Sandstone peaks of the Fanau rise to 2,600 feet.

This romantic spot once attracted a surprising resident – none other than Adelina Patti, the Victorian *prima donna,* who by the age of forty had amassed one of the largest fortunes ever earned by an opera singer. Born in Madrid and brought up in New York, she could command fees of £1,000 per performance. Her early married life had not been as successful as her financial investments, and by 1878 she was looking for a refuge, between concert tours, that would be safely out of reach of the fashionable world.

On the advice of Lord Swansea, she bought the estate of Craig-y-Nos (Crag of the Night) for £3,500. She found happiness here for the last thirty years of her life, first with the French tenor,

G. Douglas Bolton
Craig-y-Nos Castle, now a hospital

Ernesto Nicolini, her second husband, and then as Baroness Cederström with her third husband. Craig-y-Nos, it has been said, became her Shangri-La. She improved the castle – a Scottish Baronial dream set among Welsh mountains. To Craig-y-Nos she returned by special train after each triumphant tour. She had a private road cut up the hill-side to the station at Penwyllt, where her own private waiting-room was luxuriously furnished. When she drove down to Swansea or Neath to sing for charity, she had a military escort and civic receptions all along the way. To the music-loving people of South Wales, Adelina Patti was always the Queen of Song.

In 1891 she opened her own private theatre at Craig-y-Nos. The theatre is still intact and is used regularly by local opera groups. Patti died in 1919, and the castle was handed over to the Welsh National Memorial Association to be converted into a hospital. The continued existence of this hospital is under discussion. The elaborate Winter Gardens, where Patti walked on the rainy days that are common enough at Craig-y-Nos, was dismantled and has now been re-erected in Victoria Park, Swansea, as the Patti Pavilion.

About $\frac{1}{2}$ m. beyond Craig-y-Nos Castle is the white-walled Gwyn Arms, guarded by large fir trees, with the Tawe tumbling among its vast rounded boulders near at hand. The Gwyn has become an important centre of pot-holing, for this limestone country is riddled with vast cave-systems. One of the most remarkable of them is now open to the public. The Danyrogof caves are close to the Gwyn Arms, at the point where the stream comes out of a fissure in the mountainside. They were first explored by the brothers Morgan in 1912. Now they have become a popular tourist attraction, well lit through the first section of the system. They contain a fine selection of stalactites, natural bridges, caverns, and underground lakes. The caves and lakes continue beyond the section shown to tourists, and new discoveries are continually being made.

In fact, the whole of this limestone country that fringes the northern part of the coalfield is now under intensive exploration, and is recognized as one of the most important caving territories in Britain. Pot-holing, it must be emphasized, can be dangerous for the inexperienced. The caves and passages that honeycomb the crags of Craig-y-Nos, the Cribarth, and the other limestone crags of this fascinating valley should be tackled only by properly equipped experts.

Above ground, the Cribarth – the crag immediately to the W. of Craig-y-Nos Castle – is traversed by a ridgeway that leads to the Saithmaen, a group of seven standing stones. Nearby are the remains of hut circles and a cairn known locally as Bedd-y-Cawr (Giant's Grave).

CRICCIETH, *Caernarfonshire.* In the NE. section of Cardigan Bay, the village of Criccieth has one of the pleasantest stations on this coast. It is in the angle made by the arm of the Lleyn peninsula as it thrusts westward towards Ireland from the shores of Cardigan and Merioneth. Northward from Criccieth the mountains of Snowdonia pile against the horizon, but they do not overwhelm the village. It is sited towards the wide gap made by the estuary where the Glaslyn river and the Dwyryd join; and across the Glaslyn sands it looks at Harlech. Each place has its castle; each castle, in its present form, was shaped by the builders of the Edwardian Conquest to hold this angle of Wales. But Criccieth had its fortress before the last Llywelyn fell; his predecessor, Llywelyn known as the Great, son-in-law of King John of England, suffered the indignity of having a son of his made captive in Criccieth Castle during the long series of wars between himself, as Lord of Gwynedd, and the Princes of Merioneth, Powys, and the South. Edward I in fact did no more than strengthen and encase the towers, two of which still stand. Criccieth Castle remained occupied down to the time of Elizabeth I. The first founder of it as a medieval stronghold is not certainly known; but the site was used as a position of strength from very early times. It is said that Criccieth is a name derived from Crug Aeth (Sharp Hill-Top).

Behind the town, and higher than the Castle, the hill called Mynydd Ednyfed shows where some much more ancient earthwork was thrown up to overlook the coastline; and we need go no further than Ystumcegid Isaf, with its cromlech, or the little place Dolbenmaen and its hill, Craig y Garn, to find evidence of the ancient peoples who lived on this estuary. To the NE. of

Criccieth a road leads into the depth of the Snowdon mountains, ending at Cwmystradllyn, where the lake lies under Moel Hebog (Hill of the Hawk), whose steep eastward face takes you to the waste of tumbled rocks that hide what was traditionally the cave of Owain Glyndwr. And, more directly N., the road to Dolbenmaen runs into the Pennant Valley and the long and narrow channel of the Dwyfor, where old coppermines stand idle, and ancient houses contemplate the past.

Criccieth itself is a most pleasant place, with good hotels, an unspoilt beach, and indeed an unspoilt character of its own. It is still village-like in the best sense. As the long road strikes steeply up the hill, you pass the police station, with its cells boldly marked Lock Up.

At the end of the rise, where the road turns suddenly into lanes, the home owned by the late Earl Lloyd George, and called Bryn Awelon, is plain to see.

CWM EINON, *Cardiganshire.* Of great interest to the tourist and the historian, this is advertised as Artists' Valley. Certainly it has for 100 years been the resort of painters attracted by the neighbouring waterfalls, the oak-crowded hillsides, and the opening to the umber beauty of the long and rolling waves of the Plynlimon moorland and the ancient homesteads grouped under the rocks of Foel Fawr. But its true name is worth greater respect.

Set at the mountain-gap into which the old Roman road falls as it patrols the sea-edge from Taliesin northwards, the valley of Einon has a dominating position in the control of the Dovey estuary and the passes over the heartland of Wales. The estuary was the apex of the power of Powys, once regarded as a kingdom, then through the Middle Ages dwindling into a principality, and in Tudor times to an earldom, and now revived in the name for the centre of Wales. Its days as a kingdom go back to the first emergence of Britain into independence after the decline of Rome. Wales traces its national ancestry to a commander on the Roman Wall about Carlisle who bore the title of "Cunedda". Wearing, we are told, the torque and accoutrements of Roman-British military tradition, he first laid an iron hand on the district from Carlisle to Chester, and on Strathclyde, which remained "Welsh" until well into the 7th and 8th cents., then moved to establish his rule from Chester to the Severn. This line across the English Midlands he supported by thrusting his power directly to the Dovey estuary, seizing a triangle of strength that has always been the key to the domination of the whole island. The capital that he possibly and his successors certainly possessed was Pengwern, near Shrewsbury.

He has always been identified with a Romanizing purpose, and there is much in the obscured account of those dark Arthurian days to suggest that Roman culture, town- and villa-administration, military organization, and sense of identity persisted stubbornly in Britain, at least as long

Plate 8   The church at Dixton, near Monmouth   Pix Photos

G. Douglas Bolton

*Cwm Einon: the falls of the Einon stream
at Furnace*

of the later emblems used by the imperial legions, and thus as the oldest flag in the world.

In the confused chronicles of the period some hint can be found to illuminate the history of the British Dark Age and the importance of the valleys running to the Dovey river.

If Einion of the House of Cunedda did in fact set up his point of control here, most probably it would be somewhere near the farmstead of Bwlch Einon standing high on the hill behind Foel Fawr. Facing it across the valley is the steeply dropping chine, filled with woods, down which the Roman road from Taliesin makes its way to rise again by Bwlch Einon on a green track, which clearly shows how its edge was fortified against the hill-slope by a stack of slates driven into the earth. In its present state, this is probably the remains of a pack-way of later times; but it is worth following on foot, at this point from Bwlch Einon, for the view it gives of the 18th-cent. Dol-goch lying below by the stream and the tarens, now much afforested, stepping upwards towards Plynlimon Fawr. If the stream is followed to its source at Blaeneinon, a long steady slope of about 600 ft takes you to Llyn Conach and Llyn Dwfn, and so to Hafod Wnog, one of the centres of the sheep-raising community in these hills, and the brilliant view of North Wales from the summit of Rhiw Goch.

Another way, but only for the hardy, is from Cae Mardin to the hill Pencarreg-gopa, from which, with care, the old pack-way can be traced to the Llyfnant Valley. The untrustworthy remains of ancient and rustic bridges can still be found, but the deserted little valleys and the strength of the torrents forcing through them makes the expedition hazardous. This section of the Plynlimon moorland is the wildest. The long rolling combers of hill hold between them deceptive bog, and sudden turns of slope, to confuse all sense of direction. To the E., the skein of lakes, famous for their trout, spill their streams in ragged cataracts overgrown with whin and heather; and the "Hill Plinlimon, whereof I spake," as Saxton writes, "raiseth itself to a wonderfull height" much as it did in the year 1610. But, as you make your way across the peat-hags, you see the several deep clefts made into the edge of the upland by the rich valleys of farm and field, their trees clambering the rifts to stand at eye-level with you. "By reason of plentifull vallies," continues Saxton, "it is a good country as well for corne as pasture: and in old time a fruitfull breeder of the best kind of horses, which, as Giraldus saith, by nature's workmanship pourtraying, as it were, in a picture their noble shapes, were very commendable as well for the Majestie of their making and big limmes, as for their incomparable swiftness." Here and there, on the windy crest of these valleys, descendants of those horses take the air with the same confidence in their majesty as their breed had in Saxton's day, or when Giraldus Cambrensis in 1188 traced that majesty to Spanish sires introduced by Roger de Belesme, Earl of Shrewsbury.

as it did in the continental parts of what was known as Rome's Gallic Prefecture.

According to tradition, the Cunedda set his "sons" the task of holding the disturbed region between Powys and the sea by conquering native unrest and affording protection from Irish raids. His "sons" – Meirion, Ceredig, and Brychein, among others – gave their names to the still-existing districts of Merioneth, Cardigan, and Brecon. And one who was either his "son" or "grandson" was called Einion.

The "sons" (by some accounts as many as eight) reflect an important point in the later development of the Roman legionary organization. As an ethical basis on which to hold their empire together, the Romans introduced the Mithraic military discipline, in which the General was Pater, or Father, of his subordinate officers. Of the Cunedda himself the word is used; and many dominant characters in the Arthurian legend fall into categories representing the junior ranks of the Mithraic system. The Roman walls in the N. of Britain are studded with Mithraic temples, and indeed we know that London itself honoured the name of Mithras. Nor should we forget that the griffin (often called dragon), the red badge of Wales, is claimed as a descendant

Top: *The promenade and Castle, Criccieth*   Peter Baker
Bottom: *High moors in Denbighshire*   J. Allan Cash

The little black mountain fox is particularly fond of this area and the deserted overgrowth in its small ravines. If the ancient, indigenous grey fox comes this way, he keeps himself well hidden, though the view of him is sometimes reported. And, hearing such reports, one is again reminded of Saxton. The sheep, he says, can graze without fear of wolves. But, although such creatures were officially exterminated in the time of the Saxon King Edgar and of Ludwall, Prince of these Welsh countries, "Yet a long time after this there remained some still, as appeareth for certaine, by irreprovable testimonies of Record".

In the reign of Queen Elizabeth I, Cwm Einon was apparently better known to the world than it is now. The poet Michael Drayton thought it worth including in his epic *Polyolbion*. He added to the number of variations on the word Plynlimon by writing of the district: "So all the neighbouring hills Plynillimon obey". Nor is he much surer of Foel Fadian, which he refers to as Moyluadian, though he correctly gives it a craggy top. But the phrase "Cletur next and Kinuer making head with Enion" gives these streams as much prominence as the Severn or the Wye or the Rheidol.

CWRT, *Merioneth*. This charming spot is worth singling out for the exceptional beauty of its surroundings and its own unspoilt character. It is no more than a small group of cottages on the main road towards Aberdovey from Machynlleth. Known more correctly as Cwrt Pennal, it confesses its original dependence on the ancient community of Pennal close at hand. "Cwrt" means court, and the village seems to have been a successor to the military and administrative centre that stood at Pennal in medieval times. A high mound near the road, and easily seen from it, suggests a fortification. It marks the junction of the Aberdovey with the Cwm Dyffryn road, and also gives access to Ynys Pennal and the approaches to the Dovey through pleasant fields. Cwrt itself is picturesque with flowers in the summer on the scale generally found in this district.

CYNWYL ELFED, *Carmarthenshire*, a village 5 m. NW. of Carmarthen, lies in a narrow wooded valley of considerable beauty. The A484 traces this valley up from Carmarthen, following the course of the Gwili river. After Bronwydd the valley closes in. The Gwili and the abandoned railway line turn right at the old Cynwyl station. Cynwyl itself is 1 m. higher up at the junction of the little rivers Duad and Nant Coch (Red Stream). The village is neat, with some houses that still retain their colour-wash. The church is mainly Victorian and has characteristically Victorian glass. Cynwyl Elfed has rather surprisingly yielded Roman relics, including a small golden figure of Diana. About 1 m. W. is Y Gangell, the small farmhouse where the Rev. D. H. Elved Lewis was born. He lived to be ninety-four – one of the great hymn-writers of modern Wales and a beloved figure at every National Eistedd-

fod. Y Gangell has been bought as a memorial to him. He is buried at Blaencoed. From Cynwyl a fine road strikes off the A484 by the chapel at the top of the village. This goes over the open moorlands at a height of 1,403 ft down to Newcastle Emlyn.

Higher up in the valley of the Gwili, and best reached from Bronwydd, is Llanpumsaint. This secluded village, with some pleasant white-washed houses, is grouped round the church, which was rebuilt in 1882. It is dedicated to the same saintly quintuplets who keep guard over Pumsaint. The five saints – Ceitho, Celynnen, Gwyn, Gwyno, and Gwynoro – are associated with five "wells", or pools, in the river. These were still places of pilgrimage and cure as late as 1710, when Archdeacon Tenison noted that over 200 people gathered yearly on St Peter's Day to wash and bathe in the pools.

DAROWEN, *Montgomeryshire*. Standing just over 600 ft above sea-level, Darowen is typical of a Welsh countryside that the 20th cent. has barely touched. The walker can make his way to it from Penegoes by following the old green-track or drove-road along the Ffridd Wyllt (Wild Forest) and Bryn Wg (Rising Hill) and descending from Bryn y Brain (Hill of Ravens, 911 ft), as the regular traffic did when it moved between hamlet and hamlet in the 17th and 18th cents. Darowen is today better reached by car, turning off the Mallwyd-Machynlleth road at Abergwydol.

The village is set on the hill-top round a church of medieval foundation but built on a site probably much older. The name Darowen is assumed to mean Owen's Oak, but the origins of the place appear to be shown by two ancient stones, each given on the Ordnance Survey map as Maen Llwyd (Grey Stone). By tradition they once marked boundaries for the jurisdiction of the church, and they may very well have come to serve this purpose later on. The one to the N. is set, $1\frac{1}{4}$ m. from the church, on the sloping side of a field below a farmhouse. It has to be reached on foot by a lane, now overgrown and neglected, but still showing how carefully it was tooled from the rock, stepped, and drained. It passes the ruins of a 16th-cent. farmhouse. The Maen Llwyd is pear-shaped and inclined to point towards the stone on the S. This in turn is reached by a lane impassable for cars. But a visit to it is well worth while, since this second stone is a monolith standing perhaps 7 ft high and square to the cardinal points of the compass. Archaeologists are aware of such paired sitings of "male" and "female" stones. Together they lie on a direct line passing through the site of the church and bearing accurately on one of the Five Heads of Plynlimon above the magnificent ravine of Bwlch Gwyn (White Gorge). From this point the eye is led, again in direct line, to the cairn, Carn Gwilym (1,852 ft), facing the breast of Plynlimon Fawr itself across the River Rheidol.

At the foot of the Carn Gwilym stands the old farm of Hyddgen.

The stones at Darowen suggest that they form part of a complex of pointer-stones whose remains are widely spread over the Plynlimon moorlands, and that Darowen itself was originally a principal place for controlling the system. The extent of the Wessex Culture (about 2000 B.C.) that built the last stages of Stonehenge is still argued. As a trading society it did undoubtedly have direct contacts with the gold of Ireland and the amber of the Baltic. Its routes rounded South Wales and coasted North Wales to reach the Dee valley. Whether it used the intermediate passages along the valley of the Dovey is an interesting question.

No one should fail to visit the medieval church, with its many uncommon features, or (if he is athletic enough) follow the unmade track, perhaps even older, that leaves the metalled road by the church and drops down to the Ffernant valley through a tree-covered defile where the traveller must wade rough streams. The centuries-old life of this track – the one that goes by the second upright pointer-stone – is embodied in a well-spring, encased with slate slabs, that stands in the hedge beside farm buildings just below the village. The woods are haunted by the wildfowl and other creatures common in the Plynlimon country. The beauty of the surrounding district, seen from the Darowen hill, is remarkable, and the small valleys that drop below it speak still of the old Welsh country life and habits. Abercegir also has great beauty; Melinbyrhedyn – in the depth of a cwm and standing over a broad, untamed stream – shows examples of the early 19th-cent. Welsh cottage at its attractive best. The upland way from it past Ty Mawr reveals the tangle of foothills that reward you for possibly meeting on the narrow pathway, lined with gorse and bracken and walled with slate-flats, the flocks of sheep or cattle that sometimes challenge the passage of a car. Safety is found at last by the curving and, in places, precipitous descent to the lovely oak-lined valley where the road threads past isolated farms back to Penegoes.

Perhaps the most interesting hamlet in the area is Tal-y-Wern. It acknowledges the 20th cent. to the extent of having a telephone box and a post office that is many other things as well. But houses sheltering their Tudor and Stuart construction under immemorial oaks can, if the visitor is permitted access, tell him much of the old stones of Darowen, and offer wines – dandelion, elderberry, parsnip, rose-hip – that are seductive but dangerous. Here is the traditional Welsh hamlet, as yet unspoilt and unknown.

DENBIGH, *Denbighshire*. Called Dinbych in Welsh, Denbigh is nominally the county town of Denbighshire, but Ruthin has the county offices and is the seat for the Assizes. Denbigh, like other ancient towns, draws its life from the soil of its shire. Much of the county is hilly or even mountainous, and sheep provide its main income, though Wrexham and Ruabon are centres of the North Welsh coalfield along its southward

extension. The county is dominated by the plateau of hills whose topmost point is Moel Sych (2,713 ft). Into that upland platform are set three fertile valleys: the Vale of Llangollen to the SE., of Conway to the W., and of the Clwyd to the E. It is over this last rich vale that Denbigh looks. The contrast between the uplands and the green plains is sudden and striking; in the 17th cent., Daniel Defoe was greatly impressed by it and noted, in his account of his travels through England and Wales, that here one came from an unprofitable and windy district into a "most pleasant, fruitful, populous and delicious vale, full of villages and towns, the fields shining with corn . . . which made us think ourselves in England again, all of a sudden". The 17th cent. had not developed the appreciation of uncultivated nature; this was left for the more romantic minds of the 19th cent.

Denbigh Castle, on its steep limestone height towering above the town, had the history proper to a border fortress and carried the fortunes of the town with it. Before the Norman conquest of England, its story is obscure; but the Castle in its existing shape was first founded by William the Conqueror in his attempt to seize and hold the Marches of Wales. But it did not reach its present extent until 1282, when, following the Welsh War of 1276, De Lacy, Earl of Lincoln, built it under instruction from his master, Edward I of England, to play its part with Conway, Caernarfon, Beaumaris, Criccieth, and Harlech in fettering Gwynedd. The Tudor Queen Elizabeth sold it to her favourite Robert Dudley, who, besides enjoying the title of Earl of Leicester, became Baron Denbigh and Ranger of Snowdon Forest. But its most adventurous part in history came with the Second Civil War. After the first triumph of the Parliamentary forces and the imprisonment of Charles I at Carisbrook, a reaction in favour of the King stirred throughout Britain and particularly in Wales. In Pembrokeshire and the South there was insurrection against Parliament; but it was in the North that the most serious threat arose. The Royalist revival was led by Col. Sir John Owen of Clenennau, whose regiment of foot was recruited as far afield as Machynlleth and quartered itself at Pennal. He marched upon Conway and Bangor, demanding the surrender of Conway by Archbishop Williams. In the words of Carlyle, the Archbishop replied in "high, sniffing terms", and Sir John Owen retaliated with "imperious capture and forcible possession". Counter-strategy was directed from Denbigh Castle. The Royalists were defeated near Bangor, Beaumaris fell, and Sir John was imprisoned in Denbigh; a plot to seize the place and free him failed. The outcome of the event was disastrous for the King – the war in Wales had been too close and perilous for him to be allowed to live. Something of the part Denbigh played in the control of the North can be seen from the proposal by its Parliamentary Governor to extend the fortifications of the Castle to include the whole town. But the collapse of Owen's forces made this unnecessary.

The Castle keeps much of its early magnificence, and its gatehouse is a remarkable piece of architecture, with eight-sided towers carrying between them a statue; we still do not know whether it is of Edward I or De Lacy.

The mother church of Denbigh stands 1 m. E. of it, at Whitchurch. The tower is 13th-cent., and its roof is hammer-beam; some glass, which escaped the attentions of the Parliamentary troops, dates from the 14th cent. It holds monuments to many of Denbigh's worthies: Richard Myddelton, Governor of Denbigh Castle in 1575–6, father of the Sir Hugh and Sir Thomas who played so active a part in the political and economic life of the area; Sir John Salusbury of Lleweni Hall, whose son was the first to take the much-married Tudor Katheryn of Berain under protective care; and two others of note. The first is Humphry Lhuyd (as he spelt it), an antiquary of the 16th cent. who deserves wider fame than he has. Born in 1527 and dying in 1573, he was the first to put British historical archaeology on a steady basis. His maps of England and of Wales, published in Amsterdam in the year of his death, set out the succession of cities in Britain from Roman times to his own; and the map of Wales is particularly valuable not only in its printing of Latin, Welsh, and English names together, as they stand for places within the marchlands, but for marking out the divisions of Wales in the three sectors of Gwynedd, Powys, and Deheubarth (the South) from which its varied character grew. The second is the Thomas Edwards who died in 1810; he was noted by George Borrow as the Welsh author Twm O'r Nant (Tom of the Brook), who perpetuated in Wales at the beginning of the 18th cent. the traditions of interludes or morality plays, which in England died out with the growth of the Elizabethan theatre. One of these moralities is translated by Borrow, very effectively, in Chapter 60 of his *Wild Wales*. It is a dialogue between Riches and Poverty. Its poetic qualities are not so remarkable as its conclusion that the distinction between wealth and want is as inevitable as that between Sun and Moon.

Another native of Denbigh was Sir Henry Stanley, the explorer of Africa, now best remembered for his words of recognition spoken to the man he was commissioned to discover and bring back from the jungle: "Dr Livingstone, I presume?" Though the cottage in which he was born has been demolished, its photograph is shown in the precincts of the Castle. His real name was John Rowlands. The surname he took from his mother, since his father's was not available; Stanley he adopted from the New Orleans stockbroker by whom he was at last befriended.

The Town Hall of Denbigh is an Elizabethan structure enlarged in 1780. The girls' public school known as Howell's was built in 1860 by the Drapers' Company, apparently after some reflection, since the funds for such a foundation were left them by a Welshman, Thomas Howell, as early as 1540. The black-and-red cloaks worn by the girls as they move about the steep streets of the town are most attractive.

DERWENLAS, *Cardiganshire*, a small collection of houses, is about 2 m. from Machynlleth along the road to Tal-y-bont. It stands by the bend of the River Dovey, and looks across at Pennal, where it lies on the Aberdovey road, and at two houses typical of different stages in Welsh life: the half-timbered farmhouse of Cefn, and the stately home, built in recollection of 17th-cent. styles, Llugwy (Bright Water) – a

The Castle ruins at Denbigh

Peter Baker

place from which, rather more than a century ago, the shipping of timber to the port of Aberdovey and beyond was supervised. Derwenlas is very beautifully situated, and gives some of the best views of the Taren range running westward to the sea. Behind it, close to the inn, a road leads through small hills, suddenly remote, and woodlands still of native oak to Pontlyfnant and the rail junction at Glandyfi.

The inn at Derwenlas is the Black Lion. Once somewhat dilapidated, and ruefully considering its lost prestige as a stopping-place for coaches and cattle-drovers, it is now rapidly recovering its fame. Here indeed a striking incident once occurred. A wagoner left his wain in the sole charge of his horse outside the inn. He spent some hours at the bar, then remembered his horse and wagon and left the hostelry to find them. He was in no state to undergo a breathalyser test, had such a thing existed. But he had been like this all too often before, and his horse reproved him. Its language was well chosen and full of Biblical references. The wagoner never offended in this way again. The event has been quoted in many a chapel pulpit; its truth is quite beyond question. The horse spoke in the pure Welsh of the western Dovey area, recognized by its people as the royal dialect of Powys. In other places it is considered an affectation, above all in the pronunciation of the vowel *a*. Derwenlas illustrates the point, since 19th-cent. letterwriters always wrote Derwenlase to give the word its correct sound.

DINAS MAWDDWY, *Merioneth,* is a fascinating little exemplar of Welsh life. It takes its name – as its northerly neighbour, Llanymawddwy does – from the River Mawddach. This in turn creates for its estuary the description Aber Mawddach, which has fallen into the English corruption Barmouth. The distinction they share is that from the mountain-sides against which they crouch the Dovey finds its source. Higher than Cader Idris, the Aran Fawddwy with its twin crest of Aran Benllyn holds in a deep hollow the Creiglyn Dyfi; the river coming from it in its infant state is, appropriately enough, called the Llaethnant (Milk Brook).

Dinas Mawddwy can be reached from Mallwyd on the Dolgellau road. To reach Llanymawddwy, a fork must be followed from the further end of the little town. The way to Dinas takes one through a country curiously distinct from both the sharp peaks of Snowdonia and the rounded moorland shapes that roll S. of the Dovey. The hills here fall in long, steeply angled slopes set close one against the other, leaving only narrow, fissured valleys between them, and give the impression that they are all moulded to the same height. The nearest parallel in Britain is the splintered tableland in Derbyshire around Matlock. It is the kind of country that lends itself to the growth of secluded, even furtive, communities and protects their independence. The saying in surrounding parishes that Dinas has earth that is blue, air that is water, and men who

are false may be prejudiced and defamatory, but it does insist on certain real characteristics. The mining of lead was the traditional industry of Dinas, though now the hewing of slate has chiefly taken over. And the hill-formation attracts rainfall in a remarkable way; these valleys do indeed turn their air to water on occasion, and the great peaks of the Arans, close at hand, seem to act as a magnet for mist and thunderstorm. The belief that its inhabitants are not as others are is a survival from earlier days. Even now, as Borrow noted in his time, the people around Dinas show a prevalence of bright copper tones in their hair. The folk of South Wales are dark and Mediterranean in type, some of them with the crisply curled black hair that Caesar saw among the Silures; the people of Anglesey are often fair and tall. In the central area of Powys, a man may be yellow-haired until he is twenty and then steadily darken to brown. For some reason, the pocketed hills of Mawddwy have kept reserved a people noted for their distinct coloration. They emphasized their distinctiveness by warring against all comers, and were known as a band of robbers. In the days of Henry VIII, justice determined to wipe them out, and they took their revenge by waylaying and slaughtering one of the King's judges on the high road. This dramatic incident is often referred to; the result was the suppression and final dispersal of the Red Robbers in 1555. Several explanations have been suggested for the existence of this peculiar people. One is that they were descendants of intrusive Danes or even Normans; the separate section in the church at Llanymawddwy for the red men is sometimes called to the aid of this argument. "Danes", however, seem to have been disinclined to settle so far from the sea, and where they settled they were usually adventurous traders rather than spoilers; and the Norman attribution has little to support it. The more plausible theory is that the earlier occupants of the country, the Gaels (or Goidels, as Sir John Rhys called them, to set them apart from the later Brythonic invaders), were the direct ancestors of the men of Mawddwy. They would therefore be cousins of the red-haired Scots of Ireland and North Britain. The name Gwyddel is found in many parts of Wales; but by origin the name means a native of the soil, and it has no direct racial significance.

Today, Dinas is one of the most delightful villages of Merioneth, and its people are neighbourly and welcoming. It is approached from the Dovey valley and offers anglers the attraction of salmon, sewin, and trout. Where the road sharply turns for Abercywarch, it has an old, unpretentious, and attractive inn, facing a few shops typical of the remoter Welsh valleys, and set into once much larger buildings with a distinctive and traditional structure. The device of the double door facing the street is much used; the door is halved, the upper part opening to allow the owner to face and talk with the caller, the lower part remaining bolted to prevent children from invading the street. One of the most noteworthy institutions is the bank, which operates for a couple of hours one day a week, when it is visited by the sub-sub-manager from a larger township several miles away to deal with the requirements of the farmers. A recent attempt to use Dinas in the revival of the Welsh cloth-making industry has met with difficulties. But Welsh wool has many points to recommend it, particularly for shirts.

As the turn is made for Abercywarch, a steep incline opens out, showing the width of the river valley and its flat green where, by the waters of the ford, the gypsy folk from time to time find their refuge – the last heirs to the legend of the Red Robbers.

We must not leave Dinas Mawddwy without recalling the comment on itself, its neighbourhood, and its people made by Christopher Saxton, who, in the first decade of the 17th cent., surveyed this part of the world and had it illustrated in a map "performed" under his directions.

"The inland part," he says, "it so riseth with mountaines standing one by another in plumps, that as Giraldus saith, it is the roughest and most unpleasant country to see to, in all Wales. For, it hath in it mountaines of a wonderfull height, yet narrow and passing sharpe at the top in manner of a needle, and those verily not scattering, heere and there one, but standing very thicke together, and so even in height that Shepheards talking together, or railing one at another on the tops of them, if haply they appoint the field to encounter and meet together, they can hardly do it from morning till night."

The words he quotes are from the *Itinerary of Wales* by Gerald de Barri in the 12th cent. He adds, with caution, "But let the Reeder heerein relie on Giraldus credit". For the next set of remarks, he draws upon his own factual observation: "The inhabitants, who for the most part wholly betake themselves to breeding and feeding of cattaile, and live upon white meats, as butter, cheese, &c. . . . are for stature, cleere complexion, goodly feature and lineaments of body, inferiour to no Nation in Britain; but they have an ill name among their neighbours, for being too forward in the wanton love of women, and that proceeding from their idleness".

Mouthwy, as he writes it, was a well-known common, once belonging to the Prince of Powys but at last passing by marriage to the family of Mitton, from whom descended the notorious sporting squire, John Mytton – rake, drunkard, hard rider to hounds, spendthrift, hero, and in the 1820s High Sheriff of Merioneth.

DOLGARROG, *Caernarfonshire*. Near Caerhun, with its Roman memories, is a monument to later enterprises, the works of the Aluminium Corporation founded in 1907 and the power-generating station of North Wales. Its 10,000 kW. were derived from Llyn Eigiau and Llyn Cowlyd, dammed for the purpose. In 1925 the Eigiau dam burst, and Dolgarrog was swept to destruction with the loss of sixteen lives. The burst pipeline can still be seen. The population of the village itself was never large, being only between 500 and 600. The rural district of 6,000 inhabitants has declined in numbers steadily since the 1930s.

DOLGELLAU, *Merioneth*. This striking but small town is the capital of the shire of Merioneth. It lies in the long valley-rift of the Mawddach river that runs inland from Barmouth and under the long mountain-spine of Cader Idris. Those who appreciate austere beauty find satisfaction in the grey architecture of this

Dolgellau: the Aran stream, which rises on Cader Idris

G. Douglas Bolton

place, which seems to spring naturally from the geography of cliff-stone around it. Its own river is the Wnion, which meets the Ganllwyd and the Mawddach a little further W. at Llanelltud; and the bridge over the stream at Dolgellau is one of its best features. Built in 1638, it has seven arches, which manage to be both graceful and strong, and something of the same combination can be found in the houses flanking the narrow streets. Only the centre of the town gives traffic any width to manœuvre in, for Dolgellau is of ancient foundation and is proud of the fact.

The name has several interpretations, such as Meadow of Hazels and Meadow of the Slaves. Of its prehistoric past the soil has not yet yielded much evidence, but that it was a place known to the Romans seems proved by the discovery of coins bearing the name and title of the Emperor Trajan. Gold is found in the nearby mountainsides and has been worked in modern times, though the fire disaster at the Gwynfynydd mine in 1935 checked the enterprise. Possibly the Romans worked the gold; and the attribution of the name to slaves rather than hazels springs from the belief that forced labour may have been employed.

Near Dolgellau, and facing the pleasant village of Llanelltud across the river, are the remains of Cymer Abbey. This was founded in 1199 by Gruffydd ap Cynan, Lord of Gwynedd, the whole area of North Wales including Snowdonia, and by his brother Maredudd. It was set up as an offshoot of Cwmhir Abbey, but now only the church and some few other architectural fragments of this Cistercian foundation survive. In Dolgellau Owain Glyndwr held his last parliament of free Wales; unlike his Parliament House in Machynlleth, the original building has not been allowed to remain on its original site. In 1882 it was pulled down, and in 1883 removed to Newtown and re-erected in a park belonging to Sir Pryce Jones. An incident of highly coloured interest connects Dolgellau with Glyndwr in a different way. The church, built as it stands in 1726, nevertheless contains a memorial far older than itself, the effigy of a 13th-cent. notable named Maurice filius (son of) Ynyr Vychan. Vychan means small, and, flattering or not, the word survived for generations as the surname of his descendants, the Vaughans of the great house of Nannau, now 800 ft up against Moel Offrwm and the further backcloth of Cader Idris and Tyrau-mawr. Nothing of the house that was known to Owain Glyndwr is now standing. For it belonged to one Howel Sele, first cousin of Owain but apparently no friend of his. He invited Owain to his woodlands but, while they were hunting, deliberately turned his shaft on him. Fortunately Owain was wearing armour under his clothes, and the attempt miscarried. His revenge took two forms: he razed Howel's house to the ground, and he removed Howel from the sight of men. Where Howel had disappeared remained a mystery until, a few years later, the skeleton of a man with Howel's build was found in the trunk of an ancient oak. There

are several versions of the story, in Pennant's account of Wales in the 18th cent. and in writings by Walter Scott and Bulwer Lytton in the 19th. It is commemorated by a sundial on the spot where the tree once stood; it fell at last, struck by lightning, in 1813.

Moel Offrwm (possibly Hill of Sacrifice) can be reached by what is known as the Precipice Walk from Dolgellau. It has a hill-fort constructed of large boulders laid out on its summit; the narrow lake, Cynwch, lies close by.

The churchyard is distinguished by the grave of a Welsh poet, Dafydd Ionawr (David January). For a long time Welsh custom resisted the introduction of surnames, which did not begin to be used until the time of Henry VIII, and many famous poets are still known better by their "fig enw" (*nom de plume*) than in any other way.

Literary interest in Dolgellau did not stop with Scott and Lytton. Thomas Love Peacock, satirist and novelist, friend of Shelley and father-in-law of George Meredith, wrote in his own distinctive way on much that was Welsh; he considered Dolgellau one of the most beautiful of spots, with the most beautiful of women. Thackeray – perhaps visiting the place on this recommendation – was disappointed. His reflections on the service of the hotel he stayed at, boldly written in the visitors' book, are famous:

> If ever you come to Dolgelly,
> Don't stay at the . . . Hotel,
> For there's nothing to put in your belly
> And no one to answer the bell.

Of course "belly" does not really rhyme with the name of the town, even when spelt Dolgelly; the Welsh *ll* has, as the Introduction to this book points out (p. 54), a special pronunciation of its own. And the warning against the hotel now belongs entirely to the past.

One further incident of literary interest is less well known. The letter concerned is a little vague on one point, but either from or to another hotel, the Ship, Lewis Morris reported in the mid-18th cent. the appearance of a different kind of ship, a ship in the sky, making one of its ten-yearly visits to the neighbourhood of the Menai Straits in a way strangely like that of the 20th-cent. descents made by flying saucers. (*See* Holyhead.)

DYFI BRIDGE, *Montgomeryshire.* About 1 m. from Machynlleth and on the opposite river bank, Dyfi Bridge is a hamlet in itself. It seems to have begun as a place where water was taken from the Dyfi (Dovey) for wagon teams driven to and from the town. The cottages are old and picturesque. Behind them begins the rise of forested hills, belonging to the Snowdonia National Park, that culminate in the Taren range. One of the cottages was anciently an inn of sorts, and, at the further end of the hamlet on the way to Corris, one of the last working smithies in this part of Wales can be found. The major feature of the place is the deep pool

under the bridge, well known and much frequented – officially and unofficially – for its
salmon. At times when they are leaving the sea
to swim up the river and find their spawning-
places, the change of water begins to affect them
here, and they leap on the shingle-stones, to gasp
a little and recover. But any attempt to catch
them in this situation always fails. They double
up "like a jack-knife", one is told, and spring
again into the water.

Otters were once populous here, and otter-
hounds still come at times. From the parapet
of the bridge one can still hope to see the otter
sliding downstream, breathing with his nose just
above water and keeping it artfully under a
drifting leaf.

The bridge itself is a survival from Machynlleth's coaching days. It has bays let out from its
parapets to enable pedestrians to avoid the
wheels of coaches in the middle of the way.

Dyfi Bridge, not so long ago, was the scene of
riotous assemblies, when the right to fish the
waters was disputed between townsmen of
Machynlleth and the owners of private rights.
Such scenes of public defiance were often
inspired by previous visits to public houses.
After one successful night-raid on the pool, a
member of the poaching gang, who was also a
bard, is said to have addressed the moon with the
triumphant and extempore lyric:

Reece Winstone

A fall of the Twymyn river, near Dylife

> O lleuad wen,
> O lleuad tlos!
> Ti 'n llawn bob mis.
> Mi 'n llawn bob nos!
>
> (O moon so fair,
> O moon so white!
> You're full each month.
> I'm full each night!)

DYLIFE, *Montgomeryshire*. This was the
name of a district, before it became the name for
the group of houses set on the edge of the Plynlimon escarpment not far from Llyn Glaslyn.
It has an inn whose history goes back to the
days of the mining enterprises that delved the
Plynlimon moors in the 18th and 19th cents., and
to the coaches that passed there from Staylittle
and beyond. The way to it from Staylittle mounts
rapidly, and the way from it falls as steeply under
Bryn y Fedwen, finding no habitation other than
Bryn Dan until the junction of small roads
between Croeslyn and Melinbyrhedyn. The views
over the Dovey valley – of Cader Idris, the Tarens,
and Aran Fawddwy – are magnificent. As the
ascent from the E. is made, the gorge of the River
Twymyn and the crags of the Pennant fall away
on the right and give some idea of the mountain
wildness that the moorland here can show.

It was probably from this display of torrents
that the word Dylife (Place of Floods) was given
to the area. From the wide road just opposite
the inn, a devoted walker can find the still remaining coach-road, stacked with slates against the
bog, though now much overgrown with whin and

heathers, passing its milestones with their early
19th-cent. lettering and leading down to the
habitable valleys. Although the present life of
the inn owes much to the techniques of road-
construction that have largely overcome the
challenge of the terrain, it always had a local
importance. Here a gallows was set up over the
wide horizon, so that all the world might see the
swinging malefactor and be warned. In the 1930s
the remains of one such victim of justice were
found nearby – a skull and certain 17th-cent.
trappings.

At Dylife too, until quite recently, were
conducted the sittings of the Court of Strays,
held among shepherds to decide the genuineness
of owner-markings on the fleeces of sheep and
the true parentage of lambs.

EBBW VALE, *Monmouthshire*. About 17 m.
NW. of Newport, and straddled across the
waves of steep little hills that seem to break
from the landward on to the southern coast,
Ebbw Vale ranks as an urban district. As with
so many coalfield communities, the impetus of
industrialism in the 19th cent. made it not so
much a centre of communal life as an area where
workers and their families were widely grouped
together. Its life was concerned with the winning
of coal and with the decline of that industry
generally, and the drop in population of 12 per
cent between 1939 and 1946, and the huge steel-
works that spread their galleries and great
stacks below the houses on the hills, have become
the dominant factors. As such, Ebbw Vale has
been fitted into an overall national system that
does not prevent it from expressing a personality
of its own. This is manifested through its exis-

tence as a county parliamentary constituency; and, like Abertillery, a neighbour and closely parallel place both in size and interest, it lives through its political allegiance. It is fairly solidly of one persuasion, though the economic fortunes of Britain as a whole may yet give its spirit of independence an outlet in some other direction than the traditional one. It will probably always be famous as the seat held by Aneurin Bevan, himself a strongly independent spirit, who was a real representative of the area in the strong convictions, witty intellect, and chivalry towards gallant opposition, that South Wales has always shown.

In the 1950s, the population dropped by 10 per cent to rather over 29,000, a little better than Abertillery's fall of 12 per cent, and that of Tredegar with much the same extent. Tredegar stands between Ebbw Vale and Merthyr Tydfil, forming part of the same conurbation, with the same interest in coal, but having lost to Ebbw Vale its once considerable steel industry. S. from it lies New Tredegar and the chances of a new South Wales.

EGLWYS-FACH, *Cardiganshire,* a most beautiful spot, can claim to be the chief centre of the parish of Ysgubor-y-coed (Barn in the Wood). It lies a little S. of Pontlyfnant, where the Aberystwyth road crosses the Llyfnant stream. Since the Llyfnant marks the boundary here between Montgomeryshire and Cardiganshire, the village is administratively over the border; but its history belongs to the economic activities centring on Machynlleth.

Gareg – spelt Garick on the old coaching maps, and Garreg on the tombstones in the churchyard of Eglwys-fach – stands close to the Dovey, though the railway more recently cut it off somewhat from the water. It was the last port-stage in the journey up the river from Aberdovey, and coals from South Wales were landed there in the early 19th cent., to be taken by wagon on the road to Glasbwll and Machynlleth. At the end of the journey, the coal was sold at an average price of 18s. a ton, though, if special quality was demanded, it might rise to 22s. Culm, a mixture of clay and coal, was of course cheaper, although it burnt longer. It was from Gareg that timber, mainly from Glasbwll and the fine oaks that filled its valleys, was shipped to Aberdovey and abroad. The interest of Gareg is that its houses, built in terracing from the road, show the original character of the village as a wharfing-place.

A little below Eglwys-fach, the famous falls of Furnace thunder close to the road, with an old mill-building still nearby. But the charm of the place is general. The church is an appealing 18th-cent. survival, and may well be older. Its graveyard monuments do not go further back than 1700; a study of them shows how important a place it was for so wide an area. Names from Penrhyn Gerwyn, far down the road to Taliesin, and from the homesteads of Cwm Einon, the Llyfnant Valley, and the moor-land communities to the westward side of Plynlimon show that it was a link between the upland farmer and the wider world of the Irish Sea. The skull and crossbones over one such grave do not necessarily imply, as local tradition says, that a pirate lies below. Such cheerful ornaments were common on memorials in the 18th cent. The situation of the church is delightful, and a road leads from the main highway, dropping along its side, to a pair of the islanded points characteristic of the Dovey estuary even as far inland as this: Ynys Edwin and Ynys Hir. The richness of the soil and the strength and dignity of the woodlands express the character of the district, and indeed of its people. From Eglwys-fach the way to Cwm Ere is easily found. The way to Cwm Einon lies to the S., and takes you not only to one of the most lovely valleys in the area but on to the line of the road, silent among remote hills, that carried the wheels in coaching days and, long before them, the feet of Rome's legionary auxiliaries.

Beyond Ynys Edwin and close to the Dovey banks stands the Domen Las, one of the ancient monuments to the area's past.

ELAN VALLEY, *Radnorshire.* The River Elan rises on the vast moorlands S. of the Plynlimon range and, after uniting its waters with the Claerwen, flows down into a wild, romantic valley to join the Wye at Rhayader. Perhaps one should use the past tense about the Elan's flowing, since Birmingham picked the valley as the source of its water supply and built a series of great dams to form the lakes that are now a major tourist attraction. Before the building of the dams, the valley was renowned for its remote beauty. Here Shelley brought his girl-wife Harriet to the old mansion of Cwmlan. He astonished the natives by his unconventional behaviour. They long remembered how he alleviated his boredom by sailing paper boats on the river; in one of them he put a cat and used a five-pound note as a sail. On his side, he wrote some revealing letters to his friend Hogg: "I have been to church today; they preach partly in Welsh, which sounds most singular. A christening was performed out of an old slop-basin!" But he was enchanted by the scenery. He decided on one of his recurrent schemes for retiring from the world with a community of ideal friends. He planned to buy Nantgwyllt in the Claerwen Valley, where he would settle with Godwin, the philosopher, and certainly with Godwin's daughters. The scheme came to nothing, and Shelley never returned.

Instead, at the end of last century, the water engineers from Birmingham arrived and began the construction of the magnificent series of dams that ended in 1952 with the final dam across the Claerwen. It must be admitted that these grey walls of heavy stone seem to fit into the landscape, and the lakes behind them are glorious when full to the brim after rain. The Claerwen alone is of concrete.

The earlier series of dams was begun in 1892 and completed in 1907, after being formally

Peter Baker

Elan Valley: the Penygarreg dam

opened by Edward VII in 1904. The first dam is Caban Coch, built at a narrow part of the valley, with impressive crags and tree-clad hill-sides all around. A fox once escaped the hounds by running half way up the centre of it. The dam impounds a lake of nearly 500 acres, and much of the water is allowed to flow for compensatory purposes into the Wye. Caban Coch becomes a show-piece after heavy rain in winter, when the whole face is covered with the overspill water.

At Garreg-Ddu a submerged causeway runs across the lake. All the water above this goes direct to Birmingham. As Birmingham has a scheme for running some of its waste water, after usage, into the River Trent, it can be claimed that water from these wild Welsh moorlands ends up in the North Sea. The topmost dam on the Elan is Craig Goch, enclosing over 200 acres. The highest part of the Elan Valley becomes wild, open, and bare, with the infant stream meandering over the peaty valley-floor. The great sheep-walks that surround the road leading eventually over to the steeply trenched valley of Cwm Ystwyth were originally in the possession of the monks of Strata Florida. Indeed, the monks possessed most of this central moorland country by the gift of the Lord Rhys, the powerful Welsh ruler of South Wales in the 12th cent. Like true Cistercians, they introduced sheep farming on a big scale. The present-day farmers of these hills are therefore the heirs of an old tradition.

The branch valley of the Claerwen was dammed after the Second World War. The dam was opened by Queen Elizabeth II. It is the largest of the dams and impounds a lake of over 600 acres. The farmhouse of Cerrig Coupla is placed immediately under the vast concrete wall, and the farmer goes about his business unaffected by the thought of the immense weight of water poised so near him.

The older farms in these valleys were of the ancient long-house pattern, with the quarters for animals at one end and the domestic quarters at the other. One of these long-house farms was dismantled when the Claerwen dam was constructed and re-erected in the National Folk Museum at St Fagan's, near Cardiff.

ELERCH, *Cardiganshire.* From Taliesin, whose name conveys the mystery of the learning kept alive along the Irish Sea in the shadowed "Arthurian" days that followed the fall of Rome, or from Bow Street, whose decorous cottages, they say, maintain the tradition of law and order that the Bow Street runner upheld before Peel thought of a police force for Britain, you can take the road at Tal-y-bont and go eastwards into the hills. Elerch, which you reach along roads much as the Bow Street runners would have known them, is still a place where the old crafts of the countryside are kept alive among flowered hedges, narrow lanes, and fields of sheep. In the village centre it has an immense stone that serves fittingly as a war memorial.

From Elerch you run high to find, on trackways that once led to the old mines about Drosgol and the Fainc Fawr (Great Bank), the lake of Syfydrin watched by the cairns and tumuli of vanished peoples, and then go further to see the greater lake of Nant-y-moch and its barrier dam flooding the heaped valley of the Rheidol. This is a desolate and beautiful place, and the chain of pools, islanded among the heave of the moorland, is not only the habitation of trout that offer athletic challenge to the angler, but a haunt for the still prolific wildlife of bird and beast. The pools have a traditional name; they are the Pools of Gogerddan, so called after a great house some way out of Aberystwyth and beyond the ancient church of Llanbadarn-Fawr, a house that stands by the Allt-derw (Oaken Height), to the N. of the Rheidol valley and that other ancient seat, Goginan. It was celebrated enough to have a song composed in its honour, "I Blas Gogerddan". Its other connection with the arts is through the name of Dafydd ap Gwilym, the great Welsh poet of the 14th cent. whom some European critics have claimed to be the greatest lyric poet of the Middle Ages in the West. It is no direct connection, but his friend and fellow poet, Rhydderch, was born at Plas Gogerddan, and one of Dafydd's poems is an elegy on Rhydderch's death; no doubt the two spent much time together in the mansion by Allt-derw. Brogynin and Goginan nearby are the places where Dafydd himself had his personal origins, though the homestead of Brogynin was not built till some time after Dafydd died; its date was 1460.

Plas Gogerddan was an outstanding example of the homes belonging to the squires of old Wales. Its family, the Pryses of Gogerddan, could claim descent from the rulers of sub-Roman times, one of whom, by a perverse legend, was said to be responsible for the drowning of the mythical land of Gwaelod beneath the waters of Cardigan Bay. The black lion badge of Gwaethfod continued in the family through all its history. They were lords of Ceredigion, wearing the brow-fillet that served for a crown; one of them became lay abbot of Llanbadarn, and Gerald de Barri met him in 1188 on his way through Wales. A bad habit it was, says Gerald, that some of these remoter Welsh places continued the custom of appointing such laymen to ecclesiastical office. It was quite a usual custom with the ancient Celtic Church of the 5th and 6th cents., and many of their saints were such lay protectors of the priests. Gogerddan is for us a most interesting example of the survival of the usage almost into the 13th cent. But Gogerddan has earlier and darker memories. Many of the mounds and camps that lie upon the hill-sides over the Pools of Gogerddan are from the Iron Age. But several of them belong to the days of the Black Army, when Welshmen and Saxon had wasted each other in a civil war of religion, and the Dane took advantage of it. He came in his ships to Aberystwyth, and from there landed and took horse and set up his fortresses, demanding tribute, supplies, and the payment of a silver penny per head from all the inhabitants. It was a skilful plan of conquest and annexation. The Rheidol valley gave the Dane control of the western approaches to the hill-bridge between Dovey and Severn at Caersws from which the way lay wide into England. The camp by Gogerddan and the one by Buttington were strategic points from which all Britain was at his mercy. Wales under Rhodri the Great was able to escape the menace, and Alfred of Wessex to save at least some of England; but Canute succeeded in annexing England for a while to his empire of the North Sea.

In the reign of Mary of England, the Pryse of that day became a member of the Council of Wales and the Marches, and sat in Parliament in that capacity both at Ludlow and Westminster. "I Blas Gogerddan" seems to have been composed at that time by one of the harp-men whom he patronized. A grandson of his married the widow of the painter Van Dyck in the 17th cent. Gogerddan supported Parliament in the Civil Wars, an unusual thing in Wales; but when the Old Pretender planned his descent on Scotland in 1715, and, even after that, the Jacobites were in touch with the house; for a letter remains, dated 1717, from the exiled Earl of Mar asking for continued support. There were stirrings in Wales of sympathy for both the Pretenders; the Society of Sea Serjeants, formed among the Welsh gentry in the 18th cent., seems to have been devoted to the Stuart cause. And a persistent legend says that the Young Pretender, Bonnie Prince Charlie, found refuge in Plas Gogerddan after his flight from the Scottish Isles. The house is now largely of 1860, when 15th-cent. buildings were brought down.

South of Goginan, lonely in the moors, are more of the Gogerddan Pools by Fron Goch.

ESGAIRGEILIOG, *Merioneth.* The village of the Cock Rock is a picturesque place on the old road from Ffridd Gate to Corris. It stands in a sharp dip of ground where the Glesyrch stream runs through its little gorge to join the Dulas. That Esgairgeiliog was once principally a place for slate-quarrying and slate-enamelling is very obvious, since the cuttings are piled high against the hill-sides, into which, however, they effectively merge. Now, the very considerable development of forestry projects in the area has turned the attention of the village to timber in all its aspects: planting, trimming, falling, and tushing – to use the technical terms for tree-felling and drawing the great logs down the hill-breast for stacking. The hutments of the Forestry Commission are now a dominant suburb of the village. Here and there some modernization has been carried out, but the village still keeps its individual character.

The Glesyrch vale can be reached by taking a small footpath behind the cluster of houses near the bridge. The hills drop into it from a height of 1,000 ft, and it is a very pleasant and secluded example of the valley community Wales in this area so often provides. Close to the village, and set on small hillocks in deep woods, are two or three outstanding farmhouses of early Stuart-type architecture, beautiful in themselves and beautifully sited.

EWENNY, *Glamorgan.* This little village lies 1½ m. S. of Bridgend on the northern slope of a low hill. The small pottery industry is still established here, and Ewenny ware is still for sale. But the great attraction of the place is Ewenny Priory, which can claim to be the best example of Norman ecclesiastical architecture in Wales. The conventual buildings and church overlook the meadows of the Ewenny river, which joins the Ogmore close at hand. The Priory was founded by Maurice de Londres and was linked with the Benedictine Abbey of St Peter's, Gloucester, by a deed of gift dated 1141. Little remains of the Priory buildings, but the impressive circuit defensive walls, built mainly in the 13th cent., still stand encircling an area of over 5 acres. The principal gateway preserves its portcullis grooves. The modern mansion stands inside the circuit walls, which have recently been restored by the Ministry of Public Building and Works. There is a large columbarium in the mansion grounds, which remain private.

The church, in spite of alterations, is still wholly Norman in character, with powerful cylindrical columns and rounded arches. The N. transept was demolished in the last century, after falling into ruin, and the plain W. wall was built at the same time. The porch is a Tudor addition. Otherwise the Priory's whole atmosphere is of the 12th and early 13th cents. The font is Norman. An 8-ft wall separated the nave from the monastic church. The choir is beneath the vaulted tower. The S. transept is unaltered, with a fine arcaded gallery leading up to a door in the tower. This transept contains sepulchral slabs, including one of the founder, which gives an excellent example of a Norman-French inscription in Lombardic characters, reading: "Here lies Maurice de Londres, the Founder. God reward him for his services". The transept also has an altar tomb to a member of the Carne family and a touching memorial to John Carne (died 1700, aged fifteen): "Ewenny's hope, Ewenny's pride". Ewenny Priory is now undergoing a prolonged restoration, and the nave is visible only on occasions. When complete, the Priory will be restored to its former splendour.

From the churchyard, the military character of the building can be easily appreciated. The tower is strongly embattled, and battlements also run round the whole roof of the S. transept. On the outside S. wall is a Mass dial, which gave the time of the four principal monastic services. The churchyard yews are venerable, and a sunken path between cypresses leads to the porch. In the churchyard are supposed to be buried a native of Ewenny who was cook to Charles I and another who was smith to Cromwell.

On the hill leading to Colwinston is the small Methodist chapel associated with the Victorian preacher Edward Mathews (Mathews o'r Wenni). He was one of the great practitioners of that dramatic oratory which was the glory of the old Welsh pulpit.

Barnaby/Mustograph

Llyn y Fan Fach, looking down from the Carmarthen Van

FANAU, *Breconshire.* The high Fanau, or Vans, stretch E. across the Fforest Fawr to the Brecon Beacons. Fan Fawr, or Carmarthen Van, with its heights of Fan Foel and Fan Hir; Fan Gyhirych; Fan Llia; and the other Fan Fawr; range from 2,000 to 2,600 ft. Westward they run into the Black Mountain of these parts, and over their shoulders the Roman road goes between Gyhirych and Llia. The motor road from Craig-y-Nos Castle to Cray finds an ancient stone circle by the reservoir below Gyhirych; it is an area where lake and broad pasture, and the uplift over the valleys dense with woods, attracted men in the earliest ages to settle and study the working of stars and sun and know that they were in the hands of an ordered Universe. It is therefore a place where legend keeps the memory of these forgotten societies, their strange wisdom and peaceful innocence.

Llyn y Fan Fach (Little Van lake) lies under a steep circuit of Old Red Sandstone at 1,600 ft. The bed of it is also of the same stone, and once it gave good trout – daily taken in great store, it was said in the 17th cent. But it was even more famous for its eels, many of which were trapped when the reservoir was built; and, when it was the practice to set traps for them at the influx of the streams, they were said to reach 10 ft in length. The memory of the old lake-dwellers was long preserved in the tale about one of the Other People (*see* Black Mountain). Some 4 m. E. from Llandeilo, beyond the Black Mountain, is the cave called Llygad Llwchwr from which the Afon Llwchwr (Loughor) flows that has

been supposed by some to rise from the Fan Fach lake.

But of Llyn y Fan Fawr a less pleasing tale is told. Something tremendous hangs about the Fanau; once, it seems, their high walls of ancient, dark sandstone marked the primordial shore of the Atlantic. But, though the Fan Fach lake was remarkable for its fish, the Fan Fawr had no fish at all; when trout were put there, they died at once. In 1687 the head of Fan Foel fell thunderously into the pool. According to the legend, whenever death was threatened to a member of the house nearby, called Bwysua, from the waters always came a lady of the lake prophesying woe.

FARMERS, *Carmarthenshire.* This unusually named village lies, as you might expect, in deeply agricultural country; it is in the Twrch valley, near Pumsaint and 5 m. SE. of Lampeter. There is some uncertainty about the origin of the name. The village inn cannot be responsible for it, since this is the Drover's Arms, a friendly hostelry with an elaborate inn-sign. The fat Herefords depicted in the painting, however, would never have lasted more than a few miles on the long roads to England over which the drovers of the district herded their tough Welsh Blacks to market. The village is scattered. The 13th-cent. church with its heavy tower has been greatly restored, as is usual in these parts. The smithy at the top end of the village is still in business for pony-trekkers, although it has kept up with the times by adding petrol service and car repairs.

Bethel Baptist chapel dates from 1740, with rebuilding in 1820. Note the house at the entrance to the graveyard still carrying the frame for the old oil-lamp.

The Roman road from the gold-mines passed through Farmers on its way over into the upper valley of the Teifi. A more spectacular, narrow modern road into the Teifi valley goes to the top of the Twrch valley and thence, over the moors, to Llanddewibrefi. It reaches a height of 1,482 ft at the summit. Here you are on the southern edge of the great and lonely expanse of mountain land that runs without a break to Plynlimon 30 m. to the N. The wilderness is usually marked on the map as the Cambrian Mountains. Of recent years the Forestry Commission has acquired large areas of the old sheep farms, and plantations are changing the whole character of the country.

About ¾ m. due W. of Farmers is Ffaldybrenin (King's Fold). The hamlet is merely a crossroads with some pleasant houses, one of which proudly preserves an old hand-pump in the front garden. The farms hereabouts have remained faithful so far to the old custom of coating their walls with colour or whitewash. The Ffaldybrenin Independent congregation was famous in the religious history of Wales in the 18th and early 19th cents. The big Independent chapel at the crossroads was rebuilt in 1873, from the original foundation of 1833. The celebrated preacher "Kilsby" Jones was a schoolmaster for a short time (1833–4) at Ffaldybrenin, where his father was born. "Kilsby" was one of the great eccentrics, a powerful preacher who broke every rule, a wit and an "original". It was long remembered in Ffaldybrenin how he marched his pupils down to the laying of the foundation-stone of the first chapel, and gave every one of his scholars a caning to make certain they would remember a historic occasion – but only a gentle tap to the younger ones. He earned his fellow countrymen's gratitude by editing the works of William Williams of Pantycelyn.

Opposite the chapel, on the other side of the crossroads, is a low building, now in decay. This was once the village smithy. A tablet in Welsh on the wall proclaims that it was the birthplace of Timothy Richards, who became a Baptist missionary in China in 1869. This remarkable man was also a distinguished scholar and an able administrator. He so impressed the Chinese that they called him Li T'i Mo Tai and created him a mandarin of the highest rank and a member of the Order of the Double Dragon. He died in 1915.

A little to the N. of Ffaldybrenin is Llanycrwys (Church of the Cross). The church, dedicated to St David, is basically 19th-cent., but it stands on an ancient site. The old parish pound is close by. Among the hills, 1 m. NW. of the village, is the Hirfaen Gwyddog, a 15-ft-high monolith that marks the boundary between Carmarthenshire and Cardiganshire. It is a little difficult to find, but it deserves mention as it is the tallest monolith in the county and the boundary-stone with the longest historical record in Wales. It is noted on the margin of the Book of St Chad and in the 12th-cent. charter of Talley Abbey.

FERRYSIDE, *Carmarthenshire,* is a village built round a station at the mouth of the Towy estuary. Its architecture is limited to villas, a hotel or two, a Victorian church, and the main railway line to West Wales hugging the shore. But what a site! The Towy widens here, and the long line of sand-dunes guard the estuary exit. Llanstephan lies across the water, with its castle perched on the high, wooded bluff fronting the sea. Behind are the green hills. No wonder the view was a favourite subject with Morland Lewis, the distinguished Welsh painter and a follower of Sickert. Boats can be hired to cross the river at high tide. The River Towy Yacht Club stands over the railway line on the sea-front.

From Ferryside the Towy winds inland and is tidal to beyond Carmarthen. Sir Thomas Picton departed for Waterloo and his death from the now-abandoned mansion of Iscoed, 1 m. to the N. To the S., on a magnificent position overlooking the estuary, is the old Church of St Ishmael. The church is 13th cent., with a saddleback roof and a fascinating mixture of porch, turrets, and building at odd levels. It is more attractive without than within. All the gravestones very correctly turn their backs to the sea, whence came the great storm that took away the upper storey of the old tower.

Inland from St Ishmael, and reached by a narrow road turning up from the Kidwelly-Ferryside coast road at Tan-y-lan, is the very Welsh village of Llansaint, full of small stone houses gathered round the heavily restored church. The main industry of the place used to be cocklegathering, and long processions of sturdy women, their donkeys slung with enormous panniers, marched out in all weathers to the long sands at the mouth of the Towy estuary. The cockles and their gatherers are now things of the past.

FFESTINIOG, *Merioneth.* Some 3 m. from the slate-quarrying town of Blaenau Ffestiniog, this most attractive village stands at the head of the beautiful vale of the same name. It looks down towards Maentwrog, a place of equal attraction, and on the road that will take you to Bala under the slopes of the Migneint moor and the tops of the Arennigs on either side. It inspired among others the enthusiastic comment of Lord Lyttleton, many years ago, that it was a paradise of which Omar Khayyám would approve. At least it offers various mountain walks and several lakes with good fishing. The Cynfal falls are worth a visit, if only for the curiosity known as Hugh Lloyd's Pulpit, a tall column of rock rising out of the stream said to have been used by a magician in the time of James I for summoning spirits. About 3 m. further on are the Rhaeadr Cwm cataracts and the falls known as Rhaeadr Ddu and Raven Falls, in the Prysor river, now harnessed for the distribution of electrical supplies all over North

Wales and into Montgomeryshire, Cardiganshire, Shropshire, and Cheshire.

Tomen y Mur (Mound of the Wall), to the S., is an important relic of Roman days. Two Roman roads meet there, and the site was occupied by a station, or military garrison, dating probably from A.D. 100. But the mound itself was thrown up to carry a medieval castle, built by William Rufus, son and successor of William the Conqueror of England, as a holding position during his raids into Wales about 1095. The village of Maentwrog is close at hand. Llyn Conwy, on the road to Ysbyty Ifan, is a lake magnificently set among hills that give extraordinary views of the Snowdon area. Its trout are excellent.

FFRIDD GATE, *Montgomeryshire.* This is an attractive though tiny place lying at the opening of the Corris valley where the River Dulas runs into the Dovey. It was an important point on the coach-road in the days when the main highway ran to the N. of the Dovey and not along the S. side, as it does now. It has an old bridge, a good salmon pool, and pleasant houses, including what was once a mill, sheltered from what has become the major road to Corris, and the place remains much as it was 150 years ago.

It is the junction for the two ancient roads – one going northwards to Esgairgeiliog and Plas Llwyngwern, the other to Llanwrin and Mathafarn – that not only take you through outstandingly pleasant and varied scenery, but through a living picture of the past, in particular of the past of Powys.

Above Ffridd Gate rises the bluff of a solid hill whose footways and passes lead to Aberllefenni, Corris, and Cemaes.

Until about twenty years ago, the Corris section of the Tal-y-llyn and Corris Light Railway ran its toy engine and carriages from the yards at Machynlleth station to Corris and beyond through Ffridd Gate, setting its bridge over the Dovey at this point. The river bluff rises somewhat steeply here over a pool excellent for salmon. In the wall-like sides of the stream the holes that martins make when nesting can be readily seen, and their weaving flight to and fro, skimming the water through the evening, is attractive to watch.

The Corris railway is now a thing of the past; only the uprights bearing its bridge remain, shouldering through the flow of water. The open sides of its carriages used to give remarkable views of the miniature gorges of the Dulas river. The way to Corris is now most usually taken on the motor road sweeping through the very beautiful Dulas valley up the steady rise to Upper Corris and down to the lake at the foot of Cader Idris. This is a convenient route, and in no way to be despised for what it brings. It passes some pleasant groups of houses claiming some sort of village status, including Pantperthog. This spot gives a footnote to railway history. One of its few sons gallantly volunteered for military service in the First World War and went through

his basic training in Scotland. On his first week's leave he was provided with a railway pass duly made out for Pantperthog; for, look you now, Pantperthog was indeed on the line of the Corris railway. He had so little English, and guards, inspectors, ticket-collectors, and (one might add) engine-drivers had so little awareness of a place called Pantperthog, that his whole leave was spent in the effort to arrive there.

Beyond this point, the bridge crossing the Dulas can be found as it leads to Llwyngwern and the much older coach-road that takes you to Corris. This historic route can be travelled from Ffridd Gate, but at that end is far more suitable for the horseman or the walker than for cars. It is a road in the natural state of roads, accepting the rise and fall of the ground, finding its way round cliffs of slate, running through woods now rapidly being supplanted by conifer forests but still surviving between the road and river, and giving several opportunities to see the river close at hand in its wildest beauty.

This is the road as it was when Romans travelled it. What earlier history it had is, for the moment, unestablished. But certainly it formed part of their inner system of patrol. At Ffridd Gate it swung to find a convenient fordage, and found one at Dyfi Bridge, keeping westward to reach Pennal and turning S. across the river for Machynlleth, from which it joined the extension of its system of communication coasting the sea down to Taliesin and Tal-y-bont and further. From Ffridd Gate, too, it most probably thrust an arm towards Mathafarn and so to Cemaes and Mallwyd.

FISHGUARD, *Pembrokeshire.* In Welsh called Abergwaun, Fishguard is a scattered township looking out over the wide Fishguard Bay, with the slopes of the Mynydd Preseli behind. The place seems to turn its back on the rest of Britain and gaze constantly westward. This is not surprising, for Fishguard has become the terminus for the Irish boats to Rosslare and Cork. Irish money circulates here. The great breakwater, built in 1907, shelters the modern harbour with the railway station and quay. This expensive work was undertaken in the expectation that the Atlantic liners would make Fishguard their first port of call, and thus allow passengers to be whisked up to London by fast trains. The Atlantic trade faded with the outbreak of the First World War. Fishguard is now exclusively an Irish ferry terminal.

The place is really divided into three. The quay and terminal are placed near Goodwick, under the steep headland of Carncoed. Goodwick itself was a small fishing village until the harbour was built. It looks out across a sandy beach to the line of the breakwater and the fine headland of Dinas on the other side of Fishguard Bay.

Upper Fishguard stands back a little from the sea about 1½ m. from Goodwick. The houses are mainly grouped round the small square, where the Royal Oak Hotel has historical associations. From the square the road drops steeply down to the winding creek that shelters Lower Town, in Welsh "Y Cwm". Here the River Gwaun enters the sea. The place has the air of a Cornish or Breton fishing village, with one narrow street that is a terror for summer tourists with caravans, and a picturesque quay. Lower Town is now the headquarters of the flourishing Fishguard Bay Yacht Club. The pier was originally built by Samuel Fenton, to service the then flourishing pilchard fishing. The pilchards (adult sardines) have now ceased to visit Welsh waters in shoals, and the fishery has died out.

During the American War of Independence, the celebrated privateer Paul Jones appeared off Fishguard and seized one of Samuel Fenton's ships. He then landed a party and under threat of bombardment demanded 500 guineas from the lower and upper town in return for release of the ship. The ransoms were paid, but warning shots damaged the town and lamed Mary, the sister of Richard Fenton, Samuel's neighbour.

Richard Fenton was an attractive character. He built the charming house of Glynamel that still stands at the mouth of the Gwaun valley. Here he lived with his French wife, to whom he had been introduced by Oliver Goldsmith. In 1811 he published his vivid *Historical Tour Through Pembrokeshire*, from which later writers have delighted to quote, although modern historians treat it with caution.

The big event in the history of Fishguard, inspiring from the inhabitants a response in which they still take legitimate pride, was the French Invasion of 1797 (*see* p. 45). This was the last time any hostile foreign force landed on British soil, and one local heroine, Jemima Nicholas, is said to have rounded up several Frenchmen with a pitchfork.

FLINT, *Flintshire*. The county of Flint has the distinction of being in two parts, separated by a wide arm of Denbighshire. The larger and western section was known in Welsh as Tegeingl (or, as Giraldus Cambrensis wrote it in the 12th cent., Tegengel), in which has been found a perpetuation of the name of the Celtic people the Romans found in North Wales, the Deceangli. The smaller and eastward part the Welsh call Maelor, sometimes Saxon Maelor. There is some interest in this word, since it has been thought that Malory, the knight who immortalized his own name by writing the *Morte D'Arthur*, drew it from the area in which his family was founded. The division was created largely by the bitter fighting from the 7th cent. onwards between Wales and England for control of this key sector, a contest in which it can be said that neither completely won.

Flint, the town, has given the whole county its name, though no longer the most important of its townships. Mold has succeeded it as capital. As a town, Flint seems to belong more to the England of the industrial belt than to the Wales of the North. Chemical-works, artificial-silk factories, and ranks of tall chimneys affect its skyline; for it is close to the North Welsh coal-

Barnaby/Mustograph

The forlorn remains of Flint Castle

field, whose products are admirably suited for that kind of industry. We must not suppose, however, that this is in any way a breach of long tradition. The coaching-maps of the early 19th cent. record the district as rich in lead-mines, as it still remains, and in the 12th cent. Gerald de Barri, the Welsh cleric already mentioned as Giraldus Cambrensis, noted that it was a country rich in silver, where money was sought in the bowels of the earth. He also mentions a place he terms Coleshulle (Mountain of Coal), which was worked there at the same period. He was not able to note the castle, still set on the strand of sea, though now in much ruin, for it was not established until 100 years later than his visit to the North when, in 1277, Edward I made it the easternmost and first of the chain of strongholds he built, from Flint, through Conway, Denbigh, Rhuddlan, Caernarfon, Beaumaris, and Criccieth to Harlech, as a means of subjecting the territory he had wrested from the last Llywelyn. The simple, four-square plan of Flint Castle, with its drum-towers at each angle, is remarkable for one thing: the keep, or main system of defence, is not, as in all other such fortresses, centred within the enceinte or walled surround of the place. It is outside the battlemented square on a separate islet of its own, and was connected with the rest of the fortifications by a drawbridge of its own. As a point from which the passage to Ireland could be maintained and controlled, Flint played its part in the politics of Britain, first when it received Piers Gaveston, the suspect favourite of Edward II, on his recall as Lord-Lieutenant of Ireland, shortly before both he and his master were removed from all authority; and again when Richard II, attempting a dictatorship against the principles on which Magna Carta had been issued, was forced to surrender to the man chosen by the Parliament of England – his supplanter and successor, Henry Bolingbroke, the fourth Henry to reign. Shakespeare's reference to this event, in his *Richard II*, makes the King speak of the Castle's tattered battlements. This may have been some sort of poetic foresight, since the Castle was not reduced to its ruinous state until the Civil Wars of the 17th cent. Sir Roger Mostyn held it for the King, Charles I, but was starved into surrender in 1643. Royalists recaptured it in 1645, but it fell again in the following year. Since then, Flint has turned its attention to unwarlike matters. But, in view of its earlier history of conflict, a further note from Gerald de Barri is worth making.

He points out that Henry II of England, actuated by youthful and indiscreet ardour (as Gerald puts it), made a hostile irruption into Wales through the Tegengel, and suffered signal defeat. Indeed, both in 1157 and 1165 Henry was driven back from the North, as he was in 1162 from the South. Gerald blames him for not taking advice from those skilled in the matter of Welsh wars, in which the Welsh long-bow, drawn back to the ear, far surpassed the English weapon, which in the 12th cent. was still taken back only to the breast. But during these campaigns an incident occurred that is best recounted as Gerald himself wrote of it.

In the wood of Coleshulle, a young Welshman was killed while passing through the King's army. The greyhound that accompanied him stayed by his master's body for eight days, though without food, faithfully defending it from the attacks of wolves and beasts of prey. What son to his father, asks Gerald, would have shown such affectionate regard? As a mark of favour to the dog, the English, though bitter enemies of the Welsh, ordered the young Welshman's body, now nearly putrid, to be buried with the accustomed offices of humanity.

FORGE, *Montgomeryshire,* is a group of cottages strung along the roadside about 1½ m. SE. of Machynlleth on the way to Dylife. A bridge crosses a steep and narrow river-bed to follow the major road, but a practicable way avoids crossing the bridge and leads to the remote upland farm of Tal-y-bont Drain and the loveliest of the valleys cut into the side of the Plynlimon range. The narrowness of the route demands the utmost care, and the steadily rising hills provide a variety of scenery; and at Tal-y-bont Drain the heads of the Aran Fawddwy and Aran Benllyn, Cader Idris and Taren y Gesail, make themselves evident. It is possible to drive down into the valley of the Hengwm, but perhaps not advisable. To make the venture is to have the opportunity of following the ancient drove-routes towards Hyddgen and the Rheidol valley through the fir-plantations set by the Forestry Commission during the past twenty years and climbing the precipitous slopes. In the Hengwm valley itself, however, the road-surface does not make the experiment advisable, as yet. A little before making the descent, good forestry roads, turning to the left, lead to the farms and woodlands surrounding Cefn Modfedd (the curiously named Inch Hill). The Rhiw Goch (Red Slope) sheers upwards on the eastern side to the right, rising for 1,000 ft in a regular incline to a point. This regularity is too marked not to suggest the possibility of an artificial construction. The peak dominates the whole area to the S. of the Plynlimon escarpment, and for generations has been accepted by shepherds as the principal marking-point for their way from valley to valley. Ancient cairns and tumuli are scattered over the ridges nearby. At the further end of the Hengwm valley the river falls in a steep and sliding cataract.

Forge village is more properly named Fforg, and there is some dispute whether this name derives from a Scandinavian *force* (stream), or from the plain English "forge". The industry associated with it in the past is that of woolmaking and weaving, characteristic of the whole district, particularly in the 1850s. Water-mills were essential for the preparation of the product, and the centres of production were called "pandy". In Forge it is difficult now to find evidence of such fulling-mills; but between Forge and Penegoes, and in Penegoes itself, the water-wheels can still be seen, unturning and overgrown, in streams over which the mill-houses remain.

The approach to Forge from Machynlleth passes under a miniature slate quarry, worked on the face of the hill. Always small, it was operated by no more than a pair of men. Unluckily, some mishandling of the crane threw the cutter to his death, and the machinery and rails needed for the working now stand rusted and unused. A deep, water-filled hole, however, gives evidence of much earlier and deeper mining. Slate is the typical feature of the Plynlimon country, and, as you mount the sheep-tracks over the waterfalls of Rhaeadr or Hengwm in particular, the buckled formations, crumbling to loose shale, give a cross-section of the rock-structures that were strained into their present shape by the earth's upheaval from the seas millennia ago.

If you go down the Rhiwlwyfan road late at night, you become aware that the valley is haunted by the great white barn-owl; its ghostly shape and voice urge you on your way as it makes its comments on the world.

GLASBURY, *Radnorshire*, stands 4 m. SW. of Hay-on-Wye in a curve of the Wye river. Its church is in Breconshire, and belongs to the parish of Tregoed and Felindre. At Clyro is a Roman camp, recently confirmed as being large enough to accommodate an entire legion: a Roman military station that seems to stand like an isolated outpost thrusting westward into the Ellennith from Kenchester, which was Magnis, unconnected with anything between the station at Llandrindod and the Gobannium

Top: *The harbour at Lower Town, Fishguard*   Jane J. Miller
Bottom: *Hilly country near Glyndyfrdwy*   Peter Baker

we now call Abergavenny. The camp at Clyro, which from its size must have been for settled use, has a definite connection with the one at Glasbury. This was found more recently. It appears as an enclosure with two straight sides and rounded ends, typical of its kind, and set close to Glasbury railway upon a spur of hill that runs out into the valley, and from which the site of the camp at Clyro can in fact be observed. The place is called Heol y Gaer (Fort upon the Roadway); it always has been. And there are still indications that the Roman troops laid down along the valley a highway that took in the camp as a matter of course. That signals could be passed in direct line of sight from one to the other is evidence of the care with which the whole alignment was planned; similar examples can be found along the old lines of communication about the Dovey valley and elsewhere. Heol y Gaer was as large a station as the one at Clyro; either the Clyro fort could send its men out on expedition as an entire body or, more probably, another legion could encamp further down the Wye, and the two together co-operate in whatever their task might be. Both sites are set on a projecting spur of hill above the stream, for the river was liable to flood, and no commander could accept such a risk in such a country.

The dates for the two stations have yet to be fully confirmed. But the important thing is the strategic movement they represented, and the shaping of the history of Wales, and of Britain as a whole, that they initiated. The Wye at this point gives the best opening for the way into the West from the English plains; the Llynfi valley takes the route from Herefordshire down to Talgarth and Llangorse under the Black Mountains, and so to Brecon and the Usk valley to march past the Beacons. Only from such a southward point could you strike effectively into the hills of Ellennith; for towards Builth the way was blocked under the Begwns by a narrow river gorge. Heol y Gaer apparently served its turn. The campaign was effective, and it was left without further development to stand in squared ridges of green to watch the valley unsentinelled. But the long Roman road that followed on the other side of the valley reached to the towns of Moridunum, Alabum, and Bremia (Carmarthen, Llandovery, and Pontllanio), and to the networked system called the Sarn Helen that reached through the moorlands and the iron, copper, lead, and silver they concealed. This was the beginning of the settlement of Wales, and the birth of its valleyed communities in which its spirit was born.

Clyro and Glasbury are now pleasant places of woodland and water tamed to man's use. This angle of the border saw men-at-arms of many sorts succeed the Roman troops, but the work they did is as much monumented by the farm and the quarry at Heol y Gaer as by the grassy ridges that once bore their palisades.

GLASBWLL, *Cardiganshire*, is a small but highly interesting group of houses and cottages about 3 m. from Machynlleth, and best reached from that direction by turning off the Aberystwyth road at Gelli Goch (Red Grove) and following the way past Garthowen. It can also be reached, though less directly, from the Llyfnant Valley.

Its name means Grey Pool, and it lies in the hollow of a group of hills clustered about the foot of Plynlimon and at the junction of the rocky Llyfnant (Flood Brook) stream and the waters from Cwm Rhaeadr.

In former days it was a place of quite considerable industry, in timber, fulling, and even lead-mining; and, from a very distant past, it stood on the main route between Machynlleth and the busy river-ports on the Dovey, at Gareg and Glandyfi. Now it is dominated by agriculture, sheep-raising, and the growth of softwoods, which are gradually replacing the crowded and stately oak-woods spreading across its streams. Records of the houses set upon the hill-sides go far back into the 18th cent. One of them, Caersaer, seems to preserve in its name (Saw-Wood Field) a memory of the local industry that shipped logs as far afield as Canada, though later records show it to have worked as a unit in the woollen and cloth-making industry.

A cottage, Ty Mawr (Large House), recently modernized in its upper storey, and facing Caersaer across the stream, is worth noting as providing one of the most illuminating incidents in George Borrow's travels through the district on his way to the Potosi lead-mines about Plynlimon. In his *Wild Wales* he describes his walk from Machynlleth to Glasbwll apparently over Y Wylfa, and past the ancient farms of Bwlch y Groes Faen (Stone-Cross Gap) and Cae Bobion (perhaps Baker's Field). After stopping on the wayside to talk with a field-worker who, significantly, preferred to talk to Borrow in English rather than reply to Borrow's version of Welsh, he approached Ty Mawr to ask for further directions. Two Welsh women in the native dress of the district appeared. He used Welsh to talk to them, but was taken aback by their reception. The door was shut in his face, and he went his way, noting that they were probably Celtic intransigents, hating the sight and sound of an Englishman like himself. But the incident was also preserved in the memory of the family at Ty Mawr. His inquiry was unintelligible to the Welsh women, and his large stature, white hair, and piercing eyes filled them with terror.

He pursued his path towards Cwm Rhaeadr (Valley of the Waterfall), and a similar journey can be made now by a good road that ends, in effect, at Plas Cwm Rhaeadr. You can take a mountain-track some way further as it rises to the left, but it is better to go on foot up to the shoulder of Rhiw Goch. From this point, three ancient cairns, marked on the Ordnance Survey map, can be made out against the skyline. They stand high over the dangerous falls of Rhaeadr and overlook a steeply sided valley of great beauty. These cairns lie in direct line between Glasbwll and the Carn Gwilym, which faces Plynlimon Fawr at Hyddgen. In this way an

Plate 9 "Snowdon from Llyn Nantlle", c. 1766, by Richard Wilson   *Walker Art Gallery, Liverpool*
Plate 10 "Waterfall in Cardiganshire", 1947, by Ceri Richards   *National Museum of Wales*

ancient route-system was organized between Darowen and Machynlleth, in its turn connected with the trackways following the Rheidol and the Severn.

The valley of Cwm Rhaeadr itself can be approached on foot past Plas Cwm Rhaeadr farm. From the shoulder of Rhiw Goch a way can be made – again preferably on foot – to the old sheep-drove route, picking up the new Forestry Commission roads either to Llyn Pen Rhaeadr or to Hyddgen. Part of the interest of this difficult approach is that it takes you directly to the relics of the Potosi lead-mining enterprise visited by Borrow. Several of its driving-levels, pumps, and wheels remain, disused and in some cases dangerous to approach, about Hyddgen itself and at the foot of the Rhaeadr fall, at Cwm Byr (Short Valley), at the foot of Mawnog (Peat Hollow) close at hand, and elsewhere.

Alternatively, it is possible from this point on Rhiw Goch to find a way down to the road running from Ceniarth to Tal-y-bont Drain, past old farmsteads neglected through the modern need for quick-growing softwoods, and to a tiny group of cottages including one of the smallest chapels ever built.

From Glasbwll itself, starting from the cottage known as Ty Gwyn (White House), a sharply inclined and cornered road leads to Cefn-coch (Red Ridge) through a pleasant run of thickly wooded slopes and to the ridge at the head of the falls. This has particular interest for archaeologists because of the "twmps" or mounds set around Pen Creigiau'r Llan.

Another way from Glasbwll, again rising steeply and roughly, is equally interesting. It leads to Bwlch and to Rhiwlwyfan (Platform Hill), and at last to Forge. Both Bwlch and Rhiwlwyfan are now farmhouses; but the evidence is strong, from the working of the sites, that they were at first created as observation-posts during the late Roman occupation. Rhiwlwyfan in particular is an outstanding example of Welsh farmhouse-building, and preserves the features of 16th- and 17th-cent. architecture.

Above the stream dividing Ty Mawr from the cottage Ty Gwyn, the half-timbered face of Caersaer can be made out. This old and charming residence is better seen from the bank of the Llyfnant, as it forces its way through the rocks towards the Dovey to the W. Higher still above it, on a prominent hill-head, is the house Garthgwynion. The site is very beautiful, and the valley beyond it, filled with green, justifies the contention that Glasbwll gets its name not from the blue-grey of the water pool but the bluish green of the rich grass. Set close to Caersaer are some of its equally old out-buildings. They include a small chapel, built, as was the custom several generations ago, by the landowner solely for the use of the valley people. Completed about 1853, it had just over 100 years of life before, through lack of use, it went for sale.

Beautiful walks can be made from the older road to Machynlleth lying on the eastern side of the valley. They lead to Bryn-glas and to Glan-meryn. The Bryn-glas track is particularly interesting, since it takes in a relic of an earlier pack-horse route, or perhaps a road that dates back even further. It can be seen from the surrounding hills as a green continuous line still with the edge towards the hill-drop stacked close with slate-shale wedged in the soil for support.

The farm at Glan-meryn overlooks what is called Glan-meryn lake. This artificial pool, made by draining from the boggy land around it, was many times stocked with fish and equally often surreptitiously cleared of them by unknown persons. It can be easily reached from Machynlleth on foot. The area is very lovely. The lake is visited in great numbers by the type of dragonfly known as demoiselle; its blueness fits with the range of colour in the wild flowers that, since the reduction of rabbits, have spread considerably there. Gorse, whin, and heathers flourish in the small valleys round about. The woodlands are still mainly of oak trees, and the local Hunt spends much time and energy among them. So broken up are these valleys, and so considerable is the cover and the number of streams, that a pack can spend an entire day in the area, and not always with success.

GLYNDYFRDWY, *Merioneth.* This small village lies a little above the main road between Corwen and Llangollen on a steep rise through gathered woods. It is a famous name, and it has taken several forms. It means no less than Valley of the Dee. In the 14th to 15th cents. one Owain, son of Gruffydd the Younger, had the estate lying around Glyndyfrdwy as part of his patrimony, which included a still larger area around Sycharth and its castled hill, in the Tanat valley on the other side of the Berwyns. Owain, student of law and courtier in London, felt himself wronged by the Lord Grey of Ruthin, and the whole of Wales was ready to revenge both his wrongs and its own. For fifteen years Owain maintained a war against Henry IV of England that for a moment seemed likely to result in an independent Kingdom of Wales. From this place he took his name of Glyndyfrdwy, often contracted to Glyndwr, and turned by the English into a more manageable Glendower.

At the nearby place of Carrog, with its beautifully balanced bridge dated 1660, a small green hill called the Mount of Owain, close to the road, may have been the position of a fortalice belonging to him, though its woods keep that secret hidden. On its eastward side, about 200 yds away, are ruins of a moated grange that tradition calls his "Plas" or Palace. There is a memorial hall to him in Glyndyfrdwy, and Machynlleth shows the place where he held the Parliament of all Wales that declared him King. But the lonely grasses of the mount and the Plas speak more eloquently of his triumphs and his ends.

GOGINAN, *Cardiganshire.* The road from the southern foot of the ridge of Plynlimon Fawr goes to Aberystwyth over the long moorlands

J. Allan Cash

*South of Goginan: the triple Devil's Bridge
over the Mynach stream*

in two forks that divide the valley of the Rheidol river between them. They separate just beyond Ponterwyd, where the one to the S. goes to Devil's Bridge; the other runs straight forward on a level nearly 1,000 ft high, the crouching head of Plynlimon behind you, the deep cleft of the valley below. Suddenly the woodlands that crowd the lower slopes climb the hill-sides, and set to overlook them is the village of Goginan. Several old mines lie about the road; and Goginan had a recent existence as a hamlet where miners for lead lived among the farming folk who used the valley. But the reservoir near the road under Esgair Gorlan is fed by a stream called Nant yr Arian, and the woods across the stream from Goginan are the Cnwch yr Arian. In neither case is the word "arian" (silver) used as poetic description. Long forgotten, it seems that the lead of the hills around was once worked for silver too, as much as the area of Eglwys-fach and of Holywell. As yet there is no definite evidence that the Romans, whose activity among these mines has been established in other parts of the Plynlimon region, came to Goginan; but the place is very old. There is another Goginan lying about 1 m. away to the N. on a lane through woods of its own, called Old Goginan.

It was once near to a moorland pool, the lake of Brwyno, now dry and forgotten, though a small farmstead called Cwm Brwyno preserves its name. Somewhere in the neighbourhood of Goginan and Brwyno pool, the great poet of medieval Wales, Dafydd ap Gwilym, is said to have lived. Details of his birth, life, and death are obscure. Born about 1340, perhaps near Llanbadarn-Fawr by Aberystwyth (though his poetry speaks of the Dovey directly), dying between 1370 and 1388, and perhaps buried at Strata Florida, he is the subject of conflicting accounts.

The Vicar of Llanfair Dyffryn Clwyd wrote that, in 1572, he met a very old lady who had talked with someone who had met Dafydd in his life. Her description was of him as handsome, tall, and fair, his long locks banded with gold. From other sources it appears that he was slight and dark. The tale is still told of how he had to hide in a tree to avoid the many women who demanded his love; but this is the kind of tale that later generations invent. Certainly he wrote of love with charm, but also with strict application to the intricate rules of native Welsh poetry, and his name is forever linked with that of the beautiful Morfudd, married to another and lost to him. But it was the unrelenting requirement of the troubadour of his times that he must preferably love a woman who was a wife, though not his own. Dafydd is inescapably himself when he writes of nature, of the lark rising from the heather, of the nightingale in the woods, of the great encampment of stars about the heads of hills. To read his verses is to see again the thickets of the Rheidol valley, to hear the skylark above the lonely whins and ling of the Plynlimon upland, and the broad and jewelled field in which the moon moves silently above the streams that find their voice only at night around Goginan. The views of hill and sea along this road are magnificent, and the valley is one of the most beautiful in the area. It is difficult not to believe the tradition that Dafydd did live there.

GOWER, *Glamorgan,* or Gwyr in Welsh, is the delectable peninsula that runs some 18 m. W. from Swansea. Historically, Gower also embraced the country between the lower valleys of the Tawe and the Loughor, and this area is still included in the Parliamentary constituency. The Gower of the tourists, however, is now peninsular Gower: that unique landscape composition of limestone headlands, sandy bays, ruined castles, cromlechs, and downs, that has deservedly been set aside as an area of outstanding natural beauty. It is a surprise to find such unspoilt country neatly isolated from the industrial coalfield of South Wales. In spite of the encroaching suburbs of Swansea in the E., and the caravan parks that have inevitably planted themselves on some parts of the coast, "the Gower" remains basically unexploited, thanks to the vigilance of the admirable Gower Society.

Geologically, Gower is formed by two rocks – limestone and Old Red Sandstone. The limestone forms the cliffs and coastline on the S., the Old Red Sandstone heaves up from within the limestone in the humpback downs of Cefn Bryn, Rhosili, and Llanmadog. The limestone plateau lies at a level of 200 ft, cut by the sea about 1,000,000 years ago and then lifted to its present site. In the Ice Age, the whole area was covered by the glaciers that overrode Gower and Pembrokeshire from the Irish Sea. The final melting of the ice, and the corresponding upliftment of the land, have left their mark in the raised beaches that ring the coast. As the ice disappeared, early man appeared.

Gower had yielded impressive evidence of early man in the famous bone caves in the limestone of the S. coast and on the open site of Burry Holms. Later, somewhere around 3000 B.C., the westward-moving colonists of the megalithic tomb-builders settled in Gower. They left their memorials in the great cromlechs, from Arthur's Stone to Giant's Grave, that lie all over the peninsula. The Copper and Bronze Age folk came later and built the fine mound at Cilibion. Then, by 300 B.C., the warlike overlords of the Celtic tribes were in possession. Now the Iron Age was in full sway. The conquerors thus had superior weapons and a knowledge of fortification. The most impressive Iron Age camp in Gower is at Cil Ifor, about $\frac{3}{4}$ m. E. of Llanrhidian, looking out over Llanrhidian marshes. The Bulwark on Llanmadog Hill is another fine example. There is a whole series of small promontory forts along the headlands between Porteinon and Rhosili.

The arrival of the Romans put an end to the Celtic power, but they may have by-passed the peninsula. There was some sort of Roman building at Oystermouth – a fragment of the mosaic is preserved in the church; but Gower, as a whole, has no important Roman remains. The Celtic Church arrived after the collapse of Rome. The most favoured of the Celtic saints in Gower are Cattwg, Dewi, Teilo, and Madog. Llangynydd was the site of a small monastery.

The Normans came in the 11th cent., and henceforth S. Gower ceased to be Welsh. In fact, after the Norman invasion, Gower was divided into two: Anglicana and Wallicana. In S. Gower, as in S. Pembrokeshire, the Welsh were driven out and the place became a miniature "little England beyond Wales". The place-names and the language changed. Englishmen were settled, mainly from N. Devon – the theory of an intensive Flemish settlement after the drowning of the Zuider Zee lands seems to be unfounded. The Gower dialect, which survived until recently, had strong affinities with the West Country, although the speakers had a Welsh lilt. Words like "dumbledory" (cockchafer), "bubback" (scarecrow), "glaster" (buttermilk), "inklemaker" (busy man), "kerning" (ripening), "nipparty" (perky), "z'snow?" (do you know?), and "rying" (fishing) are typically Gowerian.

S. Gower folk for centuries felt themselves a race apart, and certainly, in the Middle Ages, they were under constant threat from the Welsh in the back country. Hence the numerous small castles and fortified manor houses that occur all over the peninsula. There is also a protective ring of "commons" – Clyne, Fairwood, Bishopston, and Pengwern – that cut S. Gower off from the N. and E. Gower churches tend to have fortified towers, and graveyards filled with Tuckers, Mansels, Groves, and other interrelated settler families.

Apart from Penclawdd and its cockle industry on the N. side of the peninsula, Gower is basically an agricultural area. Farming and tourism make the life-blood of the place. Before the arrival of

the motor-car, sheep and cattle were driven into Swansea every Saturday throughout the winter. The farmers at the further end of the peninsula would keep their cattle for the night at Penrice Home Farm. The farmers' wives on the coast specialized in producing laver bread – that black, treacle-like substance made by boiling for twelve hours a special seaweed that grows between tides on the limestone rock. Laced with oatmeal, it is still on sale in the rebuilt Swansea market, although in these days not all the laver weed is harvested in Gower itself. Laver bread tastes delicious when fried with bacon fat.

In the 1930s Gower joined Pembrokeshire in using its favoured position as a comparatively frost-free area for the production of early potatoes.

But, increasingly, tourism has become an important part of the Gower economy. There is no railway, no large hotel, no cinema. Gower appeals to those who are in search of a simple holiday – and long may it remain so. But visitors are warned that the week-ends see heavy traffic blocks along the Gower roads in high summer. The S. coast is the main attraction, because of the wealth of bays, with their golden sands, that are dotted along the whole length of the peninsula. On the S. side they are safe for bathing. On the W. and NW., the strong current from the Loughor estuary imposes caution. It is possible for strong walkers to follow the coastline from Rhosili and Worms Head round to Mumbles by cliff-paths and across the sands. This is one of the most attractive walks in South Wales.

Starting at Mumbles Head, a wide path leads from the road, round Limeslade Bay and Rotherslade Bay and Rotherslade, to Langland. Langland Bay is now almost a suburb of Swansea, with hotels and new flat developments, but the sands are still fine and safe. The castellated, mock-Gothic pile that is now a hotel was built by the Crawshays, the Merthyr ironmasters, as a seaside home. The sea-path leads over the golf course to Caswell Bay.

Caswell marks the limits of the borough of Swansea. Again the sands are magnificent. Pine trees fringe the bay in the centre, and the building developments on the fields in the background have not yet intruded on the scene. The great slab on the far side, under the stump of the windmill, is a challenge to rock-climbers; only experts should attempt it. Now the coast shakes itself free from all building exploitation. The path leads round the cliffs for $\frac{1}{4}$ m. to the tiny inlet of Brandy Cove, with its legend of smugglers. Here the raised beach can be well seen. The path then continues to Pwll-du (Black Pool), where the Bishopston Valley comes down to the sea. A fine storm beach has dammed the stream to form the black pool. Pwll-du is one of those lucky beaches that have to be reached on foot. The impressive headland is seamed by trenches, the relic of 19th-cent. quarrying for limestone.

The coastline beyond Pwll-du Head is rich in caves. The cliffs slope rather than plunge, but a steep path leads down to Bacon Hole. This fine cave yielded an important collection of bones, prehistoric animal remains, and evidence of occupation by early man. The remains are preserved in the Royal Institution at Swansea. There has been much discussion about certain red streaks on the cave wall. It has been suggested that these might be traces of cave paintings, the only ones in Britain. Equally firmly, other experts maintain that they are natural oozings of red oxide. Michin Hole is even more impressive, and has yielded an important collection of remains, including bones of elephant, bison, soft-nosed rhinoceros, and hyena. Take care in scrambling down the steep cliff-face to the entrance.

The fine sweep of Oxwich Bay is now in sight. This is the biggest indent on the S. Gower coast. It begins with the sands of Three Cliffs, a jagged headland, by a cave, pierced with the Pennard stream entering the sea around it. One of the cliff-top bungalows was the home of the Welsh poet Vernon Watkins. Above the dunes behind the Three Cliffs is Pennard Castle, a ruin that looks magnificent but when entered proves to be a mere shell. It was built in the 13th cent. and ruined in the 16th, and had little history in between. The settlement of Pennard is modern, and can boast only a golf links. The old church here was buried by blown sand, and a new one was built about 1 m. back from the sea. The Church of St Mary thus dates from the 15th cent.; and maybe parts of the old building, including the moulding of the two lancet windows, the font, and the great beam supporting the gallery, were incorporated in the new. The tower has an embattled parapet.

The coastline continues westward from Pennard, past Pobbles Bay under the Great Tor of Tor Bay. Hereabouts, in places best left unspecified, grows the yellow whitlow grass (*Draba oides*) found in Britain only in Gower. The face of the Great Tor has been climbed, but again a firm warning must be given about climbing on Gower limestone. The handholds look magnificent, but they are most unreliable. Only experts should venture on these plunging rocks.

The wide sweep of sands now leads on past Crawley Woods to Oxwich. Oxwich Point separates this fine bay from that of Porteinon. In between is the small cove of Slade. From Porteinon the coast takes on a new splendour. Some 5½ m. of cliff-walk from Porteinon to Rhosili must be reckoned one of the finest stretches Wales can offer. The cliffs become more precipitous after Overton, and are intersected with small, dry hollows that run down to the sea. The further W. you go, the more continuous becomes the cliff-line. At Paviland, under the small hill-fort of Yellow Top, are the famous bone caves. The entrance to them is possible from the E. at very low water only; great care must be exercised in climbing down to the caves from the headland. The grass slope is slippery, and the turn round the cliff-edge to the caves involves some rock-climbing. There have been several accidents here in recent years.

The first cave, Goat's Hole, is one of the most famous bone caves in Britain. It was first excavated by Dean Buckland in 1823, and is one of the earliest and richest finds of this sort. A headless human skeleton was uncovered and named the Red Lady of Paviland because the bones were dyed with red ochre. Later excavations by Professor Sollas in 1913 proved that the "Red Lady" was a man, of the Cro-Magnon (Old Stone Age) period. The red ochre may have been deliberately placed on the bones as symbolic ritual designed to ensure immortality.

Beyond Paviland the coastline continues to offer splendid cliff scenery to Mewslade Bay. Here a small valley comes down to the sea between high limestone bluffs. Thurba Head encloses the bay to the E. It is 200 ft high, crowned with an Iron Age fort and owned by the National Trust. Mewslade sands are exposed at low tide. The bay is accessible only by foot, and can claim to be the most spectacular in Gower. Westward is Fall Bay, in the shelter of Tears Point. Here the raised beach of the Pleistocene Age is well seen. The sands join those of Mewslade at low tide. On the bold cliff of Lewes Castle is an Iron Age promontory fort, one of the many that lie on these narrow headlands of the S. Gower coast. They enclosed small hamlets, and the banks gave some protection in the warlike age that preceded the coming of the Romans to Celtic Britain.

From Fall Bay the coast sweeps round to the magnificent climax of Gower's southern coastline, Worms Head and Rhosili Bay (*see* Rhosili). Rhosili faces W., and the broad, open sands receive the full force of the Atlantic gales. After Burry Holms islet, the coast starts to turn NE. and changes in character, although there is a final cliff display beyond Burry Holms, with the curious enclosed water of the Blue Pool. This is accessible on foot over the burrows at Llangynydd. The pool is 15 ft across and was once reputed to be bottomless. The natural arch of the Three Chimneys lies W. of the little cove of Bluepool Bay. Gold moidores and doubloons have been found here, but it is doubtful whether they came from any Armada galleon. Whiteford Point marks the northernmost point of the peninsula (*see* Llanmadog).

The northern shore of Gower differs dramatically from the S. coast. The original limestone cliffs can still be traced behind Llanmadog, Cheriton, and Llanrhidian, but they now lie inland. The Burry estuary has slowly silted up over the years, and the N. coast of Gower consists of marshland and saltings, with the treacherous sands of the estuary beyond. After the cockle village of Penclawdd, the country changes. The limestone disappears and the coal measures begin. Gower is still the official designation of the countryside, but it is no longer English, peninsular Gower. It belongs in character to the rest of industrial South Wales.

The Gower Society publishes by far the best guide to Gower, which every visitor should obtain.

GOWERTON, *Glamorgan,* 6 m. NW. of Swansea, rather belies its name. It is outside the main Gower peninsula in the centre of an industrial area. The Gower peninsula is English-speaking, but the inland area is still Welsh. The two parts of Gower are in the same Parliamentary constituency. Nearby is Gorseinon. Both townships have steel-works and collieries near at hand, although, in common with a great deal of West Wales, the whole industrial picture here is rapidly changing. The Parish Church of St John at Gowerton has a fine, modern marble reredos.

GRESFORD, *Denbighshire.* On the E. of Offa's Dyke, Gresford makes no doubt of its Welsh nationality. Its name is truly "Croes-ffordd" (Cross Road), and it lies on the route from Wrexham to Chester. It has been much overtaken by the demands of modern industrialism, and its activities have been identified almost exclusively with the North Welsh coalfield. Here in 1934 one of the worst disasters to any mining operation struck Gresford with the explosion and fire at the colliery, killing no fewer than 261 of its workers. It was an ironic comment on man's improvement of nature that this should happen in a place where nature had devised the beauty of the River Alun; and that Gresford itself should hold so much that speaks of another and older way of life. The church is a living monument to it, and the peal of its bells was listed as one of the Seven Wonders of Wales:

Gresford church

G. Douglas Bolton

Pistyll Rhaeadr and Wrexham steeple,
Snowdon's mountain without its people,
Overton yew trees, St Winifred wells,
Llangollen bridge and Gresford bells.

The church belongs to the later class of Welsh buildings, being dated about 1460 and in the Perpendicular style; but the font and the aisle end-windows are thought to have come from the Basingwerk Abbey known to Gerald de Barri in the 12th cent. Stalls and woodwork belong to the 16th cent. But the yew trees may have been thought worthy to rank with those of Overton among the Seven Wonders. Those in the church-yard were, for the most part, planted in 1714. But one growing at the SE. of the church is said to have dated from 1400.

GROSMONT, *Monmouthshire.* The name may mean Great Hill and be, not Welsh, but Norman. If so, it makes clear the character of much of Monmouthshire. It lies by the Monnow river and close to what is now the border with Herefordshire. A little further N., Pontrilas, in spite of its Welsh name, belongs to Hereford; Abbey Dore is also technically English. Between them lies Ewyas Harold, a small village that keeps alive two facts of history: that this region formed part of the wholly Welsh province of Ewyas, and that, before the Norman came, Harald – Earl of Hereford, successor to Edward the Confessor as King of England – drove into the Deheubarth in the middle of the 11th cent. and seized much of its territory. The Herefordshire village of Kilpeck, with its church as an outstanding example of the architecture of the mid-12th cent., is a monument to the second fact. For its detailed sculptural decoration, inside and out, with grotesques of men and beasts, including some that are wholly pagan, seems to be inspired not by Welsh or Saxon ideas but by the tradition of the Norse settlers in Kent and Sussex whom Harald transferred to Ewyas for the purpose of keeping the natives in subjection.

Although reckoned an English village, Abbey Dore is again of Welsh name and connection. It stands in the Golden Valley, which is in fact the Water Vale, for it was the Norman who mistook the Welsh "Dwr" (Water) for his own "D'or" (Golden). Its church is the successor to the original Cistercian monastery founded by a great grand-nephew of Edward the Confessor, and is another startling example of intricate decoration. But Grosmont represents another chapter in the history of Monmouthshire. It belongs to the Trilateral, or three-pointed stronghold, set up by Norman Lords of Abergavenny to maintain their grip on the country.

Grosmont is now no more than a quiet and reminiscent village; yet it ceased to be a borough only in 1860. In medieval times it was a place of great importance, and the 14th-cent. church confirms this. It is an ambitious structure, not of the kind that would suit a simple village, but with transepts, aisles, chancel, and chapel. The tower is octagonal, with a beautifully balanced spire; the nave arcade is massive but unfinished.

Grosmont Castle mounted guard over the Golden Valley with its two companions, Skenfrith and the White Castle. It was the most carefully considered of the three; but its stormy history has left only the inner ward gateway, the keep or central strong-point, and the containing wall with two drum-towers. These are not original, but date from a rebuilding by John of England or Henry III, the first structure having been demolished by the Welsh. Even so, the remains are magnificent, and the chimney of the banqueting hall is a remarkable evidence of its garrison strength. It was in fact occupied by Henry III himself; for the discontent of his baronage with his preference for foreign favourites encouraged Llywelyn the Great to invade, supported by several Border Lords. Henry had his wife with him, since he felt the needs of the war required his personal presence there for a long time. Llywelyn made a surprise attack by night and captured the Castle, driving the King and Queen with their noble supporters out into the darkness in their nightshifts. But time has its revenges; at Grosmont 170 years later Rhys Gethin, holding the place on behalf of Owain Glyndwr, was signally defeated by Harry of Monmouth, later Henry V of Shakespearean note. That encounter, in 1410, may be said to have conclusively destroyed the work of the King of Wales. Owain never fought again, and the rest of his life is said to have been spent in hiding at Monnington Straddel, not far from Bacton, protected by his son-in-law, Sir John Scudamore.

Skenfrith, second in the great Trilateral, is still a place of substance. The third, the White Castle, stands by itself. It can be reached either from Llantilio Crossenny or from Llanvetherine, in the first case by car and the second by foot. It is, outwardly at least, in a state of almost perfect preservation. It is of Edwardian type: a six-sided enclosure within deep walls, a drum-tower at each angle, the N. wall being short and drawing its towers close together, covering the main entrance. The curtain wall seems to have sheltered the sleeping-quarters of the garrison, since this was no place for residence but a strictly military outpost. Its isolation, and the effect it gives of remaining much as it was when first built, make the White Castle exceptional even among the always romantic castles of Wales. Carreg Cennen is remarkable for its site on an impregnable crag above its river; this castle, in a gentler region and on smoother slopes, makes its own strength and defiance of time even more manifest.

GUILSFIELD, *Montgomeryshire.* Perhaps more properly known as Llanaelhaearn, after the saint to whom the church was dedicated, this place is well worth making a detour of barely 2 m. from Welshpool to visit. The roof of the church is panelled, and beamed with flowered bosses at the intersections of its ribs. The tower is of the Early English style, the upper part Decorated. The clock-face is inscribed with the warning note familiar in many languages and in many generations: "Be diligent. Night cometh".

GWENDRAETH VALLEYS, *Carmarthenshire.* There are two Gwendraeth rivers, which unite below Kidwelly and join the Towy and the Taf estuaries to enter Carmarthen Bay. The Gwendraeth Fach valley – the small Gwendraeth – is pleasantly rural, a pattern of dairy farms with whitewashed walls on low green hills. There is a hint of industry with limestone quarries around Llangyndeyrn. About 3 m. N. of Kidwelly, on the side of the valley, is the hamlet of Llandyfaelog, with a churchyard, full of conifers, that holds the grave of Peter Williams (1723–96), one of the earliest Methodist leaders in Wales. He was born near Laugharne, and came under the influence of George Whitfield. He became a noted preacher, but his most important work was his great edition of the Bible, the first to be printed in Wales, and accompanied by a commentary. His later years were disturbed by religious controversy, but his Bible, published in 1770, has ensured him the gratitude of the Welsh people. Inside the church a plaque commemorates Dr David Davies, who attended the Duchess of Kent when she gave birth to the future Queen Victoria. He became the first Professor of Medicine at University College, London.

Beyond Llandyfaelog the valley turns NE. to Llangyndeyrn, which on older maps is spelt Llangendeirne. The 13th-cent. church has been partly rebuilt, but the general effect, within and without, is pleasing. There is some woodwork dated 1676 separating the chancel from the N. aisle. The Gwendraeth Fach crosses the main Swansea-Carmarthen road at Porthyrhyd, from its source in the high ground, generally called Mynydd Mawr, that lies N. of Cross Hands.

The Gwendraeth Fawr – the bigger valley – is the more easterly of the two. The river flows across the edge of the coalfield. It also rises in the Mynydd Mawr area just N. of Cross Hands. A string of small colliery villages mark the course of the valley to the sea – Tumble, Pontyberem, Ponthenri, Pont-iets, and Trimsaran. There has been some scarring of the country near Pontyberem by opencast mining, and a new pit, one of the few new collieries in South Wales, sunk at Cynheidre. The shaft had to be constructed by a German firm that alone retains the techniques required. The coal is hard anthracite. The new pit will eventually supply all the anthracite needed, and one by one the other Gwendraeth collieries are closing. This valley is no narrow Rhondda. The houses are generally scattered, many in their own gardens. Apart from the tips, the valley still has a country feel about it.

HARLECH, *Merioneth.* Anciently, Harlech was the county town of Meirionydd. "They have but few townes," observes Saxton in his 17th-cent. way, when speaking of the people of Merioneth. But Arlech, as he writes it, deserved his special mention: "Hard by the sea in the little territory named Ardudwy, the Castle Arlech, in times past named Caer Colun, standeth advanced upon a very steep rock, and looketh down into the sea from aloft, which being built as the inhabitants report, by King Edward the First, took name of the situation. For Arlech in the British tongue signifieth as much, as upon a Stony Rock. Whiles England was disjointed with civill broiles, David Ap Ienkin Ap Enion a noble Gentleman of Wales, who took part with the House of Lancaster, defended it stoutly against King Edward the Fourth; until that Sir William Herbert Earle of Pembroke making his way with much adoe through the midst of these mountains of Wales, no lesse passable than the Alpes, assaulted this Castle in such furious thundering manner that it was yeelded into his hands. Incredible it is almost what a cumbersome journey hee had of it, and with what difficulty, hee got through, whiles he was constrained in some places to climbe up the hilles creeping; in others to come down tumbling, both he and his company together. Whereupon, the dwellers thereabout call that way at this day Le Herbert".

This incident occurred in 1467; the Dafydd (David) mentioned was a man of great strength, bodily and moral, and when summoned to surrender made the famous reply that he had held a castle in France till all the old women in Wales talked of it; and he would now hold Harlech till all the old dames of France would know of it. He yielded at last, in spite of what Saxton reports, through pressure of famine. From this tale originates the equally famous song "Gwyr Harlech" (Men of Harlech), known probably all over the world; it does not matter that its writing cannot be traced to any date before the 18th cent.

Saxton's account is otherwise correct in its details. The area is very rich in antiquities; the original name for the fort set upon the sharp and inaccessible point of rock was Twr Branwen (Tower of Branwen), a title that recalls the heroine of one of the most mysterious tales in the *Mabinogion*, buried, they say, at Amlwch in Anglesey, where in fact an ancient mound when opened showed an urn of the Iron Age filled with cremated bones.

The present Harlech Castle is a monument to Edward I, and is one of the well-known series of garrison points he established to complete his mastery of Gwynedd. The building was finished in 1283. It is quadrangular in plan and strengthened by round corner-towers with a wide moat at the landward side. After Henry VI was defeated at Northampton in 1460, his wife, Margaret of Anjou, took refuge there with her son. In 1468 it was the last castle to hold out against the triumphant Yorkists and their leader, Edward IV. Owain Glyndwr took it after overcoming fierce resistance in 1404; but his whole movement for the independence of Wales came to an end when Henry of Monmouth, Henry V of England, stormed it and captured Owain, his wife, and his family. It was also the last castle to hold out for Charles I, surrendering in 1647.

Inside the Castle today are preserved six centurial stones, records of the Roman command at Tomen y Mur at Maentwrog nearby; their faces are 15 in. by 8 in. and bear the commander's name. At Harlech itself, a looped palstave and a bronze axe-head of the type known as Celtic were found; they can now be seen in the National Museum at Cardiff. The evidence they give of habitation in the area by a Bronze Age civilization long before the Roman is supported by a bronze palstave found at Llanfair and – one of the most remarkable finds of its period – the gold torque, a curved rod-like collar 4 ft long, in the possession of the Mostyn family.

Coleg Harlech (Harlech College) is recognized as one of the most efficient centres for adult education, providing summer schools and year courses.

About ½ m. from Harlech, a small hillock, Glas Ynys, shelters an old farmhouse, Lasynys Fawr. In it was born Ellis Wynne, the author of *Y Bardd Cwsg* (The Sleeping Bard), who, Borrow states, wrote that prose-poem in Abercywarch. He died in 1734, and is buried under the communion table in Llanfair church, 1½ m. from Harlech. In 1934, his bicentenary was celebrated in the old parish church at Llandanwg.

Harlech is noted for its healthy climate, and the commanding beauty of the area is proved by the fact that at Llandanwg the National Trust preserves the view across Tremadoc Bay to the rugged line of the Lleyn peninsula.

The Morfa (Marsh) of Harlech, where sea and land intermarry, leads to Portmadoc and contains the link of the Royal St David's Golf Club, by many considered the best in Wales.

HAVERFORDWEST, *Pembrokeshire*. Haverford, insists the topographer Saxton in 1610, is a good British name and is the same as Hereford. Both should be Henffordd (Old Road), signifying their joint foundation by Roman power and the line of communication turning upon each. Humphrey Lhuyd, about thirty years before, certainly calls Hereford by that name, but the only concession he makes to Saxton's theory is to write on his map Herford West for Haverford and add the Welsh word accepted today for it: Hwlffordd. At some time, Saxton's guess that Romans founded the town may be proved correct; but no evidence has yet been found to confirm it. Except for a remote station at Castell Fflemish, and a few scattered finds about the coasts, the Romans do not seem to have left anything to show they occupied Pembrokeshire as a whole.

Today, Haverford makes no doubt of its position as a centre for the Englishry, that part of the county of Pembroke which calls itself "Little England beyond Wales". It is true that Paterson's coach-road directions of 1811 pause to note that 1 m. out of Haverford there is a place named Merlin's Bridge. But Harford (to use the local pronunciation), the centre of county administration and for the Assizes and Quarter Sessions, is as sure of its Englishness, though ranked as a Welsh borough, as Monmouth is sure of its Welshness, though still reckoned as English in some quarters. Its unique privilege of having its own Lord-Lieutenant, the only town in Great Britain to enjoy the distinction, summarizes its situation. It was a palatinate, a border outpost, more detached from the seat of government than any other palatinate earldom — Chester, Lancaster, or Durham. It was an island, in fact, cut off from England by the storms of war that stirred about the long valleys of the South. But almost in geographical fact it is an island, since the two long arms of the Cleddau, the W. and E. branches of water than run from inland to strike due S. and pour into Milford Haven, cut a deep and double trench across the country and almost take in Haverford with an arm from the sea. "Cledd" is a word given various meanings, from sword to left-hand; but here the name seems to spring from the great cleft the rivers and their submerged valleys make. Their significance for the geography and therefore the strategy and politics of the area is shown by the village in the N. of Pembrokeshire, almost on the coast, called Scleddau, on this side of the forked entrenchment they create. If the Norman adventurers and the Flemings sent by the first two Henrys to settle in this part of Dyfed, as Pembroke is called, felt themselves cut off from English bases, much the same was felt by the native Welsh who grew into a sense of their separate development apart from the rest of Wales.

The steepness of the main street of Haverford emphasizes its situation on a height above the Western Cleddau, and its growth around the high, square-walled fortress built in the 13th cent. by one William de Valence. It seems typical of the history of the place, and the efficiency with which its Flemings possessed it, that the Haverford Castle, until well into the 20th cent., was used as a police station. Gerald de Barri had much to say of it when he went there in 1188. The effectiveness of the sermons that he and his Bishop preached on behalf of the Third Crusade was such that, by a miracle, a young man, inspired to volunteer, gained the sight that he had never had. But the sermons were preached in Latin and French; no word of Welsh was used. Gerald was himself a deeply patriotic Welshman, and wished for nothing more deeply than to see Wales re-established in the pride of its own independent Church; what is more, he knew Welsh. But the inhabitants were Flemings still in blood, speech, and manners. Their customs, particularly that of divining the future by means of rams' bones, he discusses at length, and he praises the character of these alien people who were fitted both to wield the sword and to handle the plough and held the isolated country in their charge with consummate skill and courage.

Not that they were subject to much Welsh assault. Elsewhere in Pembrokeshire, the Norman adventurers were met by local rulers with the choice of two things, war or intermarriage; and most of them seem to have chosen the second. Relations between the new half-Welsh, half-Norman lords and the people were excellent and

undisturbed; Gerald de Barri was himself the offspring of such an alliance. But, in Haverford, the Fleming knew himself to be a thing apart, and to find a Welshman there was something to marvel at. Gerald, however, speaks of one event that showed that conditions were not always idyllic. The Governor of Haverford Castle arrested a Welsh raider and held him prisoner. The captive, with his tales of bold archery, naturally excited the boyish interest of the Governor's small son; and the two were allowed to meet and talk every day. But the prisoner had suffered wrongs at the hands of the Norman, and he suddenly took the boy to the top of the Castle tower. The anguished father promised everything if the man would free the child. But, after playing with the Governor's fears and hopes for a while, the man threw the boy to death from the tower and then flung himself down as well. It is a cruel tale; but the Governor had put out the eyes of his captive and had done him other physical damage of a kind no man could forgive. The Governor set up a monastery for the soul of the child, and called it Sorrowful. There is another tale with which Gerald is connected, of a different sort. Near Haverford is a place called Poorfield, where, until a generation or two ago, a regular fair with cakes and ale was annually celebrated around St Caradoc's Well. The fair included horse-races. The saint in this case was of relatively recent sanctity, for he had died only in 1124, a little before Gerald's time. He had a hermitage at St Ishmael's, not the one set on the shore of Milford Haven, but close to Haverford. Born in Brecon, the good man left the world and followed his contemplations, among other places, on the Isle of Ary, from which he was seized by Norwegian pirates, who, either affected by his saintliness or finding there was nothing to be made out of him, let him go. It was Gerald who persuaded the Pope to canonize the hermit.

The Governor whom Gerald met was Richard FitzTancred, the youngest of his father's sons and somehow protected by Providence from many perils. So, it seems, was Haverford; for, in the days of Owain Glyndwr, the French Kingdom took up again its policy of helping Wales to reassert the independence that, half a century before, it had attempted in the cause of that Owain of Wales who is said to sleep under Carreg Cennen Castle. In 1405, 800 men-at-arms, 600 crossbowmen, and 1,200 infantry landed from 120 ships that sailed into Milford Haven. They took and burnt the town; but the Castle withstood all attack. It surrendered to Parliament in the Civil Wars; but, after the revolt of Pembroke against the Puritan dictatorship, Cromwell ordered that the Castle should be "slighted". The keep, however, remains as a stately landmark dominating the countryside. The waters of the Cleddau go by, and men go by too.

Once Haverford was the main link with Ireland, but in the 19th cent. Milford Haven, nearer the outlet to the open sea and more specifically developed, outdistanced it, though in 1811 people said that not much future could be expected for a place so far from London. Haverford is still an outstanding market centre. It has its own small port, and Withybush and Brawdy are nearby airfields. But its abiding charm is in that sense of islanded resistance to threat and even disaster which has marked its history. The Old Butter Market is a reminder of its past, and its churches are three. St Mary's, in the High Street close to the Butter Market, has most interest. It is in every sense an English church in architecture and plan, particularly in the arcade and clerestory. The tracery and capitals of the columns are distinguished, and the roof of oak is one of the finest in existence.

HAWARDEN, *Flintshire*. The village is set on the head of a slope of 1 in 16. It is still remembered for its most famous resident, William Ewart Gladstone, Prime Minister of England under Victoria, an office in which he alternated with Benjamin Disraeli. Like every other town along this border, Hawarden has its castle – a Marcher foundation captured in 1282 by Dafydd, brother of Llywelyn the Last, betrayed to Parliament in the Civil Wars of the 17th cent., retaken for Charles I in 1643, and, when finally seized by the Roundhead troops, "slighted" in 1647. The present castle was built in 1752; and to it came Gladstone in 1839 to be married to its Welsh heiress, Catherine Glynne. He had visited it a little earlier when he was still courting her, but had no time to do more than casually mention the fact in his diary, among notes on classical philosophy and English tariff-systems. For sixty years he made the place his home, founding one of his most cherished institutions, the St Deiniol Hall and Library, and running an estate from which he said he gained the experience needed to master the economics of Great Britain. He made a comment worth quoting in the present age of discontent: "It was always a matter of sailing near the wind in running the estate, and from that I have learned much of benefit to my present administration".

His memorial is in the parish church, with a window by Burne-Jones.

Connah's Quay, a trading harbour of picturesque interest is close by; Ewloe Castle, hidden in woods, dates from 1257. It was a Welsh fortress put up against the probability of English invasion, and it imitated Norman construction; but the holding Edwardian keeps of Flint and Rhuddlan displaced it. History has since ignored it, to the benefit of the present time. But it recalls the victory over Henry II achieved by the sons of Owain Gwynedd in 1157, when the chances of Welsh unity and independence seemed bright.

Hawarden R.A.F. air station is 4 m. SW. of Chester, and there are important aircraft-works in the area.

HAY-ON-WYE, *Breconshire*. "On Wye" is included in the name of this town to mark the fact that it stands directly over the river that Gerald de Barri in the 12th cent. had no doubt was the frontier between Wales and England. Hay can be reached either from Kington in Welsh Radnorshire or from Hereford by road. But in either case you have to pass Whitney, with its old wooden toll-bridge, a reminder of days when that frontier meant rather more than it does now, and Clifford, with its castle ruins, once Norman and later strengthened in the time of Edward I, each of them standing directly on the border. Hay itself was traditionally divided by the river into the Hay that was Welsh and the Hay that was English, and the town as a whole looks to the E. over the area falling between the Wye and the Monnow, in which places like Llanveynoe, Pontrilas, the Bage, and Moccas; and the three Maes-Coed villages, Upper, Middle, and Lower; insist on their Welsh character while being administered by Hereford. Here, too, the people bear names like Beddoes (Meredith), Benians (Ab Einion), Gittins, Watkins or Hopkins, Lello (Llewellyn), and many others of direct Welsh derivation and even maintain other names, like Cadwallader or Gethin, that are equally Welsh and ancient but have died out among the Welsh themselves.

Hay is set on a height and gives a steep ascent to the roads into it from Clifford and from the Brecon side. To the N., the Wye, shallow and broad at this point, lies below, crossed by the Clyro Bridge, and on the southern side the Black Mountains raise what has proved to be the untakeable parapet of Wales. Its site is most beautiful, and it is the best of centres for going by car among the many border castles and churches, the relics of medieval war, and the lost Roman sites that fill the area; or for going on foot across the heathered hills to Llanthony Abbey and the Vale of Ewyas.

Hay Castle, which marks its earliest foundation, is now an impressive house in the early 17th-cent. Jacobean style attached to remnants of a Norman castle, represented by a gateway and a tower. But this castle was not the first. The original Norman invader made a knight's castle here, of which the motte can be seen between the town and the church, rebuilt, except for its tower, in the 19th cent. Revell was the name of the knight who built it and endowed the church, a man of Henry I of England. Under John, the place came into the hands of William de Braose, a Marcher Lord whose name was a by-word among the Welsh for his ruthlessness and treachery. The fragmentary castle that survives was set up by him or, as tradition says, by his wife, Maud de Valerie. She too has passed into Welsh legend, but with a more favourable if in some ways more alarming character than her husband's. It was alleged that she built the castle entirely by her own hands. That she was strong-minded is certain; she alone among the Norman aristocracy had the courage to accuse King John openly of murdering his nephew, the young Prince Arthur whom Shakespeare paints so movingly in his *King John*. She was seized and imprisoned in Corfe Castle, where she died miserably of starvation, while her husband made his escape to the France from which he had originally come. Of the two who perplexed the inner politics of Wales so much in their time, it is she who is remembered with a degree of affection, as the almost-magical Maud Walbee. But the castle and the walls of the town were laid low by Glyndwr about 1400.

Hay is busy as a market town, and has the pleasantness of traffic and of people that is associated with such places. Its inns are busy, and among them is the Three Cocks, which has earned itself a place on the maps. It is about 4 m. out of the town, beyond the village of Glasbury, with its lovely bridge over the Wye. In coaching days the Three Cocks was an important place. Daniel Paterson's *Direct and Principal Cross Roads* (1811) sets it by Glasbury on the way to Hay and calls it simply the Cock Inn. But Paterson makes it an important stage in the route, with its own schedule of distances between point and point. It retains its ancient inner layout of yards and rooms, its doors worked by bobbin-strings, and with gates to its stairs; it leaves no doubt that it is properly the Three Cocks by showing them in gilt. The cock, however, was never a bird. It meant the supply-horse (cock-horse) necessary to help the team to climb the steep ascents that lay along the route. That three cocks were necessary at this point emphasizes how Hay lies at the foot of the steep and dark red barrier of Wales.

From Hay you can most conveniently reach another frontiered monument of history, both at Clifford to the N. and at Longtown to the S. Clifford is near Whitney, and is a village memorable for its castle. Whether this was first founded by FitzOsbern, Earl of Hereford, as a knight's castle in the early days of the Norman penetration, is a little doubtful. The present ruins are of Edward I's time, with the construction characteristic of the day. But it certainly became a seat of a Marcher Lord, owned by a De Clifford. In the reign of Henry II, that vital King of England who was equally King and Overlord from the Scots border to the Pyrenees and had Aquitaine and Ireland as his fiefs, Walter de Clifford fathered a daughter who became the King's mistress. She is long remembered in song and story as Fair Rosamund, Rose of the whole World. "A rare and peerless piece", the *Chronicles* of Holinshed call her. But Henry's wife did not see with the same eyes as her husband, and Rosamund died of poison. The church has 13th-cent. monuments, but may be older.

Longtown on the Olchon brook is a straggling village with another motte-and-bailey castle, the tower, still largely intact, standing guard now over nothing more than a quiet lane. Dorstone, where FitzOsbern may in fact have settled his strength rather than at Clifford, is a prosperous agricultural village with a church entirely new and modern. But it has in it some 13th-cent. relics worth note, and an inscription dated 1256 recording the virtues of an endower of the original church, one John Brito, whose name seems to

insist that he was a Briton, or Welshman. But Dorstone also shows a Stone of Arthur, actually the bared inner stone of a long barrow, belonging to pre-Roman days; and on the return to Hay, Mouse Castle, a prehistoric earthwork that gives most beautiful views into the horizon of the Black Mountains and, more distantly, of Radnor Forest.

Clyro, with its Roman recollections, can be reached in minutes from Hay, and Painscastle lies beyond it over the Begwn hills.

HIRWAUN, *Glamorgan.* This small town with a long industrial history lies high up on the N. outcrop of the South Wales coalfield. Aberdare is a few miles to the E. Hirwaun (Long Meadow) was the site of some of the earliest ironworks in Wales. The ironworks have long disappeared. Hirwaun now has an industrial estate, and open-cast mining is marking the district.

Yet Hirwaun is nobly placed, in spite of the scars of industry. The great moorlands of the Brecon Beacons and the Fanau stretch away to the N. – there is a particularly fine view of the summits from the top of the hill leading down to Glyn-Neath to the W. The steep escarpment to the S. has the highest point in Glamorgan, Craig y Llyn (Crag of the Lake, 1,969 ft). Two small lakes lie below the summit. Llyn Fawr, the big lake, yielded one of the most remarkable archaeological finds recorded in Wales. When the lake was drained in 1911, to become a reservoir, a deposit of peat was found that contained felled oak trees marked by axe-cuts. This gave rise to an early speculation that Wales had produced evidence of lake-dwellings on the Swiss pattern. There is still some doubt about this, but no doubt at all about the rich hoard of metal objects that next came to light. These included two great cauldrons of riveted bronze sheets with cast ring handles, bronze breast ornaments, bronze axes, a crescent-shaped razor, an iron spearhead, and a wrought-iron sickle – twenty objects in all. They seem to date from the 6th cent. B.C.

Was the hoard the spoils of a raid by the hill people on the rich farmers of the Vale of Glamorgan? And were the objects cast into the lake as an offering to the gods? Similar offerings in lakes and peat-bogs have been found throughout Europe. The hoard gives interesting evidence of the coming of iron – the new metal that gave power to the first of the invading Celts. The objects are now preserved in the National Museum of Wales at Cardiff.

A finely engineered road leads up from Hirwaun, past Llyn Fawr, over the escarpment, and down into the head of the Rhondda valley. The views from the summit of the road are impressive.

HOLMS, The, *Glamorgan.* Flat Holm and Steep Holm are two islands in the Bristol Channel between Brean Down in Somerset and Lavernock Point in Glamorgan. They are well seen from the sea-front at Penarth. Geologically they are composed of carboniferous limestone and form part of an outfold of the Mendip Hills system. The Steep Holm, as its name implies, is the higher, with a summit over 400 ft above sea-level, and is under 2 m. in circumference. The remains of a priory are reported, and this seems possible, since the islands are mentioned in the early chronicles as places of religious refuge. They were also a natural base for Scandinavian raiders, hence the name "holm". The Anglo-Saxon chronicles record that the great host that ravaged South Wales in A.D. 917 was eventually repulsed, and that the remnants held out on Flat Holm until they could make their escape westward into Dyfed.

For administrative purposes, Flat Holm forms part of the Adamstown Ward of Cardiff. It contains the lighthouse of the Channel Light, a powerful occulting beam, with a fog-signal in addition. There has been a light of sorts on Flat Holm since 1738. In 1860 the Parliamentary Committee on Coastal Defence recommended that the Severn estuary defences should be strengthened, and accordingly four batteries were constructed on Flat Holm, all armed with 7-in. muzzle-loaders. The batteries were dismantled in 1910. Three guns can still be seen, toppled over from the lighthouse battery. In 1883 the Cholera Hospital for Cardiff port was built on Flat Holm, but it has long since been out of use. In 1897 Guglielmo Marconi chose the island as the site of some of his earliest experiments, and on the 11th May transmitted the first wireless message ever sent across water. It was received at Lavernock Point by Marconi's partner, George Kemp. It consisted of the short words "Are you ready?", and is now preserved in the National Museum of Wales at Cardiff. At present the island is not farmed. A monastic site is marked on the Ordnance Survey map just N. of the farmhouse. The site is overgrown, but tradition maintains that there are two graves here that hold the remains of two of the murderers of Thomas Becket.

HOLT, *Denbighshire.* On the bank of the Dee opposite the Cheshire bank, the village of Holt is built round history, which, at this strategic hinge between Wales and England, is long and significant. Something of it is shown by the eight-arched bridge, dating from shortly after 1400, that spans the Dee and connects Holt with the Cheshire town of Farndon. As a border town, it had its castle, built by John de Warenne, Earl of Surrey, at the time of the Edwardian settlement of the marchlands towards the end of the 13th cent. Only slight remains of this persist, but the Church of St Chad, another of the saints of the Dark but Heroic Age of Christianity, built about 1400, is very beautiful; and pictures of the local gentry who rode out with Charles I to the siege of Chester in the Civil Wars can be seen over the bridge at Farndon church.

Holt, however, is remarkable for another and much earlier border strongpoint. Thomas Pennant, the Welsh traveller and scientist, in his discourse on the Wales of the 18th cent., supposes

that De Warenne's castle was built on the site of a Roman fort. For the Antonine Itinerary – which, in the last days of the imperial power, set out in detail the roads and military organization of Britain – states that 10 m. from Chester on the way to Wroxeter lay Bovium, a station subsidiary to the Deva or Castra Legionis that was Chester on the Dee. In the 17th cent., a gentleman named Crewe unearthed on his farm lands various coins and tiles showing plainly that a Roman position lay somewhere underneath. But his records were lost, and it was only by fortunate deduction that the site was recovered, about 1 m. N. of Holt on the Dee in fields known as Wallock and Hilly or Stony Croft. Earlier references had spoken of a Castle Lyons lying thereabouts. The fact that this was also given as Caer Lleon, the traditional Welsh name for Chester, caused some difficulty; but it has been resolved by evidence showing that Bovium was a supply-station for the much larger military garrison at Chester. Its position on the southward route to Viroconium (Wroxeter) is revealing. It was a centre from which the mining operations in the heart of Wales could be drawn together and the garrison at Deva could be supplied; it was the first stage of communication directly S. from Chester to that equally important strongpoint of Caerleon and Caerwent in the Severn area which established military control not only over Wales but over the whole of England.

The station at Holt, when excavated, showed it as a considerable place. Legionary control was obvious; the stamps of the Twentieth Legion, its base at Chester, were found on the prepared products that it was the business of Bovium to produce. This same Twentieth Legion controlled Caersws and held the important passageways over the shoulder of Plynlimon to the Dovey valley and the mines around Dylife. The site can be seen from Holt Bridge in flat and sloping plainland, to which led what was either the original course of the Dee or a canal for transport cut by the Romans, 9 ft deep. It seems that transport to and from Bovium was by waterway in preference to the road, It was a works depot planned with skill; pottery and bricks and tiles were among its chief preoccupations. Kilns for this production were set close to dwelling-houses, bath-houses with hypocausts, and scientifically constructed latrines, all for the artisans. In its care for the labourer, it was in some ways an anticipation of the Welfare State. Bronze Age remains were also found on the site, which suggests that the usefulness of Holt as a depot was realized long before the eagles of Rome reached Britain.

Probably not only labour but military recruitment was drawn from the local population. At the closely connected station at Caersws, the business of exploiting the raw material of ores in the hills was farmed out by the Legion to local workers; and, when the Antonine Itinerary was compiled, the influx of auxiliary, native troops into the legions and the turning over of military organization to local communities was steadily increasing. The Twentieth Legion had

South Stack lighthouse, Holy Island

G. Douglas Bolton

the special duty of overseeing the system of output and communication in Wales; but it was given other duties as well. It was sent to hold down the province between the Walls in the north of England when Valentia became for a short time another province of Britain. At the time of the Antonine Itinerary, the legions were still in Britain. More than any other country within the Gallic Prefecture of the West, Britain had interfered in the larger politics of the Empire. Constantine, who is blamed by certain chroniclers for having denuded Britain of troops and left it bare to Saxon invasion, took British legions with him to possess and pacify the crumbling Empire; and for a while he made himself Emperor in the West. But the Notitia, or Civil and Military List, of the time does not mention the Twentieth Legion. When the document was compiled, Rome itself was threatened by Germanic invasion; and, though it had long ceased to be anything more than a provincial town remembering the past, its moral significance was so great that the Empire hurriedly summoned its best troops to save it. The Twentieth Legion was actually on the march to save Rome when the annotator of the Itinerary made his report on Britain. Had it been sent sooner, the history of the world might have been changed.

HOLYHEAD, *Anglesey.* The English name of Holyhead – like that of Holy Island itself, which stands offshore from the main island of Anglesey and is almost joined to it at low tide – emphasizes the origin and special nature of the town and the district of which it is the largest modern centre. Holyhead is the point at which the ancient Irish road from London, a route that the Romans maintained as a principal line of communication, still finds its terminus before it crosses by boat to Dublin. This ferry-service operates from two harbours, the inner and older dating at least from the days when Daniel Paterson in 1811 made Holyhead the terminal point for no fewer than fifteen routes out of England across Wales, warned readers against the dangerous tides at the crossing-point at

Llanynghenedl, and referred to "Parry's" (Parys) Mountain, a hill rich in copper and very profitably mined; the outer and more recent harbour, protected by a breakwater over $1\frac{1}{2}$ m. long, was built by the old London and North-Western Railway in 1873.

The neighbourhood, rather than the general layout of the town, is the main attraction for the sightseer. Holyhead certainly has its charm; and the church is of outstanding interest. But it is on the outskirts of the place, particularly on Holyhead Mountain, that its long life and particular character can be best understood. The mountain is no more than 719 ft high; but it looks sheerly down at the sea over magnificent cliffs, and over the sea it commands 1,500 years of history. On this islanded top, the Isle of Man, Ireland, the Snowdon peaks, and the mountains of Cumberland come together within sight. Eire and Eryri, Mon and Man, Cambria and Cumbria, reassert their ancient association. It is true that, from those remote days when the waters of the world lay open for the first time to men through scientific navigation, and the seas were safer than the land and easier to cross, this section of the Irish Sea drew its shores together in a common culture. Part of the earliest history of Holyhead can be seen close to the South Stack, a small rocky point in the sea with a lighthouse, tethered to the shore by a bridge, fissured with caves and loud with sea-birds. Hut circles show there how, in the period that has left no written records of its own, human settlement was made, and perhaps the finest products of the axe factories of Ireland (about 2000 B.C.) or the mined gold of a culture about 500 years later, also brought from Ireland, were handled for transport into Britain.

But it is to the days of early Christianity that Holyhead owes its present shape and character. The Age of Saints founded itself upon the circle of sea that can be observed from Holyhead Mountain. From the 6th cent. onwards the simple oratories of missionaries set themselves in and around Anglesey, following the example of St Patrick's Isle near Man; of Bardsey by

Caernarfonshire; and of Ramsey near St David's, and Caldey, both in Pembrokeshire. Of these, the earliest were St Seiriol's (Puffin Island) off the eastern corner of Anglesey; Llangwyfan, the remotest and least changed of all; Llantysilio in the Menai Straits; and Llanddwyn Island on the western shore. The foundation of the church at Holyhead belongs to this period, being an upgrowth from the oratory of Cybi, a saint who has also left his name in the Dovey valley further S., on a little hill looking along the estuary near Machynlleth. The existing church, however, is expanded from the primitive rectangular chamber type into a four-armed cross pattern and is mainly in the Perpendicular style, showing an influence that followed the Edwardian victory over the independent Prince of Wales and continued until about A.D. 1500. Parts of the structure, all the same, suggest that Norman patternings were used; the parapet of the S. transept carries figures of men and beasts, including the emblem of Wales, the Dragon, done in a fashion and with symbolic purpose reminiscent of the tympana, or decorated over-lintels above the entrance doors of such small churches as survive at Llanbadarn-Fawr in Radnorshire or the Anglesey Penmon. The S. doorway at Holyhead church shows the same kind of workmanship, the result either of deliberate archaism or perhaps the survival of designs that had become traditional. Above it, an even more traditional form is shown in the arms of Llywarch ab Bran, a benefactor of the church, whose shield bears a chevron between three crows or ravens, a battle-sign that can be traced to the first founders of Wales in the 5th and 6th cents. A.D.

A further monument to days that were already old when Cybi first had his oratory built is the churchyard wall of St Cybi itself, a rectangular construction averaging 10 ft in height and about 5 ft in thickness, and with the remains of round towers at its angles. This was a fortress wall built by the Romans in the last century of their occupation of Britain to guard against the incursions of sea-raiders on the coasts, in the way they had to adopt in South Wales at Carmarthen and along the eastern coast of England, which they called the Saxon Shore. It was probably in this refuge that the saint set up his oratory. The font in Holyhead church is interesting; the fonts of Anglesey are, more directly than the surviving structures of its churches, living descendants of the first days of Christianity. It was the holy well or sacred spring of Celtic heathendom that the missionaries sought out. The font was their successor, brought within the confines of a new and deeper belief. At Penmon, Llanidan, and Llangeinwen, the fonts show this continuity of belief in the sacredness of nature. The two last plainly confess the influences of classical art; for in Wroxeter, Shropshire, as in places along the Roman walls in northern England, the bases of columns from Roman stations were used for this purpose. Penmon seems to have adapted the base of a Celtic cross in the same

way. But the Holyhead font has later recollections. It has the words "Robert Lloyd, Robert ap Hu Probert, Wardens", with the date 1662. This is not necessarily an indication of the date when the font was made, but possibly of its rededication. The Puritan domination of Wales after the Civil Wars caused many such Church appurtenances to be destroyed or rejected as idolatrous, particularly those that were worse than Catholic or Anglican, being survivals from the dubious faiths of Roman-British times. Several fonts of this sort were thrown out, and recovered long after from pigsties or farm kitchens. The Restoration, as at Holyhead, rescued some of them.

Religious contention affected Angelsey throughout its history. But it has always retained in its remoteness an air of innocent sanctity. This goes back beyond the Romans; the island was sacred in the religion of those Druids who dominated the Celtic peoples, Brythonic and Goidelic as they are still called, before Julius Caesar made his first incursion across the Channel from Gaul. Perhaps before Rome had any of its later greatness, this sanctity may have belonged to it; for it is from Greek rather than Latin authorities that we have the first record of organized belief in Britain. But in A.D. 58 Suetonius Agricola – as recorded by his son-in-law, the historian Tacitus – first attacked the island from the newly established Roman base at Segontium (Caernarfon), to be followed by Julius Agricola twenty years later. For it was from this island, apparently, that the British people received their sense of cultural identity and distinct belief. The Anglo-Saxon Aethelwald, High King of the English, won a victory in the Irish Sea over the Welsh and made his supremacy clear over their naval base there, giving it the name of Angles-ea, or Isle of the English. Hugh the Wolf, Earl of Chester under William of Normandy, set his knights' castles there in the course of a temporary occupation. The Puritans routed the Royalists at Caernarfon and Bangor and took Beaumaris with little trouble. But Mona (as he calls it) remains essentially as Gerald de Barri described it when, at the end of the 12th cent., he visited the place to call on men to justify the faith Cybi had set there, by going on the Third Crusade. It was a place rocky and hard, even a little repellent, but still of an amazing fertility and outstanding sanctity. Neither fashions in architecture nor changes of faith seem to have affected its simplicity and strength as it survives in its unique and remote churches.

Near the town of Holyhead lies Peibio, the scene of a recurrent phenomenon, well confirmed by contemporary evidence, that perplexed the sages of the 18th cent. as much as it does those of our own day.

Some time in 1743, Lewis Morris, an experienced mining engineer, master of many languages and eminent antiquarian, had a report from Anglesey. This was made by a farmer whose steading lay near Peibio, a little place only a stone's throw from Holyhead. "Plowing" (as it was written) "with his servant boy in ye fields", he saw bearing down upon him a ship of 90 tons, rigged like a ketch, with its fore-tack at the cathead and its pennant and "antient" flying. The day was described as indifferent and cloudy, but the detail of the ship could be clearly seen. It was "coming from ye mountains of Snowdon", not by sailing on the waves around Holy Island, but moving "about a Quarter of a mile High from ye Ground". The farmer called his wife. She ran from the farmhouse in time to see the ship in the sky retreating, its pennant lowered to the deck and all sails furled. It was steering "stern foremost", making for whence it had come, the mountains of Snowdonia.

Lewis Morris was not a man to leave such a thing unconfirmed. He hastened to Holyhead and interviewed first the wife and then the husband, separately. Neither had any doubt about the circumstances. The wife had no acquaintance with sea terms, but was quite sure of what she had seen; her only doubt was what the neighbours might think if she allowed Lewis Morris to publish the affair. Lewis Morris found the husband at an inn, visiting Holyhead on farm business. He had no doubt that the man was sober and sincere, with no trace of the "melancolick" disposition that might have led him to exaggerate or imagine. The ship had been plain to see, exact in every detail; the keel could be observed from below; the sails were distended with the wind; when the foresail was lowered, it hung in a natural way over the bow. In the end a cloud hid the vessel from sight, but not before the farmer, his wife, and his boy had had their observation supported by a flock of birds that assembled to examine the phenomenon and flew round it from all directions. When the vessel began its backward journey, the birds with one accord flew from it northwards in the opposite direction.

What finally persuaded Lewis Morris was the way in which the farmer – whose name, William John Lewis, is worth recording – assured him that he had seen another such ship exactly ten years earlier in much the same place, and that, ten years before then again, he had seen just such another.

The ships were in each case very like the old packet-boats that plied between Holyhead and Ireland; the very ropes of the rigging could be counted one by one. Lewis Morris was afraid that this series of phenomena foreboded some great calamity, and he strove to remember events corresponding with the ten-year intervals. His letter about this matter is hurried, not to say startled, and is either written from or addressed to the Ship Hotel in Dolgelley (as he spells the name of the town).

What attracts the modern inquirer is the recurrence of the visitation at such regular dates. No explanation can be found in early attempts at balloon travel; the first aeronaut to use this means was Montgolfier, and he did not make his first flight until fifty years later. The modern method of communication between earth and outer space is by flying saucer; and the appearance of these vehicles is also at regular intervals of ten years. It seems that extra-terrestrial visitors move with the times and have abandoned "Holyhead Packuet boats" for more advanced methods of flight. But, since the hill at Holyhead is the only height in Anglesey to face the distant loftiness of Snowdon, some trick of refraction may have been responsible for picking up vessels plying the Menai Straits and setting them, pennant and antient and all, to steer the skies above Peibio.

HOLYWELL, *Flintshire*, is Treffynnon in Welsh. On his scroll-map of the district, John Ogilby, the 17th-cent. surveyor of the road-systems of Britain, finds nothing more to say of Holywell than "Lead Mines". By way of afterthought, he puts "Sea", to mark how Holywell stands at the end of the route from Llyn Tegid, or Bala Lake. Earlier travellers, Gerald de Barri among them, made little note of the place except as a kind of adjunct of St Asaph or Basingwerk Abbey. It is now an industrial town with a wide main street; but it maintains the very ancient tradition of the healing well from which it has its name.

This was included among the traditional Seven Wonders of Wales, and was most probably one of the reasons why both pagan interest and Christian sanctity were centred upon the region. It is now named after a St Winefride or Winifred, earlier known as Gwenfrewi, celebrated in the 7th cent. for having defended her virginity from a certain Caradoc, who cut off her head, the holy spring gushing from the ground where her body fell. The most remarkable thing was that her

The healing well of St Winefride at Holywell
G. Douglas Bolton

uncle, St Beuno, himself widely remembered by churches throughout Lleyn, was able to reunite the head with her body, so that she later became Abbess of Gwytherin, near Llanrwst. Some Celtic and pagan myth concerned with the life-giving waters that sprang from earth has been received into the record of the Celtic Church, and has passed into a modern sanctity. The Catholic community honours the place as it does Lourdes, and for the same healing qualities. The church is of Norman and Early English style. The spring once flowed with a supply of 20 tons a minute; but the Halkin lead-mines tapped its source for drainage, and the water now comes through a disused shaft. But the water still keeps its qualities. The works of nature are a wonder in themselves, whatever man may do.

HYDDGEN, *Cardiganshire*. This considerable area of lake and sheep-walk is of outstanding interest for the study of Welsh history and social and economic life. The name itself is now chiefly attached to a slate-pile dwelling surrounded by penfolds on the banks of a stream that lies between Bryn Moel and the Carn Hyddgen, which sets its foot on the rock-strewn banks of the Rheidol to face the heap of Plynlimon Fawr. The stream itself is called Hyddgen (Deer Skin). Some say the name was originally Hyddgant (Stag), so that Carn or Mynydd Hyddgant would signify the Stag Hill. If deer of any sort once roamed these hills, no evidence of their existence is known; and the prevalent marshy nature of the moors hereabouts is not likely to have attracted them. The real origin of the name may well have lain, as its population of shepherds insists, in the actual shape of the valley as seen from the top of any one of its guardian heights. Its green and boggy grasses, thrusting up among the slopes covered with the grey contrast of flax-grass and whin, take the shape of a deer-skin laid out to dry.

It was somewhere here that in 1402 Owain Glyndwr achieved the victory over the troops of Henry IV that is celebrated in the Institute at Machynlleth by Urquhart's mural. It was an overwhelming victory, and several sites are claimed to show where the slaughtered conquered were buried; among them are the Bryn y Beddau (Hill of Graves) close to Nant-y-moch and the Mynydd Bychan (Little Hill), which stands directly over the beautiful falls and the magnificent scree-sweep of Bwlch Hyddgen. As the traditional tale of the victory attributes it to the failure of the English troops to scale the height of a precipitous waterfall, it may well be that Mynydd Bychan is correctly connected with the event. Bryn y Beddau and the area close at hand give – or rather gave – a strong indication that it was connected with even earlier generations than those of the 15th cent. Hut circles and rings of stones of a kind now identified with the mathematically accurate time-recording systems of the Stone Age – as shown in Professor Thom's remarkable work *Megalithic Sites in Britain* – were reported by engineers preparing the con-struction of the new reservoir filling the Rheidol course at this point. They are now lost to view.

The question why a place so remote – and, until the introduction of modern road-surfaces, so inaccessible – was chosen as the site for a decisive battle is answered when you look a little above the farmstead of Hyddgen and see the double cairn upon the hill above it, the Carn Gwilym (William's Cairn). The name is very probably a corruption of a Welsh word meaning watch-place. Other derivations are possible, as usual, but this one is supported by several facts. The twin stacks of piled shale stand out as a landmark for the tracks along the Hengwm, the Rheidol, and the Clywedog. Among the shepherds whose life and work is centred on this place, it is obliga-tory, whenever near them, to place a fresh piece of slate-stone on each of the piles; the cairns have a special importance, and the custom has con-tinued for centuries. They stand in direct line on the one hand with the standing stones at Darowen, with the cairns overlooking Bwlch Hyddgen by Rhiw Goch on the other, and with the carn of Hafan Hill leading to Elerch on yet a third flank. This can not only be checked by references to the Ordnance Survey map, but confirmed by sight from point to point. This was a system of routes guiding the traveller between the Roman station at Caersws and the Roman road past Tal-y-bont and Taliesin. If it was important for Glyndwr in A.D. 1400, it must have been equally important for the builders of hut circles and settlers of marking-stones in 1400 B.C.

The Hyddgen penfolds are, in this section of the Ellennith, or central moorland of Wales, the one remaining focus for its major industry of sheep-raising. Welsh farming life here was divided between the "hendre" and the "hafod"; between the main homestead, usually in the valleys, and the summer dwelling among the hill-tops. Sheep would be driven down the steep flanks of the "bwlchs" from summer to winter pasture, and back again when gentler weather made it possible to leave them without harm wandering on the hills. But summer pasturage was much less available for the number of flocks requiring it than the wide opportunites of the open moorland. Several of them had to remain to take the chance of winter, and herdsmen would remain with them. A tiny cottage, Hengwm Annedd, can still be seen by the Rheidol not far from Hyddgen farm. Not long ago a shepherd, much honoured for his skill in handling three dogs at a time in herding, lived there with his wife without ever thinking of removing to the valleys. He grew rye and made his own bread over the peat fire, and he had little need for entertainment in the winter months since he wrote his own poetry – in Welsh. But Hengwm Annedd has now joined similar crofts sagging to ruin under the rains. Hyddgen itself, however, is still the place not only for gathering sheep for such healthy exercise as dipping, but also for the shearing. The sheds are filled with workers, male and female, recruited from the valleys; and the work goes, in every sense, with a swing.

Reservoirs, afforestation, and the roads they have brought with them during the last two years are changing and contracting the area in which sheep may be raised in the traditional way. Hyddgen has seen many kinds of change already; the empty skeletons of lead-mines are hidden in the slopes nearby. Marginal farming may even work its agricultural way into these uplands. But, as one ploughman said as he stopped at the turn of his horse team at the end of the furrow: "These hill-sides have been worked before for corn. *I* can tell you that". But, in the meantime, Hyddgen can still conduct its formal shepherds' courts from time to time in the matter of deciding which stray sheep belongs to which flock, as has been done on a larger scale near Dylife.

There remains one incident of particular interest, worth telling since it has haunted the memory of Hyddgen shepherds for half a century. When Hyddgen was still a place for living in all the year through, a lonely couple of some age inhabited it. The man, coming back on his cob from his work in one of the valleys, was overtaken by sudden snow at the top of Bwlch Hyddgen. About ½ m. further on he fell exhausted from the saddle and stayed in the driving snow. The cob managed to make its way to the farm, and the old wife was roused. She took a lantern and went, well over 1 m., through the drifts to find her husband. She found him unconscious. She took him on her back and, without help from any other, brought him home. He was dead when he reached there. She too died not long after. Shepherd after shepherd will tell you that at the fall of the day a light comes from the empty house at Hyddgen and wavers to the place where the man fell and died. No one who knows this place well and at all seasons will deny, with any real sincerity, that certain things may be possible there as nowhere else.

To mark what happened and keep it in constant memory, the community of shepherds revived the ancient custom and set a circle of white stones round the spot where the woman found her man. A Forestry Commission road has driven itself close by. The white stones, once scattered, have now been replaced.

KENFIG, *Glamorgan*, a straggling village of modern bungalows and old farmhouses, confronts the largest wilderness of sand-dunes in South Wales. Even the vast steel-works that lie in the distance at the foot of Mynydd Margam cannot take away the air of mystery surrounding the miles of blown sand and tussocky grass between modern Kenfig and the sea. Under this desolation lies buried the ancient borough of Kenfig, with its castle and town walls, overwhelmed by the sand that crept steadily in off the coast from the 13th cent. onwards. The castle was probably founded by Robert, Earl of Gloucester, and by the end of the 12th cent. a flourishing town had grown up under its protection. The few ruins of the castle stand near the railway line, but have been excavated to reveal a castle mound, which supported a square keep, with walls

11 ft thick. The foundations of the exterior bailey and gatehouse were also uncovered. By the 14th cent., the threat from the encroaching sand had grown so severe that stern orders were issued penalizing any act that might aid its advance. The final disaster occurred in the early 16th cent. with a tremendous sandstorm that buried the remaining walls and houses almost overnight. When Leland visited Kenfig in 1540, he described it as "almost shokid and devourid with the sandes the Severn Se ther castith up".

Legends gathered around the site. Most of them are now centred on Kenfig Pool, the small lake that lies near the edge of the sea of dunes. This is the largest naturally formed body of water in Glamorgan, and it remains fresh and unsalted in spite of the proximity of the sea. Not so long ago it was famous for its big pike. Beneath the waters, the legends say, is the actual city of Kenfig. On still days you are supposed to see the roofs and chimneys of the old medieval houses. When the wind stirs the surface, the old bell tolls sadly from the depths. The pool is also supposed to be unfathomable in the centre. Unfortunately, the latest survey puts the depth as 12 ft at its deepest point.

The borough portreeve, recorder, and aldermen survived as an independent corporation until 1886, and the records and charters were preserved in the "Guildhall", the upper portion of the present village inn. For over a century, Kenfig Sunday school has met in the upper chamber, probably the only Sunday school in Wales that meets in an inn. The silver mace of the borough is in the National Museum of Wales at Cardiff.

About 1 m. inland from Kenfig, Maudlam church stands on a hill overlooking the wastes of the dunes. The chancel arch is restored Early Norman. The Norman font has a cable-moulded rim. In the graveyard is the tomb of Elizabeth Francis, who lived to be 110.

Nearer to Porthcawl and the sea stands Sker House, now fallen from its high estate. R. D. Blackmore, the author of *Lorna Doone*, made it the setting for the once-popular and lachrymose romance *The Maid of Sker*. The house was originally a grange of Margam Abbey. Father Philip Evans, the Jesuit priest, was arrested at Sker at the height of the Popish Plot scare of 1678. He was tried at Cardiff and hanged, drawn, and quartered after the barbarous manner of the time. The sands run unbroken from Sker point to the mouth of the Afan river, nearly 5 m. to the NW.

The modern village of Kenfig Hill, together with Pyle, lies 1 m. further inland from Maudlam, around the main road between Bridgend and Port Talbot. It is a somewhat haphazard collection of mining cottages and municipal housing, embellished with overhead power-lines.

KERRY, *Montgomeryshire*. Kerry can be reached from Newtown by going a short distance along the road to Church Stoke and Craven Arms in Shropshire. But the best way is by the moorland road that runs from Bridgnorth, following the course of the Clun river to its spring under Castell Bron among the woods that fill the valleys to the northward. You cross Offa's Dyke as you do so, leaving Llanfair Hill on the left and the Shropshire town of Llanfair Waterdine on its further slopes, and pass over the Black Mountain that looks S. over Beguildy in Radnorshire. The names make it clear that this is the country of Powys, where the Clun and the Teme run through a disputed borderland; what is Welsh and what is English can hardly be distinguished. To the E. of Kerry lies Montgomery. From the top of Kerry Hill is one of the most beautiful views of a country that has not changed since time began. These unfrequented hill-sides bred two things: rivers and sheep. The Teme and Clun have as companions the Ithon, Mule, and Lugg, which all have Welsh names, though they are at least half Anglicized. And the sheep – Radnor, Kerry Hill, Clun Forest – are also Welsh mountain sheep, though crossed with Shropshire strains. To anyone who knows the flocks that graze over the Plynlimon highlands, the small, long-tailed, short-eared sheep for whom no fall of scree is too steep and no wind or weather too hard, the breeds over the Kerry hills seem altogether different, larger, Roman-nosed, and llama-like. They answer the point made by Peacock's *War Song of Dinas Vawr*: "The mountain sheep are sweeter, but the valley sheep are fatter"; and they combine the best qualities of both.

Kerry church is a most interesting structure, consecrated in 1176, with remarkable Norman arches. It is famous as the scene of a bitter contest, at the moment of its foundation, between the Bishop of St Asaph, who claimed it as part of his see, and Gerald de Barri, Archdeacon of Brecon, who considered it to belong to the bishopric of St David's. At his home at Landeu (so he wrote), Gerald heard that the Bishop of St Asaph was travelling to Kerry with armed men to support his argument. Gerald had no doubt that Kerry fell within the district of Elfael, and so could in no way be transferred to dominion from the North. Kinsman as he was to the noble families of Welsh blood in the area, he summoned Einion and Cadwallon, chiefs of Elfael and his own cousins, to raise their forces and ride with him to Kerry. Gerald arrived first; two of Kerry's clergy, who had hidden the keys to the building, were forced to produce them. And the Archdeacon entered the church, held Mass, and caused the bells to be rung to tell the distant Bishop that the day was already lost. But the Bishop arrived, determined on annexing the place to himself. Warned from the door, he began a ceremony of excommunication against his opponents; but they were undeterred. They advanced from the church with candles and crosses against the Bishop's party, and excommunicated him and them in turn. Of the two ceremonies, the one conducted by Gerald was considered the more effective, for he was master of the bells and had them rung in triplets, which was the only way to establish an effective rite of excommunication.

Baffled, the Bishop withdrew. But there was more in the affair than appeared on the surface. Gerald the Welshman, as he proudly called himself, did not see in St David's only a rival bishopric to St Asaph. Knowing the history of the Church in Wales, and anxious to preserve its essential character, he dreamt of an independent Church within its frontiers, and of St David's at the head of it. He reported the affair to the King; he was himself at that time a candidate to fill the vacant see of St David. The English court seems to have treated the affair with some amusement; but Gerald never realized his ambition, and the Church in Wales had to wait 750 years before it had separate recognition.

Beguildy church lies at the end of the mountain road from Kerry that runs southward over the Black Mountain. The roads here are high. They give the impression that you are travelling over the heads of the woodlands; then you drop into Beguildy from open moors. The village stands on the Teme; the church has a 13th-cent. rood-screen with exceptionally good panelling and tracery and furnishings of the Jacobean period. Although it means making a considerable detour, the way to Beguildy in Radnorshire from Kerry in Montgomeryshire is best taken through Betws-y-crwyn, in Shropshire. The church here clearly belongs to the people, irrespective of what they consider to be their race. It is and has always been a church of shepherds. Over the backs of the hills surrounding it lie the stone circles and cairns of earlier faiths. It is set high, looking above Clun Forest and Radnor Forest, with a beautiful roof and screen and a chalice dated to the 17th cent. But its name describes it well; it is the Chapel of Fleeces, and in winter men would come there from their daily work wearing the coats that were the sign of their occupation.

Kerry is no longer in dispute; its hills now seem to mark the fusion of men and their interests. The Colonwy, which English call Clun, runs down to the terraced and ancient town of Clun in Shropshire with its equally ancient bridge, where Scott retired for a while to consider his novel *The Betrothed*. The castle is in ruins, and today the fortalice-church has no alarms. Hopton Castle retains only its keep, the rest of the Norman structure having gone in the Civil Wars, when its Cavalier defenders were slain to the last man for offering so tenacious and hopeless a defence. But the Kerry hills have seen these things come and go. It is the sheep and the men that remain; and they live in peace.

KIDWELLY, *Carmarthenshire*. The character of this ancient township, 8 m. W. of Llanelli, can best be summed up in the manner of an ancient Welsh triad: a contradiction, a castle, and a court case. The contradiction first. Kidwelly is the only town in Wales where you pronounce the Welsh *ll* as a single *l* in the English manner. The name was misspelt on the early Ordnance Survey maps. The correct Welsh spelling is Cydweli.

The little town grew up at the mouth of the

From Kidwelly Castle: the Gwendraeth Fach river

Gwendraeth Fach river in the days of the Norman invasion of South Wales. Just S. of the town the bigger Gwendraeth Fawr joins the smaller stream, and the united waters meander out to sea over flat marshy land. An R.A.F. aerodrome was built on these flats during the Second World War. Beyond the aerodrome, fir-plantations seal off the long sands that run almost without a break from Burry Port to Towyn Point.

Kidwelly Castle stands on the higher ground overlooking the flats; it firmly controlled both the exits from the Gwendraeth and the important road to the W. as it crossed the rivers. The Castle is the pride of Kidwelly. The first castle was built by Roger, Bishop of Salisbury, and a Minister of Henry I. It was one of a string of castles that grew up along the coast road and within easy reach of reinforcement by sea. Henry I's reign saw a great advance in the Norman control of South Wales, but after his death the Welsh rallied. Gwenllian, the wife of Gruffydd ap Rhys, led the Welsh, but she was heavily defeated by the Normans under Maurice de Londres, the new Lord of Kidwelly in 1136. She herself was captured and killed with her son Morgan. Gwenllian was long regarded as a heroine by the Welsh, and the site of the battle, 1½ m. from the town in the Gwendraeth Fach valley, is still known as Maes (Field of) Gwenllian.

The Castle, however, fell repeatedly into the hands of the Welsh. Rhys Grug, one of the sons of the Lord Rhys, captured it in 1215. Llywelyn the Great forced him to restore it to the English. In 1225 Hawise, the heiress of Kidwelly, married Walter de Braose, one of the great Marcher family of De Braose. But the Castle was many times lost to the Welsh. At last Hawise, left a

widow, married Patrick de Chaworth. De Chaworth succeeded in holding the Castle during the Welsh Rising of 1257. He was killed in the following year, and Hawise's son Payn became the heir. He and his brother Patrick took the Cross. They both died soon after their mother. The long-suffering Hawise died in 1274. By the marriage of Patrick's daughter Matilda to Edmund, Earl of Lancaster and brother of Edward I, Kidwelly eventually passed wholly into the hands of the Crown under Henry IV. By this time the Castle had lost its importance, and it fades out of history. Henry VII granted it to his supporter, Sir Rhys ap Tewdwr. Finally it came into the possession of the Earl of Cawdor, who placed it under the guardianship of the Ministry of Public Building and Works.

The present ruin stands on a steep bank on the W. side of the Gwendraeth Fach river. The Castle consists of an outer ward that runs in a semicircle from the S. to the N. gatehouse. Between the two gatehouses the curtain wall is guarded by three strong towers. The eastern wall rises from the steep bank above the river; on the western side the curtain wall was protected by a deep ditch. The S. gatehouse is an imposing three-storeyed building. Two semicircular towers flank the entrance, with a projection on the E. side to give command over the river-front. The turret was added in the 15th cent. to give convenient access to the upper floors. The N. gatehouse is very much ruined.

The inner ward is rectangular and is entered by a simple gateway immediately before the S. gatehouse. The ward has a circular tower at each angle. The original great hall, with the solar, stood alongside the E. wall of this inner ward. Later it was replaced by a new hall, built in the outer ward probably by Sir Rhys ap Tewdwr. The chapel is in two stages, with a semi-octagonal eastern end supported by massive buttresses. The clerestory had a range of trefoiled lancet windows. The three drum-towers that mark the other corners of the inner ward are well preserved and impressive.

A small town grew up before the Castle. A ruined gateway of the early 14th cent., not far from the Castle entrance, marks the southern end of the town defences. The circuit was probably not altogether surrounded with stone walls.

A second settlement grew up across the river around the priory. The Benedictine priory was founded in 1130 as a cell of Sherborne Abbey in Dorset. The priory was dismantled at the Dissolution of the Monasteries, but the fine priory church remains, the best example of the Decorated style in the diocese of St David's. It is especially notable for the large span of the nave, the spacious chancel, and the lofty spire, which was later added to the 13th-cent. tower. The W. window is coloured, but most of the other windows contain clear glass, which gives a light, airy effect to the interior. The 14th-cent. alabaster statue of the Virgin and Child was once so venerated by Kidwelly women that it had to be buried in the churchyard. It has now been restored to the church. There are numerous monuments, including the 14th-cent. coffin-lid in the S. chapel. The section of the town around the priory contains the Town Hall and some old houses, although Kidwelly is rapidly losing some of the more ancient dwellings.

The two townships are connected by a 14th-cent. bridge. At the eastern end of the bridge, a large house, now a Sunday school, brings us to the memories of the famous court case that fascinated both Wales and England in 1920. Harold Greenwood, a prominent local solicitor, was accused of poisoning his wife. He was acquitted after a memorable speech in his defence by Sir Edward Marshall-Hall at Carmarthen Assizes, which was long regarded as a classic of the Bar.

NE. of Kidwelly lie the ruins of Lechdwmy, the ancestral seat of the Dwn family. Lewis Dwn, the Herald who made an important "visitation" of Wales in 1585, was descended from this family; so was John Donne, the poet and Dean of St Paul's. His family used the same coat of arms as Sir Edward Dwn of Kidwelly.

KNIGHTON, *Radnorshire*. The county has many small and secluded towns set in the long valleys that run from Radnor Forest towards the Herefordshire levels. Of these, Knighton is one of the most charming. The coach-road guides of the early 19th cent. give little about it except – whether they describe the route to Presteigne, Ludlow, or Kington – the advice "Cross the Teme river". For this is where Knighton lies, in the meadows of the young Teme with low and rounded hills on both sides. It is a steep descent and rise to and from the town, by way of Cwm Whitton Hill or Bailey Hill, for Pilleth or Bleddfa. Knighton itself is on a small rise between the hills; its church, double-naved and with a Norman tower, has the timbered belfry typical of Herefordshire villages. The cluster of houses lies close, still with a native solidity of companionship in no way disturbed by the lift of new houses along the further hill-slopes. For Knighton belongs to its valley and to the prosperous farming community between the Teme and the Lugg. It is notable for its stock-sales and its inns. Walton (Welsh Town) and Bleddfa, with its 13th-cent. church; the Shropshire side of the Teme, with Leintwardine and its lovely old bridge; Clun Forest and its valleys folded against time; Pilleth and Casgob, with their recollections of history – all these lie within easy reach of Knighton. But it is a place where a man can simply choose to stay without any other concern.

LAMPETER, *Cardiganshire*. This name should properly be Llanbedr, to which is added Pont Steffan, since for the village of St Peter some builder set a bridge across the Teifi. He was certainly an early worker, since Gerald de Barri in 1188 preferred to mention Lampeter under that title alone. When he describes how he made his way to it from Cilgerran, he mentions that he had on his left side the Crug Mawr (Great Hill). There in 1134, shortly before his own time, Gruffydd, son of the powerful Rhys ap Tewdwr, had signally defeated an English army that had already lost its leader, Richard de Clare. With the delight in local legends he always showed, Gerald speaks of the tumulus on top of the hill: a relic of Celtic times, which was supposed to adapt itself to the measure of any man who slept on it but had the less convenient habit of breaking his armour to pieces.

At Lampeter Gerald was met by the Abbot of Strata Florida, and Lampeter seems always to have had this character of being a place mainly preoccupied with ecclesiastical affairs. Although wars and alarms occurred all about it, the nearest it got to involvement in them was when, after the Civil Wars, its local troop was assembled in the market-place for disbandment and pay-off. Although its name is now generally known in English as Lampeter, the careful Daniel Paterson, in his *Direct and Principal Cross Roads* of 1811, refers to it still as Llanbeder, spelling the other Llanbedr in Merioneth with an *i* to make the difference clear. He had nothing to say of the place, though Saxton's 17th-cent. maps mark it as a point of importance on the border between Cardigan and Carmarthen. Had he published his book eleven years later, he would have noted that Bishop Burgess of St David's had just founded in Lampeter the College of St David for training students to holy orders. It was and is an institution very much on its own, devoted to the Church as the Church of England defines it. The college preceded by a long time the foundation of the University College of Wales, with its Methodist outlook, and does not now form part of the Welsh University system. It is modelled on the colleges of Oxford and Cambridge, and indeed is affiliated to each of them with the right to confer degrees of B.A. and B.D. In architectural and internal arrangements, it is not so much a Welsh college as a college in Wales. But, against the background of the Teifi river and the wooded hills of the fertile valley, it inevitably recalls the Backs, which Cambridge men know so well. Its membership remains around 200.

Lampeter is the Assize town of Cardiganshire, and was famous for its annual horse market every May Fair day. It is still a principal market centre, and some may find this its greatest attraction, for the area of S. Cardigan is still a place of harvest and sheep-raising and of haystacks that catch the eye. For you do not see the sloping-roofed structures familiar in England before machinery substituted hay-bricks of straw. Here the round, beehive type is perpetuated, of the kind that recalls the earliest architecture of Celtic tribesmen. They are striking and of beautiful craftsmanship, and one can only hope they will never die out. But the wool-weaving of Lampeter and Cardiganshire generally has largely vanished. It calls for revival.

The even course of Lampeter's history has been marked by one happening of blood. In contrast with the story of medieval warfare belonging to its neighbours, this event, of the 17th cent., does not spring from the curiously decorous nature of the First or Second Civil War in these parts. Then, Lampeter was a very small town looking across the river at the stately home of the Lloyds of Maesyfelin. Beyond the hills lay Llandovery, where Vicar Rhys Prichard (*see* p. 59) was born in 1579, and to which he returned first as incumbent of Llandingad and Llanfair-ar-y-bryn and then in 1613 as Chaplain to the nephew of the knightly Devereux of that place, the Earl of Essex. While at Llandovery, Prichard had a son. The Lloyds of Maesyfelin had a daughter. The young man rode by, and the young woman watched him from her window. Before long, she began to flutter a kerchief from the window and he began to look for it. When he saw it, he knew her brothers were away and he might enter. One day, the brothers returned unexpectedly and found nothing to recommend the behaviour of the Vicar's son. They tied him head downwards on his horse and lashed it into fury. It galloped headlong over the hill-road to Llandovery and came into the town carrying a dead man. It is said the brothers followed him all the way and at Llandovery threw his body into the river. The Vicar prayed a curse upon the house of Maesyfelin; and now it is not even a ruin, for its stones have been taken for building elsewhere. The curse was on every stone and tree, and it seems to have been effective.

At Castell Hywel, about 9 m. W. of Lampeter, was founded in 1775, and continued till 1827, one of the most influential Nonconformist teaching academies in Wales. With the academy at Neuaddlwyd, founded in 1810, also in Cardiganshire, it had a profound effect on overseas missionary effort and even contrived to have certain of its students ordained at St David's.

LAMPHEY, *Pembrokeshire.* The Church of Tyfai, as some believe it to be, or of Fydd, saint of the Faith, lies in the region of Manorbier, Stackpole, and St Govan's Head. It has a neighbour, Hodgeston, that illustrates how near together the Welsh and English traditions stand in Dyfed. The church at Hodgeston is remarkable for its Decorated beauty; but Lamphey possesses, although in ruins, the prouder proof of its importance as one of the seven palaces of the Bishops of St David's. The W. and E. wings, dating respectively from 1250 and 1330, are joined by a gate of later design. The chapel has an outstanding window of Perpendicular craftsmanship, and the place is noted as the youthful home of Robert Devereux, Earl of Essex and favourite of Queen Elizabeth Tudor. Stackpole Court, not far from Bosherston, was a seat of the Earl of Cawdor. Its beautiful gardens and sea-cove may be visited during the week. Even more attractive for many is the small chapel wedged in the cliffs by St Govan's Head; it is now a 13th-cent. structure, but still preserves the altar, bench, and other fitments hewn from stone, and the rock-cut cell that legend ascribes

G. Douglas Bolton

St Govan's Chapel

to a 5th-cent. Cofen, perhaps the wife of a king, who chose to dwell here by the well, which in the 20th cent. preferred to run dry.

LAUGHARNE, *Carmarthenshire.* The name of this ancient borough – one of the most charming small towns in Wales – is pronounced "Larn"; its Welsh name is Talycharn. It stands at the mouth of the River Taf, at the point where it widens to join the estuary of the Towy. Southwards are the distant sand-dunes of Ginst Point, where the united rivers meet the sea. Across the water rise the green hills of the Llanstephan peninsula. Laugharne, for years, has lived happily out of the modern world. It still carries out the provisions of the original charter granted to the borough by Sir Guy de Brian in 1307.

Laugharne consists of a long street that starts at the northern end with the church, and runs past Georgian houses between a row of pollarded elms to the Town Hall, and on down to Laugharne Castle and its foreshore. This foreshore is of mud and shingle, and can be used only at high tide.

Basically English, the town stands on the very edge of the "Landsker" – that strange, invisible boundary that separated, and still separates, from the rest of Wales those parts of Pembrokeshire and southern Carmarthenshire settled by Normans and Flemings in the 12th and 13th cents. The Castle may have originally been founded in 1100, but the early buildings suffered the usual fate of border fortifications, and were repeatedly destroyed by the Welsh and recaptured by the Normans. Sir Guy de Brian held it securely at the beginning of the 14th cent. The present building was largely reconstructed as a mansion, out of the old castle by Sir John Perrot in the reign of Henry VIII. It was captured by the Parliamentarians during the Civil War. It is a romantic ivy-clad ruin, memorably painted by Turner. The remains are a shell within, though they have a fine view seawards. The Castle is in private hands, but is open to the public on application.

The Town Hall, built in 1746, has a white tower and belfry. The building is still the centre of town life, for Laugharne has a Portreeve, who wears a chain of golden cockle-shells, with attendant halberdiers, mattockmen, flagbearers, and guides. The Corporation guards its traditions, and piously toasts its founder, Sir Guy, at the annual Portreeve's banquet. The Town Hall still has a prisoner's cell, 10 ft sq., with an uncomfortable wooden pillow.

The church stands somewhat apart from the town. It is a cruciform church, dating from the 13th cent., but heavily restored in the 19th. The stained glass has received some harsh criticism, but the church makes its effect, standing on the slope of a wooded hill. In the annexe to the churchyard is the unpretentious grave of Dylan Thomas – a plain wooden cross bears a brass plate inscribed with the poet's name. It is simple, in accordance with his own wish. Laugharne has always had its attractions for writers. Edward Thomas lived here, and Richard Hughes occupied the Castle house between the wars. Dylan Thomas, however, is now the chief literary attraction of the place. He lived in the Boat House, a Georgian house perched between the hill-side and the river-bank along the narrow Cliff Walk behind the Castle. It is private, but alongside the path you can see the little shed in which so many of the later poems were written, and then look out over the poet's "heron-priested shore". His memory is cherished, not only in his favourite Brown's Hotel in the main street, but in the triennial performance of *Under Milk Wood* in the town. The poet stoutly maintained that Llareggub was not in any way based on modern Laugharne. St John's Hill, the subject of one of Dylan Thomas's happiest poems, is just S. of the little town. There is little to show of Roche Castle at its foot, near the main road westwards to Pendine.

From the open space before Laugharne Castle, a road leads up through the dingle with the ancient name of the Laiques, for just over 1 m. towards the secluded hamlet and church of Llandawke. The church is small, tucked away in a hollow behind a house. Its most interesting features are an Ogham stone, with a Roman inscription and the 14th-cent. effigy of a woman, probably Margaret, sister of Guy de Brian of Laugharne.

Llansadurnen is placed on the hill-side behind the big limestone quarry to the right of the Pendine road out of Laugharne. The limestone bluff contains the Coygan cave, which is noted in the early history of Welsh archaeology for its rich deposit of mammoth, woolly rhinoceros, and other long-extinct animals. The church was rebuilt in 1859. There are fine views out over the cultivated levels of the East Marsh, protected by its sea-bank and sand-dunes, to the Towy estuary and the Gower peninsula beyond. Peter Williams, the Welsh commentator on the Bible and a prominent figure in the Methodist Revival of the 18th cent. in Wales, was born at West Marsh, Llansadurnen, in 1723.

LLANAELHAEARN, *Caernarfonshire,* is 6 m. from Pwllheli on the Caernarfon road, and rather over 300 ft above sea-level. About 2 m. further on, the village of Trefor and the place of Morfa (Sea-Town and Sea-Land) show by their names how close they are to Caernarfon Bay. Between Llanaelhaearn and the coast, however, is Yr Eifl, falling to the water from its height of 1,849 ft over the dark and quarried crags that strike into the sea at Trwyn y Gorlech (Head-Point, or Nose, of the Great Declivity). The church at Llanaelhaearn shares its dedication to a 6th-cent. saint with the place known as Guilsfield in Montgomeryshire. But the present building is a restoration made in 1892, when its early chancel was considerably enlarged. But in that restoration various inscriptions were discovered on the walls; they are attributed to pilgrims who sought the sacred well near the church. This is now roofed in, and the waters from it are piped to supply the village. The screen is wooded and of the 15th cent. In the wall of the N. transept is a stone carved in a way that has puzzled many antiquarians.

Yr Eifl, as Llanaelhaearn's mountain is called, has had its name transformed into English; its triple peaks are often referred to as The Rivals, though the word really means either a fork or a stride – an apt description for the sharp and separated thrust made by the heads of Yr Eifl against the sky. The ascent is to a magnificent view over the bay, with Anglesey like a map at your feet and the great shoulder of Snowdonia like a wall above your head. But some care should be taken, because, at least for the second half of the way, tumbled boulders lie loose and ready to be dislodged.

The most interesting of the peaks is the eastern height, which looks over Llanaelhaearn to Gurn Ddu (1,712 ft). For here is Tre'r Ceiri, the most important relic of its sort in Wales. It is a collection of "cytiau", or hut circles, whose stone surrounds no longer carry their poled and bracken-covered roofing, but still give a striking impression of the organized town-life there in ages before history. This settlement covers more than 5 acres. The huts vary from small cell-like structures to circular ones 16 ft across. A usual interpretation of its name is Town of the Giants; but this seems to be an 18th-cent. fancy, and "ceiri" more probably means circle-enclosures. Walls once surrounded the entire site; although they have to a great extent collapsed, in places they still rise to 15 ft. Protected by the difficult ascent from the land, and by the sheer escarpments dropping to the sea, the place must have

Yr Eifl, above Llanaelhaearn

been secure and used for some important purpose. A store of gold is mythically supposed to lie in it, and the tradition may well perpetuate a memory of the seafaring folk who traded for gold across the Irish Sea, and for amber in the Baltic, and had their main centre off the Bristol Channel, in Wessex, 4,000 years ago. It certainly belongs at least to the Iron Age. A channelled ravine runs from this point down to the sea. It is called Nant Gwrtheyrn, and has attracted a more recent legend. Gwrtheyrn is a title that was applied to the Vortigern, or Great Prince, now implicated in the folklore of the period of Saxon incursion in the 5th cent. A.D. – the Prince who summoned Hengist and Horsa to his aid, was seduced by the beauty of Rowena, and so led to his country's downfall. In a large tumulus on the E. slope of this valley, skeleton remains were discovered and attributed to this sub-Roman personality. Modern opinion is that Tre'r Ceiri was re-used in the last days of Roman rule, when native levies were encouraged to defend Britain.

LLANALLGO, *Anglesey,* stands near the sea on the north-eastern edge of Anglesey. Its church has the early and simple plan that marks the island as the site of Christianity's first emergence in the seas of the West; it has also the relic of a rood-screen belonging to the Middle Ages. But about Anglesey is a touch of mystery, which was already old when the eagles of Rome stared across the Straits of Menai at the priesthood gathered to prevent their landing. A tradition of exceptional knowledge had belonged to Britain as a whole since the Wessex Culture built the circles of Stonehenge to study the mathematics of the stars; and it was that highly developed civilization which made the Irish Sea a main route for its

traffic. Caesar himself, on first raiding Britain, ordered an inquiry into the unusual character of tides and days in a place so far N. of the Mediterranean; for centuries Britain had hung like a cloud of rumour on the western limits of the world. Llanallgo seems to have had a special part to play when the earliest of civilizations, steering by the stars, found the seas opened to exploration.

It has a large burial-chamber. A rock-fissure, apparently natural, was used to make a room for the dead, two-thirds below ground level, with low uprights of stone supporting a coverstone 18 ft long, 15 ft wide, and 3 ft 6 in. deep. The chamber could hold a man 6 ft tall standing erect. When it was opened, the bone-fragments of thirty people were found. Bones of animals and mussel-shells were also scattered in it; the animal ones were possibly food for the journey of the dead, the mussel-shells possibly a token of life and fertility even beyond death. There was some pottery in the chamber, probably to contain these offerings. That the site was long a holy place seems proved by the fact that much of the pottery style belongs to the New Stone Age, when tools had reached great refinement and efficiency and men possessed arrows, axes and adzes, knives and needles, spears and hoes, good enough to make them masters of nature; and that at least one shard is from the Bronze Age, when men had learnt to find and smelt metallic ores and were no longer limited to mining for flints. There are several sites to show that, in the Stone Age, Anglesey was inhabited by people who knew of the axe factories of Ulster and Caernarfonshire and the trade they carried on throughout the British Isles. But, for the Bronze Age, Anglesey must have had special interest because of its deposits of copper in the hill Parys not far from Llanallgo; its own hill is called Bodafon (Dwelling by the Waters).

The next Age, of Iron, is one identified with the Celts whom Caesar encountered. At Llyn Cerrig Bach (Lake of the Little Stone), near Valley on the other side of the island, excavations for an airfield brought to light a hoard of beautifully executed objects; a bronze bridle-bit that may have come from Ireland, and a chariot-bit of expert workmanship; swords, spears, and a "hir-las" (battle-trumpet); and, regrettably, a series of linked iron neck-rings, imported from SE. England, for a chain-gang of slaves, perhaps criminals. At the same time bars representing currency appear. These were objects reflecting in their design a Celtic interpretation of the motifs then known to Europe and the eastern Mediterranean; for Celtic civilization was widely travelled. But Llanallgo's share in all this was limited to a hut-circle group a short way S. at Marianglas – hutments of stone walls roofed probably with some sort of thatch, where the Celtic settlements continued throughout the Roman period and men found employment in the agriculture and mining that the Romans organized. In the 3rd cent. A.D. Britain became independent for a short while. There was a mixture of movements, partly those inspired by Carausius, the British Emperor, to reorganize the island and re-align its defence-system; partly those due to raiding neighbours, above all from Ireland.

About 100 years later, Rome left Britain to look after its own defence. At Llanallgo, the hut town of Din Lligwy was remodelled into a five-sided fortalice set round a group of inner buildings sufficiently large and elaborate to suggest that it had become the palace of a local ruler. Its outer walls are linear and angled, showing direct Roman influence, 5 ft thick, containing an area of $\frac{1}{3}$ acre and nine buildings that still stand 6 ft high. Neighbouring sites have given evidence that they continued in occupation into the 6th cent. All these ancient monuments are grouped within a radius of $\frac{1}{2}$ m. from Llanallgo church. There was a well, the Ffynnon Allgo, which must have attracted early settlers; but the place seems to have been suitable for traffic in that pool of sea between Anglesey, Man, and Strathclyde, from the earliest period down to that in which Roman-British power confirmed itself around those shores. The grandson of Cunedda, Cadwallon, won a victory over the Irish at Trefdraeth in Anglesey in 500, and this established the basis on which Wales was to grow. The Norman did his best to conquer the island; but he lasted in it only eight years, and the fortress at Aberlleiniog was occupied by the British, under Gruffyd son of Cynan. The last of Llanallgo's monuments was built about 1125: the chapel with its rounded Norman-style doorway arch, its walls, rebuilt in the 14th cent., lifting to roof height still and standing on the earlier bases built for them.

Perhaps no other site than Llanallgo shows so clearly and compactly the succession of history. Above all, the great blocks of the palace at Din Lligwy makes the strongest effect. The woodlands that crowd upon it, shielding it from the world, give it a silence proper to a place that is a rare piece of evidence for centuries that have grown silent – the unrecorded centuries that saw Rome decline and withdraw and Britain come to birth.

LLANBADARN-FAWR, *Cardiganshire,* is the first place of importance on the road through the Rheidol valley, and is now almost linked with Aberystwyth 1 m. away. The church was founded by St Padarn, a contemporary of St David, who, according to the researches of Canon G. H. Doble, probably came from South Wales and not from Brittany, as is usually stated. Wherever he originated, his church became a prominent centre of early monasticism and retained an abbot as late as the days of Giraldus Cambrensis. The early church was destroyed by the Danes, and the present building dates mainly from the 12th cent. It is a strong, spare church, one of the largest in Wales, and dominated by a powerful, square tower. Within, it seems rather stark. There are monuments by Flaxman to the Gogerddan and Nanteos families, but the pride of the church is the Celtic crosses, one of which, with its complex interwoven patterning, must be accounted among the finest of its kind. Set into the chancel floor is the memorial slab to Lewis Morris (1706–65), one of the distinguished family of literary men from Anglesey, a hot-tempered scholar and a somewhat unsuccessful man of business who came to Cardigan to make a fortune out of the lead-mines. The fortune eluded him, but Wales is in his debt for keeping bright the flame of literature in the bleak years of the early 18th cent.

Although he has no memorial here, one other Welsh literary figure is inseparable from Llanbadarn. Dafydd ap Gwilym, the greatest poet of medieval Wales, was by tradition born in Brogynin near Penrhyncoch, a few miles NE. over the hills. Dafydd paints an unforgettable picture of himself in Llanbadarn church, taking more interest in the lovely women than in the service:

> My face turned to the glorious girl,
> My back to the Divine God.

He had little success, for the girls laughed at the lanky youth with his long yellow hair; he was as bedecked with clasps and rings as a modern youthful poet. No wonder he begins his poem with the exasperated cry:

> I am bent with wild desire,
> Plague take the girls of the whole parish!

His poetry bears constant witness that he had better success elsewhere.

LLANBADARN-FAWR, *Radnorshire.* This should not be confused with the Llanbadarn-Fawr close to Aberystwyth. The Llanbadarn of Radnorshire, dedicated to the same St Padarn

Top: *Dolbadarn Castle, Llanberis*   W. A. Poucher
Bottom: *Looking towards the Snowdon range from Moelfre, near Llanallgo*   Peter Baker

Overleaf: *Plate 11   The Mumbles lighthouse (see p. 268)*   Colour Library International

One of the Celtic crosses in the church at
Llanbadarn-Fawr, Cardiganshire

(or Paternus), lies in the lowland of the River Ithon, rather to the W. of Penybont and Radnor Forest and to the N. of Llandrindod Wells. Its major attraction is its church, which holds a great deal of Welsh history unmarked elsewhere. Its foundation may go back to the first days of Christianity in these islands; for a centurial stone inscribed "*Valflavini* . . ." is built into its porch. Such inscriptions were set up by detachments of 100 men, commanded by a centurion, to identify some building erected for their use as local garrisons. The probability is that this concerns the recruitment of native auxiliary forces that Rome relied on to an increasing extent in the later years of occupation. Like so many other early churches in Wales, this Llanbadarn shows the influence both of alien architectural styles and the reformed beliefs that supplanted the doctrines of Celtic Christianity. The porch is surmounted by a tympanum, an exceptional example of the carved Norman style rare in Wales but with a parallel at Penmon in Anglesey. On its face are two emblematic creatures whose tails end in the form of a cross, facing each other with a plant set between them, the plant most probably the lily-pot that was often used as a symbol of the Incarnation of Christ. It is a convention typical of Norman craftsmen.

In 19th-cent. prints, this place is called Llanbadern to distinguish it from the Aberystwyth village.

LLANBEDR, *Merioneth*. Between Barmouth and Harlech the sea-coast stretches under the standing hills of Ardudwy in a long and silent reach called the Morfa Dyffryn. It is land, but not land available to men, being still possessed by the sound and the sands of the Irish Sea. It reaches round to Morfa Harlech. Salt marsh and sand-dune are the haunt of the strange flowers that seem to be still half way through the emergence of marine growths into life upon the land; sea-birds are predominant even over the noise that comes from the airfield close to Llanbedr, the small village on the Artro river north of Llanenddwyn, and Llanddwywe.

Both of these show points of interest in their churches, Llanddwywe having a late structure of 1593, but also a circular churchyard that is a Christianized successor to the stone-circle monuments perhaps from before even the Age of Bronze. The church has attached to it a chapel, which Inigo Jones, the famous Welsh architect of the 17th cent., has left as a memorial to his skill. Llanenddwyn church, close to Dyffryn Ardudwy railway station, has the grave of Col. John Jones of Maesygarnedd, who married Cromwell's sister Catherine and was executed for his part in the death of Charles I.

But Llanbedr looks past these things altogether. Apart from being one of the best fishing centres in Wales, it is surrounded by spaces of sea and land and even of time itself that make it one of the most rewarding places to visit. It must have been significant for ancient peoples, since the neighbouring hills are scattered with standing stones, calendric circles, cromlechs, and encampments following the sea-coast under the Rhinog Fawr and its several lakes, traversed by the long trackway that passes over the Roman Steps. Out to sea, Llanbedr looks across the pebbled peninsula known as Mochras Island, famous for the variety of sea-shells that can be gathered there. Even further out to sea is the Sarn Badrig (Patrick's Causeway), a parallel formation to the one near Towyn, the Sarn-y-Bwch. These twin perils for navigators (*see* Aberdovey) may have contributed to keeping this stretch of coast in its pleasant state of relative non-development. The original name of the 14-m. ridge of stones that at low tide lays bare 9 m. of its length was Sarn Baddwryg (Shipwreck Reef).

The old sand-locked church at Llandanwg, about 1 m. N. of Llanbedr, can be reached by the field-tracks from the station or by an equally unmade road from Llanfair. Its age and interest are now protected under the Society for the Preservation of Ancient Monuments. This lonely spot marks the foundation from which Harlech sprang. The neglect of the 19th cent. has been remedied, and the place has been re-roofed. The font has been taken for protection to Harlech, but several stones dating back to the 6th cent. are preserved in it. The inscriptions on them include some with spiral ornamentation; and at Llanbedr church, which was once the Chapel of Ease for Llandanwg, there are more. Such stones are unique; they date back to the Bronze Age of about 2000 B.C., and there are few in Britain, though several in Ireland. They represent a theme that originated with the dawn of civilization and yet continued deep into classical times. At Chilgrove in Sussex, not long ago, a Roman villa when excavated showed mosaic flooring with the same design, one that is found as far afield as the eastern Mediterranean sites of Bronze Age culture. It is the serpent of stars known to many ancient mythologies – the form of movement that the constellations seem to make about the Pole Star, the one unchanging mark in the heavens by which early navigators steered. There are upstanding pillar stones of equal antiquity at Llanbedr, and a cromlech under Hafod-y-llyn that in the late 1890s was being used as a pig-trough. The long stretch of land about the Artro may well remember men who plied the Irish Sea in the first ships ever to sail it, and raised in the sister island across the waves the White Mound at Tara.

But Llanbedr also offers some of the most exciting walks to be had anywhere. The way up the Artro valley is easy of access, and cars can be taken as far as Dolwreiddiog farm, but no further. At the end of the woodland-walled route that ends by old working levels of manganese-mines, you reach the lake of Cwm Bychan. This Little Hollow Lake is wild and lonely and stops at the sharp crest of Craig y Saeth, said to have been, in days when deer roamed these heights, a place from which the arrows of hunters had their quarry to the best advantage. From here, on the eastward side, ride the Roman Steps, a fascinating trackway laid with marshalled stones and taking you between Llyn Gloyw (Rainy) and the lake called Llyn y Morynion (Maidens).

Legend has been active here. The Roman Steps are nowadays assigned to a later period and accepted as a pack-way for traffic from one valley to another; but such tracks usually went where earlier feet had gone, and the activity of Romans in search of raw materials in these mountains is too well established to be overlooked. It is a striking and well-designed path, and at the top of the Bwlch Tyddiad, which they reach, part of the way is paved (people say) with 2,000 flat stones, on which a sentinel-guard was placed. The Maidens lake has the same name and the same story to account for it as the one near Ffestiniog. The route leads to the Bwlch Drws Ardudwy, the gateway to that section of Merioneth which lies S. of Harlech. This lies at 1,255 ft and separates the Rhinog Fawr hill from the Rhinog Fach. Under the head of Rhinog Fawr spreads another lake called simply Du (Black). It is locally thought to have been formed and to be maintained by dew-fall only. As in Morynion, fishing in it is free. The trout are a little undersized, perhaps from the nature of the waters in which they swim. But at both lakes the views are magnificent.

The peak of Rhinog Fawr, like that of Aran Fawddwy, is a scrawl of tumbled boulders; but you have half Wales at your feet. The Craig Wnion over Cwm Bychan is most impressive in the way it rears itself ledge over ledge; and, further on, Moel Hebog stands behind the wide waste of the Trawsfynydd moors, and the Arennigs on one side and Cader Idris on the other make a room of the sky. Rhinog Fawr is rather over 2,000 ft up, and its head is an oval plateau steeply scarped on all sides. A little lower towards the W. are the continuation of this shape, the stepped descents of Foel Ddu, and to the S. the splendidly sited Bodlyn lake and Llyn Irddyn, which is worth a special visit. Another half-hour is required to get to it, where it stretches, deep in its midst but with shallow shores that must, it is said, be avoided. Here one should keep to the grassy footing, for that is the only protection against the Other People who live there still. Again, this is a lingering recollection of the first inhabitants of such places, the mild people of the hills who worked with stone tools and shunned contact with iron. On its W. shore are the remains of an ancient, possibly Celtic, township of stone-based hutments. About 1 m. to the N. stands the fortified height called Craig y Dinas. It is supposed to have some connection with the Druids, the priests of an ancient faith that has left permanent memorials on these slopes and by the sands of the Artro.

LLANBERIS, *Caernarfonshire.* There is an old Llanberis and a new one. The first is now called Nant Peris after the river that runs through the famous Pass of Llanberis, the bouldered ravine that shoulders through Snowdonia to the twin lakes, Padarn and Peris, under the Elidir Fawr and Fach (3,029 and 2,564 ft). On one side of Llyn Peris rise the very considerable slate quarries of Dinorwic, thought to be one of the greatest in the world. On the other side stands the single, round peel-tower called Dolbadarn Castle. The history of the present structure is disputed. But it is fairly certain that the Princes of Gwynedd had a fortalice on the site. Owen the Red was held prisoner there for twenty-three years by his brother, Llywelyn ap Iorwerth (otherwise called the Great), to cure him of his presumption in challenging the right of inheritance. This seems to have established a precedent, for Owain Glyndwr used it as a prison for his enemy, Lord Grey of Ruthin, until the ransom of 10,000 marks was duly paid. Between the days of the Llywelyn ap Iorwerth and those of Glyndwr, it was a stronghold of Dafydd, brother of the last Llywelyn, and was captured for Edward I by the Earl of Pembroke. Padarn is 2 m. long and 94 ft deep; Peris, 1 m. long and 114 ft deep. Both hold excellent fishing.

From Llanberis the most accessible route to the height of Snowdon is reached.

LLANBOIDY, *Carmarthenshire.* The derivation of this name is a mystery. Llanboidy lies 5 m. N. of Whitland in green, rolling country. The church is one of the many in West Wales consecrated to St Brynach, and the usual legend says that the saint fulfilled a prophecy by building his church here, where he saw a "beudy" (fold).

The village must in the past have been very much in the shadow of the local big house, Maesgwynne. There are some strange names around, including a Piccadilly Square. The Village Hall was built out of money won by a Powell of Maesgwynne in backing a horse called Hermit. Maesgwynne once had its own racecourse, but the glory of the house has long departed. The church is heavily restored. The family vault of the Powells in the churchyard has a figure of Grief by Sir W. Goscombe John to the memory of William Rice Powell, M.P. for the county during many years.

Some 2 m. N. of Llanboidy is the now abandoned church of Eglwys Fair a Churig. The church was built in 1770, and the churchyard is now a wilderness. The dual dedication is rare. The Norman clergy usually re-dedicated Celtic churches in their area of influence to one of their favourite saints, St Peter or St Mary. In this case St Curig has survived, linked with St Mary.

LLANBRYNMAIR, *Montgomeryshire*. Some 8 m. from Machynlleth, Llanbrynmair (Hill Church of Mary) lies in the valley of the River Twymyn. Though a small and quiet village, it has attractions of many sorts. The falls of the Twymyn from the crags of the W. Plynlinom slopes are impressive; the church is ancient and has an unusual roof. From Llanbrynmair is the most accessible route to the stone circles and prehistoric hutments that have been allowed to survive in the upper Rheidol valley.

Generations ago, Llanbrynmair was important as a market centre for the sheep-raising industry, and played its part in the Civil Wars of the 17th cent. One of its older and larger houses keeps a reminiscence of Cromwell's days. Beneath later panelling were discovered the portraits of the former owner and his wife, supporters of the Royalist cause. Both pictures were riddled with musket-shot. The Ironside soldiers, having failed to capture the family, had the satisfaction of executing them at least in effigy.

LLANCARFAN, *Glamorgan*, lies 2 m. S. of the main Cardiff–Cowbridge road. To reach it, turn off the main road at Bonvilston. Although a certain amount of new building is going on, the old village has not yet been overwhelmed by the latest addition of "desirable" residences. The Carfan brook still runs untrammelled down the side of the road, and the church lies undisturbed in its wooded hollow in the centre of the village.

Llancarfan, or more correctly Nant Carfan, has a high place in the early religious history of Wales. Here came St Cattwg (Cadoc) to set up his monastery in the 6th cent. Cattwg was the son of Gwynllyw, the chieftain of Gwent who was converted to Christianity and is commemorated in the cathedral church of Newport under the Anglicized name of St Woolas. The present church may stand on the site of Cattwg's original monastery. It is one of the largest in the Vale of Glamorgan and possesses an embattled tower, an aisled chancel, and a nave with a S. aisle, to which a chapel is annexed. The S. door is early 13th-cent. work, but most of the church dates from the late 13th cent. The screen in the S. chapel may have been part of the original screen of the former rood-loft. The chapel itself has been

most successfully modernized. The rough medieval oak chest on the right, as you enter, formerly held the church plate and valuables. There are other remains of monastic settlements scattered around Llancarfan, mainly incorporated in the walls of farmhouses. There are also some curious names to local landmarks, including Cwm-y-Breeches and Coed-y-Breeches. In the days when Llancarfan was famous as a centre for producing such useful articles of apparel, at fair time customers used to retire to these secluded spots to try the breeches on.

At Pennon, close to Llancarfan, Iolo Morgannwg (Edward Williams) was born in 1746. This remarkable man, a stonemason by trade, entirely self-taught, became at once poet, historian, enthusiast for the French Revolution, and literary forger. He was a great collector of Welsh MSS., but was not above adding to and amending much of the valuable material that passed through his hands. For this he has been well and truly anathematized by modern historians and literary researchers. But Iolo was a poet of great gifts, and the motive behind his dubious activities was a fierce local patriotism, a determination to glorify his native Glamorgan at all costs.

Out of Iolo's imagination and his romantic dream of the remote past of Wales came much of the ritual of the modern Gorsedd. Iolo and his London colleagues held the first Gorsedd in the somewhat unromantic purlieus of Primrose Hill in London at the end of the 18th cent. It was intended as a splendid revival of the glories of the ancient Druids. Its ceremonies have now been happily grafted on to the National Eisteddfod, where the Archdruid and his white-robed colleagues form one of the most important parts of this great Welsh national festival of song and poetry.

Iolo could claim that there was something in the air of Llancarfan that tempted chroniclers to take liberties with historical facts, for, as far back as the 12th cent., Geoffrey of Monmouth was claiming Caradog of Llancarfan as a worthy colleague. The works of Caradog have proved as difficult to untangle from the truth as those of Iolo. Iolo himself is buried in the church at Flemingston, 2 m. to the W., his forgeries now forgiven him and his real achievements remembered with gratitude.

The hill to the E. of Llancarfan is crowned by the hill-fort known as Castle Ditches.

LLANDAFF, *Glamorgan*, has now been officially absorbed into the boundaries of Cardiff, but this village-city and its cathedral have retained a strange, secluded charm. Llandaff must possess some secret of indomitable survival. The settlement has been sacked by the Norsemen and burnt by the Welsh. The great church has been ruined by its own bishops, and blasted by German bombs in the 20th cent. The suburbs of Cardiff creep ever closer to the W. Yet Llandaff remains a place apart – a small corner of quiet and contemplation, away from the rush of modern life. It lies on the banks of the River Taff 2 m.

Janet March-Penney
Epstein's figure of the Christus in Llandaff Cathedral

from the centre of Cardiff, and forms the climax to the long line of parklands, gardens, and playing-fields that lead so splendidly northwards, out from the heart of the city along the riverside.

Approached from the W., Llandaff Cathedral, like many of the great ecclesiastical buildings of Wales, lies half hidden in a hollow. The Cathedral green is the first pleasure offered to the visitor. None of the buildings that surround this large green plot are especially notable from the architectural point of view, but they all seem to fit in together. The Victorian houses, the whitewashed walls of the deanery, the plain white 18th-cent. façades of the canons' residences surround what, in essence, is a village green that has given itself a grandiose title. At the S. end lie the ruins of the gateway to the old episcopal palace, a 13th-cent. fortified mansion that was sacked by Owain Glyndwr in 1402. It is the garden entrance to the present palace, a large, late 18th-cent. building that, in 1958, became part of the Cathedral school of Llandaff. The miraculous well of St Teilo lay on the right-hand side of the steep road leading down from the gatehouse ruins to the Cathedral, but was sealed up many years ago.

On the Cathedral green are three interesting monuments. The first is the cross, with a restored shaft on an ancient base. Here, according to tradition, is the spot where Archbishop Baldwin preached the Third Crusade in 1188. He was accompanied by Gerald de Barri, who left a vivid description of the scene as many came forward to take the Cross, "the English standing on one side and the Welsh on the other". Further up, on the green, is the statue of James Price Buckley, Vicar of Llandaff and Archdeacon until 1924: "A man he was to all the country dear". At the far end of the green is the war

memorial to those who fell in the First World War: "Llandaff remembers her own sons".

Near the cross, the path leads down, past a tower ruined in the 15th cent., to the Cathedral itself. This tower was once the detached belfry. Llandaff can pride itself on a foundation going back to the 6th cent. St Teilo, the great West Wales monastic leader, is credited with visiting the spot in A.D. 500 and with founding a monastic settlement on the site. The "llan", or monastery, he founded took its name from the River Taff. The clergy of Llandaff were always proud to be known as "Teulu Deilo", the family of St Teilo. Nothing remains of the early Celtic churches, although a 10th-cent. Celtic cross was discovered in 1870 and now stands in the SW. presbytery aisle. The history of the present building really begins with the Normans, when Bishop Urban (in office 1107–33) began building a cathedral far more ambitious than the "little minster" that previously stood here. The work went steadily on through the next century. The completion of the inner walls of the nave was the work of Urban's successor, Bishop Henry of Abergavenny. The six western arches of the nave followed, in the style typical of the Gothic work of the West of England. The W. front was constructed around 1220. This early period of construction fitly closed with the great dedication service held in 1266, when the new Bishop, William de Braose, was enthroned. He lies buried in the Lady Chapel, an elegant 13th-cent. addition to the Cathedral. The 14th and 15th cents. saw the fabric of the Cathedral perfected; Bishop Marshall (1418–96) was one of the great benefactors. His tomb is on the N. side of the presbytery, and the painting on board, which once formed part of his bishop's throne, was saved from destruction at the hands of Cromwell's soldiers by being covered with black lead. It is now in the Euddogwy Chapel in the N. aisle of the nave.

The last of the medieval additions to the building was made by Jasper Tudor, uncle of Henry VII, who built the NW. tower, now known as the Jasper Tower.

Then followed centuries of appalling neglect. The Bishops of Llandaff were generally absentees. The revenues of the see went on everything except the upkeep of the fabric. Cromwell's soldiers used part of the nave as a beerhouse. The chapter library books were burnt. The climax of neglect was reached in 1723 when the SW. tower was blown down during a great storm. No wonder the clerics talked of "our sad and miserable cathedral".

The 18th cent. saw the first attempt at restoration, when James Wood, the architect of Bath, created a classic temple amid the ruins. Luckily funds ran out before the whole of the remaining Gothic work was buried under columns and cornices. The two large Classical urns now placed on the pathway of the old prebendal house are relics of the "Italian temple". In 1835 a movement began for a complete restoration of the Cathedral under the devoted inspiration of Dean Conybeare and later Dean Williams. The second great thanksgiving service in the history of the Cathedral was held in July 1839. The restoration was largely in the hands of a local architect, John Pritchard. He was responsible for the SE. tower, with its French-style spire and the pepper-pot roof over the 13th-cent. chapter house. The row of heads of British sovereigns that circles the S. wall is also his work. King George VI and the present Queen are on the N. side.

On the evening of the 2nd January 1941, Llandaff Cathedral was almost destroyed by a German landmine. Of the British cathedrals, Coventry alone received worse damage. Once again, the Cathedral of Llandaff rose from its ruins. The chief architect of this resurrection was Geoffrey Pace of York, and for the third time a great thanksgiving service was held in 1958 to celebrate the restoration of Llandaff to its ancient glory. And a most successful restoration it has proved to be. The Cathedral, as we see it today, is a harmonious mingling of various centuries and styles.

As you enter through the great W. door, you are confronted by the most challenging part of the new restoration. A bold parabolic arch of reinforced concrete separates the nave from the choir, and yet leaves the W. to E. vista open at floor level. Surmounting the arch is a cylindrical organ-case, bearing the sixty-four Pre-Raphaelite figures that originally stood in the canopies of the old choir-stalls. On the side of the cylinder fronting the W. door is the deeply impressive figure of the Christus by Sir Jacob Epstein, cast in unpolished aluminium. It dominates the whole Cathedral. The restoration included the replacement of the ceiling. The wood of the panelling is hardwood from Central Africa and Malaya. The font, the seating, the John Piper window over the high altar, the organ-cases, and console gallery are all new. One final and important addition has been made to the Cathedral. The officers and men of the Welch Regiment raised the funds to build a chapel in memory of their comrades who fell in two world wars. The chapel was dedicated in 1958. It fits perfectly into the texture of the N. side of the Cathedral, since the stones are river-washed stones that originally came from the bed of the Taff. Within, a great effect of simplicity and light has been achieved with the use of a barrel-vaulted ceiling. On the wall is the impressive roll-call of the regiment's battle honours.

Llandaff still holds some of its older treasures. Among them are the Rossetti triptych *The Seed of David*, now placed in the Chapel of the 53rd (Welsh) Infantry Division – St Illtud's – on the ground floor of the Jasper Tower immediately to your left as you enter through the great W. door; the Mathew tomb near the modern pulpit; the traditional site of St Teilo's tomb beneath the 13th-cent. effigy in the sanctuary; the fine Norman arch leading from the sanctuary into the Lady Chapel; the tomb in the Dyfrig Chapel of Sir David Mathew, who was

Edward IV's standard-bearer at the Battle of Towton, and the Norman S. doorway.

So Llandaff Cathedral has been reborn. Today, with little of the 19th-cent. stained glass left, it seems full of light and life – a cathedral for today as well as for the past.

Llandaff "Village" – as everyone locally calls the "City" – is also the home of the Theological College of St Michael's and All Angels and of Howell's Glamorgan School for Girls. Howell's School has a romantic origin. Thomas Howell, whose name it bears, was a merchant who traded with Spain. In 1540 he left 12,000 ducats to be "desposed unto foure maydens, being orphanes, to their marriage". Over the years, the income from the investment has been diverted from the marriage of the young maidens to the equally important business of their education.

B.B.C. Wales also has its headquarters in Llandaff, in a notably successful modern studio, concert hall, and office complex designed by Welsh architects.

LLANDDAROG, *Carmarthenshire,* is a village 4½ m. E. of Carmarthen on the Swansea–Carmarthen road. It makes a pleasant picture, with the thatched and white-walled White Hart Inn set alongside the church. The church is Victorian, built by R. K. Penson, and has an original spire, all angles and complex planes. The churchyard is surrounded by yew trees of impressive bulk and age. There is a rough-hewn lych-gate and a notice-board announcing services in Welsh. The lamp-post before the church door is a fine piece of Victoriana. The main road now by-passes the village, and there has been some new building. Enough remains to show how beautiful rural Carmarthenshire must have been in the late 19th cent.

Llanddarog stands on the ridge that separates the Gwendraeth Fach valley from the Towy. There are extensive views hereabouts over the pattern of green hills backed by the distant moors of the Black Mountain to the NE.

LLANDDERFEL, *Merioneth.* Lying to the E. of Bala Lake, and SW. from Corwen along the valley of the Dee, Llandderfel was once very prominent. St Derfel, in the 6th cent., belonged to the Celtic form of Christianity that spread among the British people with great success after the Empire of Rome – and its Gallic Prefecture in the West of Europe, including Britain – had been resolved into native government. His image, once contained in this church, was greatly revered, and pilgrimages were constantly made to it throughout the Middle Ages. Gerald de Barri wrote of how the saints of the Celtic Church were honoured throughout Wales by the careful preservation of relics; and St Derfel's horse and staff were kept in the porch of Llandderfel. Gerald's 12th-cent. approach to such questions was not shared by the Reformation, which had the image of Derfel burnt by the public hangman at Smithfield. The church and the name of Derfel, however, remain.

LLANDDEWIBREFI, *Cardiganshire,* a small village in the Teifi valley, stands 1 m. back from the river at the point where the Nant Bran comes down from the mountains. It holds a secure place in Welsh history as the spot where St David preached in A.D. 519 to combat the Pelagian heresy. The big, rather bare church dedicated to St David stands on this mound. Bishop Bec of St David's established here in 1287 a college of a precentor and twelve presbyters. The building was originally cruciform, but the transepts were removed and the tower now looks somewhat top-heavy. The interior is pleasing. The modern statue of Dewi Sant (St David) is by Frederick Mancini. The long connection of the site with Celtic Christianity is proved by the presence of no fewer than five stones with Celtic crosses, some of them inscribed. In the W. wall is a stone commemorating Idnert, the last Bishop of Llanbadarn-Fawr, who was murdered in A.D. 720.

Mary Roberts, the great-great-grandmother of Harriet Beecher Stowe, author of *Uncle Tom's Cabin,* was born in Llanddewibrefi. A fine but narrow road goes SE. over the mountains and through the new plantations of the Forestry Commission to Farmers.

Across the Teifi is Pontllanio, the site of the Roman military station of Bremia. The fort stood on the river-bank near the point where the A485 runs alongside the old railway line. From Llanio the road N. towards Aberystwyth follows the line of the old Roman road, known to Welsh tradition as Sarn Helen. There are other stretches of Roman roads in Wales similarly named after Helen, who was claimed to be the Welsh wife of the usurper emperor Magnus Maximus. He denuded Britain of Roman troops in A.D. 383, and, after setting up his court at Trèves, was eventually slain. Helen ("Helen of the Legions") was supposed to have returned to Wales, and was regarded as a saint. The line of the Roman road to the N. runs from Llanio across to Llanbadarn-Fawr near Aberystwyth and to the Roman fort at Pennal in Merioneth. Some 3½ m. along the road S. to Lampeter is Llanfair Clydogau, where three streams rejoicing in the name Clydogau come down from the hills. The Roman road, Sarn Helen, crosses the hills from Farmers and comes down into the Teifi valley here, on its way to Pontllanio. There are traces of Roman mining for silver and lead. The church has been rebuilt, but stands in the midst of an oval, prehistoric earthwork.

LLANDEGAI, *Caernarfonshire.* This is a point on the map about 1 m. from Bangor, but worthy of note for two remarkable things. The first is the lofty Penrhyn Castle. Porth Penrhyn, close by, ships the slates direct from the Bethesda quarries, and the owner of them, Lord Penrhyn, in 1836 commissioned one Thomas Hopper to set up an exercise in the Gothic style that is the present Castle. The exterior is imposing, but the architect managed to give his towers their sky-searching effect only from one angle; from elsewhere, they look just a pile of bricks. The interior is vast and theatrical, with a marriage of Norman styles as in the Castle of Otranto, and with Oriental flourishes inspired by Gustave Doré. The most astonishing feature is a bedroom that has a bedstead carved solidly out of slate and weighing 4 tons. It was offered to Queen Victoria, who replied: "It is interesting but uninviting" – a statement that, in the records of royal repartee, is worthy to rank with the more famous "We are not amused". The cellars, however, when recently explored, suggest that some far earlier site was used as a base for Hopper's Folly. Not far away another but smaller elaboration of the 17th cent. seems to have been made of a medieval house traditionally belonging to Llywelyn the Great. Penrhyn Castle is now under the ownership of public authority and houses a museum of early locomotives.

Almost exactly opposite the drive into Penrhyn Castle is a cricket field shortly to be developed as a building site. Urgent excavations are being carried out there to examine unexpected evidence of a Megalithic stone-circle system that may prove to be as great as Stonehenge. Only the base-sets of the stones can be traced, as in some of the sites on Salisbury Plain.

LLANDEGFAN, *Anglesey.* Not long ago, this was a group of scattered cottages and farms between high, trimmed walls of stone and far from any aspect of the world. Today it is a rapidly expanding residential town, which owes its sudden emergence to the setting up of the atomic power station in Anglesey at Wylfa. It is typical of the change that is rapidly overtaking so many of the provinces of Wales in the latter half of the 20th cent. Without having yet acquired a character essentially its own, since work and interest lie elsewhere, it is worth particular notice since, lying immediately opposite Bangor across the straits, it commands the best view of the full width of the Snowdon range. When the light is clear and the skies washed with recent rain, the summit of Snowdon and the gathered peaks of the Glyders, the Carnedds, and Moel Hebog can be sharply distinguished. Even Yr Eifl (The Rivals), where the coast falls away to the S., are visible. Here, not only can you see Menai Bridge above the straits standing parallel with its twin structure carrying the railway, but also the striding pylons of the power-line from the atomic power station at Wylfa. They make a new kind of bridge, bringing a new kind of civilization to Anglesey. They will shortly be reinforced when the aluminium factory at Amlwch is fully developed, and the town's ancient industrialization is renewed in the service of mankind.

LLANDEGLEY, *Radnorshire.* St Tecla in the 6th cent. came this way, it seems, and found the sulphur springs to her taste. The church is of interest, with a font and screen that speak of traditional faiths. The healing waters, however, no longer attract visitors, and it is the rocks

Llandegley church

G. Douglas Bolton

standing due S. of the village at about 1,400 ft, with their magnificent view of Radnor Forest, that give Llandegley its main appeal. The moor, which runs level to Betws Diserth, is strewn with the earthworks and stone circles of ages before history; for the valley running to Llanfihangel Nant Melan was clearly a passageway in Neolithic times. The tomen castle there dates to some half-recorded Norman incursion. The Pales, a thatched stone structure whose door bears the date 1745, stands in Llandegley as the oldest meeting-house in Wales of the Society of Friends.

LLANDEILO, *Carmarthenshire.* Properly speaking, this is Llandeilo Fawr, or the seat of St Teilo, the third after David to hold the primacy of St David's; Gerald de Barri called him Eliud or Teilaus. There are other Llandeilos in Wales, but this is known as the Great. The town, however, is more renowned for its military than its religious significance. And this is made plain by the presence of the Castle of Dynevor, spelled Dinefwr in Welsh, which takes for its footing an isolated hill apart from the town, and observes the valley of the Towy with the indifference of a long-established past. The town is a stretch of two-storeyed, barracked houses devoted to the business of the thriving valley, which, while it does not have the more romantic beauty of other valleys parallel to it in the South gives an even stronger impression of deep-rooted fertility. The woodlands have a golden light in their branches, which is no doubt why the great house standing among them not far from Llandeilo was called the Golden Grove.

The first appearance of Dynevor in recorded history is in 876, when Rhodri the Great, descendant of the House of Cunedda, who held his land against the Danes and united all Wales under his rule, made at the Castle the disposition that he hoped would enable Wales to keep that unity. He divided his kingdom among his three sons, one to hold the North, or Gwynedd, another to hold the South, or Deheubarth, and the third to have Powys, the Kingdom of Central Wales, stretching from Severn to Dovey, which Cunedda in the 5th cent. had first established. It was a partition that, however, did not make for unity but for a series of rivalries from which Wales was never free. Yet this was not the beginning of that division. It was one that the natural structure of Wales imposes; the desert of mountain and moorland called the Ellennith was then, and to some extent still is, an effective barrier to communication. Gwynedd, the upland mass of the Snowdon range with Anglesey, is cut off from any direct approach to the South except by sea through Cardigan Bay, and only with difficulty could Powys build itself along the line of the Dee and the Severn and the Wye and reach the Dovey valley. Gerald de Barri, visiting Dynevor in the 12th cent., states that in ancient times Wales had three capitals: the princely seat at Aberffraw in Anglesey, the one at Pengwern (Shrewsbury), and this last at Dynevor. But, as he well knew, he was not writing of the days of Rhodri the Great. Even in the 9th cent., Shrewsbury had been lost to Powys; it had been taken by the Saxon in the 7th cent. Gerald was looking back to the time before Rhodri when his ancestor, Cunedda, from the line of the Severn, had placed Roman-British control over both the North and the South. Rhodri in 876 was reviving a political system adapted to the geographical necessities of Wales. Dispute between the sons of the House of Rhodri and Cunedda lasted into the 11th cent., on the eve of the Norman incursion into Wales. In 1080 Dynevor was held by Rhys ap Tewdwr, one of the ancient line, and the North by Gruffydd son of Cynan, who was another of the same descent, and the Castle became concerned with the long resistance to the Norman invasion of Brecon and Carmarthen and Pembroke. This Rhys of 1080 was the first of the Lords Rhys to rule in the South, with their heraldic badge of the raven, which had come to them from the auxiliary legions led by Cunedda. They are still the badge of the family of Lord Dynevor.

But the last magnificence of the Castle belongs to the days of the last Llywelyn. Before it Llywelyn in 1256 fought and won his battle against Rhys the Less, who had turned to Edward I of England for help in making good his claims against Maredudd of Dinefwr. For a while, Llywelyn was secure; he had two successive victories against the English forces, which resulted in his capture of the Castle at Dynevor from another Maredudd, who had called in the Lord de Sayes of Carmarthen. Twenty-five years later, another battle was fought at Dynevor; and the result was the wayside tragedy at Cilmery.

The ruins of the Castle dominate the river from a high bluff. They consist chiefly of the keep, standing alone at the E. side of what was an irregular and many-sided curtain wall, adapted to take the lie of the land. The work of the Lord Rhys who died in battle with the Norman Bernard of Neufmarché in 1091, and of the Rhys who was sovereign enough to ally himself as Justiciar with Henry II, was completed by the Rhys whose support guaranteed the success of Henry VII and who built the N. front of the present Castle in a brilliant military design. The moats are carved directly from the native rock.

The more stormy side of events in the Towy valley thereafter passed to Golden Grove. It became the seat of the Vaughans, patrons of agriculture and the arts. In the Civil Wars of the 17th cent., the family, Earls of Carbery, were active Royalists. The strictly constitutional nature of the reasoning used by Parliament is illustrated by the way in which it indicted the Earl of that day, who was also Lieutenant-General of the King in the South, for taking up arms against both Parliament and the King; for it held the view that the ancient Constitution of Britain recognized not a personal monarch but only a corporate King-in-Parliament, and Charles I was executed as a traitor to his own constitutional position. But the Earl went unharmed. Cromwell, putting down the Second Civil War, which was almost entirely a Welsh affair, sent a troop of horse to take him; but Vaughan escaped in time from the Ironsides and took to the woods, while Cromwell sat down to dinner with the Earl's Countess.

But Golden Grove was not quite finished with the Civil War. Jeremy Taylor, Chaplain to the Royalist forces, was captured at Cardigan. When released, he found no refuge except at Golden Grove, where for ten years he occupied himself with writing *Holy Living and Holy Dying*. The great house is now burnt out. Its successor is the County Agricultural College.

LLANDOVERY, *Carmarthenshire,* called in Welsh Llanymddyfri, is an attractive little market town in the upper valley of the Towy. The hills are all around, and the valley dairy farms flourish. Llandovery exudes an air of quiet satisfaction with life. On summer week-ends it can get crowded with the mechanized migrants from England, on their way down the A40 to the western coastline. Normally it gets on with its business of being a very Welsh market town serving an unspoilt countryside. It has a castle. Only the ruins of the shattered keep remain, perched on the motte overlooking the cattle market and the little Afon Bran. The Castle Inn is nearby, with a modest square before it. Here George Borrow stayed, and he was loud in his praise of Llandovery as the "pleasantest little town in which I have halted in the course of my wanderings". The main street is indeed an attractive mixture of unpretentious Georgian and Victorian shops and houses. In the centre is

The climb into Llandeilo

G. Douglas Bolton

the Market Hall, with blocked-up arches beneath. Next to it is a delightful cream-and-white building completed with pepper-pot cupola and clock. Small public houses are scattered with Irish profusion through Llandovery. Historians point out that this arose from a charter of Richard III, which gave the town the sole right of keeping taverns throughout the area. A busy market day will convince the visitor that all are still needed. A modern bank occupying a pleasant Georgian house in the main street is the successor of the famous Bank of the Black Ox, founded by David Jones in 1799. Llandovery was then a great centre of the cattle trade. Drovers set out from the town with their great herds of black cattle, driving them over the mountains to the English markets. The trade flourished until the coming of the railways.

Three of the chapels in the town have architectural merit, including the well-proportioned Baptist Chapel of Ebenezer in Queen Street. Curiously enough, an English chapel – the Methodist chapel in the High Street – is the one that commemorates the greatest of hymn-writers in Welsh, William Williams of Pantycelyn. Pantycelyn is the farm in which he lived after his marriage. It lies in a secluded valley of the Mynydd Epynt range about 5 m. from Llandovery, and can be easily reached by turning off the main Llandovery–Brecon road at the hamlet of Ty-gwyn. The farm is still occupied, although it has become almost a place of pilgrimage for Welshmen. Williams was converted by Howell Harris after a sermon in Talgarth churchyard. He eventually joined the Calvinistic branch of the Methodists and travelled through Wales as an itinerant preacher from 1743 to his death in 1791. Williams was a literary artist, and his hymns have a lyrical power that made them irresistible. They played a vital part in generating the wave of religious enthusiasm that swept over Wales in the 18th cent. The two English hymns by which he is best known to the world outside are "Guide Me, O Thou Great Jehovah" and "O'er the Gloomy Hill of Darkness". His hymns still retain their power. As proof of this, the Memorial Chapel contains an oak communion table and chairs presented by the people of the Khassi Hills in Assam, who were converted by Welsh missionaries and who still sing the hymns of Pantycelyn in a far-off land.

Llandovery College stands among trees on the road out of town to the W. It is one of the two recognized public schools in Wales. The other is Christ's College, Brecon, and great is the rivalry on the rugby field between them. Llandovery owes its foundation to the deep interest in Welsh affairs shown by Thomas Phillips, a doctor who returned from India with a fortune in 1817. When he died, he left £11,000 to provide the Church boys of Carmarthenshire with a public school in which the Welsh language was to be the principal medium of instruction. The school was duly built in the Gothic style then fashionable. The first Warden was Archdeacon John Williams, a remarkable teacher, who had made his reputation as Rector of Edinburgh Academy, where he had "achieved a success, in many respects even more remarkable than that of Arnold at Rugby". After the departure of Archdeacon Williams, the original intention of the founder was modified, and Llandovery became an English-type public school. In our own day, Welsh has been restored to a more prominent place in the scheme of teaching. The college possesses two important paintings, a St Peter by Guercino in the hall, and a Crucifixion by Graham Sutherland in the chapel.

Llandovery Castle

G. Douglas Bolton

About 2 m. NE. of Llandovery at the house called Ystradwalter, one of the oldest Nonconformist academies in Wales, contemporary with the foundation at Brynllywarch, was conducted by Rees Prytherch from 1658 to 1698. During the period of persecution he held his ministrations in a cave called Cerrig-y-Wyddon, but was later able to buy Ystradwalter, and have there, and at Abercrychan nearby, a successful educational establishment.

The two principal churches of Llandovery are both on the outskirts of the town. To the S. is the parish church of Llandingat, in the meadows along the Towy. Llandingat was somewhat ruthlessly restored by W. D. Caröe in 1906. There is much Munich glass in the windows. The modern glass is by Leslie Walker. A vast Gothic font has been constructed around the original simple Norman one. The grave of Vicar Rhys Prichard is somewhere in the churchyard, although some accounts declared that it had been washed away by floods. Rhys Prichard was Vicar of Llandovery between 1594 and 1616. He died in 1644. His fame rests on a book of popular verse, published after his death, entitled *Canwyll y Cymry*, in which religious exhortation was combined with homely wisdom. *Canwyll y Cymry* had much the same influence in Wales as *The Pilgrim's Progress* in England. Popular legend declares that the Vicar wrote from his own experience. He led a dissolute life as Vicar, before a sudden conversion set him rhyming to admonish himself and his countrymen. The old house in which the Vicar lived was demolished by the Council in recent years.

Llandovery's second church stands on a small hill 2 m. to the N. of the town; hence its name of Llanfair-ar-y-bryn (St Mary's Church on the hill). Llanfair also was restored by W. D. Caröe. The church has been compared to a large tithe barn. The nave is covered by a fine tie-beam roof, and the whole interior gives an impression of antiquity. Some fragments of thin red brick in the external wall below the E. window may be Roman; they have caused speculation on whether a pagan Roman temple might have occupied the site. The Roman camp was certainly here on the hill at Llanfair. At the W. end of the church are the hatchments of the Gwynne family. Williams of Pantycelyn is buried in the churchyard, on the site marked by an unhappy monument.

The village of Llanfair-ar-y-bryn lies further up in the narrowing Bran valley, which continues the line of the main Towy valley north-eastwards into the hills. The village itself is unremarkable, but the ruins of a large mansion stand on the valley-floor. This is Glanbran, which was accidentally destroyed by fire some time ago. In the late 18th cent. it was occupied by a branch of the well-known Gwynne family, whose most interesting descendant was the feckless but attractive Sackville Gwynne (1751–94). He eloped to Dublin with the daughter of one of his father's tenants and was disinherited. He returned as a somewhat prodigal son and subsequently remarried. He is remembered as a passionate devotee of the harp. He himself was a skilful player, and he made Glanbran a centre and a place of patronage for the harpists of the day. He was one of the men who kept alive the long tradition of Welsh harp-playing through difficult times.

The valley ends dramatically beyond Cynghordy (the Meeting House), where the railway tunnels through the hills and the road zigzags around a little pointed peak called the Sugar Loaf. The Forestry Commission have planted large tracts all around, but there are still narrow, lonely little side valleys left to explore in the tangled country to the E. where the Mynydd Epynt ends.

LLANDRINDOD WELLS, *Radnorshire.* The Ithon river comes down its narrow valley from the highlands S. of Newtown, and the Aran runs from Radnor Forest. Just above their junction and the outfall of the Wye from Rhayader, Llandrindod, the Church of the Trinity, was built on a green hill in the Middle Ages. In 1696 the neighbourhood became well known for the virtues of its springs, and the farms about it were much frequented by those who were advised to try the waters. But in 1749 a Mr Grosvenor from Shropshire considered that something more might be done with the thirty wells and their varied salts and sulphurs. It was then that the fashion of Bath was introduced, and a pump-house set up with accommodation for hundreds of guests in its ballrooms, dining-salons, and gaming-places.

Now, through the coming of rail travel and the great new development of roads throughout Wales, Llandrindod has grown into an international resort. Apart from spa-treatment, of which every sort is available, Llandrindod is a busy excursionist centre. Llanbadarn-Fawr of Radnor; the Forest and Abbeycwmhir; Nantmel, associated with the legend of Gwyn ap Nudd, lord of the underworld; and the Elan Valley lakes and Rhayader can be all reached by road. Those with an interest in history can find just above Llanyre a well-preserved Roman fort called Castell Collen (Place of Hazels), and to the S. shortly before the inn that stands above Crossway, what is probably another fort, the Caer Du (Black Fort). Castell Collen seems to have been the place from which Llangollen sprang, and the standing stones that marked the old pathways over the hills towards the Clywedog and the Ithon can be traced at Llanfihangel Brynpabuan, Llanafan-Fawr, to the E. around Betws Diserth and to the W. in considerable numbers from Caban Coch lake to the hills that look down at Llanwrthwl.

LLANDUDNO, *Caernarfonshire.* The place where St Tudno set his church was apparently unknown to Daniel Paterson in 1811, when he compiled his *Direct and Principal Cross Roads* for the use of travellers by coach. In his day, it was nothing more than a tiny hamlet on the shore of the Irish Sea between Conway Bay and Colwyn

The beach and Pier Pavilion, Llandudno

Bay. It was set around Great Orme's Head, a bold promontory 700 ft high of carboniferous limestone sheering the waters above the eastward end of Anglesey. St Tudno's small church, founded in the 7th cent. by the early Christian missionary whose name it bears, still stands in its place on the head of Orme. Crowds of holiday-makers who flock to Llandudno in the summer attend its open-air services, most of them brought to the top by the cable-railway; and they can understand why the saint chose that spot. The views over Anglesey and into the great massif of Snowdonia, the shore of Strathclyde, and the coast of Conway, are such as to inspire man with a sense of the divine. Below, at the foot of Orme, a motor road, naturally called the Marine Drive, allows drivers to have a panoramic procession for a small charge.

At the end of it are the slight remains of Gogarth Abbey and the hotel that was once known as Pen Morfa (Sea-Land Height), and was the home of Dean Liddell, whose daughter, in her youngest days, was the original of the Alice famous as the explorer of Wonderland and the worlds beyond the looking-glass. "Lewis Carroll" (the Rev. C. L. Dodgson) is popularly supposed to have stayed here with the Liddells, but in the light of available evidence this belief has been questioned. On the West Shore is the memorial to Carroll, erected in 1933 and showing the White Rabbit studying his watch. It was designed by W. Forrester, a local sculptor. The Orme has become a nesting-place of guillemots.

The eastern side of Llandudno is contained by Little Orme's Head. Its height is only 463 ft, but its cliffs are wilder and more precipitous. The sands in this bay are excellent for bathing, firm and safe; those on the further side of the Great Orme, on the West Shore, are inclined to be muddy, and the intake through the Menai Straits draws the tides far out, so that various inland swimming-pools have been constructed.

Since 1850, Llandudno has grown to its present shape by careful town-planning and with an architecture that responds to the beauty of its setting.

It was, however, a place of very ancient human settlement. The principal street, called Mostyn, running towards the Great Orme, touches the system of great natural caves that are found in it. In 1879 one Thomas Kendrick, who used one such cave-entrance for a workroom, decided to enlarge it. His excavation disclosed some broken stalactite formations and, buried with them, bones both animal and human. Short-horned oxen of very ancient type, brown bear and boar, and four human skeletons were mingled together. It is assumed that the New Stone Age people may have used the place for burials; but the presence of bones belonging to men and beasts in so many caves along the sea-coasts of Wales and elsewhere is a mystery of archaeology for which some find the answer in natural cataclysms. Earlier than this, in 1849, men working the copper-mines on the Orme broke into a large cavern from whose roof stalactites hung in brilliant colours. But they had not been the first to enter it. Romans had been there before them; and wooden benches and tools for mining were found as they had been abandoned. Even mutton-bones from the lunch-boxes of the workmen remained, impregnated with copper by the long passage of the centuries.

Near Llandudno is Pabo Hill, again with magnificent views and again a memorial to a saint, contemporary with Tudno, who came to worship and convert.

Conway with its noble castle and recollections of half-forgotten wars is within easy reach; and the small holiday resort of Deganwy, or Dinas Conwy (Fort on the Conway), should be visited by anyone interested in the history of Wales.

Its half-vanished castle is a monument to Welsh resistance; one expedition after another of the Anglo-Norman forces came to a halt here as they attempted to drive into Gwynedd, and its latest Norman structure was destroyed by Llywelyn the Last in his triumph over the forces of Henry III in 1260 – which was to be reversed some twenty years later near Builth.

In a green valley, on the other side of the hills over which Llandudno sprawls away from the sea, is Gloddaeth, a remarkable survival of the late medieval great house, with perfect floors, windows, and ceilings. It was the home of that Archbishop Williams who had some difficulty in deciding for which side he held the Castle of Conway during the Civil Wars. It is now an excellent school for boys in the old tradition. But the lovely step-gabled roof of its 17th-cent. dovecote can be seen from the highway.

LLANDWROG, *Caernarfonshire,* lies on the road from Pwllheli about 4 m. before it reaches Caernarfon. It is an ancient site; but its original church has vanished under the rebuilding undertaken at great expense in recent years. Twrog must have been the saint who first settled in the district to leave his name upon the place; but it is the same name as that associated at Maentwrog with a giant who threw into that valley the "maen" (stone) still bearing his finger-marks. But the Twrog of this tale is said to have died about A.D. 610; and the title of Cawr (Giant) was in fact applied in those days to men of outstanding significance. Llandwrog is of great interest to the historian and those who care to see for themselves traces of the generations who founded our civilization.

Perhaps 1 m. from Llandwrog, set on a mound by the sea-strand, is Dinas Dinlle. Its name of Fort keeps alive the importance it had for those who built its double rampart. For here ended the great Roman road from London called Watling Street, and its stony surface can still be followed as it runs to the coastguard point on the shore. It is a road of first importance for the strategic control of Britain; and the early medieval legend that it was a construction due to mythical sons of a Waethel overlooked the fact that it was a Roman work, perhaps on even earlier foundations, and that its name seems to have been British. The road of the Wyddel – the road towards the West and Ireland – is its correct derivation. That it remained of first importance in the sub-Roman period is suggested by its association with one of the three Merlins or commanders whom Gerald de Barri names. A causeway connected Dinas Dinlle with the Caernarfon that the Romans knew as Segontium; a little below Llandwrog on the straight road that runs along the coast stands a "maen llwyd" (grey stone) such as was used on the old routes to mark the mileage and serve as a direction-post. Inland, between Pontlyfni and Llanllyfni, rises a hill-fort, Craig y Dinas, and further towards Nantlle lake at the end of a farm-track is another, Caer Engan. Dinas Dinlle is now a seaside resort.

LLANDYBIE, *Carmarthenshire.* The final *e* in Llandybie is pronounced, approximately, as "er".

This village on the road between Ammanford and Llandeilo has recently been enlarged, and the brewers have neatly eviscerated the centre to make room for a modern streamlined public house with attendant car park. There are, however, some things left. The church has a fine military-style tower and a curious interior with a line of whitewashed arches down the centre, after a rather clumsy enlargement in the 14th cent. The barrel roof is medieval. The chancel has a cluster of good memorials, including a well-carved if somewhat self-satisfied bust of Sir Henry Vaughan of Derwydd. In a lane near the bridge over the Marlais stream is the Plas, a 17th-cent. mansion that is now in a ruinous condition.

Outside the village, on the Llandeilo road, are the limestone quarries that now provide the most important industry of the area. The kilns are an interesting Victorian survival. They were designed by the church architect R. K. Penson, and have the massive quality of a Gothic castle. About 1 m. beyond is the old house of Derwydd, one of the manors of Sir Rhys ap Thomas, the great supporter of Henry VII. It has never passed out of the possession of his descendants.

To the E. of Llandybie is the limestone country rising to the high ridge that ends the line of the Black Mountain of Carmarthenshire. The Loughor river flows from a cave high on the hill-side, known as Llygad Llwchwr (Eye of the Loughor). The valley is attractive, and contains a fine waterfall at Glynhir. The fall is hidden in the grounds of the mansion. Glynhir was formerly the home of the Huguenot family of Du Buisson, who were credited with pro-French sympathies in the Napoleonic Wars. The dovecote, with its internal ladder revolving on a central shaft, is now neglected, but the locality was convinced that the Du Buissons were using it to convey secret messages to France. The story that the first pigeon bringing the news of Waterloo homed here is unfounded.

At Llandyfan, in the little side valley of the Gwyddfan brook, the rebuilt church and the light colour-washed house beside it make a charming composition against the wooded hill-side. This area still holds out against the spreading practice of covering the walls with pebble-dash, which is now making too many of the old cottages of Carmarthenshire and Pembrokeshire look like inhabited mud-pies. The miraculous healing well of Llandyfan lost the last shreds of its reputation after the Methodist Revival of the 18th cent.

The country due W. of Llandybie is largely quarried, with the edge of the coalfield not far away. The most interesting place is the rather bleak little tarn of Llyn Llech Owen, $1\frac{1}{2}$ m. N. of Cross Hands, a colliery village on the main Swansea–Carmarthen road. It derives its interest less from its appearance than from the legend about its origin. Here stood a magic well, which never ran dry as long as a "llech" (stone slab) was replaced over it after the water was drawn. One of Arthur's knights drank from the well, then fell asleep after failing to replace the slab. He awoke to find the waters pouring out and threatening to drown the countryside. He mounted his horse and rode furiously around the spreading waters. The waters stopped when they touched the hoof-marks. The same story is told about other small lakes in Celtic countries.

LLANDYSUL, *Cardiganshire*. Eastwards from Newcastle Emlyn the road touches the river-bank at Henllan, where the single-span bridge stands over teeming rapids of water, one of the most attractive views in this part of Wales. On the Teifi bank, the church of Llandysul stands like a sentinel watching the flow of water from behind the wall of its churchyard as if it stood over a castle moat. It has a battlemented tower of the kind that was needed in days when war could come at any moment from any direction. It is an ancient structure showing its growth from a simple squared chamber into cruciform chancels and side chapels. The interior is a grey and solemn walling of slab-stone, impressive in its solidity, with strong pillars and pointed arches. It is Norman, though late in style, and can look back to the sub-Roman period, for some forgotten great lady of that day is commemorated on a stone inscribed in Latin "Velvor, daughter of Broho".

Llandysul is a market town, quiet and with a great reputation for fishing in the Teifi water. Still remote, it was until recently famous for keeping many old Welsh customs. Bradley, in his classic *Highways and Byways in South Wales*,

Near Llandysul: the River Teifi

G. Douglas Bolton

records how the country wedding ceremony of the bidding, the invitation to all the neighbourhood, was conducted there with the congregation of gambos and gigs from all the farmsteads and the colourful smocks and steeple-hats of the valley community. Parry-Jones, in his *Welsh Country Upbringing*, tells the same tale. Another custom that Bradley noted was the annual challenge to combat between Llandysul and its neighbour Llanwenog up the river, in a game of football with the ball set for play on top of a ridge 3 m. from each village, the teams made up of the entire inhabitants of each place, and the goals the porchways of the church at Llanwenog and the church at Llandysul. There was a similar contest within Llanwenog itself, parish against parish – a survival of religious traditions that go far further back than Christianity, of the idea of a dual society that must honour with contests of this sort the balance of Creation between day and night, life and death, good and evil. Belief in the Other People who would haunt the house and do its work for the simple reward of a saucer of milk lingered around Llandysul later than in other parts of Wales. And between Llandysul and Pentre-cwrt stands a great mound. We need not ask whether it was put there by Iron Age Celt, Roman, Dane, or Norman. Everyone knows that the Devil himself had decided against Pentre-cwrt's too virtuous people, and took a gigantic spadeful of earth on his shoulder to fill the Teifi and so drown them. But, on his way to do the deed, he met a cobbler from Llandysul who was carrying a sackful of worn shoes to mend. The cobbler, being told of the Devil's purpose, pointed out that it was a very long way to Pentre-cwrt; he himself had worn out all those shoes in getting there. So the Devil cast down his load of earth and left it in disgust. And, if you doubt the tale, the mound is there to see for yourself.

But Llandysul sounds also a more modern note. It is the home of that Caradoc Evans who in the 1920s wrote with passionate indignation about his own Welsh people, and made a bitter attack not only on the superstition shown in such folk-tales, but on the kind that corrupted the chapels. His novels *Capel Sion* and *My People* are drawn from the life of the district in which he was born. Judgment of his novels is one thing; judgment of the people themselves must be made by finding this remote spot and considering the tower of the church against an evening sky.

About 3 m. N., on the direct road between Newcastle Emlyn and Lampeter, is Rhydowen, with its pleasant chapel and attendant stables over the way, a typical Welsh country chapel of the early 19th cent. At Llwynrhydowen, Gwilym Marles (William Thomas, 1834–79), a celebrated and controversial Welsh Unitarian minister, was evicted from his chapel through a bitter dispute with the local landowners. He was an ancestor of Dylan Thomas, who derived his middle name of Marlais from an Anglicized version of Marles.

The Teifi makes a great bend among the low hills eastwards of Llandysul. Some 3 m. upstream is Llanfihangel-ar-arth. The name is a corruption

of Llanfihangel Ioreth. The church looks out over
the Teifi valley. It is divided by a four-arched
arcade, but, as usual in these parts, has been
treated to a 19th-cent. restoration making a clean
sweep of the older features. A fine yew, with a
stone seat encircling the trunk, graces the
churchyard.

Llanfihangel parish includes Pencader, 2 m.
due S. in the valley of the Tyweli stream. The
railway from Carmarthen used the valley to cross
the high country between the Teifi and Towy
valleys, and Pencader grew with the railway. The
line is now closed, but Pencader still continues,
with its red-brick houses and its Congregational
chapel glorious in apricot and cream with gold
lettering. Although the buildings of Pencader are
modern, it has a place in Welsh history. Gruffydd
ap Llywelyn, ruler of Gwynedd, here defeated
Hywel ap Edwin in 1041 and carried off Hywel's
beautiful wife. The village also contains a memorial – unveiled by Dr William Lloyd George,
brother of Earl Lloyd George – to the celebrated
Old Man of Pencader (*see* p. 24), who prophesied that in Wales the speaking of Welsh
would never die out. Welsh is still firmly spoken
at Pencader.

LLANEGRYN, *Merioneth*, lies SW. of
Dolgellau towards the sea along the run of the
Dysynni river. It is most noteworthy for the
church, and its remarkable cruck roof of timber,
its rood-loft of the most dexterous carving, and
its font. In the centre of the village is a monument
to Hugh Owen, a minister ejected in 1662 on
points of religious principle. The font is in the
Norman style that lasted to the 12th cent., and
its rood-loft is said to have been brought from

Cymer Abbey near Dolgellau. From the mansion of the Wynnes of Peniarth, whose monuments stand in the church, a priceless collection
of ancient MSS. was transferred to the National
Library of Wales at Aberystwyth.

LLANEILIAN, *Anglesey*. This is one of the
most interesting of the Anglesey churches, since
it summarizes the whole history of religious
development in its area. As it stands, it is an
excellent example of the Perpendicular style that
began to be introduced into Church architecture
just before and after the Reformation. But this
building, of about 1500, is set on the site of a
church of the 12th cent., which now exists only
as a foundation for its successor. A further
feature is that Llaneilian has a detached chapel
at the SE. end of the nave. The chapel has a
different line of orientation from the principal
building; and this is significant. Setting the
cardinal points of the compass was looked on as
perhaps the chief work of the Deity; and much
religious dispute turned on the correct interpretation of them. The chapel stands on the site of
the original foundation, which seems to have
belonged to the first establishment of Christian
belief in the 5th and 6th cents. It was the church
of the 12th cent. that replaced both the original
structure and the original form of Christian
interpretation it represented by finding a new site
a little way off. Although that original structure
was destroyed, the ground on which it was built
was still apparently recognized as hallowed; and
the present chapel records its history.

Llaneilian is remarkable, among other things,
for its battlemented parapets, and for its retention,
after so many changes, of the simple rectangular

Llaneilian church

G. Douglas Bolton

plan derived from the earliest oratories of the missionary saints. Its interior is a masterpiece of craftsmanship in oak.

LLANELLI, *Carmarthenshire.* The name comes from that of St Elliw, a disciple of St Cadoc. The two *ll*s in Llanelli are a little hard to pronounce, but practice makes it easier, as long as the abomination of "Lan-elthy" is avoided.

This is the largest town in Carmarthenshire, with a population of just on 30,000. It stands on the estuary of the River Loughor, and grew with industry in the 19th cent. As a result, it has few buildings, or even associations, with a more distant past. But its long rows of artisan houses are of interest to specialists in the early history of town-planning. Their arcaded fronts may look a little seedy in places today, but they were ahead of their period when first built. Llanelli has taken the imprint of its industries, and at one time it was the heart of the tinplate world. The port, now closed, was concerned with coal. Both coal and tinplate have lost their old glory. The newer methods of producing tinplate in a long strip destroyed the old craft of individual plates on which Llanelli flourished in the past. The town, however, has obtained a share in the new development when a department of the Steel Company of Wales plant (now nationalized) was established at Trostre, between Llanelli and Loughor. Here the impressive, light yellow workshops stretch for nearly ½ m. With the change in industry, Llanelli has turned to other activities. But one thing has not changed. Llanelli is a town of strong local patriotism – a Welsh and heartwarming place, with an inner vitality that survives all industrial vicissitudes.

There was, apparently, a Norman castle here, but all trace of it has been lost. The early township had borough status; the present charter of incorporation was granted in 1913. The real growth of Llanelli began in the early 19th cent., when Alexander Raby settled in the district still known as the Furnace. He set up ironworks and later developed interests in copper-smelting and coal-mining. He built the first modern dock. The tinplate industry began with the building of the Dafen works in 1847. The last of the smaller mills closed after the Second World War with the building of Trostre.

The parish church stands in Bridge Street. The body of the church has been practically rebuilt, but the tower is old. There are some interesting mural monuments to old Llanelli families, including the Vaughans and the Stepneys. Two of the Stepneys commemorated won military fame. Sir John Stepney served under Wellington at Salamanca and Quatre-Bras. His son was killed leading the Coldstream Guards in the Battle of Inkerman in 1864. Llanelli has also commemorated the Stepneys with streets named after Vittoria, Salamanca, Inkerman, and Coldstream. The Stepneys first settled in Wales in 1552. Their town house still stands near the church, and has a fine Georgian façade with a row of vases on the balustrade.

The Town Hall, in the centre of the town, is neo-Jacobean, surrounded by gardens and flowerbeds. There are several attractive chapel fronts near at hand. Tabernacle, built in 1873, has strong Corinthian columns and a well-designed pediment. The Baptist chapel, also near the Town Hall, is perhaps more modest but still pleasing. In the streets behind stands the bold, red, angular Roman Catholic Church of Our Lady Queen of Peace, built in 1938, with a statue of the Madonna in painted Carrara marble and tall lancet windows. Opposite this church is the commendably modern police station. Welshmen will be interested in Capel Alis, towards the docks, with its complicated front and its memories of David Rees, preacher, editor, and eloquent radical.

Llanelli has been lucky in its parks. Parc Howard was presented to the town by its first Mayor, Sir Stafford Howard. The house in the park is now a reading room, museum, and picture gallery. The museum has exhibits from the history of the tinplate industry, and the gallery shows examples from the work of the South Wales pottery, which was active in Llanelli from 1840 to 1925. The famous "seaweed" designs are, however, better represented in the collections at Swansea and Cardiff. The pictures include paintings by J. D. Innes and his sister. Innes, a friend of Augustus John, is Llanelli's best-known artist; he died early in 1914, before he could fulfil his promise. He left memorable evocations of the landscape of North Wales, especially of the Arennig mountains.

The literary associations of Llanelli are also interesting. The luckless Richard Savage came here in 1740 and addressed poems to a charming young Llanelli widow, Mrs Bridget Jones. George Meredith often came to stay with his son in New Street. But perhaps the most famous verses ever associated with the town should not be classified as literature at all. Rather are they a rousing battle-cry, sung now by every rugby crowd in Wales and beyond, but originally associated with the Llanelli club. "Sospan Fach" (Little Saucepan) is a piece of nonsense verse about a saucepan that boils over and the mishaps that follow to the family. Exhaustive and learned researches have been undertaken to settle the various claims to authorship. The song may be based on a poem by the Victorian bard Mynyddog, revised and added to by a Swansea Eisteddfodwr, Talog Williams, and sung to a tune invented at Llandrindod Wells in 1895 by a Bangor student. Scholarship cannot convey the spirit in which "Sospan Fach" is sung by a true son of Llanelli. It can best be appreciated on the stands at Stradey Park when Llanelli are playing old rivals like Swansea. Then rugby almost becomes Llanelli's second religion. Stradey Park lies in the western suburbs of the town. Llanelli Castle is 18th-cent., with a wing added in 1874.

The immediate suburbs of the town may not be inspiring, but the country to the N. rises to over 800 ft at Mynydd Sylen. There are fine views over the wide sands of the Burry Inlet to the Gower coast. About 2 m. NE. is Llangennech, an industrial village where the River Morlais joins the Loughor.

LLANERFYL, *Montgomeryshire.* About 16 m. W. of Welshpool, and not far from Llanfair-Caereinion, Llanerfyl is not only an excellent place for anglers in the streams running into the river with the double name Banwy neu Einion, but has a church of exceptional interest. It has been rebuilt in modern times. But it attracted the attention of Daniel Paterson, who published his *Direct and Principal Cross Roads* in 1811. Of Llanerfyl he wrote: "In the Church-yard, a Monument with a Roman inscription. On right of Llanerfil, Llwysin, a seat and extensive park of the Earl of Powis, formerly the seat of the Lords Herberts, ancestors of the Earls of Powis. Cann, or Cannon Office, now an Inn, was so called either from having been an Ecclesiastical or else a Military Office, from the fortifications around it. Here is a noted Tumulus or Barrow, supposed to have contained the body of a British Chief, and is surrounded with the remains of an ancient fortification. About three miles from Cann Office, the Roman Causeway, which formerly led from Caerwys in Flintshire to Caerleon in Monmouthshire, crosses the Roman road, which formerly led from Wroxeter in Shropshire to Caernarvon. . . . Beyond Cann Office the river Twrch must be forded twice and after heavy rains is sometimes too deep; the traveller will do well to make an enquiry at Cann Office Inn".

The Roman monument is today more accurately described as Roman-British, its phrasing and the child whom it commemorates being Christian: *Hic in tumulo iacit Rostece filia Paternini ani xiii in pace.* To judge from its grammar, the Latin was not done by a Roman scholar. But the father's name is Roman enough; the little girl's name seems to be British. The use of the Christian phrase *in pace*, "that she might rest in peace", is one of the earliest known examples of its kind.

A point that the careful Paterson did not have space to mention was that the graveyard is circular. This is characteristic of several churches in Powys, or Central Wales; the church at Ysbyty Cynfin not far from Devil's Bridge explains the form by lying within what is left of a once complete stone circle of the Megalithic period. The "llan", or church enclosure, was built inside the boundaries of such earlier structures in recognition of the fact that, as recording-places for the apparent motions of the sun and stars, they were temples to the intelligence of Creation. Churches in Wales are, in their direct descent from earlier faiths, perhaps unique in Britain and western Europe. But its tolerance brought the Celtic Church into discredit with such prelates as the 6th-cent. Gildas, and has obscured its teachings well into the 20th cent.

LLANFAIR-CAEREINION, *Montgomeryshire.* Half village and half town, Llanfair on the Banwy river is a most pleasing place. It has the indefinable quality produced by a long and tenacious history, but little in the last century or so has come to disturb it, although the light railway connecting it with Welshpool has been revived by a group of enthusiasts. It has a completely 18th-cent. air, yet is unique. In the 19th cent. it was a place of professional quietude, and it continues this into our own time. Anglers resort to it, to the stream and the bridge, for there is no place where the spirit of Izaak Walton is more contemplatively present than here; and the beauty of the vale of Meifod is best seen from Caereinion. The most ancient part of its name is worth dwelling on, for, although it keeps its memory of the fact secret, Llanfair-Caereinion was the site of a Roman fort, a smallish outpost set forward from the triangle

The sea-front, Llanfairfechan

G. Douglas Bolton

between Lavrobinta (now Forden), Mediomanum (now Caersws), and the rather larger outpost at Cae Noddfa. From Mediomanum a road can be traced heading for Caereinion, but its last passages have not been recovered. Neither can the Roman name for Caereinion be confirmed with any certainty. But it seems to have watched the major way from Viroconium (Wroxeter) to the important lead-yielding area of Caersws, and it probably had a westward reach to Pennal. That it should have continued in active life to the present day suggests that, as a guard-point on the land-bridge between Dovey and Severn, it was used in the sub-Roman period. If Einion is to be reckoned, as Sir John Rhys asserted, among those successors of Cunedda who stabilized the centre of Wales between A.D. 400 and 600, it may have been here, and on a Roman foundation, that he built a useful fortalice eastwards from the valley Cwm Einon that lies off the Dovey estuary on the Roman road going from Taliesin to Machynlleth.

LLANFAIRFECHAN, Caernarfonshire. Little St Mary's suggests by its name that its foundation was either late or overtaken by the 13th-cent. conquest of Edward I. Nowadays it is a seaside resort with a character dominated by the great stretch of firm sands over which at low tide you can cross dry-foot almost to Anglesey. The bathing is excellent; it is the last place of its kind along this coast, and is for the more selective visitor. Modern housing development has made attractive advances on the hill-sides above it.

Abergwyngregin, or simply Aber, has relatively greater historical claims, mainly as a place of passage across the Lavan Sands. The sides of the valley leading from Llanfairfechan to Aber are held in by Moel Wnion (1,902 ft) and Ffridd Ddu (Black Way, 1,187); but at its head tower Foel Fras (3,091) and Yr Aryg (2,875). It is one of the best places for the walker to find his way over Foel Grach (3,195) to the heights of the Carnedds, Ddafydd and Llywelyn, and the mysterious and haunted Llyn Ogwen.

LLANFAIR-YN-NEUBWLL, Anglesey. On the NW. shore of Anglesey, the church represents in a still detectable way the first form of the missionary oratories built to mark the establishment of Christianity about the Irish Sea. These were plain little chapels, rectangular in plan, single-roomed at first but later developing a double structure, a screen dividing the congregation from the priest when, at the altar in the inner sanctuary, he offered the Holy Sacrifice. There was neither aisle nor chancel; no buttresses, no porch, no windows on the N. or W. side, and no tower in which to sound the bell. Indeed, such bells as were used seem to have been rung by hand; the Venerable Bede mentions such a practice.

Here at Llanfair-yn-neubwll, the ground-plan remains what it was at first; but the small gable to hold the bell has been added to this church in a way very characteristic and noticeable in many of the older church buildings of Anglesey and Caernarfonshire. Windows have been added in the N. wall. But no porchway was ever set over the entrance door.

The font, probably of the 12th cent., has a simple decoration round its bowl of saltire (Andrew cross) design. A similar motif is found on the font at Llangaffo. This form of cross characterizes what is known as Celtic Christianity.

LLANFECHELL, Anglesey. This small place in the N. of Anglesey has the distinction of being, with the exception of its near neighbour, Llanrhyddlad, the only spot in the island with good lake fishing. The small, weedy sheet of water called Geirian used to be a resort of salmon, who sought it out from the sea close at hand; but, in their own interests, they have been discouraged from lying in such a place, and the lake is now mainly for trout. But they have excellent cover in the weeds, and wading out is hindered by screestones under the water. Geirian is a supreme test for skill and determination. The legend of this lake is unusual. Cemlyn Bay, along the coast, was once a haunt of smugglers and pirates, to whom the caves gave shelter. So, apparently, did an ancient and deserted monastery upon the cliffs. Men came to Cemlyn Bay in the 16th cent., perhaps Spaniards from the Armada, and found refuge in the monastery, about 1 m. from the coast and in a place called Geirian. After some years, they decided to move another 3 m. inland, and they settled at the lake, building a house called Plas Mynydd. The present ruins with this name are of a building set up about 1650 on the site of the strangers' house. They had treasure in a cave at Cemlyn Bay, which they could reach, as they found, very easily from the Monastery of Geirian by way of a subterranean passage. The new house they built by the lake, and the lake itself they called Geirian too. No one knows what happened to these men. But about 1830 three others came to find the treasure: a Spaniard, a Negro, and a Catholic priest. They entered the cave at Cemlyn, for it seems they had accurate information. They even set to work upon the wall that hid the riches they were seeking. But they were never seen again. The rumour is that the wall collapsed and buried them.

Llanfechell itself has one of the original churches of Anglesey. The square, austere foundation can still be noted; but a chancel has been added, showing how the congregation, after some hundreds of years following the 5th or 6th cents. in which the church was built, had increased and the faith itself broadened. It has been further enlarged by work in the 16th cent.

About 450 yds to the N. of the church is evidence of a still earlier system of belief. A standing stone, isolated in this position, has companions in a field a little further away. Llanfairynghornwy, another church very close to Llanfechell, has a similar grouping. In both cases the primitive Christian church was erected on the site of the megaliths set up to observe the working of sun and star.

W. of Cemlyn Bay, above Carmel Head, the group of rocky islets called the Skerries carries a lighthouse, a rendezvous for sea-birds and a warning to seafarers.

LLANFYLLIN, *Montgomeryshire.* Not many modern travellers have found reason to dwell on this small town; only the traditional sweetness of its church-bells has been remarked by them. The industrious Christopher Saxton, however, making his notes for the mapping of the counties of Britain to be "performed" and published in 1610, writes of it as Lan Vethlin, or Vethlius' Church, a "little mercate town", and gives it an imperial ancestry. "That Mediolanum, a towne of the Ordovices, which both Antonine the Emperor and Ptolomee spoke, stood in this shire [of Montgomery] I am in a manner perswaded upon probabilitie. The footings whereof I have sought after with all diligence but little or nothing have I found of it; for Time consumeth the very carcasses even of cities. Yet if we may ground any conjecture on the situation, seeing the townes which Antonine placeth on either side be so well knowen, to wit, Bonium now Bangor by Dee on the one side, and Rutunium now Rowton Castle on the other side . . . the lines of position, if I may so term them . . . do cut one another betweene Matrafall and Lan Vethlin and show demonstratively the site of our Mediolanum".

Lan Vethlin, he argues, comes very close in name to Mediolanum. "For of Methlin, by propriety of the British tongue, is made Vethlin, like as of Caer Marden is come Caer Verden and of Ar-mon, Arvon". This is a reference to the Welsh practice of "mutation" (*see* p. 54), by which, according to strict rules, certain consonants are reduced to others so that the tongue can run more easily over the succession of words. And Methlin, which he therefore suggests was the true form of Vethlin, did not, to his way of thinking, "more jarre and disagree in sound from Mediolanum" than the parallel examples of Milano in Italy or Le Million in France, which no one ever doubted were originally known as Mediolanum. He goes on to state that the meaning of the Latin name Mediolanum had been found to be "in the mids betweene Lanas or little rivers", and his Lan Vethlin was indeed sited upon a plain between two riverets.

Something in this argument may belong to the form of archaeological deduction, by no means dead today, that Shakespeare attributed to his Fluellen: "There is a river in Macedonia, and there is a river in Monmouth". We now know that Medio*l*anum was in Cheshire. What Saxton was looking for was a Medio*m*anum. But Saxton lends some strength to his supposition by pointing out that "Matrafall" (Mathrafal), the seat of the early Princes of Powys, was close at hand and that Machynlleth itself was "haply" that which the Romans called Maglona, where, he says, under the General of Britain in the time of the Emperor Theodosius the Younger the captain of the regiment of the Solenses lay in garrison to keep under the mountaineers. Nothing has yet been found to give Saxton any support; but his deductions are worth considering, as they concern one of the mysteries perplexing modern research. The Antonine Itinerary, to which he refers, is a detailed document, published in the later years of the Empire and setting out the road-system of Roman Britain and the towns, supply depots, and military stations that they serviced. Between Chester and Wroxeter there is considerable doubt about the precise siting of many of the positions set out in the list, although distances in Roman miles are carefully allocated to the routes between one place and the next. Saxton may in time be proved right, even if for the wrong reasoning.

In later centuries, Llanfyllin had a reputation for its ale and ale-drinking. "Old ale fills Llanfyllin with young widows" was a phrase often quoted. The town is a centre from which the Pistyll Rhaeadr – one of the great waterfalls of Wales, once counted as one of its Seven Wonders – and Lake Vyrnwy can be reached.

LLANGADOG, *Carmarthenshire.* The Dyffryn Tywi (Vale of Towy) lies where the Towy river, striking due S. from its spring in the high Ellennith, turns away from the feet of the Black Mountain and the Fforest Fawr, and finds a channel to the SW. It is a fertile lowland, a pleasant riverine peninsula cut into the high moorland that is much less travelled today than it was by the Romans and those who went before them. The vale begins with Llanfair-ar-y-bryn (St Mary's Church on the hill), and holds first Llandovery and then Llandeilo before it works its way to Carmarthen. And between Llandovery and Llandeilo is Llangadog. Across the river to the N. the road from Llanwrda leads to the parallel valley of the Teifi, to the towns of Lampeter and Tregaron – a road that, as far as Dolaucothy, follows the causeway laid by the Romans to connect over the bare hills one civilized clearing and the next, between their station at Llandovery and their other one at Llanddewibrefi, and so to Aberystwyth. It can still be taken, and it still carries the name of Sarn Helen, the Causeway of the Helen who was a British lady of rank and became the mother of the first Christian Emperor of Rome, Constantine the Great, who was born at York, launched from Britain his successful campaign to master the world, and played his part in founding the medieval legend of Arthur. Whatever the real origin of the name the road carries, Helen and her memory are now inextricably bound to it.

Llangadog, also spelt Llangadock, keeps alive another memory, that of the Cadoc who was a saint in the Age of Saints following the ebb of Roman power. History has itself ebbed from the town. Once it was important, and it is still at least as large as Llandovery. It had a castle to guard the strategy of control from the S. and over the roads to the valley of the Teifi, but all trace of it has vanished. It is not known whether the Romans had an intermediate station there; the Normans do not seem to have chosen it as a site for one of their strongholds. The castle was

Welsh-built, and chiefly concerned with inter-necine Welsh feuds until Edward I, warring with the last Llywelyn, seized the town, burnt out the church, slew the priest, and tethered horses at the altar. It was an act that recognized not only the strength of the national feeling in Wales but the distinctive tradition of religious belief that sustained it.

The most curious incident in the story of Llangadog, however, occurred in the 1770s. Standing apart from the world under the shadow of bleak highlands, a place like Llangadog may well let the less rational instincts of mankind gain the upper hand. At Glanareth, not far from the town, lived William Powell, the son of a well-to-do family. At Llandovery lived a merchant, William Williams. The wife of Powell, it seems, became the mistress of Williams; but this was not the beginning of the relationship between the two men. For Williams had the idea that he was the illegitimate son of Powell's father, an elder off-spring, by custom entitled to take the lands and possessions of Powell. Possibly the wife, in Williams's eyes, was no more than a weapon to use against his younger half-brother. Williams took his time. The campaign against Powell, a matter of whispers and calumny, was long and surreptitious. Apparently the whole community was aware of this conspiracy in ale-houses and the like. There was no active feeling against Powell, but a fear of Williams's vindictiveness. On a snowy winter's night, Williams led a band of his cronies, all drunk, to the house of Glanareth, where Powell was stabbed to death in his own living-room. Only one man, his steward, made even a feeble attempt to save him, although the house was filled with Powell's kinsmen, friends, and servants. Some of the murderers were caught and hanged. But Williams escaped over the moors and was never brought to justice. Powell was buried in the chancel of Llangadog church. The site of his house, Glanareth, is in dispute. It was left to fall into ruin and oblivion. But the gang of men who gathered at Cilycwm to murder him set out on their mission over the hills towards Llanwrda, and Glanareth apparently stood some-where near Llangadog's sister church there. The two saintly places look across the river at one another in mournful recollection of a tragedy that stirred all Wales in its day.

Some 3 m. S. of the town is the Garn Goch (Red Cairn), the site of one of the most con-siderable prehistoric encampments in Wales. It is over 2,000 ft long and about 500 ft wide; its stone ramparts are in places still 20 ft high. The richness of the Vale of Towy made it worth holding against all comers.

LLANGAMARCH WELLS, Breconshire,
lies almost exactly half way between Llanwrtyd Wells and Builth Wells, where the Cledan river joins the Irfon. The Mynydd Epynt rises above its well-wooded and hidden valley, for it stands on what is relatively a by-road. The spring is unique, as it has barium chloride in it, not often found anywhere, and reckoned to be a sovereign remedy for heart diseases. The hotel has in its grounds buildings that derive from earlier days of greater fashion and populousness; but it now relies on those who come to it for seclusion and peace. The lake in the grounds gives good sport to fishermen, and the scatter of cot-tages among the hedge-lined lanes add a touch of human nature at its best to the fields of cattle and crops. The place has its name from the Camarch stream, which runs into the Irfon; and, though its founder-saint seems to be forgotten, it is famous for one of the later kind, John Penry, who lived for no more than the years 1563–93, yet managed to stir up trouble for himself by his passionate denial of the supremacy of state over religion, and who may have been responsible for some at least of the famous Martin Mar-Prelate tracts in that cause. He was an equally passionate lover of his native country, and combined the two enthusiasms in pleas for a special missionary effort among the Welsh people. He loved his three little daughters, too, and his last letters to them contains some of the most moving passages in English literature. His works, however, are housed in the United States.

Llangamarch churchyard has the grave of that Theophilus Evans, Vicar of the church, who not only discovered the rival qualities of Llanwrtyd waters but contrived to be the grandfather of Theophilus Jones, historian of Brecon and its shire, who stands among Welsh immortals.

LLANGATHEN, Carmarthenshire. A Roman road runs to Carmarthen from Llandeilo, and rather to the W. of this place is the village of Llangathen. It is reached from Llandeilo by crossing the bridge over the Towy river. Its noteworthy 13th-cent. church has a tower much influenced by Edwardian models of fortification. It looks away from Llangathen towards a hill of 234 ft, with ruins of an earlier and more purpose-ful castle built by the Lord Rhys of the South about the same time as he possessed the magni-ficent fortification of Carreg Cennen, 5 m. S. of Llandeilo. The church has a considerable monu-ment to Bishop Rudd of the early 17th cent. But perhaps even more remarkable is another monu-ment at Llangathen: the house of Aber Glasney, where John Dyer was born and made his home. He lived from 1699 to 1758, and, though well known, he has never had the fame that he deserves. His life was dominated by the country-side of his birth and the cultural traditions of Wales that he perpetuated. He first came upon the English public with the poem *Grongar Hill*:

> Ever charming, ever new,
> When will the landscape tire the view!
> The fountain's fall, the river's flow,
> The woody valleys, warm and low,
> The windy summit, wild and high,
> Roughly rushing on the sky;
> The pleasant seat, the ruined tower,
> The naked rock, the shady bower,
> The town and village, dome and farm,
> Each give to each a double charm
> As pearls upon a Ethiop's arm.

This was done in 1726, after a version, put out a year before, had displeased him. In the fashionable couplets of the time, it is a literal description of the Grongar Hill (410 ft) that rises to the W. of the village. It is wholly different in style and approach from the artificial writing of the classical schools of writing then dominant. But he was not content either with staying in his native place or with practising only poetry. True to the customs of the harp-men of Wales who at that time were prevalent on the roads and hill-tracks, he went off through Wales and the Marches, earning his bread not merely by verse but as an itinerant painter. He went as far afield as Italy, and when in 1740 he returned to Britain he published his *Ruins Of Rome*. The genuine appreciation of nature, directly seen, broke through the conventions of his day and made him a precursor of Wordsworth. The later poet was deeply struck above all by Dyer's poem *The Fleece*, produced in 1757, which was an epic statement of the work of the shepherds about the hills of Wales, catching their intimacy with man's brother-beasts in a way no other Augustan poet could have achieved.

He at last took orders, and carried himself and his writings to Leicestershire and Lincolnshire. *The Fleece* was his last work; but the sincerity and charm of his writing makes him still one of the Anglo-Welsh poets most worth reading. Carmarthenshire is in every one of his lines.

From Grongar Hill – on the crest of which, perhaps unknown to Dyer, stood a Roman legionary marching camp – it is only 1 m. to another place he knew: Dryslwyn. This tiny hamlet looks upwards at the castle, which set its deepest mark on history only after the conquest by Edward I. Its earliest record, wholly Welsh, is of a castle commanding the Towy from its hill and built to serve the purposes of the Princes of the South, which were mainly to confirm their power over their rival Welsh lords. In the 13th cent., it was held by Rhys son of Maredudd, and this Lord Rhys extended the tradition of Welsh feuding into a determined effort to overthrow at last the Princedom of the North. He allied himself with Edward against Llywelyn the Last. What part he played in the tragedy at Cilmery is doubtful; what ambition he hoped to serve by his allegiance to Edward can only be guessed – perhaps he thought he could play a role of allied but independent sovereign such as had been the good fortune of the Lord Rhys of the days of Henry II. But he found himself put under the jurisdiction of Edward's Justiciar, Robert of Tibetot, and everything taken from him but this one castle of Dryslwyn. He refused such an indignity, raised his men, and in 1287 rallied them to the cause of Welsh independence he had three years before betrayed. He captured both Dynevor and Llandovery, avoided an English force, and besieged Emlyn. Driven from this, he escaped to Ireland, returned in 1290, and headed a great army of revolt. But his Welsh peasants were untrained, and he was taken, carried to the King at York, dragged at the tail of a horse, and

beheaded. Dryslwyn Castle made his effort possible. It was too strong to be taken by the Earl of Cornwall who beset it, and, when one of its towers was mined, it fell expertly on Lord Stafford and his staff, putting them for ever out of action. It stands now, rather like Castell-y-Bere over the Mawddach valley, a melancholy monument to the loss Wales suffered through its internal factions.

Overbearing it on the other side of the river is another monument, set up 150 years ago to Admiral Lord Nelson, not so much for his remote Welsh connection through Greville and Lady Hamilton, and the sale of favours that founded Milford Haven, as for the victory that gave Britain a century of undisputed command over the sea.

LLANGEFNI, *Anglesey*, is a modern town of around 2,000 inhabitants. It is set at the centre of the island of Mon (Anglesey), and it has at least this much resemblance to Rome, that all roads lead to it. The valley of Cefni where it stands is one of the most fertile in Anglesey, and it is the market capital, as well as the seat of the County Council. Apart from this, it is in a position to command one of the most unusual views of Snowdon. In spite of the richness and remoteness of its setting, it does not seem to have invited early settlement; most Anglesey villages have standing stones, burial chambers, and the like dating from the first organized exploration of the Irish Sea about 2000 B.C., and the ancient churches of the island are world famous for the still living examples of the first Christian missionary effort in the 5th and 6th cents. But all these monuments appear to congregate about the sea-coast; for both the Bronze Age seamen and the holy men of Christ preferred to settle near the safety of the sea. Llangefni had one of the old foundations as its church, but of this only the site can now be traced within the churchyard of the present building, which dates from 1824. But at Tregarnedd, now a farmhouse, is a castle mound that remains where Ednyfed Fychan, counsellor to Llywelyn the Great at the opening of the 13th cent. and forebear of Owen Tudor, had his residence.

From Llangefni the ancient monuments of the island can be most adequately explored – the Tudor recollections at Penmynydd, the relics of the first Welsh Princes at Aberffraw, and the castle of their Edwardian supplanter at Beaumaris, together with the Newborough founded at the same time to mark the Conquest. The ways about the island, however, should not be allowed to leave aside the monument to the Morris brothers, not far from Moelfre Bay. They were devoted 18th-cent. exponents of the Welsh heritage in bardic lore – in the great poetry that culminated through the Middle Ages in the work of Dafydd ap Gwilym – and equally sturdy seekers-out of any Welshman of literary promise in their own day. Llangefni is almost equidistant between the unique burial chambers at Llanfair P.G., Llangaffo, Bodorgan, Llanfaelog, Bode-

dern on the one side and Din Lligwy on the other.
But those who find interest in the evidence of
those companions of Colomba, Patrick, and
David who preached about the wide waters when
the Empire of Rome was dissolving, will find it
the best base from which to discover the earliest,
simple cells of rectangular plan at Llangwyfan,
Llanfair-yn-neubwll, Llanfair-yn-y-cwmwd (St
Mary's in the Commote), Llangwyllog, Llechylched, Rhoscolyn and Rhosbeirio, Gwredog,
Cerrigceinwen, Coedana, Tregaean, and many
others, or to follow the later developments at
Llanfair Mathafarn Eithaf, Llanerchymedd,
Llangristiolus, Llaneilian, Tal-y-llyn, and
Gwalchmai. There is in fact no church in the
island, however remote (or however much over-
built, as at Llanfair P.G.), that does not rest
solidly on the foundations of faith made firm
when the whole known world was in doubt.

LLANGEINWEN, *Anglesey,* is an interesting
example of early Church architecture, where the
first single-chamber plan was extended, probably
in the late 15th cent., to meet the needs of what
was then a new devotional attitude to Mary,
mother of Christ. Lady Chapels were added,
some to the N., as here, some to the S.;
occasionally a chapel was added in both
directions, giving a cross form to the structure.
The present interior was treated, just before the
Second World War, to a restoration that it
badly needed. This was done under the direction
of Harold Hughes of Bangor, an expert who wrote
extensively on these ancient churches; and the
result is admirable.

It is a tiny interior, with tall oaken pews, but it
touches the feelings more intimately than many
other and greater structures. The font has a
design datable to the 12th cent., but showing in
its patterned relief-carving the influence of classical Greece.

LLANGEITHO, *Cardiganshire,* lies 7 m. NE.
of Lampeter at the upper end of the Aeron valley.
The village is now in a centre of pastoral peace, but
in the late 18th cent. great crowds used to
assemble here, many camping out for days. They
were drawn to Llangeitho by the overwhelmingly
powerful preaching of Daniel Rowland (1713–90).
Rowland was one of the great names associated
with the rise of the Methodist movement in
Wales. His style of preaching with its vivid evoca-
tion of the terrors of Hell and the power of Divine
love had an immediate effect on his hearers.
He began as an orthodox Church of England
curate under his father, who was Rector of Llangeitho. Later he served under his own son, after
incurring the disapproval of the authorities. In
1763 he was ejected from the Church. His followers built a special chapel for him. The present
chapel at Llangeitho is not the original one. It
does, however, retain the outside back door to the
pulpit, through which Daniel Rowland used to
appear suddenly, high above his congregation.
A somewhat uninspired statue of him stands
beside the chapel.

The church, dedicated to St Ceitho, has been
restored and has lost its interest. There is some
good modern stained glass. The village is mainly
grouped round the green, which has at its centre
the war memorial and a fine tree, and lies next to a
traffic roundabout. It has twice won the award as
the best-kept village in Cardiganshire. About 1 m.
to the E. is the little church of Llanbadarn-
Odwyn, one of the churches dedicated to the cult
of St Padarn, with its centre at Llanbadarn-Fawr
just outside Aberystwyth. Padarn was a 6th-cent.
saint and a contemporary of St David, patron
saint of Wales.

LLANGOLLEN, *Denbighshire,* belongs to
the Wales of the Dee, not to the Wales of the
Severn; to the pleasant hills and valleys, not to
the moors and crags. But it has, on its own scale,
a mountainous feature of great interest, the
Eglwyseg Rocks. Placed to the NE. of the lakeland plateau that possesses the central parts of
Wales, and sundered by it from others of its
ancient provinces, Llangollen has had a distinctive history and a distinctive challenger in the
raiding earldom of Chester. This aspect of its
past can be summarized in the name of the
most predatory of the Lords Marcher who held
Chester: Hugh Lupus, the Wolf. There are
several outstanding monuments to history in the
Llangollen area, more than in the place itself.
Among them, rather unexpectedly, is Plas-yn-
Ial on the Corwen–Chester road, the seat of the
family from whom sprang the founder of Yale
University in the United States. Ial is the name of
the princely Welsh region in the N. that numbered
Llywelyns among its possessors. Oddly enough,
Harvard may also trace its origin to a family of
Cambro-Britons on the Cheshire border. In 1832
the idea of a North Welsh University was
imagined by the Rev. W. Jones, Baptist minister
at Holywell. Thirty years later the idea was
realized at Llangollen in an academy with six
students. After forty years of endeavour, the institution was removed to Bangor.

That Llangollen itself is a product of late
Roman-British times seems to be established by
its name. It is dedicated to the memory of Collen,
a saint of what is known as the Celtic Church, and
was in being before the Anglo-Saxon assault.
He is remembered in legend as the one who was
singled out by "fairies" to be tempted by beautiful clothing and song. Their apparel was red and
green; and he reproved them by pointing out
that such was the dress of condemned souls,
since one side burnt with the fires of Hell and
the other froze with the ice of outer darkness.
Like most legends, it is largely metaphorical;
Gildas, the outraged cleric who chronicled the
shortcomings of Britain in the 6th cent., condemned its rulers and indeed its Churchmen for
indulging in such wanton pleasures and in having
sophisticated ladies at the dining-table. And,
what is more, the sub-Roman society he attacked
took red and green as dominant colours for their
military symbols.

However, the present church, though old,

Plas Newydd, the home of the Ladies of Llangollen

Reece Winstone

belongs to a much later date, and its main feature is a carved roof that came from the nearby Abbey of Valle Crucis (Vale of the Cross). Llangollen stands on the Dee, and bridges it with a structure of four arches, for a long time included in the Seven Wonders of Wales. It is said to have been built in Henry I's reign, but in 1346 it was widened and extended by John Trevor, Bishop of St Asaph and Chancellor of Chester. It has now been further widened and enlarged by construction undertaken in 1873 with an eye to the needs of the railway. It was then that a more definite date could be added to its tale, for workmen found a stone in its arches with the figure 1131 and the initials W.S.

Flannel was once the chief industry of the town. Now it is more renowned as the site of the International Eisteddfodau to which countries all over the world send dance and song teams to compete. It is a curious commentary on Collen's puritanic zeal.

One cannot mention Llangollen without including the Ladies and their house. They were two unmarried women of Irish connection, Lady Eleanor Butler and the Hon. Sarah Ponsonby, who decided to elope together – the expression is apt, since they conducted the affair without telling their families. They settled first in the town of Denbigh in 1776. From there they removed to a cottage in Llangollen, which they enlarged into the present Plas Newydd (New Place). They dominated what was then a village, and summoned various men of distinction to their Place, demanding forms of tribute in the shape of curios, particularly pieces of oak, carved if possible. One visitor, William Wordsworth, went so far as to offer a sonnet as a gift, but unfortunately he referred to the Place as a low-roofed cottage, which debarred him from ever having another invitation. It is certainly a curious house, over-timbered rather than half-timbered, and there is nothing else quite like it anywhere, except perhaps the monstrously romantic dwelling Victor Hugo chose to elaborate in Guernsey during his exile.

Llangollen can be readily reached from either Wrexham or Oswestry, and, though the town has many points of interest (its beer was famous), the surrounding area is more attractive still.

To the N. of the Vale of Llangollen, coming in a curve round the point of Cefn y Fedw (Birch Ridge), are the Eglwyseg Rocks. Their name is said to mean rocks that fell within the domain of the Church. They are a stepped and broken formation of limestone of under 2,000 ft, but dominating the valley by sudden contrast. The impression of barren wilderness they give is increased by the name World's End given to their final bluff. The road beneath them passes a Tudor house, Plas yn Eglwyseg, replacing a medieval lodge to which, in the days of Henry I, was brought a lady of Wales who has earned the title of its Helen. About 1108, Rhys ap Tewdwr, who could claim to be the independent Prince of the Deheubarth, or South, of Wales, had a daughter whose fascination must have been irresistible. She attracted Henry I himself, who made her his ward; and from their mutual feeling sprang the distinguished family of FitzHenrys. Her name was Nest. In due course Henry had her married to his Constable at Pembroke, Gerald de Windsor; from this alliance sprang the family of FitzGeralds. They lived at Cenarth Castle in Pembrokeshire and, as it happened, were invited to some celebration by Cadwgan, Prince of Powys, who had extended his power over Ceredigion or Cardiganshire. His son Owain fell in love with the wife of Gerald, and at the first opportunity raided Pembrokeshire, burnt the Castle of Cenarth, and abducted Nest to his remote hunting-lodge near Llangollen. Gerald narrowly escaped death, and he swore revenge. The subsequent tale, almost as long as the Tale of Troy, involved for many years the confused politics of Wales and the marchlands. At one time Owain escaped to Ireland, threatened as much by his father and brothers as by any other enemy, for only on condition that his son never returned was Cadwgan allowed to keep Cardigan as part of his principality. But

Owain did return, and, by a stroke of poetic justice, he died in the Dyffryn Tywi at the hands of Gerald, the husband he had outraged, through a chance encounter when neither knew he had met the other. When Gerald died, Nest married Gruffydd ap Rhys, and founded yet another of the great families of Wales, Ireland, and the North of England.

The mysterious Hill of Bran (about 900 ft) watches the Vale of Llangollen under the S. escarpment of the Eglwyseg Rocks. It is held by a castle called Dinas Bran, whose architecture is not Norman or a Welsh imitation of Norman battlemented structure. Apparently the original Celtic system of fortification, depending on wooden palisades and earthy mounds and ditches, remained much the same into the early Middle Ages. But Castell Dinas Bran has a character of its own. Its 13th-cent. occupation by Gruffyd ap Madoc, who took the side of Henry III against the Welsh, noticeably affected its architecture. But the foundation of heaped rock seems to belong to the earliest days of the sub-Roman power of Powys. The name Bran strictly means Crow, although in the extended form of Cig-Fran it means Raven, and Bran sometimes takes that sense. Bran is also the name of a great figure in the *Mabinogion*, which reflects a romanticized 14th- or 15th-cent. version of much older memories from the dark "Arthurian" times. Much of the associated literature – in particular the Graal story of the 12th cent., on which Malory founded his romance of the Grail 250 years later – shows the adapted form taken by the Mithraic legionary faiths, which set their temples around the northern walls of Britain in Roman times. And the raven was the first of the Mithraic grades. Considering the ravens of Owain that haunt the dream-like record of Rhonabwy, soldier of Arthur, and the standard round which they manœuvred, the direct descent of this castle from the 5th and 6th cents. is clearly possible.

The impression is confirmed if you take the way by car or on foot, or by barge along the canal, to Valle Crucis Abbey. This is only 2 m. from Llangollen and – though without the sense of awe that, even in its ruins, still possesses Tintern – is the most interesting example of its kind in the North of Wales. Founded in 1189 by Madoc, son of Gruffydd (Griffith) of Maelor and Lord of Bromfield and Ial, it suffered under Henry VIII. In the style known as Early English, it preserves the nave with aisles, a choir, and two transepts, and a piscina or fish-pool. The monastic buildings themselves were for some time used as a farmhouse, but have now been cleared. The main door and the lancet window are particularly worth noting. Not far away, a most interesting stone monument stands lonely in a field. This is Eliseg's Pillar – a memorial not only of its own distant times but of reasonless destruction by man. It had already stood for 1,000 years when, in the middle of the 17th cent., and at the height of the Second Civil War between Parliament and King that vexed Wales in particular,

Puritan fury despoiled it as some sort of Popish idolatry. In 1779 it was re-erected by a Mr Lloyd of Trevor Hall. The inscription on it – a restoration due largely to him – now reads: "Concen, the son of Cateli; Cateli, the son of Brochmael; Brochmael, the son of Eliseg; Eliseg, the son of Cnoillaim. Concen, great-grandson, therefore, of Eliseg erected this stone to the memory of his great-grandfather, Eliseg".

The names recall the entries made by scribes in the Anglo-Saxon Chronicle. Eliseg was indeed a historical person; he was King of Powys in the days of the final Saxon assault on Britain that burnt down Pengwern at Shrewsbury, the capital of Powys, and by a victory at the Bangor hard by Chester, which stood at the northern strategic limit of Powys about the Dee, finally severed the British of Wales from the British of Strathclyde. Eliseg took part in this battle, and must have seen the massacre of many of its 2,500 monks as they stood under the banner of their church praying for the victory of their faith. The song they sang, as they were cut down to the last man, is said to be the one known as "Ymdaith y Mwnc" (The March of the Monks), the saddest and noblest of the traditional tunes of Wales.

There are a few other survivals from this period in British history confused by ideological disputes that led, among so many other things, to the Puritan demolition of the Pillar. Uotiporius, an even earlier British King of South Wales, had for his own memorial the massive stone now in Carmarthen Museum; but it is an inscription in Ogham, the non-alphabetic writing used around the Irish Sea between A.D. 350 and 550, that honours him. The Eliseg Pillar is a direct and unique transmission to our own day of that lost time in which the legend of Arthur was created.

Some further recollections of the past in the Vale of Llangollen may be had by visiting Llantysilio and its restored church, and by making the journey to the village of Glyndyfrdwy.

LLANGORSE, *Breconshire*. This is the name of a village and a lake – both lie southwards from Talgarth; and of a line of hills running almost due N. to S. into the Usk valley. The village has an ancient church, and so has each of the Tal-y-llyn (Lake Head) hamlets, Llanfihangel and Llangasty, at the side of the water. Strangely enough, as there is a Tal-y-llyn under the wall of Cader Idris in Merioneth, so there is a Gader Hill here above the two Tal-y-llyn villages and Llangorse. Again the churches have ancient stones inscribed in a way familiar to students of these remote places. Nearby is the Llandewi where Gerald de Barri had his home, and the site of Peytyngwyn to which Owain Glyndwr set the torch in revenge for the betrayal of him attempted by its owner, Sir David Gam. And, at a farm now known as Troed-y-Harn, is the place once called Tref Trahaiarn, from which the young Trahaiarn rode to meet De Braose, to be treacherously beheaded and to start the war of revenge that ended in disaster at Painscastle.

But Llangorse is famous above all for its lake,

called Syfaddan in Welsh, which was once swum by pike and perch and by eels so tremendous that they have inspired the description "cyhyd a llyswen Syfaddan" (long as a Syfaddan eel). It is a reeded, shallow stretch flocked over by fowl of many wild sorts that, as Gerald de Barri stated, acknowledged by their rising and crying only the true blood of the Kings of Wales. This, he recounts, was a salutation they refused to give to the Norman Marcher Lords who passed that way. It has a legend of a sunken city. In 1650 a special Parliamentary survey was given to its richness as a fishery; in 1695 this note was made: "In the greate poole called Llyn Savathan once stood a faire citie which was swallowed up in an earthquake and resigned her stone walls into this deep and broad water, being stored most richly with fish in such abundance as is incredible. And indeed the fishermen of this place have oftentimes taken up goodes of severall sortes from the very hart of the Poole but whether these might be goodes that were cast away in crossing the water is onknowne but we have never heard of any such mischance in our time".

Tales abounded of roofs and walls that were seen in certain lights below the water. The legend is an example of the genuine folk-memories that linger in this exaggerated form. About 1925 a "cafn unpren", a primitive canoe made out of a single tree-trunk, was recovered from the lake, dating to the period, several thousand years ago, when settlers built stakes out into the water and raised hutments upon them.

From Penyfan above Llangorse village is a beautiful view of the lake, 5 m. in circumference, and of the hills that stretch S. towards the steel and mining towns. On the top of Mynydd Troed are scattered the hut circles of earlier and vanished civilization.

LLANGUNNOR, *Carmarthenshire.* On the line of the Roman road between Llandeilo and Carmarthen, which the modern road follows, are two villages. One is Llangathen, near Llandeilo; the other is Llangunnor, close to Carmarthen.

As you near Llangunnor, you pass close to the farmhouse Ty-gwyn, where Richard Steele, the friend of Addison, co-author of *The Spectator*, poet, playwright, and Member of Parliament, spent much of the last three years of his life. He had the place through his second wife, the "Dear Prue" whom he called his constant monitress and whom he begged always to see that he acted with some kind of order and good sense. His life had been one of work and worry; the excellent judgment with which, in the House of Commons, he opposed the operations of the South Sea Bubble did not always serve him in his own business or even in running a theatre. There was tragedy for him in the small-pox that struck down his children and killed his son; but he had some peace for a while at Ty-gwyn, though towards the end he had to remove to a house in King Street, Carmarthen, which later

became an inn, the Ivy Bush. There he died in 1729. But two years previously, at Ty-gwyn, he had made his Will; and it was witnessed by John Dyer, the wandering poet whose home was at Llangathen. The Richard Steele of verve and adventure who had written so many letters from the Devil Tavern, Temple Bar, found his best happiness and his best friend in the valley of the Towy. There is a monument to Steele in Llangunnor church, as well as one to Lewis Morris, the author of the *Epic of Hades.*

Immediately opposite, across the Towy, is Abergwili and the palace of the Bishop of St David's.

Llangunnor and Abergwili share a curious descent from days more ancient than the 18th cent. Near Llangunnor was the Maridunum of the Romans, the original Carmarthen, though now a place of fields by the river a little to the E. of the modern town. Ty-gwyn stands between this site and the earthwork put up by those who lived in Maridunum before the Romans made it theirs. It is close to Pen-sarn, a hamlet that in its name preserves the memory of the Roman roadway that bore upon it. And Abergwili, where the Bishop of St David's removed his palace in the 16th cent., is overlooked by Brynmyrddin (Merlin's Hill), on which there is a standing stone to mark the routes followed before the legions marched that way. Beside it, a Welshman can remember that in 1020 the first Llywelyn, son of Seisyllt, won a battle at Abergwili that confirmed his position as Prince in South and North, a generation before Harald the last Saxon drove westward into Wales.

LLANGURIG, *Montgomeryshire.* From Llanidloes you may go towards Machynlleth or Aberystwyth over some of the remotest hills under the sky. If the road to Staylittle and Dylife is taken, you reach a height of just under 1,700 ft and pass, deep in the moors of the Ellennith, the Van mines that were worked for lead. If the alternative route is taken, you follow a lift of land no more than 900 ft up and come to Llangurig; but there too you have the lead-mines of Van close at hand. Llangurig belongs to the Wye where it first falls from Plynlimon Fawr into narrower and deeper folds of earth. It is an old place that has a church much restored but still with signs of medieval interest.

The fortune of the town, however, largely turned upon the development of the Van mines in the 18th-cent. phase of their history. Roman workings for lead have only recently been rediscovered about Dylife; in the 18th cent. the industry had a new impetus mainly due to the enthusiasm of Lewis Morris, the Polymath, or master of all arts and sciences, as he was proud to call himself. The long history of lead- and silvermining in this area, and the peak of effort it reached in the 19th cent., have caused the Van mines to be taken over by the Institute of Industrial Archaeology, and the shafts, levels, and working structures are to be preserved and made available to the public. The remains are very

Plate 12 The Pembrokeshire coast west of St Govan's Head   Pix Photos

extensive, and are by no means confined to the area immediately S. of Llangurig; they extend far across the peatland hanging over Glasbwll and Hengwm and Bwlch Gwyn, places where in the mid-19th cent. the Welsh Potosi Company prospected hopefully for silver, and Lewis Morris in the 18th advised his employers generally about the best method of sinking exploratory shafts. His letters are particularly concerned with the area about Bwlch Gwyn, in the parish of Llanbadarn-Fawr, as he puts it – the wild and empty cleft 1 m. broad, that is now mainly a resort for buzzards in the Plynlimon escarpment to the N. His recommendations are practical and detailed. He is also concerned about the difficulty of maintaining good relations with the workers, or "navigators", who were inclined to riot alarmingly over their wage-rates, and with local farmers owning the sheep-walks in the district, who were equally violent in pressing for compensation.

It is clear that in those regions, as wild and remote then as now, overseers and managers like Lewis Morris had to bear their own burdens unassisted by law. Nevertheless, Morris was able to ride his cob over the moors where Montgomeryshire, Cardiganshire, and Radnorshire met, and to cogitate on profound matters, which he expounded at length to his many correspondents. These matters included the derivation of Greek and Latin civilization from Celtic sources, the true meaning of the diatribes of Gildas against the rulers of Britain in the sub-Roman period, the Druidic lore and bardic alphabet, the significance of standing stones and ancient crosses found on the way. Included also were the varying merits of Welsh as spoken in different parts of Wales. For Morris was not only an industrious antiquarian; he holds, with his brother and with such associates as David Lewis, the distinction of being the first to found some organized attempt at establishing a Welsh Academy of Letters and to find in Welsh culture a bridge between the ancient and the modern world. That his conclusions were confined within the limits of the 18th-cent. knowledge in archaeological matters is only half-criticism. It is to be hoped that any monument to the ancient mining industry of the Ellennith will include a memorial to him. In his practical working life, Lewis Morris of Anglesey carried on the tradition of Rome in these parts. In his philosophic discussions, he maintained the learned curiosity of Camden and Saxton and many others who knew that the recovery of past history was the accumulation of human experience and a guide to the future.

The way onward from Llangurig passes and leaves the Wye and picks up the Tarenig river. It rises to 1,359 ft, and Eisteddfa Gurig (Rest Place of Curig the Saint) is reached. Here you are on the broad back of Plynlimon, and, from the Dyffryn Castell inn some way further ahead, the most usual route for walkers to reach the height of Plynlimon Fawr is followed. Posts are conveniently and wisely set to mark

the way; for the wide level of the moorland can not only gravely mislead but even create the impression that Plynlimon too is featureless. Lovers of mountains will avoid this route and take the ascent, long and demanding as it is, from Forge through the Hengwm valley. The creation of the Hafren (Severn) Forest, stretching from the E. up to the head of Plynlimon, has added much variety and indeed beauty. And the Nant-y-moch and Clywedog reservoirs have set jewels in Plynlimon's crown, greatly helping to dispose of the unfavourable reputation that the northern head of the Ellennith has suffered, which only the approach from Eisteddfa Gurig gave it and it never otherwise deserved.

LLANGYFELACH, *Glamorgan,* a village on the northern boundaries of the borough of Swansea, has in recent years become rather involved with newly built villas, but the church is still attractive, placed on a hill-side looking northwards to the moors of Mynydd y Gwair. It is the only church in Glamorgan with a detached tower. The story goes that the Devil, envious of St Cyfelach in building the church, started to make off with the tower. The imprecations of the saint forced him to drop it before he had gone 100 yds. The old church, however, was demolished for structural reasons, and the new one built on a safer site slightly to the N. The new church is well proportioned and contains some unusual items. An ancient, interlaced Celtic wheel-cross is inset on the N. wall of the nave. It bears the inscription *Crux Xri* (Cross of Christ). Here also is a fine stained-glass window by the students of the Swansea Arts College to the memory of one of their colleagues of promise who died young. The painter Evan Walters was born at Llangyfelach, and he presented one of his paintings to the church, in memory of his parents. The organ is rather surprisingly placed under the N. window. There is the base of another Celtic cross in the churchyard, decorated with fret designs and plaitwork interlacing.

Llangyfelach was renowned in the old days for its hiring fair. It fell into disrepute, so it was said, because the prospective mistress was "too often mistaken for the maid".

The most distinguished son of the parish was Col. Philip Jones (1614–74), who was born at Pen-y-waun farm near Clase House. He took the Parliamentary side in the Civil War, became Governor of the Swansea garrison, and was present in the Battle of St Fagan's in 1648. He became a trusted friend of Cromwell, and was a member of his Council. He it was who arranged Oliver's funeral with impressive dignity. Throughout the Commonwealth, Col. Philip Jones was the real power behind the scenes in South Wales, where he succeeded in amassing a fortune. What was more, he succeeded in keeping most of it after the Restoration. This subtle, indispensable administrator died in peace on his estate at Fonmon in the Vale of Glamorgan in 1674.

To the N. of Llangyfelach are the Felindre

tinplate-works of the Steel Company of Wales, now nationalized. These streamlined workshops are part of a great industrial complex. The other units are at Trostre, near Llanelli, and Margam, near Port Talbot. The three form an integrated plant for the production of tinplate by the most modern methods. These works have displaced the numerous smaller ones that made South Wales the seat of the tinplate industry.

LLANGYNFELYN, *Cardiganshire.* This very small scatter of houses, a little over 1 m. from Taliesin and set well into the flatland known as the Cors Fochno, is notable because so much of the character of this part of Wales has been formed round it.

The Cors Fochno is an estuary land, half soil, half water, and that water more than half salt. It is a wide stretch of reeded marsh lying behind the level reaches of sand that make the principal feature of Borth and Ynyslas. This extent of seaboard is properly called the Traeth Maelgwn, after the British King addressed as Maglocunos by the 6th-cent. cleric Gildas, but referred to by later chroniclers as Maelgwn. It was on these sands that he was proclaimed war leader of all other kings in Britain; the occasion was the suddenly launched, though long-prepared, Anglo-Saxon assault on the country led by the House of Wessex and Ida of Northumbria. An account of the ceremony, as detected by Sir John Rhys in the MSS. known as the Welsh Laws, states that the choice of chief among kings was left to the waves of the sea; through the cunning of one Maeldaf, Maelgwn was seated on the shore in a chair "made of birds' wings", and thus he was the only one of the several claimants to be borne above the oncoming waters. The tale need not be taken at its face value as myth. Some traditional ceremony associating the kingship of this island with the sea may have lasted long enough for Canute to repeat it, with the result we all know. And the birds' wings that bore Maelgwn aloft may have sprung from the military eagles, larks, and hawks distinguishing the Roman legions whose auxiliary forces remained in Britain when the Empire fell.

From the earliest times, the mouth of Dovey had a dominant position in the economic as well as the strategic control of West Wales. To the N. of it stands the legend-haunted site of the Carn March Arthur and, not far from Llangynfelyn, the equally legendary Bedd (Grave) of Taliesin, set on the S. side. The names both of Arthur and of Taliesin have become associated with the troubled times that followed the retreat of imperial Rome; and for the frontier state of Powys, with its centre at Pengwern, near Shrewsbury, the control of the way from the Midlands to the sea through the Dovey valley was essential.

The houses at Llangynfelyn centre about the modest but ancient and beautiful little church. Cynfelyn, whose name was given to the place, is believed to have been a saint of the Celtic Church that preceded Augustine of Canterbury in the Christianization of this island. The present church is not so old as those associated with the names of similar saints, particularly in Caernarfonshire; a pleasant house facing the church appears to be of 16th-cent. architecture, and gives some clue to the present structure of the church itself. But the Cynfelyn who left his imprint on this district – thrusting into the sea some 5 m. SW. of Llangynfelyn is a landmark for ships called the Sarn Gynfelyn – may have left a more immediate and factual monument to himself.

No one who uses the road skirting the Cors Fochno can fail to notice the series of small hills standing sheer above the level fields like so many islands against the reeds and ditches of the plain. That they once really were islands is more than a guess, for they are expressly so named. The word Ynys (Island) is attached to no fewer than eight such places on the Ordnance Survey map; and Llangynfelyn itself is clearly one. It has to be reached by a road, passing among the reeded fields of the fen, dipping low into a hollow once boarded against the flow of water but now only rarely flooded, and rising sharply to a hill-top. Until recently, this was indeed an island, though modern skills in road-construction have attached it firmly to the mainland.

On the turn of the road at the head of the hill, you can see, low against the skyline of marsh and water, a small prominence set about with trees. Trees of any kind are alien to the stretches of the Cors Fochno, and these are birches. The spot is wholly isolated; against the sunsets that form such a striking feature of the Dovey, the birch-tree clump and the tiny knoll on which they seem to stand are given a surprising prominence.

Such remote areas were for many generations the refuge of those who wished to live in peace. Ancient food-gathering communities often sought them out; to surround themselves more effectively, they laid mats of birch twigs and branches on which to build their huts. Nearby, this knoll, a piece of relatively solid earth thick with stunted birch, reveals that a walled dwelling was once built upon it. With its wide night sky, it would be an ideal resort for a hermit in the days of Cynfelyn, as such recluses were much concerned with the works of God as manifested in the apparent motion of the stars. All travel by sea or land depended then, as it still basically does, on the accurate record of such phenomena.

If you wish to explore this lost habitation, a local guide is essential. The Cors Fochno is gradually being reclaimed. But the place in which the knoll is set has not yet suffered this change. And, even where it has been made, there are deep, mud-filled ditches, covered with green scum against the peaty black sides, that look temptingly like lanes. Wherever the bog stretches, the greatest care must be taken to stay on the recognized route and endure even the most primitive of branch-laid bridges.

A relatively safe channel runs from Craig y Penrhyn to the river-course among the sands and salty creeks. Shellfish and crabs, and the fowl that fish for them, exist along these uninhabited beaches where the ranges of hills enclosing the

Dovey valley on both sides can, by the lover of solitary nature, be seen in all their beauty.

LLANGYNWYD, *Glamorgan*. This little village, on a high ridge above the Llynfi valley, 1½ m. S. of Maesteg, has a fame in Wales out of all proportion to its size. The tragic story of the Maid of Cefnydfa near Llangynwyd, and her unhappy passion for the poet and thatcher, Wil Hopkin, is familiar to most South Walians, and has invested Llangynwyd with an air of romance. The modern village of Llangynwyd is largely a housing estate on the main Macsteg–Bridgend road. The old village lies 1 m. up in the hills to the W., through narrow lanes. The church is dedicated to the 6th-cent. St Cynwyd, who was connected with the celebrated monastic establishment of Llancarfan in the Vale of Glamorgan. It has a fine embattled tower, with a peal of eight bells and a porch with the figure of the patron saint, bearing the model of the church in his hands. A sundial is fixed on the S. exterior wall. The Latin inscription proclaims that it was a gift of E.P. (probably a member of the Powell family) of Tondu in 1686.

The interior has been so thoroughly restored that little remains of the original church furnishings, except some of the old oak benches. There are unusual multi-foiled openings on either side of the chancel arch. The font dates from the 15th cent.

Locally, Llangynwyd is known as Yr Hen Plwyf (The Old Parish). Legend, which has been particularly busy in this locality, asserts that the name arose because a carpenter had to make a coffin for a man who died aged twenty-eight. The carpenter was uneducated and thus uncertain how to write the figure 28. He put down four sevens in a row, since he knew that these added up to the required number. At the burial service, the clergyman happened to be a stranger to Llangynwyd. He saw the extraordinary number and was informed that the man had spent all his life in the parish. Said the cleric in astonishment, "This must indeed be a very old parish!" The name, however, probably arose because of its connection with the old Tir Iarll (Earl's Land), when the whole area formed part of the estate of the first Norman conquerors of Glamorgan. There are scanty remains of an early castle. Higher up on the mountain-side are the large earthworks known as Y Bwlwarcau (The Bulwarks) and a square enclosure that has been claimed as a Roman camp. Beyond, in land taken over by the Forestry Commission, is the mound known as Twmpath Diwlith and the site of the Bodvoc Stone. The whole area is rich with prehistoric remains.

It was the 18th cent. that brought romance to Llangynwyd. The popular story relates that Ann Thomas was the heiress to the estate of Cefnydfa. Her mother had ambitious plans to marry her to Antony Maddock, the son of substantial people in the locality. Ann had secretly lost her heart to Wil Hopkin, the local poet and thatcher. Ann was forced into marriage;

she died two years later, so the story goes, of a broken heart. Wil never married, and he died fourteen years later. He is supposed to be buried near the westerly yew tree of the churchyard. The favourite song "Bugeilio'r Gwenith Gwyn" (Watching the Wheat) is supposed to have been written by Wil Hopkin, and it carried the fame of Wil's romance round the world, wherever Welshmen have settled. Ann Thomas certainly existed. Her marriage contract is still extant. Wil Hopkin is known to have taken part in an Eisteddfod in Cymer in 1735. Beyond that, all is conjecture, and much of the tale did not stand up to the critical examination of Prof. G. J. Williams. But the old story still goes marching on. A memorial column to the celebrated men of the district stands on the cross-roads outside the churchyard, near the charming thatched inn of the Old House Tavern, which Wil is reputed to have patronized. Among the other names commemorated on the column is that of Cadrawd (T. C. Evans), the village blacksmith, who wrote the history of the parish and made a celebrated collection of old farm furniture and implements, which is now in the National Museum in Cardiff.

Llangynwyd was one of the last places in Wales to maintain the old custom of the Mari Lwyd around Christmas-time. The origin of the name is uncertain. Mari Lwyd may be a corruption of the Welsh for "Hail, Mary", and the custom is a survival of the medieval religious interludes; or it may even be associated with some ritual of the first horse-using Celtic aristocracy. At Christmas, a band of singers tours the countryside, led by a man dressed in a white cowl, topped by the skull of a horse bedecked with ribbons. The Mari Lwyd party stands outside the doors of the houses they visit and sings impromptu verses, which must be capped by the people within. When the verses fail, the Mari Lwyd party enters in triumph, to be regaled with good things, a general chasing of the girls, and a drinking of toasts.

At Brynllywarch, a prosperous farmhouse in Llangynwyd, Samuel Jones – who had been born at Chirk Castle and entered at All Saints, Oxford, in 1647 – founded the first Welsh Nonconformist academy, having had the living at Llangynwyd from no less a person than the Lord Protector, Oliver Cromwell. It was a Presbyterian foundation inspired by the Cromwellian Acts for propagation of the Gospels in Wales and the redress of grievances there. On the death of Samuel Jones the academy was removed to Abergavenny.

LLANGYNYDD, *Glamorgan*. The name is pronounced locally as Llangenny.

This village, 16 m. W. of Swansea, shares with Rhosili the distinction of being the most westerly of the Gower villages. More than anywhere else in the peninsula, the old Gower traditions and dialect have survived in Llangynydd. Here lived Phil Janner, most famous of the Gower folk-singers. He sang at the King's Head Inn, and he lies buried in the churchyard. The good folk of Llangynydd and N. Gower have always been independent. When the government introduced summer-time during the First World War, N. Gower held a public meeting and finally decided to give this dangerous innovation a month's trial.

Three hills surround the village: Llanmadog Hill (609 ft), Rhosili Down (632), and Hardings Down (500). All are of Old Red Sandstone, rising out of the limestone plateau that forms the rest of Gower. The church is dedicated to St Cenydd, and was probably built by Henry de Newburgh, on the site of the old Celtic "clas" (monastery). It is the largest in Gower, but has been drastically restored, leaving as points of interest only the worn tomb of one of the De la Mare family and three coffin-lids, one of which may have belonged to the tomb of St Cenydd. The village well on the green opposite the lych-gate has a worn cross on its cover.

Llangynydd is 1 m. from Rhosili Sands over the burrows, and past a large caravan site. To the N. is Broughton Bay and its fine sands. Bathing is notoriously dangerous here because of the estuary tides, but the situation is impressive. Behind, on Hardings Down, are the embankments of an Iron Age fort.

LLANIDLOES, *Montgomeryshire*, lies on the Severn a little over 15 m. from Newtown. The reaches of the river here run from a narrow valley out of the Plynlimon hills, and the way W. to Machynlleth takes you at once over the empty spaces and wide outlook of the moorland, which afforestation is now beginning to change. Southwards the road will lead to Rhayader and the drowned valleys by Elan Village whose waters form the Birmingham reservoirs, lying under hills still largely unchanged since the days when peoples now forgotten raised their tumuli and cairns upon them. By the rocky escarpments of Cerrig Gwalch (Falcon Crags), the way will lead to Newbridge on Wye and the Radnorshire hills about Llandrindod Wells. But Llanidloes is still very much shut in and somewhat isolated. The centre of the town is distinguished by one of the pleasantest examples of a market cross, or timbered meeting-place for market, anywhere in Wales; this one was built in 1609. The lower part is an arcaded space for stalls; the upper, a set of council chambers. Proposals for its removal as an obstruction to traffic were bitterly opposed before the Second World War.

Lead-mining was once a major interest; but the place remains a market centre for the surrounding villages, and a producer of wool. It also has some business in the tanning of leather.

Its most serious intervention in history occurred in 1839. This was the time of Chartism, the demand for reforms that would bring Parliament more directly under the control of the people, and introduce a system of economic justice more favourable to the factory worker and more generous to the poor. Llanidloes was then a considerable centre for the weaving of wool; and close by was Newtown, where Robert Owen,

the philosopher and originator of the Co-operative Societies, was born and where he returned to die in 1858. The wool-weavers, working in loom-sheds transformed from cottages already old, in Llanidloes as throughout this area of Central Wales, were particularly discontented with their conditions of labour and their wages; the privations of the poor in the district were extreme. The local Press reported several instances of lonely old women found dead, eaten by rats.

In the 1830s the expectation of revolution, such as had occurred on the Continent, was acute in Britain. Plans for a concerted march on London from all over the country alarmed the authorities sufficiently to arm the constabularies with cutlasses and hold the militia in constant readiness. An address was published from Newtown and displayed in Caersws and Llanidloes: "Helots of England! Toiling husbandmen and despised mechanics! Be firm. Boldly demand your long-forgotten rights. . . . Once divided, you must inevitably fall a sacrifice to the merciless foe!" It concluded, all the same, with an appeal for peace, law, and order.

The reaction was a panic summoning of militia and hasty swearing-in of special constables all over the Severn valley. But the reaction at Caersws was chiefly from the Methodist interests that were dominant in these parts. The populace was adjured not to desert their places of worship on the Sunday for which the revolution was fixed, and reminded that the agitators were men who lived by the tongue rather than by toil and were seekers after power at the expense of the multitude. Neither Caersws nor Newtown answered the call to revolt. In Llanidloes, however, some who were found carrying guns were arrested and imprisoned, in spite of their protests that they were bent only on a mild afternoon's sport in the hills. Llanidloes weavers were noted for discussing political affairs as if they were Members of Parliament; and their drilling and marching in the streets of the town had for some time been anxiously watched. Clumsy intervention by constables and militia resulted in a short but damaging scuffle in the centre of the town, when railings were torn up and fences broken, and the Mayor distinguished himself by emerging, long after the fight was over, from underneath his bed.

The incident was provoked by the introduction of London police, a precaution that illustrates how serious the authorities considered the threat from the "mad mobs" who might set the Severn valley ablaze. It began with the arrest – without warrant, by a London policeman – of a native, one Abraham Owen, who was walking through the main street with a spade over his shoulder. The weapon was by no means proof of revolutionary intent; but official alarm is shown by the fact that troops had been landed at Aberystwyth from Ireland to march upon the place. The riot ended at Montgomery Assizes and gaol, the strongest evidence against the forty accused being an appeal by the local Chartist lodge that

Llanidloes: the old market hall

headquarters should send them a speaker to explain the purpose of the movement. But as drilling and marching in unauthorized groups was a penal offence, some of the condemned were sentenced to fifteen years in Van Diemen's Land, Australia.

The church here dates partly from the 13th cent. Its N. arcade is notable, and the hammer-beam roof is said to have come from Cwmhir Abbey in Radnorshire, when it was demolished at the Dissolution.

The Museum of Local History and Industry was founded in 1933.

LLANMADOG, *Glamorgan,* is tucked away in the NW. corner of the Gower peninsula. It looks N. over the marshlands of the Burry estuary, but immediately behind rises Llanmadog Hill, with limestone crags that overhang in places. Up against one of the crags is the church, dedicated to St Madog, a pupil of St Cenydd at nearby Llangynydd. The church was restored in 1865. It is Early English, with a small tower and a saddleback roof and parapet. The church possesses a Norman font, and traces of wall paintings were found during the church restoration. Inset, in a window-sill on the S. side, is a stone with an early Roman-British inscription, probably 7th-cent.: "Guan, son of Duectus, lies here". A Celtic pillar cross stands against the outer S. wall.

Llanmadog Hill (609 ft) rises behind the village. It is prominent in all views of Gower from the other side of the estuary. At the NE. end is the Bulwark, forming a complex defence-system of Iron Age date, with the ditches and banks well preserved.

N. of the village, and reached by walking across the extensive Whiteford Burrows, is the sandy spit of Whiteford Point, the most northerly point of Gower. The lighthouse is now mechanized, and the whole area is a Nature Reserve owned by the National Trust.

About ¾ m. E. of Llanmadog is the tiny village of Cheriton, with its attractive little church. The choir-stalls, altar rails, and altar are all the work of a former Rector, John David Davies, who died in 1911; a skilled wood-carver, he was also an authority on the history of Gower. North Hill Tor, locally called Nottle Tor, is the prominent limestone spar overlooking the marshes ½ m. N. of Cheriton. The massive earthworks are not pre-historic but are probably connected with the Norman occupation of Gower.

To the S. of Llanmadog, about 1½ m. off, is Burry Green, with its white walls and old house. The road linking N. and S. Gower at its far western end twists southwards between Cefn Bryn and Rhosili Down. It joins the S. road at Landdewi, with its small and conspicuous church, which has nave and chancel out of line.

LLANRHAEADR - YM - MOCHNANT, *Montgomeryshire.* About 6 m. by road from Llanfyllin, this village is reached by a road passing through some of the finest scenery in Montgomeryshire, offering both the pleasant views along the Tanat valley and, by way of contrast, the sight of Gyrn Moelfre (1,707 ft). The fall, Pistyll Rhaeadr, from which the village gets its name draws visitors to the place, following the way taken by George Borrow. The church, which has no saint's name, is described simply as being by the Falls of the Swift Brook (though some translate it as the Brook of Pigs). A special object of interest is a grave-slab, probably of the 10th cent. It is inscribed: +*XPI Con Filius De-teh Fecit.* Perhaps it is an invocation of Christ, recording the name of the man who had it set there, and also the name of his father.

It was here that William Morgan, born about 1540, translated the Bible into Welsh and so gave the language the basis for the modern forms it has developed. The work was published in 1588, twenty-one years after permission to use Welsh in this way had been granted by Queen Elizabeth Tudor. Her father, Henry VIII, had banned

Welsh from all official usage, and so William's undertaking was most important. It included a revision of the version of the New Testament put out in 1567. He later became Bishop of St Asaph, and he has a monument to his memory there before the Cathedral, several of his co-workers in this field being commemorated with him.

There are almshouses behind the church, and in a small hollow among the hills above the village is a holy well, more ancient than the church and perhaps known to the inscriber of the stone.

LLANRHIDIAN, *Glamorgan.* This village, in N. Gower 11 m. W. of Swansea, looks out of the wide expanse of Llanrhidian Marsh and the sands of the Burry estuary. There has been a certain amount of new building, but the place has not lost character, and one of its inns is still pleasantly named the Welcome to Town, Gentlemen. The church has been built under the steep scarp that must have been the cliff-edge before the silting-up of the Burry Inlet. It is 13th-cent., with a Late Gothic E. window. In the S. porch is the "Leper Stone", a strangely carved slab whose exact meaning has yet to be deciphered. It probably dates from the 9th cent. A.D. Other curious stones can be found near the church, including the remains of the old cross on the green, which is reputed to have been used as a pillory. The village mill has ceased to work, but the large mill-pond is still there.

About 1 m. W. of Llanrhidian on the road to Cheriton is Weobley Castle. It is more of a fortified manor house, mainly built in the 13th and 14th cents. by Henry Beaufort, Earl of Warwick, and then the De la Bere family. Later it passed into the hands of Sir Rhys ap Thomas, Henry VII's favourite, and eventually to the Mansels. It is now under the Ministry of Public Building and Works. The site is impressive, and the building is worth the visit for the glimpse it gives of domestic life at the end of the Middle Ages.

Just to the E. of Llanrhidian is the hill of Cil Ifor Top, crowned with an Early Iron Age fort (1st cent. B.C.). The earthworks are among the largest in Gower and cover nearly 8 acres. There is a deep scarp towards the N.; the entrance is on the S. side. From Cil Ifor Top you look S. to the whole line of Cefn Bryn. The pond near Cilibion, at the point where the road over Cefn Bryn joins the Gower North Road, is Broad Pool. It is rich in water plants and insect life. The area is now a permanent Nature Reserve – a good place to see the wild ponies that are a feature of Cefn Bryn and the Gower commons. Cilibion has a youth hostel, one of two in Gower.

LLANRWST, *Denbighshire*, is a smallish market town on the Conway river. It is supposedly dedicated to St Restitutus, under a Welsh form of his name, Grwst. The church, in the dominating position inevitable throughout this land of early sainthood, is of comparatively Late Perpendicular form, owing much to the expansion of ecclesiastical architecture in Wales that followed the accession of Henry Tudor to the English throne. But it contains, from earlier times, the great stone coffin holding the stone effigy of the Llywelyn known as the son of Iorwerth, a prince who wrested control of the province of Gwynedd – or, as the 18th cent. began to call it, Snowdonia – from all competitors and asserted himself equally in the politics of England. He married the daughter of the unlucky King John, and set his signature on Magna Carta in 1215; for that document established the rights of Welshmen and Scotsmen no less than those of English barons, burghers, and freemen, under the doctrine of the natural justice they were all entitled to claim. The Gwydir Chapel, built under the direction of the Wynn family in 1633, has monuments of its distinguished members, but is of greater importance through being attributed to the great Welsh architect, Inigo Jones. To him also is attributed the bridge that spans the Conway and is dated 1636; it has an unusually bold and balanced structure. It rises

Llanrwst on the River Conway

G. Douglas Bolton

sharply, almost to a point at the centre height, as was customary in his day, and yet the harmony between its length and the span of its three arches is too striking to be assigned to some merely competent designer.

The attribution has, as sometimes happens, no more than traditional support. The same tradition insists that he came either from Llanrwst or its immediate district. Much of his early life is obscure. Born in 1573 and dying in 1652, he is first mentioned in a document of 1603 as an artist; his earliest employment seems to have been as a man skilled in antiquities, for he acted as adviser to the Earl of Arundel, and his journeys in France, Italy, and Germany to discover and buy objects of the sort seem to have laid the foundation for his achievement as an architect. The Banqueting House at Whitehall, the recasing of the nave and transepts of Old St Paul's in London, the Queen's House at Greenwich, and the town-planning designs for Covent Garden and Lincoln's Inn Fields are some of his better-known works. But, before these, he designed the settings for the production of Ben Jonson's *Masque of Hymen* in 1606. His importance as the first and perhaps the greatest British architect is recognized; he is less well appreciated as the earliest practitioner of stage design, moving from the bare boards of Shakespeare's "wooden O" to the re-creation of the living world within the theatre.

On the opposite bank of the river, what was once the Tudor mansion of Gwydir Castle (1555), burnt out in the 1920s, stands restored. The Gwydir Uchaf chapel has a painted ceiling.

About 2 m. to the W. of Llanrwst is another church, that of Llanrhychwyn. This spot lies in Caernarfonshire; it has some connection with Llanrwst, since its church is called Llywelyn's Old Church. It is of very early type, and relates to the earliest of Christian foundations in this area. But its font, a square tub set on a pair of stone steps, dates it to a period shortly after the Norman conquest of England when such things first began to be used.

LLANSANTFFRAED, *Breconshire.* Under the Brecon Beacons that rise to the W., and on the Roman road that runs to Brecon town over the Bwlch that is traditionally the gateway to Wales, the village of Llansantffraed, in spite of its old Christian church, perpetuates the memory of Brigid, a bride who was a Celtic spirit of the hills before she became blessed with the charity of a new faith. The antiquity of the place was noted in 1811 by Daniel Paterson in his *Direct and Principal Cross Roads.* A small hamlet of Sgethrog is still noted on our modern maps, and Paterson, pointing out that "Llansanfraid" was 2 m. from the main road and near the lake called "Langor's Pool", adds that at "Skythrog" was a Roman stone that stands like a milestone close by the highway side, with an inscription down the front. There is unfortunately no means of confirming that it stands there still.

The church has a particular interest in the fact that it holds the memory of two distinguished natives of the village: Henry Vaughan, the Swan of Usk (as he was called in his day), and his brother. They make a parallel to the two other great brothers of the 17th cent., Lord Herbert of Cherbury and George Herbert. For George Herbert was both divine and a poet, and his brother was a poet and philosopher as well as diplomat. Henry Vaughan was a poet, and Thomas, his twin, was an alchemist and mystic; he held the living of Llansantffraed until his death. They came from a family originating in Tretower, close by. Of the two, Henry had the more outward-looking life, studying at Jesus College, Oxford, and then reading law in London, but turning to medicine and becoming a doctor at "Newton by Usk", which seems to have been Llansantffraed under its Anglicized name of Newton St Briget. Both brothers were Royalist in sympathy, and in 1649 Thomas lost his living through this. Henry had seen something of the battles, but by then had returned to his birthplace. He is buried in the churchyard beside which runs the Usk he loved. He foresaw, or intended, this end; for he wrote:

Isca, whensoever those shades I see
And thy loved arbours must no more know me,
When I am laid to rest hard by thy streams
And my sun sets where first it sprung its beams,
I'll leave behind me such a large, clear light
As shall redeem thee from oblivious night.

That large, clear light seems settled in his valley, and his return to it must have been a compensation for his long term of imprisonment as a Royalist. Of his poems, one called *The Retreat*, which means no flight from battle but a going back to his own home and the things of nature that he loved, gave Wordsworth the idea for his *Intimations of Immortality.*

On the way to Brecon is another church, Llanhamlach, in which are ancient sculptured stones and a 13th-cent. effigy.

LLANSAWEL, *Carmarthenshire*, is a village at the junction of the Melindwr and Marlais rivers 8 m. N. of Llandeilo. The united streams join the Cothi around the quarried hill of Pen y Dinas. A quiet place, devoted to fishing, with a 13th-cent. church, two pleasant inns, and a Methodist chapel that disputes with Cilycwm the honour of being the earliest chapel of the denomination in Wales. Little Llansawel produced in succession two principals of Jesus College, Oxford: John Williams from 1602 to 1613, and Griffith Powell from 1613 to 1620.

The road N. out of the village goes through Rhydcymerau and the outlying plantations of the Brechfa Forest over the mountain to Llanybydder in the Teifi valley. The road W. joins the Cothi valley in 2½ m. at Abergorlech. This hamlet has a fine three-arched bridge, reputed to be the oldest in Carmarthenshire, over the Gorlech stream; a restored church; and an old reputation for quoit-playing, the quoits being fashioned out of the flat stones of the river-bed. This is forestry country now, with woodlands in the hills to the right of you all the way to Brechfa.

LLANSILIN, *Denbighshire*, is a place still as remote as it was when George Borrow, making his way from Llanrhaeadr to find Sycharth, the hill made bare of the mansion of Owain Glyndwr, found he was also close to the spot where Huw Morus lay buried.

A village or townlet Borrow called it, having at a short distance to the W. some high hills, which form part of the Berwyns. He reached it, as he notes, after passing the stream where that Owain, King of the Welsh, had had his corn-mill. The church, he observed, had several enormous yew trees around it, probably as old as the days of Henry VIII. The main body of it was ancient, but the steeple, for Borrow, was modern. By the innkeeper he had brought with him, he was led to the southern wall, and to a broad slab set in the ground. Beneath it lay the remains of Huw Morus.

Some miles away at Pontymeibion, Huw Morus was born in 1622. An obelisk there now marks his birthplace. He died in 1709. Although, apparently, he never wrote in English, he belonged by temperament and in his literary skills to the school of Anglo-Welsh writers outstandingly represented by Donne, Herbert, Vaughan, and Traherne. An innovator in the writing of Welsh verse, and a leader of the free system of metre and rhyme, he had a blend of intellectualism with lyricism typical of the Metaphysical poets. He wrote of love much as Lord Herbert of Cherbury did, with a sense of beauty transcending physical attraction. He was Cavalier in sympathy, and this may have done something to prevent him from achieving a wider fame. But Borrow was right to remember, among Morus's works, the *Addewid ddyfal ddianwadal* (Dialogue between Life and Death), and his elegy on Barbara Middleton. Huw Morus also wrote political verse, such as the *Lamentation of Oliver's Men, on the Restoration of Charles II.* But he was no sycophant of royalty, and he supported the interest of William of Orange against James II. He died when Queen Anne was on the throne.

LLANSTEPHAN, *Carmarthenshire.* Seen from the other side of the Towy estuary, Llanstephan has a charming air of tranquillity. The whitewashed houses of the Green are mirrored in the waters at high tide. Behind the Green the narrow streets climb the hill towards the church and its tower set against tall trees. Ruined Llanstephan Castle looks everything an ancient castle should be, on a high bluff fronting the sea. It was a favourite with the Romantic painters. Llanstephan can claim to be the best-sited village in Carmarthenshire. It benefits from its isolation on a small peninsula formed by the triple estuaries of the Gwendraeths, Towy, and Taf.

The road from Carmarthen to Llanstephan passes the scanty remains of Green Castle, on a hill at a sharp bend in the highway. This particular stronghold was built by the English family of Rede. The ruins of the castle of the Welsh Princes lies 600 yds S. The road dips down to follow the widening river. To the right is Pantyrathro, a new riding centre planned on a big scale to attract the leading show-riders of the country, and surrounded by an unspoilt pattern of green fields and small hills.

The waterfront of Llanstephan, the Green, lies separated from the rest of the village along the sands of the estuary. The main street slopes pleasantly up to the church, which possesses an imposing military-type tower and a nave mainly of the 13th cent. The building was restored in 1872. Within are numerous early 19th-cent. memorial tablets, besides the tombs, dating from the 17th and 18th cents., of the Lloyd family in the Laques Chapel. The Meares family of the local big house, the Plas, are commemorated by their elaborate hatchments. The E. window has some fine stained glass.

The main street forks at the church. The left branch runs towards Llanstephan Castle, and is a dead-end for traffic, leaving a walk up to the Castle gates. On the right is the splendid 18th-cent. mansion, the Plas, with a pillared portico. The Castle is now in the charge of the Ministry of Public Building and Works. The defensive value of the site, with its southern and eastern sides formed by abrupt slopes falling 150 ft to the low cliffs fringing the water, made it attractive to the Iron Age folk long before the coming of the Normans. The hedge of the field to the W. of the Castle marks the line of the bulwarks of the Iron Age fort.

The present approach to the Castle is up a steep track, with the Castle ditch running round to the W. tower from the great gatehouse. The gatehouse is an imposing structure, with its two drum-towers and some features suggesting that its builders derived their inspiration from the castle in Caerphilly by Gilbert de Clare in the mid-13th cent. The actual gate has been walled up; a new entrance was opened in the 15th cent. Over the old blocked gateway is a curious chute down which boiling water could be poured on to a storming-party. The inner ward of the Castle slopes steeply uphill towards the upper ward, where the first Castle stood; it was built at the end of the 12th cent. The ruins consist of the inner gate and a stretch of the original wall beyond.

The early history of the Castle is obscure. When the Normans began their penetration of South Wales in the late 11th and early 12th cents., they soon appreciated the advantages of having firm bases on the coast from which they could support their penetration inland. They built Kidwelly Castle to control the mouth of the Gwendraeth. Llanstephan Castle performed the same function for the Towy. The exact date of construction of the first Castle is uncertain, but it was certainly captured by the Welsh princes Cadell, Maredudd, and Rhys in 1146, and thus received its first mention in history. The courage of the young Maredudd, who flung the English scaling-ladders down when repulsing an attempt to recapture the works, was long celebrated by the Welsh chroniclers. But by 1158 the English had reoccupied the Castle. The Lord Rhys, the most powerful of the Welsh Princes of South Wales, retook it when he broke with Richard I. It fell again to the Welsh under Llywelyn the Great in 1215, was recovered by the English, and again passed for a moment into Welsh hands in 1257. When the tide of Welsh independence finally ebbed, the Castle was greatly strengthened in the new style of fortification that marked the era of Edward I. The Welsh may have captured it in the Glyndwr Rising. After that its importance declined. The Crown held it for two centuries and granted it to various owners. Jasper Tudor received it from the hands of his nephew, Henry VII, and the final alterations to the structure may have been made during his tenancy. Then it sank into oblivion and picturesque decay.

Beyond the Castle is St Antony's Well, which still receives its offerings of pins as a healing well and as a wishing well for the lovelorn. The woodlands are known as the "Sticks", a rough translation of the Welsh "coed" (wood) by the local town crier. The fine bluff of Warley Point (358 ft) separates the estuary of the Towy from that of the Taf. The coast curves round to Black Scar, where the Ordnance Survey map shows a ferry to Laugharne. Would-be crossers are likely to be disappointed today, as the long lane down to the sand-spit is now overgrown. About 1 m. inland, N. of Llanstephan, is the hamlet of Llanybri. The houses are grouped round a church, which was designated the "Marbell" Church in an inventory of Edward VI, but later passed into the possession of the Dissenters. The church, with its curious tower, is now in complete decay.

N. of Llanybri the country is well wooded, and among the trees is Coomb House, once the home of the founder of Morris's Bank in Carmarthen in 1784. It is now a Cheshire Home. A narrow lane meanders SW. to the ruined church of Llandeilo Abercowin (more correctly Abercywyn), near the banks of the Taf. The farm called the Pilgrim's Rest, near at hand, dates from the 15th cent., but the church is an utter ruin, with the churchyard buried in weeds.

LLANTHONY, *Monmouthshire*. The remote and beautiful Vale of Ewyas forms the valley of the Honddu river as it runs under the Black Mountains of Talgarth, W. of the hill-top known as Mynydd Myrddin (Merlin's Mount). It holds the remains of what was a priory of Austin Canons, founded between 1108 and 1136 by Hugh de Lacy, the Marcher Lord of Hereford. The Black Mountains here stretch between Abergavenny, the Roman station of Gobannium, and the Roman fort that was set at Clyro. Humphrey Lhuyd, in the 16th cent., set "Euas" as a district a little E. of Hay within the Deheubarth, or South province of Wales, and on the border of the principality of Powys. The Welsh rulers who succeeded to the Roman controllers of Britain in these parts were harried by the Saxons under Harald, and by the Norman border barons who followed him. Clyro has, not far from it, the remains of a Norman stronghold. Llanthony shows the same historical succession. Before the present structure was built, there was a chapel on the site dedicated to St David of Wales, called Llanddewi Nant Hodni. De Lacy, in the midst of his wars against the Welsh, suddenly had a transformation of spirit, and became an anchorite; together with Ernisius, Chaplain to Henry I, he retired to Llanddewi Nant Hodeni. They rebuilt the chapel and created a community of forty canons that Queen Maud was pleased to patronize. Something in the air of the place seems to have had a profound spiritual effect; for Walter de Gloucester, Constable of England, joined the community, and under Robert de Bethune, who succeeded Ernisius as prior, the present structure was completed. In the beginning, its influence must have been great; for near Gloucester was created a second Llanthony, whose remains were later embraced by the railway sidings of a more enlightened age.

The very remoteness of the place seems to have attracted men who wished to escape from the evils of the world; but this same remoteness was its downfall. Gerald de Barri visited it in 1188 on his tour of Wales, and he tells us how the first anchorites who settled there would not clear the woods or till the soil in case the place should lose its solitude and wildness. "Here the monks," he says, "sitting in their cloisters enjoying the fresh air, behold the tops of the mountains touching the heavens and herds of wild deer feeding on their summits; the body of the sun does not become visible above the heights of the mountains, even in a clear atmosphere, until the hour of prime. A place truly fitted for contemplation, a happy and delightful spot, fitted to supply all its own wants!" But, he adds, the extravagance of English luxury, the pride of a sumptuous table, gradually corrupted the inhabitants of the priory. The first De Lacy who discovered the place had prayed that it might never become wealthy, since the faith decreased in virtue whenever it increased its riches. Gerald takes occasion to inveigh against the desire for creature comforts that he saw was already inclining the monks to turn from the beauties of nature that surrounded them. Perhaps Gerald may have been a little prejudiced, since he himself lived remotely and poorly, as he says, close by in a little place called Landeu, which he dearly loved.

By the reign of Stephen, most of the monks felt no longer inclined (in their own words) to sing to the wolves, and they preferred to migrate to the daughter house at Gloucester. Only a prior and four canons remained, and it had no more than a shadowy existence until the Dissolution under Henry VIII.

Gerald insists that the name was properly Llan Nant Honddu, after the river that runs there. Of the great effort in building, from 1180 to 1200, not much remains. There is now among the ruins an inn, which was once the prior's own

Ruined Llanthony Abbey

lodging. The whole is in the late Norman style known as Transitional, having magnificent walls with tall and pointed doorways and windows; the gatehouse has been used in the 20th cent. as a barn. A small parish church close by is a contemporary of the priory. The ruins have a strange beauty, and they give a sense of strength and determination, unfortunately lacking in the monks, but reflecting the character of the hills and meadows around them, the things that Gerald so much loved. A century ago, as old prints show, much more remained.

The priory, now known as Llanthony Abbey, was bought in 1811 by Walter Savage Landor, the poet and friend of Browning and Swinburne. His early writings – which included his verses to Rose Aylmer, his first love – were done in Wales. But Landor's grace in writing was not matched by his temper, and his attempt to revivify the priory failed largely because he could not adjust himself to his neighbours, who combined to make life there impossible for him. In 1814 tenants, local authority, and county society together drove him in disgust to live abroad.

Some 4 m. higher up the valley is Capel-y-ffin, where Llanthony Monastery was built in 1869 by Father Ignatius (Joseph Leycester Lyne) for the Order of Anglican Benedictines. The building was the property of Eric Gill, the sculptor, and in 1935 was converted into a girls' school. The road to it from Llanthony is along a valley of solitary beauty.

Other places of similar interest in the near neighbourhood are Llantilio Pertholey, with a church apparently built by spontaneous inspiration in Decorated style; and Llanfihangel Crucorney, where stands a lovely Tudor mansion once magnificent with trees; and Alltyrynys, a farmhouse claiming to be the original seat of the Sitsilts, a Welsh name Gerald gives several times

as Sissul, and which became further Anglicized as Cecil. This was the family that attained high position through the Robert Cecil who became Lord Burleigh and Queen Elizabeth Tudor's most trusted adviser.

But Gerald de Barri contributes another tale to the interest of this part of the Vale of Ewyas. For, as he left Landeu and proceeded to Talgarth, he passed through the narrow wooded tract called Coed Grono (Wood of the Gronwy river). And he recalled how one Richard de Clare, Norman Lord of Cardiganshire, under guard from Brian de Wallingford, lord of the district, had come that way, and, when he entered the wood, had dismissed his companions and gone forward only with a minstrel and a singer, the one accompanying the other on the fiddle. Perhaps De Clare had been won too much by the beauty of the Vale of Ewyas; and he paid the penalty. The Welsh were waiting for him under the command of Iorwerth, brother of Morgan of Caerleon; they slew him and fell upon his escort, with great slaughter. The place where this happened is still called Coed Dial (Wood of Revenge). For Richard was the first of his line; he had arrived under the Norman Conqueror, and was set by William I to the task of invading Wales and destroying its inhabitants. He paid for this temerity, as Gerald relates, in the year 1136.

There are gentler memories to be found at Cwmyoy, lower down the Honddu river, where, under an old bridge that may have taken the pack-trains of the past, the river runs slow and deep and the trout sleep grey against the stones.

LLANTRISANT, *Glamorgan.* No other township in Glamorgan has so splendid a site. Llantrisant is perched in the saddle between two steep hills 8 m. NW. of Cardiff. The church and the ruined tower of the castle dominate the picturesque huddle of houses that cling to the hill-side. To the S., Llantrisant looks out across the valley of the Ely over the whole of the Vale of Glamorgan. Behind are the bare mountains guarding the coalfield. No wonder Richard de Clare, about 1246, deposed the last Welsh ruler, Hywel ap Meredith, and built a castle here. In 1326 the unhappy Edward II, driven westward by his own consort Isabella (the "She-Wolf of France") and his rebellious barons, was finally trapped near Llantrisant and brought to the castle on his way to disgraceful death at Berkeley in Gloucester ten months later. The little borough received a charter from Hugh le Despenser in 1346. Llantrisant men are known to have served under the Black Prince in his French Wars. Hence, according to local legend, the nickname "Black Army" given until quite recently to men of the town.

After all this, it is something of a disappointment to climb up the steep hill that leads to Llantrisant and enter the place itself. The houses are rather utilitarian, although there are indeed some narrow, twisting lanes that plunge alarmingly off the summit of the hill. The church has a splendid situation, but has been heavily restored. A pre-Norman slab marked with three crosses is set into the outside N. wall. Within, on the N. wall of the nave, is a worn effigy said to represent Cadwgan Fawr of the lordship of Miskin, who was a pillar of Welsh resistance to the encroachments of Gilbert de Clare. Near the door is a large and decorative hatchment, with the motto *Resurgam*. The only noticeable relic of the castle is a fragment of the drum-tower, which may be the Ravan Tower mentioned by Leland as being still in use as a prison in Tudor times. Even the Corporation of the ancient borough was dissolved in the municipal reforms of 1888, although the silver mace of the Portreeve has fortunately been preserved.

Nevertheless, Llantrisant re-entered history startlingly in 1884. Llantrisant had been selected as his home by the celebrated Dr Price, one of the great eccentrics of Victorian Wales. After a stormy youth as Chartist and exiled rebel, he returned to stalk through Glamorgan as a living protest against the vulgarization and industrialization of the country. Healer, sunworshipper, and despiser of convention, he dressed in trousers and coat of green and a fox-skin cap with tails hanging down behind. He felt himself to be the lineal descendant of the Druids, and therefore above the ordinary Anglo-Saxon laws of the land. Marriage he despised, and he set up house at Llantrisant with a young girl by whom, at the age of eighty-three, he had a child named Iesu Grist (Jesus Christ), who died in infancy. To the horror of the inhabitants, he proceeded to cremate his son in Caerlan Field, on the hill-top outside Llantrisant. A mob gathered. Price had to run for his life to his house, where the mother appeared at the door with a shot-gun at the ready and defied the infuriated crowd. Price was taken into custody and tried at Cardiff Assizes in 1884. He was acquitted by Mr Justice Stephens on the payment of one farthing costs. As a result, cremation became legal in Britain. The Doctor lived to be ninety-three, and was then himself cremated, before a huge crowd, on the same Caerlan Field where he had defied public opinion so dramatically. A tablet in honour of Dr Price has been set up at Llantrisant by the Cremation Society and the Federation of British Cremation Authorities.

To the E. of Llantrisant lies the 550-ft hill of the Caerau, with impressive Iron Age earthworks of a hill-fort showing elaborate triple lines of defence.

Llantrisant has been chosen as the site of the new Mint, and most of the lower ground surrounding the saddle-shaped hill of the ancient borough is being earmarked for extensive industrial and housing development. The whole character of this neighbourhood is bound to change very soon.

LLANTWIT MAJOR, *Glamorgan.* A little S. of Cowbridge, and close to the sea, is Llantwit, which must be called Major because there are two other villages of the same name, near Caerphilly in the same county. This is the Great Church of St Illtud, as the name was spelt by Christopher Saxton when, inquiring about the place, he wrote in 1610 that it stood on the foundations of some much older and greater town, for the signs of what were formerly streets and houses lay all around it. Roman coins had been discovered both here and not far away at St Donat's Castle, a fair habitation, then, of the ancient and notable family of the Stradlings, first conquerors of Glamorgan. He was much concerned to know whether this area might contain the site of the Roman city of Bovium, which the Antonine Itinerary set 15 m. away from Nidum, or Neath. He was inclined to think that Cowbridge might be the lost site. And, since he argued from the similarity of meaning between the Cow and the Bovium of the Latin, he reminded himself that the village of Boverton, set 1 m. from Llantwit, might afford an even better clue.

Llantwit is undoubtedly a very ancient place. On the coast, another 1 m. from Llantwit, is a camp on the cliff, perhaps from the Iron Age, and ditches of earthworks suggesting that at some early time the small river mouth was fortified by those who used the sea. This is possibly evidence of Roman work, for in 1888, at Caermead, just outside Llantwit, was found a very large example of the Roman villa settlement, which in later days would be called a manor, farming the countryside and organizing its labour and life in the way that so profoundly influenced the economy of the Middle Ages. Its mosaic floors had survived, and they showed it to be a considerable structure, built in the 2nd cent. A.D. and lasting into the 4th, the time of the first breakdown of Roman order under the attacks of what they called the Conspiracy of the Barbarians. It seems to have outlived this period of disaster, and to have continued its life, but in lessened form.

To this point upon the shore came Illtud, a man of Brittany, to found at the end of the 5th cent. what was to be a major centre of learning for the Church that built itself within the society left by Rome to be governed by its own native cities. He was, it is said, great-nephew to St Germanus of Auxerre; and the school he founded belonged to that interpretation of the faith which was accepted, before the 7th cent., by both Britain and Gaul. Dewi, who became the St David of Wales, Samson of Dol, and the Pol of Léon otherwise called Paulus Aurelianus, were thought to have received instruction here. Even the Gildas who, from Brittany in the mid-6th cent., wrote of sub-Roman Britain the one contemporary account that has survived for us, and made unsparing attack on the doctrines of Christianity received there, was one of Llantwit's scholars. He frowned on the Celtic Church in Britain for its study of the Classical sciences as expounded by Neo-Platonic philosophers who studied the heavens in relation to the mathematics of space and time. The ancient poems of Wales, preserved in the Book of Taliesin, can claim connection with Llantwit at the same period; for Taliesin, no less than Gildas, is traditionally entered on its roll.

From the time of Gildas darkness falls over the history of Britain. The ships of Cerdic attack the southern coasts, are beaten off, and come again. The villas of southern England defend themselves; the men with Roman names and the men with British ones stand together under Gildas's fierce summons to give way. One of them, Gerontius, defends Devon and Cornwall and the Bristol Channel, perhaps from what had been the Roman naval base in the Severn Sea. Bedford, Bristol, Chester fall in succession. Llantwit, like the rest of Wales, has as defence only the line of Powys, the double line of dykes from Dee to Severn that would not give way. Not until the Normans came does the School of St Illtud return into the record of history. The FitzHamon who took Glamorgan from the two rival Welsh rulers contesting it converted Llantwit into a monastic cell of Tewkesbury Abbey, and not only the kind of Christianity it taught, but also the stock of its inhabitants, seems to have been changed. A thorough colonization of the Cowbridge area took place, and the people are now English in feeling.

From the original foundation, no structure remains that you can see. What does stand, here or there invaded by picturesque but destructive ivy, is a double building, part belonging to the monastic, part to the parochial uses. The tower joins what are called the western and the eastern church, the old and the new. Parts of the old, originally Norman, are as they were first put up, the S. doorway in particular; but as a whole it was reconstructed in the 15th cent. The new is built in the style of the 13th cent. and stands much as it did. About the same time, on a site for long called the Palace, a medieval build-

ing was set up. Excavation proved it to be a very large building, scattered about with pottery and other domestic relics dating between 1200 and 1400; it may well have been what tradition said it was, the palace of a great Church dignitary.

But it is the old church that houses the uniquely interesting crosses and memorial stones dating from the dark days when the Celtic Church was besieged by the Saxon who had taken the Cross from St Augustine. In the new church the Middle Ages placed its own memorials of charming simplicity: the font, the carved rood-screen, and the Jesse niche in which is set the sculptured tree of the descent of Christ from the family of kings. But the old building protests the Celtic cross, now without its head, on which the name of Illtud is carved. If not dating from the 5th or 6th cents. in which he lived, it is certainly a memorial made for him at least as early as the 8th. Beside it is another, smaller cross, still headed with the quartered circle that gave the Christian faith the symbol of the four points of time and space that, for the Celtic Church, proved the mathematics of Creation. It is not the memorial of a saint, but of a king who is named in the chronicles of the Book of Llandaff: Hywel son of Rhys – or, as lettered here, Houelt whose father was Res. The delicate tracery of the design is one fit for a ruler and protector of his people. He lived about 890. Llantwit Major, or Llanilltud Fawr, seems to have been a burying-place for the great in those days. There is a 13th-cent. coffin nearby, on which, among knotted loops that show the undying influence of the Celtic sense of ornament, the face of a young woman looks up at those who pass by with a plea that she be not trodden on. Illtud is not alone in his memorial, for the Samson of Dol whom Gerald de Barri singles out as a distinguished Bishop of St David's has close at hand his own cross of A.D. 800. Some 700 years later, one Matthew Voss was buried in the church, having died at the age of 129, and so deserving some relative form of sanctity.

The town itself is a monument to its distinguished history. The Town Hall of the 15th cent., sometimes called the Church Loft, has two storeys and a pre-Reformation bell-turret, inscribed with the plea that Illtud might always pray for the place. A large tithe barn remains, and on the W. side of the church a round dovecote and the old monastery gateway. The Tudor house, whitewashed and gabled, is a pleasant example of its period, and is called in recollection of its distinction the Ty Mawr (Great House).

From the Llantwit shore, abandoned and barriered with rocks, the shores defended by Gerontius with his legendary fleet stand clear from Devon and Cornwall. Around them were the seas that Samson and Illtud crossed, seas that joined Britain and Brittany in one faith, and of which in the 5th cent. Riothamus – the man with the best claim to be the historical origin of Arthur – tried to make a military bridge, so that his sturdily undisciplined troops might yet save the Empire of the West. Illtud and Riothamus laid the foundations on which the most powerful influence in medieval times worked for the ideas of chivalry and justice, with real effect upon the growth of civilized values. Gildas in his own way sought the same things. Without disrespect to St David's, Llantwit may be reckoned as the most important point from which the West revived its learning and its beliefs.

Aerodromes now dominate the neighbourhood, from Llantwit to Cardiff.

LLANUWCHLLYN, *Merioneth*. The Church above the Lake is 1 m. SW. of Bala Lake. The village is of ancient foundation, for between it and the lake is Caer Gai, a 17th-cent. manor house built inside the ditches of a Roman fort; legend has associated it with Sir Kay, one of Arthur's noblest knights. The roads that led to the fort have not yet been traced; so far, it must stand isolated at an angle from Pennal to the W. and Caersws to the E. Meanwhile, we may suppose that the legionaries, whatever their sterner work, found time to angle for the gwyniad, the whitefish member of the salmon tribe that is found only in Bala Lake, and to follow the Lliw, the Dyfrdwy (Dee), and the Twrch for the trout that are plentiful in the streams. The Twrch valley is outstandingly beautiful, with its view of the eastern flank of the Arans; and the Lliw, a short way along its course, takes you to the Carn Dochan and its gold-mine that the legionaries must have been most concerned with, and the heaped structure of stones called a Castle. You must walk from the Roman fort if you wish to take the mountain footpath to the Llyn Arennigfawr. Its gloomy loveliness is unique, and the crags of Arennig rise majestically; but the lake has not much fish, unlike its neighbour, the Arennig-fach. The graveyard of the church commemorates with its wrought-iron gate Sir Owen M. Edwards, the famous Welsh educationalist of the early 20th cent.

In the neighbourhood, Llanfor is worth a visit for the ancient church (*see* Bala). At Llanycil, the original parish church of Bala holds in its graveyard the tomb of Thomas Charles, one of the founders, at the end of the 18th cent., of Calvinism in Wales. Inside the church appear the words addressed to the memory of the pastor, Evan Lloyd, poet and rebel. Curate of Llanymawddwy, he set himself against sin among the people whom Saxton in the 17th cent. had described as wanton beyond all others in Wales. His zeal made him suspect of Methodism, and Church authority could find no other living for him. He did indeed sink into Methodist ways but, we are assured, his heart was always with the Church.

LLANWNDA, *Pembrokeshire*. Daniel Paterson's *Direct and Principal Cross Roads*, published in 1811 for masters of stage-coach services and their passengers, pauses on the coast of Pembrokeshire. "Fiscard," it says, having no truck with those who would call it Fishguard: "Near this place, 1200 Frenchmen landed in 1797 under a General Tate; who shortly after surrendered to Lord Cawdor at the head of the yeomanry and peasants, without firing a shot."

This note was made barely a dozen years after the event. The story of the French landing at Carreg Wastad, just N. of Llanwnda, is famous (*see* p. 45). It gives the impression that France expected little of the landing except to be rid of persons who were something of a burden; and that the galley-regiment itself was looking for better accommodation than it had at home. There were, however, a good many Irish among the invaders. Little damage was done, except that the Irish-American leader of the French commandeered a dinner laid for a neighbouring landowner; and the only shot fired went through a grandfather clock in the same house, because it chose an unfortunate moment to strike. Even the communion plate at Llanwnda church, which the French seized, was returned unharmed. But the sequel at Llanwnda was more serious.

The Nonconformist tradition in Wales was still, at the end of the 18th cent., as suspect as it had been in the 17th; religious dissent was thought capable of becoming political dissent. Since the Restoration, Pembrokeshire, where the castle at Pembroke had been the only one in all Wales to declare at once for the King, was particularly under suspicion. It was even rumoured that in the Risings of 1715 and 1745 the Pretenders to the throne of Britain, Old and Young, had had active sympathizers there; the Young Pretender was even supposed to have made his escape from Scotland by finding refuge in Cardiganshire, just to the N. of Pembroke. And a curious society, calling itself the Sea Serjeants and prevalent among the gentry of Wales, was suspected of revolutionary and anti-Hanoverian sympathies. With this in mind, after the surrender of Tate's forces, the authorities arrested two men in Llanwnda, curiously enough named Thomas William and William Thomas, for fraternizing with the enemy; two others, Thomas John of Little Newcastle and Samuel Griffith of Pointz (or Punch) Castle, were sent for trial. Both were prominent Nonconformists in the district. They were imprisoned in Haverfordwest on charges of having incited the enemy not to surrender, and betrayed the fact that only women were paraded against them. But both were discharged in due course, the only evidence against them coming from French prisoners.

There is a monument to the occasion on the cliffs at Carreg Wastad, where they drop to a sea that besieges them more effectively than the French fleet. From the lonely but flowered cove of the hills that stand at the entrance to Fishguard Bay, a magnificent view can be had. But Llanwnda church itself, old and isolated, recalls days long before 1797. One of its vicars was Gerald de Barri, the Welshman of the 12th cent. who deeply loved his birthplace in Pembrokeshire, loved his little home at Landeu even more, and loved all Wales both well and wisely. Beyond Llanwnda, along the hill-tops are the stone circles and hut dwellings of people who, legendary even in his day, had seen the ships that brought back gold from Ireland and carried it again to the Mediterranean, that transported the stones of Preseli to Stonehenge, and were the merchant fleets of the Age of Bronze.

In the near area, one of the most interesting of these remains is the settlement known as Gaer, or Garn, Fawr on the topmost point of hills by Strumble Head overwatching Cardigan Bay and the promontory of St David. A modern lighthouse stands offshore; but some may find the house of Sealyham, between Fishguard and Haverford-west, of even greater interest. It was there that the breed of Sealyham terriers was first intro-duced. Today these small and wiry dogs are recognized as one of the four kinds distinctively Welsh, the others being the corgi, or cattle-dog, whose short legs and brown, underslung body were developed to avoid the back-kick of resent-ful cows; the Welsh terrier, a smaller and smoother variant of the Airedale type, a black-and-tan; and the Welsh foxhound, whose distin-guished ancestry comes from the Middle Ages, when the strains used at St Hubert's Monastery in Champagne, by the Counts of Brittany and the Kaids of Barbary, were mingled. The sheep-collie, though found everywhere in Wales, is of a sort common in Scotland and England and has the same hardihood and intelligence. The lurcher, faithfully following the gypsy caravan with his muzzle close to the bucket slung behind it in which he is trained to put such game or poultry as he may find by the roadside, is an altogether international type.

It is at Narberth, however, 10 m. due E. of Haverford, that such considerations come most to mind. It is not its old castle of squared Conquest type, with its impressive main gateway, that stirs one's thoughts, but the older recollections in-spired by the first pages of the *Mabinogion*. For that late medieval version of far more ancient philosophies makes Narberth the chief seat of Pwyll, Prince of Dyfed, Lord of Days, who met while hunting there the hounds of the Under-world cried to the hunt by Arawn of the Silver Tongue, Lord of Hades and of Night. Hounds they were such as man did not know, for their hair was of brilliant white, and their ears were red; and, as the whiteness of their bodies shone, so did the redness of their ears. Somewhere below the Preseli hills to the N., that Under-world may yet be found, or imagined, with its beautiful buildings and its youths and maidens in rich apparel of red, green, and yellow.

LLANWRIN, *Montgomeryshire*. This small place stands 2½ m. from Ffridd Gate to the E., following the Dovey river by the old coach-road. Llanuoring is the name the scrolled coaching maps give it in the script of 150 years ago. Once a principal place, it is now mainly a fine church with a fine rectory set close beside it against the wooded hill. The church is of the style called Early English, with ancient stained glass and a very fine rood-screen. The rectory has a mainly

18th-cent. appearance. The farms on the road leading to it are some of the best in the area, and the stream-fall behind the village leads to the tops about Cae Adda.

LLANWRTYD WELLS, *Breconshire*. On the road between Builth Wells and Llandovery, at the point where the Irfon river runs due S. from its source in the wide uplands of the Bryn Garw (Stag Hill) and the Drum yr Eira (Snow Ridge), past old Llanwrtyd with its mill, to meet the Cledan stream, the Wells of Llanwrtyd made one of the most beautiful watering-places in Wales. As a healing spring of the modern kind, it had been active since 1732, when the Vicar of Llangamarch, Theophilus Evans, dis-covered the properties of its water by observing (people say) the remarkable agility of frogs about a spring in the valley. Llanwrtyd has strong sulphur, chalybeate, and saline springs from the igneous rocks around it, and hotels with every other convenience once added pump-rooms to the number, but these are no longer in opera-tion. Fishing and boating are available on the Abernant lake, and there is an excellent golf course.

Old Llanwrtyd, at the foot of Garn Dwad (1,500 ft), has an outstandingly good viewpoint where the edges of the Great Desert of Wales, the rolling moors that stretch unbroken to Rhayader and Elan and the Ystwyth valley, stand against the sky, and the walls of the Irfon glen contract about Abergwesyn. This has a church of exceptional interest and an ancient inn. It is still famous, but now attracts anglers, not the men who crowded there in earlier days, the drovers who came with cattle from over the hills and passed through Llanwrtyd on the way to places like Llandegla and the open ridgeways of Berkshire and Hampshire. It is a curious illustra-tion of the continuity of history that the paths across the moorlands, laid in many cases by Roman legionaries supervising the transport of ores, created such places as Abergwesyn, and that the drovers, following where they had led, largely founded the modern banking system, by use of the paper-token credits passed between them as they went about their traffic.

LLANYBYDDER, *Carmarthenshire*, is a small but flourishing market town on the River Teifi 4 m. SW. of Lampeter. The river here is the boundary between Carmarthenshire and Cardi-ganshire. Most of Llanybydder is in Carmarthen-shire. The houses are spread out along the main roads, with the Cross Hands Inn and its pointed arched windows prominent at the cross. The heart of Llanybydder remains lower down near the church and the Teifi bridge. The church is a heavily restored building with a fine tower. Next to the churchyard is the Mart, Llanybydder's pride. This is one of the few places left in Britain that hold a monthly horse fair on a grand scale. The time to visit Llanybydder is the last Thursday in the month. Dealers from all over the country pack the bar of the Black Lion. The horses are mainly hunters and ponies, but there is also a demand for other breeds, surprising in this age of the motor-car. Just S. of the town, on a low hill, is the earthwork of Pen-y-gaer.

At Pencarreg, 1 m. to the N., the river takes a wide bend, leaving a small lake at the foot of the wooded hill-side.

The prominent cross at the roadside, on a low bridge 1 m. outside the town towards Llandysul records nothing more important than the satisfaction of the parishes of Llanybydder and Llanllwni, together with that of the Turnpike Trust, at the decision of the County Surveyor to pass the structure as a county bridge in 1822. Llanllwni is the next parish downstream from Llanybydder. It has a bridge across the river and a 13th-cent. church, well restored in the 1930s.

Mynydd Llanybydder, the moorland to the S. of the town, reaches a height of 1,340 ft. It has been extensively planted by the Forestry Commission. A lonely road leads across it southwards to Llansawel in the Cothi valley.

LLANYMYNECH, *Montgomeryshire/Shropshire*, is a genuinely Welsh town in all its aspects, yet the boundary between Montgomeryshire and Shropshire runs through its main, one might say its only, street. Its houses and inn have a shapeliness standing over from the early 19th cent. It is on the River Vyrnwy, not far from its junction with the Severn, and also on the railway link with Llanfyllin; it stands in an arm of a wide valley on to which tall hill-bluffs thrust themselves. Near at hand are relics of the frustrated Potteries and North Wales Railway which failed for want of subscribers.

But Llanymynech is of great interest historically, for a lost route of Roman times lies in its neighbourhood.

When Rome first set foot in Britain, under the Emperor Claudius, the period from A.D. 75 to 140 saw the establishment of Deva (Chester) – the Caerleon of the N. upon the Dee – and Isca, still called Caerleon, in the S. upon the Usk, holding between them the essential strategic points that have shaped the history of Wales. Segontium (Caernarfon), Canovium (Conway), and Moridunum (Carmarthen) made major points in the control of the W. Between these points various stations studded the routes that pushed into the mountains, aimed particularly at the exploitation of mineral resources. One of these was called Mediolanum; and its site is still a mystery. There was a Roman station at Caersws, with which Mediolanum has been tentatively identified. But the Castle Lyons at Holt in Cheshire, a supply and production point both for the Caerleon at Chester (whose name it seems to have shared in the native tongue, though its Roman name was Bovium), and for the Viroconium now known as Wroxeter, has been firmly identified and excavated; and the recorded distances between point and point made by the Antonine Itinerary do not fit with Caersws as the lost Roman site of the 3rd cent. A.D.

Meifod near Llanfyllin, Llanfyllin itself, and Llanymynech have at various times been suggested. This adds interest to the persistent local report that, a few years ago, a farmer ploughing a field left for generations untilled turned up the foundations of a fort of Roman construction – then covered it again, thinking the land should have a better use than to amuse archaeologists.

Evidence of even earlier economic development has been discovered in old workings in a hill close by, a mining operation that, perhaps in the Bronze Age, was abandoned, leaving in the depths of the tunnelling a pair of arm-bracelets.

LLANYNYS, *Denbighshire*. About 5½ m. SE. of Denbigh, this small village is distinguished by a striking church. Its foundation is presumed to have been during the period of missionary activity by the Celtic Church, in the 5th or 6th cent. Its outer appearance seems to substantiate this, though it certainly confesses later development in style. It is double-naved; it has a bell-gable, also double, and the bell is worked by wheels. It was once recognized as a principal centre of Church administration, and therefore had the name of Llanfor (Great Church). Set at the junction of the Clywedog and the Clwyd rivers, it is liable to be flooded in the rainy seasons; this added to it the name of Llan Ynys (Island Church). Medieval field-systems, typified by baulks between the sections of the communal land, can still be seen nearby. It was damaged by the troops of Edward I, but was sufficiently restored to be visited by Edward Lhuyd, the Welsh antiquary (not to be confused with the Humphrey Lhuyd who was a native of Denbigh close by), shortly after the Restoration.

The walls may date from about 1220; the main door, carved with Tudor roses, bears the date 1554 and a sanctuary ring. The furnishings are mainly of the 17th cent., and include the pulpit, built in 1633. The original pillars of the nave, made of stone, were replaced by wooded columns in 1768; only the bases of the earlier pillars now remain, except one, which stands complete.

The church is dedicated to St Saeran, whose effigy is carved on a memorial stone. It was moved inside for shelter in 1961.

LLANYSTUMDWY, *Caernarfonshire*. The name of this delightful village means "Church at the Bend of the River", it is rather over 1 m. from Criccieth to the W. The river is the Dwyfor (Great Water), which reaches the village from the N. through a steep and heavily wooded ravine. There is a bridge carrying the main road over the river, and from it the track can be taken to where, high over the tumbling stream, stands a memorial deliberately shaped like a cairn. It is a simple structure, and commemorates Earl Lloyd George of Dwyfor, who is buried in that place. As you come from Criccieth, and before you reach the bridge, you pass an inn called the Feathers. Opposite is a pair of cottages, the further one being that in which Lloyd George lived as a child. Against it is a wooden lean-to

The early home of Lloyd George at Llanystumdwy

G. Douglas Bolton

building, in which the uncle who brought him up, Richard Lloyd, carried on his business as shoemaker.

The young Lloyd George and his brother both practised as solicitors, David Lloyd George in Manchester. He entered politics, and was elected M.P. for Caernarfon Boroughs in 1890. His political outlook was influenced first and most strongly by the Welsh nationalism that was then blossoming under the guidance of such men as Tom Ellis and Owen M. Edwards. Together with this, he had a keen sense of the need for social justice, a reaction against the policies that in the 19th cent. had increased the English and Anglicizing preponderance of landlordism and industrial ownership begun in the 18th cent. His most momentous effect on British politics came when he was Chancellor of the Exchequer under the Asquith Liberal administration; his Budget introduced the broad social reforms that later grew into the concept of a Welfare State. The opposition to these proposals from the House of Lords precipitated the General Election of 1911, and the result was a fundamental change in the English Constitution. For, by the Parliament Act of 1911, the power of the Lords to act at least as an equal partner with the Commons in the control of legislation was abolished. Since then the very existence of the House of Lords has been called in question, and the House of Commons has become in effect the sole authority. It was a suspended revolution whose final effects are still to come.

Lloyd George's further activities in social reform were interrupted by the First World War, during which he emerged as the national leader for victory, displacing his former Prime Minister, Herbert Asquith, by way of a palace revolution. His energy was largely responsible for the outcome of the War. But, although the Government under his leadership won the General Election afterwards, he could not control the period of peace. The Treaty of Versailles, with which the constitution of the League of Nations was closely bound, raised problems that led to the Second World War and still remain unsettled.

The economic dislocation, and reduction in the industrial supremacy of Britain, that followed the War were matters too complex for him to resolve; in any event, his leaning towards social reform alarmed traditional minds yet did not satisfy the new Marxist views on the evils of society and how they should be cured. It was, however, his conclusion of a treaty with the Irish Free State in 1921 that was his downfall. Irish nationalism had risen during the resistance to English domination, and attempts to suppress the revolution by irregular forces (Black and Tans) had failed. An Irishman and a Welshman, Arthur Griffith and Lloyd George, arrived at the settlement between England and Eire that set up the Irish Free State, as it was in the beginning. The next General Election, in 1922, defeated Lloyd George, and, although his incursions into politics remained lively and forceful, he never again attained power and was never able to reunite the Liberal Party he had led under Asquith. As an orator, he was greatly distinguished; as an author, he wrote among other works his war memoirs, which, like those of his close associate during the First World War, Winston Churchill, will always be a source for future histories of the most dramatic and fatal period in European affairs since the fall of Rome.

He never lost his facility in Welsh, and during the War his personal staff was composed of Welsh-speaking Welsh people.

LLAWHADEN, *Pembrokeshire.* A little N. of Canaston Bridge, and on the bank of the Eastern Cleddau, is a castle that reflects the history of the Church of St David's in its own way. For the medieval bishop was a fighting man, even though he used not the sword, but the spiked and weighted ball slung from a chain and called a "morning star"; this excused him, at least technically, from the charge of letting blood. Llawhaden Castle was for the use of the Bishops of St David's, but presumably as a place of refuge from sea attack. The exposed position of Pembrokeshire in the wide waters around it not only caused the sack of the first buildings there, but

Top: *The bridge over the Afon Dwyryd, Maentwrog*   G. Douglas Bolton
Bottom: *The Menai Straits, with the suspension bridge and the Snowdon range*   Peter Baker

made such an inland point of security advisable. The slope to the Castle is steep, and further protection is given by a moat. The ruins date from just after 1250, and rise against the empty spaces of the land that lifts towards Foel Cwmcerwyn with the studied symmetry of that great age of castle-building. The gate towers are cylindrical and joined by an arch-span, backed by the southern curtain wall with its own two towers. Its chapel was made in 1510, but still has the touch of the earlier century upon it. The church of the village was rebuilt in the 1380s, but retains the basic structure of the earlier chancel and tower. The bridge over the Cleddau, which lies between the two, the Castle and the church, is itself interesting and ancient.

LLAWRYGLYN, *Montgomeryshire.* The name means Valley Floor; and it seems to have a special significance. The place is now no more than an area of valley-head 4 m. from Trefeglwys to the W., where the Trawsnant and the Trannon come down from the moors underlying Staylittle and Dylife to work their way into the Severn valley at Caersws. Llawryglyn can be reached by car on the mountain road that runs towards the remarkable rock-fall and torrents of Pennant. But it is the walker who will get the greatest interest, by taking the grassy drove-tracks that lead from Llawryglyn over the Trannon moor.

The moor is largely a level plateau with broadly separated points rising from it to about 1,500 ft. To the W., the height of Foel Fadian rises to mark the shoulder of the Plynlimon escarpment. The drove-tracks are bold and discernible through the bogland, for they have been used for centuries. One of them moves towards Carno almost directly N., and the other to Pennant, finding a way over the crags to drop into its valley.

Along the route, you go past milestones of the 19th cent., for part of these tracks was used as a coach-route about Dylife, and the still solid causeway lifts steadily above the peats and heathers. But away from this road, old enough in itself, the ancient cairn of Twr Gwyn (White Tower), stands in the centre of the moor to remind us that it was a highway for traffic long before coaches were invented.

Llawryglyn, in fact, is at the end of the Roman road that goes into the little valley from Caersws. Its object was to reach the lead-mines, worked over many centuries, that pit the upland between Dylife and Hyddgen, and to bring the product back to Caersws for handling into pigs and stamping with the sign of the administering Legion. Standing stones mark this Roman road into Llawryglyn, but though Romans used them, we do not know the Romans set them there. The Empire was built on a succession of earlier cultures, and its lines of communication were laid down long before them.

The Trannon moor is perhaps the most important area in the story of those dark ages in British history. Only a few miles wide, it connects the Dovey valley, and its estuary opening on the Irish

Sea, with the Severn valley opening into the Bristol Channel, which has its entrance-gate at Llawryglyn. Strategically and economically, the Dovey and the Severn have affected the shaping not only of Wales but of Britain as a whole. At Darowen, a little beyond the Pennant valley, the line of pointer-stones begins again. Of the two that hold between them Darowen and its church, the northern one is pre-Roman. Similar pointer-stones run along the Dovey valley westwards past Penegoes to Machynlleth and lie in the folds of hills reaching to Hengwm.

Sir Cyril Fox, in his *Life and Death in the Bronze Age,* has pointed out that the brilliant Wessex Culture that built Stonehenge in its surviving form, and traded widely with the Mediterranean, Ireland, and the Baltic, sent its seagoing craft over the Irish Sea to bring back gold. The routes they used to return to whatever social centre they possessed have been traced first to the mouth of the Dee and so southwards along the Severn, and from the Pembroke coast to the area of Bristol and Salisbury Plain. Ancient cultures, skilled in navigation, originating in the Mediterranean, were inclined to think of the Irish Sea as an extension of the Biscay waters, using Brittany and Cornwall as landmarks on the way. The Dovey, which is the deepest valley-entrance into the interior and the one that offers the easiest transit to the head of Severn, is something they would not overlook. With river-portage at least as far as what is now Glandyfi, the land-way could be followed to Tal-y-Wern by Darowen, over which the S. stone stands, and Pennant and the Trannon moor open the short trail to the Severn at Caersws.

Apart from the natural beauty of the area, and its wide views over the central peatland of Wales and the sharp ranges of the North, it is a place where you can feel the feet of a hundred generations walking beside you.

An equally interesting road leads S. towards Llanidloes and Llangurig.

LLYFNANT VALLEY, *Cardiganshire/Montgomeryshire.* The Afon Llyfnant, falling from its source in the Plynlimon uplands, marks the boundary between Montgomeryshire and Cardiganshire. At its juncture with streams at Glasbwll, it makes a determined thrust due W. through a steep, narrow gorge until its outfall at Pontlyfnant reaches a wide and grassy flat where the Dovey winds broadly to the sea. To follow its course over smooth grey boulders under leaning oaks, and see nothing but hill-farms rare on the mountain-sides, is to find its former importance as a highway of commerce quite incredible. But it was once the most direct way from the busy ports and ship-making yards at Gareg, with subsidiaries at Derwenlas and Eglwys-fach, to Machynlleth. Timber, bark, hides, and wool from the "pandys" by the streams went one way for export, and coal and culm came the other. In even earlier times, the lead-mines found their transport routes down to Glasbwll from the hills, and so to the Dovey

Plate 13   Tintern Abbey (see p. 333)   *Picturepoint*

yards, the Welsh Potosi mines that George Borrow found over Cwm Rhaeadr from Glasbwll 100 years ago was the successor to ventures the Romans and many generations after them had made.

Now the Llyfnant Valley is an accredited beauty-spot, and new motor roads high along its northern side lead above the river to the timbered woodlands about Garthgwynion and the ancient house of Caersaer over the Llyfnant pool. Walkers may be recommended to take the southern track, though half way along it the river should be crossed to reach the modern road and follow the green courses that go to the levels of the Cwm Rhaeadr and the sight of the steep falls.

LOUGHOR, *Glamorgan,* in Welsh Llwchwr, lies 7 m. NW. of Swansea on the banks of the Loughor river where it turns and widens out into the Burry estuary. The countryside around is somewhat industrial, but the demolition of the old steel-works at Bynea across the water has opened up the view northwards where the Loughor winds among the marshes, with green hills beyond. The Loughor river forms the boundary between Glamorgan and Carmarthenshire, and Loughor town is the lowest point near the sea where the river can be bridged. It thus became a Roman station on the road to Moridunum (Carmarthen). There are few remains of the Roman Leucarum, and the actual outline of the fortifications is in dispute; but pottery, coins, and traces of a bath-house were revealed when the railway was being constructed immediately S. of the castle ridge. The fort, however, may well have stood on the higher ground. A Roman altar with Ogham markings stood in the rectory gardens; a cast of it is now in the National Museum of Wales. The Normans built a small castle at Loughor to command the river-crossing. It was destroyed in 1115 by the Welsh prince Gruffydd ap Rhys. The present few remains stand on the mound to the left of the busy main road that carries the traffic down to the wide bridge over the Loughor. They consist of some walls and a broken tower at present being restored under the Ministry of Public Building and Works. The church stands on a second mound between the castle tower and the river; a lane lined with old cottages runs in between. The church is dedicated to St Michael and is in the Early Perpendicular style, rather heavily restored. The house known as the Sanctuary was formerly part of the property of the Knights of St John.

MACHYNLLETH, *Montgomeryshire.* This fascinating market town stands inland, on the S. side of the Afon Dyfi (Dovey), some 10 m. from Aberdovey and 18 m. from Aberystwyth. Although the town itself has not many more than 2,000 inhabitants, its part in Welsh history has been considerable.

It was once thought to have been founded as a Roman military station, Maglona. But the late Prof. Fleure, digging at a site on the hill Pen-yr-Allt just above the town, discovered an Iron Age "Celtic" encampment, and undoubtedly from very early times the position occupied by Machynlleth was of first importance. The Dovey estuary makes a deep bite into the coastline of Wales from the Irish Sea, and the river-valley carries far into the run of hills at the centre of Wales, offering the shortest and easiest approach to the valleys of the Dee and Severn and the English Midlands. The Roman administration must have realized the significance of the area, since its roads have been traced leading to Machynlleth from the N. through Corris and Esgairgeiliog and through Tal-y-bont and Taliesin from the S. A series of steps, now much reinforced with concrete but still largely hewn from a slope of rock, can be seen at the rear of the Plas Machynlleth on the Aberystwyth road; they are called the Roman Steps. The rock-hewn portion does not in fact date from before the 1870s, having been made for travel by horse into Machynlleth from the house near Glasbwll now known as Garthowen. All the same, the rock-slope itself probably belongs to a very old track leading to the town along what is now a pathway through the Plas parkland; it was originally the highway into Machynlleth, and was incorporated in the park by its owner about 1840. The hill from which the Roman Steps descend is called Wylfa (Watch-Place), and it may well have been connected with a military installation as far back as the Romans.

A later association may be with the Roman-British commander Maglocunos, who by tradition was proclaimed leader of the Cymric forces rallied to oppose the Anglo-Saxon attack on Britain from the South and East in the middle of the 6th cent. He is known in Welsh legend as Maelgwn. His installation was carried out on the sands of the Dovey estuary. Whether there is really a connection between the names Maglocunos and Machynlleth, we can only guess. The accepted derivation is from "maen" (stone-block, particularly a pointer-stone) and "cynlleth" (wetness, in this case probably a river).

Later still, Machynlleth was chosen by Owain Glyndwr to be the capital of the Wales he had succeeded in freeing for some years from the rule of Henry IV. Dolgellau, Harlech, and Machynlleth were made in succession the place of assembly for his parliaments; but it was at Machynlleth – in 1404, when he had reached the pinnacle of his success – that he was proclaimed King of Wales. This sealed the traditional importance of the town as the centre of a distinctive Welsh culture.

His Parliament House, much extended and restored, now stands in the centre of Maen Gwyn Street immediately opposite the ornamented park gates of the Plas. The original structure is confined to the low and narrow run of rooms forming the Library. In the 19th cent. it played its part in the dominant economy of Machynlleth as a storehouse and carding-room for wool. The present building is known as the Institute, founded not only as a monument to

G. *Douglas Bolton*

The Clock Tower, Machynlleth

the memory of Owain Glyndwr but also to serve the town as municipal offices and a place of rest and culture – the local sense of humour at once renamed it the Restitute. The Library contains mural paintings by Murray Urquhart, commemorating Glyndwr's achievements at the siege of Caernarfon Castle and the battle on Mynydd Hyddgant, associated with the Plynlimon moorland around Hyddgen. On the Council Room floor, and set into the corridor walls, are slate slabs that until fairly recently could be found in Machynlleth streets, particularly the street rising from the railway station to the Clock Tower and called Doll (or Toll) Street, on which are listed the tolls for the passage of sheep and cattle into the town. This system of tax-extortion was, however, tempered with mercy; for an early 19th-cent. document points out that "Sheep going to water are exempt from toll unless they pass more than two miles on the turnpike road". As the centre for the wide range of upland sheepfarms covering the foothills of the Plynlimon moor, Machynlleth streets are still often filled with flocks from the surrounding valleys. Stock-sales and grading take place regularly, though at times some of this activity moves to Cemaes. But the grounds of the Plas remain unrivalled for their sheep-dog trials, at which the standard of performance is invariably high both for dogs and men.

Apart from the Toll in Doll Street, another toll-house until recently stood at the end of Maen Gwyn Street, where the road to Mallwyd and the mountain road to Dylife meet it. It has now been demolished; but at least one of its companions, though somewhat restored, remains standing.

Machynlleth sprang from a combination of three hamlets, Pen-yr-Allt, Pentre Rhedyn (Fern Village), and Maen Gwyn; and the town grew steadily as a vital focus for the traffic of the day. The crags and morasses of the area northwards from the Dovey valley allow passage, N. to S., only through the defiles from Corris and Dolgellau, and along the narrow coastal strip following the line of Cardigan Bay; and, E. to W., along the river-line. This geographical problem is still only gradually being overcome; earlier centuries concentrated on the coach-roads clinging to the banks of the "Douey Fluvius" and converging mainly on Machynlleth. As a result, in the middle of the 19th cent., the town had no fewer than twenty-four thriving inns.

Of these not many are left. The 18th-cent. White Lion and Wynnstay Arms (originally the Herbert Arms) largely keep their traditional character. They stand about the road-junction in the heart of the town now marked by the Clock Tower. Another inn enjoys a wholly ghostly existence; although it was demolished to make way for a side road out of Maen Gwyn Street, the space it once occupied is still affectionately known as the Cross Pipes. The Red Lion, facing the Wynnstay Arms, is a smaller and perhaps even older hostelry; the Skinner's Arms is another such. The glory did not depart until the coming of the Cambrian Railway, but, with the decline of the railway system as a whole, the glory shows signs of returning.

The three original villages had their common centre at the Market Cross, replaced in 1873 by the Clock Tower, commemorating the family of the Marquesses of Londonderry, who had become owners of the Plas. A photograph of the

Market Cross on its original site can be seen in the Owen Glyndwr Institute. This building is celebrated in literature through the visit of George Borrow, who, about 1860, entered it to observe various trials before the magistrates, mainly of local townsfolk for the heinous crimes of poaching salmon from the Dovey waters. Whatever his views on the legal points involved, Borrow had no great opinion either of the offenders or of the keepers who gave evidence against them. It must be admitted that this matter of poaching is another age-old tradition of which Machynlleth is proud. The Dovey is noted for its salmon; in the 1920s the war between private owners of fishing rights and the town, a constant series of night battles between gangs and wardens, culminated in open riot by day. The municipality has now acquired control of rights in fishing the waters and issues licences for the appropriate fee. Whether under these changed conditions poaching has been given up is a delicate question. Besides salmon, the rivers and streams in the immediate area provide excellent trout.

At the upper end of Maen Gwyn Street stands a genuine survival of Machynlleth's Jacobean prosperity, a typical early 17th-cent. building that gives the effect of half-timbering although the front is worked in local slate. It appears to be inscribed "1628 OWEN PVQH IO VXOY". The lettering really means that the house was the property of one Owen Pugh and his wife (UXOR); that is, of a Machynlleth notable who, it seems, acquired the property through his wife. If permission is obtained, a visitor may be shown, inside the house, a striking example of the family tree, worked in plaster over the chimney-breast as a many-branched apple tree with the names in line of descent painted on each branch.

A little further into the town, now set against a house wall, is the ancient monument from which the street takes its name: the Maen Gwyn itself. It is in two fragments, but its first shape as a single direction-stone is clear. As such, it belongs to the remotest history of the Dovey valley. Its companions can be traced on the bank of the Dulas at Penegoes; at the road-junction at Abergwydol, lying beyond Penegoes; and, shattered, along several remote lanes winding through the Plynlimon foothills. Such early signposts of a pre-Christian and pre-Roman society were often deliberately broken as pagan symbols. Most of such destructive efforts, however, were made in the reforming days of Henry VIII and the even fiercer period of Cromwell. The Second Civil War, as it is called, which followed the execution of Charles I in 1649, took place mainly in Wales; after the Protectorate had succeeded in pacifying the country, it was heavily garrisoned, and much of its memoried past enshrined in monuments and language was suppressed. The name Staylittle, found as small villages here and there in the district, is said to mark the establishment of such temporary garrison outposts. In Machynlleth itself, the names of side streets, such as Garsiwn (Garrison) and Barracks, belong to this period.

Maen Gwyn has a remarkable line of houses from the 17th, 18th, and early 19th cents., outstanding in a country that has not in the past been greatly concerned with town architecture, but has preferred to concentrate on village and farm. Several of the houses admittedly need preservation; but the street is a living whole.

Threatened by floods that still at times fill the Dovey valley from side to side, Machynlleth took the precaution of building, particularly against the low-lying fields now occupied by the modern school, a series of high slate-pile walls intersecting each other at right angles. Once very evident, they are now largely dismantled, but one at least can still be seen running alongside the road as it passes below the railway bridge by the station.

A little below the site of the Clock Tower, at the corner of a steeply dropping line of cottages, stands Royal House. Its street-front in later years was converted into a shop; but it is a house of late medieval construction with rooms and fireplaces and narrow windows typical of its period. Tradition says that it was the resting-place of Henry Tudor on his way to Bosworth Field and the winning of the Crown of Britain as Henry VII of England; it is respected as commemorating the achievement of an ambition that inspired Owain Glyndwr and the Princes of Powys long before him. It may also have associations with the Royalist cause during the Second Civil War, since the royal visitor is alternatively taken to be Charles I. A persistent legend insists that a tunnel runs from beneath it, under the Dovey itself, to emerge as far away as Pennal, also the site of a Roman military station.

Machynlleth Plas is now the property of the town and houses its offices. It was given to the town by the late Marquess of Londonderry shortly before the Second World War. It was owned in the early part of the 19th cent. by one Sir John Edwardes and passed to the Londonderry family by way of marriage. It is mainly 17th-cent., with considerable 19th-cent. additions, but a portion of the fabric at the rear is 16th-cent. The grounds are extensive and take in the hilly woodland known as Llynlloedd that rises between Machynlleth and Glasbwll. Beneath these hills, and close to the Dylife road, is another Plas called Llynlloedd. Both Plas Llynlloedd and Plas Machynlleth house between them the kennels of the Plas Machynlleth Hunt.

This is a foot-pack, the nature of the country making the use of horses in following hounds inadvisable – unless (people say) you are prepared at times to get off your horse and carry it. The breed of hound is distinct from those known in England, and the purpose and method of hunting are equally distinctive. The hounds are bred short of leg and encouraged to "babble" or throw tongue, since otherwise the huntsmen would find it difficult to trace them or follow their line in such broken country. Their ancestry is from the medieval breeding between the French black hound of Hubert, the fallow hound of Brittany, and the white hound bred in Barbary (Morocco). The narrow valleys of the Plynlimon foothills, thick with native oaks and ash, were from time immemorial an enviable shelter for the fox. The rapid introduction of Forestry Commission fir-plantations, closely set, has not only extended the cover for the families of foxes, but has made it impossible to deal with them, since they are secure from pursuit. As a result, local farmers are now inclined to organize shooting-parties of their own rather than call in the Hunt; and poison and trapping are frequent forms of defence. Depredation by foxes is a serious matter among the isolated hill-farms and lonely sheep-walks in the area. Moreover the Hunt has always regarded itself as a policeman rather than a commando force; its objective is, by constant patrolling, to scare the fox from his forays. Here the fox has the upper hand over the hound, and in the fastnesses of the Five Summits of Plynlimon he has an ultimate sanctuary from which it is almost hopeless to dislodge him. The chief occasion for the meets of the local pack is on New Year's Day by the Clock Tower. That day is in fact a public holiday in this part of Wales, and its celebrations are at least as important as those of Christmas.

A picturesque tradition in Machynlleth is the maintenance of the seasonal fairs. They are held in Maen Gwyn Street, where for many generations the "stondings" were set around its ranked trees, which still insist on their privilege of growing well away from the kerb in the road itself. Nowadays such practices as the hiring fair – at which labourers offered themselves for service by sporting a wheat-ear in their caps, and contracts were concluded by the simple ceremony of the hand-clasp – no longer persist; although in certain parts, for example Radnor-shire, the custom is said to have continued into the 1940s. But the huckster fairs are a regular institution; travelling traders, of many nationalities, offer their bargains in clothing, crockery, and sweetmeats by way of Dutch auction. This is a system of putting a price on a set of goods and adding another and another item at the same general price until the invitation to buy is accepted. The cry of "Un etto! Un etto!" ("And another! And another!") can still be heard, where the vendor is Welsh or has learnt Welsh in his travels. On these occasions the gypsies (locally known as sipsies) make their appearance. Both gypsies and tinkers with cart and caravan pass from time to time through Machynlleth. Against them, however, official pressure has gradually asserted itself; even the device of finding a patch of waste ground off the main road, and shifting the wheels once every night to maintain the claim of having "moved on", is of little avail. In living memory, Machyn-lleth was a centre of resort for the "Egyptian" tribe. On a triangle of ground at the fork of roads by the old Toll House, where now new council houses stand, the caravans met, the fires were built, and the full gypsy marriage ceremony was carried out. The flames leaping, the bridal pair leaping across them, the torches tossing, the fiddles playing, created a picture now unfortunately dimmed. The refuge for the unwelcome vagrant folk was for a while in the unclaimed patch close to the bridge of Felin Gerrig; but little by little they have drifted away to the less vigilant bailiwick of Dinas Mawddwy.

Notable in present-day Machynlleth are the church and Dyfi Bridge. The church, grey and dignified, has a set of houses by its entrance, built typically of the local slate-stone and dating to the days of Machynlleth's earlier prominence. The churchyard is filled with graves of the late 18th and early 19th cents.; the banker, the merchant, the gentleman, the naval surgeon who were aware of Nelson and Napoleon as contemporaries still lie there side by side. And for us the occasional lines of verse contrive to make them live again:

Before the Infant knew his mother's name
Or seemed to know her only by her smile,
Unsparing Death with speed relentless came
And snatched him from his mother's arms
    awhile.

The separation was not long endured
Ere they again did meet in love more pure,
Where they an everlasting life will lead,
From death, from sorrow and from pain
    secure.

MAENTWROG, *Merioneth.* In the Vale of Ffestiniog, Maentwrog can be reached from Portmadoc, 7 m. away, on the road to Traws-fynydd. The descent from Portmadoc into the valley is one of the most striking sights on any road in Wales, and passes an old mansion that later became a roadside hotel. Routes from Bala, Dolgellau, and Betws-y-coed meet at the village. The name is taken from the great stone to be found in the churchyard; it was probably set beside the Roman roads that met here by Tomen y Mur, but it has been adopted into the legend of a giant called Twrog who threw it down from the surrounding hills. The church has been thoroughly modernized, but may well date from A.D. 610, when the giant is reputed to have died, and be in fact a sister foundation to Llandwrog not far from Caernarfon.

The great reservoir of Trawsfynydd is in the hills to the S. of the village.

MAESTEG, *Glamorgan.* Fairfield, as it would be known in English, is a typical upgrowth in the South from the economic circumstance affecting the great coalfield. It is both town and urban district, but is better thought of as the latter. The communities around it within the conurba-tion find it convenient as a shopping centre, and all roads lead to it. But its prosperity de-pends on that of the neighbourhood's activity. When bituminous coal commanded a world market from the South, Maesteg on the Llynfi river grew to a population of 25,600. The depres-sion of the 1930s affected it as severely as it was felt throughout all the South. In twenty years, the population had dropped by 10 per cent, and its future depends on the efforts made to introduce

Cottages at Mallwyd

new light industries and plans to reclaim the South once more for woodland. In many ways, Maesteg can look to a brighter and cleaner life in the 21st cent., and the bustling spirit of its people already promises it.

MAGOR, *Monmouthshire.* The name is derived from the Welsh word for wall, and may be an echo of Roman reclamation work in these parts. Caerwent is not far away. The village of Magor lies on the edge of the Caldicot Level and looks out over the Level to the Bristol Channel. The big church is known as the Cathedral of the Moors. The tower is 13th-cent. and has a high-roofed chancel. A fine 15th-cent. two-storeyed porch makes an impressive entrance. The arcades that link the nave with the aisles are decorated with angel figures. There are interestingly carved corbels on the wall of the S. aisle that formerly supported a vaulted roof.

The ivy-covered ruins in the churchyard are the scanty remains of the old priory. The main railway line runs right below the churchyard wall to the S. The village square is surrounded by pleasantly colour-washed buildings, including the post office. In the centre is the very large war memorial, set up in 1924 by Lady Rhondda. It commemorates the dead of Magor and the surrounding villages. It also has a bronze medallion with a portrait of Lord Rhondda and the inscription "For he, too, died, serving the nation as Food Controller".

To the eastern side of the village, on the Undy road, stands the old age pensioners' homes, for which the Chepstow Council is responsible. They are small houses, well grouped, with white walls and Welsh slate roofs – a model of what housing schemes can be when imagination is boldly used.

From Undy a long lane, ending in a footpath through private land, leads out to an unspoilt stretch of the sea-wall that guards the levels along the Severn shore. The path passes the house of Pennycloud, which is the Monmouthshire way of writing Pen-y-clawdd (Top of the dyke).

MALLWYD, *Merioneth.* This small town lies on the road between Machynlleth and Dinas Mawddwy. That it had some importance as a point on early communication routes is suggested by the probable derivation of its name, from Maen Llwyd, a phrase associated all over this area with the pointer-stones by which travellers found their way. It stands back from the road, with a wide stretch of common land before it. The church has a porch to its door with the date of 1641, though the foundation must be much older: considerable yews still stand around it.

It was a place through which Borrow chose to pass without much comment. It is attractive in particular to anglers. Here the slate-building in the lower Dovey area begins to give place to the stone structure of the N.

MANORBIER, *Pembrokeshire.* Some 6 m. from Tenby, as the road goes, where the limestone crags change abruptly to Old Red Sandstone, stands the shell of Manorbier Castle, still overlooking the village that from old time gathered under it for shelter. When Henry I of England was encouraging a forward policy into Wales that was doomed to lack of success, the Lord de Barri, of the place now called Barry, found a small and convenient bay upon which to set his strong-point. The present structure is the work of one of his descendants, John de Barri, who initiated it in 1275; fifty years later the work was finally done. The speed with which such great constructions as Caernarfon Castle could be carried through throws light on the disturbed conditions that held back the completion of Manorbier. But these were political rather than military; the Castle never had to withstand siege, and, in its outer face, it remains as at first. The inner ward, an imposing example of the firmly balanced architecture of the time, is surrounded by the curtain wall with the twin towers of its gatehouse contemplating the fall of land without any afterthought from the 13th or 14th cent. The chapel and the great hall and its solar wings have been domestically rearranged since then.

But this grave and, as it turned out, largely beneficent structure, is notable because of a man who never saw it as it appears now. He was born in the earlier Castle about 1146, and sprang from the family that possessed it. He was Gerald de Barri, who treated his half-Norman descent as nothing in comparison with the soil of his birth. He called himself Giraldus Cambrensis; for he used, as educated men throughout Europe did in his day, the international language of Latin, representing the broad base of European culture of which British, French, or English "race" meant nothing other than a local variation. Gerald the Welshman was one of the most brilliant minds of the Middle Ages; as he wrote in Latin and read extensively in it, he could draw upon the experience and sophistication, as well as legal logic, possessed by the great classical scholars, and his work reads with a modern tone rare among his contemporaries. An active Churchman, he was Archdeacon of Brecon Priory; an intelligent clerk, he was used to advise on the state of affairs in Ireland; an excellent speaker, he went with Archbishop Baldwin on the recruiting campaign for the Third Crusade that resulted in his most famous work, the *Itinerary of Wales*.

Apart from his international work, he was passionately devoted to the cause of an independent Church in Wales, its head at St David's and its outlook toned to the Christianity David the saint had represented (that "Celtic Christianity" which, as so many of its foundations show, built upon the honour of the works of nature – sun, star, bird, and beast) that pagan peoples in their simplicity accepted. His ambition to become the Archbishop of that independent Welsh Church was never fulfilled. His attempt, through his writings, to maintain the distinctive culture of Wales in verse and song, and the national pride he both praised for its virtue and blamed for its excesses, as part of a common fabric between Welsh and English and Norman, was not immediately successful. But a man who could think of his "little place" at Landeu as he did, who could see with so eager an appreciation the work of the beavers in the streams, the stately stride of deer upon the hills, and the waving beauty of corn and woodland, is assured of his position among great writers. It is of Manorbier that he writes in a way that shapes the whole man for us: "It is excellently well defended by turrets and bulwarks and is situated on the summit of a hill extending on the western side towards the sea-port, having on the northern and southern sides a fine fish-pond under its walls, as conspicuous for its grand appearance as for the depth of its waters; and a beautiful orchard on the same side inclosed on the one part by a vineyard and on the other by a wood remarkable for the jutting-forth of its rocks and the height of its hazels. On the right of the promontory between the Castle and the Church near a very large lake and mill, a rivulet of never-failing water flows through a valley, sanded over by the strength of the winds. This country is well supplied with corn, fish from the sea and wines brought in from abroad. What is preferable above all is its nearness to Ireland. It is mild with healthy air. Demetia (as the Romans called Pembrokeshire or Dyfed) with its seven cantered-divisions, is the most beautiful as well as the most powerful part of Wales; Pen Broch the finest part of the province of Demetia; and the place I have described the most delightful part of Penbroch. It is evident, therefore," he adds with a slight touch of amusement at himself, "that Manor Pirr [Manorbier] is the pleasantest spot in Wales." He rounds off the passage with an apology for speaking so warmly of the place where he was born.

The church he writes of, on the other side of the valley, seems to be still in some part the church he knew as already ancient. But the nave and tower were refashioned in his time, the transepts a century later. Additions and elaborations have been made since then. Remoter origins for Manorbier are found at the edge of the bay $\frac{1}{2}$ m. from the Castle, in a dolmen with a capstone 15 ft long and 9 ft broad, called locally the King's Quoit. The mound that once covered it has vanished.

MARGAM ABBEY, *Glamorgan*. Between the busy dockland of Port Talbot and the sands of Porthcawl runs a stretch of untrammelled shore called Margam Burrows. Looking down on it from a height of rather over 1,000 ft is the Mynydd Margam, standing beside its twin, Moel Ton-Mawr. Christopher Saxton, going that way in the first decade of the 17th cent., thought better to write the name Margan and so emphasize its possible meaning of sea-margin. Between Mynydd Margam and the shore are early camp sites; and near to them is Margam Abbey. It was old enough in Saxton's time, but he looked for something older. He found an old stone by the wayside between Margam and King's Henge, obviously Roman, for it bore an inscription, which he sets out in his book; though worn by time, it seems to say that it commemorated one Pompeius Carantopius. "The Welsh Britons," he comments with an unusually acid note, "by adding and changing letters read and make an interpretation" that altered it to an account of the murder of Prince Morgan, from whom this country took its name, "who was slaine, as they would have it, 800 years before Christ's nativity. But Antiquaries know full well that these Characters and forms of letters be of farre later date".

But on the exact watershed of Margam hill he noted and illustrated the famous stone, squared and on its upper side incised with a cross, which reads: *Boduoc hic iacit filius Cato Tigirni pronepos Eternali Uedomau.* The script is as strange as the Latin in which it is written. The *a*s are in fact upside-down to our modern eyes. It clearly belongs to the sub-Roman period in Britain and is assigned to A.D. 520. *Pronepos* means great-grandson; who Eternalis was we cannot be sure, but, as at least four generations must have passed between Boduoc and his great-great-grandfather, Eternalis must have lived about A.D. 390, when Rome still kept effective footing in Britain. Cato Tigirn is unlikely to have had a Roman name. On the contrary, he has a title of Tigernos that takes us back to native Celtic royalty and later resulted in Catigern and similar forms. "War leader" is the meaning of what for him was probably a personal name. What other memorial that family of rulers may have had upon this shoreline, as vital to the 5th and 6th cents. as it was in Norman times, is most probably lost like the city of Kenfig, buried by Margam Burrows in a catastrophe of the 16th cent., under the sands for which, as Saxton puts it, Neath in his day was infamous.

Nor is there anything left to show whether the Abbey had a forebear of the time of Catigern and Boduoc; it was founded in 1157 by the Norman Robert of Gloucester, and his work persists in the nave of the church and various fragments of the monastic buildings. The chapter house is 13th cent., a lovely structure twelve-sided from without but circular within, rounded about a central pier, its vestibule beautifully vaulted. Some evidence of Margam's earlier history is preserved with a large collection of crosses and inscribed stones from the area in a separate building. But the church is remarkable for the memorials it keeps of the Norman family of Mansel. One of them was involved in a tale as romantic as that of the Nest whose abduction by Owain son of Cadwgan, Lord of Ceredigion, set Wales afire with flames like those of Troy. Oddly enough, the heroine of this tale was also called Nest. It is a tale of Sir Walter Mansel of Margam who loved the daughter of Elidr the Black, but who, unfortunately, was himself loved by her cousin Gwladys. The love-affair between Walter and Nest was not only seen with disfavour by this other woman but also by Griffith, Nest's brother, who loved Gwladys without hope of return – except at a price. The price was the death of his sister and of her lover, which he brought about by finding them near the cliffs above the sea and sending an arrow through Walter's heart. Nest threw herself into the waters after the dead man. Her white ghost haunts the bridge at Pont y Gwendraeth (White Sands), close to Kidwelly.

MATHAFARN, *Montgomeryshire* (or Math-avern, as the coaching maps insist), lies about 2 m. beyond Llanwrin into the valley of the Dovey. The same maps sketch a noble house by the side of the name. The place now chiefly consists of this one house, which is worth observing, though it has diminished slightly since its

early association with the Princes of Powys. Some connection is also claimed with Owain Glyndwr.

It stands where the modern version of the coach-road now swings suddenly to go by the Iron Bridge across the valley and join the major Newtown road at Cemaes Road and its station. In coaching days the way went to the N. of the river to reach Cemaes village itself by what is now not too good a route, however pretty.

From Mathafarn an interesting archeological expedition can be made to Cae Adda, a very old farmhouse that for long resisted the demands of authority for afforestation. Somewhat to the W. of the farmstead are two parallel rows of "twmps" (mounds). Their significance is unknown. For want of better attribution, they have been named respectively the Saxons' and the Britons' graves. They have never been excavated. The highly educated man who attempted to carry out the operation was, at the first attempt, driven away by a fall of heavy rain from an unclouded sky. Some days later, at the second attempt, he was forced to run under an equally unexpected fall of hail. At the third, a flash of lightning finally deterred him. On the two earlier occasions he brought his spade and mattock back home with him. On the third, he left them behind. He has never returned to claim them.

MATHERN, *Monmouthshire*, is tucked away at the end of a no-through-road 3 m. S. of Chepstow. Although the motorway from the Severn Bridge passes near it, Mathern has retained its seclusion and surprises. It has a palace hidden among the trees near the churchyard. For over 200 years Mathern was the chief country residence of the Bishops of Llandaff. The palace is partly 15th-cent. It has a low tower and some charming oriel windows. The palace garden is a masterpiece created in 1890 by H. Avray Tipping, the authority on Grinling Gibbons, the 17th-cent. carver. Tipping lived in the palace and carefully restored it. The house is private, but the grounds can be glimpsed from the churchyard.

The church is dedicated to St Tewdric, a 6th-cent. Welsh chieftain who died in the hands of the pagan Saxons. The Bishops of Llandaff used it for ordinations and as a consistory court. It is a richly decorated little church, with arcaded aisles, wall monuments, and a fine 15th-cent. tower. The nave is 13th-cent., with one window that still possesses fragments of the original glass.

There are other old houses in Mathern, including Moynes Court, rebuilt in the 17th cent. by Francis Godwin, Bishop of Llandaff. The gatehouse has two square towers on either side and is much older than the rest of the court. Moynes Court can be seen on the left hand as you drive down to the M4 towards Newport.

MENAI BRIDGE, *Anglesey*. The village, Porthaethwy in Welsh, is a street of houses on

Top: *Manorbier Castle*   G. Douglas Bolton
Bottom: *Llanfair P.G. station nameplate, preserved in Penrhyn Castle Museum*   Peter Baker
Overleaf: *Plate 14   St David's Cathedral (see p. 312)*   Colour Library International

the Anglesey side of the bridge built by Telford and completed in 1826. It is in every sense a bridgehead township for the gathering and distribution of supplies between Anglesey and Caernarfonshire. The bridge can properly be called remarkable, since, apart from an earlier experimental construction in the North of England in the mid-18th cent., it was the first suspension-structure to bear heavy traffic. The problem of allowing for expansion of the steel bearers is solved by cunningly concealed rollers; and it is built so well that no vibration-waves from the motor traffic are felt by foot-passengers crossing the water by the side lanes. The pedestal-towers are of a curiously Egyptian design. The bridge is 1,000 ft long, 579 ft between pier and pier, 28 ft wide, and rising 100 ft above the highest level of tide, which can swell as much as 20 ft in height and come in with great speed. Years were spent in its construction, and at the church of Llanfair P.G. is a memorial tablet to the men whose lives were lost in the work. The view from the bridge is splendid, both downwards to the water pressing against the rocky islets and forward along the straits themselves. A little further on the Holyhead road, which the bridge was made to serve, is the village of Llanfair Pwllgwyngyll to which the name of its twin, Llantysiliogogogoch, has been humorously added. St Mary's by the White Aspen over the Drobwll (Whirlpool) and St Tisilio's by the Red Cave, are now represented by a small church with an ancient font and a graveyard below which the statue of Nelson peers out to act as a landmark for sail over the water by the Britannia Tubular Bridge that carries the railroad and was designed in imitation of Telford's Egyptian style. Standing high above it all is the column for the Marquess of Anglesey, who was on Wellington's staff. His absorption in the art of war is proved by the loss of his leg by a cannon-ball at Waterloo. "By God," said the Duke, "you have lost your leg." "By God," said the Marquess with surprise, "so I have."

Llanfair should not be left without reference to the very unusual burial chamber at Bryn-celli-ddu. This cairn has now been re-covered by a mound of earth to protect it and give some idea of its original appearance; but the modern mound shows only a portion of the monument's full area. It was once 160 ft in diameter, covering a many-sided chamber 8 ft across and roofed with two large capstones, approached by an open outer passage 6 ft long, entering by a roofed portal into an inner passage 20 ft long. Four concentric circles of stones surround the inner area. A pillar and a bench also of stone stood by an inscribed slab that has been removed to the National Museum at Cardiff, a cast of it being left at the site. This patterning, with those at Barclodiad y Gawres near Aberffraw, are the only two examples yet found in Britain of a series of Bronze Age monuments, dating from the second millennium B.C., left by early peoples in Brittany and Guernsey. That this area was of particular importance to those who set this

burial chamber in position is shown by the fact that Llanddaniel-fab, close at hand, has two other such monuments, the Plas Newydd chamber and the Burial-Place of Hen Bobl (the Ancient Folk) as well as a standing stone at Tyddyn Bach. Others are scattered widely throughout Anglesey. Apparently Maglocunos the High King was building on foundations laid centuries before him by those pioneers of the first technological civilization who sailed from the Levant to the islands of the Irish Sea.

MERTHYR MAWR, *Glamorgan*, is a well-known beauty-spot near the mouth of the Ogmore river SW. of Bridgend. Beyond the by-pass round the town, the river runs through fine woodlands under an old four-arched bridge with apertures through which farmers pushed sheep at dipping-time. The river continues towards the sea past Merthyr Mawr House. In the private woods behind the house stand the ruined oratory of St Roque's Chapel, with a collection of stone fragments collected from the locality, including the Conbelanus Cross and the Dobitaucus Cross, locally known as the Goblin Stone. An enormous cavern near at hand is the result of subsidence in the limestone caused by an underground stream.

The village of Merthyr Mawr is a picturesque collection of thatched cottages, although slate roofing has now appeared on one of the largest. The Church of St Teilo is modern; traces of the old foundations are visible inside. The churchyard cross is mutilated, but there are some interesting stones here including the Paulinus Slab and some worn medieval effigies of Churchmen. The road continues for $\frac{1}{2}$ m. beyond the church until it runs to a dead-end among the sandhills of Merthyr Mawr Warren. There is a car park under the trees near the ruins of the fortified manor house of Candleston Castle, built in the early 15th cent. The name is a corruption of Cantelupestown, since the Castle was owned by a branch of the powerful Cantelupe family. It was inhabited up to Victorian times, but is now in complete decay, with the lands to the S. overwhelmed by the dunes.

Merthyr Mawr fills the whole area at the mouth of the Ogmore – an expanse of lonely sand-dunes, some of which are among the highest in the country. Sand is driven by powerful winds from the Atlantic across this section of the South Wales coastline all the way round to Swansea. The movement of the sands at Merthyr Mawr occasionally uncovers material of great archaeological interest, and it has revealed the place as the site of what was probably an important Neolithic settlement. There are various tumuli, one of which yielded remains of the Beaker folk. This tumulus was 500 ft in diameter and 21 ft high; it contained six burials. The results of the excavation are now in the Museum of the Royal Institution at Swansea. Later finds have been made; without question the area is archaeologically rich. To the W. of the Warren is the hamlet of Tythegston, more easily reached from

Top: *The burial chamber at Bryn-celli-ddu, close to Menai Bridge*   Peter Baker
Bottom: *Broad Haven on St Bride's Bay (see p. 263)*   J. Allan Cash

the Porthcawl side. The rebuilt church has a 14th-cent. bell and a round-headed cross-slab that may date from the 7th cent. There are traces of a Roman-British camp near the edge of the sand-dunes. Tythegston Court was reconstructed in 1769. It was the scene of a notorious 15th-cent. abduction when Lewis Leyshon forced Margaret, Lady Malefaunt, to leave Upton Castle in Pembrokeshire and held her prisoner at Tythegston in an attempt to marry her. She made her escape and brought Leyshon to justice before Parliament in 1437.

MERTHYR TYDFIL, *Glamorgan.* Its name is explained by a legend that takes Merthyr, as it is generally called, back in time to the emergence of Wales as a national entity from the last days of the Roman world. For Tudful, they say, was a British princess, daughter of the Lord of Brycheiniog (Brecon), the Brychein after whom his province was named and "grandson" of the Cunedda who marched from the North to hold the centre of both Wales and England with the state of Powys. She was a Christian, and she was martyred for her faith. Martyrdom and faith have occupied a large place in the history of the town.

It played its part in the wars that resisted the Norman penetration from the southern coastline along the deep valleys descending from the Ellennith; 2 m. away on Morlais hill, a Norman castle that was never finished makes its ruins a monument to those times. But Merthyr has been shaped by a different kind of history. It is a county and parliamentary borough, set in the valley of the Taff rather below the junction of its two major tributaries, the Taf Fechan and the Taf Fawr. Southwards from Merthyr stretches the once mighty coalfield, but, although the town owed much to its association with the coal industry, its own former greatness was due to ironstone deposits and to iron-working. "Former greatness", regrettably, is correct. In 1831 it was the largest town in Wales, with a population larger than those of Newport, Cardiff, and Swansea put together. In 1931 its people numbered 71,000; in 1951, 61,000. In the 1930s, one-fifth of its inhabitants were unemployed, and the burden of rates contributing to their support was the highest in all Great Britain.

When the Industrial Revolution first launched itself into an expanding world, large ironworks were built to exploit Merthyr's natural resources to the full. They were built at Dowlais, Cyfarthfa, and Penydarren; Merthyr grew to be the greatest iron and steel manufacturer in the world, linked by rail and canal with Cardiff. In 1811, Daniel Paterson's *Direct and Principal Cross Roads* takes care to emphasize this point, and it adds the remarkable fact that a regular post was established between the two places, operating five days in the week. The Dowlais works were laid down in 1759, and had the distinction of being the place where the chemical and engineering innovations introduced by Josiah Guest were followed by Bessemer steel-rail rolling in 1856. The Cyfarthfa

works were founded in 1765 by Bacon, managed after 1794 by Crawshay, and became steel-foundries in 1883. This prosperity continued to grow into the 20th cent. up to the First World War; then, apart from other factors affecting South Wales as a whole, heavy industry in the Merthyr area preferred to move towards the coastline and the ports. As a result, Merthyr found its lowest level of depression, with half its working population unemployed. Nor was there anything in the town or its neighbourhood to offer much consolation. The hurried demand for exploitation of its iron called in thousands of workers who were housed in barrack-like terraces against the steep hills without plan; solid and cramped, they did well enough to act as sleeping-bunks, but Merthyr was nothing more than a narrow warren along the roads of the South, indistinguishable from neighbouring areas. Slag-heaps and spoil-tips invaded the green flanks of the countryside. The native spirit of Merthyr that had managed to produce, on the one hand, the first steam-powered locomotive, invented by Richard Trevethick in 1804, and on the other the musical genius of Joseph Parry at the end of the century, was neutralized. The over-specialization of Merthyr in iron production, like that of the whole South Wales coalfield in its own product, relied on the assumption of a world that would continue in the pattern of British predominance over the international routes of trade. Before 1914 these were mainly controlled by ocean-lines of traffic and communication. The rapid development of continental and inter-continental motor roads opened areas of economic potential formerly unreachable, and upset the balance between nations and continents, and places like Merthyr that had had a sudden uprush of energy under one set of conditions were as suddenly left empty when new ones intervened.

The Special Areas Acts of 1934–7 and the Special Areas Reconstruction Association of 1936 were formulated to deal with those congregations of life like Merthyr that had been called into being by the 19th cent. and that the 20th cent. had left derelict. The Distribution of Industry Acts of 1945–8, and the continuous legislation that has followed, applied to Merthyr the benefits of the new age of discovery that opened after the Second World War, the new freedom brought by modern transport and synthetic processes of production. The ironworks that closed in 1930 have been succeeded as the main staple of Merthyr's life by the production of what the home market has been induced to require, the washing-machines, and similar convenient substitutes for physical labour, that hire-purchase makes readily available. It is an economic situation that depends for its ultimate success on productive policies much wider in application than Merthyr can provide. But conditions of labour and facilities for health and recreation are such as the past generation did not dream of.

Southward along the Taff river is Aberfan, where the disaster of the 21st October 1966 took place.

MILFORD HAVEN, *Pembrokeshire.* The haven opens with two smaller bays, Angle Bay and West Angle Bay, the second at the mouth, the first an inlet, of the haven itself. The inlet is muddy; West Angle is a reach of broad sands; and both lie about the charming village of Angle, so named because it was In Angulo, or at the junction of these doors that opened from Milford. Angle Bay clearly shows what importance was attached to the entrance to this fine natural harbourage, which Defoe, on his 17th-cent. tour, described as one of the greatest and best inlets of water in Britain. "Mr. Camden," he adds, referring to an even earlier traveller and antiquarian in these parts, "says it contains 16 creeks, 5 great bays and 13 good roads for shipping, all distinguished as such by their names; and some say a thousand sail of ships may ride in it and not the topmast of one be seen from the other." This was the principal feature that made Pembrokeshire an object of desire to the Norman adventurers, and the settlers sent by the first two Henrys of England were concentrated along the N. of it. The great Castle of Pembroke commands the landward creek that runs into it; today on the S. shore is Pembroke Dock, and on the other side is Milford Haven the town. The more westerly approaches were watched by Angle, where Henry VIII built block-houses to defy all possible assault, and the ruined peel-tower still stands over its moat. Its West Bay holds an island, the Thorn, with an obsolete fort upon it. The last military service the haven performed in British internal history was to shelter the Parliamentary fleet from storms just at the time when Royalist attacks might otherwise have taken Pembroke Castle.

Milford Haven is an interesting town to those who have an eye for the unusual. In spite of the military and naval importance of the area it commands, it was famous in the great days of the British fishing industry for being fourth among the reapers of the seas' harvest. Skate, hake, and conger were its customary catch, which it varied with beasts peculiar to the place, if not in kind, then certainly in description, for "megrims" and "witches" are surely rare enough. The town is set against a smooth but steeply rising hill, and its houses are ranked rather like barracks, in a square, low series of terraces that seem generally to date from the days of Nelson. He is in fact remembered in the Castle Hotel, since he came that way in 1808 to lay the foundation-stone of the parish church. And Lady Hamilton stayed in Milford too; as Emma Hart, she was mistress of one man who bargained her away for a price that was laid out in founding Pembroke Dock, the once important base for the Navy and for seaplanes. The area is now important for its oil-refineries; one working plant strikes against the sky over the low hills that face Milford across the water. There are monuments to former Sea Lords at the bottom of the hill below Milford town; but the place seems now to have withdrawn itself into the magnificent geography of the whole haven.

This is a submerged and sunken valley, widening to a breadth of 2 m. and 20 m. long. There are no bridges, though a car-ferry is available towards the upper reaches of the haven, plying from Neyland (New Milford) to Hobbs Point. Going that way, you can turn westward again for St Bride's Bay, a remote and beautiful area with more wild flowers and sea-birds than it has humans, with astonishing scenery of ocean and cliff and the long beaches of Little Haven, Broad Haven, Nolton Haven, and Newgale stretching N. towards St David's. The bay can be seen from the pleasant village of Dale and the road that goes from Dale Bay to St Ann's Head, itself at the head of the haven. Close to it is Mill Bay, where Henry Tudor first landed in 1485 and waited for the word that the Lord of the South, Rhys ap Thomas, would come to his aid. After the fatal Battle of Tewkesbury, Jasper Tudor had fled with his young nephew Henry for shelter to Pembroke Castle. There they stood siege, till they were rescued by the brother of the man who was investing the castle with Yorkist troops. The young Tudor was recalled from his exile in Brittany by his former tutor in arts and sciences, Dr Lewis, a Welshman who now proposed to teach him politics too. Master of South Wales was Rhys ap Thomas, a man who had sworn deep fealty to Richard III of England; never would Henry come to claim the Crown of England through Wales, he swore, except over his body. But when Henry and his Uncle Jasper landed with their 2,000 men, Pembrokeshire rose to greet them, and the Bishop of St David himself informed Rhys that he was free of his oath, since Richard was himself perjured, a murderer of an infant king, and a usurper. Rhys, with all his following, went to meet Henry, and (it is said) thought it as well to make his own interpretation of the oath by lying before him and inviting him to step over his body. The result was that the army of liberation moved in two parts, one under Rhys through Brycheiniog (Breconshire) and one under Henry through Ceredigion (Cardiganshire), pausing a night at Machynlleth. The two sections conjoined at Shrewsbury, the old capital of Powys. From there the way to Bosworth was short. From Shrewsbury, Henry bore before him the rouge and passant dragon standard of Powys, and all Wales felt that the House of Cunedda was at last justified. The leaping song "Tros y Gareg" is a shout of praise for him.

Marloes, 2 m. from Dale, has memories of even earlier days in the Rath of Marloes, a prehistoric fortress with a triple bank of defences and, out from the ideal sands of its bay, the small island of Gateholm, once much inhabited, since on its narrow area more than 100 hut circles are to be found, but now mainly possessed by primroses in early spring. It is companion to the remoter and larger islands of Skomer and Skokholm, the first of which is also covered with relics of ancient hutments of a population much larger than its resources could ever have supported. The industry it engaged in does not seem to have been the usual one of tool-making or copper- and gold-prospecting; it may have lived as a centre of ship-masters, a harbourage for navigators in the dawn of

West of Milford Haven: Marloes church

seamanship. Now the only sea-steerers are kitti-
wake and cormorant, petrel, puffin, razorbill and
guillemot, shearwater and fowl more familiar to
land, buzzard, peregrine, raven, and chough.
The still further island of Grassholm, wholly uninhabited, is abandoned to the gannets, whose
families make it a solid drift of snow upon the
grey waters. Marloes village has a name that
seems to echo the parallel names of Morlais in
Cornwall and Morlaix in Brittany – the Sea-
Stretch; and, apart from its fisher interests, it
still carries on one of the ancient food-gathering
practices of ancient Wales. There the tide leaves
on the rocks the long, bubbled strands of seaweed,
brown and leathery, that are gathered and boiled
into the green mass called laver bread. It is a
delicacy peculiarly Welsh, and much enjoyed
about Gower and points W. and E. Its full flavour
can be appreciated only when taken with bacon
or gammon, though some say it is even better
with porridge. In either case it has to have the
condiment of custom; for at first one's reaction
is doubtful. Its delicacy is the reward of courage;
and courage is needed.

MOLD, *Flintshire*, the county town of Flintshire, the centre for this part of the North Wales
coalfield, and the marketing-place for the agricultural district in the Alun valley, stands 6 m. S.
of the town of Flint. Its main attraction now is
the picturesque High Street and the parish church,
dating from the 15th cent. with its interesting roof,
glass, and animal frescoes. To the N. of the town,
on Bailey Hill, the Norman Lord Robert de
Monte Alto set his motte-and-bailey knight's
castle on a mound. Nothing of either remains,
but it is supposed that a contraction of Mont-Alt
gave Mold its present name. It is called in Welsh
Yr Wyddgrug (the Forest Heath).

Today Mold is a busy meeting-point for many
traffic routes, and seems always to have been one.
The Roman road to Canovium, now Caerhun,
near Conway, and Verae, probably St Asaph
rather than Bodfari, passed close by Mold; and an
obelisk at Waun, 1 m. to the W., shows where,
about A.D. 430, a victory was won by the British
of the neighbourhood against some enemy
advancing along this route from the N. It is known
as the Alleluia Victory, since Bede records an
account of it in which a St Garmon, sent to
propagate the Catholic faith in Britain, routed
the opposing forces by hiding his troops until,
with a great cry of "Alleluia!", they startled the
enemy into flight. Some doubt has been thrown
on this story by eminent Welsh scholars, who
point out that the very name Garmon seems to
be not much more than the Welsh word for an
outcry, "garm". But we can safely believe that
along the Roman road a battle was fought at that
time between supporters of one Christian belief
and those of another.

SW. of Mold, at Llanarmon-yn-Ial, is a church,
double-naved in the usual style of this part of
Wales, with a figure of the Virgin possibly brought
there from the Monastery of Valle Crucis at the
time of the Dissolution. It contains the tomb of
Gruffydd ap Llywelyn (about 1350) and a monument to one Evan Lloyd (1639). A little beyond
Llanferres is the Three Loggerheads Inn, with a
signboard allegedly painted by the Welsh artist
Richard Wilson. It was near here that he died in
1782 in Colomendy Hall, a house he had inherited
from his brother. He began his life at Penegoes in
Montgomeryshire and, after years of struggle and
success in Italy and London, returned here to
end his days in peace. He is buried in the churchyard at Mold, and has a window dedicated to his
fame.

In Mold itself there are memorials to a great
name in the native Welsh literature of the 19th
cent. The inn called the Mostyn Arms bears a
notice of the National Eisteddfod of 1873, of
which Daniel Owen, the novelist and social critic,
was Chairman. The troubles that accompanied
the industrial development of the country and
the birth of the new trades union movement were
deeply felt in Mold. In his novels, written in
Welsh, Daniel Owen reflected the changes of the
time with the shrewd character-sketches he made
of his contemporaries. But in his writing there is
always a strong sense of the simplicity of life his
generation seemed to be leaving behind. Opinions
vary, but for some *Gwen Tomos* is the best of his
works. He can be called the Thomas Hardy of
Wales, but a Hardy without the pleasures of
despair.

MONMOUTH, *Monmouthshire*. The town
stands where the Monnow river flows into the
Wye, and both it and the county to which it gives
its name occupy a most important strategic
position. It holds the lower hills between the
moorland heart of Wales and the wide fields of the
Midlands; it masters the outfall of the rivers
whose upper reaches lead to the central passes
between Severn and Dovey, and whoever holds it

can control the whole Deheubarth, or South of Wales. It was this line between the Wye and Severn on the one side and the mid-point of the western coast of Wales that decided the political pattern and the succession of wars that at last gave the country its character. The Romans were aware of how natural features must dictate the lines of strategic advance; they had their station near Monmouth and they called it Blestium, an important link in the chain that went one way through Caerwent and Caerleon, another way to Wrexham, Caersws, and Chester. Humphrey Lhuyd, antiquarian of Denbigh, in the 16th cent. set Monmouth, to which he is careful to add the "British" name of Mynwy, firmly on the W. of the Wye and in the territory of the Deheubarth, leaving the principality of Powys to run down the other bank of the river and include the Forest of Dean, now reckoned as English and part of Gloucestershire, though still retaining some vestiges of its separate identity. For Humphrey Lhuyd traced the division of Wales into its three provinces – Powys, Gwynedd, and the South – to sub-Roman times long before the sons of Rhodri the Great in the 9th cent. resumed that division of territory.

From positions that they established in the angle between Severn and Wye, which the Welsh call Gwent, the Normans under FitzHamon and his twelve knights conquered Glamorgan, and Bernard of Neufmarché, the illegitimate son of William the Conqueror, advanced to seize Brycheiniog (Breconshire). Norman power in Monmouth town is now shown only by the Norman chapel close to the famous gateway and the bridge over the Monnow that must be crossed to enter the town. It is a prized and unique possession, and the remarkable architectural harmony achieved by the builders is typical of the work of the 13th cent. to which it belongs. At the end of the 13th cent., after the fall of the last native Prince of Wales, Edward I of England took Gwent, alone among the territories administered by the Lords Marcher, into the Kingdom of England. It was a recognition of the extreme military importance of the area. But, more than anywhere else in the borderlands known as the Marches, Monmouthshire has remained mostly Welsh, not only in place-names but in the use of the language. The legislation of Westminster increasingly during the 20th cent. had to refer to Wales and Monmouthshire together, in educational and Parliamentary matters and for recruitment of the Welsh Guards. It can be truthfully said that Wales has recovered at least one of its lost provinces.

The most famous of its natives is Geoffrey of Monmouth, sometimes known as Geoffrey ab Arthur, Archdeacon of Llandaff in 1140 and consecrated in 1152 as Bishop of St Asaph, a place he never visited before his death three years later. Although Henry V of England was also, in due course, born in the castle at Monmouth, Geoffrey can claim to be the founder of the great Arthurian legend that spread through Europe in his time and inspired Malory and Tennyson and many others with what came to be known as the "Matter of Britain". Geoffrey alleged that he got the details of his historical romance from a "very ancient" book in Welsh that came from Brittany. The history that Geoffrey wrote of Britain before the days of Henry II was based partly on a medley of legends into which the tale of Britain's unruly participation in the affairs of the Roman Empire had fallen. Carausius, who had made it independent in the 3rd cent.; the military commanders who supported the other provinces of the West in setting up the short-lived Gallic Empire in the next; the Maximus who followed a similar path in the 5th cent. and won a place for himself in Welsh legend as Macsen Wledig; and the Riothamus (wrongly assumed by later historians to be a Breton) who attempted to restore the Gallic Prefecture in the 5th cent. were all pressed into service to create a British hero who was intended to act as a precedent for the Angevin Empire that, under Henry II, ruled from Scotland to the Pyrenees.

Geoffrey's fellow Welshman and fellow cleric, Gerald de Barri, writing some forty years after the appearance of Geoffrey's book, summed up its authenticity by telling the tale of a dying man oppressed with various devils who danced on his chest (see p. 24). This is not to deny that Geoffrey's tales contained a kernel of truth; modern archaeology has even found a basis for the legend he accepts that Britain was first colonized by the Brutus who came from fallen Troy, though not for the way in which Geoffrey retails it. Geoffrey's sources were both philosophical and allegorical. But he created an epic in prose of the constant battle men have to fight for the sake of civilization, and it has made both him and his visionary king immortal.

The Monnow bridge in Monmouth

G. Douglas Bolton

The Henry of Monmouth who was born about 250 years after Geoffrey's death did in some way realize the ideals of which he had written. As Henry V he owes a great deal to Shakespeare's patriotic handling of his deeds and reputation. The Welsh Fluellen whom the dramatist attached to King Harry represented the considerable and important part Welshmen from Gwent played' in the victories of Crécy and Agincourt. It was not simply that the David Gam (David the Wry) who had attempted to assassinate Owain Glyndwr at Machynlleth distinguished himself on the field; the archers to whom Henry V owed his success were the bowmen from Monmouthshire. The special skill of the Welsh with the long-bow was in drawing it back to the ear, an art the Normans never knew. It was said to have been made possible by the unusual suppleness of the yews that grew in Gwent, from which the bows were made; but in any event Welsh archery was recognized as being superior to that of all others.

Gerald the Welshman makes a strong point of this matter. The people of Venta (Gwent) were more famous for war and for their archery than any other in Wales. He cites an instance in which Welsh arrows went through the oak portal of a tower, four fingers thick, and in memory of so remarkable a feat the arrows were left in the gate. He quotes William de Braose, of evil memory, as saying that one of his men-at-arms was struck through the armour of the thigh, the thigh itself, and the flap of his saddle by a Welsh arrow that killed the horse under him. But Gerald disposes of the idea that it was the yews of Gwent which made such feats possible. The wild elm is the tree that he praises.

It was to mounted Welsh archers that Strongbow, the Clare who was the Norman Lord of Pembroke about 1170, owed his nickname and his successful invasion of Ireland. Richard II of England maintained himself with a special force of Welsh archers; and there seems to have been a readiness in Wales in the 15th cent. to accept Henry V as a Welshman since he was born at Monmouth.

Nothing now remains of Monmouth Castle, though some relics of the town walls can be traced. The 14th-cent. church with its tall tower is largely a restoration. But there is a museum with mementoes of Admiral Lord Nelson, and the pleasant hotel at which he stayed keeps, with its cobbled approach, a Regency-style charm. The Shire Hall is 18th-cent., and has before it a statue to the Hon. Charles S. Rolls, founder of Rolls-Royce and the first person to fly the Channel both ways without landing.

Monmouth received its charter in 1550, and since then has been happy to be a borough and a market town for its neighbourhood. In Monmouthshire, wheat and milk production have steadily increased; two-fifths of its area is grass, and the production of cattle and sheep and of cider-apples is flourishing. But coal-seams also are still important, and the county produces up to 15,000,000 tons of coal a year from the centres at Blaenafon, Pontypool, Cwmbran, Nantyglo

and Blaina, Abertillery, Abercarn, Ebbw Vale, Tredegar, Rhymney, and Bedwellte, where there are also most important steel-production units. Newport on the Usk is a busy port with many industries of its own.

MONTGOMERY, *Montgomeryshire,* is a long way from its railway station, and the roads from the nearest town of size and commercial importance tend to leave it to one side. This is typical of a place with a great name but not yet recovered from its dwindling into the status of a village, where between 1799 and 1939 no new buildings were erected, but where the spirit is strong. Most of the surviving houses are Elizabethan, Jacobean, Queen Anne, or Georgian. But one of the best known of the houses connected with Montgomery, the half-timbered dwelling built in 1675, called Lymore and once part of the property of the Earl of Powis, no longer exists. In spite of protests, it was demolished in the 1930s. But there are various contemporary survivals, particularly towards the Dovey valley. Although they originated as a device known to the Romans against the dangers of settlement in softish soil, they are an importation from Shropshire, and apparently not of Welsh production.

As the traditional capital of Montgomeryshire, the town seems to stand a little apart from the history of the rest of Powys. Its name is that of a conqueror, Roger of Montgomery, a Norman appointed to serve as a Lord Marcher in the reduction of the bastion of Wales. Welshmen call the place Trefaldwyn (Baldwin's Town), because a successor of the earlier Normans, one Baldwin de Boller, built the second castle in the days of Henry I by way of reasserting alien supremacy over the natives. This too led the precarious life proper to a border castle, and it had to be replaced by a third, built by Henry III in 1223.

Only a few fragments of this, in turn, now remain. It was the home of the Herbert family (connections of the family holding the earldom of Powis), including two of its most distinguished members, Lord Herbert of Cherbury and his brother George Herbert. The first, being among other things a distinguished diplomat, attempted to keep a philosophic neutrality during the Civil Wars of the 17th cent., and surrendered the castle on demand to the Sir Thomas Myddelton who did so much to uplift the cause of Puritanism and Parliament in these parts of Wales. His reward was to see the castle destroyed, five years after its surrender, in 1649.

The church, like some others in this still rural area, has a magnificence that seems out of proportion to the size of the town. It dates from the middle of the 14th cent., and one of its more important features is the rood-screen of great beauty, which was brought there from the place that gave Lord Herbert his title, the small town of Chirbury. When in position there, the screen belonged to the abbey church, demolished at the Reformation. The seating-stalls have misericords; the font is Late Norman. One of the memorials is to Richard Herbert, the father of the famous brothers mentioned above. In the graveyard is the well-known spot where one John Newton Davies was buried, convicted of murder in 1821 but always protesting his innocence. As proof, he swore that no grass would grow on the grave of a man wrongly condemned; and for a long time it was said that no grass grew on his own. Now, however, some apparently grows there after all. This does not necessarily mean that John's protestation of innocence is disproved; perhaps after more than 100 years he has forgiven his accusers.

Montgomery lies in the lowlands not far from pleasant places like Llanmerewig, Sarn, Kerry, and the valley in which Llanidloes stands. It can look S. to the two Black Mountains and the passes that will take you to Radnorshire and its forest; or westward to the moors of Carno and the shoulder of the Plynlimon escarpment above Dylife. But its memories belong rather to the E. – to that long marchland in which Chirbury stands.

Although only 3 m. from Montgomery, Chirbury is 2 m. across the border. It is a very charming village; and it is not only part of the history of Montgomery the town, but part of the land of Powys from which Montgomeryshire claims to descend. On his map published in the last quarter of the 16th cent., one Humfreydus Lhuydus (Humphrey Lhuyd) of Denbigh insists that Powys should still be shown as a division of Wales setting a triangle from the Dovey mouth to Chester and to Neath upon the Severn, running its English frontier between the two latter points along the courses of the Dee and Severn. In this he had some justification, since, until its abolition under the Protectorate, there was some revival of the idea of Powys in the setting-up of the Court and Council of Wales, with its capital at Ludlow. After the turmoil of the Middle Ages had settled into the strong, centralized government of the Renaissance with the accession of Henry VII after Bosworth, the whole country was subdivided into these councils, and Wales and the marchlands found, under the common government of Ludlow, an end to their internal disputes. To mark what he considered to be the Cambro-British origin of the place, Lhuyd wrote it down on his map as Lhudlow. The quiet place of Clun in Shropshire he marks under its Welsh name Colynwy; Church Stretton is Strethon; Bishop's Castle is Tre Escop; and Oswestry, Croys Oswald. Shrewsbury is Ymwythig; Worcester, Caer Frangon. Each place of significance has its original Latin name attached; for Powys was proud to be the direct heir of Rome not only against the invading Saxon but also against recalcitrant Britons of North and South. Indeed, this largely forgotten fact is one of the keys to the politics of medieval Wales. If the Princes of Powys appeared from time to time to seek allies among the Normans against the Welsh, and among the Welsh against the Normans, it was because they were conscious of their distinct cultural and national identity. Cultural especially, perhaps; for, as the heirs of the Cunedda who in the 5th cent. first set on foot the attempt to unite and organize the Roman-British province after the decline of the Empire, they were aware of a sense of a civilization that, in the Roman tradition, was superior to races, and the Welsh name for the Welsh people today is Cymry, meaning allies or combined peoples.

The marchlands that succeeded to the lost Kingdom of Powys, with its capital at Pengwern, have been made by this sense into a community that is half Welsh, half English; and its poets and other writers have been masters of a special kind of literature, combining subtle Welsh literary forms – the unexpected adjective that carries a whole set of associations, the quick transference of thought from image to image – with a nervous and concentrated English phraseology. The last master of this Anglo-Welsh poetry was Dylan Thomas; his predecessor was George Meredith. But among the earliest who so used the English language with a Welsh mind were the so-called Metaphysical poets of the 17th cent. And of these the brothers Lord Herbert of Cherbury and George Herbert count among the greatest.

Allegedly the family was at first of Norman blood, since it was founded by a Herbertus Camerarius who came over as a close attendant of the Conqueror. In the 13th cent. a descendant of his had lands granted to him in Wales, and he began the praiseworthy practice of marrying a Welsh heiress that has been consistently followed ever since. The closest connection the family had was with the House of Pembroke. But in his famous *Autobiography* Lord Herbert, who is full of tales about the accidents at arms of his ancestors, is proudest of his great-great-grandfather, Sir Richard Herbert of Coldbrook in Monmouthshire, who "passed through the army of the northern men twice with his pole-axe in his hand and returned without any mortal hurt". Not even that hero of romantic fantasy, Amadis of Gaul, says Lord Herbert, could surpass such a feat; and the tale strangely echoes Hamlet's description of his own father. Next in prominence was Herbert's great-grandfather, "steward in the time of Henry VIII of the lordships and marches of North Wales, East Wales and Cardiganshire, a man of power but also of true justice".

The *Autobiography* of this Edward, Lord of Cherbury, is fascinating. It presents him as Shakespeare's Friar Laurence might have presented Romeo's companion Tybalt. For the way in which the duels, the insults and challenges duly repaid in the streets of London, the gallantries in foreign courts and the activities of war and intrigue, are described reminds one that his brother George was a priest. There is a curious note in Lord Herbert's account of his meeting with lovely women; though by no means a Puritanical one, it suggests that his admiration of beauty was too sincere to ask for possession. He had indeed a Platonic frame of mind,

and was welcomed in his day as the successor
and equal of Francis Bacon. Like Bacon, Lord
Herbert attempted a new view of all philosophy;
he embodied it in *De Veritate*. More luckily
than Bacon, he established himself as a true
poet. George Herbert, the priest, could write:

> Sweet day, so cool, so calm, so bright,
> The bridall of the earth and skie;
> The dew shall weep thy fall tonight,
>   For thou shalt die.

> Sweet spring, full of sweet dayes and roses,
> A box where sweets compacted lie;
> My musick shows ye have your closes,
> And all must die.

His brother Edward, asking whether love
should continue for ever, wrote:

> So when one wing can make no way,
>   Two joinèd can themselves dilate;
> So can two persons propagate
> When singly either would decay.

> So when from hence we shall be gone
> And be no more, nor you nor I,
>   As one another's mystery
> Each shall be both, yet both be one.

The mixture of intense feeling with ruthless
logic, characteristic of the Metaphysical school
of writing and so much in tune with an age of
scientific discovery and speculation, is stronger in
Lord Herbert in these extracts than in his more
frequently praised brother George. They are
from a poem worthy to stand with those of
Donne, also a Welshman of Powys and the
master of them all.

MOUNTAIN ASH, *Glamorgan.* About
18 m. NW. of Cardiff, the small village of Aber-
pennar on the Cynon river, tributary to the Taff,
grew in the 19th cent. into the town and then the
urban district of Mountain Ash, one of the most
important of the coal-mining centres in the
South. But the economic collapse of the 1930s,
and the general decline in the importance of
coal in world economy, affected Mountain
Ash rather more severely than most of its neighbours. Nearly 20 per cent of its population
evaporated. But in its heyday its choir was famous
and its skill in bandsmanship unexcelled.

MOYLEGROVE, *Pembrokeshire.* In Welsh
Trewyddel, Moylegrove spells itself with or
without the *e* in the middle, according to the
whim of the cartographer. The place is 5 m. SW.
of Cardigan, and has kept itself astonishingly
neat and colour-washed, a worthy entrant for
the title of best-kept village in Pembrokeshire.
It is small. Two chapels confront each other
with a line of low houses on either side. The
Ceibwr stream runs happily under the bridge
on its way down to the sea at the Ceibwr creek,
1 m. away. The road dips down to Moylegrove
and then rises in an alarmingly steep and twisting fashion. Moylegrove, down in its secluded

valley, is a lucky place. A little higher up the
Ceibwr valley is Monington, which has a church
with some frescoes in ochre and the 18th-cent.
house of Pant Saeson.

SW. of the village, up on the plateau above the
valley, are two fine cromlechs, Llech-y-Drybedd
and Trellyffant.

MUMBLES, The, *Glamorgan.* The term
"the Mumbles" has in recent years been popularly
extended to include the whole of the limestone
peninsula that shelters the village of Oystermouth
and dramatically terminates the curve of Swansea
Bay on the western side. The Mumbles themselves
are the two islands that lie at the very tip of the
curve. The derivation of their strange name is
uncertain; it may possibly be an Anglicization
of the Welsh Mynydd Moel (Bare Mountain).
On the outer island is the lighthouse, first built
as far back as 1794 and surrounded with a complex
of storehouses, signal stations, and fortifications,
which are now largely disused since the light
has become automatic. Underneath the cliff
on which the lighthouse stands is the cavern
known as Bob's Cave. In the late 1870s, a popular
poem by Clement Scott – a favourite at dramatic
recitals – made famous the heroism of the sisters
Ace, the daughters of the lighthouse-keeper,
who rescued a drowning sailor. They waded
into the boiling surf and pulled him ashore
with a rope made from their knotted shawls.
Inevitably they became known as the "Grace
Darlings of Wales". The lighthouse is needed,
for the shoals of the Nixon Sands extend to the
westward, just off the outer island. Both islands
can be reached on foot at low tide. The Mumbles
lighthouse was also the scene of the early experiments of Wheatstone and Dillwyn Llewelyn,
which led to the development of the electric telegraph.

The Mumbles pier runs out from the headland
opposite the islets and contains a special slipway
for launching the Mumbles lifeboat. Together
with the Winter Gardens, now a hotel and dance-
hall, the pier was built in 1898, at the same time
as the celebrated Mumbles Railway was extended
from Oystermouth to Mumbles Head. This
railway could claim to be the oldest passenger
one in the world. The track round the bay from
Swansea to Oystermouth was constructed in
1804, and passengers were first carried in 1807.
The carriages were, of course, horse-drawn. In
the steam era, from the end of the 19th cent.,
engines drew a string of open-sided carriages,
with seats on top. These "Puffing Billies" had an
atmosphere all their own, with the passengers
clinging like limpets to the outside steps, and little
boys turning cartwheels at every stop to earn
pennies. The line modernized itself, with electric
cars, in 1929. Finally the all-conquering bus
displaced the whole railway, and the world's
oldest passenger trains ceased to run in 1960.

The road cutting now leads back from the
pier, under the steep cliffs of the headland. To the
left, after you leave the cutting the gabled and
turreted Bristol Channel Yacht Club, with two

brass cannon at the door, is a connoisseur's piece for anyone interested in Edwardian survivals. The village of Oystermouth now occupies the space between the steep hill-side and the sea. There are some picturesque lanes that climb up between the houses along the front. They are reminders of the day when the popular rhyme had it that:

> Mumbles is a funny place,
> A church without a steeple,
> Houses built of old ships wrecked,
> And a most peculiar people.

The great days of Mumbles seafaring are over. The oyster-beds, for which the place was famous since the days of the Romans, are now finished, although remains of the "perches" can sometimes be seen at low tide. Instead, the Mumbles and Oystermouth have become a stronghold of week-end yachting and sailing. Oystermouth started to expand as a dormitory for Swansea at the end of last century, and contains only two monuments of antiquity. The church, which is rather hidden back among the houses near the little open space of the Downs, is dedicated to All Saints. It is an attractive building, some of it modern, but with an ancient core. The square font has the date 1251 inscribed on it. There are three 17th-cent. bells on the floor at the W. end. The present bells in the tower come from Santiago de Compostela in Spain. The church has, however, acquired fame – or perhaps notoriety – from the fact that Dr Thomas Bowdler is buried in the churchyard. Dr Bowdler of Bath published in 1818 his expurgated edition of Shakespeare, from which he had excised all passages "calculated to deprave the youthful mind". He performed a similar service for Gibbon, and died leaving the verb "to bowdlerize" as an indispensable part of the English language.

The second ancient attraction of Oystermouth is the castle, finely placed on a hill that in recent years has had difficulty in shaking itself free of housing projects. Oystermouth was regarded as one of the "Keys of Gower".

The earliest castle on the site was burnt by the Welsh in 1285. It was probably built by William de Londres, who seems to have been the first holder of Oystermouth. The present remains all date from the reconstruction after the Welsh Rising of 1287. The castle is somewhat irregular in plan, with a gatehouse, an open courtyard or ward, and a keep, all connected by high curtain walls without towers. The gatehouse did indeed possess two circular towers, but they have been demolished. The keep contains the domestic buildings. To the left were the great hall and the principal apartments. To the right, on the top floor of the three-storeyed building, was the chapel, which still preserves its piscina and a traceried window. The castle is now in the care of Swansea Corporation.

From the castle, but even better from the 250-ft summit of the hill behind the headland, you can enjoy the whole panorama of Swansea Bay. Walter Savage Landor once compared it to the Bay of Naples. This, frankly, was going too far. But even now, with heavy industry established around so much of its shore, the sweep of the bay is memorable, as it curves from the distant point of Porthcawl under the dark mountains of the coalfield, past the terraced houses of Swansea and round to the white isles of Mumbles Head. It is even more impressive at night with the shore lights reflected on the full tide.

Immediately to the W. of the headland are two small coves known as Bracelet Bay and Limeslade Bay. They are rather cluttered with car parks, and there is even a shanty town hidden in the little combe at Limeslade. Beyond

Oystermouth Castle

G. Douglas Bolton

them the cliff-path leads round to Langland Bay. This is the start of the most attractive cliff-walk in Wales – the south coast of the Gower peninsula.

MYDDFAI, *Carmarthenshire*, lies 3 m. S. of Llandovery in fine scenery. The main point of interest is the church. This is partly 14th- and partly 15th-cent., and is dedicated to St Michael. The interior has seen some curious alterations. There is a partition across the E. end of the N. aisle, which hides a medieval window. There are pieces of ancient glass in the window next to it. The S. aisle has become the nave. The octagonal font is a curiosity. The roofs are barrel-vaulted, and there are numerous painted panels. The hatchment of the local grandees, the Gwynne Holfords, hangs over the chancel arch. Their Georgian house at Cilgwyn, 2 m. to the W., once abandoned, is now reoccupied.

Myddfai was famous for its long line of physicians, who claimed to be descended from the Lady of the Lake (*see* Black Mountain). The first of the line was Rhiwallon, who lived about 1200; and the last, Sir John Williams, who died in 1926.

MYDRIM, *Carmarthenshire*, is a village 7½ m. due W. of Carmarthen in green, unfrequented, pylon-free country. The trout stream of the Dewi Fawr flows under the bridge in the dingle near a row of pleasant cottages. Here, too, is the new children's playground, partly surrounded by high wire fences that conjure up totally unjustified visions of the destructive powers of the children in this gentle place. The church stands among the trees above the Dewi. It is approached through a line of yews, but was rebuilt in a rather unexciting mid-Victorian manner. The form of the churchyard is more interesting. It is oval and may indicate that the original church was deliberately built on a pre-historic site. Stephen Hughes (1622–88), a leading Dissenter who first collected the works of Vicar Rhys Prichard (*see* Llandovery) in 1659 and was a man of influence under Cromwell, held the living here in 1654.

Up the road is the Methodist chapel with a remarkable pillared front. On the main A40, 4 m. out of Carmarthen near the Mydrim signpost, is Cana Chapel, with its long, clear windows, which from certain angles give you the illusion of seeing clean through the building. Cana is now a model of how a chapel should be decorated. It has no vulgar pebble-dash, but an elegantly planned scheme of olive and white.

NANTLLE and the **SIX LAKES,** *Caernarfonshire*. Where the mountains of Snowdonia drop and divide between Penygroes and Llanllyfni, Nantlle stands on the motor roads leading towards Snowdon. Rather than any other place, it can be taken as a starting-point for the discovery of the chain of lakes looped round the neck of Snowdon, since it is set on one of them, Llyn Nantlle Uchaf. Each of these lakes is inti-

mately connected with the heights that gather round Yr Wyddfa, or Snowdon summit. Each of them has a distinctive beauty.

Cwellyn takes the road from Caernarfon to Beddgelert under its arm, and even had a station of the Welsh Highland Railway on its shore. The most probable explanation of its name (as suggested by F. H. Ward, whose work on lake-fishing in Wales is indispensable) makes it a contraction of Chwech Llyn. Six lakes lie in a group about the head of Snowdon: Ffynnon-y-gwas, Nadroedd, Cwm-Glas, Coch, and Gader, with Cwellyn itself making up the number. A little further out from this group, Nantlle, Cwm-Silyn, and Dywarchen lie about Trwm Ddysgl; Glaslyn and Llydaw are sheltered by Snowdon; Gwynant and Dinas watch the road from Capel Curig to Beddgelert, and Cwm-Dulyn lies apart under its screen of rock where the hill that bears its name looks down at the Pennant Valley.

In earlier days Cwellyn was called Tarddeni, which seems to mean Outpouring. About 1¼ m. long and ½ m. wide, it gives an exceptional view of Snowdon, not of the summit at its most grimly impressive, but of the sunlit morning mists about the mountain's shoulders. Yet even Snowdon has to give place here to Mynydd Mawr, hanging over the NW. of Cwellyn. It is a spur of very ancient rock – relics of Snowdon's remote volcanic origin, felspar crystalled with quartz – that catches the clear light of morning and the silver bars of rain, so that the whole mass floats against the blue of sky and the blue waters like a cloud of ice. The lake has been sounded to a depth of about 150 ft; the relatively shallow parts run out from the shore for 5 to 30 yds. Once salmon and sea-

Llyn Gwynant, one of the Snowdon lakes, with the mountain Yr Aran

Jane J. Miller

trout were able to ascend the rivers into Cwellyn, using the strength and arts that Gerald de Barri, nearly 800 years ago, was delighted to watch and describe. But a dam across the Gwyrfai river thirty or forty years ago has since prevented them.

Prehistoric dwellings neighbour the lake above the crags of Craig Cwm Bychan; and here, as in some other places, the story is told of a wife, belonging to the Other People, who must never know the touch of iron. In this case she was accidentally struck by a stirrup-iron, and so vanished for ever. These recollections of pre-Celtic folk living close to waters that fed and protected them are, for Cwellyn, supported by the tale of one who came upon the Other People dancing on the shore at evening. He joined their circle and was taken by them to their strangely different world. Seven years passed like one night; and he returned to find his parents dead and his promised wife married to another. The interest of this tale is in its striking parallelism with the one Gerald de Barri heard at Swansea in 1188, the details of which, as set out in his *Itinerary of Wales*, are today curiously suggestive.

Ffynnon-y-gwas is only ¼ m. long. It lies almost directly under Snowdon and against the Clogwyn Du'r Arddu, dark and peaty and overseen by an ancient standing stone. Its name is explained by the fact that a shepherd was accidentally drowned here while washing sheep. But the "gwas" that can mean a servant can also mean a youth, and some pre-Christian ceremony of appeasing the spirit of the depths by sacrifice of one of the community's fairest youths may possibly be remembered in the word.

Small, deep, and black in marshy ground, Nadroedd has a shore walled with rocks. No fish swim there. The name means Lake of Adders, it is said; and, as the terms of art associated with 18th-cent. Druidry include Adders as a priestly title, the lake has been connected with rites of which no reliable particulars have survived. It is curious that "gwas y neidr" means "dragon-fly", and perhaps both Nadroedd and Ffynnon-y-gwas take their names from the colourful and strange creatures that haunt lake-waters.

The small and fishless Llyn Cwm-Glas has a minute island. The lake is severed from Glaslyn by walls of rock that sheer from a ridge so narrow that its width at times becomes not much more than a foot. The legend here speaks of hidden treasure – jewels, coins, and the golden throne that went with the crown of Britain and was hidden by Merlin in Cwm-Glas until the Saxon should be driven from the island.

The Coch (Red) lake is so called because so much iron lies in the bed of the lake and the stream feeding it that the dominant hue is purple-scarlet. Here again we find a legend of the bride from the Other People and the evil of iron.

Llyn y Gader, with dangerous boggy banks but an exhilarating view of the Snowdon summit, has many trout and can be visited without much danger that its legends will prove true. As it is told of the Llyn y Cau on Cader Idris, so here in

the 18th cent. a young man swam in the deep waters. But, as he reached the centre, a long and trailing beast rose from the depths, wound him in its coils and dragged him into a hollow under the banks. Another story is of a yellow creature that dwelt in the lake and was hunted up the Bwlch Drws-y-coed and killed; 100 years ago this lake was known as Cadair yr Aur Frychin in consequence.

An exceptionally interesting lake is Dywarchen, by reason of a natural feature that attracted the notice of Gerald de Barri. It is called the Lake of the Turf Island because it still has in it a floating islet, now little more than 1 yd across, but recorded in 1698 and again in 1798 as being much larger. The astronomer Halley recounts how he actually swam out to satisfy himself that the island did in fact float and could be steered by hand. A similar phenomenon is found in Mynyllod near Bala, where it was noted that, if the island drifted towards Corwen, the market there would be good and at Bala bad, and vice versa. Floating islands of the kind have been noted all over the world and in all periods of history; they seem to have had a special sanctity in pre-Christian days.

Glaslyn offers beauty instead of fish. The valley in which it lies is one of the most impressive in all Snowdonia. Cliffs around it stand straight at heights of up to 1,000 ft, and the water is of an unusual bluish green that catches all colours of weather and season. Here the monster Afanc was destroyed by Hu the Mighty in days of old – though one should add the caution that, since the time of Hu, sheep and goats are reported to have vanished mysteriously at night from its banks.

Though in a milder and more pastoral setting than any of the others, Llyn Gwynant gives an incredibly beautiful view of Snowdon as you come upon it from Penygwryd. At this point the terraced and gigantic precipices of Lliwedd and Wyddfa are seen in their fullest magnificence. If possible, the time of sunset should be chosen, for then the beacons of the sun are lit on the summits for a moment that is never forgotten.

Between Beddgelert and Penygwryd lies Llyn Dinas. It is very lovely in itself, but it also falls into line with the legends surrounding the Snowdon lakes. For here not Merlin but Vortigern left the throne of Britain in hiding, and here one day a youth will come and tread upon a secret stone, and the recess will open and Britain will be itself again.

Llyn Cwm-y-llan adds a third to this series. For here, after the Battle of Tre Galan close by, Arthur the King, wounded, asked to be brought that he might find shelter. He was placed in a cave closed over with great rocks, and lay sleeping until a farmer chanced upon the place. For a moment the King woke, and his companion knights stirred in their slumber. But the farmer told them the time was not yet ripe for them to come again and save Britain. They sleep there still.

In Llydaw you find a castellated lake, battlemented with the crags of Grib Goch and the cliffs of Lliwedd. They rise from 700 to 1,000 ft above

Porth Dinllaen, west of Nefyn

the deep, jade water. For geologists it has exceptional examples of glacier working; archaeologists record it as a place where one of the earliest boats made was recovered from the peat. It was a canoe fashioned from a single trunk by hollowing it out – about 9 ft long, the stern square, the stem blunt and with a rudimentary keel. Originally it was 18 in. wide. Probably lake dwellings were once built out into the water.

If any of the lakes of Snowdonia can be said to have continued into the present the customs and traditions of their early population, it is certainly Ffynnon Lloer (Lake of the Moon), one that has the extraordinary quality of taking the full moon into the rounded crater within which it lies. Until a generation ago it was the custom among the mountain farms on May Day Eve to hold ceremonial dances on its shores.

NASH POINT, *Glamorgan*, is not the most southerly point of the coastline of the Vale of Glamorgan. This is at Rhoose, between Aberthaw and Barry. Nash, however, is the most interesting and impressive of the vale headlands. Two lighthouses stand sentinel over the cliff-edge, which is here steep-cut in strangely regular, layered rocks. Out to sea stretch the dangerous sandbanks that are marked, far out in the channel, by the Scarweather lightship. Near in is the Tusker Rock. The narrow, navigable passage between the sands and the point is the "Gutter Fawr", a notorious place for seamen, especially in the days of sail. It was the tragedy of the wreck in 1831, when eighty-one lives were lost, that convinced Trinity House of the need for a lighthouse on the spot. In a later shipwreck, of the collier *Ben-y-glo*, the gale was so violent that the ship was thrown clean against the cliffs and the crew were able to walk off the vessel on to the shore. The Admiralty experts who were sent down to examine the lighthouse site in 1840 were themselves nearly drowned. Of the two lighthouse towers, only one is now in use. The architecture of the lighthouses, the subsidiary

buildings, and the white-walled enclosure at the cliff's edge is in the best tradition of early 19th-cent. Trinity House, which combines simplicity and elegance with fitness for the job. N. of the lighthouse is a dry valley, with an Iron Age fort on the cliff-edge. Cars park at the top of the cliff near the lighthouses. About 1 m. inland is the rather forlorn little church of Marcross, with a 12th-cent. chancel and nave, a slender tower with a saddleback roof, and a Norman moulded doorway in the S. porch. The font is curiously large for so small a church – almost a hip-bath for baptizing outsize babies.

The Bristol Channel starts to widen out at Nash Point, but there are fine views over the water to the heights of Exmoor in Devonshire.

NEFYN, *Caernarfonshire*. Little more than a fishing village in recent years, Nefyn has developed as one of the most attractive resorts of the Lleyn. It stands between the sea with its stretch of firm and moulded sands, the sea-land called Morfa Nefyn, and the hill of Garn Bodfuan (918 ft). Facilities for sport include riding, fishing, and golf. Its past was magnificent. It was specially favoured by Edward I of England, who may well have been attracted by its level and gentle beauty. After the fall of Llywelyn the Last, the English King held a tournament to celebrate his triumph as part of a general festival at Nefyn in 1284; and the site of the lists can still be traced. To confirm Nefyn as a place he chose to honour, his successors created Nefyn in 1355 as one of the ten Royal Boroughs in North Wales. The woods on Garn Bodfuan are beautiful, and hidden in them are the "cythiau gwyddelog" or stone-built circular hut sites frequent in Lleyn and marking a settlement of people pre-British or even pre-Celtic. Bodfuan village, a little way off, has a hall with a lake and well-laid-out grounds. The house itself is a pleasant example of 18th-cent. architecture.

Nefyn is separated from the wide bay of Porth Dinllaen by a small promontory, the Penrhyn.

This bay, too, offers excellent bathing and sea-fishing, and is shut in from the broader seas by its own promontory, where there is an inn and the remains of an old fortress site.

NEVERN, *Pembrokeshire.* When the Norman Martin of Tours landed at Abergwaun, or Fishguard, in 1087, among the earliest of the Conqueror's adventurers into Wales, he settled in effect a kingdom for himself, inter-wed with the equally distinct and independent Welsh rulers; and it was Nevern that he chose as his capital. His son moved his seat to nearby Newport, which was more conveniently set upon the coast; and to a large extent he identified himself with the native traditions of his lordship. The exceptional character of the two towns and the area they commanded is reflected in the sense of continuity and peaceful growth they give.

Nevern is hidden in a valley some 300 ft below the road that crosses the hills and seems to have dropped out of time as steeply as it drops in space. The church is no longer specifically Norman, for its battlemented tower, typical of the time when the church had to be a fortress against sea-rovers as well as serving other purposes, is of the Late Perpendicular fashion of the 12th and 13th cents. It is deeply beset with old yews, which make an avenue of approach to it. But it holds with great care many early Welsh stones, inscribed both in Latin and in that Ogham form of lettering which came into being about A.D. 400, when Rome declined, and faded away by A.D. 600, when the first unlettered attempt of the native peoples of the Severn Sea and of Ireland to communicate in writing was replaced by the more learned skills of the Celtic Church. The Norman Church saw no difficulty here in accepting the memorials of the Dark Age of Britain, and one very large stone, intricately ornamented with Celtic incisions, which must be as old as the high cross lifting itself 12½ ft above ground and called after the Celtic saint to whom the church is dedicated, St Brynach. Dominating the skyline is the height of Carn Ingli (or, to use its real name, Carn Engyl Lle, the Place of Angels), where Brynach is said to have retired to talk directly with visitants from Heaven; perhaps upon that stark volcanic height, 1,138 ft up, the saint had his first hermitage. On its slopes lie the walls and ruined towers of one of the best preserved prehistoric camps in Wales. This point of land, with this hill overlooking the small bays of the coast, was a place of planned settlement long before Christianity; and the hills of Preseli, of which Carn Ingli forms part, were holy to the men who built Stonehenge.

But it was St David who became the dominant figure of belief, particularly when Rome allowed pilgrimage to his shrine at St David's at least half as much importance as one to St Peter's. About 100 yds W. of the church is a cross cut into the face of the wayside rock, and before it a carved kneeling-place for pilgrims. The pilgrim routes to St David's had their principal point of departure from Abercywyn in Carmarthenshire, not too far from St Clear's, a place to which men took sail from Cornwall, Brittany, and the shores of Biscay. Here at Nevern, on the last track of their journeying, they stayed to pray.

NEWCASTLE EMLYN, *Carmarthenshire,* Castell Newydd Emlyn in Welsh, is a pleasant, friendly, and very Welsh little market town on the Teifi 10 m. E. of Cardigan. Basically, Newcastle Emlyn consists of one street that turns to the right and left before dropping down on to the bridge across the river. Over the bridge you are in Cardiganshire. The Teifi forms the county boundary along the whole stretch of the river between Lampeter and Cardigan, and fierce has been the county pride of the little towns and villages on either bank. Newcastle Emlyn is in Carmarthenshire, but Adpar, over the bridge, refused to be included in the urban district of Newcastle Emlyn, when this was formed in 1897. It still remains separate. The first printing-press in Wales was set up here by Isaac Carter in 1718, a fact commemorated by a tablet on a house near the bridge, set up by the Newcastle Emlyn Happy Winter Evening Entertainments Committee in 1912.

The Castle of Newcastle Emlyn stands on a grassy knoll, with the Teifi flowing round it in an S-bend that makes a natural moat. The New Castle was so called to distinguish it from the old castle built earlier downstream at Cilgerran. The New Castle was first constructed by the Welsh prince Maredudd ap Rhys of Dinefwr (Dynevor). His son, Rhys ap Maredudd, rebelled against Edward I, after his conquest of Wales. The fortress was finally captured for the King in 1288, when the walls had been pounded by a "military engine" dragged across country from Dryslwyn in the Towy valley. In 1343, Llywelyn ap Gwilym was Constable of Newcastle. He was the uncle of Dafydd ap Gwilym, Wales's greatest medieval poet. The Castle and town suffered severely in the Glyndwr Revolt and fell into decay. Henry VII granted it to Sir Rhys ap Thomas after the Battle of Bosworth. Sir Rhys largely rebuilt it as one of his residences. During the Civil War it changed hands repeatedly. It was the last castle in South Wales to hold out for the King. The Parliamentarians then "slighted" it, leaving it a complete wreck. The ruins today are ivy-grown and romantic.

The church is comparatively modern and stands at the end of an avenue of lime trees. It was built in the 1840s, and enlarged eighty years later by W. D. Caröe. It is not unattractive; it makes remarkable use of slate from the quarries of Cilgerran. The material seems to be everywhere in the church. The interior is paved with large slabs of it. Slate-stone is used for the square pillars supporting the roof and for the chancel arch. The font is of slate, and so is the sundial outside on the S. wall.

The Magistrates' Court, decorated with the lion and unicorn crest, is near the church. Bethel Methodist Chapel, near at hand, is well proportioned. The church, court, school, and chapel form a pleasant enclave off the main street.

The miniature Public Hall and Library is a gay Victorian fantasy, complete with clock. Perhaps none of the buildings of Newcastle Emlyn are very distinguished individually, with the exception of a well-built bank in the main street and the old hotel near the bridge. But the general effect is attractive, especially when the town is busy on market day.

The road that runs S. from Newcastle Emlyn direct to Cynwyl Elfed passes through unfrequented country and rises to over 1,000 ft on Moelfre. To the W. of this high point, narrow lanes twist down to the few houses of Cwm Morgan in the wooded valley of Cwm-cych. This is a countryside of small farms on high, hard ground.

NEWPORT, *Monmouthshire*. Casnewydd-ar-Wysg (Newcastle-on-Usk) is the proper name for a town that leapt into international prominence as the export centre for the hinterland coalfield of Monmouthshire, and the vast iron and steel productivity the 19th cent. developed. In 1801, Newport's population was just 1,135. One hundred and thirty years later it had leapt to 89,198, and in 1935, by judicious extension of its boundaries, it included a total of over 100,000. Its chief significance was as a port, and in 1842 the docks, with 6 m. of quays, were initiated. When Newport's boundaries were widened, the Alexandra Docks, acquired by the Great Western Railway, could claim to have the largest water-sheet held in by locks anywhere in the world: South Dock 95 acres, North Dock 29. The Transporter Bridge had then been nearly thirty years in service. Times and the affairs of men have brought their changes. In 1938, Newport's exports of the range of products its hinterland supplied amounted to 3,250,000 tons, of which coal totalled over 3,000,000. By 1956, exports had dropped to 1,333,000 tons, of which coal represented just under 1,000,000. Imports in the same period rose from 354,500 tons to 1,350,000.

The town still has evidence of its origin in the attempt of the Normans to extend their Conquest into the West. Robert FitzHamon, the invader of Glamorgan, with his following of twelve knights and their troopers, founded the castle in 1171. It survived the Border Wars well enough to be remodelled in the 14th and 15th cents. when England was at war within under the contending banners of the Roses. Its siting is a monument to the planned tactics that attempted to push the frontier of Powys and Gwent from Severn to Wye and then to the Usk over which it stands. Its central tower served both practical and spiritual needs; for above is the chapel and below is the water gate, and the bridge tower has windows that are a remarkable example of the 15th-cent. Decorated style.

The castle is under the care of the Ministry of Public Building and Works; but the castle's contemporary, the Church of St Woolos on Stow Hill, has had a more living destiny. The church is largely as FitzHamon had it made, the nave

G. Douglas Bolton

The Church of St Woolos, Newport, Monmouthshire

Norman of the 12th cent., though the chancel belongs to the later time when the castle was refashioned. The two outstanding features of St Woolos are its Galilee (or Mary) Chapel, between the nave and the ponderous square tower, which belongs to the emergence of an English style from the Norman, and the door to the nave, which is Norman in its stern balance of arch but with two columns at its sides carved in another fashion and believed to have been brought from the Roman town of Caerleon, the Isca that had its name from the Usk. The word Woolos may mark a similar transition or amalgam between Roman and Celt: it hints at the science of seamen who may well have had an earlier shrine here than the one that the Norman chose to establish. The font is particularly worth examining; but the church has the distinction that in 1921, following the disestablishment of the Church of England and the creation of the Church in Wales, it became Pro-Cathedral to the new diocese of Monmouth.

Although the town is not very distinguished in architecture, being a rapid and utilitarian growth of the 19th cent., the Museum in Dock Street houses much of what has been recovered from the Roman settlements at Caerleon and Caerwent. And that it maintained the deep tradition of Welsh culture is shown by birth in it of William Henry Davies, whose fame as a poet belonged to the 20s of this century, but who is certain to outlast the century altogether. He had the detached, wandering spirit that was the heritage of the harp-men who sang their way from place to place in the 17th and 18th cents. and who could still be found even in the industrial South well into our own time. His penurious and adventurous life in the U.S.A. in 1890 he has immortalized in his *Autobiography of a Super-Tramp*. But his verse combines the direct simplicity and detailed observation of Wil Hopkin together with the metrical craftsmanship and unexpected image-association of the great Welsh "Metaphysicals", from the Herberts to Meredith and Dylan Thomas. The "time to stand and stare" is something the harp-men sought as determinedly as he; and, like them, he could find a world of meaning in a butterfly upon a stone.

NEWPORT, *Pembrokeshire.* The Nevern river rises from its source in the Mynydd Preseli (Prescelly Hills) and flows almost due W. into Newport Bay, which curves under Dinas Head to reach the small sea-harbour of Cwmyreglwys, with its crumbled church on the sea-walls and tiny craft lolling on the wave. It runs through a close-sided valley and, as it meets the sea, leaves standing on the slopes of hills the town of Trefdraeth, a "city on the sands", as the name implies, though in English it is known as Newport. A great deal of history has concentrated around Newport, and it had its time of fame and even power; but from all this it has chosen to resign and have nothing but the wind upon the hills and sea.

Parts of its history are obscure, though they have left permanent memorials. From the Preseli tops the thirty-three dolerite stones were taken by those who built Stonehenge, for it seems this curve of Pembrokeshire had some special importance for the shipping that went back and forth between the coasts of Wessex and Ireland. Whether they used Newport Bay at any time for their landings is a matter of guesswork; but, in the valley on the other side of the Mynydd Preseli near Mynachlog-ddu, is a stone circle, Gors Fawr, of the kind meant to serve the same purpose of time-count as Stonehenge.

Of Roman times there is little direct evidence in other parts of Pembrokeshire, but the old track now called the Ffordd Ffleming is a trackway, perhaps older than Rome, but leading to the one military station with its short, straight relic of roadway that has been discovered, the fort at Castell Fflemish. The possibility that Newport and its bay were not overlooked by them rests on the fact that Newport seems to have had a special strategic importance. At one time, its seagoing business was great enough to make it a serious rival to Fishguard; then under Elizabeth Tudor the place suffered a plague, from which it never recovered.

Before that, it had played a fatal part in the development of Welsh history. After the defeat of Harald of Saxon England, the rulers of Wales had some breathing-space in which to recover from the series of successful attacks he had made across the border. The Normans were for twenty

years too much occupied with completing their conquest of Harald's kingdom to be able to consider a serious assault on Wales. The opportunity was not taken. A strong personality of the House of Cunedda, Rhys ap Tewdwr, Prince of Dinefwr in Carmarthenshire, emerged with sufficient ability to establish himself as master of the South and make common cause with Ap Cynan, Prince in the North. By 1079 there was a possibility that Wales might recover a unity it had not had since Hywel the Good in the previous century and Rhodri the Great in the century before that. But in 1081 the Norman had taken both Chester and Shrewsbury, and with that considerable advantage the Conqueror himself advanced into Wales and struck as far as St David's. Beyond founding the castle at Cardiff, his campaign had no success. He died in 1087.

But the feuds among the Welsh between the rival provinces of Powys and Gwynedd and Deheubarth were always irreconcilable. Rhys was disturbed by the revolt of one of his sub-rulers, Einion, Prince of Dyfed, as the Welsh call Pembroke. In 1088 Rhys marched to St Dogmael's, and there he overcame the troops of Einion with heavy slaughter. Einion fled into Glamorgan and persuaded Iestyn, its overlord, to carry on the feud against Rhys by calling in the Norman. This was the opportunity that FitzHamon and his twelve knights took to conquer the South. William Rufus, the second Norman King, played his part personally in extending the grasp of the Conquest to S. Pembrokeshire. But the castle at Newport was not built until the 13th cent., and was built by William de Turribus. Its gate, with one flank-tower remaining, its outer wall and another isolated round tower, were incorporated into a mansion built in 1859.

The original castle has a unique history in relation to the Norman adventure. In 1087 Martin of Tours (or de Turribus) landed at Fishguard with a detachment of men that seems to have made its conquest by parley and not force. Although it was reckoned a fief of the South, Dyfed had always a certain separateness, and this part of it not only allowed a peaceful settlement by its new master but welcomed his marriage into the local princely family. The lordship of Kemes kept its distinct character; southern Pembroke was directly owned by the King of England, but the northern part remained Welsh in language and thought and in the independence it persuaded its only half-Norman lords to keep. Martin's descendant, William, founded Newport with his castle, and the succession of his line was unbroken. From 1100, the Lord Marchership of the Barony of Kemes continued into the 20th cent., and its holders exercised the unique privilege of appointing the Mayor to their borough of Newport. For a brief period, early in the 13th cent., Llywelyn the Great seized the castle; but its later history seems to have been disturbed only by rumours of the landing made by the French invading force at the end of the 18th cent. near its old rival Fishguard.

One of the most interesting successors to

Martin of Tours was the George Owen of Henllys who, in the days of Queen Elizabeth Tudor, wrote an account of Pembrokeshire filled with detail of the countryside and the customs of his native place. Like his remote connection, the 12th-cent. Gerald de Barri, he has praise and blame for both: horse-breeding neglected, but the trout and salmon superb; too little fencing of fields done, and too many trees wantonly cut, but the soil fruitful and pleasant; the men unsoldierly and neglectful of archery, and idling with bowls instead but engaging in the game of knappan at risk of life and limb. This knappan was one of a kind anthropologists delight in studying: a leather ball was sewn and stuffed, perhaps in some forgotten pagan ritual of head-hunting, and pursued with sticks by horsemen in a mixture of polo and lacrosse. It is probably from similar games, played on foot, that football in both its forms, association and rugby, has been derived. No pleasanter note is sounded in Welsh history than in the journals of George Owen and in the tale of the lordship of Kemes.

NEW QUAY, *Cardiganshire*. In Welsh Ceine-wydd, New Quay is a rather Cornish-looking little seaside town climbing up a hill overlooking Cardigan Bay 12 m. N. of Cardigan. It grew up in the 18th and early 19th cents. in the days when shipbuilding was an important part of life in every little inlet along the bay. New Quay actually looks E., with a sturdy stone pier curving round to protect the anchorage. The harbour dries out at low tide, leaving a fine stretch of sand, which has made the modern fortune of New Quay. In high summer the town bursts its bounds, and caravan parks sprout along the wooded slopes above the water. But New Quay has retained its charm. The houses are mainly Georgian and Victorian, making a fine effect as they line the lower slopes of the 300-ft Pencraig hill. Yachting is a major occupation. The high bluff of New Quay Head stands out seawards from the harbour. New Quay church, dedicated to St Llwchairn, was rebuilt in 1863, with only the Norman font and a carved beam over the W. door left from the old building.

The sands curve round to Llanina, where the old church, at the sea-edge in the grounds of Llanina House, has been completely rebuilt.

Inland, at the point where the road to New Quay turns down from the main Aberystwyth–Cardigan highway, is Llanarth, with a church that can boast a Norman font and a standing stone with Ogham marks. At Wern Newydd, Henry VII is reputed to have stayed on his way to Bosworth. According to local tradition, he also visited Llwyndafydd, where he had a brief affair with the daughter of the house. The Parry-ap-Harrys of Cardiganshire long claimed royal blood. At Llanarth the Gilfachrheda farm became a stud after the Second World War, for breeding Palomino ponies. The ponies in most of the famous circuses came from this Cardiganshire village.

NEWTOWN, *Montgomeryshire*. Y Dre-newydd (the New Town) can be said to justify its name in an unprecedented way. For it was not only, by deliberate purpose, a new town in planning and political policy when first founded, but the proposal now is to revolutionize the whole area in which it stands and incorporate it and the town of Caersws further to the W. in the upper Severn valley into a new town of considerable proportions.

Not very much of its origin is reflected in the present Newtown, a busy and prosperously archi-tectured centre, once a leading manufactory for flannel and tweed, but more recently a market for the agriculture and sheep-raising of the district. The most important situation of the land lying under the Kerry hills at the junction of the Mule and the Severn, as commanding the strategy of approach between England and Wales, decided Llywelyn the Last to build a town and fortress to protect it at Abermule. He began the project in 1273; but unfortunately it came to the attention of Edward I of England, who was equally aware of the strategic significance of the place. He ordered the destruction of the Maiden Castle Llywelyn had set up, and, in a sense, this dispute caused the war in which Llywelyn lost his life and Wales its independence.

In 1279 the victorious King of England was able to grant a charter for the founding of a new town that would control this vital passage between the two countries. But the grant concerned land not in the position Llywelyn had chosen, but somewhat further E., around a small village, Llanfair in Cedwain, which commanded a ford across the Severn where it looped almost in a circle giving space for the creation of a much larger community.

For some time Llanfair retained its name un-changed; but by the 16th cent. it is referred to as the Nova Villa (New Town) *par excellence*. A map preserved in the National Library of Wales, dated 1798, shows its original layout: the tradi-tional system, used by the Romans but long antedating them, of a chessboard pattern, the streets running into each other at right angles. It was then still enclosed by the loop of the Severn, but now the river is built over by the extension of the town.

In the present church, new at the end of the 19th cent., a relic of the old church of Llanfair can be seen in the reredos that was the screen of the older structure.

But perhaps Newtown is better known as the birthplace of Robert Owen, who, after spending much of his life and socio-political activity in the United States, returned here to die. Born in 1771, he left Newtown to become a master spinner, taking the main industry of his native place to Lancashire, where, marrying the daughter of the partner of Richard Arkwright, he was able to bring to the business the new methods of machine production. He never forgot, however, the con-dition of the workers in the weaving industry, such as he had seen in his native town, and his life was devoted to the spread of education and the reform of society. On this subject he published his famous work *A New View of Society* in 1813, giving it the significant sub-title *Essays on the Formation of Character*. For he traced the evils of the human condition to the advance of capitalism, and anticipated Karl Marx in demanding a new form of community in which co-operation should replace competition, surplus profits should be returned to the workers in the form of social services, and the returns on capital severely limited. He did not restrict himself to theory, but applied these principles first to his own business and then, on a wider scale, to an attempt to relieve the distress following the end of the Napoleonic Wars in 1815 by a plan to settle the unemployed in "villages of co-operation" instead of giving them poor-relief. By active co-operation he believed, all men could produce enough to support society as a whole, and they could then live in harmony together by sharing the profit and the produce equally. Such a system would, he thought, reform all men's moral character. He carried his principles into the New World and formed the settlement of New Harmony, in Indiana, to set them in practice. His influence on the development of modern thought in these matters is very great, but largely unacknowledged in relation to other claimants. He returned to Newtown in time to know of the collapse of the Chartist movement among the local weavers at Caersws and Llanidloes in 1839.

The Museum dedicated to his memory and to relics concerning him, in Newtown, is housed in the premises of a modern bank. This housing of his memorials he might well consider with a sense either of the irony of things or the generosity of his opponents.

OFFA'S DYKE is the remarkable earthwork that runs, with some gaps, from the shores of the Dee in North Wales to the banks of the Severn near Chepstow. For centuries it marked the actual boundary between England and Wales. The political boundary has now been profoundly altered, and only at a few points is the Dyke the actual demarcation line. But Welshmen still speak of going "dros Glawdd Offa" (across Offa's Dyke) as if it were a great and indeed a desperate adventure. The Dyke does not appear to have been a completely defended barrier like the Roman wall in Northumberland, although it must have been a formidable affair to cross. In some places, even today, the ditch facing the Welsh side is 12 ft deep, and the rounded bank is 60 ft broad. There is no doubt that it was constructed during the reign of the powerful Mercian King whose name it bears. It is a defiantly Saxon undertaking. It cuts across all Roman roads at right angles, and all the ancient Celtic backways are ignored as the Dyke goes steadily on over hills and across valleys. Sir Cyril Fox, the authority on the Dyke, suggested that it could only have been constructed after negotiations and treaties with the Welsh, since at some points the line taken by the Dyke leaves tactical advantages on the Welsh side. But the Dyke certainly had its ditch towards Wales. No doubt Offa was striving to fix, once and for all, the demarcation line between English and Welsh,

as well as to make it difficult for raiding-parties to cross back with their booty from the fertile lands to the E. of the Welsh hill country.

The Dyke starts at the sea near Prestatyn. It follows the ridge of Halkyn Mountain, crosses the high ground to the W. of Wrexham, and comes down into the valley of the Dee E. of Llangollen. It is clearly visible in the grounds of Chirk Castle and on the hills near Selattyn. The main street of Llandysilio, near Four Crosses, runs on the site of the Dyke. The Dyke crosses the Severn at Llandrinio and runs along the Long Mountain of Welshpool. A good stretch of it can be seen alongside the road from Knighton to Montgomery. At Montgomery it is well seen in the grounds of Lymore Park, and this is one of the very few places where it still forms the political boundary. Then it runs over Clun Forest to the Knighton area, where once again there is a good section to be seen. Hence the Welsh name for Knighton, Trefyclo or Tref-y-Clawdd (Town of the Dyke). It can be followed clearly to Presteigne.

When it enters the present county of Hereford, the Dyke becomes intermittent, although again there are good stretches. The Dyke fades out for a quite long distance after crossing the Wye. Maybe the woods and high moors of this Black Mountain type of country were sufficient defence. It finishes in fine style with entrenchments on the cliffs of the lower Wye and a final earth wall in Sedbury Park, overlooking the Severn estuary.

At the North Wales end, there are good views of another earthwork known as Wat's Dyke, which runs somewhat E. of Offa's Dyke, from the Dee estuary near Basingwerk to the Dee valley near Ruabon. At this northern end it may sometimes be more impressive than Offa's Dyke, particularly in Wynnstay Park outside Ruabon. The space between the dykes can be as much as 3 m. There is no foundation for the theory that this intermediate terrain was designed as a common trading-ground between the Welsh and English. Wat's Dyke may simply have been an earlier version of the scheme that Offa later carried to such an impressive conclusion. There are traces of Wat's Dyke further S., near the Severn.

Offa's Dyke is a moving reminder of that long, bitter struggle between Briton and Saxon through the mists of the past in which the Welsh won their right of survival as a nation.

OXWICH, *Glamorgan*, a showplace of a village on the S. coast of the Gower peninsula, is almost overwhelmed by its own popularity on week-ends in summer. The houses shelter under the bold headland of Oxwich Point (280 ft). This has been seamed by old limestone workings, but makes a fine show, tree-clad and dominating the splendid sands that run E. to the limestone crags of Tor Bay and Three Cliffs. The church is built on a ledge over the sea, at the start of the headland. It is sheltered by a grove of trees. The chancel is barely 3 yds long, which makes it the smallest in Gower. It may be based upon a Celtic cell. On the other hand, the W. tower is surprisingly massive. The font is very old, and tradition maintains that it was brought to the church by the patron saint, Illtud. The tomb-recess in the N. wall of the chancel contains 14th-cent. effigies that probably represent members of the De la Mare family.

The small houses of the village preserve their charm, in spite of caravans and new buildings. John Wesley stayed in one of these houses during his missionary tour of Gower. Behind the village, near the narrow road that climbs over to the tiny bay of Slade, is Oxwich Castle, a fortified manor house built by Sir Rice Mansel about 1541 on the site of an earlier Norman castle. The Mansels were the powerful Gower family who owed their rise to the Tudors. They tended to live dangerously. Anne Mansel was killed at Oxwich by a stone during a local fight in 1557. The ruins have been recently restored by the Ministry of Public Building and Works, and consist of a gateway with the Mansel arms above it, a tower, and the remains of a massive columbarium.

Oxwich Bay is shallow and safe for bathing, and has a large car park among the barrows near the village. But behind the dunes lies a large area of salt marshes, lily ponds, and woods that offers a variety of plant and bird life rare in southern Britain. The area is now a Nature Reserve. In the wooded parkland behind it stands Penrice Castle, the largest castle in Gower. Like many other Gower strongholds, it was built in the 13th cent., a forerunner of the style later perfected under Edward I. The gatehouse and curtain wall are intact. S. of the gatehouse is the complex group of buildings that comprise the tower of the keep, the main hall, and two projecting towers. The columbarium on the curtain wall was added in the 15th cent. In the 16th cent. the Mansel family abandoned Penrice in favour of their newly built manor house, Oxwich Castle. The modern Penrice Castle stands below the old ruins, and is the only large county house in Gower. Its nearest rival is Stouthall, 1½ m. to the NW. on the main South Road. Stouthall, the seat of the Lucas family, was built in 1754 and is now a convalescent hospital. Penrice is Georgian, with a Victorian wing, and was originally built in 1775. The village of Penrice is hidden away in a tangle of narrow roads W. of the Castle grounds. The stump of a cross decorates the village green, with the old pound close at hand. The rounded hillock is the old motte of the first Norman castle of Penrice. The Church of St Andrew has been restored – no Gower church escaped its 19th-cent. restoration. It has the usual embattled tower and a surprisingly large porch, with a strange inner doorway independent of the jambs of the archway and set in a thick oak framework. Penrice, now so quiet, once had the reputation of being Gower's rowdiest village, a great centre for prize-fights, dancing, and cock-fighting.

From Penrice the narrow road goes S. to Oxwich Green and on past Pitt, a fine 17th-cent. farmhouse, with corbelled chimneys, numerous windows with drip-stones, and a glorious view over the whole sweep of Oxwich Bay and Cefn Bryn.

PAINSCASTLE, *Radnorshire.* S. of Radnor Forest, and above the Vale of Ewyas and the Wye, Humphrey Lhuyd sets his mountain district of Elfel with one important place marked in it on his 16th-cent. map: Payn. Elfael (to spell it more correctly than he did) is for him a sub-province of the "Kingdom" of Powys, and one that holds the key to South Wales by defending the Wye valley from attack by way of Hereford. The outliers of the Ellennith, the vital heart of Wales, run down here to Hergest Ridge, and the importance of the area is emphasized by the way Offa's Dyke is held firmly to the E. of it. Both the country and its people are things apart, for Elfael is neither peat-land like Plynlimon nor crag like Snowdonia; nor is it moor like Radnor Forest, nor open pasture land like much of Cardigan and Carmarthenshire, but a network of valleys under wooded hills, fertile and removed from traffic with what is called the world. After Harald, the last Saxon, had come and gone again to die at Senlac in 1066, the Norman raided it, and Bernard of Neufmarché, who had seized Brecon from the S. set up a large knight's castle on a mound under the command of Payen FitzJehan to hold the Elfael. Of this structure only the mound remains, but Payen's Castle is still the name of the village. Like all the small places about it, Painscastle in its network of lanes has a unique charm. But it deserves a further note since it was the site of what can be taken as one of the most decisive battles in the history of Wales.

In 1197, the position between the Welsh Princes and the Norman invaders had reached a stage of uneasy balance. Sixty years earlier, the Welsh under Gruffydd ap Rhys had gained a significant victory at Cardigan; Henry II found it politic to take the Lord of South Wales, another Rhys, as ally against his own ambitious baronage, and, as a result of the apparent settlement of affairs, the Lord Rhys called together the bards of all Wales to hold the first contest of music and song in honour of their common heritage at Aberteifi (Cardigan) in 1176. But the Norman Marcher Lords were still eager for plunder, and, in spite of Rhys's efforts, the three divisions of Wales – Gwynedd, the North; the Deheubarth, or South; Powys, the separate and distinct princedom of the Centre – were still following rival traditions of policy and purpose. The unity of all Wales, which for a moment Owain Gwynedd had been able to assert successfully against Henry II at Corwen and the Lord Rhys had been hopeful of confirming at Aberteifi, was in doubt.

In the same year that the first Eisteddfod of bards was held, William de Braose of Abergavenny, the cruellest of the Marcher Lords, invited the Welsh rulers of the South to his castle for a feast of peace and reconciliation. His men-at-arms fell upon his guests and killed at least seventy of them, men and women. Welsh reaction was felt throughout all Wales, but, although several of his accomplices were destroyed, De Braose survived. Twenty years later, he was able to commit a similar act of treachery by seizing Trahaiarn Fychan (the Younger), against whom he bore a grudge, tying him to a horse's tail, dragging him through the streets of Brecon, and then beheading him. Trahaiarn was a cousin of Gwenwynwyn, son of Owain Cyfeiliog, the poet and Prince of Powys. Gwenwynwyn swore oaths of blood, and took his men to besiege the fortress at Painscastle, De Braose's main strongpoint. But the castle was efficiently held. And the Princes of Powys had been extending their power into Cardigan and the South in a way that the family of Rhys resented. The Normans found one of them to raise the South against Gwenwynwyn; and at Painscastle the men of the Deheubarth and the Marcher Lords destroyed the men of Powys utterly. Trahaiarn went unavenged; and worse, the hope for a united Wales received its death-blow.

PARKMILL, *Glamorgan*, is a village on the main S. road through the Gower peninsula, 7 m. W. of Swansea. Parkmill is crowded into the wooded valley of the Ilston stream, where the Gower Inn, the Victorian Gothic school, and the cottages line the road. It is a popular pull-up for tourists in summer. A working mill, the last in Gower, is tucked away in a side valley. The Ilston stream joins the Pennard Pill as it leaves the woods and goes down to the sea into the fine bay of Three Cliffs. Pennard Castle stands, a mere shell, on a rock overlooking the Pill and the extensive sandy burrows. It looks imposing from a distance, but it played little part in history, since it was in trouble with sand rather than enemies from the 13th cent. onwards.

Inland, away from the crowded road, Parkmill can offer surprises. The Ilston stream rises on Fairwood Common and flows down through fine woods. At Trinity Well are the foundations of the first Baptist chapel established in Wales. An open-air stone pulpit and a plaque stand as a memorial to the founder, John Myles, Rector of Ilston, who eventually led his followers to New England in 1663, where he founded the Baptist church at Swansea, Massachusetts. Ilston hamlet lies at the top of the valley. It has a much-restored but still interesting church dedicated to St Illtud, the leader of the Celtic Church in the 6th cent. and founder of the celebrated monastery at Llantwit Major. The massive tower has a saddleback roof and three bells, two dating from the 18th cent. and one from the 15th, inscribed with a prayer to St Thomas. The churchyard yew is claimed to be 600 years old.

The Green Cwm, the most westerly of the two small valleys that unite at Parkmill, runs up through the woods of Parc le Breos, which used to be a hunting-lodge of the De Breos family who held the lordship of Gower in the 13th cent. A walker's path leads up to the fine megalithic tomb of the Giant's Grave, first excavated in 1869, when the remains of two dozen human beings were found in it. This important chambered long barrow (*c.* 2500 B.C.) has now been carefully preserved by the Ministry of Public Building and Works. Cathole Cave, a little further up the valley, is one of the well-known Gower bone-caves. The Green Cwm finally opens out on to Pengwern Common at Llethrid. Here the stream disappears underground and forms Llethrid Swallet, the finest cave-system yet explored in Gower, complete with stalactites and rare mud formations. It is for expert pot-holers only.

PARTRISHOW, *Breconshire*. The Black Mountains of Brecon lift to the height of Rhos Dirion (2,338 ft), though the greater height is Pen y Manllwyn (2,660 ft). It is a country of hidden valleys and hills that have been smoothed by time

Partrishow: the church among the trees

G. Douglas Bolton

into broad reaches between woodlands and chequered with flock-walks of deep and rainy green. Many feet must long ago have trodden the tracks that wind upon the slopes dividing Llanthony from Talgarth, for the Manllwyn means that a pointer-stone was set to show the way over the hills; but very few go there now.

There is a smaller height among the mountains called Partrishow (1,500 ft), from which the dark barrier between Wales and England unfolds into blue distances of peace. Partrishow has a church, which time itself has forgotten and history, fortunately, has lost. People say that the Roundhead troopers who thought fit to stable their horses in ancient houses of God, and to destroy all pagan devices set therein, looked for this church but were deceived by the hill-paths winding round it. The small structure is now Early Tudor in style, with a very beautiful rood-screen and a timbered loft excellently carved. But it also has a font of curious interest, dating from the 11th cent. The writing cut into it reads: *Menhir me fecit in tempore Genillin*. Who Menhir was no one can truthfully say; but Genillin has been identified as a Prince of Powys whose authority reached to the border on which the Norman was shortly to press.

The place has another name, which claims to be older than Partrishow; it is Patricio, and this word, which might otherwise suggest a direct Roman-British origin for its founder saint, is sometimes elaborated into a corruption of Merthyr Isho, to provide an alternative account of a hermit with the unparalleled name of Isho and his martyrdom at the hands of an unidentified pagan potentate. An anchorite did inhabit this spot, which invites men of strong and lonely spirit to live uncomplainingly through the long silence of its summer days. But the cell, which is within the church and walled apart on the W. side, is not considered older than the 13th cent. It has a stone altar, apparently of that period, cut into with crosses of consecration; there are two similar altars in the church. On the walls are the remains of paintings such as the late Middle Ages used to beautify their holy buildings; one, a figure of Time with hour-glass and scythe and accompanied by a skeleton, stays visible. Whatever admonition this figure was meant to convey, it now seems to say no more than that time, in certain places, manages to stand still, and that hills and trees are immortal, while men live effectively only in legend.

PEMBROKE, *Pembrokeshire*. This town gets its name from its position at the head of the inlet-harbour of Milford Haven. In modern Welsh it is Penfro; but Gerald de Barri, who had a personal feeling for the area, believed the correct spelling was Pen Broch (Head of the Inlet). The town gives its name to the county, though officially the county town is now Haverfordwest. There are several divisions into which Wales naturally falls; the main ones are the provinces of Gwynedd in the North, Deheubarth or the South, and Powys with its eastern boundary from Chester to the Forest of Dean and its inner angle

stretching to the mouth of Dovey. But Gwent, known as Monmouthshire, has its separate history and its distinct people; Anglesey has its own individual island story of 4,000 years. Pembrokeshire, too, has been something of an island apart from the rest of Wales. The trading civilization called the Wessex Culture, which gave Stonehenge its final and surviving shape, and sent through Biscay to the Straits of Gibraltar a line of ships, one of which has in modern times been recovered from the sandy death-trap of the Landes, brought the sacred stones of Pembroke's Mynydd Preseli up the Bristol Channel to stand at Stonehenge and at further places, like Tangley in Hampshire.

How far the Romans penetrated is doubtful; one of their great roads pushed from Neath to Carmarthen and went N. to Llanio, but the coastline and hinterland of Pembroke show little of their presence. This is strange, as Pembroke bears every sign that the area was favoured by human settlement, with a population that has left its mark upon every hill-top in cairns and cromlechs, standing stones and hut circles. In some ways, apparently, Pembroke was an islanded part even then. Lack of mineral riches may have made it unattractive to the imperial power; neither were the Romans themselves an actively seagoing people, however ready they were to hire native skills to police the coastline. The only ocean-based Roman naval force so far discovered was in the Bristol Channel; and it must have been manned by natives who had inherited the practical knowledge of seaboard traffic dating from the days of the Wessex Culture, 1500 B.C.

Perhaps much of the unexplained history of the sub-Roman period in Britain turns upon the relatively unassimilated Pembrokeshire people, equipped with navigational skill and in contact with the offshore Irish coast. The task of those who succeeded to the rule of Rome, the "sons" of Cunedda of the North, was to carry his military organization seawards and to rule the shores of the West from Anglesey. In Pembrokeshire David, the saint, settled his centre for propagating the Christian faith on the basis of the earlier and simple beliefs of the native races. Perhaps it was from Gwent that Patrick sailed to do the same for Ireland, from the same Roman-British region that Columba went as missionary to the Eubedes (Hebrides). The Saxon did not reach effectively so far W., though the Viking made his raids here and there when the state of Cunedda at last fell. It was the Norman, however, who chiefly created its present shape.

Pembroke Castle stands at the head of a small creek out of Milford Haven, as the town lies at the end of the long street running from the railway station. In 1090 Arnulf of Montgomery, son of the Marcher Lord of Shrewsbury, made his expedition westwards and raised what is now one of the most impressive castles to survive from those days of conquest. It was an island outpost even then, a narrow headland away from Wales, but an excellent vantage-point for reaching Ireland. In 1148 Richard known as Strongbow, with his force of mounted Welsh archers, set out

G. *Douglas Bolton*

Pembroke Castle

from here for the further conquest of the sister island. William Marshal, who died in 1219, strengthened the Castle for its better use as headquarters of the border county, or palatinate; and his work was completed by the end of the century. This character of an outpost that grew into self-sufficient independence was maintained by Pembroke throughout its history. Henry I and Henry II settled colonists in the county, perhaps contingents of Flemish mercenaries hired to maintain it as a military stronghold. Their descendants, and those of Norse traders who had put their own strongholds on the coastline and left their names for them in Hasguard, Fishguard, Ramsey, Grassholm, Goodwick, and Milford, have made the area non-Welsh in language and somewhat non-Welsh in feeling. But this latter aspect is confined to a preference for churches with slender towers and corbelled parapets, rather than the traditional bell-towered churches of the Welsh villages, and a reluctance to accept Welsh-speaking neighbours as neighbours at all. It is not so much a pro-English feeling as a sense of Pembroke independence; rather as one finds the natives of the Forest of Dean confident that the Foresters are a nation apart.

But in Pembroke Castle the man was born whose mission was to attempt to build a national unity on the basis of these local prides in independence. In the 15th cent. it was held by Jasper Tudor, Earl of Pembroke, and Henry Tudor grew there into manhood. To Milford Haven and the Castle he returned in 1485 from his exile in Brittany, to take the Crown of England from the thorn bush at Bosworth and found the dynasty that built modern Britain. The system of regional government that he founded broke down when the Stuarts attempted to make it the groundwork for a centralized monarchy. Pembroke again asserted its individual character. In the First Civil War, it was the only strong-point in Wales to declare for Parliament. When Parliament was dissolved in 1648, Pembroke was the first and most determined to declare against Cromwell in the Second Civil War. The revolt of Sir John Owen in

the North was an affair largely of cavalry skirmishes and counter-marches outside the walls of the great northern castles. In Pembroke, in 1648, it was a very serious matter for Cromwell, since it was a Parliamentary stronghold that had turned against him on a point of principle; Poyer, the Mayor of Pembroke, and Laugharne, its General, had not only rallied throughout Wales the feeling for the King rather than for what had proved to be a single-party dictatorship, but had drawn to their cause those whom Cromwell himself described as gentlemen of purpose and gallantry. The defences of the Castle were great enough to hold off Parliamentary assault for weeks; only the betrayal of its water-supply brought its surrender. The traitor was discovered and buried in the water-pit; but Poyer and Laugharne were captured. They were allowed to draw lots to decide which of them should pay the final penalty. It was Poyer who was shot in the Piazza at Covent Garden.

The Castle is surrounded on three sides by the tides of the haven, and shows at its best during high tide. On the landward side it is protected by a ditch. Isolated and strong, its gatehouse is magnificent, set upon a green sward with a cross-arch connecting its two drum-towers, and opening the outer curtain into the inner ward, where a unique four-storeyed cylindrical keep rises to 75 ft with walls varying from 7 to 20 ft in thickness. Its domed stone roof is also unparalleled. The prison tower and the spiral stair leading to the water gate are particularly remarkable. The dominant circular construction evidences a keen eye to all-round fields of fire.

Over a bridge close to the Castle, the way goes to the place called Monkton, now a suburb of Pembroke but formerly the outgrowth of Arnulf's first colonizing. There he set the Benedictine priory that was to confirm the right way of thinking among the people. Its long, barrel-vaulted nave seems to carry on the ideas embodied in the circular keep. But it is worth noting that its outer, northern wall is the relic of an earlier church belonging to an earlier expression of faith. The tall tower of the Pembroke power station, set among green fields and grazing sheep, expresses a faith of the 20th cent.

PENCLAWDD, *Glamorgan,* whose name means Head of the Dyke, is the last village of N. Gower before the peninsula merges with the mainland. N. lies industry and the coalfield. Penclawdd itself is industrial, long and straggling, but its fame in South Wales is based on its indomitable cockle-women who for centuries have driven their strings of donkeys over the sands out to the great cockle-beds of the Burry estuary. The donkeys are not so much in evidence nowadays, and the cockle industry has been modernized, but Penclawdd is still the centre of "Cockle Land". Immediately N. and E. of Penclawdd stretch the marshes and lowlands that fringe the Loughor river.

PENDINE, *Carmarthenshire,* stands where the hills return to the sea beyond the burrows and flatland that extend westward from Laugharne. It is 14 m. SW. from Carmarthen. The village has been overwhelmed by caravan sites, cafés, and car parks, all drawn to the spot by the presence of the magnificent 5-m. beach of firm sand. The military have also arrived, and the greater part of Pendine Sands are shut off by the fence of the rocket-range. The attendant village among the dunes is the usual architectural chaos created by the Services. But enough of the sands remain open to the public to make them a magnet for holiday-makers. Cars seem proper on these sands, for Pendine was a famous course for record-breakers during the heroic years of speed attempts after the First World War. The Welsh ace, Parry Thomas, was killed here, and his car is buried in one of the sand-dunes. There is a strong movement among enthusiasts to exhume it and place it in Pendine as a memorial to an important era in British car development. A charge is made for driving cars on to the beach, and motorists must be careful of the tide and softer patches of sand.

The church, with its saddleback roof, is at the top of the hill above the village. It was built in 1860. About 1½ m. inland, N. of Pendine, is Eglwys Gymyn, on the road to the charmingly named hamlet of Red Roses. The church is small but interesting. It stands within a triple circular earthwork that may be pre-Christian, and is surprisingly re-dedicated to St Margaret of Scotland, probably because Guy de Brian of Laugharne, who claimed descent from Margaret, repaired it in the early 14th cent. Within, the floor is stone flagged, the roof vaulted, and the walls plastered white. Two treasures are a first edition of Peter Williams's Bible – Williams was a curate here for a short time – and a remarkable stone with Ogham markings and a Latin inscription to *Avitoria Filia Cunigni* (Avitoria, daughter of Cunignus). Cunignus was Cynin, a son or grandson of Brychein Brycheiniog, the ruler who gave his name to Breconshire. It forms a direct link with the earliest days of Celtic Christianity in these parts. The church also possesses an ancient pilgrim's bottle, and the Ten Commandments in Welsh painted over a 16th-cent. English version on the N. wall.

About 2 m. W. of Pendine, on the road to Amroth, is Marros, with a Victorian church and a war memorial in the shape of a trilithon, rather reminiscent of Stonehenge. The hill on which the village stands is 453 ft above sea-level. The land to the S. plunges steeply down to the sea and protects the lonely beach of Marros Sands. You must walk and scramble to get here. It is one of the few places left on the coast where the motorist is not in evidence.

PENEGOES, *Montgomeryshire,* is a small village about 3 m. due E. from Machynlleth on the road to Cemaes and Mallwyd. Its interest is considerable. It is reached from Machynlleth over an ancient bridge, Felin Gerrig (Mill-Stone), beneath which can still be seen the even more ancient ford over the rocks through which the stream passes. The antiquity of this road is established by the name of the group of cottages that act as a kind of suburb to Penegoes; Craig yr Henfordd (Stone of the Old Street). The road, leading ultimately to Newtown, is said to be of Roman foundation, and its length and directness support this belief. A drive to the left here leads to the old mansion Gallt y Llan standing half way up the side of the "gallt" (wooded hill). This house, together with another mansion close by, Dol Guog (Fastness Field), shares a legendary connection with the vanished fortress of a ruler famous in Welsh history, Owain, known as Cyfeiliog from the name of the area he ruled, but in his day recognized as Prince of Powys. This division of Wales, originally the triangle lying between Chester, the mouth of Dovey, and Monmouthshire, was the front line of Welsh resistance against English encroachment during the Middle Ages, and, in name at least, it has been revived as the comprehensive title for the counties of Central Wales under the new grouping. Dying in 1197, Owain left a considerable reputation both as a poet and as an economic administrator, for to him the introduction of hill sheep-farming, still a vital industry to the district, is attributed. Probably his residence was on the top of the hill of Gallt y Llan; broad approaches up its sides can still be seen, and the native rock shows signs of artificial dressing. The site is of strategic importance, commanding the outlook towards the Dovey estuary to the W., the approaches through the narrow defile of the River Dulas from Corris to the N., the passage from Mathafarn to the E., and the routes from the Five Summits of Plynlimon to the S. Like Machynlleth, its near neighbour, Penegoes stood in earlier days at the focal centre of warlike manœuvre.

Its name has been traditionally said to mean Head of Egoes, a Celtic chieftain of mythical proportions, whose buried head is said to lie beneath a grove of oaks whose remains still stand a few yards beyond the church. So strong was the legend, that as recently as the 1950s an attempt to fell the grove was defeated by protests from the villagers. The truth is perhaps even more interesting, since Egoes appears in fact to be the plural of "ag" (an opening), and the name of the village to mean a place set at the head of the five valleys that open from the northern escarpment of the Plynlimon range.

Undoubtedly the village, though in an area made available to modern transport, keeps alive many ancient traditions. On the southern side of the road, almost immediately opposite the church, is a well, still used by the inhabitants and accepted as a wishing well. By the bank of the surprisingly rough stream lies an old pointer-stone, which suggests that the road through the village is much older than the Romans.

Of the five trackways to the S., those now practicable for cars are the four to Darowen, Aberhosan, Dylife, and Forge. Each runs through a valley with a considerable range of beauty, and each at last reaches the foot of the S. escarpment of the Plynlimon range; but only the road to Dylife can be recommended for comparatively safe ascent into the Plynlimon moorlands.

Apart from its local interest, Penegoes is distinguished by a name of international significance. At the end of a lane running S. from the church stands the rectory. This was the birthplace of Richard Wilson (1714–82), one of the earliest and most brilliant of the modern school of landscape painting. Although trained in Italy under Zuccarelli, and successful as a portrait painter of the British royalty and peerage, and noted in his day for such works as the *Coast Scene near Naples* (in the National Museum of Wales) and scenes in the Italian Campagna, the influence of the countryside where he was born, and the delight he took in it, never left him. The sharp shoulders of Cader Idris can be seen from the height of Gallt y Llan, and his painting of the mountain-crest with the lake beneath it (1774) captures the character of the mountain. His view of the Mawddach valley, running to Barmouth beneath it, is one among several of his works in the Manchester Art Gallery. His *Caernarfon Castle* can be seen in the National Museum of Wales, which has a number of his pictures; others can be studied in London in the National Gallery and the National Portrait Gallery. The rectory stands now much as it did in his day and, on application, it is possible to be shown the room in which he was born.

The old house Gallt y Llan can easily be seen from the main road, half way up the hill with its subsidiary, Bryntudur, standing high above it. Now in the shape given to it by the 19th cent., it has wide windows opening upon a lawned space where meets of hounds were held. Its foundations, deep in the rock of the hill-side, are at least of early 18th-cent. construction, and its family was connected with the large houses studding the district from Penrhyn Gerwyn, near the Dovey mouth, to Garthgwynion at Glasbwll and the manor of Dol-goch in Cwm Einon. Their record is marked in the 1720s by the tragedy of an eldest son's drowning in the lake of Tal-y-llyn. The oak-woods of great age covering the hill-top have to some extent been felled, and the thickets of

coloured rhododendron are much reduced. But they are remarkable for giving a haunt to one of the rarest creatures in Wales or the British Isles, the pine marten, whose habits of descending upon the farm fowl are as dangerous as the forays of foxes, which make the place so much their own that their courting dances can often be watched there. Until recently, the red squirrel was abundant in these woods. The hard winters of twenty years ago reduced them severely. They can still occasionally be found in the trees above Forge; the alien grey squirrel has not yet invaded the area.

On a hill to the N. of Penegoes, to the right of the stream that flows by the mill, Pen Rhos Fach can be seen. Though not mentioned in Peate's classic work, it is a unique example of the longhouse construction that persisted in Wales from the Middle Ages into Stuart times. Cattle and human beings shared their quarters to the extent that the family living-rooms led directly to the byres and were part of the same construction. It is said that warmth from the beasts, as well as convenience in providing fodder in winter, was responsible for the arrangement. It no longer applied to Pen Rhos Fach in the 19th and 20th cents.; but the place is well worth a visit for the balance and dignity of its architecture.

PENMAENMAWR, *Caernarfonshire.* Early travellers had some wariness in approaching the Height of the Great Stone that looks out from the Caernarfon coast towards the shores of Anglesey. But it was essential to undertake the dangerous ascent and no less dangerous downward route, for the Traeth Lafan (Lavan Sands) stretched far enough out from the mainland to enable you to get near enough, as Daniel Paterson recommends in his *Direct and Principal Cross Roads* of 1811, to take a ferry over to Beaumaris and so reach the important copper-mining area of Amlwch and Parys Mountain. The copper-mines have now declined into nothingness, and the roads are no longer what they were when Defoe and Pennant and Dr Johnson considered the ways there with dread. In the case of Johnson, however, the anxieties were overdrawn. He and his party, who had dared to start out only because they could not find accommodation overnight, discovered that a new way had been cut. Smooth and enclosed between parallel walls in the mountain-side, it protected the wayfarer from the "deep and dreadful" precipice dropping to the waves. But this protecting wall had been broken here and there by mischievous wantonness. The inner wall gave some protection against the frequent falls of loose rock from the hill above, liable to collapse at the smallest accident. The old road, they observed, was higher up than the new one and must have been "very formidable". Now road and railway carry round the face of the headland above the sheer drop to the sea, this last in a kind of roofed gallery. There is a similar road tunnel through Penmaenbach, 188 yds long; but the earlier way, rough but most attractive for its scenery, crosses Sychnant Pass and touches Dwygyfylchi with its lovely small valley, joining it to Penmaenmawr. This great headland, 1,550 ft above sea-level, encloses the town on one side, and Moel Llys (1,180 ft) shuts it in on the other. Gladstone popularized the place; and, whatever may have happened to throw doubt on various of his other opinions, his one on this subject stands firm.

For the archaeologist, Penmaenmawr is of exceptional interest. Close to it is the famous Craig Lwyd axe factory, one of the several that research has been disclosing in recent years, and that throw an astonishing light on the skills of a Stone Age people whom the last generation was prepared to dismiss as entirely primitive. The industry of making axes and other tools for the agriculture and building techniques of the time was widespread and expert. The products were transported between Ireland and Britain and traded from Scotland to Kent. Seaways and landways were both open to this traffic; at Craig Lwyd hundreds of these tools were discovered in various stages of preparation. At Llanarmon in Denbighshire a pair of axes, beautifully tooled in green stone, were found in the limestone caves in 1896; and these have now been traced with confidence to the factory near Penmaenmawr. The same caves gave evidence of Stone Age burial and pottery-making. But the Craig Lwyd factory is proof of far more sophisticated skills than that. A similar site can be seen at Llyn Barfog, in Merioneth. There can be no doubt that the expert manufacture was matched by an equally intelligent knowledge of trade and travel.

PENMON, *Anglesey.* This is a place with several attractions. It is distinguished by a priory church of outstanding interest, historical and architectural. It is close to the Trwyn Du (Black Nose), the eastward extremity of Anglesey in this direction. And, offshore, there is another and smaller island, now commonly called Puffin Island, after the sea-birds associated with it, but more properly known as Ynys Seiriol, the island of the saint who settled there about the 5th or 6th cent., and whose fame was enough to make even Saxon and Northman raiders call it Priestholme.

"Priestholme et Penmon" is the description given in centuries later than the 6th to what was evidently regarded as a joint institution. According to the Welsh Chronicle, the saint's original foundation on the outlying island was laid waste in 968. Both St Seiriol's and Penmon suffered by the incursion of one whom the Chronicle calls Markt ab Marallt. Before this, it says, Penmon was the fairest spot in those parts. It is hard to discover the name of this Norse raider under its Welsh form, or even to be certain he was not a Welshman. The reaction against the Anglo-Saxon success on land made many Welsh intransigents prefer to associate with those energetic Norsemen who recognized in Britain a point from which some continental power might challenge their own supremacy. Nothing is now left at Penmon but a church in Normanesque style, and at St Seiriol's a ruined structure, on a site occupied by a cottage, which gives no indication of a date earlier than Penmon shows. Gerald de Barri, with indulgent interest, noted the Monastery of Ynys Seiriol in 1188. Hugh Lupus, the Wolf of Chester, made a transient occupation of Anglesey in the early days of the Norman conquest of England; but the fortress he put up at Aberlleiniog was repossessed by Gruffydd ap Cynan of Gwynedd, then the dominant principality in Wales, in co-operation with Magnus of Norway; and in A.D. 1130 he appointed his son Idwal as Prior of Penmon. But, even so, Dugdale gives the date of the present building as 1221, and states that it was the creation of Llywelyn ap Iorwerth, the Great Llywelyn who for a while united all Wales under his control.

It is a cross-form construction, of a predominantly Norman type, and thus untypical of most churches in Anglesey. In the 13th and 15th cents. the chancel was rebuilt and again rebuilt. The N. transept is now no older than 1855; but the rest of the church retains its unique Normanesque character. The tower in fact keeps its original Norman roofing and blunt spire; and the tympanum, or door-lintel, at the S. of the nave is a remarkable example of symbolic workmanship rarely found elsewhere, apart from the church at Llanbadarn-Fawr in Radnorshire. But, although it could be said that Penmon is a Norman minster on a small scale, more interest may be taken in the remains of its earliest, purely Celtic foundation. This can be found in two places, with much the same form. There are two complete crosses of distinctive Celtic Church shape; the remains of a third exist.

One of these is in the church itself; the second is a short way off in the park. The equal-armed cross in both cases projects beyond the circular head – an extension unusual in a Celtic cross. The shaft is covered with key-pattern interlacing. But the cross in the park is made unique even among its contemporaries by an attempt to represent sculptured figures, one perhaps of Christ with a halo, others of men between beasts. This may result from an influence more Irish than Welsh. And the font is worked from an Early Celtic cross, whose intricately patterned base has been hollowed out to serve a new purpose.

PENMYNYDD, *Anglesey.* A short way beyond Menai Bridge or Porthaethwy, on a side turning from the Holyhead road, is a village that holds a church as ancient in foundation as any in Anglesey, but containing monuments associated with the revival of Welsh tradition by the Tudors. Here this family, which was to initiate the flowering of Britain in the 15th and 16th cents., first found its footing. A little distance from the village, towards Pentraeth, is the old manor house of Plas Penmynydd where Owen Tudor, squire at the court of Henry V, was born. He married Katherine of Valois – the Kate whom Henry V wooed and Shakespeare delightfully depicted – after the death of the English King. Owen's grandson Henry Tudor, Earl of

The chancel of Penmon church, with the ancient font

Reece Winstone

Richmond, asserted a claim to the throne of England that he justified by force of arms at Bosworth. His victory there not only ended the time of chaos and degeneration dominated by the Wars of the Roses, but created the new sense of Britain's unity that was to reach fruition through his granddaughter, Elizabeth Tudor.

Henry Tudor (Henry VII, as he became) was very conscious of his Welsh heritage. It was he who introduced the Rouge Dragon into the royal heraldry of Britain, reviving the war emblem carried in the 5th and 6th cents. by the House of Cunedda, which created Powys and Wales as we know it, but also from their seat at Shrewsbury kept in the English Midlands the Roman-British tradition as part of the cultural heritage left by the Empire in western Europe. As Lord Bryce points out in *The Holy Roman Empire*, the very name Welsh was given by the Germanic successors of the Romans not to any foreigner, but only to those who were directly identified with Roman civilization, so that throughout Europe the words Welsh or Wallace, Walloon or Wallach, reflect the same fact of basic European unity. The idea of that unity never died in Europe, and the Holy Roman Empire founded by Charlemagne in A.D. 800 was an attempt to perpetuate it. Britain never forgot that it had once formed part of that western Gallic Prefecture of the Empire which for some years asserted its own independence as a distinct Gallic Empire, much as Britain under Carausius at the end of the 3rd cent. A.D. had achieved ten years of independent status. The series of wars with France that Henry V ended were largely a continuation of the effort to reunite the Gallic Prefecture. With this in mind Henry VII, looking back to the tradition of Cunedda, gave the name Arthur to his first-born son, the Prince of Wales, after the legendary hero who, in the Dark Ages following the with-drawal of Rome, had summarized the endeavour to maintain the civilized values of the past. In the year of Bosworth, the name and fame of Arthur were revived once more in the *Morte D'Arthur*, by the Malory who was born within the marches of Wales. This work drew on relatively genuine sources, particularly the 13th-cent. story of the Grail, said to be based on a manuscript of the 8th cent. and written by a Welsh cleric of the time, in which the view of man and his destiny expressed in Classical philosophy was reconciled with Christian teaching.

It was in this sense that Henry VII asserted a deep and original ethic to which all the peoples of Britain belonged, and so founded the greatness of the Tudor dynasty. The Cambro-British, as the Welsh thereafter were called well into the 18th cent., were regarded in literature as a people whose contribution to the national character was unique.

The church at Penmynydd was considerably restored in 1840, Queen Victoria contributing £40 to the task of renovating the structure that housed the monuments of her remote connections. It cannot, therefore, show the same unadapted plan of the single-chambered oratory, such as may still be found at Bodedern, Rhosbeirio, Llanfachraeth, and elsewhere in Anglesey. It had a N. chapel added in the early 15th cent., and even the font may be only a century earlier than that. But it traces its foundation to at least the 7th cent.

Gronw Fychan (whose name is now usually found as Vaughan) marks the origin of Tudor eminence. Uncle of Owen Tudor through his half-brother Meredydd, he could claim to be a great-grand-uncle of Henry VII. He was a friend of the Black Prince, and symbolized a period of Anglo-Welsh reconciliation after the Edwardian Wars by becoming Constable of

Beaumaris Castle in 1381. His wife, Myfanwy, lies in effigy beside him in this parish church dedicated to St Gredifael, its first and distant founder. The Tudor arms that he bears are of a chevron between three helmets. This is not quite the original form of the arms, which were granted to his ancestor Ednyfed Fychan, Steward of Llywelyn the Great, in 1232. They were then not helmets but heads, allegedly of decapitated Englishmen. The effigy, as it now is, may represent some later and tactful emendation.

Both Gronw and his wife, as sepulchral figures, were removed to this church at Penmynydd when another member of the family, Henry VIII, in some sort of reaction against his father's policy, withdrew from Europe and its universal Church, and dissolved all abbeys and monasteries in the parts of Britain he controlled, whether their origins were Catholic or Celtic. The order affected a foundation at Llanfaes, near to Beaumaris, which was created by Llywelyn the Great, the same who gave its arms to the House of Tudor, and where his wife, Joan, daughter to King John of England, was interred. Llanfaes was also the first resting-place for Gronw and his wife Myfanwy. For safe keeping, these early Tudors were removed to their present sanctuary at Penmynydd church. Joan and her large stone coffin, with her effigy upon the lid, were not taken there. She is now in the grounds of Baron Hill near Beaumaris, well tended after centuries of neglect.

PENNAL, *Merioneth.* This lies on the Machynlleth–Aberdovey road almost exactly midway between the two points. The road itself is of unvarying beauty, rising at times over the steep ridge that falls to the curving water, and following a line of wall that exemplifies local skill in slate-pile construction. Groves of old oaks line the way, and below can be seen the series of rich fields surrounding islanded ridges that are a feature of the Dovey estuary. Pennal itself, rich with roses in summer, offers many points of interest. The old inn belongs to the coaching era, and the church is marked on 17th-cent. maps as a landmark showing the way to "Penalt". The bridge stands across the junction of streams finding their way to the Dovey nearby. Close at hand, a side road leads southwards to link again with the main road near Marchlyn. To use it gives the opportunity of seeing a house of the Tudor period and the well-marked site of the Roman fort now known as Cefn Gaer; the squared lines of its foundation earthworks are unmistakable. This was one of the five Roman fortresses in Wales, and was set to mount guard over the approaches by coast and by mountain passes to the Dovey estuary, which from before that time until well into the Middle Ages remained the strategic key not only to the Welsh area but ultimately to the English Midlands. Several Roman relics have been unearthed from it.

Some of the houses in Pennal have been destroyed to serve the purposes of modern traffic and its servicing. Let us hope the process will be halted, for Pennal still preserves a character in some ways unparalleled in Wales or England. The salmon of the Dovey and the trout of the neighbouring streams make a great attraction for anglers. But Pennal has more recently been opened up in a way that for the first time makes the hidden and ruminating valleys of the Taren range available to the tourist.

The three peaks Taren Hendre, Taren y Gesail, and Taren Cadian rise sharply above the village. They are worth a reference of their own. But from Pennal the road can be taken by car or on foot at least as far into the run of valleys as the woods lying beyond Pennal Towers, still showing the outward state of a great house. Beyond this point, only the foot-walker should go further towards Rhydygaled; but the motorist can satisfactorily travel along the right fork to find the succession of forestry roads that now climb as high as the shoulders of the three heads of the range. It was once possible to walk by way of an old packway from Pennal back to Machynlleth over cascades and precarious tracks set into the side of the hills. The peculiar beauties of that walk do not now exist. Roads on a severer and much more dominant scale now run to Twlly Nodwydd and Maesgwern Goch. The slopes of gorse, heather, and bracken remain evident here and there; but the principal view is of Alpine ranks of conifers possessing the valleys in dark majesty and presiding over rugged river-beds where the new bridges look down on worn boulders far below. From the scenic point of view, the change is not altogether for the worse; and, beside the raw roads and even upon them, the heathers and the foxgloves, the small violets and at places the sundew typical of the Tarens, are staging a counter-attack. In particular, the channelled mountain torrents are insisting on asserting their independence.

Some care should be taken, after Twlly Nodwydd, to find the proper way for Dyfi Bridge and Machynlleth if you intend to carry through the full journey. The firs are deceptive in the way they open out into avenues falling sheer down the slopes. It is possible to go by mistake over the same route several times – unless you can discover at Pant Spydded the tall slab of slate-stone set there to mark the passage for shepherds in the deep snows and, before then, for the packway from the old quarries round Taren y Gesail.

Having found this, where it overlooks a sharp and crowded cwm, you can pick up a farm-road that will take you by a steep but lovely descent, passing through farmsteads, to the Aberdovey road. Watch should be kept for the sheep that use this road for their own purposes, and the turn into the main road can be dangerous. From half way down this descent it is possible to look over the Plynlimon escarpment at the Pen Plynlimon Fawr and study the ragged fret of hills that stand over the sea towards Aberystwyth.

The way to Dyfi Bridge is reached close to Penrhyn Dyfi, one of the area's distinguished old houses. The house of Pant Lledydwr, with its isolated lake, is close at hand.

PENNANT MELANGELL, *Montgomery-shire.* On the southern edge of the Berwyn hills and lying due E. from Aran Benllyn, Pennant Melangell is about 5 m. from Llanrhaeadr-ym-Mochnant. The valley in which it lies is, during late spring, filled with wild roses in a way not often found in this part of Wales. Its main attraction lies in the church, now of Norman style, with a square, squat tower and blunt steeple. Grave monuments inside it date from A.D. 1370 onwards. The most notable of its furnishings is a rood-screen, carved perhaps about the middle of the 15th cent. and setting out the legend of the sainted Marcella, a British princess who, the story goes, took refuge in a hermitage in this remote valley to escape the advances of the ruler of the district. He found her again only by accident; for, as he took his pleasure one day in the hunting of hares, one of them ran to her and hid beneath her robes; nor would the hounds attack it or her, so much were they impressed by her saintliness. The hunting prince was equally impressed, and gave her the grant of lands for an abbey, over which she presided. The tale has parallels; Marcella may in fact have supplanted some other saint or object of veneration. But they say no hunting of the hare has been done in the district since the church was first built.

PENRHYNDEUDRAETH, *Merioneth.* The name, which means Head of the Hill-Slope over the Two Reaches of Sand, accurately describes the place. It stands upon a ridge of land that is left islanded where the Glaslyn river and the Dwyryd join to create a great estuary of sand and sea and marshland, part of which was reclaimed by the enterprise that planned Portmadoc. The wide undulation called the Traeth Bach lies below it, and to the NW. runs the Morfa Gwyllt (Wild Sea-Land). It is a bridge between the landscapes of the heaped Snowdonia of the N. and the upland massif of Ardudwy pressing upon Harlech. The site was noted in 1188 by Gerald de Barri, who passed that way coming from the Mawddach estuary

to reach Nevyn (as he spells it) on the shore of the Lleyn peninsula, where he found time, in the intervals of preaching for the Third Crusade that was about to be launched, to inquire into the legend that the Merlin of the Woods, the third Merlin who was neither Roman nor Scots but native to lower Britain, had been born there. He saw the two great stretches of tidal sands, and called them the Traeth Mawr and Traeth Bachan, the greater and the less. Two castles of stone had lately been erected there, he writes, one called Deudraeth and built by the sons of Conan, which stood towards the northern side of the estuary; the other called Carn Madryn, which seems to have meant Fox Hump, built by another family, the sons of Owen. This he sets in Lleyn, and perhaps by that he meant to place it near to what is now Portmadoc. For once, his travels seem to have confused his memory, for he is certainly inaccurate in his account of the approach through Ardudwy; but that Penrhyn-deudraeth has a distinguished history we can take as correct.

Eight centuries have obliterated the evidence, though at Minffordd, where the railway strikes the road from Portmadoc, a small but manageable way leads to a wooded spit over the sands where the maps mark a Castell Deudraeth. The small hill to the E. of the village carries the surviving proof of early occupation, where a "cistfaen" (burial-stone) stands looking over the Traeth Bach and across the Dwyryd stream towards Llandecwyn. On the height above this place lies Llyn Tecwyn Uchaf, 500 ft up and closed with lovely hills and the sight of the sea-coasts. It serves as reservoir for Portmadoc; but its isolated position and the wide skies it reflects make that fact of no account. It is $\frac{1}{2}$ m. long and supplies some of the best trout in the area. It has a legend, which may unfortunately be true, saying that in the 17th cent., when such customs were frequent, an old woman suspected of witch-craft was rolled down the hills to Llandecwyn in a spiked barrel. There is a spot, taken to be her grave, marked by a large piece of quartz-rock

The Glaslyn estuary near Penrhyndeudraeth

G. Douglas Bolton

that would have the effect of preventing her ghost from haunting the place. Her name was Dorti, they said, and anyone who passed close by had to throw a stone on the grave. The tale apparently confuses this lake with a site in the Dolcoran valley, near Llandecwyn, where more concrete evidence exists for the killing of the witch. The piece of quartz was of the sort that was set in times before history to mark the trackways over Plynlimon, much as the Greeks used a white stone for outstanding points; and the duty of casting a stone to keep the marker-cairn permanent has a living parallel in the cairn by Hyddgen. The Tecwyn lake probably belongs to the record of the first explorers of these coasts before even the Celts entered Britain.

PENTREFOELAS,   *Denbighshire.*   Some 7 m. from Betws-y-coed, Pentrefoelas lies among moors that have as their main feature the Alwen lake-reservoir. This attraction it shares with Cerrigydrudion for, as Edward Lhuyd wrote in 1698, the River Alwen sprang from the lake to run to Llyn-y-Kymer in this latter place. The geography of the area has been considerably changed by the making of the reservoir, and there is no evidence now of the Kymer lake, apart from a local place-name of Cymer. The Alwen reservoir is one of the largest of its kind in Wales, 3 m. long and averaging $\frac{1}{4}$ m. wide. It is an open lake, not dominated by great heights but lying among the slopes of Mynydd Hiraethog free to the winds. It is an excellent place for trout; so too is the Nug stream at Pentrefoelas, and the Alwen river itself. Its accessibility, however, invites attention from piratical visitors. But, like many another lake, Alwen has a protective spirit, and attempts to draw the waters with nets are said to be always defeated by sudden storms. Part of Alwen, a bowl-shaped depression at the SW. corner, was called Dau Ychen (Two Oxen). The spirit is supposed to have dragged a pair of such beasts into the depths at this point. There is no need to record this tale as possible evidence for a monster. Like the legend of Hu the Strong, who dragged the Afanc from the waters with a pair of oxen, it is a piece of religious symbolism belonging to a pre-Christian era.

PENYBONT, *Radnorshire.* No more than a large village, Penybont stands at the junction of roads from Shrewsbury and Presteigne – and Llandegley, Llanddewi Ystradenni, Llanbadarn-Fawr, and Nantmel – at the western edge of Radnor Forest. It has a comfortable hotel and much local notoriety. In relatively recent times it was called the Wembley of Wales. This was due to its being the centre for horse-racing in several forms, a very natural interest for any town of Radnorshire. Jockeys may have their colours up, or a rider may be the son of the farm on his favourite horse. Handicapping is one of the most interesting features, and has to be studied with the greatest attention by those not familiar with local rules. Sulkies are also a feature of the racing, and the specially trained horses in these

events are a delight to watch. To draw these light, sporting vehicles, the horse must adopt a smooth and regular pace far removed from canter, trot, or gallop. It must be a steady, level motion in which the paired legs on one side move forward together while those on the other flank lie back. Once in movement, it is almost impossible to rein in these animals, which go as relentlessly as a railway engine and almost as if they were on rails. To attempt to ride one over Radnor Forest raises many problems, and is recommended only to those with an appetite for the unprecedented.

PILLETH, *Radnorshire,* is a lonely village to the NE. of Radnor Forest and in the main valley of the Lugg river. That valley is a place of ancient settlement, and around Pilleth are set the marking-stones of the first organized inhabitants of these islands, with their burial mounds and places of worship.

For the modern mind, Pilleth is notable because it has had a Shakespearian dignity given to it. The dying King Henry IV heard at the Castle of Berkhampstead the news that the kingdom he had won from Richard II, and had hoped to settle under a Parliamentary régime, was in danger of destruction. The unity of Britain that Edward I had aimed at establishing S. of the Scottish border by his overthrow of Llywelyn the Last of Wales, and by his direct annexation of the border lordships, was threatened not merely by revolt in Wales under Owain Glyndwr; but by a victory that seemed at first to be conclusive, won by the "irregular and wild Glendower" against the English forces under the Earl of Mortimer, sent to suppress him. In 1401 Owain, the future King of Wales, marched to meet the English-led army at Pilleth, where its Castle stood under the Bryn Glas, or Pilleth Hill. The Welsh mountaineers with their dreaded long-bows, caught Mortimer in the flat and winding valley, and the result was disastrous for him. His men were levies from Hereford and Radnor who, some 120 years after the Edwardian Conquest, still felt themselves to be Welshmen rather than English feudal tenants, and it is said that many of them at the first encounter joined Rhys Gethin (the Terrible), Glyndwr's able lieutenant. Those who stood by Mortimer were slaughtered in their hundreds, and Mortimer himself was captured. He carried the matter further by swearing fealty to Glyndwr as King of Wales and marrying his daughter.

This disaster seemed to mean the end for the House of Lancaster and the Settlement that had done so much to confirm the constitutional development of England on Parliamentary lines. For Mortimer was uncle to the Earl of March, who, by believers in the divine right of Kings, was taken to be the rightful ruler of England. From Pilleth, key to the district of Elfael and so to the whole South, Glyndwr went on to the siege and sack of Cardiff; Hotspur and the Earl of Percy in the North of England marched to join him against the Lancastrian King. Owain – King of Wales, as he was proclaimed at Machynlleth; ally of France;

and reviver of the idea of Welsh unity that had come to grief 200 years before at the Battle of Painscastle, not far from Pilleth – stood upon a hill in England and saw the army of Percy and Hotspur routed by the Henry of Monmouth who was to be Henry V of England. Four years after Pilleth, the victory, which had seemed to make possible at last the ambitions of the Lord Rhys for the cultural unity of Wales, and those of Gerald de Barri for its independent Church, faded away and Glyndwr himself vanished into hiding.

About 1870 this hill, which had lain untilled for generations, was put under the plough. As the share bit into the soil, it turned up a heap of buried bones. The number of them and the associated objects made it certain that they were relics of the thousand men of Mortimer who died in the battle. Trees were planted to mark the spot, and the grove still stands as a memorial to those who fell that day and to the hopes that fell thereafter.

PLAS LLWYNGWERN, *Merioneth*.

Standing on the old Roman road from Corris down to Ffridd Gate, Plas Llwyngwern also marks the junction between this route and the more modern road to Upper Corris. The house, which can be clearly seen, is connected with the Londonderry family that owned the Plas at Machynlleth. It marries well with the natural beauty of the place. The River Dulas here runs at a gentler level, shaded by trees. Certain mountainous heaps of shale and slate-stacks and an overhead railing not far away show where quarries of the lesser sort have been made; but they also melt into the charm of this luxuriant valley.

Afforestation is very marked, particularly over the opposite side of the river, but it does not in any way detract from the interest of the road as you follow it. It is worth following, for very near are two remarkable natural features. One is known as the Gelligen Stone Chests, a succession of deep ravine-like depths cut from the rock through centuries by the river. The other is the cave of Hwmffra Goch. It is partly hidden by crowding ash, but the small, worn track towards it can be detected.

It is apparently a simple, caved entrance into the hill-side, but on passing through the arch you find yourself under the open sky, with a pool and a fall of water and a further cave-like formation ahead of you. It is an extraordinary place, well covered from observation on the coach-road. This made it admirable for highwaymen, of whom Hwmffra seems to have been the most distinguished, though little about him is known. From it, the odds were very much in favour of a surprise attack, and the road could not avoid passing by it. As a well-sited position for banditry, its history must be as long as that of the road itself. And it is curious to note that Hwmffra was as red of hair as the Red Robbers of Dinas Mawddwy.

PLYNLIMON, *Cardiganshire*.

This range of hills, standing above an escarpment rising suddenly 2,000 ft over sea-level from a series of foothills running to the Dovey valley, is itself a lengthy ridge nearly 2,500 ft high. Its chief heads are Pen Plynlimon Fawr (Great Plynlimon), nursing in its flanks the lake, the "Eye of Rheidol", from which rises the Afon Rheidol; Pen Plynlimon Arwystli, imaginatively linked with an Aristobulus of early Christianity; and Pen Plynlimon Cwm Biga.

Traditionally, Plynlimon is taken as marking the boundary between the stony mountains of the North and the gentler grassy hills of the rest of Wales. It is in fact much more. Writers are inclined to dismiss this magnificent range as featureless; but this is because the approach they describe is over the difficult moorland carved by narrow streams into a succession of repetitive slopes from the Aberystwyth road to the S. The real character of Plynlimon can be appreciated only if the ancient trackways are followed through the cwms and by the splintering waterfalls that pour from the escarpment to the N. Only within the last few years have roads available for modern traffic begun, tentatively, to open up this wide and beautiful area.

The name Plynlimon has always varied in its spelling and interpretation. "Plinilimmon," says the cartographer John Speed, dating his map 1610, and "Plynllymon" in another of the same year. "Plynlimon Montes," said Humphrey Lhuyd about thirty years before him. "A hill called Plymlummon, or as pronounced Plynlummon," says Lewis Morris, an industrious commentator on Welsh antiquities, and much else, writing a letter in 1742; "Pumlymmon, or as pronounced Plymhummon," is the version he preferred in a slightly earlier communication. He stresses the importance of noting this constant difficulty in spelling by asking himself what the word meant: "Whether it be derived from Pen Luman, or Lummon, the Hill of the Banner?" The Plyn or Plym has often been ascribed to a recollection of the Latin *plumbum*, since the mining of lead, as of silver, in these hills was not only undertaken by the Romans but engaged the professional attention of Lewis Morris himself. The Pum, on the other hand, is accepted as a contraction of the Welsh word "pump" (five), and the most popular assumption is that a reference is intended to the five major rivers that find their source in this upland moor: the Wye, Severn, Rheidol, Ystwyth, and Clywedog. The list, however, varies. A reference to a "Pumlumon" in the ancient text known as the Black Book of Carmarthen narrows the definition. "Llumman" is Welsh for a banner; "llumon" is a beacon and signal-fire. There are five outstanding summits along the Plynlimon escarpment: Foel Fadian, still from time to time used as a beacon site; Taren Bwlch Gwyn; Mawnog; the hill of Hengwm; and the hill of Rhaeadr. Although many summits stand along this line, these five, ranging between 1,650 and 1,800 ft, form a group dominating the whole area towards the Dovey valley; the most convenient place to observe them is on the Dylife road as it falls towards Bryn Dan. Once these are seen, the meaning of "Plynlimon" becomes clear. They are the five summits on which all the traditional trackways converge. Each presides over a valley of its own, differing in aspect and in wildlife; each has its fall of water; each has its own history. They form a kind of castellated front towards the N., and to stand on the height of any one of them is to become possessed of the whole shape and history of Wales.

The summit of Plynlimon Fawr can be easily, but unrewardingly, reached from Eisteddfa Gurig; a slightly more difficult approach is from Bugeilyn; the most impressive, though the loneliest, is by the mountain-track past Hyddgen. From this point Plynlimon Fawr rises in two stages, first over the hump called Plynlimon Fach, and then up a sheer face to the cairns at its summit. An alternative way is to cross the young Rheidol by the rock-ford short of the cataract from Llechwedd y Buarth, leaving the solitary croft of Hengwm Annedd to the right, and make the long but regular ascent up Craig y March, which brings you to the source of the Wye in a series of linked springs.

Here on the height of the ridge, the view, even with only middling weather, takes in the entire sweep of Cardigan Bay, Bardsey Island and the promontories of Pembrokeshire being clearly seen. When the air is sharp and clean, the head of Snowdon thrusts beyond the gap in the skyline between Taren y Gesail and Cader Idris. The curious shape of the Arans, always a prominent feature of this area, shows like the knuckles of a clenched fist; the Wrekin points the route to the English counties; and the Black Mountains and the Brecon Beacons stand to the S. Here Wales makes its own stand, for the upthrust of the Five Summits forming the northern bastion of the Plynlimon moors guards the considerable stretch of territory – lakeland, peatland, sheep-walk – that has determined the character of Welsh culture and developed in its secluded valleys the tenacious communal life of its peasantry. Snowdonia, the old Kingdom of Gwynedd, is an outlier with a tradition and even, to some extent, a language of its own. The coast of the Irish Sea, the farming valleys of Carmarthen, Cardigan, Radnor, Brecon, and the rest, and the marchlands along the Severn, are all a kind of deposit from the empty and impassable moors surmounted by Plynlimon. It is now possible to see along the lower Rheidol the sheet of water that forms a new reservoir, drowning the site of Nant-y-moch that housed so much of Wales's later bardic tradition, and to see across the flanks of the moulded tarens the scars made by new Forestry Commission roads, and the terraced insets in which are planted the infant firs that in due time will alter the whole ecology of the area. The peat is now much channelled and drained, and many of the traditional green-tracks that have served pony and sheep-flock for generations have been overridden by the service-roads needed for afforestation. The way is at last open for the motor-car. But a word of advice is needed for the walker.

From Plynlimon Fawr you look down on the pair of cairns known as Carn Gwilym and, to the

E. of it, bulking above the Hengwm river, one of the most difficult stretches of peat-hag and moss-pool to be found anywhere. The riversides are netted with small channels, overgrown and hidden by the long, coarse grass into which the unwary walker can fall. The peats hide under bright green scum, sinking to dangerous depths. Where there is no obvious track, it is advisable to follow the streams in their own bed along the stretches of slate-shale that they show. Trout are many, and they adventure even into the frequent falls as well as into the lakes scattered not only about the feet of Plynlimon but over the whole extent of sight from its summit. It is this proliferation of pools that gave to the moorland heart of Wales the name which has been Anglicized as Ellennith, the Land of Lakes. Giraldus Cambrensis (Gerald de Barri) was ready to accept it as a Welsh word. His *Itinerary of Wales*, written in 1188, is a brilliant study of conditions in the Wales of his day, and deserves its international fame.

What is rare, but from its danger requires special note, is the sudden onsets of mountain mist that affect these highlands. They can occur when the day is at its mildest, when the sun is steady and the wind has dropped to an occasional breath. A white and wool-like cloud gathers in the river-valleys and steals from ravine to ravine, surrounding peak after peak. It is a rapid and, it can be imagined, strategically planned advance. The swiftness with which the walker can be overtaken is surprising. The most experienced frequenter of the area is well advised, once overtaken, to remain where he is rather than risk, in that white blindness, the possibility of walking over one of the sheer gaps, dropping for perhaps 700 ft, that suddenly appear under the feet even by day.

It is best to choose clear weather, and from the cairns striking the sky above the Eye of Rheidol to follow the spine of the ridge along what proves to be the springy and trapless heather stretching steadily to Arwystli, to Cwm Biga (the source of the Severn, disguised for the English-speaker under its true name of Blaenhafren), and the crags of Garn Fawr. Close at hand is the cairn called Garn-fach Bugeilyn. On Plynlimon Fawr, you look down at the separate part of the moors that centres on Hyddgen. On Plynlimon Cwm Biga, you overlook a second and again distinct section of the area. Between them, the Llechwedd Crin stretches a barrier of bog that seems always to have insisted on preventing effective communication. Bugeilyn takes its name from the lake gathered below the cairn. To the E. of it a way can be made to the head of the River Clywedog and, ultimately, to the standing stones beyond Llawryglyn, which appear to mark a route older than the Romans, linking itself with the Carn Gwilym above Hyddgen. But at this point one can stand and think of Kay and Bedwyr (Bedivere), companions of Arthur, who, in the words of the *Mabinogion*, once stood there together "in the highest wind in the world".

PONTARDAWE, *Glamorgan.* The name means the Bridge over the River Tawe, and the village lies in the Tawe valley 8 m. NE. of Swansea. The steel-works that started the township are closed and dismantled, and Pontardawe is becoming a dormitory for workers in industry nearby. Hills stand all around; the site is not without beauty, although the place contains the usual stone-faced, two-storeyed houses characteristic of the western coalfield. The modern Church of All Saints stands over the town. The Church of St Peter has an unusually tall tower. From Pontardawe a road runs up through the valley of the Upper Clydach to Gwauncaegurwen and Cwmgors. The National Coal Board has sunk a fresh shaft here, and Abernant colliery is one of the few new developments in the South Wales coalfield. On the hills (1,018 ft) to the W. of this valley is Carn Llechart, a fine megalithic stone circle consisting of twenty-four stones, with a chambered tomb in the centre. The circle can be reached from the narrow road that leads up on to the mountain-side from Rhyd-y-fro. This whole area is rich in prehistoric remains. About 1 m. S. of Carn Llechart is the little chapel on Mynydd Gellionnen, which has a figured stone, thought to be pre-Christian, built into the side of the wall. The road from Rhyd-y-fro continues up over the moorland to Penlle'r Castell (Summit of the Place of the Castle), where a pre-Roman earthwork is finely placed. This is a notable viewpoint in spite of the new power-lines. The view runs from Mynydd Preseli (the Prescelly Hills) in the far W. to the summit of the Brecon Beacons in the E.

The hills to the N. of Pontardawe behind Llangiwg also hide antiquities. Llangiwg church has an embattled tower and is a prominent landmark perched on its hill. It has been heavily restored. Some 2 m. N. along the road over the ridge of Cefn Gwryd is an area containing numerous cairns and one large stone circle of the same age as that on Carn Llechart (about 2000 B.C.). The remains comprise three concentric rings of flat stones.

Opposite Pontardawe to the E. is Mynydd Marchywel (1,350 ft), with its forestry plantations. This mountain separates the Tawe valley from the Vale of Neath (Nedd). Cilybebyll church has a 13th-cent. tower.

PONTARDULAIS, *Glamorgan*. An industrial township 8 m. NW. of Swansea, Pontardulais lies on the River Loughor (Afon Llwchwr), which here forms the boundary between Glamorgan and Carmarthenshire, a matter of some interest to the thirsty on Sundays, since Glamorgan is "wet" and Carmarthenshire "dry". Most of Pontardulais is in Glamorgan. The village expanded rapidly in the 1870s with the coming of the tinplate-works. There are thus few antiquities, beyond the old church of Llandeilo out on the river marshes, near the site of an old castle motte. Pontardulais was a centre of the Rebecca Rioters during the agrarian troubles that beset Wales in the 1840s. The Hendy gate was destroyed with some bloodshed, but the attack on the gate near the Fountain Inn on the E. side of the village was more successful. The lane down which the rioters

rode can be seen near the old Goppa Chapel. Pontardulais has always been proud of its musical tradition. The Pontardulais Choir was the finest in Wales between the two world wars. The present male voice choir carries on the tradition. The brass band is also notable. The tinplate-works have recently closed with the development of the great modern complexes at Margam, Trostre, and Felindre, but Pontardulais retains its vitality. Northwards the river runs in a pretty valley at the foot of Graig Fawr (906 ft). The Dulais stream comes down from the hills behind Graig Fawr, and is charming in its upper reaches, once beyond the colliery. The lonely Chapel of Gerdinen marks the point where the narrow road goes over the moors down into Cwm Cathan.

Some 3 m. E. of Pontardulais, in the tangled country on the edge of the moors, is Felindre, which has given its name to the new tinplate-works (now nationalized), although they are nearer Llangyfelach. On a sharp corner of the village stands Nebo Chapel and the graveyard that contains the show-piece of the place. Set in the hedge is the Murder Stone, erected by public subscription to record the unsolved murder in 1832 of Eleanor Williams in a lonely farmhouse not far away. The stone is reputed to turn red on the anniversary of the crime. The eye of faith can certainly detect a rust-colour. And who can be certain of its origin? Behind Felindre are the valleys that held the old Blaen-Nant-Ddu reservoirs of Swansea's water-supply. There is good walking country up to Mynydd y Gwair (1,099 ft).

PONTYPOOL, *Monmouthshire*. About 9 m. NW. of Newport, Pontypool represents one of the earliest of towns in the South Wales area to adventure on a career of industrial production. Its interest in iron goes back, perhaps, even to the times of the Roman government of Britain, which put a military post at Caerleon and a civilian settlement at Caerwent. In 1720, it was the first place in which tinplate was successfully produced in Britain. It was an active producer of tinplate and steel, though its collieries have become of more importance to it. The traditionally industrial nature of its history gave its workers a leading part to play in the Chartist risings of 1839 (*see* p. 47). In 1811 Pontypool was a thriving place and, like the other Monmouthshire town of Usk, a great and busy centre for japanning work. What now distinguishes Pontypool from other South Welsh industrial centres is that, being a Monmouthshire town, it has never abandoned its interest in farming. While its urban population dropped in 1951 to 43,000, from 44,000 in 1931, its rural-area inhabitants increased from just over 5,500 by a little more than 5 per cent in the same period.

At Trosnant, near Pontypool, from 1732 to 1770 a Baptist seminary of education flourished, founded by John Griffith, who was also in charge of local ironworks. He concentrated on the spread of education in the farming community and carried his enthusiasm as far as America, where he emigrated in 1759.

PONTYPRIDD, *Glamorgan*. Like all the centres of 19th-cent. industrial development in South Wales, Pontypridd suffered a loss of activity and population after the disastrous 1930s, 10 per cent of the latter dwindling away within twenty years. Its position at the junction of the Taff and the Rhondda rivers, however, makes it still an important road and rail centre. The single-span bridge over the Taff, built in 1746, is a remarkable feature. Coal-mining is still an activity; but the present population of a little under 40,000 looks for the future to the development of light industries connected with the great Treforest Industrial Estate.

PORT DINORWIC, *Caernarfonshire*, is a small village between Bangor and Caernarfon, lying on the mainland side of the Menai Straits. It is an upgrowth from a long and narrow creek, which offers shelter from the run of tide and the storms that distress the straits; traditionally, it gets its name from Northmen who made it an anchorage during the Viking raids that began in the 8th cent. The row of houses was once the home of fishermen; it always served as a port for the shipping of slates from the Llanberis quarries. Now it is largely a base for local yachting, and during the off-season a dock for the larger ocean-going yachts that include the West Indies as a port of call. The men who live there are full of reminiscence of their travels, and are an altogether remarkable community. A convenient inn gives every opportunity to make their acquaintance.

PORTEINON, *Glamorgan*, an attractive village on the S. coast of Gower, possesses one of its best beaches, and the arrival of the car parks and caravans has not spoilt it. There are still thatched cottages, whitewashed walls, and narrow lanes that defy any car. The place gets its name from the 11th-cent. Welsh prince Einion, but Porteinon has long since become part of English-speaking Gower. The church, dedicated to St Cattwg (Cadoc), has been heavily restored. The life-size statue at the corner of the churchyard shows Billy Gibbs, the coxswain of the lifeboat that met disaster in a rescue attempt in 1916. The lifeboat was then withdrawn. Tradition has been renewed with the establishment in 1968 of a new, inshore lifeboat at Horton, the twin village of Porteinon across the Burrows. Westwards, Porteinon Point protects the bay. Here, at the curve of the shore that leads out to Skysea, an islet at high tide, is the old lifeboat house, now a youth hostel. At the Point is the ruin of the Salt-house, once a mansion of the Lucas family. Here John Lucas settled in the middle of the 16th cent., a man of "furious and ungovernable violence" who seems to have been a sort of local Robin Hood. The succeeding Lucases maintained the family tradition until the great storm of 1703 finally wrecked the Salthouse.

In the cliffs on the other side of Porteinon Point is one of Gower's great curiosities, Culver Hole. A 60-ft wall of rough masonry has sealed off a deep cleft in the rocks, into which the waters rush at high tide. The path down is slippery. The construction has never been adequately explained. It could have been a columbarium when pigeons were bred for food, or a stronghold built by the same buccaneering John Lucas who built the Salthouse. There is the usual story of a secret passage between the two. It is a mysterious place.

PORTHCAWL, *Glamorgan*. This breezy seaside place, on a low limestone promontory 7 m. SE. of Port Talbot, began its resort career as a favourite with workers in the industrial valleys of the western coalfield. It is now more widely known and patronized. On the W. side of the promontory is a fine waste of sand-dunes and open sand. To the E. of the promontory are equally sandy dunelands along the mouth of the Ogmore river. Across the wide Bristol Channel, the high tors of Exmoor are visible on clear days.

In the early days of the industrial development of South Wales, Porthcawl made a bid to become an outstanding coal port, but failed because of the greater facilities developed at Barry. The former dock basin has been filled in as a car park, and the old piers enclose a little harbour for yachts and an occasional pleasure steamer. The harbour divides Porthcawl in two. To the W. stretches the Esplanade, with the Grand Pavilion and the main shopping centre behind it. The Esplanade and the West Drive lead out to the fine, open spaces of Locks Common fronting the sea. Here, among low limestone rocks, is the bathing-place of Rest Bay, with The Rest, a large convalescent home, immediately behind it. Here too is the Royal Porthcawl Golf Club, one of the finest courses in Wales. Inland, now linked to Porthcawl by recent housing developments, is Nottage, a village that has still preserved some of the whitewashed walls and cottages that used to be such a feature of the Glamorgan scene even thirty years ago. From some angles, in fact, Nottage seems to be nothing but white walls. Embedded in many of the walls are fragments of the old Chapel of Ease, which fell into disuse after the building of the parish church at Newton, 1 m. to the E. Nottage Court – the "ty mawr" (great house) – has now been designated as a building of special architectural interest. It is a restored Tudor manor house. It contains Tudor fireplaces, a reputed priests' hole, and tapestries of the 15th cent. that formerly belonged to Tewkesbury Abbey. R. D. Blackmore, the author of *Lorna Doone*, stayed at Nottage Court when writing his romance *The Maid of Sker*. Westward from Nottage the sand-dunes of Kenfig begin. The Pyle and Kenfig Golf Club has an eighteen-hole course here.

E. of the harbour, Porthcawl changes character. This is the popular day-tripper side of the resort. Coney Island, built along the sands of Sandy Bay, has a giant fun fair with big dipper, round-abouts, and everything you expect from a modern mass-entertainment centre. The fine sands of Trecco Bay are separated from Sandy Bay by the low headland of Rhych Point. A vast caravan

park, densely packed, has covered the sea-front here. But further E., where they begin to curve past Newton Point to Merthyr Mawr Warren, the Burrows are largely untouched.

Inland from the Burrows, and now part of the town of Porthcawl, is the village of Newton, with its ancient Parish Church of St John, standing before the neatly mown village green. The tower is impressively strong, built for defence as well as for the use of the church. Within, the main points of interest are the altar, one of the few pre-Reformation altars left in Glamorgan; the 15th-cent. pulpit with its strange carvings of the Flagellation of Christ; and the octagonal font. S. of the church, across the village green, is th famous spring of St John's Well. It is now covered in, with steps leading down to the clear water. The well owes its fame to the remarkable relationship with the rise and fall of the tide on the shore $\frac{1}{4}$ m. away. When the tide is out, the well is full; when the tide returns, the well is practically empty. An inscription on a slate fixed in the outside wall reminds the visitor of this phenomenon, and also of the Latin verse by Sir John Stradling (d. 1637) of St Donat's Castle, who interested the learned antiquary Camden in the curious behaviour of the well. Sir John's equally curious English verse expresses the feelings of the Nymph of the Severn face to face with the Spirit of the Well:

Called though he be, he lurkes in den, and
  striveth hard againe;
For ebbe and flow continually by tides they
  keep both twaine.
Yet diversely, for as the Nymph doth rise,
  the spring doth fall:
Go she back, he com's on, in spite and fight
  continuall.

PORTMADOC and **TREMADOC**, *Caernarfonshire*. The road from Maentwrog and the road from Trawsfynydd pass from Minffordd towards Criccieth along the edge of the Traeth Bach, the little stretch of sand facing the Morfa Harlech across the estuary of the Dwyryd. At Minffordd, toll must be paid to cross the embankment, 1 m. long, that was built in the 1820s to reclaim 7,000 acres from the sands and sea. This is now known as the Traeth Mawr; it extends across the greater estuary of the Glaslyn river. It cost £100,000, which today would represent a value many times larger. Along the embankment the serrated outline of Snowdonia and the long arm of Lleyn can be seen in their entirety and to better advantage than from anywhere else. In 1821, as a result of the reclamation scheme, Parliament consented to the construction of a harbour; and it is to this fact that Portmadoc owes its existence. It was named after a William Alexander Madocks, M.P., whose initiative was responsible for the entire undertaking; and he followed it up with the development of the small town of Tremadoc on the western side of the Traeth Mawr.

Both places are relatively modern. Portmadoc is a business centre, well built and even picturesque in response to its setting, which gives beautiful views of Cardigan Bay and the uplands of Merioneth. The harbour is very good, and, besides its activity in slate-shipping, makes a centre for exploring the bay. Its twin, Tremadoc, is a remarkable example of early 19th-cent. town-planning; it seems to have been intended for far greater expansion than it actually gained. Town hall, market square, and theatre (which has decided to become a chapel) show that Mr Madocks looked into a future that was never realized. His enterprise commanded the enthusiastic support of the poet Shelley, who brought his wife Harriet and her sister Eliza Westbrook to live, it is said, at Tan-yr-allt, a long, white house with a veranda, 1 m. from Portmadoc on the Beddgelert road; it is set over the highway with its back into the wooded hill-side, as its name describes. More probably, he and his companions may have lived in another house in its grounds. Near Tremadoc, in any event, he wrote much of his early *Queen Mab*. Here, too, the mysterious attempt on his life was said to have been made. His friend Thomas Love Peacock, who wrote many novels and poems celebrating Welsh legend, thought Shelley's account of the affair no more than fantasy. Peacock's summary of the evidence for the attack with pistols in the dead of night sets it beside Shelley's other escapade of coming into the dining-room stark naked to assert before his guests his belief in man's natural virtue. Later, substance was given to Shelley's account by a local shepherd who confessed that he and some of his friends had been annoyed by the poet's habit, on his walks, of putting sick sheep out of their misery without attempting to save them, and that they had therefore let off a few shots at him to scare him away from the district. The affair remains a mystery. Peacock writes of Wales and its scenery, particularly round Dolgellau, with the enthusiasm of a tremendous walker who did not always find Shelley as energetic as himself. *The Misfortunes of Elphin*, a romance based on the legend of the cities of Cantref Gwaelod, drowned in Cardigan Bay, is Peacock's best-remembered work.

Another connection with Tremadoc is that T. E. Lawrence was born there in 1888. His first enthusiasm was for the medieval castles of the Crusaders in Syria, the Kingdom of the Franks, with its capital at Jerusalem, set up in the 11th cent. They are the most perfect examples of the kind of military architecture that in this country is called Norman; and, as he was born in the area commanded by Harlech and Criccieth Castles, Tremadoc may well claim that it inspired the visit to the Middle East that interested him in the future of the Arab peoples.

Echoes of earlier wars can be found in Penmorfa, 3 m. from Portmadoc, where the ancient little church has a memorial tablet to Sir John Owen, Royalist leader of the Second Civil War against Parliament in the 17th cent. Condemned to death, he somehow secured a reprieve; report has it that he and his fellow prisoners were given the chance to draw lots, and that Sir John was fortunate. The Latin tribute eloquently records his courage and loyalty; and at least he had the satisfaction of living long enough to see the Restoration of Charles II.

About ½ m. S. of Portmadoc is Borth-y-gest, a hamlet joined to Criccieth by a stretch of firm clear sand. It is an outstanding resort for bathing, trout and salmon fishing, sea fishing, and golf. Portmeirion is on the spit of land between the estuaries of the Dwyryd and Glaslyn.

With all their attractions, Tremadoc and Portmadoc seem forced to renounce any claim to being the place from which Madoc, son of Owain of Gwynedd, sailed to discover America. Their origin is recent, though Borth-y-gest has been put forward as the harbour from which the 12th-cent. prince set out for the fabled lands of the West. In 1584 the historian David Powel suggested the possibility that was supported by Thomas Howell in the 17th cent. and was turned into an epic poem by Southey in the 19th. Although efforts to find actual descendants of the Welsh colonists in America have all failed, the legend may hide a truth more interesting than itself. In recent years American scholars have become convinced of communication across the Atlantic far earlier than the voyages of Columbus; indeed, Turkish sources have revealed a chart of the eastern coasts of the two Americas said to be derived from Alexandrine sources and known to Columbus years before he set sail. The skills of early Mediterranean seamen were far greater than is generally realized; and recent archaeological research has shown a contact between Wales and the Mediterranean that persisted through the Middle Ages.

PORTMEIRION, *Merioneth*, is a marvellous "exotic", a tiny Italianate dream-town full of colour, columns, and cornices, boldly planted amid the slaty rocks and estuary waters of one of the wildest parts of North Wales near Portmadoc.

The dreamer was the distinguished Welsh architect Clough Williams-Ellis. In the years between the two world wars, he had been a doughty battler against the spoliation of Britain's landscape. He determined to prove that the "development" of an old estate need not mean wrecking it. He found the site he wanted in the small rocky peninsula that juts out between the estuary of the Glaslyn and that of the Dwyryd. Southward the views are incomparable, with the whole line of the Rhinog mountains rising above still waters as the tide floods in. He purchased the old mansion of Aber Ia, added Castell Deudraeth and its grounds to the property, and in 1926 began the transformation of a corner of Wales into something resembling Portofino or Sorrento.

Portmeirion has grown through the years and is still growing. The area itself has become one of the showplaces of North Wales. The starting-point for the scheme is the early 19th-cent. house at the water's edge, now converted into a hotel. The waterfront ends with an elegant white tower. The hotel contains a massive Renaissance fireplace, an 18th-cent. fireplace, and a library, removed complete into the house from the Great Exhibition of 1851. This delightful eclecticism is the keynote of the whole architectural complex. The campanile that crowns the rocky hill behind the hotel is Italianate; the houses clustered alongside it come from 18th-cent. England. There are cunningly planned vistas, flights of steps leading to viewpoints over the sands and tidal channels of the Traeth Bach, and gardens set with cypresses around the green. A dome floats above the eastern part of the village and confronts a town hall, which contains a splendid 17th-cent. plastered ceiling rescued from a demolished mansion in Flintshire. Mr Williams-Ellis cannot resist picking up any discarded architectural elegance in danger of demolition. Hence the presence at Portmeirion of a lovely colonnade from Bristol and a Norman Shaw façade. A President of the Royal Institute of British Architects, when confronted with the view from the chantry high above the main part of the village, remarked: "Ah! the mixture as never before". Portmeirion has been called the last nobleman's folly, a Welsh Xanadu, and a home for fallen buildings. No matter what it is called, it remains a triumphantly successful piece of architectural romanticism.

In addition to these building delights, the Portmeirion estate has one of the finest wild gardens in Wales, called the Gwyllt (Wild). Much of the small rocky peninsula is covered with a dense growth of rhododendrons and exotic plants introduced into Wales by Caton Haigh, one of the great authorities on Himalayan flowering trees. The rhododendron and azalea blossoms are at their best around mid-May. Hydrangeas flourish in late summer and autumn. In addition there are palms, cypresses, and gingko and eucalyptus trees.

Portmeirion has naturally been used as a film set on many occasions, and Noel Coward wrote his comedy *Blithe Spirit* in the Watch House, between one Saturday and the next. Deudraeth Castle itself has been converted into flats. Earl Russell's country home is near the estate.

A charge is made for day visitors who come to explore the Gwyllt garden or to see the village.

PRESTATYN, *Flintshire*. What is now a small market town and a popular seaside resort, particularly for those who come from the opposite shores of the Liverpool inlet, was in the 18th cent. a busy industrial centre for the lead-mining district of North-East Wales. Before that, it was the site of a castle built before the days of Henry II and held by the Prince of Powys, Owain Cyfeiliog, acclaimed by Gerald de Barri in 1188 as one of the three wisest and best of the native Princes of Wales. Although Prestatyn offers much interest further afield in its closeness to Rhuddlan and Holywell, St Asaph and Caerwys, it is in the site of its own castle that it preserves one of Wales's saddest memories. For it was the aim of Powys, the central province and old Kingdom of Wales, to draw the North, which was called Gwynedd, and the South, known as the Deheubarth, into one strong state that might preserve Welsh culture and religion intact. Against Henry II, when he invaded the North through Flintshire, Welsh forces gained three considerable victories in succession. But the Welsh rulers used the opportunity only to challenge the position of Owain Cyfeiliog, who, from the main base of Powys (in what is now called Montgomeryshire) had advanced his strength to control Rhuddlan and Prestatyn northwards and had also pushed his power southwards towards Brecon and lower Cardiganshire. The Owain who was Lord of Gwynedd and the Rhys who was Lord of the South combined against him, and Prestatyn and Rhuddlan were wrested from his control. There had never been a better opportunity to weld Wales into one state; and that opportunity was never fully recovered.

PRESTEIGNE, *Radnorshire.* The population of Presteigne is fewer than 2,000, and it gives the impression that this is as it should be. It is the county town of Radnorshire, where Assize Courts are held and the County Council has its seat. It does not doubt its distinct identity, and it lies in a country of gentle slopes and wide vales, luxuriant in a sturdy peace quick with growth. Here the Lugg river makes the boundary between Radnorshire and Herefordshire, between Wales and England. Llanandras is the Welsh name for Presteigne; Offa's Dyke lies some way to the N. of it on Llan-Wen Hill, and again to the S., where Walton has a name that marks it as the Welsh Town. As with the rest of Radnorshire, little or no Welsh is spoken in it; it prefers its own variety of English. The Welsh name for the shire is Maesyfed, sometimes translated as the Sinking Meadow because in dry weather one of its streams, the Somergil, vanishes into the soil. Another explanation is that it means Easily Conquered, by reason of the contrast between its open lands and the wave-like curves of the Radnor Forest that bear upon it. But the word "fed" in Welsh means a limit or confine, and for the old Kingdom of Powys Radnor may have been the SE. March.

Presteigne confirms that sense of being nothing but itself which is typical of the border population. The houses are of a fairly uniform Georgian kind, with those used for professional purposes drawn round the church, which, Norman in origin, was remodelled in the Decorated period, the 15th cent. But, as the Welsh for the town implies, its foundation must have been parallel with that of Old Radnor. What was once the castle now lies in a public open space called the Warden. The inn, a genuine half-timbered house of the 16th and 17th cents. was in his day owned by a relation of the Roundhead Bradshaw who signed the death-warrant of Charles I. But the later history of Presteigne does not seem to have been much disturbed. Owain Glyndwr had one of his first great victories at Pilleth in the early 15th cent., not far from the town, yet its pastoral life

G. Douglas Bolton

The church tower, Presteigne

was in Tudor and Stuart days distracted only by the meeting of priests and officials to inquire into and condemn the operation of white witches and their incantatory rites in the neighbourhood. In other parts of Wales, especially in Montgomeryshire, the white witch was still at work well into the 20th cent., and there are living people who can vouch for the efficacy of their recommended remedies, a raw potato in the pocket for rheumatism and a handful of earth for curing warts. But authority in Radnorshire may have been inclined to take a severe view of such activities for two reasons: the magician John Dee, who seems to have been no more than a man interested beyond his time in the scientific analysis of Nature, was a man of Radnorshire descent and perhaps of the princely family of Llywelyn Crugeryr. Born into the service of the household of the Tudors, Dee escaped burning by Mary to act as secret agent for Walsingham and trusted adviser to Elizabeth Tudor. His reputation, however, has never recovered from the accusation of dabbling in black magic. And about the hills of Presteigne roamed – perhaps still roams – the black and ghostly hound, attached to a local family, whose tale was used by Conan Doyle for his Sherlock Holmes adventure *The Hound of the Baskervilles.*

PUMSAINT, *Carmarthenshire.* This hamlet lies on the main road between Lampeter and Llandeilo at a bridge over the Cothi river. The pleasant inn where George Borrow stayed while he tramped Wild Wales overlooks the trout stream. For the rest, Pumsaint consists of a few scattered houses, an old smithy, and the overgrown entrance to the decayed estate of Dolaucothi. Dolaucothi was the ancestral home of the Johnes family, who owned it from the reign of Henry VII. The old house was the scene of a celebrated late Victorian tragedy when Judge Johnes was murdered in his study by a discharged butler who afterwards committed suicide.

Pumsaint must be distinguished from Llanpumsaint, a small village 15 m. to the W. in the Gwili valley (*see* Brechfa). "Pump" is Welsh for five, and the same five saints were connected with both places. Ceitho, Celynnen, Gwyn, Gwyno, and Gwynoro were apparently quintuplets – one of the earliest cases on record. Legend relates that they came under the spell of an enchanter who laid them to sleep in a cave near Pumsaint. There they lie, waiting to return when a truly pious bishop shall rule the diocese of St David's. It is no reflection on the Church in Wales that, so far, the saintly "quins" have not reappeared.

Pumşaint has magnificent and unfrequented country to the N. The upper reaches of the Cothi are particularly attractive.

About ½ m. E. of Pumsaint are the celebrated Roman gold-mines. Nothing is visible of the Roman bath-house marked on the Ordnance Survey map, over the bridge E. of the village. The mines, however, can be seen ½ m. N. of the main road. The land is now National Trust property. The Carreg Pumsaint, a stone with five hollows for the five saints, is close at hand on a low mound. The Romans worked partly by opencast and partly by driving adits into the lodes. The opencast section looks like an overgrown modern quarry, but the adits honeycomb the wooded slope beyond. Some of them have Roman chiselmarks clearly visible. Exploring the galleries is dangerous, and a fence has recently been erected to prevent the public from entering certain areas. Gold has been worked here in recent times, until 1939.

From the gold-mines the road runs up the Cothi valley, which becomes increasingly beautiful. The aqueduct that brought water to the mines from the head-waters of the Cothi can be traced on the S. side of the valley. It requires expert eyes to follow its full course, but it must have been one of the most impressive works of its kind in Britain.

Some 3 m. up from Pumsaint beyond the goldmines is Cwrtycadno (Fox Hall). Cwrt Methodist chapel stands at the crossroads, with its name curiously spaced among the windows. The National Trust owns the fine natural woodlands that clothe the hill-side. The National Trust area includes the farm that was once the home of "Dr" John Harris, the "dyn hysbys" (wizard) and astrologer, who was famous throughout Wales in the 1830s. People came to consult him from all over the principality. He had received some medical training, was a distinguished herbalist and healer, but was also credited with practising the black art in the woods around Cwrtycadno.

The valley closes in about 2 m. beyond Cwrt.

The Cothi comes down from its mountain source in a fine ravine and a series of falls among the thick woods called Pwlluffern (Pit of Hell). A miniature pass, Bwlch-y-Rhiw, takes the road over to the tributaries of the upper Towy valley. Just over the top, amongst the trees on the side of Mynydd Mallaen, is the Baptist chapel of Bwlch-y-Rhiw, built originally in 1717. It can claim to be the most romantically situated chapel in South Wales. The road drops down to Rhandirmwyn under the crags and woods of Mynydd Mallaen.

PWLLHELI, *Caernarfonshire*, is the capital of Lleyn (Llŷn), the long peninsula that runs out from Snowdonia into the sea towards Ireland. Philologists have been inclined to see a parallel in the words Lleyn and Leinster. Certainly the Welsh of this part of Wales differs from that of its other provinces, and has many words in it closely akin to Erse. Pwllheli is the Salt Water Pool, as some translate it; and its fine and land-locked harbour, sheltered from winds and exceptionally safe for boating, justifies the name. Others find in it a corruption of Porth Heli, the Port of a lord of the district called Heli.

Its status as a corporate borough goes back to the time of the Black Prince, son of Edward III, who created it as "free", that is, self-governing. Formerly the harbour was much used, but gradual silting of sand needed a Government grant of £70,000 to clear it, and it is now a refuge from storms out at sea. This, however, has increased its usefulness as a boating and fishing centre. The amenities of Pwllheli have also been more recently added to by the holiday camp at Afonwen, once a remote railway stop lost among green lanes and flowered hedgerows with beautiful views over Cardigan Bay, used as a naval training base during the Second World War. There are two Pwllhelis. One is the old town, N. of the railway terminus at the head of the harbour, with town hall and market hall, and a parish church that, round the core of a church typical of the ancient foundations of Anglesey and Caernarfonshire, has developed into the Early Decorated style. The other Pwllheli consists of two seaside suburbs, South Beach and West End. The county school rises high above the town, and Penrhos aerodrome, 2 m. to the S., brings Pwllheli well into modernity. There are many facilities for sport and recreation. They include shooting – geese, widgeon, teal, plover, and also rabbits. Students of nature have excellent opportunities to study the flowers of the sand and of the moors above it.

From Pwllheli the Lleyn, with its many ancient churches set along the pilgrim ways that sought the holy places of Bardsey and Anglesey, the many sites of interest to the archaeologist, the cliffs and uplands bright with flowers and loud with seabirds, and above all the massive range of Snowdon and its foothills can be seen to best advantage. St Tudwal's Islands, with their Early Christian sanctuaries, were bought by Clough Williams-Ellis, the architect and founder of Portmeirion, creator of so much new beauty in the neighbouring villages, to save them from development. Llanbedrog is a charming village 4 m. away with an excellent beach and the mansion of Glyn-y-Weddw, once a pleasure centre with an art gallery. Close by is Mynytho and the Ffynnon Arian (Silver Spring), one of the holy and healing wells of this favoured part of Wales. The villages of Abersoch and Abererch are delightful; Clynnog Fawr is exceptional in its closeness to Yr Eifl (The Rivals) and the mysterious prehistoric city of Tre'r Ceiri. The Nanhoron valley, wooded and rich, leads to Garn Fadrun (1,217 ft), the next highest point to Yr Eifl in the Lleyn. This has on its summit a prehistoric fortress of curious interest, since it contains a stone known as Arthur's Table. By some it has been supposed to play as important a part for the Welsh as the Stone of Scone in Scotland; but its significance is probably more religious than political. A Tudor mansion, Madryn Castle, has become a fully technological school for the farmers of the 20th cent.

About 6 m. E. along the coast of Lleyn is Llanystumdwy, where the 1st Earl Lloyd George of Dwyfor has his memorial and the chapel uniquely designed by Clough Williams-Ellis. Criccieth, 8½ m. from Pwllheli along the same road, has its castle, the ascent through Dolbenmaen of Garnedd Goch (2,301 ft), and the Craig Cwm-Silyn, sheering down to its lakes; the tall peak of Moel Hebog (Hill of Hawks), over-topping the Llyn Cwmystradllyn; Dolbenmaen with its ancient church; and the long loveliness of the Pennant Valley.

The Lleyn is noted for its cromlechs. Here are the striking ones of Cefn Isa and Ystumcegid Isaf: ribs of long barrows that once shielded the bodies of men powerful and honoured in the Iron Age, but now stripped of their covering. The capstone at Ystumcegid, supported on its uprights, is 5 yds long and must have roofed something more than a grave, perhaps a ceremonial temple. About Cwmystradllyn lake is told the legend of how a bride of the Other People was won from the waters by a young farmer, but stipulated, as her kind did, that she should never be asked to touch iron. For years the young man carefully obeyed; then at one harvest he threw her the last sheaf, forgetting that a sickle was buried in it. At once she vanished, never to reappear. This story is typical of many lakes in Wales. It is a folk-memory of the Bronze Age people who dwelt in these secluded hills, tending their beasts and raising their crops apart from the invading Celtic race from Europe with their tools and weapons of the strange new metal, iron. In this case, the ceremony of casting the last sheaf is a recollection of the ceremonies of propitiation and sacrifice to the fruitful Earth in return for its yield of corn. And the Cwm-Silyn lake also has its legend of the small people, clad in green, who possessed it but came only in the twilight and vanished if they saw a mortal near them; again a memory of the shy and timid race that lived in the high hills and built their dwellings on stakes driven far out into the lake-bed.

RADNOR, OLD and **NEW,** *Radnorshire.* These two places – New Radnor a small township, Old Radnor now mainly a site, but one of great historical interest – are little more than 3 m. apart. New Radnor has a hotel and pleasant small inns that make it an excellent centre for riding or walking the forest hills or fishing the streams. To the N. of it lies Radnor Forest, and to the S. the equally interesting Hergest Ridge and Caety Traylow, holding the hamlet of Gladestry between them. The immediate front to New Radnor in this direction is the curiously rounded hill called the Smatcher, from which it is possible to look down into the flat meadows running E. to Evenjobb just within Offa's Dyke and Walton (Welsh Town). This level vale of the Summerhill Brook is marked with standing stones marching from Kinnerton on the N. to Old Radnor on the S., marking a line of communication that seemingly belongs to Old Radnor's pre-Christian past.

The plan of New Radnor is still set out as old prints describe it: a simple chess-board pattern suggesting some recollection of Roman town-planning. It is attributed to the Harald, Earl of Hereford, who became the last Saxon King of England, who destroyed Old Radnor in his campaign into Wales in the 11th cent., and set up New Radnor in its place as a stronghold of English power. But no real evidence establishes the surviving pattern of the town beyond the 13th cent.; the layout has a parallel in that of Winchelsea in Sussex, and the attribution may possibly be better made to the notorious De Braose (or Bruce) family of Norman conquerors who seized Radnor about 1200. Nothing remains of the castle but its grassy foundations; Owain Glyndwr destroyed it after the victory at Pilleth, perhaps by way of retaliation for Harald's "slighting" of the Welsh castle at Old Radnor over 300 years before. Local memory is tenacious of the event, but inclined to confuse it with what occurred in the Civil War, when New Radnor was held for Charles I, and the Cromwellian batteries smashed the place into submission. The church, however, still stands much as early 19th-cent. prints show it, with a pleasing square tower not far from the cattle-watering stream that runs through the streets of New Radnor.

For the remoter history of the place, one must go to Old Radnor, now a church upon a hill and very little else. There are legends, and still some visible evidence, that New Radnor once extended far beyond its present limits; but for Old Radnor, apart from the vanished castle, the church seems always to have been the focal point. Some assert that Roman legionaries set a camp there; and it is true that Charles I visited it after his retreat from Naseby. But its origin is probably in pre-historic times. The existing church is reckoned one of the finest in Wales. From 840 ft above sea-level, it looks over the plain between the circled hills down to the standing stones by Kinnerton. It is large, in the Late Decorated style; it has a considerable W. tower and 15th-cent. linen-fold panelling, a noteworthy screen and ancient stalls for seating. Its font is supposed to be the oldest in

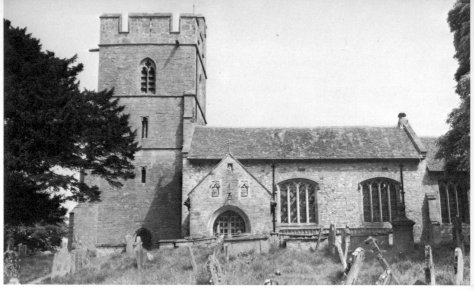

Old Radnor church

Britain, and is a remarkable memorial to the growth of the Christian faith in these islands. As far back as the 6th or 7th cent., when the Roman Empire decided to leave defence of its western provinces to such native auxiliary forces as the cities might organize, and the official adoption of Christianity was challenged by the resurgence of older faiths, this font is believed to have served a Christian purpose in a church on this site. But that was not its original character. It seems to have been an altar-stone, or some other important object connected with the N. to S. line of standing stones that still follows the road from Kinnerton to Old Radnor, marking what must be one of the oldest traffic routes in Britain.

RADNOR FOREST, *Radnorshire*. The well-known gibe at Radnorshire and its lack of rich estates and flourishing squires is quoted under Abbeycwmhir. A more recent comment was that of a Radnorshire policeman who, while he attempted to deal with local traffic, said per-spiringly that you could count 900 sheep to one man. Much of this character is imposed on Radnorshire by Radnor Forest. Although in many parts heavily treed for a long time, and subject to further afforestation in latter years, it is still a forest in the ancient sense – not of a wooded area but of a wild one. The reputedly highest point in it, the Black Mixen (2,135 ft), is actually topped by a neighbouring hill, the Great Rhos, with another 30 ft. Bache Hill, the Whimble, and Vron Hill stand a little lower and mix their half-Anglicized names with others still defiantly Welsh: Esgair Nantau, Mynd Maes Melan, Rhiwiau. Mostly it is an area of rounded green backs, a last dying fall of the Ellennith, but the Great Creigiau shows where the land can still break into a rocky scramble such as you find on the northern face of the Plynlimon escarpment.

The Forest can be said to lie between New Radnor and Penybont. Unlike the moorland of Montgomeryshire, of which it forms a south-easterly extension, it is a dry and sweet-grassed place with its own brand of sheep. But above all it is ground to ride over. Horses are native to it. The wild pony is as traditional in the Forest of Radnor as in the New Forest of Hampshire.

The best point to ride from is possibly New Radnor. From here the tracks will take you to the Shepherd's Well and the tumulus over the woods of Llethr-ddu, or a little further over Fron Wen (White Breast) hill to the Rhiw Pool. Another tumulus looks out over the valley to Cefn-y-crug (Heather Back) and the Shepherd's Twmp standing at the same height of just over 1,500 ft.

Other beautiful rides or walks will take you to Llandegley and what is called the Sulphur Spring, or between the Water-Break-Its-Neck falls to Llanfihangel Nant Melan with its old farms, or to the curious declivities of Cowlod and the Foel. The choice is between the opportunities offered by Harley Dingle, with its gradual incline upward to the side of the Great Creigiau and the Black Mixen, both lovely and straightforward, or those that lie in the direct route from Penybont to New Radnor, which is an adventurous route alternating rapidly between the grassy field and the screefall, the mountain-top and the wooded valley-level. By horse or foot is the only way to see Ednol Farm, with what was once a church, though the pretty place of Casgob can be reached by car, and from there the run of the Lugg as it passes under the hill behind the site of the castle of the famous Pilleth.

Radnorshire is full of Welsh names not only for hills but also for villages and farmsteads, and yet no Welsh is spoken there. You will find, of course, a similar state of things in Shropshire, Herefordshire, and Cheshire; and in Gloucester-shire the new crossing of the Severn laid by the most modern techniques of bridge-building goes by the ancient ferry town of Aust, the Welsh form of the Latin Augustus whose imperial name the Romans gave to the ford so vital to their system of control.

But Radnor Forest remains solidly an island, a dry lift of soil at the extremity of the central peat-moors of Wales, a spur of Powys still thrusting itself eastward of the Dyke in defiance of Offa, a country where the horse maintained its 3,000-year-old supremacy perhaps longer than any other part of Britain, and where the wheelwright, smith, and saddler still follow their ancient crafts.

RAGLAN, *Monmouthshire.* The town is most remarkable for its castle. It was the latest of the medieval strongholds; indeed, its creation can be said to mark the end of the Middle Ages. William Herbert, Earl of Pembroke, had it made and intended to use it as a fortress in the Yorkist interest during the Wars of the Roses. It was that long-drawn and bloody feud between the Yorkist and Lancastrian Houses for the throne of England which destroyed the whole system of faith and law upon which medieval Britain was built. The Earl was captured and executed by the Lancastrians in 1469, just twenty years before Henry Tudor, afterwards Henry VII, ended the Wars and reconciled the badges of the two opposing sides by uniting the White Rose and the Red in the new symbol of the Tudor dynasty. The curious fact is that Henry was at one stage in his career imprisoned by William Herbert in this same Castle of Raglan. During the later troubles of the Civil Wars, Charles I was a guest in the Castle after the rout of Naseby, and it was defended against Fairfax, Cromwell's General, for ten weeks in 1646 – the last castle to hold out against Parliament in the First Civil War. Charles II on his restoration rewarded the family by raising it from an earldom to a marquessate; and the 2nd Marquess distinguished himself further by writing a treatise on the use of steam and water-power in which he anticipated the steam-pump in the 17th cent. It is said that he had already turned his inventiveness to use by driving off the Roundhead attack with water-hoses, but there is no contemporary evidence for this. The great hall and the six-sided central keep attract most attention; the outstanding feature of the Castle, however, is its great length of surrounding wall. Raglan stands alone, commanding a wide countryside. Between it and Monmouth, Craig y Dorth is supposed to mark where Owain Glyndwr took to the hills after his allies, Hotspur and Percy of Northumberland, had been overthrown at Shrewsbury.

REYNOLDSTON, *Glamorgan,* in the centre of the Gower peninsula, is 10 m. W. of Swansea. The rather straggling village runs along the southern slopes of the central part of Cefn Bryn. The church has been heavily restored, but the public house, the King Arthur, looks out over a village green that merges into the bracken-covered hill. Reynoldston is very much the Gower crossroads, the place where you go for the doctor and everything else.

The Old Red Sandstone ridge of Cefn Bryn, which is the backbone of Gower, runs over 4 m.

from Penmaen to Burry Green. The highest point (609 ft) is at the eastern end, and the track of Talbot's Way, named after a 19th-cent. squire of Penrice Castle who used it to return from hunting, runs the whole length of the ridge. Just off the centre, near the point where the road from Reynoldston to N. Gower crosses the ridge, is the celebrated cromlech Arthur's Stone. The huge capstone is estimated to weigh 25 tons and still roofs the burial-chamber, although the stone has been partly split – according to legend, by King Arthur's sword. The structure was once covered by a mound and dates from somewhere around 2500 B.C. Arthur's Stone is probably the Maen Ceti of Welsh tradition, a pebble cast out of King Arthur's shoe. Like many of these huge prehistoric stones, it was supposed to go down to the sea to drink on New Year's Eve.

RHAYADER, *Radnorshire,* lies between Plynlimon and Radnor Forest, and between the Ellennith and the Melienydd, the great moorland desert of Wales and its south-eastern extension that dropped to the pasture lands of the Usk and Wye. How old it is as a place of habitation we do not know; the church preserves a font with rough designs of human heads, but it does not date further back than 1200. The name of the place is taken from what were once the great rapids of the Wye by which it stood, but the creation of the Elan Valley dam, and a great chain of reservoirs, formed between 1893 and 1904, diminished the rapids. It is a market town noted for its sheep fairs, and with exceptional facilities for fishing both in the Elan reservoirs and various natural lakes in the area and also in the moorland streams. The miles of uninhabited country around it make it most attractive for walkers and geologists; there are outstandingly good roads, much needed in so wild and exposed an area.

Perhaps no better description of the region can be had than the words of John Leland, created King's Antiquary in 1553 and commissioned to go on an itinerary of the country and make an inventory of everything of interest and value in it. W. of Rhayader are the lakes known collectively as the Teifi Pools, most of them close to each other. The trout – of fine, bright quality – are from a strain said to have been introduced there by the monks of Strata Florida. To a modern eye the scenery in which they are laid is wild and austere, but beautiful and with wildlife, particularly fowl, of rare interest. To Leland, it appeared very differently: "Of all the pooles none stondeth in so rokky and stony soile as Tyve doth, that hath within hym many stonis. The ground all about Tyve and a great mile of towards Stratfler is horrible with the sight of bare stonis, as cregeryri mountains be". By "cregeryri" he meant the Snowdon range Welshmen still prefer to call Eryri. Of the "rokks" he refers to, one well repays a visit; it is the Craig Naw-Llyn (Nine-Lake Rock), from whose height the sheets of water can be counted in their series across the moorland, which reaches the horizon in a heaving, umber stretch without trace of man. There is, however, a mountain-track made none knows when but running on the eastern side, where the stream-cuts have brought down masses of the rocks that Leland so much feared. A section of this track is marked on maps as an ancient road; and it has one feature of great interest. Part of the way is cut through rock, 2 ft deep and extending some 30 ft. It may even have preceded the trackway. Locally this is known as the Pedolfa (Shoeing Place), and so seems to fit with the use of these peatlands of the Great Desert as ways of transit for cattle-drovers making the long journey from Wales into the lowlands of England for the sale of cattle. It was essential to give them shoes for feet that would have to travel 200 miles; and, whatever the origin of this path, it was adapted in this place to serve that purpose.

A road, suitable for motor-traffic, runs to Teifi from Pontrhydfendigaid, going to Ffair-rhos and there becoming rather more inconvenient. Perhaps it is here, even more than above Bwlch Gwyn on Plynlimon, that the Great Desert impresses one with the sense how well its name is deserved. Teifi is isolated in an area of emptiness 30 m. from N. to S. and up to 15 m. from W. to E. The great Cors Goch Glan Teifi, or Bog of Tregaron, now a Nature Reserve, reaches towards it; coot and heron find their haunts there, and seagull and hawk make it their hunting-ground. In this region, it is said, alone among places in Britain, the black adder has a home. Around Plynlimon, a red adder is supposed to live, though experience suggests that this is no more than the peaceable slow-worm. Adders infest the hills above Aberdovey, without doubt, and the black adder of Teifi should not be dismissed as a legend. For some observers, Teifi is a place of dignity and wonder; others may prefer the opinion of Leland.

RHONDDA, The, *Glamorgan*. This is an area made famous in the 1930s by the long disaster of decline that squeezed its energy into the realignment of welfare conditions. It is a whole district, an urban district council area, into which are compressed the conurbations of the Rhondda Fawr river valley – Treherbert, Treorci, Tonypandy, and Porth; and those of the Rhondda Fach – Maerdy, Ferndale, and Tylorstown. Of its early economic organization, it is Ton y Pandy (as it should be written) that states its nature: the Untilled Land Where the Fulling Mills Are. The streams once turned the wheels of the "pandys" in which wool was worked into cloth.

It was at one time a green and beautiful district, without towns of any note, for Christopher Saxton in 1610 leaves it empty of names except for the town of Aberdare, some distance away, and 200 years later Daniel Paterson had no reason to include any of the names of the Rhondda in his careful study of British roads. Partly, this was due to the fact that the Rhondda Fawr valley was a cul-de-sac ending in the bleak uplands of the

Brecon Beacons. The names of other places than Tonypandy show that they originated in the tremendous drive for coal production that boomed throughout the 19th cent. It was, and still has to be, one of the most densely populated areas. In 1931 its population of more than 140,000 was packed 23,000 to the sq. m. As coal advanced, so were the terraced ranks of houses built in and between the valleys, with no thought of attuning their plan to the nature of the country; the streets lie like the prongs of a fork stabbed into the soil. The present and the future of the Rhondda is summed up by the drop in population, 141,344 in 1931, and twenty years later 111,357; the 8-m. group of conurbations was reduced in density by between 20 and 25 per cent. Its thrustful development had been due to its possessing seams of the best steam-coal anywhere. But, in the production of power, steam has found competitors that have far outdistanced it. While its economic vigour lasted and for some time after, the Rhondda bore men distinguished in music as in boxing and football. Coal used to be the most important industry, and its export was carried on through Pontypridd by way of Cardiff and Barry. But the Depression of the 1930s turned the Rhondda into a depressed or special area, and attempts were, and still are, being made to introduce light industries to maintain the level of employment. The Rhondda awaits its share in the new opportunities of the 20th cent.

RHOSILI, *Glamorgan*, is the climax of the 16 m. of sandy beaches, bright limestone headlands, and plunging cliffs that form the S. coast of the Gower peninsula, W. of Swansea. The village is just a collection of houses that seem grouped round the church for shelter from the wind that comes straight up the channel from the Atlantic. Lying 200 ft below is the splendid stretch of sand, 5 m. of unspoilt sea-coast, that runs from the extraordinary headland of the Worm to the island of Burry Holms. The Church of St Mary is a typically simple Gower church, with a fine Norman doorway. It contains modern glass and a memorial to P.O. Edgar Evans, the Rhosili man who died with Capt. Scott on the return from the South Pole. The adjacent hamlets of Middleton and Pitton are included in the parish, but are much more sheltered than Rhosili.

From the church a grand cliff walk goes out to the Worm. On the left is the "Viel", which is the local name for the ancient open-field system, the strips of arable land that are a remarkable survival of the farming methods of the Middle Ages. Worms Head winds out to sea like the serpent the Norseman named it after. The islands are cut off at high tide. The Inner and Outer Heads are connected by the arch of rock called the Devil's Bridge, and in high wind the hollow of the Blow Hole, on the N. face of the Worm, makes a strange booming that is carried a long way inland. The Worm is now a Nature Reserve.

The sands run to the N. from the promontory

G. Douglas Bolton

The Church of St Mary, Rhosili

of the Worm, backed by the bare hill of Rhosili Down (632 ft), the highest point in Gower. The hill has numerous prehistoric remains, including the ruined megalithic tombs of the Sweyn's or Swine's Houses, which date from the same period as Arthur's Stone, roughly 2500 B.C. The views are magnificent. The Old Rectory is the lonely house at the foot of the down, 1 m. from Rhosili facing the sands. It is reputed to be haunted.

The sands of Rhosili also hold curiosities. The bones of the ship that appear at low tide are the ribs of the *Helvetia*, wrecked in 1887. The most famous of the Rhosili wrecks is that of the "dollar ship". This is thought to have been a South American ship bringing back the dowry of Catherine of Braganza. Quantities of silver coins were uncovered in 1807 and again in 1833. Rhosili Bay was invaded by a silver rush; claims were frantically staked as the tide rose among the diggings. Fortunes were made by the find. One of the Lucas family was reported to have got away unfairly with the bulk of the silver and then fled the country. His ghostly coach is supposed to traverse the sands on wild nights. The bay looks its best when the long line of surf comes rolling in, driven by the south-westerly gales.

The limestone islet of Burry Holms ends Rhosili Bay on the northern side. The island has an Iron Age earthwork across the middle. There are also traces of a medieval monastic cell; the 6th-cent. St Cenydd, whose church is in nearby Llangynydd, is connected with it. The automatic lighthouse has replaced the old light on Whiteford Point.

RHUDDLAN, *Flintshire*. "A noble castle called Ruthlan" was recorded by Gerald de Barri in 1188, journeying through Wales on behalf of the Third Crusade. There he was nobly entertained by its owner, David, eldest son of Owain Gwynedd, Prince of North Wales. The place was then, as now, set on the Clwyd river and was a sea-port. But the interest of the reference made by Gerald is that it speaks of a castle not of English building, but of Welsh. The existing ruins date from the Edwardian Wars and their conclusion in an English victory, for Rhuddlan was one of the chain of strongholds built in 1277 to keep North Wales in subjection. Apparently David possessed a castle of the kind still remaining, not far away, at Ewloe, a Welsh structure on the Norman model, antedating the Conquest and forming the scene of Owain Gwynedd's rout of the forces of Henry II in 1157.

For the Welsh, however, Rhuddlan has a sadder significance. Here a total disaster was inflicted on their forces, under Caradoc, by those of the Offa, King of Mercia, who is said to have later set up, westward of the Severn, the Dyke containing the Cymry that today bears his name. The defeat is still remembered; Morfa (Sea-Land), the Marsh of Rhuddlan, gives its title to a lament, magnificent in its music and a masterpiece of its kind. At Rhuddlan Edward I chose to dictate the terms on which the Welsh recognized defeat through the Statute of Rhuddlan (1284), holding court there for three years while he prepared the control and administration of the territories over which English suzerainty should at last be direct.

Rhuddlan Castle is similar in type and plan to the rest of Edward's North Welsh fastnesses; quadrangular in plan, with two gatehouses and six round towers. Until the Civil Wars of the 17th cent., it kept itself much to itself; neither the Rhys, son of Maredudd, who in 1287 raised a national revolt in the South, seizing both Dynevor and Llandovery, nor the nearer war with the Madoc who claimed to be son of the dead Llywelyn and captured Oswestry in 1295, in any way disturbed it. Held for the King in 1646, it decided to surrender to the Parliamentary commander, General Mytton, and was almost immediately "slighted", or dismantled, by order of Parliament.

The parish church has an old tower designed to serve as a mark for ships at sea; whatever its

Rhuddlan Castle

Peter Baker

date of first foundation, it is now a characteristic double-nave structure of the kind familiar to the Vale of Clwyd and belonging in type to the 15th cent. But it is peculiar in having its twin naves divided by an arcade internally and fitting them each with a separate roof.

Three m. SE. of Rhuddlan, at Bodelwyddan, is another church, but one dating from the middle of the 19th cent. Built of limestone relieved with Belgian marble, it was set up by Lady Willoughby de Broke in memory of her husband. The sculptures and windows reflect the taste of 1856.

RHYL, *Flintshire*, stands at the mouth of the River Clwyd, also called the Foryd, and as an estuary town has sands of very considerable extent, creating its great popularity. The architecture of the place is subordinate to its attraction as a family holiday resort and the crowded interest of its inland surroundings. They are relatively flat, as becomes a riverine area. But within a short distance you can come upon Rhuddlan and Prestatyn, points of fame in the troubled story of the battle for Welsh independence; St Asaph with its cathedral and holy well and its history going back well into the 12th cent.; Treffynnon (Holywell), with its equally ancient traditions that have persisted in making it a place of pilgrimage to this day; Offa's Dyke, which served as frontier between Saxon and Cymro in the Dark Ages and lies a short way due E. from Rhyl; and the Roman road close to it that still goes to Llanelwy, as St Asaph is otherwise known, on the way to the copper-, lead-, and silver-mines that from ancient times have studded Denbigh and Flint.

RIVERS. Gerald de Barri, the great Welshman of the 12th cent., Churchman, statesman, diplo-

mat, lover of men and dogs and of his home at the foot of the Ellennith moors, saw Wales as fashioned by its rivers. No better account of them can be given than in his own words, though in the 20th cent. something can be added.

"Wales is divided and distinguished," writes Gerald, "by noble rivers, which derive their source from two ranges of mountains in the Ellennith, in South Wales, which the English call Moruge, as being the heads of moors or bogs; and Eryri, in North Wales, which they call Snowdon, the latter of which are said to be of so great an extent that if all the herds in Wales were collected together they would supply them with pasture for a considerable time."

"The Severn," he continues, "takes its rise from the Ellennith [Plynlimon] and flowing by the castles of Shrewsbury and Bridgnorth, through the city of Worcester and that of Gloucester, celebrated for its iron manufactures, falls into the sea a few miles from the latter place and gives its name to the Severn Sea. This river was for many years the boundary between Cambria [Wales] and Loegria [England]. It was called in British, Hafren."

He goes on to repeat the tale of Geoffrey of Monmouth, who invented the Arthurian romance, that Hafren was a British princess of ancient times, drowned in the Severn tide. But apparently the name has more to do with "hafn" (haven), or "haf" (summer), than with a woman who was as unlucky after death as she was in life; for "hafren" became in later Welsh a trollop or wanton, perhaps from the recollection that she was originally a goddess of the river and thus unchristian.

Gerald points out that Shrewsbury was the capital of Wales when the Kingdom of Powys stood firm upon the line from Chester and

The River Usk at Crickhowell

Strathclyde to the Severn and Wessex. The poet Drayton in the 17th cent. supports this with Welsh authority to show that Powys belonged to the early period before the Saxon turned his weapons to the West, and allows his Severn to claim an ancient British right to the green fields of Hereford, the hills of Malvern, and the Forest of Dean. But now the Severn, rising on the breast of Plynlimon Fawr, and falling into the green and narrow valley by Caersws, with its recollections of the Roman legions, goes from its bridge at Newtown into English territory and passes at last by Aust, where the Romans had their ferry across the river, to find a sea that is one part Wales and one part England: the Severn Sea, which the Norman took, to settle on the shores of Pembroke and Glamorgan, Monmouth, and Carmarthen, and where piracy was such that the business of the monastery at Margam was largely to provide sea-rovers with sanctuary from pursuit. Now, the Severn is less a barrier than a bridged means of access between Wales and England. But at Newtown and Llanidloes the fish still rise; and, by the Long Mynd, Caer Caradoc looks down on the road built by the Roman conquerors of Caratacos.

"The river Wye," reports Gerald, "rises in the same mountains of Ellennith and flows by the castles of Hay and Clifford, through the city of Hereford, by the castles of Wilton and Goodrich, through the Forest of Dean, abounding with iron and deer, and proceeds to Strigul castle below which it empties itself into the sea and forms in modern times the boundary between England and Wales."

Of all the Welsh-born rivers, the Wye is the most beautiful. Its valley is a long and wavering course of meadow and woodland; and its salmon are known all over the world. From Plynlimon

Fawr, a spring close to the source of the Severn now finds its way through the young upshoots of conifers to wander through a territory where Wales and England become one. Between Wye and Severn, Humphrey Lhuyd in the 16th cent. set the long protective arm of Powys, that ancient province of Wales whose princes followed the policy of affirming, between themselves and whatever power held England, a relationship of equals that earned them little sympathy from the other ruling houses of Wales. But they retained the identity of their people by becoming almost Lords Marcher of the borderland themselves, and so nominally avoided the incorporation into England that Edward I proposed for the northern princedom of Gwynedd. This quality still lingers among the people, English-speaking with names like Blew, Prothero, and Cadwallader and villages like Pontrilas, Breinton, and Dilwyn. Among such persons must be counted the poet Traherne in the 17th cent., a Herefordshire man who nevertheless, by his name of Trahaiarn and his verses in the language of John Donne, showed how deeply ran the Welshness of his blood.

The Wye is a river of peace. From Builth and Rhayader, where it still goes under the austere skyline of the Epynt and Radnor Forest, to Hay, where it leaves the long dark wall of the Black Mountains and passes N. of the Golden Valley to enter England; and so to Welsh Bicknor and English Bicknor; to Tintern Abbey, whose walls seek the sky; to Chepstow and the Caldicot Level, where Caerwent looks, from the Roman streets on which the children of the legionaries played, towards Penhow, whose Norman keep is fragmented into a farmyard – throughout its course the Wye has made beauty out of generations of war. The monuments to this achievement can be seen in the quiet beauty of small churches –

Mitchel Troy, Rockfield, and Dixton – not far from Monmouth, and such a place as Dingestow Court, whose Elizabethan splendour housed for so long the MS. treasures of Wales's history.

The Usk, Gerald says, "does not derive its origin like Severn and Wye from Plynlimon, but flows by the castle of Brecon, or Aberhonddu, where the Usk is joined by the river of that name, by the castles of Abergavenny and Usk, goes through the ancient City of Legions, or Caerleon, and discharges itself into the Severn Sea not far from Newport." This was the last boundary fixed between England and Wales – strangely enough, by Henry VIII of England, a Tudor king who in 1534 made a number of curious dispositions. The separate Council of Wales that Henry VII had set up for his son Arthur, Henry VIII's elder brother who died before their father, to be administered by him as Prince of Wales, remained until the Roundhead Parliament abolished all such councils in Britain in the 17th cent. It included not only the Marcher Lordships, but Shropshire, Hereford, Worcester, and Gloucester, with a connection through the Prince with Cheshire and Cornwall. Of all the territories Humphrey Lhuyd claimed for Wales in 1579, only Monmouthshire was formally linked with England. The original Act of Henry VIII provided, as his later ones did, for English legal administration; the Welsh language was not encouraged for official use. The Act is often read as an annexation by England of Wales; but the separate title of Dominion and Principality of Wales was used then and afterwards; and the one area between Wye and Usk – Gwent, now known as Monmouthshire – that was attached to England has stayed largely Welsh to this day. The legislation continued the policy of Powys, for which Gerald de Barri strove all his life, and which the Wye seems to confirm: that Wales and England, each with its own identity, should work harmoniously together.

Now, westward of the Usk, the great area of coal and iron that was suddenly upthrust by the Industrial Revolution smoulders into the green revival of afforestation and light local manufactories. Newport is entering a new phase in the development of its out-going trade. This change it faces with confidence. For Wales the 21st cent. holds no fear.

Other rivers of the South, Gerald takes in order. The Rhymney and the Taff, which "goes its way to Llandaff and its great episcopal See, and then to the castle of Caerdyf". The Afan river that "rushes impetuously from the mountains of Glamorgan between the famous monasteries of Margan and Neth". The Neath itself that, descending from the mountains of Brecon, falls into the sea not far from the town of Neath, forming a long tract of dangerous quicksands. The Tawe that flows to Abertawe, "which the English call Swainsey", as he spells Swansea. The "Lochor" (Loughor) and the "Wendraeth" (Gwendraeth); the Tywy (Towy), "another noble river that rises

Across the Wye to the Severn estuary

G. Douglas Bolton

in the Ellennith mountains and passes by the castle of Llandovery and the royal palace and castle of Dynevor, strongly situated in the deep recesses of its woods; by the noble castle of Caermarddin where Merlin was found, and runs into the sea near the castle of Llanstephan", to be seized in 1254 by Llywelyn the Last. The Taf that "rises in the Preseli mountains not far from the monastery of Whitland", where Hywel the Good had codified the laws of Wales 200 years before Gerald wrote, "and passing by the castle of St Clare, falls into the sea near Abercorran and Talacharn [Laugharne]. And, from the same mountains, the rivers Cleddau, encompassing the province of Daugleddau [Pembrokeshire] and giving it their name, one passing by the castle of Haverford and the other by that of Lahaden [Llawhaden]. And in the British language they bear the name of the Two Swords".

The Teifi too he names, pointing out that it was the only river in Wales that had beavers; but also it exceeded every other river in the abundance and delicacy of its salmon. From the same Ellennith came the "Ystuyth" (Ystwyth). He does not mention the Rheidol, in whose lower valley Dafydd ap Gwilym was to find the source of his great songs. And he thought that the Dovey must rise in Snowdonia, unless in his day the Arans were included in the area of the Snowdon range, as they are today in the National Park of Snowdonia. Nor was he accurate in supposing that the Mawddach formed the great Sands lying below the Vale of Ffestiniog. But he knew how the Conway met the sea "under the noble castle of Deganwy", that isolated and hillocked structure from which the armies of the Henrys and the Edwards fell back, and which now looks over the heads of caravans, chalets, and the terraced sea-front of Llandudno. The Clwyd, guarded at its mouth by the Castle of Rhuddlan, he knew as well. He had studied the Dee closely, from "Penmelsmere" (Bala) and through Chester; it leaves "the wood of Coleshill, Basinwerk, and a rich vein of silver in its neighbourhood far to the right and by the influx of the sea forms a very dangerous quicksand. And thus," he concludes, "the Dee makes the northern and the river Wye the southern boundary of Wales."

ROCH CASTLE, *Pembrokeshire.* This small castle is perched on an undercut and isolated rocky outcrop overlooking the wide sweep of St Bride's Bay. It is a prominent object for miles around, with its air of having been drawn by a monk to illustrate a medieval chronicle. The original castle is claimed to have been built by a Norman knight named Adam de Rupe (*rupe* is charter Latin for a rock). Legend further relates that Rupe built his castle on the rock to avoid the prophecy that he would die from the bite of a viper. A viper was, however, carried by mistake into the castle with a bundle of firewood. It bit Adam de Rupe, and killed him. The Roches were one of the important families in the English conquest of southern Pembrokeshire, and held big estates in its northern section.

Roch Castle (the "e" was dropped during the 19th cent.) was built on the edge of "Landsker" – that invisible boundary which, to this day, separates Welsh-speaking from English-speaking Pembrokeshire. The direct line of the Roches ended in 1420. By about 1601, the Castle was in the hands of the Walter family. During the Civil Wars the Castle changed hands several times, and Walter wisely took refuge in London. Lucy, the daughter, entered history after the family had fled still further to the Hague. She became the mistress of Charles II, and gave birth to a son who afterwards was acknowledged by Charles as the Duke of Monmouth. The Castle was in ruins for over 200 years. It was restored in 1900 by the Viscount St David, and has been further restored since then, especially by the present American owner. The interior is small. The ancient tower is entered through a guardroom, from which a stairway in the thick wall leads up to the main or "court" room. A small chapel is housed in a jutting tower. The upper storeys contain small bedrooms. A new wing was added in 1902. The present furnishings were chosen to reflect the living conditions of the periods during which the castle was actively defended. Roch is not generally open to the public.

RUABON, *Denbighshire,* is a feature of Wales that identifies itself with modern progress. Although small in population, it is an important railway junction; it is a manufacturing centre for the production of chemicals, fine ceramics, bricks and tiles, and forms part of the North Welsh coalfield. Like the iron-working towns of Cefn-mawr and Acrefair, it introduces a hard and practical note into the harmonies of the Vale of Llangollen. Its church can look back to the 14th cent., and shows monuments of the period and a faded wall fresco.

It is adjoined by Wynnstay, the seat of the family of baronets, Watcyn Williams Wynn, that played so great a part in the social life of Wales through the 19th cent. The house is relatively modern, being rebuilt after a fire in the latter part of the last century; but the park is recognized as a beauty-spot, and is distinguished by monuments set up to commemorate members of the famous family, above all the Nant-y-Bellan Tower set up to the memory of the Fencible Regiment, known as the Ancient Britons, which took part in the Irish troubles of 1798, when the ideas of the French Revolution spread to Ireland, and an attempt was made to anticipate the freedom it achieved in 1920. Several of its officers were killed under the command of the contemporary Sir Watcyn. It is right to refer to him so, since, generation after generation in the minds of Welsh people, the wealth and influence of the family put it on a level with the greatest powers in the land. Indeed, in the 19th cent., it was said that the Welsh worshipped only one trinity: Victoria, Mr Gladstone, and the Sir Watcyn of the time.

Wynnstay and its troop of Ancient Britons are today most distinguished for counting among their number the famous "Nimrod", the

The Castle, Ruthin

Peter Baker

C. J. Apperley, born in 1777 at Plas Gronow in Denbighshire of landed but impoverished gentry, who not only wrote the *Life of John Mytton* but also works on hunting and horse-racing that became classics of their kind.

RUTHIN, *Denbighshire*. This is a town that still contrives to keep the sense of its medieval origin, since it stands on a hill with its houses grouped round the market square. The rise in the centre of the town is 1 in 11, and the Council House and the timbered houses of 16th- and 17th-cent. pattern take you back to when Ruthin was of much importance to the woollen trade. This was in the days of the Tudors; a charter was granted to it in 1507, and its grammar school, typical of the educational impulse that played so great a part in Tudor policy, was founded in 1594.

Its history goes back even further, as a rough block of limestone set at the W. side of the square close to Exmewe Hall makes plain. This ancient stone is traditionally said to have been the execution block on which, by order of King Arthur, one Huail son of Kaw was beheaded. The tale need not be taken literally; the stone is a relic of the Roman-British society for which "Arthur" was the symbol, and Huail was recorded by later chronicles as being the brother of Gildas, the 6th-cent. British cleric who wrote his famous though biased history in Brittany. The legend is a metaphorical rendering of history. But interest of a more recent date is attached to Ruthin. The uprising of Owain Glyndwr began here when he surprised the town in 1400 and made an attack on the castle. It was then held by a Lord Marcher, Grey of Ruthin, whose family had had the grant of Dyffryn Clwyd in 1282 following the fall of the independent principality of North Wales; between him and Glyndwr there was a personal enmity. The town was burnt, but the castle held out. Glyndwr had better fortune two years later when, in his victory at Vyrnwy, Grey was captured and imprisoned in Dolbadarn Castle. He was, however, later released for a ransom of 10,000 marks; a fitting conclusion on both sides, since the feud began with a treacherous move on Grey's part to acquire Glyndwr's property in the valley of the Dee. The Welshman had been trained as a lawyer at Westminster.

The town of Ruthin is said to get its name from the castle, built of red stone and so having, perhaps, the Welsh name of Rhudd Ddin. It shared the fate of its fellow 13th-cent. Edwardian structures in North Wales during the Civil Wars; held for the King, it was taken by the Parliamentary general Mytton in 1646, and was dismantled by order of the Protectorate. It is now mainly a ruin, but its ground-plan, moat, and curtain wall defended by five drum-towers can still be seen. St Peter's Church, once a monastic foundation, was made a collegiate church about 1310 by the Grey of Ruthin of the time. Its N. roof, intricately carved, was done by order of Henry Tudor, Henry VII of England, when he purchased the Marcher Lordship from the Earl of Kent.

In the Ruthin area are many places of great interest. Llanrhaeadr-yn-Cinmerch has a church whose lych-gate, porch, and elaborate chancel roof are masterpieces of woodwork. It is ancient, but with the double-nave construction to which native Welsh churches turned in their later development. Its Jesse window, dated 1533, is an excellent example of Tudor glass-colouring. During the Civil War it was hidden from the Puritan troopers in a chest, which in turn was buried in the churchyard. Both it and the chest, restored to its due place, are worth examining.

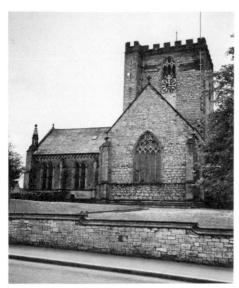

G. Douglas Bolton

St Asaph Cathedral

ST ASAPH, *Flintshire.* The road from Bangor, leaving its fork to Rhuddlan on one side, drops with a descent of 1 in 14 and comes to Llanelwy, better known to English ears as St Asaph. It is a quiet and detached place on a hill between the Clwyd and the Elwy rivers. Its one feature is the Cathedral, to which it subordinates every other interest. The name, said to be either Asa or Asaph, belonged to a grandson of a ruler called Pabo in the days when the Church followed the Celtic form of belief. He was not the first founder; that distinction belonged to a Kentigern who took refuge from persecution in Wales and originated a monastery that Asaph was appointed to administer after Kentigern's death. Since Asaph himself is presumed to have died about 596, at the time when St Augustine entered Britain to summon it to the Catholic faith, the foundation must be reckoned among the earliest. The Cathedral is, nevertheless, the smallest in the country and also the plainest, keeping the austerity proper to the early saints. It is only 182 ft long and 68 ft wide; Owain Glyndwr burnt the building out in the early 15th cent., though the exterior keeps its 13th-cent. style and structure. In 1715 the tower was repaired; in 1875 Gilbert Scott refashioned the whole of the Cathedral. Literary monuments are a tablet to the memory of Mrs Felicia Hemans, who did much to imprint her version of Welsh romantic legends on the English mind, and the dictionary of Welsh-Greek-Hebrew compiled by Dic Aberdaron, who lies buried here.

But the modern mind is more likely to recall that Gerard Manley Hopkins spent much time in the neighbourhood of St Asaph, and took up the Welsh language and Welsh verse-structure. He wrote to Robert Bridges telling him what interest he found in this unfamiliar language and what difficulty in mastering it. The rules of metrical form in Welsh poetry are ancient, subtle, and strict; the simple rhyming and alliteration familiar to the older schools of English verse in no way compare with the sain, llusg, croes, traws of cynghanedd, which call on the poet to exercise the utmost skill and ingenuity. William Barnes, the poet of the West Country, attempted one of these Welsh devices in his well-known lines:

> And there for me the apple-tree
> Do *lean down* low on *Linden Lea,*

in whose last phrase the consonants *l, n, d, n, l* are repeated in parallel order and only the vowels are allowed to change. Difficult as this is to apply, it is perhaps the easiest of the rules to follow; yet the even more difficult art of "penillion" – of alternating not only words but also musical successions – can be seen to be done at any small village Eisteddfod in rural Wales. The art of Gerard Manley Hopkins, which has transformed the style and mental content of English poetry for all time, deliberately adopted the methods and manner of these Welsh traditions, particularly in the case of *The Wreck of the Deutschland,* as Professor Bell has shown.

Hopkins may well have been chiefly drawn to study what was to revolutionize English poetry by finding the work of the tramp, Dic Aberdaron. But he was also influenced by the work of William Morgan, the former Bishop of St Asaph, who translated the Bible into Welsh twenty years after permission to do so was granted by Elizabeth Tudor in 1567. Bishop Morgan is commemorated – together with William Salesbury, Bishop Richard Davies, and Thomas Huet, who in that year put out their Welsh translation of the New Testament – by a monument outside the Cathedral. Between them, they shaped the Welsh language into its present form.

ST BRIDE'S MAJOR, *Glamorgan,* is a village on the road to the coast 4 m. SW. of Bridgend. The road enters the village through a fold in the limestone downs of Ogmore Down and Old Castle Down. About ¾ m. across Old Castle Down are the slight ruins of Castle upon Alun, an outpost of Ogmore Castle. Nearby is Coed-y-Bwl, famous as the "daffodil wood", one of the glories of the area in spring. In 1818 workmen digging on Old Castle Down discovered what must have been one of the most remarkable archaeological finds recorded in Wales – bronze helmets and daggers of the Late Celtic period, richly inlayed with gold, silver, and blue enamel. The finds were mysteriously lost when they were sent to the Society of Antiquaries in London. The description remains to tantalize archaeologists.

The entrance to St Bride's Major itself is guarded by a fine grove of trees, on the left-hand side as you come from Bridgend. They were planted to commemorate the visit of General Picton in 1815. Picton was staying with his brother-in-law, then Rector of St Bride's, when he received the news of Napoleon's escape from Elba. He took his last Holy Communion in St Bride's Church and set out immediately to join

Wellington in Belgium. He met his death in the Battle of Waterloo.

St Bride's Church stands on the slope of a small hill to the right. The effect has been somewhat spoilt in recent years by the amount of villa-building that has gone on in the village, but the church itself retains its charm. It consists of a chancel, nave, and N. porch with the usual massive tower and battlements so characteristic of many Glamorgan churches, built, one feels, as much for defence as for the service of God. The chancel arch and N. door are Norman, the rest of the church mostly in the Decorated style. The Butler family, who held the nearby manors of Dunraven and Ogmore, have numerous monuments in the church. In a recess of the N. wall is the tomb of a knight in plate armour with his lady. The effigies probably represent John Butler and his wife, Jane Basset of Beaupre, through whose daughter the manor of Dunraven passed into the hands of the Vaughans. The canopy is enriched by carvings, and on the front of the tomb are "weepers", in this case the sons and daughters of the deceased couple. The church contains many other memorials. The churchyard is dominated by a fine cross.

On the Beacons Down, behind St Bride's, are numerous tumuli. The ancient trackway known as Heol-y-Milwr (Soldier's Way) crosses this high ground from Ogmore Castle.

ST CLEAR'S, *Carmarthenshire*. In Welsh this is called Sancler.

It is a township 8 m. W. of Carmarthen, with a station on the main railway line to Fishguard harbour and the W. It is also on the busy A40 road, and in the holiday season the traffic through the main street is intense. St Clear's, in fact, is a road junction even more than a town. But it can claim to be a town rather than a large village, since it was once granted a charter of incorporation. In the main street, beside the bridge across the Cynin river, is the war memorial, with a mosaic set up to the memory of Group Capt. Ira Jones, a Welsh flying ace in the First World War. The most interesting part of St Clear's lies on the road that leads out to Laugharne. Here is the church, originally the church of the Cluniac priory founded by the first Norman Lord of St Clear's as a cell of St Martin-des-Champs. The only other Cluniac house in Wales was at Malpas in Monmouthshire. The priory was never important. In 1441 it was held by the Archbishop of Canterbury, among others, on payment of a red rose in midsummer. There are no remains of the priory except some grass-covered mounds, but the church is worth study. It has the usual massive military-type tower, so common in South-West Wales, but its chief surprise is a fine Norman chancel arch with rich carvings, rare in any part of the country. Near the lych-gate in the churchyard are the remains of a cross. There is nothing left of the small castle except the castle mound.

The St Clear's district was one of the centres of discontent during the Rebecca Riots that convulsed rural Wales in the 1840s and led to the reform of the toll-gate system of road maintenance.

About 1½ m. E., on the main road, is Llanfihangel Abercywyn, with a modern church at the roadside. The 13th-cent. church was abandoned in 1848, and the Norman font removed to the new church. The old church is roofless and buried in ivy near the banks of the Taf. There are some roughly carved slabs in the churchyard, popularly but erroneously believed to be the graves of pilgrims to St David's; hence the local name the Pilgrim Church. It is also believed that, if the graves are left undisturbed, the parish will always be free from snakes. An annual pilgrimage takes place on the last Sunday in July.

Llanddowror, some 2 m. SW. of St Clear's, is famous as the centre of the "circulating" schools of education in the Nonconformist cause begun by the Rev. Griffith Jones in 1730 under the patronage of Sir John Philipps of Picton Castle, Haverfordwest, whose sister he married. Although it was not the first, it was the first to defy successfully the legislation that in effect outlawed Nonconformity and, with it, the Welsh language in the 18th cent.

ST DAVID'S, *Pembrokeshire*, is a village, with only 2,000 inhabitants. It is set on a small stream called the Alun, somewhat inland from the sea and the promontory that thrusts its arm between the Irish waters and the reaches of the Severn Sound.

"Once a considerable place," says Daniel Paterson in 1811, "the Cathedral is a pretty good structure containing several ancient monuments, among which are those of the Father and Grandfather of Henry VII." This curiously insufficient summary would have been only half accepted by Gerald de Barri, who visited the place with Archbishop Baldwin on their journey through Wales in 1188 to preach the Third Crusade.

The antecedents of the village are bound up with those of its famous Cathedral, and of the man who in the 6th cent. is said to have made it the principal seat of Christianity in all the West – David, patron saint of Wales. He is better known to the Welsh as Dewi, and the place as Tyddewi (House of David). But Gerald says: "St. David's is the head and in times past was the metropolitan city of Wales, though now, alas, keeping more of the name than the effect". He adds that the name of the province was Demetia; and of St David's, Menevia. For so, he believed, the Romans named them. But no evidence has yet proved Roman occupation of this point, though the Antonine Itinerary, along the S. coast of Wales, does speak of a Menapia, from which one could sail "ad Hibernias", towards Ireland. The garrulously misconceived Chronicle of Nennius (9th cent.), in telling us how, after the withdrawal of direct rule by Rome, Cunedda of the North came to Wales and drove out intrusive Irishmen who had seized this coast, echoes the truth – which Bede records – that, for fifty years after Britain became a self-possessed Roman-British

The Bishop's Palace, St David's

state, the House of Powys stabilized the situation under the imperial emblem of the Tufa, the three ostrich-plumes of sovereignty.

It was then, Gerald believed, that Dubricius, Bishop of Caerleon, resigned the see of the West to David, who may have been the uncle of the Arthur whom, a few years before Gerald wrote, Geoffrey of Monmouth had taken as King once over Britain, Scandinavia, and Rome. David can be safely attributed to that period. But the glory, by Gerald's time, had departed. Menevia, he says, is situated on a remote corner of the land by the Irish Ocean, the soil stony and barren, ever exposed to the winds and to attacks by Flemings on the one side and the Welsh on the other. But he points out that, as to soil and climate, the site was deliberately chosen by its founders; for they preferred to be hermits rather than pastoralists.

Gerald gives the names of twenty-five Bishops who had followed David in control of the see – Welsh names including that of Asser, the great scholar who worked with Alfred of Wessex, and of the Morgeneu who was the first Bishop of St David's to eat flesh, and who, in judgment, was killed by pirates there. He appeared that same night as a vision to a brother bishop in Ireland, and confessed that, because he had broken the rule of the Order and had eaten flesh, he had lost his soul's salvation. Gerald proudly recalls how, when the Latin Church converted the Kentish Kings to its interpretation of Christianity, the Celtic Church was summoned by St Augustine to do reverence to Canterbury as the chief Christian seat in Britain. The seven Bishops summoned to meet him noticed how, with "Roman pride", he did not rise to greet them but

remained seated. They therefore returned, feeling that so arrogant a man could not have a better faith than their own.

Gerald's comments on the comparison between St David's and Canterbury in his own day are bitter. In Canterbury there was opulence, learning, and intelligent handling of law; in St David's, poverty, resentment, and a total lack of justice. Gerald's ambition was to save St David's by persuading the English Kings who claimed control of Pembrokeshire to reinstate its independence and so have greater guarantee of Welsh loyalty than force could ever effect.

He makes two further points. First, the spot where the Church of St David stood was in the Glyn Rhosyn (Vale of Roses), where the first sanctuary was set up in the 6th cent. No roses could be found there any longer, says Gerald. And the first foundation was dedicated to St Andrew. Indeed, he insists that the church of his day was of Andrew and David together. Several places are suggested as the birthplace of Patrick, both in Wales and Strathclyde, but the case for Caerwent is very strong, because the founders of early Christianity in Wales, Scotland, and Ireland all had their origin in a concerted effort that sprang from the Severn Sea.

The other tale Gerald tells is of the visit made by Henry II after his descent on Ireland to the St David's that, about 1120, had been raised by Pope Calixtus II to the position of a holy place of pilgrimage; two journeys to it would be worth one to St Peter's in Rome itself. So Henry came, clad as a pilgrim, to St David's shrine. But, as he passed over the great stone that served as a bridge over the Alun stream, a woman shouted to him

In St David's Cathedral: medieval carving on a misericord

in Welsh. The stone, though cracked, was of beautiful marble, 10 ft long and 6 ft wide. Marble, says Gerald, was a feature of the Valley of Roses. Who had set the stone there none knew, but it had a special sanctity from times before David's; and, at moments of urgency, it would speak aloud. Its name was Llech Lafar (Stone of Speech). It had prophesied that a King of England who attempted to conquer Ireland would try to pass across it and would at once be slain (as Gerald interprets it) by a man with a red hand. When Henry was told what the woman warned him of, he boldly stepped on the stone and passed over it unharmed.

The interest of the story lies in the Welsh woman's belief that some one would come to revenge the loss of the ancient faith and nationhood of Wales, much as the Arthur of legend was expected to do. The title Red Hand was actually applied to the grandson of Llywelyn the Last who went to France in the 14th cent., the Owain of Wales who planned a French descent on the coasts to recover what Llywelyn had lost and Owain Glyndwr later tried to regain. Like Arthur, he sleeps in a cave until the summons shall come. But Gerald, learned though he was in Welsh, may have erred. The Llawgoch (Red Hand) was more probably Llawchog (Protector). And of the one man who can be said to survive from the old "Arthurian" days that followed Rome in factual record, the Uotiporius who stands not only in the record of Gildas but has his name inscribed upon a memorial stone, the title of Protictor (Protector) also remains. He was ruler of the Demetia in the 6th cent.

Today in Tyddewi the ancient cross, its head-circle renewed, stands in the middle of the small town at the top of a street of pebbles known as the Popples. Beyond it rises the present Cathedral; to reach it, you leave the cross for the Tower Gate, which has in its flank a bell-tower, eight-sided and the relic of an earlier structure. The gate and the walls enclosing the precincts of 18 acres was the work of Gower, Bishop from 1328 to 1347. The Cathedral is at least the third to stand on this site, and in 1188 Gerald saw the work that had been started to replace the older one eight years before. The Cathedral, the ruined Palace that Gower built, and the equally ruined St Mary's College lie together in the Vale of Roses, so that the tower, seen on approaching the town, shows only its head. Thirty-nine steps drop from the gate to the door of the Cathedral.

The original foundation was destroyed by raiders along the coast, and rebuilding undertaken in 1180 was not finally concluded until 1522. It was begun by Bishop Peter de Leia, a Norman who has left a nave mainly of his design. Outwardly, the Cathedral of sandstone from Caerfai is dull by day, but under the glimpses of the moon takes on a silver beauty. Inside, the decoration is unusually elaborate. The contrast, they say, was deliberate. The tower hides below the hills so that no other attackers from the sea should know it was there; art and wealth to make it a thing of splendour were reserved for the interior. The austerity of the solid Norman nave is balanced with the warmth of the stone used. But, despite the skill of the builders, the foundations of the N. side of the nave had to be buttressed in the 16th cent. to prevent collapse. No such device, however, could prevent the fall of the first tower in 1220; and in 1248 an earthquake demolished large parts of the structure, so that the choir, transepts, and presbytery were set up again, following the design of the nave but moderated into a style the 13th cent. would accept, with pointed arches and no triforium.

Gower took the Lady Chapel of 1300 and added windows, a porch, and a new tower; his work was completed by his successor, Vaughan, in 1520. Nevertheless, the Cathedral suffered considerable neglect during the 17th and 18th cents. In 1775 the Palace was portrayed by Wynne and Sandby as a romantic ruin; in 1797 the Cathedral roof was stripped of its lead, so that Yeomanry and Fencibles in Pembrokeshire might have bullets to defend the coast from the French fleet that landed invading troops at Llanwnda. These matters were largely remedied by a restoration in 1800 under the direction of John Nash, and Gilbert Scott in 1862 went further with a restoration of the W. front as conjectured from what could be discovered of the original design.

The Norman structure of the nave is more intricate than anything attempted elsewhere in the period. The ground beneath it dictated that the floor should slope upwards to the altar in a 3-ft rise. The columns, alternating the customary Norman circular girth with octagonal shaping, are built to suit the eye with a perspective inclination. The same artistry that sculptured the figures standing high overhead in the entrances of Britain's great cathedrals was used here for the pillars. The roof, of the black oak of Ireland, dates from 1500. Where the screen separates the nave from the choir, the tomb of Gower who erected it is set.

Below the tower is the space where twenty-eight choir-stalls of about 1470 have, under their seats, the carved medieval "babooneries" of daily life; for the Church of those days felt that laughter was the best weapon against the Devil. On the left is all that remains of the shrine of St David himself; the stone base was begun in 1275. Not far away are the tombs of Edmund Tudor, the Earl of Richmond who fathered Henry VII; of the Lord Rhys son of Gruffydd, master of the South at the end of the 12th cent.; and possibly the tomb of Gerald de Barri, lover of St David's, who was twice nominated for the bishopric and twice found by royal authority to love it too much to be allowed to have it. But, if the shrine of David is now nothing but a bare foundation, behind the altar is what may be a more direct memorial to him. In 1866, in the recess now disclosed, human bones were found. They are preserved in a casket, for they would have no reason to be so placed unless they belonged to the first House of David. Two skeleton remains were in that place, of St David and of his teacher, St Justinian. The Andrew who shared the original dedication with David is presumed to have been interred elsewhere.

Of the neighbouring structures, St Mary's College, a tall-towered battlement set to the winds, was founded in 1365 with a chapel in the Perpendicular style preserved since 1934 with help from the Pilgrim Fund. The Palace of 1342 was remarkable in its day and is still magnificent. Very much a fortress, standing over its vaults with an arcaded parapet, a great hall and doorway, and rose-windows of considered beauty, it withstood everything except perhaps the attentions of its last incumbent, Bishop Barlow (in office 1536–48), who is said to have stripped off the leaden roof when he removed from St David's to Abergwili near Carmarthen. According to slanderous report, this was done to provide dowries for his five daughters, for whose successful marrying-off he would naturally make any sacrifice. He was rewarded – if they all married bishops, as the tale goes.

The tale of St David's reaches back to the days when the fleets of Rome had their base in the Severn Sea. The SE. promontory of Pembroke was a headland of first importance for them, as it had been for the builders of Stonehenge in their traffic with the westernmost limit of things. On the same course went the founders of a new purpose for men, using the skills of the Celtic Mediterranean to spread it wide. Andrew, David, and Patrick are real persons not because of their physical identities but because of the partnership of peoples that they represent.

ST DAVID'S HEAD, *Pembrokeshire.* The promontory of land that thrusts into the open seas at the extreme point of Wales towards the W. is named after the saint who is credited with the chief part in establishing Christianity throughout Wales in the 6th cent. A.D. But it has another interest in the name it had among navigators who supplied the geographer Ptolemy with the information he used when mapping the western shores of the world. They called it Octapitarum; and it had for them as evocative a meaning as the Gates of Hercules that opened from the Mediterranean, or Middle Sea, into the empty and shoreless waters on the edge of all things.

The promontory has a close kinship with those other buttresses – Land's End in Cornwall, Finisterre in Brittany, and Finisterra in Spanish Galicia; they all have the same ridged resistance, the same jut of rock vibrant in the winds with wiry grasses, the same flowers that breathe salt. For the ancient world, they were all towers of the same castellated shore looking across the moat of ocean to the heavens where the sun trod and the stars moved in circled company. Before Ptolemy made his notes of what the world was like, seamen whose names and language are lost had adventured into these western spaces; the men who brought gold from Ireland to trade with the East were they who carried the stones of Mynydd Preseli to frame the observatory of time and space at Stonehenge. Etruscans and Carthaginians had fought a naval battle in the Atlantic reaches to decide which should rule the sea-routes to the Cassiterides. Rome has destroyed them both, so thoroughly that Etruscan words cannot now be understood, nor Carthaginian records be recovered, except in fragments and at second hand.

Ramsey Island, beyond St David's Head

G. Douglas Bolton

But about 500 B.C. a Greek had managed to run the gauntlet and discover the islands NW. of Europe whose resources the powers of the western Mediterranean jealously kept secret from the cities of Hellas. His record has survived; and in it are names he is not likely to have invented, since they are not specifically Greek. He had found them already in use: Belerion for Land's End, and Thule for some last northerly place that modern research seems able to assign to Norway, though some authorities give it to Iceland – the Romans thought it applied to Shetland. Other names, still familiar to us, such as Eriu and Albion (old words for Eire and Britain), even the Liguria that the Welsh still use in the form Lloegr for England, seem to have been known to Aeschylus, the first of the great Greek dramatists. Probably the ocean-going commerce of days whose history has been lost had contrived a series of international seafaring terms to distinguish the coastlines that they touched. Ptolemy's showing Scotland bent at right angles to the rest of Britain has become a classic howler; he must have misread sailing directions that told him to take his bearings from the West when coasting England, but to take them from the North when making for the opposite shore of Norway. The translation of Octapitarum as the Eight Perils conveniently relates the word to the Bishop Rock and its seven attendant Clerks that ride the waves off St David's Head, and it may very well be justified. But early sailors ruled their navigation by the eight points of N., S., E., W., and their intermediates, derived from the stars and the extreme points of the sun's movements, its rise and set at winter and summer solstice. These eight points were taken to lie round the

rim of the world; and Ptolemy's informant may have meant that the promontory marked the edge beyond which men dared not travel.

This is something not to be forgotten when standing on the cliff by Carn Llidi, where the prehistoric rampart of a vanished folk and the hut circles of a community that settled here in sight of the sea give evidence that men in that forgotten time lived, worked, and travelled much as we do, and had before them the same prospect of beauty and infinity. Against this background, Carn Llidi, though only 595 ft high, rises to grandeur. But it reminds one, too, that Patrick, missionary saint to Ireland, had at its foot the vision of the distant island he was to convert, as if he had been lifted up to see it below him with an angel's eye; that David himself was born not far from here, according to the legend, by the well now marked by the ruined chapel dedicated to his mother, Nonna (St Non); that in the small wharfing-place called Porth Stinian stands another chapel – to David's teacher in the Word, St Justinian, who suffered martyrdom on the island of Ramsey, dark in the waters offshore. Beyond Ramsey, a place of seals, the Eight Perils lie awash in the waves. The description of them by George Owen, in his study of Pembrokeshire in 1603, is famous: "A-seaboord this Iland Ramsey rangeth in order the Bushop and his Clearkes being seven in number, all ways seen at lowe water who are not without some small Choristers who shewe not themselves but at spryng tydes and calm seas. They preach deadly doctrine to their winter audience". This comment is as true today as it was for Ptolemy's pilot.

The Chapel of St Patrick is at Porth-Mawr, or

St Dogmael's Abbey

Whitesand Bay. It is not legend alone that links the founders of the Celtic Church with this remote and sea-besieged place, whose chronicle goes so far back to the first navigators of these waters. Samuel Pepys wrote in his diary, when on the voyage home from Tangier, that there was nothing so convincing of an intelligent design in the Universe than the sight a man had, when alone among the seas, of the great and regular order of the stars. In the breakdown of order among men that came with the decline of Rome, when simple men looked anxiously for a belief, it was among the seafarers between the coasts of Ireland and Britain that the work of re-civilization was taken up by those we know as the missionaries of the Celtic Church. Landward, they took their message to implant it where for many generations pastoral communities had erected the stone circles that traced the swing of the sun day by day throughout the year; for the shadows cast by those sundial-markers reflected a superhuman intelligence of which all must stand in awe. Seaward, they built upon that study of the stars which men had learnt to trust in hours of peril. The first Christian faith looked directly in the face of nature, and did not concern itself with men's disputes about its interpretation. The myths and the confusions of tradition that surrounded the names of Patrick and David do not matter. The chapels, monumenting them together on the shores that watch the Eight Perils under the sky and across the sea, are wonder enough in themselves.

ST DOGMAEL'S, *Pembrokeshire.* In Welsh called Llandudoch, St Dogmael's is a large village 1 m. out of Cardigan town at the point where the Teifi estuary begins to widen to the sea. The houses climb the steep hill-side above the tree-guarded river. Salmon are a major interest. The Abbey of St Mary the Virgin was the key to the early growth of St Dogmael's. The ruins consist of the N. transept and the N. and W. walls of the nave. The N. transept is early 15th cent. The nave walls are 13th cent. Some interesting carvings are still preserved, including a stone cadaver now placed in a recess in the N. transept and various fragments collected in the infirmary. The ruins are well laid out with green lawns by the Ministry of Public Building and Works.

The Abbey was founded by Robert Martin, Lord of Cemmaes, in 1115. It was one of the rare foundations in Britain of the Order of Tiron, founded by St Bernard of Abbeville. The rule was similar to that of the better-known Cistercians. St Dogmael's possessed two daughter houses in Wales, on Caldey Island and at Pill near Milford Haven, but they never played the prominent part in Welsh history of abbeys such as Strata Florida or Valle Crucis.

The parish church, built in 1847, stands alongside the Abbey ruins. It contains a 7-ft stone pillar with an Ogham inscription on one edge and a Latin inscription identifying "Sagranus, son of Cunotamus". The date is 6th cent. Other early inscribed stones suggest that the church stands on the site of an ancient Celtic "clas" (monastery). The Ogham inscription at St Dogmael's supplied the key to the successful deciphering of the Ogham alphabet in 1848.

St Dogmael's main street twists at the Cardigan end and sets itself resolutely to climb the hill-side. Many of the houses have attractively layered walls of contrasting light and dark brown stone. Alun Owen, the playwright, lives in a house on the water's edge. About 1 m. beyond St Dogmael's towards the sea are Poppit Sands, complete with car parks and caravan sites.

ST HILARY and **BEAUPRE,** *Glamorgan.* St Hilary is easily reached by driving along the main road between Cardiff and Cowbridge. The tall mast of the I.T.A. that radiates the Harlech programmes dominates the countryside just before the Cowbridge by-pass. To the N., the whole panorama of the mountains guarding the coalfield is spread before you. Turn left at the sign of St Hilary, and you reach the village within ¾ m. The place is strangely quiet after the rush of traffic along the main road. It looks out southward over a fine view of the Vale. A thatched house gives distinction to the little open space before the church, and a thatched inn lies tucked away behind the buildings among the many dead-ends of road in which this village specializes. St Hilary's Church has a chancel with a Norman arch, some elegant arches in the nave, and an ancient rotund font of Norman origin. Two monuments attract attention. Under an arch in the N. wall of the nave lies the effigy of a youth in 12th-cent. civilian dress – a hood and a long robe. It could be the tomb of one of the De Cardiff family. The second monument is an altar tomb of a knight in armour, Sir Thomas Basset of Beaupre.

Beaupre itself ("Bewper" to the local inhabitants) is a surprisingly secluded ruin about 1 m. S. of St Hilary, tucked away down an unsignposted lane on the road from St Hilary to St Mary's Church. In spite of the unavoidable new power-lines, the countryside around Beaupre evokes the old unspoilt landscape of the Vale. The River Thaw runs through woods past the remains of this fine Tudor manor house of the Basset family, built in 1586. Two Renaissance-style porches are its special glories. The outer one bears the Basset arms and the Welsh motto "Gwell angau na chywilydd" (Better death than dishonour), which in later days was adopted by the Welch Regiment. The inner courtyard porch is in three storeys with pillars of the three orders, Doric, Ionic, and Corinthian. The inscription on the panels records: "Say cowdst thou ever fynd or ever heare or see worlldry wretche or coworrd prove a faithfull frynde to bee Richarde Bassett having to Wyf Katherine daughter of Sir Thomas John Knight Bwylt this porche with the Tonnes in Ano 1600, his yeres 65, his wyf 55". The obsolete word "Tonnes" is still a mystery. Beaupre has now been carefully restored by the Ministry of Public Building and Works. There is no foundation for the stories that have gathered around Beaupre such as that it was the original home of the Sitsyllt family, ancestors of the Cecils, or that Magna Carta was drafted here and approved by the barons before they presented it to King John. Many of these stories grew in the fertile imagination of Iolo Morgannwg, who created them for the greater glory of his native Glamorgan.

SARN HELEN. This is a name to be found on the Ordnance Survey maps for Cardiganshire, Caernarfonshire, Merioneth, and Breconshire. It marks what is, in spite of its being relatively neglected, as remarkable a monument in Wales as the Roman walls are in the North of England. It is the path of the great causeway that was the major line of communication for Rome between North and South Wales. It penetrated, as few roads have done in later centuries, the massed moorland area called the Ellennith region of bog and lake. Archaeology is gradually revealing that the chief reason for this adventurous undertaking was the exploitation of the natural wealth in the hilly heart of Wales: lead, silver, copper, and gold. Legionary stations set up along its route were posts for collecting, processing, and exporting the results. Otherwise inaccessible valleys were connected through it, and, after the disintegration of centralized Roman power, it was to the communities left stranded in them that the saints of the 5th and 6th cents. travelled to found their simple oratories. It might be said that this causeway created the Wales that was to be.

It can be followed, preferably in most places on foot, from the Lampeter area to Aberystwyth, from the Dovey estuary to Cwm Einon, from Machynlleth to Corris, and picked up again through Merioneth where it runs parallel with the long, straight road to Trawsfynydd. It seems to end at Dinas Dinlle or Segontium, near Caernarfon.

The romanticized Lord of Caernarfon, Macsen Wledig, the *Mabinogion*'s rendering of Magnus Maximus, who in the 4th cent. made Britain his own and made a bid for the Empire of Rome itself, is connected with it through the British princess Helen whom he wooed and won. Another legendary account would prefer Helen, mother of Constantine the Great, as the woman it had its name from; but what may be the true derivation of Sarn Helen would to many minds be much more appealing. The course of the Sarn can be best appreciated about the Teifi valley around Cellan and Pontllanio, which is one of the places associated with the vanished Roman Loventium. The instinct of the Roman was to lay his roads straight as an arrow's flight from point to point, as much as it was to square off the angles of his camps rather than lay them in the circular form approved by Celts. It was not possible in this difficult terrain to follow the principle for more than a relatively short distance at any place; the Sarn can be noted on the maps as striking from side to side, its short, straight arms bent sharply from point to point. This in itself would be enough to distinguish the route from any other the Romans laid. Today the Welsh for angle is "elin". Another long-established explanation of Helen (Elen) is Y Lleng (the Legion).

SAUNDERSFOOT, *Pembrokeshire.* Between Tenby and Amroth on the southern coast of Dyfed. Saundersfoot had the curious distinction of being a port for such anthracite production as Pembrokeshire used to provide. The hinterland village of Kilgetty was concerned with this activity; but Saundersfoot is now a resort for holiday-makers of the neighbourhood, being a centre for simple pleasures on the sands, promontoried coastline, and long stretches of sea that distinguish this England beyond Wales.

SEVEN SISTERS, *Glamorgan,* a colliery village, was originally named from the seven daughters of the man who owned one of the first pits sunk in the district. It stands near the top of the Dulais valley, which joins the main valley of the Vale of Neath at Aberdulais. The valley retains some of its old rural charm in the lower reaches before Crynant, but becomes industrial at Seven Sisters. The head of the valley has been ravaged by tips and opencast mining around Onllwyn and Banwen. The eastern edge of the Dulais valley is formed by Cefn Hirfynydd (Ridge of the Long Mountain), along which the Romans drove their road from Neath to the camp at Coelbren. In common with other stretches of Roman roads through Wales, it bears the Welsh name of Sarn Helen. The eastern slopes of Hirfynydd are densely forested, but in places one can still trace the course of the road. It comes down off the mountain in the N. into Banwen, where a line of terraces among the coal workings bears the proud title Roman Road. This road then went N. for $\frac{1}{2}$ m. to Coelbren, where the site of a Roman camp, Y Gaer, is clearly visible alongside the winding lane between Banwen and Coelbren. The series of farm hedges marks the defences.

Below Seven Sisters: the Henryd Falls
G. Douglas Bolton

From the Coelbren camp the road struck out NE. to cross the high range of the Fforest Fawr at the top of the valley of the Nedd (Neath). After that it ran down into the Usk valley at the Brecon Gaer. On the W., Coelbren looks down into the upper valley of the Tawe, at the point where the last collieries mark the end of the northern outcrop of the coalfield. To the N. and W. all is wild moorland rising to the summits of the Fanau. Just below the village the Nant Llech stream tumbles to the Tawe over the Henryd Falls, one of the highest and finest in the district. A small car park has now been opened nearby.

SEVERN BRIDGE. This gloriously elegant arc of steel, soaring over the wide Severn, is probably the finest architectural and engineering achievement in the Britain of our time, and is easily the most magnificent entry-point into Wales. From wherever you see the bridge, it has the beauty that comes from the perfect adaptation of means to end.

Strictly speaking, the bridge is not in Wales at all. The main section – the span across the Severn itself – is firmly anchored on the soil of Gloucestershire. This section joins the viaduct across the narrow Beachley peninsula that separates the Severn from the Wye. The road then crosses the Wye by a daringly constructed bridge to come ashore in Monmouthshire. The whole complex, with its approach ramps, is over 2 m. long.

The main bridge is carried on two tall, graceful towers of steel that rise 445 ft above the water. The main span is 3,400 ft, the seventh longest in the world. The two side spans are each 1,000 ft. Beneath the spans, the River Severn is 1 m. wide. The main cables are about 1 ft 8 in. in diameter, and each cable consists of 8,322 wires, all lying parallel. The roadway is formed of hollow steel boxes, 10 ft deep and 75 ft wide. The sides of the boxes are tapered to give a streamlined shape for winds blowing across the decks. The suspender cables are also unusual; they are not vertical, as has been usual in suspension bridges, but are inclined, forming a triangulated system with the main cables. The roadway boxes were assembled in Chepstow and then floated down the Wye and into the Severn, to be lifted into position at high tide. The revolutionary conception of the deck structure was due to Sir Gilbert Roberts. It gives to the Severn Bridge an air of incomparable lightness. All the new concepts of bridge-building embodied in the Severn Bridge were thoroughly tested in the National Physical Laboratory at Teddington, Middlesex.

The Wye Bridge has a main span of 770 ft and side spans each of 285 ft. It is of the stayed-girder type, the first to be built in Britain. This applies the cantilever in cable form. The two 100-ft towers are placed in the centre line of the bridge. The stays consist of two cables that pass over the tops of the towers. The ends are anchored to the deck of the centre and side spans at a distance of 225 ft from the towers. The united Severn and Wye bridges are the lightest for their length and loading ever built. The site survey and design work were

Peter Baker

Into Wales by the Severn Bridge

carried out between 1945 and 1949. The work on the site began in the spring of 1961, and the whole structure was opened by the Queen in 1966.

The bridge is likely to change the whole life of the people who live on either side of the Severn, and give an impetus to the planning of Severnside as a rapidly expanding economic unit. In the meantime, the bridge stands in a green, un-industrialized countryside. Crossing it is always an experience, whatever the state of the tide. At low tide a great expanse of sandbanks is revealed, stretching upstream towards Gloucester, backed by the Cotswolds and the hills of the Forest of Dean. Towards the sea, the dark mass of the English Stones run half way across the channel. The tide comes in at an impressive speed. The Severn has one of the largest tidal ranges in the world, and sometimes reaches 46 ft at the bridge site. The currents run up to 9 knots.

The Toll Plaza and the Service Area are on the Gloucestershire side of the bridge.

SKENFRITH, *Monmouthshire*, lies a short way SE. of Grosmont on the Monnow river. With Grosmont and the White Castle, it formed the Trilateral of defence set up by the Norman Lords Marcher to secure their hold on the Welsh border-land of Gwent. It is now exactly on the line that divides Monmouthshire from Herefordshire; across the stream, the village of Garway can be seen, once a seat of the Knights Hospitallers with their Chace (Hunting-Ground) on Garway Hill. Garway church is of great interest. First a church of the Knights Templar, with a round nave peculiar to that Order, such as can be seen at the Temple in London or the Temple at Cambridge, it was taken over by the Hospitallers on suppression of the Templars, probably in 1308. The Templar Knights had been formed to serve as a *corps d'élite* in the Crusades, but turned their

attention in time to banking and other worldly activities; it was perhaps their great wealth rather than the accusation of heretical practices that inspired the Kings of France and England to destroy them. The Hospitallers built a nave of more customary design; but the chancel arch is Norman. Its oak-work is remarkable; and the dovecote built by the Hospitallers with its 666 pigeon-holes still stands among farm-buildings. But what links it to Skenfrith is the tower: a square, loopholed structure apart from the body of the church. There are many such detached church-towers in the marchlands, for they were built to serve as keeps where the villagers might take refuge from the sudden assaults made on them from the Welsh hills.

Skenfrith church – not dissimilar in type, with a double-roofed bell-tower – houses the Skenfrith Cope. The castle is close to the road from Welsh Newton; again of Edwardian character, with four-sided outer fortification, round towers at each angle, and containing a circular central keep. Once it looked across the Monnow to Garway as an outpost of alarm; now it presides chiefly over anglers and the excellent trout for which the river here is famous.

SKEWEN, *Glamorgan*. The 8 m. that lie between Neath and Swansea form a stretch in which the industrial upthrust of the 19th cent. found its most vigorous expression. Skewen grew to fame by being neighbour to the refinery built by an international oil company at Llandarcy 1 m. S. Some 650 acres with 60 tanks storing 160,000,000 gallons of oil offset Llansamlet, with its spelter-works (the greatest in all Britain), and Morriston, where the foundries dominated night and day and made life impossible for every kind of vegetation. Times have now changed, and some of the ravaged areas are being reclaimed.

SNOWDON, *Caernarfonshire*. This most shapely of British mountains is the highest summit in Wales and is worthy of its supremacy. The summit carn of the central peak is 3,560 ft above sea-level. Snowdon is glorious to look at from any direction. It draws the eye like a magnet, seen from the W. amongst its fellow peaks above the wide levels around Portmadoc. It is even more impressive at closer quarters – for example, from near Capel Curig. Here you see Snowdon itself, Yr Wyddfa, with its attendant peaks of Carnedd Ugain (3,493 ft), Y Grib Goch (3,023), and Y Lliwedd (2,947). Snowdon stands in the centre of the wild mountain land of Arfon. The neighbouring ranges of the Glyders and Carnedds are not far below it in height, but cannot compare with it for mountain form. Snowdon is the Old English name for the whole range, the equivalent of the modern Snowdonia. The Welsh name Eryri (Abode of Eagles) was also applied to the whole mountain area.

Five great cwms have been carved out of the mountain mass, and finally deepened by the glaciers of the Ice Ages. Above the Pass of

Snowdon from Capel Curig

Llanberis lies the wildest and most inaccessible of these cwms, Cwmglas (Green Hollow). It holds two small lakes under the savage crags of Carnedd Ugain. The knife-edge of Grib Goch (Red Comb) separates Cwmglas from the grandest of the cwms, Cwm Dyli (probably Hollow of Rushing Waters). Seen from the favourite viewpoint of the road down into Nantgwynant, Cwm Dyli rises in three tiers. In the middle tier lies the fine lake of Llyn Llydaw, with the great crags of Y Lliwedd on the left and Grib Goch on the right. Higher up, under the very summit of Yr Wyddfa is the tarn of Glaslyn (Green Lake). The colour is probably due to the presence of copper ore. The copper was worked in the 19th cent., but the mines have long since been abandoned, leaving only a few roofless buildings around Llyn Llydaw. Glaslyn had a sinister reputation in Welsh folk-lore. It is supposed to be bottomless and the abode of the Afanc, a monster that lived in Llyn yr Afanc, a deep pool in the River Conway near the Fairy Glen. Its depredations became so terrible that the inhabitants finally took courage, and, after the monster had been lured from its pool by a beautiful maiden, they chained it and dragged it across the country past Dolwyddelan with a team of oxen and finally cast it into Glaslyn.

The waters of Llydaw are impounded in a pipe-line that drops down to a small power station in the Gwynant valley. During wet weather the Glaslyn stream still makes an impressive series of waterfalls out of the cwm. The circuit of the peaks around Cwm Dyli is a favourite expedition, known as the Snowdon Horseshoe. The narrowest part lies over Grib Goch, where there is a sheer drop on the N. into Cwmglas. From Grib Goch the track goes over the ridge to Carnedd Ugain, then up to Snowdon summit. Here is a steep drop down sliding scree to the saddle of Bwlchysaethau

(Pass of the Arrows). The final slope leads up to the summit of Lliwedd (most climbers drop the "Y" before the name). The Horseshoe is a serious mountaineering expedition, and should not be lightly undertaken. Under winter conditions it can be dangerous. One of the best, if roughest, paths to the summit is the "Pig Track", which starts from the Pen-y-pas youth hostel at the top of the Llanberis Pass and leads across to the higher cwm near Glaslyn, then up the zigzags on steep scree slopes to the saddle between Carnedd Ugain and the summit. An easier variant follows the track into lower Cwm Dyli, then over the causeway that crosses Llyn Llydaw to join the Pig Track near Glaslyn.

Southwards from Cwm Dyli, the next great hollow is Cwm-y-llan (Church Hollow). It is bounded on the N. by the back slopes of Lliwedd, and on the S. by the pointed peak of Yr Aran (2,451 ft). The cwm is deeply carved by ice, and the scenery rivals parts of Cwm Dyli. On a rock in the lower cwm is a plaque commemorating the visit of Gladstone, who made a speech to quarrymen from the spot. The Watkin path was constructed in its lower reaches in 1892 by Sir Edward Watkin, who also built the chalet at the foot of the cwm. The last stretch of the path becomes very steep as it struggles up the scree slopes to the summit.

The western slopes of Snowdon cover a wide stretch of mountain-side that can hardly be defined as a cwm. But a popular path to the summit starts at the old station of the Welsh Highland Railway at Rhyd-ddu and strikes out over the moorlands to the summit. Not far from the final slope, the character of the path changes dramatically as it comes out on to Bwlch Main (Narrow Pass), a ridge with a steep drop into Cwm-y-llan on one side and a plunge down the cliffs of Llechog into Cwmclogwyn (Hollow of the Cliff) on the other. It is also known as the Saddle.

Cwmclogwyn is the fourth of the great cwms. It is not very much frequented, as it is difficult to get out of at the head. It is rather bare, with a few bleak lakes on the lonely floor of the valley.

The last of the Snowdon cwms is the most northerly, Cwmbrwynog (Rushy Hollow). This, again, is tucked away and unfrequented, but it hides one of the most striking precipices in North Wales, Clogwyn Du'r Arddu (Black Precipice of Arddu) – it may indeed be the steepest mountain cliff in the British Isles. The crags face N. and are seldom touched by the sun. The dark tarn at the foot of the cliffs adds to the grandeur of the scene. Little wonder that the main cliffs of Clogwyn Du'r Arddu were not climbed until 1927. The West Face yielded in 1928, when Jack Longland led the successful party.

Cwmbrwynog, a long range of summits, lower and rounded, runs northwards to Moel Eilio (2,383 ft). The northern slopes of Snowdon are more gentle than those to the E. and S., and the easiest route to the summit runs up them from Llanberis. The Llanberis path is a 5-m. slog, clearly indicated all the way. It gives fine views as it nears the summit.

These northern slopes also carry the only mountain railway in Britain (the rail on Snaefell, in the Isle of Man, is a tramway). The railway starts from Llanberis, and runs on the rack-and-pinion principle perfected in Switzerland. It is steam-driven, and was opened in 1896. The maximum gradient is 1 in 5 and the gauge 2 ft 7½ in. The line is just under 5 m. long, and is open between Easter until about mid-October, depending on the weather. In its first stage it climbs up over a viaduct of fourteen arches, through the gorge cut by the Afon Arddu. In the gorge is the fine waterfall of Ceunant Mawr, over 60 ft high. It looks its best after heavy rain. After crossing the open slopes to the E. of Cwmbrwynog, the railway approaches the cliff-edge at Clogwyn Station, with a grand view into the depths of Llanberis Pass. The final station lies slightly below the summit. The buildings near the summit are not altogether worthy of the site, but they get broken into during wintry weather, and there are great difficulties in keeping the whole summit area tidy. On fine days all the world and his wife seem to crowd on to the top. There are plans for improving matters. But the view cannot be improved. Snowdon is magnificent to look from as well as to look at. On clear days, the Wicklow Hills in Ireland are visible to the W., and the mountains of Cumberland and the Isle of Man to the N. Snowdon weather is typical of mountain weather in western Europe, and the range has an extremely heavy rainfall. In Cwm Dyli the gauge has registered 200 in., which makes it the wettest place in southern Britain. But there are as many clear days. On every sort of day one should remember that Snowdon is not a mountain to be trifled with. Strong boots and sensible clothes must be the rule for all climbers, together with a modicum of mountain-sense.

The Snowdonia National Park is a tract of country taken over since 1947 under the policy by which so many countries are seeking to preserve the wild nature men have tamed and now feel in danger of losing. The area preserved here begins shortly after you leave Portmadoc and continues southwards as far as Dyfi Bridge. It includes most of the Snowdonia massif and reaches to the heights around Cader Idris. Mile after mile of excellent modern highways runs smoothly through the new shape given to the skyline by the immense forestry undertakings that disguise the sharp heads of the hills, and hold the long green valleys with their rivers and grazing cattle between the arms of grey rides striking through the ranks of conifers. The Migneint; the Trawsfynydd lake and high plateau of moorland; the Rhinogs and the Arennigs; Rhobell and the Bala hills, where the project first began; Dolgellau and Cymer Abbey; the Arans and Cader Idris; the Tarens and the hills reaching from Corris to Aberllefenni, and the ones between Pantperthog and Pennal – all these now take on this transformation where footpaths are signposted and the highways are streamlined for traffic. But lakes and farm land, and the squared stone houses that spring from the soil as naturally as the native rock from which they are made, keep the shape of Wales and its history alive.

SOUTHERNDOWN and **DUNRAVEN BAY,** *Glamorgan.* Southerndown itself, 5 m. S. of Bridgend, is a pleasant village perched on the cliff-top overlooking the widening Bristol Channel. The large Late Victorian, turreted hotel that dominates the place has now become a home for the blind. A coast road leads down to Dunraven Bay. This offers a fine stretch of yellow sand at low tide, and some rock formations of great geological interest. At Dunraven the basement beds of the lias overlie the carboniferous limestone in perfect symmetry, while westward towards Ogmore-by-Sea the carboniferous limestone is in its turn overlaid by the white conglomerate limestone known as the Sutton Beds. The appearance of these bands of rock is so regular as to seem almost artificial. The south-eastern point guarding the bay has been christened Trwyn-y-Witch from its supposed resemblance to a witch's nose, and on the bulky headland immediately behind it are a tumulus and the grass-grown outlines of an Iron Age fort.

The 19th-cent. castellated mansion of Dunraven Castle, the Welsh residence of the Earls of Dunraven, stood on a hollow overlooking the bay from the SW. It was pulled down after the Second World War, and now only the out-buildings remain, surrounded by groves of fine trees. No deer remain in the park. Dunraven has a long history and a mass of picturesque stories added to sober historical fact. In the mists of the Dark Ages the domain was supposed to belong to the British chief Caradog (Caractacus). By 1130 the Norman Maurice de Londres held the estate, and finally he granted it to one of his followers, Arnold le Boteler. The Butlers retained possession for many centuries, and left their memorials in the church at St Bride's Major, but in the 16th cent. the ubiquitous Carmarthenshire family of the Vaughans obtained it, as usual by fortunate marriage. Finally, the Dunraven family acquired it in the early 19th cent.

The legends gather more thickly around the tenure of the Vaughans. In the 16th and 17th cents., the story goes, the Vaughans tried to extricate themselves from their financial difficulties by the lucrative practice of "wrecking". The highly improbable method they are said to have adopted of luring ships to their doom was to fix lights to the heads of cattle grazing on the headland. One lurid account in particular relates how Vaughan hurried down on a stormy night to rob the dead, and was met by his desperate underling, "Matt of the Iron Hand". Vaughan himself, as a magistrate, had ordered the mutilation of Matt when he had been suspected of piracy. Matt reported the result of the night's work to Vaughan by holding up the severed hand of the unfortunate ship's captain. Vaughan, with horror, recognized a ring on one of the fingers as belonging to his only son, who had long been in search of fortune abroad. The wretched father was so shaken by Matt's horrible revenge that he immediately sold the estate. This tale was a favourite with 19th-cent. novelists and local poets, but seems to be of comparatively late origin.

STRATA FLORIDA, *Cardiganshire*, in Welsh Ystrad Fflur, is the Way of Flowers.

About 15 m. SE. of Aberystwyth, and in the midst of the great desert region of Central Wales, are the remains, at last carefully preserved, of the Cistercian foundation of Strata Florida. It was a place still in course of erection when Gerald de Barri, Archdeacon of Brecon, accompanied Archbishop Baldwin on a tour of Wales to summon men to the Third Crusade. He slept there one night in 1188, and comments on how austerely it was set amid the Moruge or Ellennith, the bleak moorlands possessing this part of the world. Not until 1201 was the building completed, though a charter was granted in 1184 by Rhys ap Gruffydd, Prince of South Wales, confirming a grant made some years previously. This may refer to an actual foundation by Robert FitzStephen, a Norman baron who had invaded the domain of Rhys, twenty years before; but, since Rhys succeeded in capturing Robert, he may well have considered he was entitled to the credit for the Abbey as well as to the rest of Robert's effects. He may have found some justification in the fact that an earlier and purely Welsh foundation had existed about 2 m. off, in a spot still called Hen Fynachlog (Old Monastery). Proud as he was of his Welsh blood, and fiercely contending that the Church in Wales existed in its own right independently of Canterbury, Gerald de Barri did not make any reference to this fact in his account of his travels (1188). John Leland, who went over much the same ground in about 1540, similarly notes the situation of Strata Florida, but adds that, though the hills were once heavily wooded thereabouts, now by neglect and short-sightedness the trees were all gone.

This in a way summarizes the story of the Abbey, which has been called the Westminster of Wales. However little Welsh the Order of Cistercians may have been through its origin in France, Gerald notes that its Abbot, who came out to meet and greet them, was called Sisillus – a Welsh name of great interest since, as Seisyllt, it seems to have fathered the name of Cecil, the borderland family that provided Elizabeth Tudor with her famous Lords of Burleigh, and was itself derived from the Roman name Sextilius. And, wherever they settled, the Cistercians were devoted to one thought: to develop and improve the land where they dwelt. Their Order was almost Puritan in outlook; the monks deliberately chose desert and sterile places for their labour, and were forbidden to wear shirts or gloves. Not only did they break up and till uncultivated soil; they built bridges and laid roads, planted trees and held open house for the traveller and the needy. The prevalence of names like Ysypytty (sometimes Spite) throughout Wales marks the many places where they set up their *hospitium* or place of comfort. In this area, the monks of Strata Florida are remembered for their practice of stocking the wild lakes with trout, apparently for the first time. The Teifi Pools, 3 m. NE. of them; Gwyn lake in Radnorshire; and the Gwenog near Lampeter are places where their work remains. Of the last, it is interesting to note that, at the end of the 17th cent., the Vicar of Llanwenog wrote to Edward Lhuyd, the antiquarian, to tell him that once that lake had bred a kind of trout distinguished by having a kind of gold or silver collar round the gills. He thought it was some extraordinary sport of nature; but setting collars round the gills of pike or carp was

The Abbey, Strata Florida

G. Douglas Bolton

a well-established medieval practice. But this record of the industry of the monks of Strata Florida disappeared, as the Vicar put it, "with the Oliverean Revolucion", Cromwell's troopers having expertly cleared the lake. Sheep, too, were introduced by the monks, so efficiently that in 1212 King John of England gave the Abbey his royal licence to sell and export wool.

Something of the Puritan spirit of the Cistercians is shown in the architecture surviving from their Abbey. They would have no images made of living creatures, though in fact during excavations earlier this century two exquisitely done pieces were recovered, one the shaven head of a monk and the other the head of a greyhound. But they responded to the artistic appeal of their native Welsh craftsmanship; the capitals of pillars, and in particular the ornament of the Norman-style W. door and the crosses that mark the graves of the monks in their cemetery, are exceptional and prove the survival of earlier Celtic art. The place has no tower; it keeps the first stern rule of the Order that bell-towers were too ostentatious. Nor are there aisles to the transepts, though each has three chapels attached to it with stone vaults, but with tiles still remaining in place around the altars, probably manufactured in Shropshire. But, among the possessions of the Abbey, the most famous was the Cwpan (Cup), the sacred instrument of healing believed to be made out of a piece of the Cross. Whoever drank his medicine from it was certain to recover. It came, after the Dissolution, to the mansion of Nanteos, and from there it was let out to sufferers who sought its aid. From 1866 onwards, the custom was followed by asking for a deposit, a sovereign or a gold watch and chain, to ensure its safe return, receipts being given when it was surrendered again and recorded with the letters of thanks for the cure. The last of these records was made in 1903. This is the Cup credited with being Malory's Holy Grail.

The plan of the building was that of a short-armed cross. Although its completion was the last in the series of buildings set up by the Cistercians, Valle Crucis (1200), Cwmhir (1143), and Margam (1147), it retains a primitive character, the walls being roughly piled but probably smoothed off with plaster. Its ruinous condition is due to a series of disasters. It was struck by lightning in 1284, burnt out by Edward I as a stronghold of Welsh nationalism in 1294, and suffered similarly in the days when Owain Glyndwr and the English soldiery who dispossessed him used it as a fortified garrison in the time of Henry IV and Henry V of England.

One of the tasks of the monks was to preserve by careful copying manuscripts and records of the past. The *Brut y Tywysogion* (Chronicle of the Princes), done by Caradog of Llancarfan, was thus perpetuated here. This history of Wales has a particular interest since Geoffrey of Monmouth, who launched the legend of King Arthur with his *History of the Kings of Britain* in the middle of the 12th cent., expressly names Caradog as the man who should most fittingly continue the story into later times. The final blow to Strata Florida came in 1539 at the behest of Henry VIII. By that time, the Abbey had dwindled steadily since the Edwardian Wars. When dissolved, it housed only seven or eight monks. The bridge that the foundation had laid across the ravine where the Mynach river joins the Rheidol can still be seen. It is a simple construction in stone, and is overlaid by two more modern bridges. It is inappropriately known as Devil's Bridge; but, like the place near at hand, Ponterwyd, it could be better called the Bridge of Staves.

At Strata Florida was buried the Rhys son of Gruffydd who claimed to be the grantor of its charter. The same Gerald de Barri who visited the place makes note of those he considered to be the wisest and most efficient rulers then in Wales. Rhys son of Gruffydd he does not set in the first three places of merit, but puts him in the second order as one not overwise but of great and adventurous spirit.

Tradition, however, makes a yew tree growing over a grave there a monument to the greatest of all Welsh poets: Dafydd ap Gwilym. The date and place of both his birth and death are in doubt; but the years 1340–1400 would certainly contain his life. He may have been a native of Cardiganshire, or perhaps of the Dyfed that is further S. and now known as Pembrokeshire. He appeared after the Edwardian Wars and began a new tradition in Welsh poetry; although he continued the subtle metrical forms of the older schools, he gave them a new impetus that acknowledged the influence of literatures beyond his native country. He was a master of lyric feeling; both for his many loves and for the things of nature, the skylark or the owl, he found words that break not only from the sterner subjects of the bards of North Wales but from the artificial themes of love for love's sake of the troubadours of France. He seems to have had contact with the literary tastes of the Normans settled as lords in South Wales who were rapidly becoming absorbed into the native peoples in blood and speech. But his poetry is his own. It gathers not only the old Welsh forms, but also the old Welsh philosophies of life and the destiny of man, into a volume of verse where energy inspires both delight and despair and has a rhythmic shape that has placed him in the front rank of European poets. He has a most modern note; and, so long as human nature remains human, he will be modern for all generations.

STRUMBLE HEAD, *Pembrokeshire*, is in Welsh called Pen Caer (Fort Head).

Some of the finest stretches of coastal scenery in Wales are hidden away in the rugged recesses of the Strumble headland, W. of Fishguard. This is a windswept peninsula where the rocks come bursting through the farm lands, and prehistoric remains are scattered everywhere. It is best entered by the twisting road that leads up behind Goodwick, and the harbour works of Fishguard, to the little village of Llanwnda, from whose churchyard you look N. to the line of coast on which the French landed at Carreg Wastad Point for their strange invasion in 1797 (*see* p. 45).

Strumble Head

Trehywel Farm, the French headquarters, is not quite 1 m. W. of the church. The actual spot on the cliff-top where the French came ashore is marked by a commemorative stone. One look at the iron-girt coast makes one marvel that they ever succeeded in landing at all.

Beyond Llanwnda a narrow road leads out to the headland of Strumble. The lighthouse, with its white walls, is open to visitors. It is an important station. There is no comparable light further N. in the whole curve of Cardigan Bay until Bardsey Island on the point of Lleyn. Westwards of Strumble lighthouse the coastline becomes even more rugged and impressive. Here is the highest point of the Pen Caer peninsula, Garn Fawr (699 ft). The second highest lies further inland, Carn Gelli (625 ft). Garn Fawr, with its rocky tor-like outcrops, has a fine hill-fort of the Early Iron Age on the summit. All around are the remains of hut circles. On the side of the sea Garn Fawr slopes down to Pwllderi. Here the cliffs are 400 ft high. The youth hostel is perched dizzily above them. At the side of the narrow road to the cliff-top is a memorial stone to Dewi Emrys (1879–1952), the Welsh poet whose verses, in the Pembrokeshire dialect, made the place memorable to all lovers of Welsh literature.

The hamlet of Trefaser, where Bishop Asser was reputed to have been born, is just inland from Pwllderi. About 1 m. southwards is the bigger village of St Nicholas, with a pleasantly restored church and a small vaulted S. transept. The sturdy farmhouses of the Pen Caer peninsula, with their roofs battened down to stand the winter storms, are still in evidence all around. There is a notable dolmen at Trellys. Pwllcrochan cove is a rocky inlet where the cliffs are 200 ft high and dangerous to climb. They continue round to Abermawr, where the peninsula can be considered to end in a bay, backed by a pebble bank, and inaccessible without a walk or parking cars in narrow lanes. One of the lanes leads back through a tree-lined dingle to the Tre-gwynt Woollen Mill, an old Pembrokeshire mill that, happily, is still at work.

SWANSEA, *Glamorgan*, still the second largest town in Wales and traditionally keeping an eye askance at Cardiff, which claims to be a place of some importance too, is known in Welsh as Abertawe, since it stands at that point by Gower where the Tawe, dropping from its source in the Black Mountain of Carmarthenshire, opens into the Swansea Bay of the Bristol Channel. It claims, indeed, that the famous air known in English as "The Bells of Aberdovey" does not truly belong to that pleasant and dignified harbour of Cardiganshire at all, but should be properly called "The Bells of Abertawe". The name the town bears in English is, however, very old. The matter had already become uncertain when Christopher Saxton passed that way in 1610. Today "Swansea" is accepted as being derived from the name of a Viking rover who plundered these coasts in the 9th cent. and somewhere made a settlement afterwards known as Sweyn's Ea (Island). While Saxton is prepared to admit the possibility of Scandinavian influence, either by trade or war, and dismisses any connection with swans, he makes a suggestion worth repeating. Seals, he points out, regularly haunted the shores and the islets out to sea, and were called "sea-swine"; therefore to call it the Swine-Sea would not be out of order. The charter granted by King John of England using the name Swinnzey may, or may not, bear him out.

Whatever remoter origin Swansea may have had, its historical record first becomes clear with the descent upon it in 1099 of the Norman Henry Beaumont of Newburgh who seized Gower and built a castle where Swansea now is. To look for it now is profitless; what now stands as Swansea Castle is the relic of a manor house, fortified as was necessary, and erected by Henry Gower,

The Guildhall, Swansea

Bishop of St David's, about 1340. It was largely destroyed by Owain Glyndwr at the beginning of the 15th cent.; to the King of an independent Wales, the cities of the South were enclaves of the enemy, and Abertawe suffered almost as much from his fire and sword as Cardiff. It was embellished with an arcaded parapet, a sign-manual of work undertaken through the good Bishop not only in Swansea but westwards towards Pembrokeshire. Up to the outbreak of the Second World War, plans were afoot to remove the screen of houses in Castle Street, Castle Lane, and the Strand, and so leave clear the sight of its tower. So, too, the Parish Church of St Mary was rebuilt in 1898 by Sir Arthur Blomfield, and again in 1955 after being bombed; but the brass memorial to Sir Hugh Johnys (1441) survived. The tomb of Sir Matthew Cradock and his Lady, however, perished. The Lady, a Gordon and daughter of the Earl of Huntly, was bidden by King James IV of Scotland to confirm the claim of Perkin Warbeck, the Pretender to the throne of Henry Tudor, King Henry VII of England, by marrying him. Henry's contemptuous treatment of the man who persuaded so many that he was indeed one of the young Princes said to have been murdered in the Tower of London by Richard III was followed by giving his bride to a Welshman who could be trusted; and Sir Matthew continued in that trust till his death in 1531. Among these historic figures one, a true native of Abertawe, is outstanding. Where College Street and Goat Street met was born Beau Nash, dictator of manners and fashion in 18th-cent. Bath.

But to stand on the height of Brynhyfryd and look over Swansea town in the days of its pre-eminence was to see the pit-heads close at hand, and the house-rows file on file, the broad back of Green Hill bare with a sulphurous yellow, and to know that in the district that took its name from that hill lived a colony of Irish ready to assert their identity against the Welsh. It was a sight of encouragement no less than of squalor. Behind the relentless modern industrialism, you could learn what men thought of in their own lives; from beyond that region of smoke and spoil, of oiled rivers and arid fields, you might catch the smell of the warm, drowsy air that belongs to the South by the Severn Sea.

The county of Glamorgan held more than half the total population of Wales before the Second World War, and may well exceed that proportion now. Coal-mining made its fortune, and South Wales was the principal coal-exporting area in the world from 1880 onwards. Some 70 per cent of its productivity was carried overseas when steam was the chief source of power and the smokeless quality of South Wales anthracite was in demand everywhere as the best steam-producing fuel. The SW. part of the coalfield yielded 90 per cent of British anthracite, and Swansea, where the field drew close to the sea, was in the best position to take advantage of the fact. The height of energy and success was reached in 1913. Before 1870, South Wales was the greatest iron-producing region in the world, and the ores lay near at hand to the deposits of coal. It was not until the 1900s, when the demand for purer ores needed in the manufacture of steel led to importation from Spain, that foundries began to be removed from the upper reaches of the valleys to the coastline. The effect on Swansea was gradual but certain. The depression that began in 1923 was a sign of the inevitable growth of industry in parts of the world starting on it much later than Britain and using new scientific knowledge. The great South had ores and anthracite and undertakings that sprang directly from them. But it had no alternative resources, and its population had no alternative outlet for its spirit. The pre-eminence of the great days ate up the lean years.

In 1801, that population in Swansea was no more than 6,099. In 1931 it had grown to 164,825. Eighty factories were busy with tinplate and spelter, produced from zinc sulphides imported from Australia. Copper-smelting gave way to copper-refining as the first process was gradually taken over by countries no longer content to produce only the crude ores. But a tremendous production was made of steel tubes of every kind, and Swansea was used as a centre for superphosphates processed from the raw stuff imported from North Africa. Six miles of quays were measured among the Docks, begun in 1859 and taken over by the Great Western Railway. The Queen's Dock of 150 acres was utilized by an oil company with the terminal of the crude-oil pipeline at Llandarcy. As an effort to combat the lingering depression that in the 1930s made one-third of the workers unemployed, a new electric power station was opened at Swansea in 1935, linked to the national grid. The subsequent tale of Swansea is the tale of the entire South Welsh industrial complex.

Over several generations, Swansea had taken the natural riches of its region and the exploitation of them very much in its stride. It had never permitted iron and anthracite to dominate its thoughts entirely. From 1814 to 1823, Swansea china was a product of exquisite charm and flowing design that make it still greatly sought after. The Guildhall of Swansea, designed by Percy Thomas and opened in 1934, was the place of refuge found for the explosive murals designed by Frank Brangwyn, an artist of Welsh origin, and intended by him for the Royal Gallery in the House of Lords in London. Sixteen great panels, a panorama of the human race and the flowers, fruits, and animals they lived among, designed to illustrate the wealth of Empire, burst through that formal commission to become an epic of the energy of life itself. The Fine Arts Commission decided that it was altogether too much for the Lords. Swansea recognized a kindred spirit and gave it welcome.

The sturdiness of the people's outlook could be seen, a generation ago, in housewives discussing grave themes of unemployment and its remedy, or, more recently, in the waves of uprising against a political opponent from the body of a hall, and the relapsing tide of laughter and cheers a moment after if the same man could touch his hearers' generosity. The Second World War shattered the architectural heart of Swansea, and the world shift in economics betrayed much of what the 19th cent. had created for it, as with all South Wales. But there have always been two strands in the life of the town. One changes and the other is immortal.

In the 1690s, the Welsh antiquary Edward Lhuyd conducted an examination of Swansea with several correspondents. They noted in the parish of Oystermouth the Roman mosaic pavement in the churchyard and the legend attached to it; the standing stones called hoarstones, or boundary-marks, ancient already when the Romans saw them, and the Early Christian chapels, some of them buried in the sands of Gower. They discussed the woodlands and wetlands that lay around the town, and the way limestone gave place to coal-veins entirely in the district. Above all they inquired from "all

kindes" of coal-miners the truth about the Maen Magal or Glain Neidr (fossil plants and animals) discovered in the workings. They were among the first to make a serious study of this evidence of a vanished world and its forms of life. They noted, too, the living plants characteristic of Swansea and its parishes. The soil they found barren generally, and fit only for small cattle and goats, for rye and barley; but "laver", the edible seaweed still eaten in Swansea, was found on the sea-coast in abundance. There were flowers: tutsan (St John's wort), key-rose, rames (wild garlic), and botchwort. But in that neighbourhood there were only coal-works and ironworks. Creeks and natural harbours made the place even then a dominant factor in the economic life of the Bristol Channel. At Oxwich, a parish of the lordship of Gower in which Swansea was the chief centre, shipments of this material amounted to about 2,000 tons in a half year. Kilvey and Clyne were the principal places from which the coal-outcrop of Swansea Bay was won; others lay along the half-circle between Loughor and Llanrhidian. The coal went by sea to Devon and Ireland from the group of harbours called South Burry, which sent out coastwise in 1699 no fewer than 7,848 tons; one pit, the Wern at Llanmorlais, sold away 2,000 tons of its own winnings in eight months.

But they also noted the presence in the area of the English language and English settlers, talking somewhat in the dialect of the West of England but using words that suggested a Norman origin: evidence of the attempts at annexation made by the Conquest Kings of England. But these foreign importations, still much alive in the days of Queen Elizabeth Tudor, were steadily dying out. In the 1920s Swansea was a firm centre of Welsh culture, not only in municipal effort but in the daily life of the people. It was the chapels that established this culture. In the pulpit, the "hwyl" (rhythm of inspiration) sounded in the epic phrases of the preacher. Men who worked at the coal-face would come to Sunday school and offer, in extempore verse and song, tributes to the Word. To an old house on the hill of Brynhyfryd, with uneven floors that had taken the tread of three centuries, and where not only the rooms but the staircases with deep window-wells were stacked high with books, the villagers of Gower came with the baskets and platters they had woven from the rushes of the marshy fields. And a blind harper also came regularly, carrying his hand-harp of the kind that Gerald de Barri described in the 12th cent., continuing the great tradition that not only filled the villages of Tudor, Stuart, and Hanoverian Wales with travelling harp-men but called some of them to honour in the court of kings.

For Swansea remained predominantly Welsh in spite of its international trade, and was a little different from the other communities lying the length of its valley; many of the pits it included had no pit-heads, but were worked by long galleries driven into the hill-sides along which men could walk; and this made a certain advantage in conditions. More than anywhere else, Swansea concentrated in itself the whole of the industrial South; it was Wales in the 19th cent. riding into the troubled 20th cent. and an altered world.

The change in the pattern of its life can be shown by selected export figures such as: 1938, coal and coke, tinplate, oil, iron, steel rails, patent fuels, cement, flour – 4,500,000 tons, of which coal made up 3,750,000; 1956, coal, petroleum products, patent fuels, iron and steel production, tinplate, flour – 4,100,000 tons, of which coal made up 1,600,000.

The copper imported from Cornwall around 1700 changed to the vast Siemens industry of tinplating at Landers between 1869 and 1888. Now at Llandarcy, 5 m. out, stands a large oil refinery. The air raids of the Second World War demolished the centre of Swansea in a crushing attack; but the opportunity to re-plan its centre has been resolutely grasped. Grey and tumultuous over its hills, the ancient lordship of Gower, Swansea and Llangiwg, Llangyfelach, Llandeilo Tal-y-bont, St John's, Llansamlet, Loughor, Llanrhidian, Ilston, Pennard, leads the South in forming a new future.

Swansea's exports, which in 1938 amounted to 4,400,000 tons of coal, steel, and fuels, of which coal amounted to 3,750,000, fell in twenty years only by a little on the overall amount; but coal itself dropped to less than half the earlier figure. Nevertheless, its grammar school, founded in 1682, has a greater successor in the University College of Swansea, opened in 1920. And, since 1923, Swansea with Brecon forms a separate diocese of the Church in Wales.

TALGARTH, *Breconshire.* Near the gap of the Llynfi where the river breaks through the barrier of the Black Mountains to join the Wye, Talgarth stands about an old bridge laid across the Ennig stream and guarded by an ancient tower. Apart from being brought into the ambit of the British railway system by the Hereford and Brecon section of the London, Midland, and Scottish line, Talgarth seems to have enjoyed the greatest happiness possible; its people had no history, in the sense of the "slighting" of castles and the slaughter of men-at-arms. Its importance was in things pastoral and the religious spirit that seems to have lingered in this part of Wales long after Llanthony Abbey dwindled into desuetude in the 13th cent.

Close to Talgarth is the tiny hamlet of Llaneleu, once possibly Llan Elwy, since the gliding river of that name is near it. Its church is of the simple kind that formed the first foundations in Wales, though it has the bell-turret that was shortly after introduced. The S. door is framed by a wooden porch, and is of medieval workmanship hasped with what is said to be the original iron. The rood-screen is also of wood, but has the curious character of being roofed by a loft-door. The loft, or upper chamber, of old Welsh cottages was of this construction. Reached by a rough ladder, it was a platform lying out into the lower

room where the occupier slept. Here the loft is walled with upright planks pierced with four-leaved openings, which may have been squints, or peep-holes, sometimes used by those otherwise debarred from taking part in the ceremonies. There is a rough cross painted on the over-arch; the date is taken to be 14th cent.

Outside by the churchyard grows an ancient yew once used as a whipping-post; the holes into which the offender's hands were thrust and secured by a tie-bar still remain.

What seems to be the relic of Llaneleu's manor house should be visited. It is within the area of a modern farmhouse whose door is protected by a porch probably of medieval building. It bears the phrase *Deus nobis haec otia fecit* (God gave us this space of peace).

Although he can hardly have seen it, Gerald de Barri would have thought this phrase most apt. He lived in a little place that he called Landeu; possibly the Llanddewi near Llangorse and some way from Talgarth. From there he went to Talgarth and Llaneleu in 1188, making as he went his sharp comment on the monks of Llanthony Abbey who, in that remote region, lusted after the fleshpots of the town.

In the opposite direction, S. from Talgarth, is Trefeca. In this place, in 1714, was born Howell Harris, son of a prosperous farmer. He was intended for the Church, the established Church of England, and with that in mind matriculated at Oxford; but his religious enthusiasm was too great for orthodox ways of thought and teaching; he retired to Trefeca, and from there pursued his mission throughout Wales as an itinerant evangelic preacher. He was never ordained; and if the Church found little to approve in him, the people at times found less, for he was much spat upon and stoned. This had the result often to be observed; his willingness for martyrdom won an enthusiastic following. At Trefeca he was able to settle; he founded and housed there a community called the Connexion. His religious ideas were based on those of the Moravian Brotherhood. Among Methodists he had one devoted supporter, Selina, Countess of Huntingdon, who rented Tredustan Court nearby and made it a college for students eager to enter the Ministry. The Trefeca house became a theological college for Calvinistic Methodism, closed in 1964, and has a chapel built to Harris's memory. His tomb is in Talgarth church.

Harris died in 1773, but not before he had assumed another militant character. The alarms of the Seven Years War reached even to Breconshire; and Howell Harris became an ensign in the local militia, bringing twenty-four of his converts with him to the colours. The Luther of Wales, as Harris is sometimes called, thought that the Word at times could not do without the sword. His brother, who had no divine inspiration, made a fortune in army supplies during the same war. Howell himself organized the economics of his community and he introduced many of the new mechanical devices that ushered in the Industrial Revolution.

Bronllys, on the Brecon road, has a detached tower to its church; like so many others, it was a place of refuge in times of stir, and cattle would be rounded up for safety in its lower parts while women and children went to the upper floor; the tower was in fact a fortalice. Bronllys has a more conventional castle as well, but it is a single keep of the knight's castle type. Gwernyfed Hall is a Tudor manor with a 12th-cent. door.

TALIESIN, *Cardiganshire.* This village deserves mention, though its existence is not recorded on the old coaching maps, which name only Tal-y-bont to the S. of it and Tre'r-ddol (Trethol, they say) to the N. It lies where the road to Ynyslas turns off to run through Llangyn-felyn. Its earlier name of Tre Taliesin meant Town of Taliesin, and the grave (Bedd Taliesin) associated with the legendary poet of the "Arthurian" period in about the 6th cent. is near at hand. The most convenient way to reach it is from Tal-y-bont, where a lane, leaving Cwm Ceulan on the right, travels directly to the site. The grave consists of a mound with a flat slab resting on four stones – a memorial of a type going further back than the 6th cent. A.D., with which the mainly 14th-cent. *Mabinogion* tales appear to connect the Taliesin who was the greatest bard of the West. What is reputed to be the actual grave is a narrow trough of stone nearly 6 ft long. The site certainly belongs to that fascinating complex about the mouth of the Dovey to which the Carn March Arthur also belongs.

The view of the Dovey valley and of the western outfall of the Plynlimon moorland is impressive. The way in which the small valleys filled with woods cleave into the upland ridges is emphasized by new afforestation, and the flat expanse of the Cors Fochno stretches broadly to the sea. Further interest is added to the very beautiful woodlands by the report that, two or three years ago, a golden eagle, escaped from captivity, made its eyrie above them and some-how found a mate. Its presence is eagerly watched for here.

Good roads now lead well into the eastern moors, and the spread of forestry roads is open-ing up the area in an unprecedented way. But much of its interest is concentrated on the old coach-road, which even earlier was a stretch of the Roman patrol route supervising the entrance to the Dovey valley. This can be picked up from Tal-y-bont and followed northward past the Bedd Taliesin where the way dips sharply into the Cletwr valley and goes past Llwyn Walter and its old lead-mine to Llwyn Gwyn. "Llwyn" means a grove of trees, and the repetition of the word gives some insight into the nature of this narrow and ancient but very good road. It runs through the heart of silent country, and its walls, stacked with slate-flats, are an excellent example of the constructional skill that, everywhere in this area, has allowed such walls to run up and down the steep slopes and remain for many genera-tions. Although once bearing relatively heavy traffic, this road is now almost deserted, and it gives an opportunity to see inland Wales between land and sea at its undisturbed best. Here and there along it still stand houses that watched the coaches pass.

Once the road may have plunged straight down into Cwm Einon for Eglwys-fach. But this, perhaps once used by pack-animals, is now possible only for walkers. The way now goes sharply to the right, finds the broad modern road that rises along the side of Cwm Einon, and strikes towards the new afforestations at its head. Only the foot-traveller can now take the path downward by Tyn-y-garth, cross the stream, and find the old pack-way again as it climbs to Bwlch Einon.

TALLEY, *Carmarthenshire.* The name is an Anglicized version of the Welsh Talyllychau (Head of the Lakes).

The place lies among green hills roughly half way between Lampeter and Llandeilo. No more peaceful spot exists in South Wales. There are two small lakes and the remains of an old abbey, set in wooded country, beautifully undisturbed. The Abbey ruins consist of the eastern and northern walls of the tower, with the two fine arches that support them. The outline of the rest of the church can be traced, but not much has escaped the demolition of the Abbey over the centuries. The Abbey is now in the charge of the Ministry of Public Building and Works, who have created amid the ruins an atmosphere of peace and privacy of which the monks would surely have approved. The white-walled and colour-washed houses of the little village, and the Georgian farmhouse beset with beeches and conifers near the Abbey buildings, seem to fit in perfectly with the well-kept lawns around the remains of the pillars of the nave. In the centre of the nave is a tablet recording the association of the Edwinsford family with the Abbey from the 12th to the 19th cent. A wire fence separates the Abbey precinct from the nearby churchyard and the parish church.

Talley was originally founded by the Welsh prince Rhys ap Gruffydd – the Lord Rhys, as he is known to Welsh history, ruler of Deheubarth and the most powerful Welsh potentate of the late 12th cent. Talley was unusual, for Rhys gave it to the Premonstratensian Order. The aspira-tions of the Order had much in common with those of the Cistercians, and both wore the white robe. But the White Canons also undertook parochial duties. Talley remained the Order's only house in Wales. By 1189 Rhys had bestowed considerable estates upon the foundation. Subse-quent rulers of Dynevor continued this patronage. After Edward I's first Welsh War in 1277, Talley was obviously impoverished, since the King took it into his own hands. He also attempted to make it more English in sympathy. Talley was subsequently placed under the super-vision of various English houses, including Halesowen. The English section of the Premon-stratensians became virtually independent of the mother foundation in France during the 14th cent. Talley led an uncertain existence, and suffered in the Glyndwr Rising. It is significant that the Welsh poets, so lavish in their praise of the hospitality and learning of Cistercian houses like Strata Florida and Valle Crucis, have little to say about Talley. At the Dissolution, the religious community of Talley consisted of eight canons. The outlying lands were disposed of, but the Crown retained the rest in the Royal Manor of Talley. The fine seal of the Abbey, for some mysterious reason, found its way to Norfolk and is now in the Norwich Castle Museum.

The monastic chancel was used as the parish church until 1772, when a new church was raised N. of the Abbey. This was subsequently rebuilt. It is now a simple bell-cote church with a flagged floor and clear-glass windows. The interior has a charming simplicity. It is filled with old pews and the quiet ticking of the clock. The churchyard runs down to the first of the lakes. Altogether it is a place to remember.

The Abbey and village lie just off the main road. It is possible to make a circuit of the lakes along the narrow road past the church. This brings you back to the main road within 2 m. after passing through a long avenue of oak trees, with glimpses of the northern lakes. The avenue is associated with the big house of the district, Edwinsford, which lies just round the hill on the banks of the Cothi. The house is now abandoned. The main road continues towards Pumsaint. About 4 m. from Talley, just off the road, is the hamlet of Crug-y-bar, a pleasant collection of whitewashed houses clustered round an equally pleasant chapel. The place has given its name to one of the best and most popular Welsh hymn tunes.

TAL-Y-BONT, *Cardiganshire*. About 10½ m. from Machynlleth and 7 m. from Aberystwyth, Tal-y-bont stands, as it has done for centuries, on what was once the narrow line of communication N. to S. along the Cardiganshire coast, wedged between hills and sea. Like many such places in this central area of Wales, it seems generally to have escaped notice by travellers. But 150 years ago it was recognized as an important place and – now that the edges of the Ellennith, or inland moor-barriers, of Wales are being broken into by new roads and the country is being spectacularly opened out – Tal-y-bont may well recover much of the interest once given to it. Several Tal-y-bonts are scattered through Wales; but this one on the coaching maps (Talabont, they call it) is distinguished as the place where silver-mines are prominent. Lead was the most widely profitable product of the district all around the southern region of Plynlimon; but it seems that Tal-y-bont was able to rely for some time on the allied metal, silver. Northward of it, at a place now rather difficult to identify but called Llanhangel by the Kinver stream, there was a silver-mill, a little below the place the maps term Garick, known now as Gareg, the old port of the Dovey.

There is nothing now to connect Tal-y-bont with industrial activity of any sort. It has an attractive inn with a front recalling the Palladian style of the early 19th cent. It is a little S. of Taliesin, for long a point of interest for tourists. But, in more modern terms, it stands at the neck of roads where they lead towards Elerch, and from there to the long and winding motorable ways deep into the heart of the Ellennith and to the sight of the new reservoirs in the Rheidol valley and the forest-plantations rising beside them. The round trip is one of the most magnificent now available.

TAL-Y-LLYN, *Merioneth*, a very small hamlet, gives its name to the lake lying at the western foot of Cader Idris. The road from Dolgellau drops steeply down into the valley where the lake lies, and the view of it from the point where the road steers away for Corris is the best one can have of the shining water. The lake, which is more correctly called Llyn Myngul, is rather over 1 m. long, its NE. end fading into shallow and reeded flats, from which an ascent can be made steeply to the head of Cader. The further end opens from the narrow Dysynni valley, and from here the two fishing hotels that constitute Tal-y-llyn village look out over the embankment water. The view of Cader is striking, but its summit is lost among the crowded heights that thrust themselves upon the lake from all sides, the slopes from Glyn Iago among the Tarens to the S. being dominant.

The church is small and stands to one side rather obscurely. It is dated only from 1600, but has kept many characteristics of style belonging to earlier days. The chancel roof is painted over with red and white roses as if to commemorate the 15th-cent. wars between the Houses of York and Lancaster. At the E. end is a painting showing the Twelve Apostles. And over the door is a Welsh inscription in the traditional verse form of the Englyn. It can be translated:

> This is a house of refuge, holy and high,
>   a kingly closure from the world.
> Let no man enter it
>   unless his heart is pure.

TARENS, The, *Merioneth*, is the name given to the mountain range of which the Taren y Gesail is the highest point. In some way, it can be called the smaller brother of Cader Idris, which it faces across the lake of Tal-y-llyn. Although by no means so rock-hewn, the Tarens (for there are several of them) have their own magnificence.

There are many names for a hill in Welsh, and each name has its distinct descriptive use. "Bryn" may be almost any hill, though it is most often employed to mean one that hems in a valley. "Mynydd" is a mountain and signifies a single upstanding block. A "foel" is a rounded and peaked eminence smooth of trees and bearing only grass. Your "craig" or "garreg" is a rocky height of varying greatness; where "carnedd" or "carn" is used, a pile of stone has been collected by men's hands to make a landmark of the place.

Jane J. Miller

The lake of Tal-y-llyn

"Llechwedd" means a scree-slope, though it is often employed only to suggest a steady hill-fall. Sometimes "banc" is applied to the simpler forms of moulding. But a "taren", like these considered here, marks a feature of the geography of Central Wales by no means so often found elsewhere. It states that the hill, after making for some distance a slow and purposeful rise to its height, sharply breaks off into a cavernous descent. This is a feature that can be seen plainly as you look at the Tarens from any point of the hills about the Dovey. They show three main heads, each sharpened to a peak against which lies the darkly shadowed slice of the boulder-ridden valley.

These three are named Taren Hendre (Hill of the Main Dwelling, 2,076 ft); Taren y Gesail (Taren of the Shoulder, 2,187); and Taren Cadian (1,981), which takes its name from the stream coursing down it. There are other Tarens: Barcut, Nant y Mynach (Monk's Brook), Cwm Ffernol, (probably the Ankle), and Taren Fach (Little Taren).

All three emphasize the accidented shape of the terrain: sudden upthrusts, equally sudden rifts, and streams cascading from unexpected altitudes. It is from Pennal that the long ranges and quartering valleys of this line of hills can best be seen. But, for the athletic, one of the best walks in Wales can be made from Aberdovey past the Carn March Arthur over Trwm Gelli by Esgair Weddan to yet another Taren, Rhos March (Stallion's Moor), and so to Hendre, the little lake by Foel y Geifr (Goat's Hill), and the pitted, peaty head of Taren y Gesail itself. From here, the heaped hills of Merioneth and the shark-like fin of Cader Idris make a striking effect. There is a long but satisfying route that can be taken to Cadian over the congregation of afforested plantations. The grasses, however, conceal numerous boulders; and in a rainy or misted season the chance of falling into the valley must be warily considered. In the depth of this valley, pine-martens are said to find a home. Foxes are certainly plentiful, and have often been hunted over these heights, usually by the pack that the farmers themselves have formed. But what is most peculiar to Taren y Gesail is the prevalence in its marshy ground of the insect-eating sundew, found here in numbers. It also frequently shows the spectacle of the buzzard hawking at the seagull, the combats being conducted by the buzzard with indignation, by the gull with aristocratic indifference. Here water and land seem to meet air. If the way is taken by Glyn Iago, the crags directly overlooking Tal-y-llyn lake can be reached. The descent is sheer; but the sight of the lake, lying like a piece of blue slate below your feet under the huge paw of Cader Idris, is worth the effort. From Taren Cadian there is a very negotiable track either to Upper Corris or, by a long and silent corridor of conifers, to Pantperthog in the Dulas valley.

Machynlleth can be reached past the old slate quarries under Gesail and the "Barns" of Ysguboriau; the whole of this descent is very attractive, and this track is better chosen for descent than for climbing to the Gesail peak, since the last stages entail a long and relatively monotonous effort. But, either descending or ascending, this route will take you to the discovery of the pack-way from Abergynolwyn, cut into the neck of the peak of Gesail and covered with spear-like rushes. It once served as an extension of the quarrying done at Abergynolwyn, northward in the Mawddach valley. But natives of the area will tell you that it was originally not only a commercial route but a military road, and supplemented the garrisons of Machynlleth.

TENBY, *Pembrokeshire*. This delicious little town on the coast of southern Pembrokeshire, 27 m. W. of Carmarthen, is a Georgian watering-place that has strayed into the 20th cent. The elegant houses, perched on the cliffs, look down on golden sands and a harbour crowded with yachts. To complete the picture, the medieval walls still encircle the town. The heart of the place lies within the walls, although Tenby has now expanded. The municipal buildings, the station, and the new housing estates are outside the circle of fortifications. Tenby is popular, and overflows in high summer. Inevitably the caravan and camp sites are growing on the outskirts. But the charm and Georgian delights remain.

Tenby has a long history. It may have started its career as a Norse settlement, but by the 9th cent. it was a Welsh stronghold, whose attractions were celebrated in a noble Welsh poem in praise of Dinbych-y-pysgod (Tenby of the Fishes):

Pleasant the fortress on the shore of the sea,
Merry New Year on the beautiful headland,
Louder the song of the bards at their mead
Than the beat of the waves resounding
    below. . . .

The Norman seized Tenby, and henceforth it became part of "Little England beyond Wales". The castle was built on the headland that juts out between the North Sands and the South Sands. The ruins still crown Castle Hill; the keep contains a museum. The statue of Prince Albert stands among the fragmented walls. Tenby became a walled town in the 13th cent. The walls were strengthened in 1457, and again during the Armada scare in 1588. The line of walls is best seen from the South Parade, where the main gate, with its remarkable five-arched entrance, is well preserved. Tenby had a rough time in the Civil War. It was captured by the Parliamentarians in 1644, and retaken in 1648 after defecting during the Second Civil War. It was twice bombarded from the sea. During the 17th and 18th cents.

Tenby was a fairly busy little port. There are some buildings that survive from the medieval period. The Tudor Merchant's House is on the narrow street of Quay Hill. It has a gabled front and corbelled chimney-breast. The ground floor is a museum. Next to it is the Plantagenet House, with its Flemish-type chimney. Both houses are owned by the National Trust. St Julian's Chapel, down by the harbour, has been much reconstructed, and at one period was Tenby's first bathing-hut. St Julian's was the place where the last special fishermen's services were held in Wales.

The finest medieval survival in the town, however, is St Mary's Church, the largest parish church in Wales. The greatest part is Perpendicular in style. Within is a splendid arcade of eight arches along the N. and NE. aisles. The chancel roof (1470) has notable carved bosses. The nave roof is also finely carved. The church is full of monuments, including a large Jacobean effigy to the wife of Thomas ap Rhys, and the tomb of Bishop Tully (*d.* 1482) in the NE. chancel, and the notable alabaster tombs of Thomas White and his son John, the Tenby merchants. Thomas helped the future Henry VII to escape to Brittany with his uncle, the Earl of Pembroke, after the Battle of Tewkesbury. The cellars in which the Earls were supposed to have been hidden still remain under a chemist's shop. The church also contains a memorial to Robert Recorde, the mathematician, who was born in Tenby in 1510. He was a pioneer in algebra, the first man to use the plus and minus signs. Augustus John, the painter, was also a native of the town.

In the early 19th cent. Tenby emerged with a new beauty. Sir William Paxton, the flamboyant Carmarthenshire magnate, descended on the town and began its conversion into one of the most charming and elegant of watering-places. The bay-windowed hotels rose along the North Walk, Castle Square, and the cliffs above the South Sands. The Sands made Tenby's fortune.

The harbour and Castle Hill, Tenby

Peter Baker

The North Sands curve round to the yacht-crowded harbour. Beyond Castle Hill are the Castle Beach and the South Sands, which unite at low tide. St Catherine's Rock has a fort converted into a house, and the sands to it dry out at low tide. A great deal of the atmosphere of the early 19th cent. remains recorded in the etchings of Charles Norris, who settled in Tenby about 1805. His house in Bridge Street is now marked by a tablet.

Tenby's vogue lasted well into Victorian times. S. P. Cockerell designed the public baths, now Laston House, in Castle Square, with a Greek inscription meaning "The sea washes away all the ills of mankind". North Bay House in High Street is known locally as the Prize House from the story that its design won a prize at the Great Exhibition of 1851.

The South Sands stretch westwards to the dunes of the Burrows, where there is a first-class golf links. Behind the sand-dunes lie the Ritee marshes. About 100 years ago it was still possible to take small boats far inland to St Florence, which has some old houses, with "Flemish" chimneys, grouped round the church. The church gives an impression of age, having Norman and Early English walls, and arches inserted during the 13th cent. There are some interesting wall monuments. Augustus John was born in Tenby.

Between St Florence and Tenby, overlooking the Ritee flats, is Gumfreston, with its secluded church, which has an exceptionally tall tower. On the N. wall of the nave are some faint wall paintings, which may represent the patron saint of the church, St Lawrence, with his grid-iron. The recess behind the grill has a pre-Reformation sanctus bell. The springs in the yard S. of the church were once places of pilgrimage. They have been cleaned, and are said to possess the same medicinal qualities as the waters of Tunbridge Wells.

TINTERN ABBEY, *Monmouthshire.* Where the Wye widens in its lower reaches, 4 m. after leaving St Briavel's on the Gloucestershire side, there is a small village called Tintern Parva. Somewhat further, in a lie of green fields in the broad valley where the hills stand apart from it and the Wyndcliff height is $2\frac{1}{2}$ m. away, Tintern Abbey stands at the point where the Wye ceases to be tidal and the sea itself withdraws. In 1131, Walter de Clare, the Marcher Lord of Chepstow, founded this abbey for the Cistercians, the monks of Cîteau in France who took themselves into the wilds of a Wales that had to be secured and settled by the new Order. The church belonging to it, which has become its chief feature, was not consecrated till 1288 and is in the later style called Decorated. It has no roof now, and stands by itself among the meadows by the river. It is 228 ft long and 150 ft wide. Sacristy, chapter house, parlour still exist as reminders of the monks' sacred duties and the places where they met in community. Kitchen and dining-place, or refectory, also survive, and the quarters where the brothers who were laymen and not in orders

could do the business the Abbey demanded. There is nothing but silence and green grass along the nave; but, in many ways, one of the architectural triumphs of Henry VIII was that he should by his Act for the Dissolution of the Monasteries have given to Tintern a state of ruin that makes its beauty all the more impressive because of its bareness. The tall grey walls seem to move upwards as you watch them, much as you get the impression, when looking at a tree growing in the silence of a woodland, that the stir of sap is singing through its trunk and the whole growth has a rhythmed energy. This is no fancy; the structure is remarkable for the artistry of its balance, and shows all the signs of that delicately managed capture of line which is the mark of great sculpture. As you move about the feet of the great arches and follow the lines of tracery in the E. window, 64 ft high, you get the sense that the place was never meant to be roofed but always to reach the sky.

TOWYN, *Merioneth.* This was originally a village set some way from the sea along the Morfa (Sea-Land) Tywyn, the flat reaches that lie S. of the estuary of the Dysynni river. The name comes from this stretch of sand and marsh, the "tywyn" that means both an extent of land and a thing that shines. The original village has now been widened into a seaside resort curiously distant from the sea, but having an exceptional purity of air and water and, from the low level on which it stands, giving an equally exceptional view of the mountain ranges enclosing it. The sands are very safe, and walks along them are remarkable for the roll of seas they show. The church gives some evidence of the age of Towyn as a place of human settlement. As it stands, it is now of Norman work, the nave, aisles, and N. transept being in that style, with rough piers of plastered rubble and without capitals. The S. transept and tower are new, and belong to the restoration done in 1882, when at last the ruin made by the fall of the tower in 1692 was repaired; but the restoration carefully reproduces the earlier workmanship. The church, however, is distinguished by having in it what the Royal Commission on Ancient Monuments described in 1921 as probably the most ancient monument in the Welsh language. It is the so-called Stone of Cadvan, one of the Three Blessed Visitors who came from Brittany in the 6th cent. to found their faith on the shores of the Irish Sea. Cadvan (better written Cadfan) was the founder and first abbot of the monastery on Bardsey Island. The Stone is inscribed with lettering once translated: "The body of Cyngyn is on the side where the marks will be. Beneath a similar mound is laid the body of Cadvan. Sad that it should enclose the praise of earth. May he rest without blemish".

Modern research does not approve this translation. Cadvan has been displaced by other suggested names, such as Cynien or Tegryn. Cyngen, however, remains unchallenged; and it is the name of more than one 6th-cent. saint.

There are other monuments worth noting: the

effigy of a knight in 14th-cent. armour, Grufydd Adda (Adam) of Dolgoch and Ynys-y-Maengwyn; and one of a priest in the same period of Edward III, showing his cloak-hood or amice drawn over the head, which is unusual. St Cadfan's Well in the Dolgoch estate nearby still keeps its ancient purity.

Towyn has several modern features to recommend it, including a school, a market hall, and the site of what was an important radio transmission station for transatlantic communications. The region around it has much to offer.

To the N., the Dysynni valley takes you to Llanegryn. On the way to it from Towyn, at Pont Dysynni, is the mound of Tomen Ddreiniog, a tumulus or burial-place according to the learned, but the site of a stronghold as is locally believed. Close by is Tal-y-bont, a farmhouse that was a manor of the last Llywelyn and of the English Kings who dispossessed him. In 1275, Llywelyn wrote letters to the Archbishop of Canterbury and others sitting in Council in London to urge his own case; and from it in 1295, Edward I, the overthrow of Llywelyn completed, dated a charter in evidence of his own undisputed rule. The Plas of Ynys-y-Maengwyn is no longer to be seen as it was. Built by the Corbett family and fortified by the Royalists in 1645, it was burnt by them almost immediately to prevent its falling into the hands of Parliament.

From the now very largely modern house, the road can be taken to Bryncrug village and for the lake and village of Tal-y-llyn. As you descend into the wide and beautiful Dysynni valley, you observe, overhanging to the N., the Craig yr Aderyn (Bird Rock), the only inland nesting-place for the cormorants that are a feature of these coasts. Further up the valley are the ruins, hidden by the growth of trees, of Castell y Bere. Once this was one of the most important and carefully executed castles in Wales. Here the last point of resistance to Edward I was maintained. For, after the stray death of Llywelyn near Builth, his brother Dafydd held out against siege. The castle was surrendered and destroyed. Dafydd escaped to the North, but was betrayed by men who thought his cause was hopeless, sent to London, and put to death with public humiliation. The attitude of the English Crown to the Welsh Princes was, in fact, strongly influenced by the insistence of the bards that the Crown of London that the Romano-British had once possessed would in time fall again into the hands of the Welsh; and the head of Llywelyn, severed after his death, was shown in London with a mock crown upon it in derision of the prophecy. The accession of Henry Tudor in 1485 was hailed as fulfilment of it.

The roads in the Dysynni valley are winding and narrow. The hill-sides are wild and sheer and scattered with rock. The wildlife of hawk and buzzard is very evident, and you are followed everywhere by their stare from the skies. In the September season particularly, an eye should be kept open for the passing of the foot-packs, the foxhounds of the local kennels, whose services are much needed for protection of the flocks.

Towyn is the starting-point of the Tal-y-llyn Railway that runs to Abergynolwyn. Opened in 1865, it is one of the few narrow gauge railways still in use.

TRAWSFYNYDD, *Merioneth,* may well have got its name from the ancient road that crosses the hills here from Dolgellau to Maentwrog and the North. For it means That Which Spans the Mountain; and the road is very ancient. The one you follow today goes straight as an arrow and almost due S. to N. across the moorland of Crawcwellt and Pennant-lliw. A little to the E. of the modern highway and parallel with it lies the track of the Sarn Helen that was the road of the Romans. Below the Mynydd Bach, a small eminence you leave on your right as you come to Trawsfynydd from Dolgellau, are the standing stones that signposted the route, and on the left, $1\frac{1}{2}$ m. below the Trawsfynydd lake, is another close to the roadside.

The town is small and ranks its houses narrowly on a steep hill; grey and reflective, it seems to enshrine the poet whose memorial stands at the centre of the place. It is Hedd Wyn who is commemorated there, shown shirted with rolled sleeves and gaitered as he was in life. He was a shepherd, and he put into his verse the mountains and the marshes, the wild and restless creatures, and the unstirring crags about him. The white peace of the mists that hang about these hills, and that were so much the companions of his daily life, was what he chose for his "fig enw", the adopted name that in Wales is so much more often the one a man is known by than any he has on official registers. His memorial was set up and unveiled in 1923. The National Eisteddfod of Wales was held in Birkenhead in 1917, and, by custom, the winning poem was there announced and the successful bard called to take the chair and the crown. But there was no answer to the summons. In the previous July, Hedd Wyn had been killed in the fields of Flanders.

The work of modern technologies has considerably affected the region round Trawsfynydd. The great reservoir by which the town stands, and the sight of which dominates the approach by road, is a drowned valley of great richness and, over 2 m. long and wide, was in the 1930s expected to hold the largest amount of water of any such place in Wales. What were hill-peaks are now a few scattered islands; but the lake is of very great beauty and is an irresistible invitation to anglers. Its main purpose, however, is to supply power to the Maentwrog hydro-electric station with a capacity of 24,000 kW. from the reservoir's 1,200,000,000 cu. ft of water. Atomic power is also being developed on the Trawsfynydd moors – not, it is to be hoped, as an expansion of the military tradition of the area where the artillery had a training range 3 m. to the SE. of the village, in use during the summer months.

E. of Trawsfynydd rise the Arennig heights, lying southwards as you leave the village for Dolgellau, and mounting to 2,800 ft. At Ganllwyd, a small place met with on that route, a bridge over

Trawsfynydd atomic power station

the Eden river marks the entrance to the upper valley of the Mawddach, now deep under the trees planted by the Forestry Commission – pine, spruce, larch, fir. Through these a rough road leads to what may have attracted the attention of the Romans to this district, an old gold-mine. It is from here that the Sarn Helen can be found, and the way taken back on foot to Trawsfynydd through bare moors framed by the shoulders of Rhinog and Arennig, and further to the Tomeny Mur, the old Roman station and, later, temporary Norman strong-point, the relics of which can be seen at Harlech.

Llyn Tryweryn, some way due E. of Trawsfynydd, is beautifully set in the Prysor valley. George Borrow was told it could yield trout of at least 50 lb. We must remember that he had this information during conversation at an inn near Rhyd-y-Fen.

TRECASTLE, *Breconshire.* On the main road between Brecon and Llandovery, this little village is surrounded by fine scenery. The Fanau form the background, and Usk is near. Trecastle (Town of the Castle) was once a place of consequence in the early days of Welsh history. The castle was probably a motte-and-bailey type, of which there are some scanty remains. The large coaching inns, that were needed when Trecastle was an important stop on the road from Brecon through West Wales to Fishguard and Milford Haven, still have their impressive entrances to the coach-yards. The village street has some good early 19th-cent. houses.

About 1 m. beyond, on the road to Llandovery, is Llywel. The modern café and lorry park, not far off, do not detract from the simple dignity of the old church among its yews. Llywel was once the seat of the Welsh Prince Ildw, who disputed the advance of the Normans under Bernard de Neufmarché. The church has a strong, battlemented tower of the 15th cent. Within are cradle roofs and a 16th-cent. screen. Three saints share its dedication: David, Padarn, and Teilo. The churchyard still contains the old stocks. Beyond the church, a wide double-tracked road turns to the right, making a strange sight in such lonely country. Visitors are warned that it leads up on to the Mynydd Epynt moors, and was constructed to give access to the extensive firing-ranges that cover the western half of Epynt.

The coach-road to West Wales continues westwards, through the hamlet named Halfway, until it runs down through a narrow, wooded valley to Llandovery. At the side of the road is a memorial pillar, put up to the memory of the coach-load of travellers who were driven over the "precipice" by a drunken driver – one of the earliest traffic warning signs in Wales. An older road to Llandovery ran over the hills under the actual slopes of the Fanau. This degenerates to a rough track, which brings you to the old Roman camp, Y Pigwn. The outline of the defences can be traced. Close at hand is the new Usk Reservoir, which now impounds the upper waters of the Usk for Swansea Corporation. This can be easily reached on a well-surfaced road leading to Llanddeusant. The whole of this area is open, high set, and inspiring.

TREFGARN, *Pembrokeshire.* The Cleddau rivers of Pembroke are, as Gerald de Barri insisted in 1188, named after the sword. The Western Cleddau runs suddenly, as it leaves Wolf's Castle, into a rocky gorge that is one of the most striking sights of Dyfed, almost due N. of Haverfordwest. To a very great extent, this Western Cleddau marks a frontier between the Welshry and the Englishry of Pembroke. Here, it is claimed, was born the future King of Wales,

Owain Glyndwr. The place of his birth was dictated by the fact that his mother was visiting her parents. Perhaps something of the wild beauty of the wooded cleft got into his spirit; or perhaps he preferred to accept Gerald's translation of "cledd" as a sword. It is the beauty, however, that remains here.

TREGARON, *Cardiganshire.* Sturdy George Borrow, on his tramp through Wild Wales in the 1850s, thought Tregaron had the air of a small Andalusian town set against dark mountains. Tregaron certainly seems a place apart, at the top of the Teifi valley, with a suggestion of the wilderness that lies hidden in the hills behind. It is proud of its Welshness. The centre of the little town is the square before the early 19th-cent. Talbot Inn, in which Borrow stayed. The square contains a statue of Henry Richard (1812–88), M.P. for Merthyr Tydfil and known as the Apostle of Peace from his work for international understanding with the Peace Union, the forerunner in Victorian days of the United Nations. Tregaron's other famous man was of a different character: Twm Shon Catti (Thomas Jones) who lived about 1530–1609. Twm, known as the Wild Wag of Wales, was born near Tregaron, and a dubious tradition made him the illegitimate son of Sir John Wynn, the North Wales magnate. He seems to have been a two-sided personality – bard, scholar, landowner on the one hand; practical joker, wit, highwayman, and general scallywag on the other. His career belongs as much to Llandovery and Ystradffin as to Tregaron (*see* Cilycwm). The children of Bartholomew Evans (Plant Bat) earned an unenviable reputation as robbers in the 17th cent., but this did not prevent their father from being buried in the church in 1684.

The church is dedicated to St Caron, now known to be a saint of Irish origin in spite of local legends. The building stands on the mound in which St Caron is supposed to have been buried. The churchyard is oval, which in Wales usually indicates the great antiquity of the site. The tower is 14th-cent., but the aisle-less body of the church has been rebuilt. The N. chancel window has good modern glass.

About 1 m. N. of Tregaron is the great local curiosity – Cors Goch Glan Teifi or Bog of Tregaron, the remarkable bog through which the Teifi cuts a deep course. The bog is 4 m. long and 1 m. wide with a depth of over 30 ft in the centre. It is claimed to be the largest peat bog in Britain. The Cors Garon was formerly two large lakes, impounded behind a glacial moraine at Tregaron. They were drained as the outlet level was lowered by the post-glacial Teifi. The bog is a Nature Reserve, white with cotton-grass in late summer.

The Iron Age hill-fort of Carreg-y-Fran stands above the town $\frac{1}{2}$ m. to the NE.

Behind Tregaron lies the great upland area that, for want of a general title, is marked on some maps as the Cambrian Mountains, although the title is never used locally, each section being given its own local name. This wilderness runs S. of Plynlimon for nearly 30 m., effectively shutting off Cardiganshire from the rest of Wales. It used to be called the Great Desert of Wales, but the desert has been tamed by the new plantations of the Forestry Commission and their rough roads. There is still some land left for the sheep, and Tregaron market is still important as a sheep and cattle centre, but the days are passing when, for example, William Williams (1698–1773) of Panty-Seri could be known as the King of the Mountains, with a flock of 20,000 sheep. Faced with an action at law, this Job of the West boasted: "I will maintain a seven years' lawsuit with only the breechings of my sheep's wool". But the mountain road eastwards from Tregaron over to Abergwesyn can still give a feeling of utter remoteness. Llyn Berwyn, the lake on the summit of the pass into the mountains, will soon be surrounded by the growing trees, but the narrow road rises and falls across the lonely heads of valleys. In the upper valley of the Camddwr, reached by a track from the Tregaron–Abergwesyn road that turns S. 6 m. from Tregaron is the solitary chapel of Soar-y-mynydd, to which the worshippers used to ride on horseback in the days when the hill-farms were still inhabited.

Riding has returned to Tregaron with the growth of pony-trekking. Tregaron is an important centre for the sport, and the town at certain times is filled with the clatter of hooves. The days when the drovers took the black cattle in great herds over the mountains to England seem to be returning. One old drover said to Borrow about Tregaron: "Not quite as big as London, but a very good place".

TRELECH A'R BETWS, *Carmarthenshire.* A cross road and a chapel with a few houses around form the core of this wide, scattered parish near the source of the Dewi Fawr in lonely country. At the crossroads stands Rock Chapel, rebuilt in 1827. It is well designed, with two entrance doors and a tablet announcing that "M. Jones, the Minister, was the first body interred here". The windows have some original colour patterns. The church is a little distance away at Pen-y-bont, with views over the Dewi valley. It was built in 1834, but has a charming benefaction board, which not only records the bequests for the Charity School but adds a painting of the schoolmaster and mistress at work with their classes. Trelech has been a prolific nursery of Welsh preachers, including Morgan Jones, ordained at Trelech in 1789, who became known as the Winner of Souls. The ruins of Capel Betws lie 2 m. W. of the church. They date from the 13th cent. and contain an old passage, 10 ft long, leading from the aisle to the chancel. The chapel fell into disuse in the early 18th cent.

The countryside around Trelech is full of small valleys, hidden woods, and trout streams. Beyond, to the N., the land is bleaker and more open, forming part of the long ridge that separates the Teifi valley from the gathering-ground of the group of streams that eventually unite their waters in the Taf.

TRELLECK, *Monmouthshire,* stands close to Tintern Abbey. Now no more than a village, Trelleck was once the capital of Monmouthshire. Its importance probably goes back further than the Middle or even the Dark Ages, as the 5th and 6th cents. are termed, since they contain the troubled period immediately following the recession of Roman rule. The name Trelleck (more correctly spelt Trellech) is derived from three standing stones inclined one towards another near the village crossroads. Their exact age is doubtful; but that they had a significance for the ancient "township" is shown by the sundial presented to the church in 1689 – its base is decorated with a representation of these stones in relief. It also carries a Latin inscription meaning "Harold was victorious here". This is due to the 17th-cent. assumption that the stones were a monument to the incursions of Harald, Earl of Hereford and last King of Saxon England, who came nearer to the conquest of South Wales than any of his predecessors. But the stones are much older than he; and the "Druid altar" in the churchyard perpetuates the memory of the time-recording systems employed in centuries before the Romans came and operated by the shadows of such monoliths.

A holy well also belongs to the village, much resorted to as late as the 17th cent. and mentioned in the medieval Book of Llandaff. The preaching-cross close to the church may date back to the Age of Saints and the 5th cent.

TRETOWER, *Breconshire,* In the upper reach of the Usk valley, and at the SW. extremity of the Black Mountains where Pen Allt-mawr and Pen Cerrig-calch overlook the stretch of river where it lies, Tretower has something more to recommend it than its unspoilt charm of water and woodland. The tower that gives it the name was built in the reign of King John of England. It is a single tower set in the angle of a previous castle built by Norman raiders, a square keep in their best style; but neither they nor John after them could prevent the ruin that overtook the attempt to plant an invading strong-point in this place. What remains is a village castellated with nothing more warlike than orchards. A Roman road runs towards it from Brecon, going to Crickhowell, and the road northwards to Talgarth is overseen by the remains of an ancient fortification on Cerrig-calch.

The claim of this place to fame rests on the fact that it was the seat of the Vaughans, the Welsh family that in the 17th cent. produced one of the greatest Welsh poets writing in English: Henry Vaughan, called from his Breconshire origin the Silurist. He was one of the Metaphysical school of writers that combined a Welsh subtlety of image and metaphor with English verse forms. In Tretower you can understand how he could write of Man:

> Weighing the stedfastness and state
> Of some mean things which here below reside,
> Where birds like watchful clocks the noiseless
>   date
> And intercourse of times divide,
> Where bees at night get home and hive, and
>   flowers
> Early as well as late
> Rise with the sun and set in the same bowers . . .
>
> I would, said I, my God would give
> The staidness of these things to man! . . .

He is buried in Llansantffraed, not far away.

Near Tretower: Crickhowell in the Usk valley

Peter Baker

J. Allan Cash

The coastal village of Abereiddi, not far from Trevine

TREVINE, *Pembrokeshire.* Between St David's and Fishguard the coast road runs through scenery of exceptional grandeur. Mathri, Abereiddi, Llanrhian, and Porthgain are places where it can be fully appreciated. But between Trevine and Abercastell, at a farm called Ty Hir (Long House), there is an exceptionally fine dolmen, 15 ft long and 9 ft broad, on six supports. The engineering ability of those who built it in the Megalithic period was remarkable. Even more so was the spirit of worship and of aspiration towards immortality that moved them. The sea and sky here make a perfect frame for it.

USK, *Monmouthshire.* On the E. bank of the river from which it gets its ancient Celtic name, the town of Usk looks over broad meadowlands. Through them the river flows with few pre-occupations other than to be a centre for first-class fishing, with suitably first-class inns. Usk is an important mart for sales of farm stock. It is in some sense the capital of the Monmouthshire that is exclusively rural. Its past is half forgotten. Formerly it was a Roman station, for Burrium has been identified with the present town; but – unlike the neighbouring Roman places, military as at Caerleon, and civilian as at Caerwent – the original has not been located. There is a castle dating from the days of the Lords Marcher, a foundation of the De Clares, set on a hill above the town and reached by a steep ascent. All that remains of it is a grassed quadrangle over which rise the main gateway and a square keep, a large round tower of Conquest type, and portions of the hall and living-rooms. It is a piece of architecture that manages, even in ruin, to keep the balance and proportion shown by medieval builders, and its detached parts retain a separate dignity.

There is also a church once attached to a Benedictine nunnery. But its history now belongs to its famous salmon and to the agricultural college 2 m. away.

VAYNOR, *Breconshire.* Its church and tavern linked together in unexpectedly impressive scenery, Vaynor lies 3 m. N. of Merthyr Tydfil. Here the coalfield is completely hidden, and the northern limestone belt begins. On a ledge overlooking the gorge made by the Taf Fechan as it flows down from the heights of the Brecon Beacons, Robert Thompson Crawshay built a strange church, with a tower that seems to combine all possible Gothic motifs. Today a small bush sprouts out of the top of the tower. The lower part of the churchyard is a forest of dock-leaves under magnificent cypress trees. But the place remains strangely evocative of a forgotten Victorian era. Crawshay was the last of the great iron kings of Merthyr, before the coming of the Bessemer process transformed the methods and fortunes of the iron industry. He and his wife attracted most of the great names of the Victorian Age to stay at Cyfarthfa Castle. He was a brilliant amateur photographer whose work is on display in the Cyfarthfa Castle Museum. He was also a somewhat unusual father, who summoned his daughters to pose by the sound of a whistle, and took a somewhat enlightened view of his marriage vows. He lies in the churchyard under a great slab of Old Red Sandstone with the inscription "God Forgive Me".

Above the crags of the quarries on the opposite side of the gorge, and approached by a separate road from Merthyr, are the scanty remains of Morlais Castle. The Taf gorge forms the boundary here between Glamorgan and Breconshire. The Castle was built by Gilbert de Clare, "Gilbert the Red", in the 13th cent. to consolidate his hold on the hill country of Glamorgan after the Edwardian conquest of North Wales. Morlais was probably the cause of the violent dispute between de Clare and de Bohun, Earl of Hereford. Edward I surprised the whole of the Welsh Marches by laying crushing fines and forfeitures of estates on the two men, who, like most of the great Marcher barons, were accustomed to think

The Garrison Tower of Usk Castle

that they were far above the law. Edward I himself came to Morlais at the end of a forced march from North Wales.

A portion of the curtain wall still stands round an oval-shaped ward. Two drum-towers stand at either end, one of which has a chamber with a central column supporting the vaulted roof. There are the remains of a well shaft in the enclosure. The ruins stand 1,252 ft above sea-level with magnificent views towards the Brecon Beacons.

VYRNWY, Lake, *Montgomeryshire.* The lake called Vyrnwy can be reached by road from Mallwyd or Llanfyllin, or on foot from the head of Bwlch Oerddrws (1,065 ft) 4½ m from Dinas Mawddwy. At the foot of the lake, Llanwddyn is a model village that replaces the old village now at the lake's bottom. In 1881 was begun the scheme for flooding the valley of the Afon Fyrnwy. "A bare and featureless valley" was the verdict on the countryside then; it was to be dammed by a wall 160 ft high and 1,200 ft long. The storage of water to be made available for Liverpool was estimated at 12,000,000 gallons. The Liverpool Corporation, however, undertook to respect the rights of riparian owners, and tunnel-sluices would be carried through the embankment. The 46 m. the water would be carried to its destination would run through underground tunnels. It is now, so far, the largest lake of its kind in Wales, 5 m. long and nearly 1 m. wide. The expectation of the planners that the scheme would vastly improve the beauty of the area may or may not be justified; but the lake is now a thing of grandeur. Little sign remains that it is not entirely natural. The hills around lie back from the waters, skirted with woodland, their summits bare peat-moor. It is best seen from a boat, for the coastline of the shores is a series of inlets and bays with little rivers pouring rapidly through them. The head of Aran gives a special dignity to the lake, its sharp outline like that of a knotted fist thrusting against

the moon or the sun as they lie upon the water.

Fishing here is among the best in Wales, and the difficulty of reaching the lake by road, still a problem today with Bwlch-y-Groes rising against you as you come, preserves its austere charm.

WELSHPOOL, *Montgomeryshire*, is in Welsh called Trallwng.

More exactly Pool and nothing more, this Welsh Pool has had a stormy history. It is now by way of being the county town of Montgomeryshire, although Montgomery itself claims that title, since the Council and the Assizes are held in it. It has another claim: Castell Goch (Red Castle) or Powis Castle – whose Earl carries on the tradition, in name at least, of the ancient Kingdom of Powys of which Montgomeryshire is the last solid fragment – is so close to Welshpool as to be considered together with it. Once concentrating like other Montgomeryshire towns on the flannel industry, Welshpool now widens its interests but still remembers its past. It lies close to the Severn, the traditional barrier between Wales and England, and the Long Mountain that, although it stands only just over 1,300 ft high, marks the frontier between Montgomeryshire and Shropshire. In the town are many reminiscences of the past. Its architecture is still largely Georgian and shows what is, in Central Wales, the distinctive character of being brick; neither the slate of W. Montgomeryshire nor the stone of its northern boundaries is found here in the valley of the Severn. Some of its shops still carry the old fire-office signs that were widespread in the later 18th cent. One among them, proudly announcing the name of the man, Gilbert Jones, who caused it to be built in 1692, and of his wife, states that they were the family of the original Joneses in the land. By the way that leads to the Castle, half-timbered houses keep alive the memory of political feuds with the nail-studded imprecation "God Damn Old Oliver". The date, 1661, leaves no doubt which Oliver was intended.

G. Douglas Bolton

The valve tower on Lake Vyrnwy

The Castle is of red sandstone, heavily modernized. It still keeps the size and shape recorded in the prints of the 1830s, and the park similarly preserves its oaks. They are a most distinctive part of the scene hereabouts, as they were intended to be. For "Capability" Brown, who founded the tradition of the British landscape garden in the early 19th cent., renovated the Castle and its grounds. They have claimed the tallest tree in Britain – a Douglas fir over 160 ft high; and oaks that antedate Brown and his capabilities by several centuries, since one was measured at 24 ft in girth and another at 31. They are oaks that probably remember the Owain ap Gruffydd who in 1250 founded the Castle, and the Sir Thomas Myddelton who in 1644 captured the place for Parliament, though it was spared from demolition by the orders of "Old Oliver". The Restoration of Charles II affected the gardens to the extent that part of them was terraced in

the style the exiled Stuarts had learned to appreciate at Saint-Germain in France. But the oaks may look even further back.

The church at Welshpool (St Mary's) has monuments to its connection with the Earls and the military matters that concerned them. It has some notable architecture in roof and tower; it also has, opposite its door, a great stone. It is known as the Maen Llog, another of the Maens that so often follow the ancient routes among the hills of Montgomeryshire. Its name alone signifies its importance, though not necessarily from its attribution as a "Druidic" altar. Whatever its original purpose, it was used as a throne by the Abbot of Strata Marcella, a Cistercian monastery 3 m. to the NE. of Welshpool that was brought down when all the monasteries were dissolved by Henry VIII, its foundations being all that can now be seen. The Maen Llog is probably the most important of such monuments in Wales.

A visit should certainly be made to the Powysland Museum. Not itself of very ancient foundation, it has succeeded in preserving some most striking relics of the Kingdom of Powys and its history. Of these the most attractive is the earliest, a shield of the Iron Age decorated with the intricate art characteristic of the "Celtic" civilization. Fossils, shells, and Roman antiquities help to give some further idea of the origins of Powys; the Castle can also show furnishings of the time of Charles II's visit, gifts from Clive of India, and work by Grinling Gibbons.

WHITLAND, *Carmarthenshire.* Here, westward from St Clear's, you can turn S. on a minor road for Tavernspite and Red Roses, whose names make them almost irresistible. But Whitland may demand more attention, not because of any surviving architecture or outstanding importance in its present quiet life, but because it is associated with one of the greatest figures in Welsh history and one of his major acts of state.

Much has vanished from Whitland; it was the site of a Cistercian abbey, founded in 1143 after the Norman had made his presence felt and a knight called St Clare had founded St Clear's. Of the Abbey little now remains; the wars of Owain Glyndwr and the Dissolution of the Monasteries by Henry VIII have effectively reduced it. But more than 200 years earlier a White House stood at Whitland – the Ty Gwyn ar Daf, where Hywel the Good, King of Wales, summoned clergy and laymen to approve his codification of laws. This was in 930. Parliamentary practice as we know it, and the concept of democracy it represents, grew out of the medieval assemblies that agreed upon the laws by which communities should live. Whitland represents one of the earliest of such assemblies within Britain.

Hywel appeared when both Wales and England had barely survived the Viking onslaughts. In 871 only his grandfather, Rhodri the Great, and Alfred of Wessex had been able to hold their territories against the Scandinavian invasion. The work of Rhodri fell to pieces after his death,

G. *Douglas Bolton*

Powis Castle, near Welshpool

and Hywel is first known to history as a petty ruler of a district called Seisllwyg, in 909. He slowly created a united Wales. He is said to have visited Rome in 928, and he appears to have laid the foundations for reconciliation between the Church of Rome and Celtic Christianity.

The code of laws made by Hywel at Whitland range from regulation of duties and precedence at court to repudiation of trial by ordeal for proof of evidence, and of simple accusation for formal statement on oath; from mutilation of thieves to enforcement to suretyship. So great was their effect that the 14th section of the Statute of Rhuddlan by which Edward I sought to settle Welsh affairs expressly accepts Hywel's code as the basis for future law in Wales.

What has earned Hywel a significant place in history is his attitude to Anglo-Saxon England when, in 937, a determined attempt was made by a league of the Scandinavian and Celtic peoples

in Strathclyde, Scotland, and in Brittany to obliterate it altogether. The schoolbook picture, popular in the 19th cent., of the Northman raids as a series of lusty piratical incursions overlooked the importance of Britain as a point of strategic control over the North Sea area; if it fell under the influence of the new Europe emerging after Charlemagne into unity once more, the independence of the Baltic peoples was directly threatened. The question remained undecided until in 1066 William the Conqueror succeeded at Senlac Hill in seizing Britain when Harald of Norway failed at Stamford Bridge. If Hywel had decided to join the combined assault on England, it is doubtful whether the Anglo-Saxon kingdom could have survived. But he thought in terms of the unity of law and religion that Wales and England shared as European peoples, and not in those of Teutonic paganism. His refusal to join the Celtic-Northman alliance made him the subject of bitter satire from the bards. Had his decision gone the other way, the whole history of Europe might have been changed – and not necessarily for the better.

The triumph of Athelstan at Brunanburgh over the powerful confederacy of peoples that confronted him is entered by the Anglo-Saxon Chronicle under the year 938, and celebrated in a song of rejoicing that is one of the greatest pieces of early English verse. But there is no international monument to Hywel at Whitland. Perhaps there should be one.

Of the White House to which Hywel summoned his learned men, it is said that it was first founded as a chapter house, for that is the real meaning of the name; in old Welsh "gwyn" is not only white but also noble. Probably it was so set up about the same time as the White House of Bangor, in A.D. 480. The learned Leland knew it only as a monastery of Cistercians established by Rhys ap Tewdwr, Prince of the South, about 1143. But then Leland was writing under the commission of Henry VIII, who was as little sympathetic to the Celtic Church as he was to the Church of Rome. The place was certainly known to Gerald de Barri, and the tale he tells of it is a commentary on the idea of justice in the 12th cent. When travelling to it, he and his Bishop were told that a young man who had set out to meet them with the object of enrolling for the Crusade had been set upon and murdered. They found his body by the wayside, and their escort was able to lay hands on the twelve archers of the Castle of St Clear's who had slain him. Some feud between castle and castle was involved. But the Bishop was not concerned with that. He prayed for the soul of the murdered man; and the twelve archers, by way of penance and expiation, were signed on for the Crusade.

WREXHAM, *Denbighshire*. Since the extension of its boundaries in 1935, Wrexham has claimed to be the largest town in North Wales – a claim presumably not to be challenged unless the projects are finally launched for some New Town about Caersws. But it is not reckoned a county town; its importance and size are due to its being the centre of the North Welsh coalfield, 40 m. long, that extends beside the Dee. Iron- and steel-works locally are fed by this means, and the cannel coal of Flint, which belongs to the same series of seams, is excellent for the production of gas. It is mainly English in speech and style of building. Its most interesting feature is the Church of St Giles, built in 1472, with a tower nearly 140 ft high. This was traditionally listed as one of the Seven Wonders of Wales. Its sculptured ornamentation is typical of its relatively late period.

It is here that Eliugh (or Elihu) Yale is buried. In 1637 his father emigrated from the ancestral mansion of Plas-yn-Ial, and Elihu was born in Boston, Massachusetts. It was his recruitment from England, where he had returned at the age of four, into the East India Company that can be said to have founded the University of Yale; for, having governed Fort Madras from 1687 to 1692, he sent to Newhaven, Connecticut, a cargo of books and of Indian goods that were successfully sold for the sum of £562 12s. 0d. The University he thus initiated has a Wrexham Tower in its Memorial Quadrangle; the tomb he rests in was restored by the University in 1874. Its epitaph on him is famous:

> Born in America, in Europe bred,
> In Africa travelled and in Asia wed,
> Where long he lived and thrived; in
>   London dead.
> Much good, some ill he did; so hope's
>   all even,
> And that his soul through mercy's gone
>   to heaven.
> You that survive and read his tale take care
> For this most certain exit to prepare.
> When blest in peace, the actions of the just
> Smell sweet and blossom in the silent dust.

There are echoes in this poem, but they are from excellent sources.

Although Oswestry, not far away, is in Shropshire within the marchlands of Wales and not in Wales itself, it must be mentioned here. In its parish church, badly damaged in the Civil Wars but restored by 1664, is a canopied monument of the Yale family, with kneeling effigies in a style that lingered into the 17th cent., of Hugh and Dorothy Yale, kin to Elihu and his father, and carrying the date 1616.

In the Ceiriog valley, south of Wrexham

G. Douglas Bolton

G. *Douglas Bolton*

The Jubilee Arch on the road to Cwmystwyth

SE. of Wrexham is Bangor-Is-Coed, the site of what was claimed to be the largest and oldest foundation of the Celtic Church, destroyed by the Northumbrian army about A.D. 615. But a visit to Llansantffraid Glynceiriog, no more than 11 m. away in the beautiful Ceiriog valley, revives American interest. In the village Memorial Hall, a tablet was set in 1934 in memory of Thomas Jefferson, who drafted the American Declaration of Independence, and whose *Summary View of the Rights of British America* had a deep influence both in the American Colonies and in Britain. Its argument applied the fundamental principles of Magna Carta to the theme that, whatever allegiance the Colonies might owe to the Crown, they were legally independent of rule from Westminster. He was born and died in America, between 1743 and 1826. But his forebears seem to have come from Snowdonia in Wales. His argument had a precedent in the institution of the principality. By contrast, Judge Jeffreys, the hanging judge of the Bloody Assizes that stamped out the embers of the Monmouth rebellion against James II in the West Country, was also of Welsh descent: he was a Denbighshire man, born at Acton, 1 m. from Wrexham, in 1648.

But Llansantffraid in the lovely Ceiriog valley has a gentler record in the memory of John Ceiriog Hughes, a farmer who was also a stationmaster but, dying in 1887, is better known as the Nightingale of Glyn Ceiriog; for he was a poet – a poet among the Philistines, as his biographer records. The village of Llansantffraid Glynceiriog has its whole Institute dedicated to him.

At Marchwiail, the modern Wrexham Industrial Estate has been developed.

YSBYTY YSTWYTH, *Cardiganshire,* whose name means the Hospice on the Ystwyth, lies 12 m. SE. of Aberystwyth on a fine site high above the river valley, which becomes narrow and heavily wooded as it plunges deeper into the hills. Ysbyty is mainly from the 19th cent., when the inhabitants worked in the now disused lead-mines at Cwmystwyth. The Victorian church is magnificently placed, with a glorious view. The old church, now empty and abandoned, lies immediately below it in a weed-filled hollow.

The road dips down steeply to the adjoining village, Pontrhydygroes (Bridge of the Ford of the Cross). The influence of Strata Florida Abbey is strong upon the names in these parts. Adjoining the bridge is the lodge gate for the Hafod estate. Hafod is now in the hands of the Forestry Commission, and the site of the old house is a caravan club. About 150 years ago this was one of the most celebrated places in Wales, visited and admired by romantic travellers. Coleridge came here, and there is a strong possibility that he remembered Hafod when he wrote of Kubla Khan's Xanadu. Here Thomas Johnes (1748–1816) planned an Earthly Paradise, with a house built by Baldwin and enlarged by Nash, and plantations of rare trees that covered the slopes of the hills. Hafod contained a fine library and a priceless collection of old Welsh manuscripts. The first mansion was destroyed by fire in 1807. Johnes rebuilt the house, but could not completely rebuild the early enchantment of Hafod. He ran into financial difficulties. His only child, Marianne, died in 1811 at the age of twenty-seven. He himself died at Dawlish, away from the tree-girt Paradise he had so lovingly created. The exotic life at Hafod has been well described by Elizabeth Inglis Jones in *Peacocks in Paradise*.

The church at Hafod – Eglwys Newydd (New Church) – stands on the road high up on the hill-side NE. of the house, with a fine view down over the estate and the ruins of the mansion, blown up as unsafe in 1958. The hill-sides, once planted with rare trees by Johnes, are now mainly under conifers. The church contained the famous monument to Marianne Johnes carved by Chantrey. Eglwys Newydd in turn was consumed by fire in 1932, and the Chantrey carving is now a calcined pile of stone. The church, which is an early creation of the Romantic Age, has been charmingly restored, with an old barrel roof and some remains of the 16th-cent. glass preserved after the fire.

At the top of the road from Hafod, over to Devil's Bridge, stands the commemorative arch built by Johnes out of rough stone to celebrate the Golden Jubilee of George III. It has been restored by the Forestry Commission.

Beyond the Hafod estate, the Ystwyth runs deeper into the hills, past the abandoned lead-mines of Cwmystwyth. The road out of the trench cut by the Ystwyth crosses lonely, treeless, wild country to come down into the upper valley of the Elan, and then past the Birmingham reservoirs into Rhayader.

YSTRADFELLTE, Breconshire. Some 15 m. NE. of Neath lies this village whose name means Way over the River Mellte, now as in former days well worth a visit for the beauty of the surrounding countryside, in marked contrast to the mining areas below it. "Ystradvellty," said Daniel Paterson's Direct and Principal Cross Roads in 1811: "A Public-house, where corn may be had and at Pont Neath Vaughan a decent little inn. At the former of these places the river Vellty loses itself underground; and about a mile to the right of the latter is the Fall of Neath, a beautiful and picturesque scene. Near Pont Neath Vaughan cross the Purthin river and enter Glamorganshire."

What is now called Pontneddfechan (Bridge of the Little River Neath) is still a centre for seeing the rugged course of the Mellte, Hepste, Neath, and Pyrddyn. One of the inns, the Old White Horse, is now a youth hostel for the area between the Sgwd yr Eira (Spurt of Snow), the Clungwyn falls, the surprising cave of Porth-yr-ogof, the Sgwd Gwladys, and the Sgwd Einion. The hill of Craig y Llyn (almost 2,000 ft) has the loftiest peak in Glamorgan. Near Ystradfellte itself is the way from which it must have taken its name, the Sarn Helen, or Roman road, by which stands the Maen Madoc, a stone with the inscription Dervaci filius Justi ic iacit (Here lies Derva-cius, the son of Justus).

A lake also called Ystradfellte, between the Fan Llia and Fan Fawr, is pleasant for trout fishing and even more so for its views over the wild mountains that stretch to the N.

YSTRADGYNLAIS, Breconshire, and **YSTALYFERA,** Glamorgan. These two villages run into each other at the top end of the Swansea Valley, but, by a curious piece of boundary-drawing, Ystradgynlais is in Brecon-shire and Ystalyfera in Glamorgan. Both are mining villages, although Ystradgynlais has developed new industries as coal has declined. The crags of Y Darren Widdon (Rock of Sighs) dominate Ystalyfera and rise to 1,160 ft. The Tawe valley opens out a little at Ystradgynlais, which stands almost at the northern limits of the coal-measures. Beyond Abercrave, the Tawe runs clear and turns the limestone corner of Craig-y-Nos, when all signs of industry disappear among the high hills.

Both villages are intensely Welsh in culture, and well known for choirs and literary men. Dr Vaughan Thomas, the Welsh musician, was born at Ystalyfera.

The Twrch valley runs into the Tawe at a point half way between the two places. The road to Brynaman runs up through this narrow, twisting valley to the mining village of Cwmllyn-fell. The Twrch itself rises on the Carmarthen Van (2,632 ft), running down off the Old Red Sandstone rocks of the summit ridge, Fan Foel, into limestone beds, through a moorland valley that is very rough indeed.

YSTRADMEURIG, Cardiganshire, is a hamlet placed in lonely country 14 m. SE. of Aberystwyth. The Cors Goch Glan Teifi, or Bog of Tregaron, lies to the S., and the hills roll away northwards to the Plynlimon massif. The church, restored in the 19th cent., stands next to the old school of St John's College, with its pointed windows and yellow walls. The school was founded in 1734 by Edward Richard, a schoolmaster of genius, who attracted the sons of many distinguished Welshmen of the early 18th cent. The school still maintains the old traditions. There is little to show of the old castle except a few mounds. It was first built by Gilbert de Clare in the early 12th cent. It passed into Welsh hands and was finally dismantled in 1208.

The Caradoc Falls are a triple cascade, which have to be reached on foot. In wet weather they are impressive.

Maps

Legend

———————	Motorway
———————	Trunk Road
———————	'A' Road
———————	'B' Road and selected other roads
– – – – –	National boundary
— — — —	County boundary

Scale

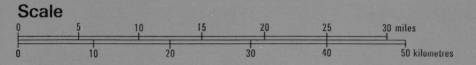

0	5	10	15	20	25	30 miles

0	10	20	30	40	50 kilometres

Key to Map Pages

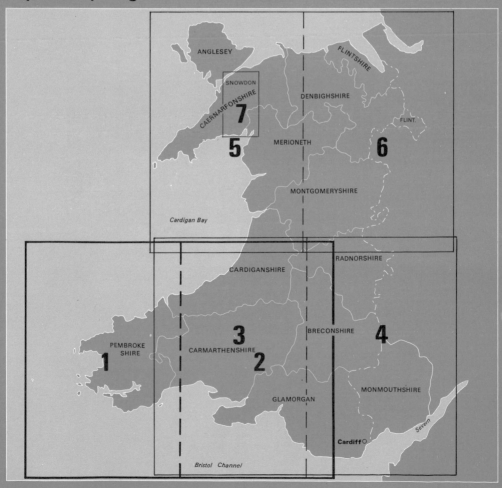

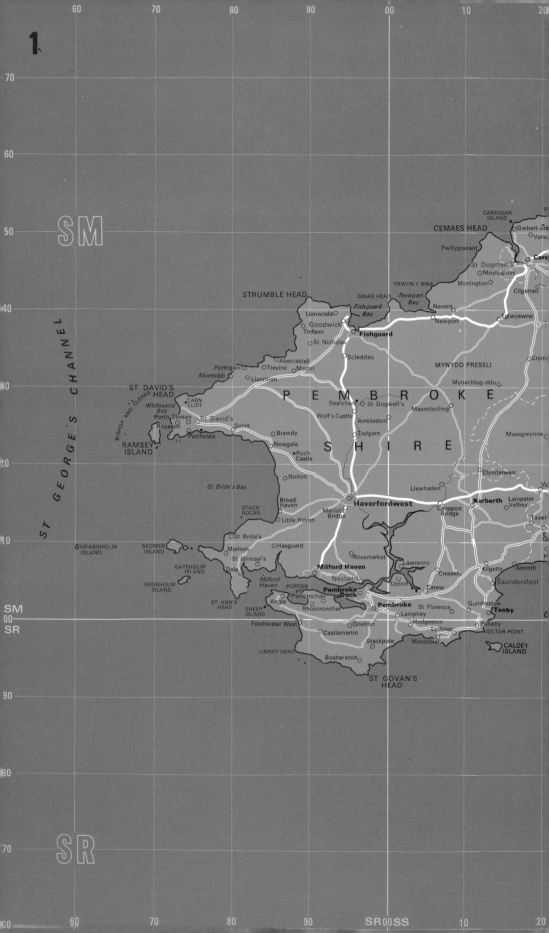

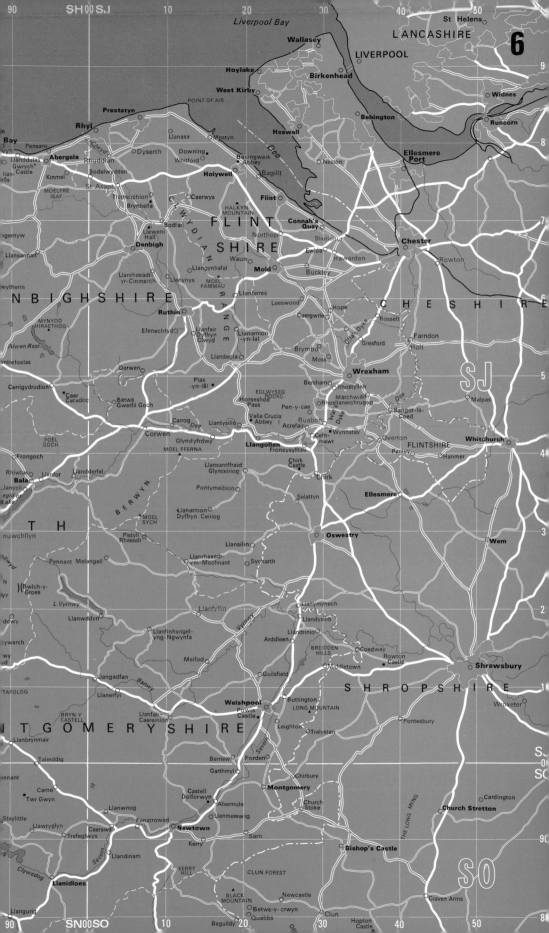

Concise Bibliography

The editions referred to are those used in the preparation of this book.

Prehistory and the Wessex Culture

Anglesea. London, H.M. Stationery Office, 1963.

FLEURE, J. H. *Gyda'r Wawr*. Wrexham, Hughes & Son, 1923.

Fox, Sir Cyril. *Life and Death in the Bronze Age*. London, Routledge & Kegan Paul, 1959.

HAWKES, J. and C. *Prehistoric Britain*. Harmondsworth, Penguin Books, 1958.

PIGGOTT, Stuart. *Approach to Archaeology*. London, A. & C. Black, 1939.

THOM, A. C. *Megalithic Sites in Britain*. Oxford University Press, 1967.

Celtic Wales

DE JUBAINVILLE, H. d'Arbois. *L'Étude de la Littérature Celtique*. Paris, 1883.

DE JUBAINVILLE, H. d'Arbois. *La Civilisation des Celtes et celle de L'Épopée Homerique*. Paris, 1884.

RHYS, Sir John. *Celtic Britain*. London, Society for Promoting Christian Knowledge, 1882.

Roman Wales

CONYBEARE, Edward. *Roman Britain*. London, Society for Promoting Christian Knowledge, 1903.

GRIMES, W. F. "Holt; Castle Lyons." *Y Cymmrodor*, Vol. 41. London, Cymmrodorion Society, 1930.

ORDNANCE SURVEY. Map of Roman Britain. 1956.

RICHMOND, I. A. *Roman Britain*. Harmondsworth, Penguin Books, 1955.

Segontium. London, H.M. Stationery Office, 1963.

WHEELER, Sir Mortimer. *Rome beyond the Frontiers*. Harmondsworth, Penguin Books, 1955.

The Celtic Church

BARING-GOULD, S. "Lives of the British Saints." *Y Cymmrodor*. London, Cymmrodorion Society, 1875.

BEDE, The Venerable. *Ecclesiastical History of England*. London, Dent (Everyman's Library).

Cambridge Medieval History, Vol. 3. Cambridge University Press, 1922.

ELLIS, T. P. "The Catholic Church in Welsh Laws." *Y Cymmrodor*, Vol. 42. London, Cymmrodorian Society, 1931.

EVANS, A. O. "Three Old Foundations." *Y Cymmrodor*, Vol. 42. London, Cymmrodorion Society, 1931.

EVANS, Sebastian. *The High History of the Holy Graal*. Translated from the medieval French. London, Dent (Everyman's Library).

GILES, J. A. *Six Old English Chronicles* (by Gildas, Nennius, and others). London, Bohn, 1901.

GREENE, Tyrrell. "Ecclesiology of Anglesea." *Y Cymmrodor*, Vol. 40. London, Cymmrodorion Society, 1929.

HUGHES, Howard, and NORTH, H. L. *Old Churches of Snowdonia*. Caernarfon, 1924.

JONES, Hartwell. "Early Celtic Missionaries." *Y Cymmrodor*, Vol. 39. London, Cymmrodorion Society, 1926.

LLEWELLYN, Alun. "Forebears of Erigena." *Aryan Path*, Vol. 39, Nos. 1 and 2. 1968.

LLEWELLYN, Alun. "Celtic Christianity." *Aryan Path*, Vol. 39, Nos. 8 and 9. 1968.

RUSSELL, Bertrand. *History of Western Philosophy*, Chapter "John the Scot [Erigena]". London, Allen & Unwin, 1954.

Arthurian Romance

Black Book of Carmarthen, The. Facsimile of original texts. Oxford, Cymmrodorion Society, 1882.

Book of Aneirin, The. Original text. Pwllheli, Cymmrodorion Society, 1908.

Book of Taliesin, The Facsimile of original texts. Pwllheli, Cymmrodorion Society, 1910.

GEOFFREY OF MONMOUTH. *History of the Kings of Britain*. London, Dent (Everyman's Library).

GUEST, Charlotte. *Mabinogion*. 1849. Revised edition by G. and T. Jones, London, Dent (Everyman's Library).

LLEWELLYN, Alun. "Mappa Mundi of Taliesin." *Anglo-Welsh Review*, No. 38. 1967.

LLEWELLYN, Alun. "Note on the Tale of Bran." *Anglo-Welsh Review*, No. 39. 1968.

Red Book of Hergest, The. Original texts of the Mabinogion Tales, the Histories, the Triads, etc. 2 vols. Oxford, Cymmrodorion Society, 1890.

RHYS, Sir John. *Studies in the Arthurian Legend*. Oxford University Press, 1901.

Medieval Wales

BARTRUM, P. C. "Noe, King of Powys." *Y Cymmrodor*, Vol. 43. London, Cymmrodorion Society, 1932.

CUNNINGHAM, W. *The Growth of English Industry and Commerce*, Vol. 1. Cambridge University Press, 1919.

EVANS, D. L. "The Principality of Wales, 1343–1376." *Transactions* of the Cymmrodorion Society. 1927.

GARDINER, S. R. *History of England,* Vol. 1. London, Longmans Green, 1896.

GIRALDUS CAMBRENSIS. *Itinerary of Wales, 1188.* London, Dent (Everyman's Library).

LLOYD, Sir J. E. *History of Wales.* London, Benn, 1911.

OWEN, Edward. "The Croes Nawdd." *Y Cymmrodor,* Vol. 43. London, Cymmrodorion Society, 1932.

STUBBS, W. *Constitutional History of England.* Oxford University Press, 1880.

STUBBS, W. *Select Charters.* Oxford University Press, 1913.

TREVELYAN, Sir George. *English Social History.* London, Longmans Green, 1949–52.

Tudor Wales

BALLINGER, J. "Katheryn of Berain." *Y Cymmrodor,* Vol. 40. London, Cymmrodorion Society, 1929.

CAMDEN, R. *Britannia.* London, 1586.

DRAYTON, Michael. *Polyolbion.* London, 1612.

LHUYD, Humphrey. *Cambria.* Antwerp, 1573.

TANNER, J. R. *Tudor Constitutional Documents.* Cambridge University Press, 1930.

Wales in the 17th and 18th Centuries

CARLYLE, Thomas. *Letters and Speeches of Oliver Cromwell.* London, Chapman & Hall, 1907.

CLARENDON, Edward, Earl of. *History of the Great Rebellion.* 1688. Reprinted by the Oxford University Press, 1843.

DEFOE, Daniel. *A Tour through the Whole Island of Great Britain.* 1724–6. London, Dent (Everyman's Library).

JONES, F. "The Vaughans of Golden Grove." *Transactions* of the Cymmrodorion Society. London, 1963.

MORDEN, R. *A New Description of the State of England.* 1704.

OGILBIE, John. *Britannia.* 1675.

PENNANT, Thomas. *A Tour in Wales.* Vol. 1, 1778; Vol. 2, 1780. London.

SALMON, D. "The French Invasion of Pembrokeshire." *Y Cymmrodor,* Vol. 43. London, Cymmrodorion Society, 1932.

SAXTON, Christopher. *The Counties of England and Wales.* With maps by William Kip and John Speed. London, 1579–1610.

Torrington Diaries, The, Vol. 1. London, Eyre & Spottiswoode, 1934.

Trial of William Spiggott and Others at Hereford, The. Gloucester, 1770.

WYNNS OF GWYDIR, The. *Collected Papers, 1515–1690.* Cardiff University Press, 1926.

Wales in the 19th and 20th Centuries

BORROW, George. *Wild Wales.* London, Dent (Everyman's Library).

BRADLEY, A. C. *Highways and Byways in North Wales.* London, Macmillan, 1893.

BRADLEY, A. C. *Highways and Byways in South Wales.* London, Macmillan, 1903.

EVANS, Owen. "Non-Ferrous Metallurgical Industries in South Wales." *Transactions* of the Cymmrodorion Society. London, 1931.

HORSFALL-TURNER, E. R. "Montgomeryshire in 1839." *Montgomeryshire County Times.* 1935.

JONES, Thoresby. *Welsh Border Country.* London, Batsford, 1946.

LEWIS, Eiluned and Peter. *The Land of Wales.* London, Batsford, 1948.

LLEWELLYN, Alun. "A Nineteenth-Century Account Book." *Anglo-Welsh Review,* Nos. 36 and 37. 1967.

PARRY-JONES, D. *Welsh Country Upbringing.* London, Batsford, 1948.

PATERSON, Daniel. *Direct and Principal Cross Roads of Britain.* London, 1811.

PEATE, I. C. "The Woollen Industry." *Y Cymmrodor,* Vol. 39. London, Cymmrodorion Society, 1928.

THOMAS, Edward. *Beautiful Wales.* London, A. & C. Black, 1905.

Literature and the Arts

ARNOLD, Matthew. *On the Study of Celtic Literature.* London, Dent (Everyman's Library).

BELL, Idris and David. "Dafydd ap Gwylym: Fifty Poems." *Y Cymmrodor,* Vol. 48. London, Cymmrodorion Society, 1942.

BELL, Idris. *Welsh Poetry.* Oxford University Press, 1936.

DAVIES, Lumley. "Contributions of Welshmen to Music." *Transactions* of the Cymmrodorion Society. London, 1931.

DOLMETSCH, Arnold. "Ancient Welsh Music." *Transactions* of the Cymmrodorion Society. London, 1936.

LEWIS, Saunders. *Welsh Augustans.* Wrexham, 1924.

MORRIS BROTHERS, The. *Letters.* Aberystwyth University Press, 1907. "Further Letters of the Morris Brothers." *Y Cymmrodor,* Vols. 49 and 50. London, Cymmrodorion Society, 1947 and 1949.

PARRY, T. *Hanes Llenyddiaeth Gymraeg.* Cardiff University Press, 1953.

PEATE, I. C. "The Welsh House." *Y Cymmrodor,* Vol. 47. London, Cymmrodorion Society, 1942.

RICHARDS, Thomas. *Antiquae Linguae Britannicae Thesaurus.* Bristol, 1759.

WILLIAMS, Gwyn. *Welsh Poetry.* London, Faber, 1952.

Sport

APPERLEY, N. W. "Mountain Hunting" in *A Fox-Hunting Anthology.* London, Cassell, 1928.

"NIMROD" (C. J. Apperley). *Memoirs of the Life of the Late John Mytton.* 1837. London, Methuen, 1936.

WARD, F. *The Lakes of Wales.* London, Herbert Jenkins, 1931.

Index, with Map References

Some alternative place-names are given, Welsh ones in *italics*. Where confusion between two places is possible, the county name is added in brackets. The principal castles are indexed under their towns. Lakes and rivers appear under their main names, but other features under their descriptive ones, such as Mynydd or Bwlch. For the map references, the first figure, in **bold** print, gives the number of the map. The two letters that follow give the large National Grid square, enclosed by heavy lines. The final four figures show the position of the place within that square; the first two measure the distance eastwards from the left-hand vertical line, and the last two the distance northwards from the base.

A. = Afon; R. = River. I. = Island. L. = Lake or Llyn.